Spirituality, Religion, and Aging

I dedicate this book to my family, who tolerated my many absences so that I could complete this project: Alex for his patience, love, and impressive cooking; Alexa for her insights and skills; Alistair for his wit and medical worldviews; and Ella and Oliver for their affection, joy, and fun.

Sara Miller McCune founded SAGE Publishing in 1965 to support the dissemination of usable knowledge and educate a global community. SAGE publishes more than 1000 journals and over 800 new books each year, spanning a wide range of subject areas. Our growing selection of library products includes archives, data, case studies and video. SAGE remains majority owned by our founder and after her lifetime will become owned by a charitable trust that secures the company's continued independence.

Los Angeles | London | New Delhi | Singapore | Washington DC | Melbourne

Spirituality, Religion, and Aging

Illuminations for Therapeutic Practice

Holly Nelson-Becker
Loyola University of Chicago

Los Angeles | London | New Delhi
Singapore | Washington DC | Melbourne

FOR INFORMATION:

SAGE Publications, Inc.
2455 Teller Road
Thousand Oaks, California 91320
E-mail: order@sagepub.com

SAGE Publications Ltd.
1 Oliver's Yard
55 City Road
London EC1Y 1SP
United Kingdom

SAGE Publications India Pvt. Ltd.
B 1/I 1 Mohan Cooperative Industrial Area
Mathura Road, New Delhi 110 044
India

SAGE Publications Asia-Pacific Pte. Ltd.
3 Church Street
#10-04 Samsung Hub
Singapore 049483

Acquisitions Editor: Nathan Davidson
Editorial Assistant: Alissa Nance
Production Editor: Veronica Stapleton Hooper
Copy Editor: Diana Breti
Typesetter: C&M Digitals (P) Ltd.
Proofreader: Gretchen Treadwell
Indexer: Wendy Allex
Cover Designer: Glenn Vogel
Marketing Manager: Jenna Retana

Printed in the United States of America

Library of Congress Cataloging-in-Publication Data

Names: Nelson-Becker, Holly, author.

Title: Spirituality, Religion, and Aging: Illuminations for Therapeutic Practice Holly Nelson-Becker, Loyola University of Chicago.

Description: Thousand Oaks : Sage, [2017] | Includes bibliographical references and index.

Identifiers: LCCN 2016040646 | ISBN 9781412981361 (pbk. : alk. paper)

Subjects: LCSH: Geriatric psychiatry. | Older people—Mental health—Religious aspects. | Psychiatry and religion.

Classification: LCC RC451.4.A5 N453 2017 | DDC 618.97/689—dc23 LC record available at https://lccn.loc.gov/2016040646

This book is printed on acid-free paper.

17 18 19 20 21 10 9 8 7 6 5 4 3 2 1

BRIEF CONTENTS

DETAILED CONTENTS

Chapter 8 • Spirituality, Religion, and Health   221

Chapter 9 • Spirituality in Emotion, Depression, and Anxiety   251

Chapter 10 • Memory, Dementia, and Spiritual Care   281

FOREWORD

SUSAN H. MCFADDEN

Starting in the 1960s, a few gerontologists began suggesting that it was time to stop treating religiousness and spirituality as taboo topics. They urged their colleagues to see that the aging process motivates many people to wrestle with questions about life's meaning and purpose that have deep roots in the religions of the world. However, although the 1971 White House Conference on Aging produced an important document about spiritual well-being in later life, the majority of academic researchers and many practitioners paid little attention. Slowly, however, momentum built as more books and journal articles appeared and as professional organizations supported the formation of groups interested in research and practice that takes spirituality, religion, and aging seriously. As this book notes, toward the end of the 20th century, a variety of cultural factors converged to stimulate fresh thinking on the roles of religious beliefs, practices, and communities in older people's lives as well as new insights into the many ways they experience and express spirituality.

I do not believe it is an exaggeration to say that Holly Nelson-Becker has written a book that represents a turning point in gerontology. Her work reflects contemporary postmodern assumptions about the intersectionality of various shaping influences on individual identity and it respects the many sources of diversity among peoples and cultures. At the same time, in every chapter, she shows how wisdom from the past can enlighten our thinking today. She also understands that research, theory, and practice related to religion, spirituality, and aging are shaped to some degree by their historical moment as well as people's positions on the relation between science and religion.

From her standing ground in social work research and practice, Nelson-Becker reaches out to colleagues in psychology, nursing, pastoral care, art and music therapy, and other disciplines and professions that study aging and serve older adults. She values interdisciplinarity and transdisciplinarity, respectfully showing how persons with different perspectives from her own have historically viewed religion, spirituality, and aging. She uses the metaphor of "leaping limits" to address how people can get out of the silos that restrict them to a particular disciplinary language and assumptive world.

One criticism of much of the work from the previous century was that it treated religion generically and showed little understanding of the actual beliefs of adherents of different religions. Nelson-Becker corrects that problem by offering detailed descriptions of eight major religions, including the religions of indigenous Americans (recognizing, of course, that there is much diversity in this group). It is also impressive to see that she paints a differentiated portrait of spirituality, and accepts that some forms of spirituality have no theistic focus. Along with adding to their knowledge about specific religious beliefs and various forms of spirituality, Nelson-Becker urges mental health practitioners to be self-critical about their biases toward religiousness, particularly when they assume that devout people are rigid and judgmental. She also wants practitioners to understand that some older adults experience profound shifts in religiousness and/or spirituality, sometimes by leaving one tradition and turning to another, or by giving up previously held beliefs and practices altogether.

This book breaks new ground in many ways. For example, it frequently addresses the spiritual and religious challenges experienced by people who immigrate to the United

States later in life to be near their adult children. With immigration such a contested political issue in our times, it is refreshing to see the compassionate approach taken in this book. She understands that many of these elderly immigrants feel helpless and hopeless and she offers suggestions about how practitioners might offer support and assistance. Whether writing about newly arrived immigrants, or Americans who have lived in one place their entire lives, Nelson-Becker lifts up the spiritual resonances of their everyday lives. For example, she pays attention to the meaning of home for older adults, including those journeying into dementia.

Although Nelson-Becker reviews the DSM-5 diagnostic categories often associated with older people, she tries to de-medicalize her approach to their suffering and speaks about their "maladies of the soul." She offers new ideas about how elders with mental health problems might be accompanied through spiritual suffering to spiritual freedom and discovery. Her compassionate view of older adults extends to those with dementia and she offers many helpful suggestions on how to connect meaningfully with people undergoing changes in their ability to remember, plan, make decisions, and so forth. Ever open to creative new approaches to authentic connections with other persons, she affirms the importance of improvisational techniques as a form of communication with persons living with dementia.

Even when she's wrestling with weighty philosophical and theological topics, Nelson-Becker always returns to the real lives of older people. She also keeps her focus on how counselors and therapists can be helpful to elders who indicate that they want to address religious and spiritual issues. Warning that practice must always be ethical, and never coercive, she suggests that for some professionals with some clients, it might sometimes even be appropriate to introduce prayer into the encounter. On the other hand, she is quite aware of what she calls the "shadow sides" of both religiousness and spirituality.

Holly Nelson-Becker is a highly skilled social worker, therapist, researcher, and teacher. Her commitment to teaching and learning shines throughout all the chapters of this book. Each one has discussion questions, assignments, and spiritual exercises that can be used in classes, and each also includes many helpful resources. People reading this book outside of a classroom setting can learn much from thinking about the questions, assignments, and exercises she provides, and all readers can take advantage of the opportunity to expand their own spiritual repertoires by reflecting on the epigraphs and practicing the meditations that appear in every chapter. This care in tending to the spiritual lives of readers is yet another example of this book's courageous, wise, and fresh approach to how we might understand spirituality, religion, and aging in the 21st century.

PREFACE

Aging is different for everyone who is lucky enough to live to older ages. Just as all persons have their own life, they will have their own death. Aging, too, though it has some common themes, is a uniquely perceived interlude of time. Thus, everyone has their own aging. No one is free, I believe, of some aches and pain that have their origin in the body, the heart, the mind, or spirit. This book is intended to teach about a somewhat neglected area in academia that is often left to theology or to pastoral care professionals, clergy, imams, rabbis, shamans, a sadhu or guru, a monk or nun, a bodhisattva, and other holy teachers. This broad area is the spiritual dimension of the aging experience.

Mental health practitioners or therapists emerging from any disciplinary venue should know how to assess, engage, and address the spiritual and religious needs of their clients. Evaluation of any interventions or helping actions is also important. In contemporary societies, the persistent problems that clients and patients encounter cannot often be solved through application of one kind of tool or approach. Instead, a holistic perspective with its multilayered and multimodal complexities provides the potential avenue for healing. Healing is not merely a one-time occurrence for many individuals. Rather, people require healing of many kinds as they travel through a lifetime. In some cases, trouble just flies in to a life from external events; in other cases, demons in the form of fears and anxieties people battle lie deep inside themselves. Invisible, they fester and smolder there. When brought to consciousness or to light, there is capacity for transformation and growth. Perhaps, if in the middle facing toward the last decades of life, individuals think about their younger selves and what they have since experienced, they might furtively wish to go backward rather than forward in time. However, the truth is that wherever clients are in a life, they do have the resources to move forward across roiling rivers, stepping stone by stepping stone, until a greater vision enraptures them. Therapists represent some of those stepping stones to the other side—to spiritual freedom. To be the catalyst for change in a person's life is powerful. This kind of power must be handled gently, and not in service of one's own self-promotion or ego.

Our lives are fleeting. We live and are then heard no more (at least in real time). From sacred text in the Christian tradition comes this question, "What is your life? For you are a mist that appears for a little while and then vanishes" (James 4:14, Revised Standard Version). Shakespeare put this idea a little more cavalierly in *Macbeth:* "Life's but a walking shadow, a poor player that struts and frets his hour upon the stage" (Act 5, Scene 5). Perhaps so, but within that space of time there is so much potential for learning, for achievement, and for imprinting the world with whatever it is we have to offer that, long after our own voices are silenced, will remain in some form and be transmitted to following generations. This may be nothing more than a word of encouragement that allows a friend to make a better decision, an idea that improves life for clients or patients, anything at all that threads out to create good on the planet we now call home. The truth is that everything matters and everyone matters. In fact perhaps a purpose of people we may deem as antagonists or adversaries is to awaken something within us. Disturbing the status quo is at times a worthy aim.

In Chinese medicine there is a fifth season, beyond the typical natural seasons in nature we know as spring, summer, autumn, and winter, all of which cycle in an endless round.

This fifth season stands in late summer, the pause when the color of trees and plants is no longer so vibrant, but carries a truer pigment of itself, the median between the bold and the dull. Technically the fifth season begins in late August and extends until the autumn equinox. This is also the time when vegetables and fruits are ripe and ready to be harvested. Earth is at the still point of time. This is the pause when everything slows. It marks the transition between yang and yin energy, from fiery reds of summer into the yellows and oranges of autumn. Similarly, the heavenly pivot is the pivot point in acupuncture that represents the point between heaven and earth. It is a point of balance between being connected to heaven and grounded on earth.

Each of these images applies to aging. The fifth season suggests that beyond the surface of what is seen as ordinary, or the four seasons that structure our years, is something deeper. When people are willing to go deep into their experience, there is something to be gained, fruit to be harvested that can last into later years—the winter period of life when passions and intensity may have cooled, but much still flows below the surface as a river runs deep under ice. The winter of life is not a time of stagnation, but can be a time of new openness to what life offers. The pause of the fifth season suggests a time and space for reflection before one enters this final phase; this interval consists of many years or few. At this still point, one considers the history that has brought one to this moment, and what may yet be available to choose. The heavenly pivot promotes the power older people continue to have at every age to change and grow and turn in new directions. It is an affirmation that no one need ever feel stuck, because even in the most physically limiting situations, such as permanent residence in a nursing care facility, there are choices that can be made about one's response. Having choice connects people back to who they are and who they want to be. Beyond decision making capacity, for instance in the experience of dementia, we can trust that people continue to be held in the hand of the universe.

Despite difficulties then, the possibility to live a life of meaning and joy is immeasurable, awe inspiring, breathtaking even. Meaning abounds through our personal reflection and social engagement. Aging is not best described by frailty, burden, or compulsory obligations, but by the opportunity for ongoing learning, volunteering, altruistic acts, and crafting a legacy of purpose in other lives we lightly and briefly join as well as our own. This is accomplished through the relational nature of linked lives and not through solitary pursuits alone. Meaning unfolds through the rhythmic departures and arrivals, exits and entrances, of people and places that structure the great dance of our lives.

The questions of aging are the questions of history. What does it mean to have life? What does it mean to be or become old? Who decides who is old? What is the value of aging? What is abundance, generosity, hospitality? How are they created and/or enhanced? What is the spiritual self? How does religion speak to the experience of humankind? What is the call of justice for everyone when the needs of the many and the needs of the few sometimes collide? How can we support diversity in its many forms and types, so that our lives and the lives of everyone else are enriched instead of diminished and threatened? When political systems fall apart, how can we stay strong in our regard for common human needs and choose to support the need of another person because it is greater than our own? And beyond the question, what am I searching for, lies the question of commitment, what do I believe? How have my beliefs changed and how or where have they remained the same, if they have?

There are also the scientific questions. How does empirical study, along with our theological or philosophical search, add to our knowledge of how to live a healthy and fulfilling life? What does the research tell us? As the positive psychologists suggest, what does it mean to flourish? How is flourishing facilitated, or does it only come from that inexpressible essence of the individual within? Under what conditions, by whom, and for whom can the pathways to healthy aging and flourishing be lit or ignited, cleared of debris, and maintained? How can the resident meaning within life challenges be accessed? These are a few of the questions I have welcomed, though not definitively answered, in the pages of this text. I pose them here for your consideration.

As an academic text, this book is written to teach students of counseling, nursing, marriage and family therapy, pastoral care and chaplaincy, psychology, social work, and thanatology about older adults, aging, and spiritual and religious issues. While mental health professionals are the primary intended audience, I also believe this book holds value for people who just want to learn more about aging, spirituality, and religion. Out of my experience teaching for 20 years, I know that individuals learn through multiple formats. So, I have adopted an integrative style of teaching here, describing and explaining aging content, modeling meditations, and providing assignments and exercises that may be surprising to some readers.

Further, this text is written to an inclusive audience of practitioners or public citizens who consider themselves spiritual, religious, both, or neither. A common category for those who choose to classify themselves outside of any religious or spiritual context is either *agnostic*, someone who believes one cannot know about the existence of God—or *atheist*, not believing in God or a god(s). However, those designations do not provide a clear definition of one's developing identity. The latter groups may resonate with the term *secular humanist* or something different. In my classes, I suggest to students that it holds greater meaning to define themselves as what/who they are, rather than what/who they are not.

Why did I write this book? I have carried within me some of the same ambiguities and contradictions that you likely live with. I have written this text to teach you from several levels/perspectives. Thus, you will at times find an academic and scientific voice, at times a spiritual voice, at places, a personal voice. Knowledge is not monolithic, univalent, and thus to learn about a thing, it is helpful to witness its multidimensionality. Achieving a balance across multiple influences and expressions is a challenge, but a goal of this book. I have added a transdisciplinary perspective in Chapter 12, while maintaining focus on the clinical or mental health professions introduced in Chapter 1. I have included important knowledge about specific aspects of aging that mental health or health practitioners need to work with clients, such as expanded or reduced emotional range, depression, anxiety, health issues, and dementia. Issues such as the social construction of identity, forgiveness, narrative work, and the meaning of home and public/private space are featured here. Brief incursions into ethnic, racial and gender/sexual diversity in aging are shown. Exploration of the arts in meeting spiritual and religious needs is discussed. However, showcasing religious and spiritual diversity and traditional and modern approaches to aging is the overarching task. As I concluded the writing of this book, I began to realize that each chapter could have been a separate book and other chapters might have been included. Those explorations must remain for a later time. Overall, I wrote this book because I discerned a need.

How did I arrive in gerontology? I have benefitted from a multiplicity of careers and interests. I loved learning languages and saw them as a way to topple walls between people. As a student traveling in Europe, I once found myself in a train car among seven other young adults. Although three or four languages were represented, we were able to hold one wonderful and profound conversation with a couple of us interpreting for others. That image remains strongly fixed in my mind. I thought I might work in an international venue, but not seeing myself as a teacher at the time, I began an eight-year career with the airlines, performing multiple kinds of tasks.

Years later, I began to experience a kind of discomfort with my perfect life. Several times I was assigned to an international flight to Mexico or South America. Spanish was not one of my languages, though it was close to one in which I was fluent. On one occasion, I overnighted from a flight to Maracaibo, Venezuela. My resort hotel room was not one of the ones facing the ocean, but instead, overlooked a hillside dotted with shacks that represented the slums of the city, and through this the poverty of the world. In a pivotal moment of deep incongruence as I sat on my balcony, I realized it was time to do something more with my life. When my schedule allowed, I began with Catholic Social Service in Mesa, Arizona as a telephone reassurance volunteer to elderly people, picking up an earlier undergraduate interest in social services that was filled at the time by a course on rural poverty. Volunteer work reaffirmed my ultimate decision to exit the airlines and obtain a master's degree in social work at Arizona State University.

My career as a social worker led to experience in the psychiatric hospital of Maricopa County, Arizona where we treated clients with a wide range of mental health issues including some of the most extreme disorders. From there I became an outpatient mental health case management supervisor and then a counselor with mostly older adult clients in long-term care who were referred to me by either their medical doctor or their psychiatrist. This long-term care psychiatric team offered great learning about the mental health and spiritual needs of older people. Fortified by the desire to learn more about spirituality and aging, I returned to academia for a PhD at the University of Chicago with a specialization in gerontology and religion within social services. From statistics gathered by Jim Lubben, PhD, University of Boston, I later learned I was one of two 1999 PhD graduates in social work with a dissertation in aging.

My spiritual story began when I was very young. It has been a life's work to try to integrate that part of my journey in a way that could be visible and would be at least somewhat acceptable to my profession. In that task I was assisted by some wise friends, particularly Dr. Edward Canda, who has been a mentor since my years at the University of Kansas, and Jim Kreider, LCSW, who also mentored me in spiritual understanding. I am grounded in a Christian faith tradition, the Community of Christ, where I was ordained and practice in the ministerial office of Elder today. I continue to learn from my Kansas spiritual group under the direction of our teacher, Renee Brown. Like some of you, I have had some extraordinary spiritual experiences of a mystical nature that have taught me something about the many streams or levels of living and the need to remain as fully awake as possible, living as congruently and truthfully as I can with my beliefs as they evolve. This involves being authentic, living with integrity, and sharing my learning and knowledge.

Each chapter in this text is organized to include beginning quotations, an introduction to the chapter, material related to the chapter theme, a chapter summary, questions for discussion, a suggested meditation, exercises to explore your spirituality, websites, and additional suggested reading material. Some chapters also have concluding cases and potential assignments. A few chapters have shorter cases within the body of the chapter.

My hope is that this book will take you, the reader, into a journey about aging and therapeutic practice with older people that relates to and reveals what they deem sacred, spiritual, or religious. My prayer and intention is that this book will open new lines of thinking and perhaps fresh responses for you in your work with older adults. Whether you stand in a spiritual tradition or not, I also hope this material will open a parallel path of dynamic discovery for yourself and your own aging, even if it is only a path to deeper and better-framed questions. Time spent in not-knowing, when you are able to acknowledge the limits of your understanding and give everything over to grace or that sustaining force which you do not know, represents the thin space, the quiet space, of readiness for radical transformation. May this book help bring you to that transformative place.

ACKNOWLEDGMENTS

There are many individuals who facilitated the completion of this book and for whom I give gratitude. One of the first was Denai Armer, a KU MSW graduate, who believed in this project and volunteered her time at the beginning to help search the literature. Other students who assisted me as graduate students across different terms include Jennifer Johannesen, Susann Ozuk, Eneke Frank Mwakasisi, Amanda Creden, Catherine Stowers, and Leanne Atwell. MSW graduates Lauren Dowden, Caitlin Maruyama, Sarah Hansen, and Mukhayyokhon Azamova provided valuable insights. I also owe my gratitude to the students who enrolled in my spirituality and aging courses, loss, grief, and dying well courses, and the social work and aging courses I taught over a number of years especially at the University of Kansas and Loyola University Chicago.

Psychologists David M. Wulff and Susan McFadden offered constructive ideas and comments on specific chapters. Loyola University Chicago doctoral student Shveta Kumaria provided feedback on a section of writing, as did Loyola colleagues Shirley Simon and Susan Grossman. Manuscript reviewers to whom I am grateful for their insightful comments include Kathleen McInnis-Dittrich, Roseanna McCleary, and anonymous reviewers.

I acknowledge the contributions of Alexa Gummow, my daughter and a medical anthropology master's graduate, who provided me with many helpful suggestions and masterful photos.

I am grateful for Nathan Davidson and the editing team at SAGE and their support of this book.

I thank Bill Creed, SJ, who provided spiritual direction for the Ignatian exercises. Finally, I received encouragement from many friends, family, colleagues, and others who helped keep me on course, who modeled some of the concepts I have written about here, and who taught me through their lives.

Holly Nelson-Becker, PhD, LCSW, Professor
& Hartford Faculty Scholar in Geriatric Social Work

More information at

https://www.researchgate.net/profile/Holly_Nelson-Becker

http://works.bepress.com/holly_nelson-becker/

http://www.hollynelsonbecker.com

PUBLISHER'S ACKNOWLEDGMENTS

SAGE wishes to acknowledge the valuable contributions of the following reviewers.

Roseanna McCleary, California State University Bakersfield

Kathleen McInnis-Dittrich, Boston College Graduate School of Social Work

Ann Verrett Guillory, Felician College

ABOUT THE AUTHOR

Holly Nelson-Becker, PhD, LCSW, is a professor at Loyola University Chicago and a Hartford Faculty Scholar in Geriatric Social Work. Her PhD is from the University of Chicago and she obtained a MSW from Arizona State University. She holds BAs in modern foreign languages and in international studies from Graceland University. She is a recognized expert in social gerontology who has investigated the pathways to resilience and well-being in older adults. Her research areas focus on spirituality and aging, with an emphasis on end-of-life concerns and diverse cultural expressions. She helped create national standards for spiritual care in palliative care as one of six writers representing multiple health-related professions, and she is past chair of the Interest Group on Religion, Spirituality, and Aging for the Gerontological Society of America. She served on the National Program Committee for the Hartford Doctoral Fellows Program in Geriatric Social Work. She was awarded fellowship in the Gerontological Society of America in 2013.

INVITATION

Come.

Leave assumptions behind and prepare

To learn what you never knew and to rediscover what you already know deep inside

about the spiritual geography of aging.

Experience the dissonance and the congruence in what is accepted and proven,

Expected, hoped-for, and given as gift,

Culminating in the aesthetic endeavor of simply living your life.

May your therapeutic practice be the art you send into the world.

PART ONE

PRINCIPLES OF SPIRITUALITY AND RELIGION FOR GERONTOLOGICAL PRACTICE

CHAPTER ONE

THE IMPORTANCE OF SPIRITUALITY AND RELIGION FOR GERONTOLOGY

There was something formless and perfect before the
universe was born.
It is serene. Empty. Solitary. Unchanging. Infinite. Eternally
present. It is the mother of the universe. . . .
It flows through all things, inside and outside, and returns
to the origin of all things.

—Tao Te Ching, trans. Mitchell, p. 25

We collect data, things, people, ideas, "profound
experiences," never penetrating any of them . . . But there
are other times. There are times when we stop. We sit
still. We lose ourselves in a pile of leaves or its memory.
We listen and breezes from a whole other world begin to
whisper.

—James Carroll

No wise person ever wanted to be younger.

—Jonathan Swift

This chapter will introduce the reader to religion and spirituality in mental health practice with older adults. It will provide statistical evidence for the value of spirituality and religion to older adults within the wider demographic portrait of aging. It discusses the history of mental health disciplines in relation to religion and religious values, and it identifies a few of the assumptions that make working with religious and spiritual beliefs difficult for practitioners. Key figures and ideas about aging consciously will be presented. The chapter will close with some clinical notes for the aging journey in life's second half.

The quote above from the Tao Te Ching suggests that the universe is purposeful and, although unknowable, has a dynamic quality of unity within it that mirrors the birth-to-death cycle of life. The second quote ponders the pace of life in postmodernity, which is so quick and full it fails to include the moments of profound experience when we begin to know ourselves and, hence, connect more deeply to the entire outside world. This is one of the benefits of aging suggested in the third quote by Swift. Although explanations for the selected quotes will not always be provided, in order to permit the reader to identify his or her own applications and meanings, examples of potential meanings are given here. Generally, you, the reader, will carry your own abundant ideas for what these quotes evoke in you.

AGING IN A POSTMODERN TIME

The founder of American philosophy and psychology, William James (1902/1961), associated old age with heightened religious involvement due to assumptive concerns about impending mortality (McFadden, 2005, 2015). It is important to recognize that old age then, when the average lifespan was about 50 years for those born in 1900, had a different meaning than old age today, when many people remain active into their 70s, 80s, and even 90s. In the early 20th century, people lived with acute illnesses that might lead to quicker deaths. Moreover, in the early part of the 19th century, the U.S. culture was permeated by a largely Protestant, Catholic, and Jewish sensibility that was well-integrated with daily life. That is beginning to change, but older adults remain the age group most connected to religious faith. The role of religion and spirituality has become increasingly recognized for older people in managing expected changes to physical health; related or unrelated challenges to mental health; social support network changes with deaths of peers, siblings, and spouses/partners; increasing awareness of mortality; questions about life meaning; and coping with other end-of-life and existential concerns (Ai, Ardelt, & Wink, 2010; Nelson-Becker, 2006; Puchalski et al., 2009).

Although aging today contains within it greater numbers of opportunities and potentials than in past decades, there are also new kinds of vulnerabilities and risks for diminishment, morbidity, and ambiguous dying. The path of chronic illness leading to death is no longer a quick pathway as in sudden death, or a downward slope as in some terminal illnesses, but by contrast is often slower and more confusing, with many small ascents and descents within a gradual downward trajectory. However, it is important not to understand the second half of life as solely a gradual downward slide into death. In fact, that slope begins at birth. Instead, the goals of the second half of life suggest a much richer differentiation in terms of finding meaning and purpose and achieving growth. The potentials for positive aging are numerous and expansive. Investigation into positive aging is a newer focus of research. Increased vibrancy, wisdom, and legacy may be outcomes of increased years. Describing this richness and diversity of pathways enhanced by spirituality and religion as perceived by individuals is the aim of this book.

There are a number of prevalent myths about the aging experience that tend to assail a holistic and realistic viewpoint. Further, myths can be one of the most insidious forms of bias, as these represent prejudice against the success of living to an older age and constitute an impression of one's future self. The following are common understandings or myths:

1. Creativity diminishes with age.

2. People become more religious as they age.

3. Depression is more widespread in older people than younger ones.

4. Cognitive decline is concomitant with advanced age.

5. Older workers are less productive and thus less valuable employees.

6. Loneliness is more likely.

7. More exercise is always better. (Breytspraak & Badura, 2015)

1. *Creativity.* In terms of creativity, experimental innovators require decades to achieve their peak potential through a process of searching (Galenson, 2010). Their work builds gradually and incrementally. As an example, the highest prices commanded in the works of Cezanne were for pieces he executed in the last year of his life. This contrasts with a second creative type, conceptual innovators, who tend to plan their work using ideas and emotions and may make important contributions early in their careers.

2. *Religion.* Older adults represent the most religious demographic group, so it may be supposed that people become more religious as they age. However, the Religious Landscape survey (Pew Forum on Religion & Public Life, 2007) demonstrated that people move in and out of religious affiliation in very fluid ways. Nearly 28% of adults leave the religion in which they were raised to join another or remain religiously unaffiliated. If switching among different Protestant denominations (joining or leaving) are included, that percentage rises to 44 (Pew Forum on Religion & Public Life, 2007).

3. *Depression.* Prevalence of depression in the community is highest among those from ages 18 to 25 (8.9%) and lowest among those over age 55 (5.5 %) according to the National Institute of Mental Health (NIMH, 2012). Those figures do not include institutionalized older adults for whom depression rates are generally higher.

4. *Cognitive decline.* Neurologically there are changes in the aging of the brain, but cognitive decline is not inevitable. Baltes (1993) suggested that there are many forms of knowledge-building, memory retrieval, and wisdom development and much variation across individuals. My father, David N. Nelson, is an example of a 96-year-old who continues to live independently and retains excellent cognitive ability and memory recall.

5. *Older workers.* Older adults in the workforce tend to remain highly productive according to labor market research by Burtless (2013). This is partly because people with higher educational levels tend to stay longer in the workforce. Those who have more fragile health and less education are less likely to continue employment.

6. *Loneliness.* A longitudinal study of U. S. older adults followed between 2002 and 2008 who were questioned about loneliness (and thus focused on it), suggested that 13% were often lonely and 30% were sometimes so (Perissinotto, Stijacic, & Covinsky, 2012). However, other research by Carstensen's group indicates that at older

ages people cull their social networks to maximize emotionally satisfying relationships (Carstensen & Mikels, 2005). Thus, while loneliness is a concern, the portrait of loneliness looks different at older ages.

7. *Exercise.* There is no question that the single most important key to ongoing health is movement. In older adults, encouraging exercise appropriate to ability is important. However, recent research suggests there may be an upper limit to the amount of exercise that returns a positive benefit. The fastest running paces or walking rates indicated a higher mortality rate for heart attack survivors (Williams & Thompson, 2014).

So, although myths about the aging experience abound, let us not carry them with us into the pages of this book. Instead, we can peek at the promise and possibility in possessing the gift of long life, one that is balanced by consideration of a spiritual perspective. In fact, viewpoints about age and aging, such as reaching for the wisdom and spiritual power of our ancestors, those known and unknown, and living in a way that respects the earth and generations to come, are also prominent narratives. Age does require physical and psychological adjustment to observable change, but it also signals a much less visible and grander opportunity for expansion and deepening through following a spiritual path.

PRACTICAL AND ORIENTING DEFINITIONS

Brief definitions will be provided here, with more expansive definitions in Chapter 2. *Religion* is defined as formal engagement in religious activity, for example, involvement in religious ritual or other forms of religious participation (Dowling, 2007). In the social sciences, religion is often viewed as a subset of spirituality (Canda & Furman, 2010), but in the theological and religious disciplines, spirituality may be seen as a subset of religion. Religion is often distinguished from spirituality by its focus on behavioral manifestations of religious belief or values and social relationships among those who hold a common faith. It is particularly salient for those in the United States who are more likely to engage in religious activity compared with others in the Western world (Coleman, 2011; Coleman, Ivani-Chalian, & Robinson, 2004).

As used in many gerontological and geriatric studies, the concept of religion is more organizationally oriented, namely an organized system of beliefs, practices, rituals, and symbols designed (a) to facilitate closeness to the sacred or transcendent God, higher power, or ultimate truth/reality and (b) to foster an understanding of one's relationship and responsibility to others living together in a community (Koenig, McCullough, & Larson, 2001, p. 18). This refers to the beliefs, experiences, rituals, and ethical code shared by a community and transmitted over time (Canda & Furman, 2010; Nelson-Becker, 2003, 2005). Physical limitations imposed by poor health may lead to the declines seen in attendance at religious services among the oldest old. A further issue that may affect religious attendance of older people in adverse ways concerns the social-psychological context. Issues of guilt and challenges to a former identity, if an older person's circumstances and identity shift, can lead to fears about lack of acceptance. Familial constraints involving multifaith families may also serve as a limiting factor. Or, sometimes older people may simply feel they have outgrown faith community. On the other hand, pursuit of faith-based sources, such as prayer, scriptural text reading, and electronic religious media such as TV and radio may satisfy spiritual needs at home. Assisted living and nursing care facilities may provide onsite services or transportation to religious services, which also mitigates the decline in actual religious participation, even if formal attendance falters.

Spirituality in helping professions has a broader orientation and includes relationships with entities that are considered sacred, such as God/Universe/Higher Power, nature, or ourselves. People are viewed as relational beings with an underlying spirituality, though this is not acknowledged by everyone. Spirituality may include whatever is important in an individual's worldview, so it can expand to include deceased relatives, angels, guides, and other energies and forces determined by cultural background and personal belief (Nelson-Becker & Canda, 2008). The quest for meaning and purpose and to determine and achieve right action form two important aspects of spiritual development. Spirituality is not limited to alignment with theistic belief; it also may be subsumed in atheistic, nontheistic, panentheistic, polytheistic, animistic, mystical, and other conceptual and heart-centered structures.

PORTRAIT OF RELIGION AND AGING IN THE UNITED STATES

Roughly 84% of older adults from ages 60 to 69 who reside in the United States have reported maintaining membership in Christian religions, with an additional 5%

Religious Attendance by Percentage and Number	Age in Years					Missing	TOTAL
	18–24	25–34	35–44	45–64	65+		
More than once a week	11.9%	13.0%	10.8%	14.1%	18.5%		13.8%
	42	66	62	148	98	5	416
Once a week	18.5%	24.0%	25.1%	27.2%	31.8%		26.0%
	65	122	144	286	168	7	785
Once or twice a month	22.4%	16.9%	17.4%	14.4%	12.3%		16.0%
	79	86	100	151	65	3	481
A few times a year	19.6%	17.5%	21.6%	18.1%	11.9%		17.7%
	69	89	124	190	63	6	535
Seldom	17.6%	16.9%	18.3%	16.4%	12.3%		16.3%
	62	86	105	172	65	8	490
Never	9.7%	11.6%	6.3%	8.8%	11.0%		9.3%
	34	59	36	93	58	5	280
Don't know/Refused	0.3%	0.2%	0.5%	1.0%	2.3%		0.9%
	1	1	3	11	12	6	28
TOTAL	100.0%	100.0%	100.0%	100.0%	100.0%		
	352	509	574	1051	529	40	3015

Table 1.1 Religious Attendance by Age (Data from the Religion and Public Life Survey, 2007)

reporting membership in other world religions such as Islam, Hinduism, and Buddhism (Pew Forum on Religion & Public Life, 2007). These percentages increase slightly for adults aged 70 and older. Of Americans who are 65 and older, slightly more than half (53%) attend church weekly. Table 1.1 shows religious attendance by age from the Religion in Public Life Survey (Pew Forum on Religion & Public Life, 2007).

Moreover, 90% of Americans report believing in God, while 80% report a belief in the afterlife (Pew Research Center, 2009). Table 1.2 provides data from the Religion in Public Life Survey (Pew Forum on Religion & Public Life, 2007) on belief in God or a Universal Spirit. As can be noted, this does not vary widely across age cohorts, with 92.6% of those 18 to 24 in agreement, compared to 94.5% of those 65 and over. Fifty-nine percent of Americans express belief in God with no doubts. Atheism is still very rare in the United States, at about 3% of Americans in 2012 (NORC at the University of Chicago, 2013). A third important variable is importance of religion. According to the same study (Pew Forum on Religion & Public Life, 2007), 69% of adults aged 65 and older report that religion is very important to them; that differs from the 45.7% of those 18 to 24 who name religion as very important (see Table 1.3, Importance of Religion by Age). A similar question asking about the importance of spirituality was not provided in this survey.

This affirms a level of religiousness in the United States that is greater than that of several other Western countries, including Germany, France, and Great Britain (Greeley, 2001). These patterns of religious activity are dynamic and changing in response to variations in ethnic and racial composition. On the Association for Religion Data Archives website (ARDA, n. d.), for example, it is possible to compare changes in denominational affiliation in the United States overall and by county for 236 world religions between 1990 and 2010, although some modifications in how particular denominations have reported numbers of adherents need to be considered in conducting these comparisons. Those who self-identify as Protestant now represent

Table 1.2 Belief in God (or a Universal Spirit) by Age (Data from the Religion and Public Life Survey, 2007)

Belief in God by Percentage and Number	Age in Years						
	18–24	25–34	35–44	45–64	65+	Missing	TOTAL
Yes	92.6%	93.3%	94.1%	95.2%	94.5%		94.3%
	327	474	539	1000	500	31	2840
No	5.4%	5.3%	3.7%	2.8%	2.5%		3.6%
	19	27	21	29	13	1	109
Other	0.3%	0.6%	0.5%	0.4%	0.8%		0.5%
	1	3	3	4	4	1	15
Don't know/Refused	1.7%	0.8%	1.7%	1.6%	2.3%		1.6%
	6	4	10	17	12	7	49
TOTAL	100.0%	100.0%	100.0%	100.0%	100.0%		
	353	508	573	1050	529	40	3013

Table 1.3 Importance of Religion by Age (Data from the Religion and Public Life Survey, 2007)

Importance of Religion by Percentage and Number	Age in Years						
	18–24	25–34	35–44	45–64	65+	Missing	TOTAL
Very important	45.7%	60.0%	60.4%	61.0%	71.1%		60.7%
	161	305	346	640	376	19	1828
Somewhat important	32.4%	21.5%	26.0%	25.2%	18.3%		24.4%
	114	109	149	265	97	9	734
Not too important	13.1%	10.8%	8.6%	7.6%	4.3%		8.4%
	46	55	49	80	23	2	253
Not at all important	7.7%	7.7%	4.7%	4.5%	4.9%		5.5%
	27	39	27	47	26	5	166
Don't know/Refused	1.1%	0.0%	0.3%	1.7%	1.3%		1.0%
	4	0	2	18	7	5	31
TOTAL	100.0%	100.0%	100.0%	100.0%	100.0%		
	352	508	573	1050	529	40	3012

49.3% of the U.S. population, while increasing numbers of Latin American and other immigrants have contributed to growth in the number of Catholics (now at 24.9% of the U.S. population; Dillon & Wink, 2007; Wuthnow, 1998; NORC at the University of Chicago, 2013). The General Social Survey (GSS) has been tracking changes in the religious landscape since 1972. More Americans report now that they have no religious preference than in previous surveys. In 2012, about 20% of American adults reported no religious preference, and this trend has accelerated since 1990 (GSS, 2012). However, this decline in people who identify with an organized religion does not indicate a decline in conventional religious belief. Although the data are given across all adults, they suggest that belief in God remains high while formal religious participation is falling off. Still, individual religious participation, sometimes described as private prayer, remains a significant activity for older persons. To a question asking what activities adults 65 and older complete on a daily basis, 76% reported praying (Pew Forum on Religion & Public Life, 2007). This ranked behind four other activities: talking with friends or family (90%); reading a magazine, newspaper, or book (83%); taking prescription medication (83%); and watching more than one hour of TV (77%).

Beliefs about religion vary even within the same tradition. It is helpful to recall that people have many reasons for joining a religious faith, and these reasons can include such aspects as geographic proximity, programs for social justice, or social connections (and sometimes status) that have little match with particular beliefs. Likewise, sometimes people's spiritual and religious beliefs evolve substantially, yet they choose to remain in their tradition. While individual beliefs evolve, the interpretation of beliefs and values in the larger polity may also develop, either in the same or a different direction. Sometimes this developmental process can be a result of cultural changes in the broader society. For instance, in 1975, the General Synod of the Anglican Church of Canada (ACC) passed legislation enabling women to be ordained as priests; the Reform movement in U.S. Judaism ordained its first female rabbi in 1972. Although seemingly occurring in the 1st-century Christian church (Phoebe is noted as a deacon and Thecla, who traveled with Paul, may have been an apostle), there have also been examples of women holding religious office in earlier times and cultures. Lysimache was a priestess of Athena in ancient Greece, and women served as oracles, such as Pythia who interpreted the will of the deities. Women now serve as priests, ministers, and rabbis in many—though not all—Christian and Jewish denominations. For many religious bodies, such as Catholicism, the ordination of women remains controversial. Indeed, some denominations have lost membership over this sacramentalized leadership.

Although belief is an important aspect of religion, as suggested above, religion also involves other important aspects, such as social connection, acceptance, common goals for social engagement, and programs for those who are poor. The Beliefnet website (see Websites at the end of chapter) offers a Belief-O-Matic quiz that asks 20 questions about religious concepts such as the nature of God, the afterlife, human capacities, and other issues. Response items are very detailed and make clear distinctions. According to responses given, respondents are provided a religious group (or none) that most closely aligns with their beliefs. In my course on spirituality and aging, I invited students to take this quiz and advised the class about the result. Among twelve mostly social work students, six were ascribed to Unitarian Universalist, two were secular humanist/atheist/agnostic, one Catholic student aligned with Mormonism, one was Conservative Christian, one was Orthodox Quaker, and one was a Liberal Quaker. This diversity led to many respectful and interesting discussions throughout the semester, from which everyone benefited.

THE DEMOGRAPHICS OF OLD AGE

Those 65 and over represent 13.3%, or 41.4 million, of the U.S. population (an 18% increase since 2000) and are expected to grow to 21% of the population by 2040. Projections indicate that they will more than double to 92 million by 2060 (Administration on Aging [AoA], 2012). Persons reaching age 65 have an average life expectancy of an additional 19.2 years (20.4 years for females and 17.8 years for males). Thus, the greatest increase in the U.S. population will be among those age 85 and older. Further, there will be large increases in very vulnerable groups, such as the oldest old living alone, especially women, nearly half of whom now live alone; elderly racial minorities living alone who have no living children; and unmarried elderly persons with no living children or siblings (AoA, 2012). There is a need to understand and develop both formal and informal supports that will be accepted by this older group. Thus, spirituality and religion, already a key part of life for many aged persons, will likely play a role for continuing generations who slip into old age.

As with definitions of religion and spirituality, it is helpful to reflect on the term *aging* or *old age*. Generally, the meaning of old age is socially constructed. Aging is relative, and what *old* means changes as one moves through time. *Chronological aging* refers to aging that uses distance from birth as a marker. However, because people age differently depending on genetic composition, health habits, gender, and other variable factors, the term *functional aging* addresses the abilities people have at different points in time that could reinforce a plan for independent living or, in contrast, establish need for living in a congregate setting with supportive health assistance, such as a nursing care facility. As people become older, biological aging does lead to increased risk of frailty.

Three categories identified by Bernice Neugarten (1974) in the 1970s defined ranges of older adulthood. Young-old included people age 65 to 74, middle-old included people age 75 to 84, and 85 and older was considered the oldest-old category. Today more individuals are living to 100 and beyond as the group of centenarians steadily increases. Although the UN has no established definition for old age, generally an age 60 or over was considered old in developing countries and was tied to receiving retirement benefits, though developing countries would often define aging by altered social roles. A survey conducted by the Pew Research Center (2009) of 2,969 older and younger respondents suggested that the average beginning of old age was 68, yet in respondents ages 65 to 74, only 21% reported they felt old. In respondents 75 and older, 35% reported feeling old.

In view of the above considerations, what is the most respectful way to refer to people on the right-hand side (upper x axis) of the aging and health curve? A nonrandom Internet survey by NPR from May 19–28, 2014 led to 2,657 responses (Montagne, 2014). As with the variability in older persons themselves, there was no consensus. The preferred terms were *older adult* (42%), *senior* (32%), and *elder* (31%). Least-preferred terms were *geezer* and *geriatric* (both 71%), followed by *old-timer* (64%), *our seniors* (63%), and *silver tsunami* (55%). The result is that those who age successfully have survived, and survival alone is something to be celebrated.

INTERSECTIONALITIES AMONG SPIRITUALITY, GENDER IDENTITY, AND OLDER AGE

We are now more deeply aware that individuals carry many kinds of identities, which intermingle in ways specific to that individual. For instance, an older person who is disabled and a member of a particular cultural or ethnic group may express his or her spirituality in a certain manner. Often this expression is shaped by patterns of oppression or acceptance in the larger community. The idea of intersectionality emerged from revisionist feminist theory that challenged the idea of gender as the organizing principle of life.

Intersecting social identities come to the foreground in work with older persons who may be lesbian, gay, bisexual, transgender, or gender nonconforming (LGBT-NC). Multiple levels of oppression affect their experience of aging. If LGBT-NC persons have been participants in a religious faith community, it is likely they have had to hide or suppress their gender identity to avoid marginalization or even religious persecution. If they are persons of color, members of the LGBT-NC community, and members of a minority or world religion, then they may feel or be thrice-marginalized.

Orthodox religions have been traditionally unwelcoming to people who are openly LGBT-NC, basing this position on a narrow interpretation of religious text, although other religious faiths have been affirming. "Sacred religious texts have been used as weapons to legitimize harm, ostracism, and make claims about one's lack of worthiness to engage the divine and supportive religious community" (Nelson-Becker & Sangster, 2015, pp. 8–9). Religious rejection has led to disillusionment by many in the LGBT-NC communities and some have abandoned traditional religious pathways. LGBT-NC individuals, in a large measure, have experienced a sense of religious loss; however, older adults, especially those aging with HIV, often find value in their spiritual and religious identities (Brennen-Ing, 2013; Fredriksen-Goldsen, 2011; Vance, Brennan, Enah, Smith, & Kaur, 2011).

Gender identity is a person's deeply felt, inherent sense of being a woman, man, blend, or alternative gender (Institute of Medicine, 2011). A few older individuals have tried to bury their gender variance from themselves, leading to great spiritual struggles throughout life. Current American Psychological Association practice guidelines recommend the need for trans-affirmative practice that is respectful, aware, and supportive of those who identify as transgender (Anderson & Kazak, 2015; Porter, Ronneberg, & Witten, 2013). Transgender older persons participate in a wide variety of religious and spiritual practices, having moved generally to a different spiritual or religious affiliation as they have transitioned identity (Porter et al., 2013). Reconciling a nonheteronormative sexual identity and a spiritual identity remains challenging for older persons.

A BRIEF HISTORY OF SPIRITUALITY ACROSS DISCIPLINES

The stance of academic professional disciplines toward religion has had a varied course from the last part of the 19th century across the 20th century and into the 21st. To a large extent, this has mirrored the inconsistent and conflicted relationship of North American society toward religion, even as the official political position has been one of separation between church and state. In early periods of the late 19th century and beginning 20th century, when some of these disciplines were developing as coherent educational programs, spirituality would have been subsumed within religion if it was seen as separate at all, so *religion* is the more precise historical term. However, in the current postmodern era, spirituality has the wider resonance across cohorts.

The mental health disciplines subscribe deeply to evidence-based research and research-informed practice. Therefore, the interlocutions between science and religion/spirituality matter. Francis Bacon insisted on employing an empirical approach to knowledge and testing propositions experimentally. Newton suggested that we lived in a clockwork universe designed and sustained by God. For them, science, nature, and religion were not incompatible. Nonetheless, there are at least four approaches to the relationship between science and religion, which are described by Barbour (2000) as conflict, independence, dialogue, and integration. The *conflict* position, emerging in the 18th-century Enlightenment period, regarded religion as an obstacle to reason and natural philosophy, known as science. At the same time, those with strong religious positions maintained that science held an incomplete knowledge. The *independence* position was a vista of separation: science and religion had two different authorities and neither could explain the other. The *dialogue* position held that both science and religion, while separate, have the potential to inform and enrich each other in an interactional manner. Finally, in the worldview of the *integration* position, religion is embedded in all human experience and thus is harmonious with science, even if all answers have not yet been discovered. These differing positions offer subtle, and sometimes unrecognized, influence in practice today.

History of Spirituality in Social Work

From the mid-20th century up until 1960 in the United States, there was very little interest in and research on the ways spiritual and religious concerns either facilitated or hindered an aging person's search for and achievement of a satisfying quality of life. Although never completely absent in social work, the field of religion and any formal relationship to social work had fallen out of favor. A few studies did emerge in the medical, social, and behavioral sciences, especially psychology (see Allport, 1950; McFadden, 1995, 1996, 2015; Wulff, 1997), but academic disciplines typically avoided this area. Religion and spirituality were considered to be less amenable to empirical validation, other than investigating people's sociological habits in religious affiliation and practice such as prayer. There were, however, some ongoing trends. Abraham Maslow wrote about religion, values, and peak experiences in his 1964 book of the same name. He contemplated the attributes of individuals that could result in their highest expression of self. Although he has been linked with humanism, his work moved solidly into spiritual considerations with its focus on searching for the sacred in the ordinary and his development of a holistic way of thinking.

Social work had religious roots in the late 19th century in two compelling but competing organizations founded by contemporaries born in Illinois: Mary Richmond and Jane Addams. The Charity Organization Society, under the direction of Mary Richmond, consisted partly of visits by *friendly visitors*, also known as caseworkers, to those in poverty with a goal of improving their lives. Religious values were motivating factors, though socioeconomic conditions were more often direct reasons for poverty than assumptive individual deficits. One of Richmond's books, *Social Diagnosis* (1917), developed a foundation and principles for the social work profession and sought to ground the profession in the scientific method observed in medicine.

The settlement house movement was established in the United States by Jane Addams from her visit to Toynbee Hall in London and her travels in Europe. At Toynbee Hall, volunteers, who were usually from a higher social stratum than those with whom they worked, sought to engender social reforms that would reduce disparities, poverty, and other disadvantages. In expressive language, Addams tells of her dream "to build a cathedral of humanity capacious enough to house a fellowship of common purpose" (Addams, 1910/1981, p. 71). Hull House in Chicago, which Addams managed, was one of the most well-known and successful examples. Addams, also the winner of the Nobel Peace Prize in 1931, was a trailblazing pioneer for immigrant integration, education, and employment, as well as local public health needs such as better treatment of sewage and improved factory conditions. Both the Charity Organization Society and the settlement houses were founded on the need for social reform and motivated by Christian values of the era.

Social work in the early 20th century moved to align itself with behaviorism and greater empiricism, causing it to distance itself from its early religious values. In an address to social workers at the University of Chicago in 1980, Martin Marty, a Lutheran historian and professor, called on social work as a profession to return to its religious roots and recapture what might be important for modern times (Marty, 1980). Edward Canda explored religious values of social work professors in his 1986 dissertation, and this led to his career focus on the value of spirituality and religion in social work. Other scholars of spirituality, religion, and social work have followed his lead; further, many social work scholars not otherwise focused in this area now include questions on religion and spirituality in their research because of their value.

Three associations in social work have lent support for attention to spiritual issues. The Society for Spirituality and Social Work (SSSW) was founded in 1990 by Dr. Edward Canda to promote connections among people holding diverse spiritual perspectives. An implicit goal is to help social workers and others understand and develop spiritually sensitive practice. A related organization founded in 2002 is the Canadian Society for Spirituality and Social Work (CSSSW). These two organizations share conference leadership and host alternately as the North American Conference on Spirituality and Social Work. A third organization, the North American Association of Christians in

Social Work (NACSW), dates from 1956 and is more narrowly designed to "integrate the Christian faith with spirituality." It also hosts a convention, promotes publications, and disseminates other resources.

History of Spirituality in Nursing

Spirituality in nursing traces its origins to ancient times and had a strong connection to religion (Paley, 2008a, 2008b). Florence Nightingale believed that a model nurse should take inspiration from both professional and religious callings. Although affiliated with the Church of England, she valued the contribution of Eastern religions. She also wrote that "Spirituality is intrinsic to human nature and is our deepest and most potent source for healing" (Macrae, 1995, cited in O'Brien, 2008, p. 45). In the 1930s and 40s, acceptable nursing practice included reading the Bible to interested patients; however, as nursing became a profession, everything that could not be subjected to scientific inquiry was seen as illusion. In the mid-1950s, spirituality began to be uncoupled from religion and boundaries between what was spiritual and nonspiritual grew murky. In fact, the concept of spirituality began to be seen as universal and stretched to the point that discussion of meaning and values was captured under the term *spirituality*.

The advance of spirituality in nursing in the 20th century somewhat paralleled that of social work, moving from early embeddedness, to greater distance, to later inclusion of spiritual viewpoints in the last two decades. Scientific inquiry, technology, education, and research were viewed as being of paramount importance (Barnum, 2006; Johnson, Tilghman, Davis-Dick, & Hamilton-Faison, 2006; O'Brien, 2011). However, in religious-affiliated universities especially, vespers (evening prayer) and other aspects of religion were included as a component of education until the 1950s (Johnson et al., 2006). Religion and belief were taught with regard to practical matters such as religious dietary restrictions. Two models developed side by side—the scientific model that addressed a biopsychosocial approach and the holistic model that more strongly embraced spirituality in the body-mind-spirit paradigm (Barnum, 2006). By the latter part of the 20th century, holistic care—especially body-mind connections—was gaining visibility and support. However, similar to the case in social work, this has not been universally adopted and some critiques have been issued about mixed or limited empirical support. The American Holistic Nursing Association (AHNA, n.d.) recognizes the totality of what is needed for healing and is particularly concerned with "the interconnectedness of body, mind, emotion, spirit, social/cultural, relationship, context, and environment" (para. 2).

History of Spirituality in Psychology

Psychology also became a distinct division of science in the late 19th century. As with other professions, its cohesiveness has been embattled and the result is pluralistic perspectives in most subspecialties. Division 36 of the American Psychological Association (APA), the Society for the Psychology of Religion and Spirituality, upholds diverse forms of research methods and interpretive frameworks in religion and spirituality. Division 36 officially took its current name in 1993, but it originated in 1946 with the advent of the American Catholic Psychological Association (ACPA). At that time this association had two primary aims, "(1) to bring psychology to Catholics and (2) to bring a Catholic viewpoint to psychology" (Bier, 1975, as cited in Reuder, 1999, para. 1). As views became less parochial, this group expanded to include other religious viewpoints and the name shifted to Psychologists Interested in Religious Issues (PIRI). After some years of debate this group was voted part of APA in 1976

(Reuder, 1999). Now, this division encourages use of outcomes and findings in clinical and other applied settings and seeks constructive dialogue and interchanges with religious perspectives and institutions. The division describes itself as "strictly nonsectarian and welcomes the participation of all persons who view religion as a significant factor in human functioning" (Society for the Psychology of Religion and Spirituality, 2014, para. 1). Most psychologists understand that the psychology of religion is not value free and operates under assumptions common to the ideological culture that may include apologetics (the defense of one's own view) and ethnocentrism (the biased judgment of other views). See Wulff (1997) for an extensive discussion.

What follows is a very brief survey of some of the key figures that emerged out of the juncture between psychology and religion. Several early proponents of the discipline of psychology (newly formed itself from philosophy) also carried religious interests. G. Stanley Hall (1844–1924) was the first president of APA and became president of Clark College. He gathered scientific evidence for the role of physiological processes in religion, leading to study on fasting and sleep deprivation. His students, Edwin Starbuck (1866–1947) and James Leuba (1867–1946), both with wide interests and achievements in the developing field of psychology of religion, studied religious conversion and whether mystical experience could be explained in terms of psychophysiological processes, respectively. William James (1842–1910) represented a humanistic tradition. Instead of seeking a representative sample as did Starbuck on his questionnaires, he looked for rare cases where religious attitude was identified as the core approach in individuals. In some ways, his use of the term *religious* more closely paralleled modern use of the term *spiritual.* Rather than reductionist, his approach was descriptive. Sigmund Freud (1856–1949) was the founder of the psychoanalytic tradition. He regarded belief in a monotheistic God as a delusion satisfying infantile emotional needs; thus, all religious belief served psychological functions and could not in itself support truth claims. C. G. Jung (1875–1961) considered religion as a source of delusion and projections of psychic processes, yet also a symbol for transformation and wholeness. Jung was considered a depth psychologist, but his views also aligned with the humanists.

In the early 20th century, the rise of behaviorism made studying religion unpopular. Proponents of behaviorism valued study of observable phenomena over consciousness. Although interest was never completely absent, Gordon Allport (1897–1967) began reigniting interest in religion with his work written in the 1950s. While focusing on immediate issues such as intergroup prejudice, Allport also held a strong interest in the effect of religion on individuals. He preferred using quantitative models to study complexities of personal and social existence, and he researched students and church members to look at religious faith in its everyday forms. He conceptualized an important distinction still in use today between intrinsic (religion valued for its inward components) and extrinsic (religion valued for its outward features, such as social support) aspects. As with other mental health disciplines, the interest in religion and spirituality has continued to expand and today there are many psychologists contributing to this field.

History of Spirituality in Counseling

The American Counseling Association formed in 1952. Prior to that, Frank Parsons's vision of counseling was primarily vocational: adapting and matching work with personal values and aspirations. School counseling evolved from the 1930s through the 1950s. In the late 1970s and 1980s, counselors moved into mental health counseling roles with the establishment of U.S. Department of Veteran's Affairs (VA) mental health centers and specialized education. Within counseling, the Association for Spiritual, Ethical, and Religious Values in Counseling (ASERVIC; Miranti, n.d.), represents interests of counselors in this area. In 1961, Catholic counselors in the American Personnel and Guidance Association (APGA) formed their own National Catholic Guidance Conference, but one with an institutionalized affiliation with APGA. In 1977, this group became known as the Association for Religious and Values Issues in Counseling (ARVIC). In 1993, the division took on its current name under the American Counseling Association as ASERVIC. Although the Catholic heritage was an advantage in providing a sustaining strength in numbers, it was also a limitation because Catholicism had been somewhat dominant. Now, that is no longer the case and this division represents many religious, spiritual, and humanistic interests.

As a proxy for interest in counseling and spirituality, Powers (2005) reviewed articles, chapters, and books published in this area of counseling. From 1879 to 1929, nothing appeared in her databases. In each decade from 1930 to 1949, three articles were published. From 1949 to 1959, 13 articles and 5 books appeared. In the decade and a half from 1980 to 1994, there were 119 publications. From 2000 to 2004, Powers found 531 publications, evidence of both expanding interest and opportunity. One caveat is that some of these articles appeared in journals focusing on both pastoral care and counseling and so were assumed to be more oriented to pastoral care. Maslow's transpersonal work, the creation of ASERVIC, and increasing interest in multiculturalism, which included discussion of religious and spiritual values, were suggested as partial explanations of this interest. Absent from her search was inclusion of the keyword *religion* with *spirituality*.

Interdisciplinary Commonalities

Subdisciplines within professional disciplines and associations that held religious interests have had to contend with concern that they might favor one religious tradition over another or evangelize. However, most clinicians perceived themselves as less spiritual and/or religious than their clients, and they were confounded about how to consider questions about spiritual suffering or religion as a resource with service users (Jensen & Bergin, 1988). Thus as more religious and spiritual issues have found their way into therapeutic sessions in diverse settings, training has become an increasing focus for practitioners both in graduate education and postgraduation. The relationship between religion and the mental health professions has been convoluted, complex, and increasingly fluid.

Across all of the mental health professions, some common elements are seen in the emergence, near disappearance, and reemergence and continuing growth of professional religious and spiritual interests. This process can be thought of in four phases: (1) *sectarian origins* for social work and nursing, and *scientific empiricism* for psychology as well as counseling, to a lesser extent (late 19th century through early 20th century); (2) increasing *professionalization and secularization* (early 20th century to mid-century and the 1970s in some professions); (3) *renewal of interest in spirituality, religion, and their effects* (mid-century through 1990s); and (4) a phase of *transcending boundaries/integration* (1990s through the present) that suggests leaping over narrow disciplinary constraints and cultivating a professional transactionality that honors everyone's work in a new manner (Nelson-Becker & Canda, 2008). This last phase might also be named *leaping limits*.

Sectarian origins suggests that both nursing and social work were founded in times when individuals were marginalized because of age, health and mental health problems, need to protect child welfare, and poverty. Philanthropic concerns and interests in social justice based on religious values stimulated development of these professions. Psychology, building on some of the claims and assumptions from philosophy, sought to explain human behavior through experience and observation. In the second phase of historical development, *professionalization and secularization,* these mostly fledgling professions moved to disidentify with religion and to gain stature through closer alignment to empirical approaches. The desire to remain a vital force in society during a time when the validity of religious faith was seen to conflict with science meant that taking the part of science was more likely to ensure survival of the profession. *Renewal of interest* was sparked by the work of a few eminent scholars, such as Allport and Maslow, publishing across professions, who understood the threads of religion and spirituality as important in human lives and thus legitimate areas of inquiry. The postmodern era suggests that transcending boundaries and collaborating across professions to discern the varying impacts of religion and spirituality can yield fruitful results. Holding slightly different lenses, each profession has a contribution to make.

Gerontology has provided a particular home for interdisciplinary inquiry and collaboration. The Gerontological Society of America (GSA) remains the foremost interdisciplinary scientific society and its interest group in Religion, Spirituality, and Aging was accepted as a formal interest group in 2003. The GSA includes anthropologists, biologists, counselors, economists, nurses, physicians, psychiatrists, psychologists, sociologists, social workers, and other behavioral and social scientists. Coinciding with horizontal transdisciplinary expansion, there has been a vertical expansion in the range of spiritual areas addressed in research and practice, such as connections between spirituality and aging in health, mental health, coping with life challenges, growth during the dying process, caregiving, collaboration with religious communities, and others (Nelson-Becker & Canda, 2008). This expansion of professional interest in spirituality and religion has mirrored increasing inquiry within the general U.S. population.

ASSUMPTIONS ABOUT RELIGION AND SPIRITUALITY

There are several reasons that providing room for discussions of religion and spirituality in the therapeutic process is difficult. As shown above, older adults are the single most religiously oriented group among all ages, but they are also usually very aware that religion and spirituality may not be comfortable to address in therapy. In my clinical work with older adults in Phoenix in the late 1980s and 1990s, I was frequently told that had I not asked the question about whether religion or spirituality mattered, patients would not have mentioned it. However, they found the freedom to talk about religion as resource or challenge valuable. Many clinical colleagues at the time would not address it because they worked for a public agency and worried about disapproval; however, my psychologist supervisor was supportive. Because of the range of the beliefs and the importance of protecting—not judging—individual belief, boundaries are also essential. The limits of these boundaries will be addressed in Chapter 3. One of the great concerns about addressing religion in therapeutic work is that clinicians who may be religious (or even those who are not) may try to proselytize (convert) others to their thinking. This, of course, violates free will and self-determination.

A second assumption may be that everyone who affiliates with certain faith traditions has fundamentalist and restrictive views when, in fact, older adults, too, may subscribe to some beliefs and not others within their tradition. In practice, local expressions of religious communities may adhere more or less closely with the larger body. If a therapist or mental health practitioner knows something about the principles of a certain religious tradition, it may or may not apply. Thus, while educating oneself generally about major religious traditions can be very helpful, it is also not definitive.

Third, some mental health practitioners may assume that many religious traditions are stifling and rigid, while most spiritual expressions are beneficial. In fact, religions are not static and are affected by time passing and by culture. Many mainline Protestant Christian communities now ordain women and some also ordain people who are LGBT-NC (e.g., Community of Christ). Spiritual groups are subject to some of the same dangers as major religious traditions. Further, people who follow their own spiritual path can sometimes misperceive reality in ways that become a danger to themselves or others. Ultimately, it is best to surrender assumptions about spirituality, about religion, and about people who may say they are nonreligious and nonspiritual, for sometimes the latter may act in concert with the most extraordinary spiritual or religious values of all.

THE LEGACY OF AGING IN MODERN TIMES

The last 15 to 30 years have seen an expansion of interest in aging, religion, and/ or spirituality. *Conscious aging* describes groups that seek to embrace aging and its potentials for both service and insight/wisdom, which can lead to expanded living. As used by H. R. Moody (2003), conscious aging stands in contrast to successful aging achieved through adaptation. Conscious aging suggests an increasing ability to be with what is as one ages and to possess equanimity. Moody (2003) saw conscious aging as a "holistic line, a pathway characterized by an increasing integration of divergent element of an individual's self, both rational and emotional, to yield a more complex structure" (p. 142). This is difficult work, however, and does not appeal to all. Another proponent of expanded opportunity in aging was Gerald Heard, who wrote *The Five Ages of Man* (1963). According to Heard, a post-individual psychological phase occurs in stage five. This signals a leap of expanded consciousness and repair of inner conflicts that leads to wisdom. Those achieving this second maturity would be recognized by society as sages. However, he assessed society to be mostly stuck at the previous (fourth) transitional age of individualism and imbalance.

Some of the key writers in this area of conscious or developmental aging include Ram Dass, Rabbi Zalman Schachter-Shalomi, Jay Goldfarb, Tom Valente (wisdom) and Roshi Joan Halifax (who teaches compassion in dying at the Upaya Zen Center). Other supporters have included Mary Catherine Bateson and Robert Atchley. H. Rick Moody, formerly education director for AARP, has written newsletters on human values in aging, bioethics, and teaching aging for many years. Retired in 2013, his plan was to complete or begin at least five books (H. R. Moody, personal communication, March 14, 2014). Rabbi Zalman Schachter-Shalomi developed a series of trainings based on the idea of "sage-ing": growing older wisely, creatively, and well. Sage-ing International is now an organization with the mission of changing society's current belief system from aging to sage-ing—that is, from simply becoming old to conscious aging. This group believes the wisdom of conscious elders is urgently needed; the goal of the sage-ing program is to support that development. Sage-ing is described as both a philosophy and a set of psychological and spiritual practices (The Vision of Sage-ing, 2012).

Huston Smith, professor emeritus and author of *The World's Religions*, wrote about his own experience of compromised aging with osteoporosis in his 2009 autobiography, *Tales of Wonder*. His life work had been somewhat directed by his birth in Dzang Zok,

China to two Methodist missionary parents. Side by side and interwoven in his small village were Buddhism, Confucianism, Taoism, folk religion, and Christianity. He became an informal practitioner of many of these, including Hinduism and Islam, but he never left Christianity. Now in his mid-90s and living in an assisted living facility, he commented that he enjoys his fellow residents, tries to do what good he can for them, and repeats a religious chant, "Jesus have mercy on me, a sinner," many times a day that for him is "better than any pill" (p. 111).

Although most of the individuals and groups above work locally and a few on a global level, there is another group of singular individuals chosen by history to live a part of their lives in very public political or social justice capacities on the world platform. This group of now-retired high-visibility volunteers was organized by Nelson Mandela in 2007 and consists of former world leaders. Called The Elders (2014), they are an independent group of global leaders who work together for peace and human rights. They are now chaired by Kofi Annan. No longer holding public office, but having earned international trust, they can act independently outside the influence of vested interests and with full integrity. Among their number are counted Mary Robinson, Jimmy Carter, Desmond Tutu, and Graça Machel. Their principle goal is to work toward peace and human rights along diverse paths consistent with their skills. Mandela summed up their mission in these beautiful words "support courage where there is fear . . . foster agreement where there is conflict . . . inspire hope where there is despair" (The Elders, 2007).

Overall, legacy need not be the known totality of what one leaves behind writ large. The danger of this thinking is that only those whose actions have been recorded in history, discovered and detailed in media, or who have garnered awards and criticism through their participation on a world stage in political or cultural processes have created legacy. Rather, legacy may be inscribed in the small gifts given and remembered, such as a grandfather showing a grandson how to hold a tool or a grandmother showing a granddaughter how to create a valued family recipe. It can be a special name bestowed or the tone of voice radiated with speech. Legacy can be given intentionally or extemporaneously. Because it is known by what is remembered, it is not always in the control of the giver. In the perceptions of the receiver, it is always present as long as the memory is held.

NEW DIRECTIONS

Internet and Other Online Interface Programs

The proliferation of online formats for connection such as Facebook, MySpace, Skype, Twitter, and other voice over Internet protocols (VOIP) have led to greater connective opportunities for older people. E-mail had its origins in a file sharing system developed at MIT in 1961 and began to be widely adopted in the 1980s. ARPANET (which sounds a bit like AARPnet, but bears no connection to AARP) is credited as being the forerunner of e-mail. (AARP is the American Association for Retired Persons organization founded in 1958 by a retired teacher which has a mission of enhancing quality of life for older adults. It has become a public policy advocate for seniors.) Increasing older adult use of computers was affirmed through a review of 151 articles published between 1990 and 2008 in 11 databases (Wagner, Hassanein, & Head, 2010). Communication and social support were deemed to be the primary uses of computer connectivity by seniors. Information about all aspects of aging, caregiving, and spiritual opportunities also reside on the Internet. Many national and local faith-based organizations have a presence there. Each chapter in this text will include some websites that might offer value to mental health practitioners or their older clients.

Although these newer formats can expand opportunities for many older adults to benefit from increased contact with relatives, friends, and other communities, some of which may be religious, there is also danger. Older people are frequently targeted in financial abuse and other scams. Many older people have succumbed to slick promises of having won a lottery or claims about a relative traveling abroad who has lost all of her money and is in urgent need of having several thousand dollars wired to her. Earlier decades brought face-to-face forms of abuse; that risk remains alongside the expanded risks of Internet abuse.

Spirituality and the Brain

The study of neuropsychological experience related to spirituality and neural mechanisms of spirituality is expanding our understanding about the potentials and processes of the brain. A number of researchers believe that the brain and body hold latent reserve capacity (Bulkeley, 2005). Essayist Michael Murphy (1992) suggests that "we live only a part of the life we are given" (p. 3). This is supported by research underway to explore brain functions and how they can be altered over time, both for therapeutic effect and for recovery from traumatic brain injury or accidents. But the process of aging superimposes additional changes to the brain that can include neurodegeneration: these changes challenge fluidity of neurocognitive processes and lead to cellular deconstruction, alongside opposite movements of cellular activity stimulated by learning. The Nun Study was a longitudinal study from 1991 to 1998 of sisters from the Notre Dame order across the United States (Snowden, 1997; Tyas et al., 2007). It was notable because the nuns had kept tests and other records from the time women joined the order and the nuns generously made available their brains for autopsy, so good data were available for comparison of factors over time. Although neurofibrillary tangles and senile plaques that are identifiers of dementia were present, many of these nuns did not exhibit features of that illness. Odds of developing dementia were shown to increase with age, but only for those with little education (Tyas et al., 2007). It may be that these nuns were superperformers and slipped into lower, but still functional, mental states as they aged. The potential of religious and spiritual practices to serve a protective effect are intriguing.

Several studies using brain scans of such diverse groups as Franciscan nuns, Buddhist meditators, Sikhs, Sufis, and yoga practitioners have been completed to map neurochemical changes using single photon emission computed tomography (SPECT; Newberg & Waldman, 2009). Results were compared to control groups of nonmeditators and nonreligious people. Some parts of the brain were activated while others become quiescent. Of note was the anterior cingulate structure of the brain that appeared to be essential for empathy, compassion, and fear reduction. Buddhist meditators and Franciscan nun study participants showed increased blood flow in certain parts of the brain compared to baseline; they could evoke God-consciousness experiences through meditation, prayer, and ritual. Separate studies by Newberg and his team have revealed that spiritual practices, even those not associated with religion, enhanced neural functioning of the brain to improve physical and emotional health. Moreover, intense and long-term contemplation of God or spiritual values seemed to permanently change sections of the brain that affected mood, perceptions of the self, and the external world. Newberg asserted that while thinking about the big questions of life that religions and philosophies typically address, the brain grew. A dualistic separation of the material body and thoughts of the mind was advocated by Descartes in his view of reality, but a holistic perspective that acknowledges the co-influences of the body and mind—and even the spirit—suggests a more functional approach for older people seeking treatment from psychotherapy and medicine. Certainly the capacity for reflexive self-awareness is one of the unique features of consciousness and what helps us all understand who we are—and how we can change if we wish.

Immigration, Religion, and Older Adults

People have immigrated to live with their families in the United States at older ages in recent years. This is likely to continue. If people have difficulty connecting to their ethnic and cultural community, then language isolation can be a concern. Along with this trend, it is likely that the numbers of older people who come affiliated with world religions also will increase. This means that the image of religion in America that has generally meant salience for Catholicism, Protestantism, and Judaism will expand to include larger numbers of adherents of Hinduism, Islam, various schools of Buddhism, Bahá'í, Zoroastrianism, and many other religious groups that most of us know little about. In the UK, this diversity has meant greater complexity and difficulty in addressing religion and spirituality in the public sphere (Nelson-Becker, 2011). However, this also provides opportunities to learn how faith can enrich as well as hinder the lives of older people.

CLINICAL ASPECTS OF LATER-LIFE SPIRITUAL JOURNEYS

We all hold an inner blueprint that diagrams and details the journey we make to become fully everything we are. However, that journey is never a straightforward path. In fact, it often twists and turns, rises, and descends or even drops at points precipitously. We achieve clarity through asking questions concerning what is our path instead of someone else's and suffering the reality of obstructions. We learn what summons us by footpath through plateau, mesa, marsh, or forest where in certain places our movements are easy, in others quite difficult. The first half of life is about learning societal rules, even laws, and forming an identity (Rohr, 2011). Further, developing security from which we can later explore and understanding the role of gender are formative tasks. Some of this is facilitated in nourishing ways by our institutions of government, education, and religion, but at some point they can each become boundaries or obstacles. In a systems view (Bertalanffy, 1969), unless we are infused by new and positive energy (Eros) we all may wind down in entropy (Thanatos). We have all likely observed people walk into a room and transform it through their laughter and inner brightness. We also witness people we might prefer to avoid because of their cynicism, criticism, and demands. In doing so we fail to see their need, much less meet it. These reactions form part of ourselves that, if we desire, we can transform.

In the second half of life, about age 50 and beyond, people have answered some of their beginning identity questions—with whom they will partner, what education or training they will receive, and what occupation or occupations they will select. Some people grow into rigidity and fail to grow out of it. In trying to achieve perfection, they are unforgiving of mistakes in themselves or others. However, as Huston Smith (2009) and Ken Wilber (2001) suggest, maturity is about drawing larger circles that contain everything that is smaller or has come before. This is where therapists can help older people connect the subparts of their narratives. Greater inclusiveness, rather than exclusivity (the ideal of perfectionism), is the goal of the second half of life. In these later decades, people may transcend the learning of the first half of life, but it is not rejected. Rather, all is included.

The great myths and legends of history are important because of their capacity to hold contradictions in relationship and to suggest we look closely at paradox. They do not often tell of historical truths, but the truths they tell are timeless. "Deep time orients the psyche, gives ultimate perspective, realigns us, grounds us, and thus heals us" (Rohr, 2011, p. xxx). Deep time is a way of speaking about an expansive view of time that unites past, present, and future elements such as psychological time, cosmological time, and Kairos (spiritual time). Here, consistent with quantum mechanics, time is not an arrow going one way into the future but is circular and recursive. At the end of life, if dying individuals discuss vivid and present time connections with deceased loved ones, they have entered deep time. By contrast, mostly we live in shallow or superficial time, which keeps us on the surface of life, dealing with practicalities of daily living, getting by. At older ages, there is always a potential to heal and go deeper. In that process of healing, environments, too, may feel the effects and respond through enhanced learning that takes the circle wider. The stories we tell to our grandchildren may just as well be for ourselves.

SUMMARY

This introductory chapter provided data on what it means to age in the United States in this decade and the volatile relationships that the mental health professions have had with this topic. It has set out a few of the current issues that will define the intersections between aging, religion, and spirituality. Finally, the chapter closes with discussion of what new things aging can open up for us in the second part of life. Indeed, the opportunity to age is a gift that not everyone receives. Whatever age you are and whatever background you bring, you can help older people to live more consciously and more fully in the life that they have.

QUESTIONS FOR DISCUSSION

1. What are some of the benefits and challenges within the changing demographic portrait of aging in the United States?

2. What are challenges to spiritual identity in vulnerable aging populations, such as those who are LGBT-NC?

3. Compare and contrast trends across the mental health professions in their relationship to religion and to spirituality. What were some of the commonalities and differences in historical connections to religion?

4. What are some reasons to be cautious in discussing religion and spirituality with older clients? What assumptions may professionals and older people typically have about religion? About spirituality? How might they be similar or different?

5. What are spiritual stories? How can we create opportunities to listen for them in therapeutic work?

6. In what ways does the growing number of aging persons suggest a need for more training and education in working with religious and spiritual issues? What do you want to learn?

INTRODUCTION TO MEDITATION EXERCISES

There are many forms of meditative practice. Some meditation styles are connected with a particular spiritual or religious tradition; some are very general and not associated with any kind of tradition at all. Some meditative practices are developed by an individual for his or her use alone. Although idiosyncratic, these can be no less effective. Through application of learning theory, we understand that some people learn best by using one type of sensory input rather than another, such as visual, auditory, and kinesthetic styles. This is apparent in classroom teaching where multiform teaching tends to have good results.

What are the potential effects of meditation? One effect most needed in our current society is stress relief and relaxation. This is one reason why Herbert Benson's relaxation response material released in the mid-1970s and generally viewed as an adaptation of transcendental meditation became so widespread: It met a growing need. Other uses of meditation beyond relaxation,

important though it is, include accessing deeper levels of information and connecting with one's truest sense of self. The purpose of this brief introduction here is not to provide background research on meditation, though some of this is available elsewhere in this text, but instead to provide experiential opportunities for students to try different kinds of practices in order to assess styles that may prove useful. A further benefit can emerge from participating in a class together and inviting students to share their responses. In my teaching, I have found that meditative exercises can have very different results among students. When they are willing to discuss their responses, it is very clear that what one student may find frustrating or difficult can be very rewarding for another. Moreover, students reported that they looked forward to and appreciated the beginning moments of this class, which often began with a meditation. Meditation can be done at the beginning or end of a class, and this text introduces many styles throughout the chapters.

MEDITATION: BREATH

This is a short meditation that can be done anywhere and often. It may be done alone or silently in the company of others. Attention to the breath can also be given for a moment at one's desk. First, one pauses to concentrate on breathing in and out deeply, just noticing the breath, relaxing into it, and letting go of all other thoughts to clear the mind. This creates space for destressing and for

change. There are many possible variations on this practice. You may breathe in and out by counting, pausing between breaths. To aid in conscious breathing, you may say to yourself, "Breathing in, I know that I am breathing in. Breathing out, I know that I am breathing out" (Hanh, 1991). This practice can produce a grateful feeling for life and for living in the present moment.

EXPLORING YOUR SPIRITUALITY: INTRODUCTION

Exploring your spirituality is a series of exercises at the end of every chapter designed to expand your understanding of who you are as a spiritual being and, at the same time, extend your spiritual repertoire. Although there are many kinds of exercises and rituals originating in different religious traditions that could be included, this text limits exercises to those that would fit under the broad umbrella of spirituality in order to help practitioners, especially those for whom this might

be like traveling to a foreign country with little fluency in the native language. The goal of these exercises is to increase presence or groundedness and present moment awareness, to offer play, and to suggest areas of creative expansion. All of this should occur within a context of curiosity. Learning to pose good questions is an art, but one that can greatly assist both ourselves and our clients. A good question can open up everything and be a fresh path to clarity.

Although most religions offer invitation to all, some religious exercises specifically build on knowledge of that tradition and would be less meaningful apart from it. Second, ethical issues can arise when knowledge is borrowed or given without permission. A caution for this is knowledge may be misapplied in dangerous ways. This can occur either when knowledge is partial or when ethical intentions are not in place. If you are a therapeutic practitioner who has a religious tradition, explore it and let it teach you all that it can. Following the mystic guides who have emerged from each tradition is often a good place to begin. A sampling of these include the Sufi ascetic, Ibrahim ibn Adham; Mohammed; the Christian convert Dionysius the Areopagite; the Buddha; Jewish mystics such as Hillel and Maimonides; Christian mystics such as Bernard of Clairvaux, Teresa of Avila, and Ignatius of Loyola; as well as many others. There are also modern mystics including Sri Aurobindo Ghose, Thomas Merton, and others living today who have chosen and shared their mystical path. Much of the mystical tradition is written and provides ancient wisdom. This wisdom offers the potential for transcendence, moving beyond the self with only the stars as constraint, and for immanence, connecting with the ocean inside your inner core.

The spiritual exercises offered here are a beginning entry to deepening experience. They are also intended to offer something to those readers who may consider themselves to be nonspiritual and nonreligious. These include those who call themselves atheists and agnostic. A positive frame for these individuals might be humanism, and thus humanists who would subscribe to a philosophy of belief in the virtues of humankind, a commonality to which most therapists would subscribe. Overall, to work with spirituality and religion in older adults it is helpful to be able to recognize their presence. These exercises are designed to help the reader see the spiritual side of life by exploring a few of its features for themselves.

EXPLORING YOUR SPIRITUALITY: BASIC QUESTIONS

The following questions are offered for self-reflection:

1. What is the greatest source of meaning in your life? Describe it. How do you contribute to this source and draw from it?

2. Do you believe in God, a Sacred Source, a Higher Power, or a Transcendent Power? If yes, try to describe this force. If no, try to describe what you do believe about the foundations of the universe.

3. Have you ever had an experience beyond your ordinary experience or an experience where suddenly all life became vibrant and colorful? Try to draw or form something about this experience, either in a representational or nonrepresentational (abstract) way. Use colored pencils, watercolors, modeling clay, or any other available medium.

4. Are you a member of any religious or spiritual group? If so, how does it add to your life or disturb you?

5. What are the sources of nourishment in your life? Discuss your connections with the natural world, friendships, or other aspects of daily life that give you a sense of peace and place in the world.

6. What does your level of physical health mean to you? In what way do you take it for granted, or does it affect how you function in life? What spiritual significance does it have, if any?

The following questions related to continua are for both self-reflection and action:

1. Think of religion and spirituality together at one end of a continuum of what gives meaning to your life. The other end can be anchored in what you define as generating your highest meaning. This latter end can be principles like love, hope, beauty, peace, goodness, or people such as family or friends, or anything else that encourages you to get out of bed each morning. Where would you place yourself on this continuum

today? At a specific time of your choosing in the past?

2. Imagine a second continuum or axis with religion at one end and spirituality at the other. Again, consider where you would place yourself on this continuum. Perhaps you would not be on it at all. Where would your place be? There is certainly a place for you.

3. Imagine a third continuum, this one representing where you are today compared to your religious and spiritual belief system at age 8. This continuum may be short or long, depending on the amount of space you want to place between yourself and your earlier beliefs. Where would you see yourself?

If you would like to do so, draw the three separately on a sheet of paper, writing your name, the place, and date. If you are in a group where trust has been established, you might do this together for each continuum and discuss, using your bodies as the markers. I have done this in a classroom by asking people to line up along the four walls according to anchor points set for all.

EXPLORING YOUR SPIRITUALITY: CONNECT WITH NATURE

Many of us live in cities and have begun to lose our connection to nature. Although the natural world is still around us, it may become invisible in the press of demanding and eventful lives. However, immersing ourselves in the natural world, soaking in all that is present to our senses there, has a capacity to nurture us deeply.

1. First, determine what your need is right now. What is it that you are missing? To learn this, you might try stilling your thoughts. See what image or idea comes up.

2. Spend time outside. It may include taking a short walk, hanging laundry and feeling the breeze in your face, or watching the squirrels or rabbits play. Smell the fragrance of fresh rain or newly mowed grass. Touch a tree and try to listen for what it tells you. Capture this tree wisdom in your imagination and try to hear what it would say.

3. Let the colors of the outdoors pop for you. Listen for the music of birdsong and imagine what you hear in it. (At https://www.allaboutbirds.org/how-to-listen-to-bird-song-tips-and-examples-from-the-warbler-guide/ you can learn what to listen for in distinguishing different bird species.)

4. If you have a garden or houseplants, notice what you enjoy about nurturing and caring for them either indoors or outside. What are the differences? How do the different seasons of the year affect your gardening?

5. What do you, in turn, return to the natural world? How do you try to live in a *greener* way? What do you conserve or recycle or what will you conserve or recycle? How do you live in a way that will enhance or preserve nature connections for others?

6. What do you know now that you didn't know before this short exercise?

7. Write or journal about your experience. What learning came out of this for you?

WEBSITES

American Holistic Nurses Association

http://www.ahna.org/

This organization promotes holistic healing across body-mind-spirit distinctions. It promotes holistic health care and learning.

Association for Spiritual, Ethical, and Religious Values in Counseling (ASERVIC)

http://www.aservic.org/

This division within counseling offers resources such as white papers, teaching modules, and well-developed competencies.

Beliefnet

http://www.beliefnet.com/

This website contains a vast array of information on many different religions and life sectors. It provides information for specific religions, for broad application of spirituality, as well as how religion may affect other parts of a person's lifestyle. This website has a strong connection to religion and is meant to serve as an online safe place to explore faith.

Canadian Society for Spirituality and Social Work

http://www.stu.ca/~spirituality/index.html

This Canadian organization supports interactions between social workers interested in spirituality, makes conference proceedings and papers available, and provides notices of events of interest to its membership.

Division 36, Society for the Psychology of Religion and Spirituality, American Psychological Association (APA)

http://www.apadivisions.org/division-36/index.aspx

This division of the APA offers newsletters, other publications, and event notification.

The Elders

http://www.theelders.org/

Described in this chapter, this website details the current work of world leaders to collaborate for peace and human rights. They bring much credibility through their former high visibility positions on the world stage and their global understanding of what is needed today to build a more just environment for all.

Human Rights Campaign

http://www.hrc.org/resources/faith-positions

This site provides an overview of faith positions on LGBT-NC status within organized world religions.

Indie Spiritualist

http://theindiespiritualist.com/

This may be of particular interest to 20- and 30-somethings as it includes musings and recommendations from a punk and hardcore music aficionado with a background of addiction that often made him his own worst enemy. He approaches spirituality in an authentic way that has much in common with traditional understandings but uses a modern lens. Though this may be surprising to some, it represents an alternative way of thinking about spirituality that may be appealing to those practitioners who are grounded in pop culture.

National LGBTQ Task Force Institute for Welcoming Resources

http://www.welcomingresources.org/multifaithlinks.htm

This site provides information about welcoming resources within many different faith traditions, with links for additional resources on spirituality.

Sage-ing International: Wisdom and Spirit in Action

http://sage-ing.org/

This website is built on the Sage-ing movement begun by Rabbi Zalman Schachter-Shalomi. It is devoted to conscious aging. It names as its purposes to

- support each other in growing into the role of sage—the wise elders so desperately needed in our families, our neighborhoods, and our world;

- offer workshops and creating inspirational and educational materials;

- empower elders to serve our communities and the world;

- and invite our members and friends to be in community with each other.

The Scale of the Universe

http://htwins.net/scale2/

This website presents the universe in a scale that humans can conceptualize, both macro-and–micro levels. A scale like this can show just how significant older adults really are (e.g., there are billions of cells in your body, and all they care about is you).

Society for Spirituality and Social Work

http://societyforspiritualityandsocialwork.com/

This site connects social workers with interests in developing spiritually sensitive practices. Resources include website links, syllabi, and other information.

CHAPTER TWO

DEFINING RELIGION AND SPIRITUALITY
Professional and Practical Philosophies

In the pursuit of knowledge, every day something is added.
In the practice of the Tao, every day something is dropped.
Less and less do you need to force things,
Until finally you arrive at non-action.
When nothing is done, nothing is left undone.

—Lao-tzu

If you bring forth what is inside you,
what you bring forth will save you.
If you don't bring forth what is inside you,
what you don't bring forth will destroy you.

—The Gospel of Thomas

The thing we tell of can never be found by seeking,
yet only seekers find it.

—Abu Yazid al-Bistami

This chapter presents definitions that will form a foundation for the remainder of this text. It begins with a broad discussion intended to underline the importance of terms. The etymology of the words *religion* and *spirituality* are identified in an introductory section. The concept of soul is developed and a diagram is shown to illustrate this model. Definitions used in academic professions are given for religion and spirituality. Research data on definitions of religion and spirituality given by older adults, their practical philosophies for living, are included in the Appendix of this book. Because they all appear in practice with clients, definitions for existentialism, spiritual well-being, spiritual suffering, and spiritual care are shared. A table illustrating spiritual concerns with examples is included. Standards related to inclusion of religion and/or spirituality for the professions of counseling, nursing, psychology, social work, and chaplaincy are detailed.

The first quote above, by Lao-tzu, suggests that learning develops through revising one's understanding, adding some ideas and abandoning others that no longer apply or have been shown to be incorrect. Through this process, greater knowledge forms and one learns better how to learn. The ultimate point of wisdom is to accomplish your purpose. When all actions are directed there, no effort is wasted. One achieves a certain symmetry in knowing what to do and what not to do in everyday living. The Gospel of Thomas, through words reportedly given by Jesus, proposes that everyone is born with a goal to complete. If individuals choose to follow through with their discerned life goals, they can experience great joy. However, if they choose to do other things, they may suffer. Implicit is the idea that everyone has a unique capacity to contribute to the collective good of humankind. If that particular contribution is withheld or changed, humanity mourns the loss. The third quote, by Yazid al-Bistami, explains that spirituality and religious belief can never be proven by seeking demonstrable scientific evidence, but, if individuals set an intention to grow, growth will happen. Knowledge will arrive.

Building useful definitions of religion and spirituality is important. Although these concepts have been a part of history from ancient times, they have not always been understood in the same way across generations. They are somewhat dependent on context, yet they also inscribe enduring principles. In this way they encompass two contradictions. They convey universal truths, but they also change from professional discipline to professional discipline and from person to person. Our language is symbolic and shapes our understanding. It sensitizes us to what we look for and see, what we come to know, and how we, in turn, express our knowledge and experience. Both of these—knowledge and experience—color our understanding of religion and spirituality. Further, without a definition it is hard to measure religion and spirituality, both subjective references in an objective world of evidence-based practice.

SHIFTING FOUNDATIONS

In the paradigm delineated by Berger and Luckmann (1971), we create or see only the reality we experience and the one approved by our friends, neighbors, and society. We socially construct this reality. Thus, although many realities may co-exist, as suggested by Davies (1995), the one that is most convincing, that dominates our thinking, is the one we accept and then exercise as our operational definition (Nelson, 2000). However, there is a deconstruction that first must occur when we move into very new terrain of learning. This might take place during a mystical experience, a ritual or moment where time pauses and we encounter the sacred. There is a sort of shock or shift both when we enter this reality and when we exit. Worship, meditation, and prayer are quiet ways of entering, but there are also violent or sudden events that can thrust us across this threshold, for example when a loved one dies in a car accident and our reality changes abruptly.

This balancing on the edge is described by Turner (1969) as "liminal space." In his thinking, liminal space was like a caesura—a pause—between poetic verses or within a line of verse. It signals a period of ambiguity and change. Liminal space is threshold space where we stand at the edge of the old—what no longer completely works— waiting to step into the new. It thus denotes a space of transformation between phases of separation from former ways of thinking and reincorporation of novel and deeper understanding. It is a time that is betwixt and between, when one may no longer feel a part of the old fabric of life but feels excited, fearful, or anxious about crossing into new territory. This liminality may represent a pause between life stages, change of health status, crises of belief, retirement, or death of key friends or companions. It is a point where something novel can enter and thus is ultimately teachable space that encourages us to think or behave differently. Religion and spirituality can help older adults access foundations of meaning for the next stage of life as they face multiple challenges, but what are they exactly?

RELIGION AND SPIRITUALITY: WHAT DO THEY MEAN?

Religion and Related Terms

The etymology of the words *religion* and *spirituality* provide some context in the historical use of these two terms. *Religion* is generally accepted to derive from the Latin term *religio*. Some writers believe this comes from the words *re* and *ligare*, which mean to connect again or bind together again, an interpretation from St. Augustine (Campbell, 1988), though there are other interpretations of this ancient term. A question to pose might be, What came loose that needed rebinding? Is it about reconnection of persons to the Divine or making connections between the inner and outer self? Is it about acknowledging the rhythmic nature of life and the need to evolve and grow when it figuratively comes apart? Is it about building community? Another central word related to religion is *inspirare*. This word is Latin for *breathed into* or *filled, inspired.* This can denote breakthrough moments of creativity, renewal, or transformation when persons are motivated or remotivated to return to life with new energy. In German, the word is *Eingebung*, inspiration, or a gift being received from inside.

Many religions discuss the need for sacrifice, relinquishing something to create space for something else. Carers/caregivers relinquish their voluntary time to give physical and social nurturing to others, often family members. The word *sacrifice* emerged from the Latin term *sacrificium*, to make sacred or holy. This implies that sacrifice has the potential to be a holy act: When one sacrifices one's own desires in the service of the needs of others, there is a divine quality that emerges. There is something of *unimpaired innocence and virtue* and *spiritual wholeness* (as expressed by the definition of "holy" provided in the online Merriam-Webster dictionary) that can emerge. In this context, many older people care for each other when one member of the friendship or partnership becomes disabled. Grandparents also are likely to care for grandchildren part-time when parents manage full-time employment, or full-time if the middle generation grapples with their own difficult problems such as alcohol or drug abuse, divorce, or health assaults.

Further, one of the goals of many religious faith traditions along with psychotherapy is healing, whether that healing is physical, mental, or spiritual. Spiritual leaders, such as Jesus of Nazareth in the Christian tradition, are often described by their acts of healing, which emerged out of a ground of deep compassion for the suffering of others. The terms *wholeness, holism,* and *holy* share the same Old English root word *hal.* The term *healing* derives from the Old English word *haelinge,* shared with the cognate word *holy.* Thus, the terms *healing* and *holy* share links with words connoting to make healthy or whole. Holistic and alternative medicine seek to nurture body, mind, and spirit as a key to reducing or eliminating the effects of illness and disease. As older adults become more frail with age and more likely to manage one or more chronic illnesses, there may be a type of wholeness that emerges as they reframe their life stories and achieve an existential maturity.

Religion is known through the major influences of world religions such as Christianity, Judaism, Islam, Hinduism, Buddhism, Hinduism, Jainism, Zoroastrianism, Sikhism, Shinto, and Bahá'í, some of which are discussed in Chapter 5. In addition, there are a variety of folk religions and new religious movements. Features of most religions are laws or a set of ethical guidelines. While some religions promote strict adherence, others consider these principles for living with a range of obedience levels. Chittister, in her text *Monastery of the Heart* (2011), describes the rule of St. Benedict as a type of vision for goals to accomplish, rather than a rule for which punishment is meted for failure. The eightfold path of Buddhism is a series of principles, while the Judeo-Christian Ten Commandments are viewed more precisely as a prescribed code of conduct. Apparent disobedience cost the Israelites more time to wander in the desert, as reported in the Bible. Some religious leaders are more disposed to interreligious dialogue (Dalai Lama, 2010) and others less so. Fred Phelps of the Westboro Baptist church of Topeka, Kansas, was an example of rigidity in holding viewpoints and taking actions that cause thoughtless pain to others, such as picketing funerals of military personnel. The key issue is that like politics, most Western religious faiths rest on a continuum point somewhere between fundamental, conservative, and liberal faith traditions.

Faith

Faith is defined by Smith (1979) as an orientation and response to oneself, others, and the universe. It reflects the human capacity "to see, to feel, to act in terms of a transcendent dimension" (p. 12). Some individuals tend to use the words *religion* and *faith* interchangeably, but belief is usually seen as one of faith's expressions, and not the only one. For others, *faith* is a term that may be perceived as believing something despite an absence of proof. It can be a difficult subject because faith is used to believe something that does not offer conclusive scientific evidence, though there may be other forms of evidence provided; for example, "Faith is the assurance of things hoped for, the evidence of things unseen" (Hebrews 11:1, New Revised Standard Version).

Within certain more fundamentalist spiritual or religious groups, depth of faith may suggest a hierarchy within the group, in which those with the most faith are deemed to be higher than others on a social scale. This can suggest that more faith equals a better or a more religiously effective person. Faith is an integral part of the religious and spiritual experience; it functions as the backbone for belief. In the secular community, the questioning of faith or the lack of faith in a higher power or deity tends to be viewed as more desirable than an abundance of faith. The concept of faith can be looked at as a spectrum (Caitlin Maruyama, personal communication, April 19, 2014), such as Table 2.1.

Table 2.1 Spectrum of Faith

Desirable for Believers	Indifferent Individuals	Desirable for Secularists/Scientists
More faith	Neutral	Less faith
Evidence if available	Neutral	More evidence

Faith is required for individuals to believe something without evidence. People may feel conflicted because they may find evidence for one argument (such as the case for biological evolution) but may be taught otherwise (creationism).

Spirituality and Related Terms

The term *spirituality* derives from the Latin expression *spiritus* for vapor, breath, or wind (Canda, 1988; Elkins, Hedstrom, Hughes, Leaf, & Saunders, 1988). In Greek, the term *pneuma* denotes breath, air, and wind, or spirit and soul in a more religious context. In Hebrew and Arabic, *ruach* or *ruah* carry the meaning of spirit. Spirit is also considered to be the animating or vital force of a person. This force is known in Japan as *ki* (used in aikido, for example) and in India as *prana* (Sanskrit). The term *spirit* is thus very closely allied to the act of breathing, which is an unconscious but fundamental process. This is the reason that many meditative practices rely on intentional breathing to connect individuals to their spiritual mind. Other meanings of the term *spirit* include strength, courage, character, and soul or psyche. What is particularly striking is that this concept emerged across many cultures through history. It leads us to imagine that the lived experience of the spiritual domain was something valued and important enough to be named and articulated over space and time.

A recent study of 95 adults (not older adults) with a greater religious diversity than reflected in the normal population concluded that four ideas might best describe perceptions of the spiritual (Ammerman, 2013). These were theistic (tied to personal deities), extra-theistic (various naturalistic forms of transcendence), ethical spirituality (focused on everyday compassion), and belief and belonging spirituality (tied to cultural notions of religiosity). This expansive view could express the perceptions of future cohorts of older people.

Intersection of the two concepts. Religion and spirituality may be viewed in multiple ways (see Figure 2.1). Some people see them as completely separate areas and may consider themselves either religious or spiritual but not both. In one of my studies described in the Appendix (Nelson-Becker, 2003, 2005), older adults for the most part identified themselves as religious only. Other age groups see these as integrated, having areas of intersection or complete equality. Still another view is that religion includes spirituality (taught by one of my professors at the Divinity School at the University of Chicago), or spirituality may be the larger part with religion just a small piece, perhaps in attending religious services two or three times a year on holy days. A last viewpoint includes those who would identify as neither religious nor spiritual. Does that mean that they have no resonance with these domains? Possibly or possibly not because some of them would happily call themselves secular humanists, existentialists, or other adopted terms that privilege the value of life and the human condition. In the larger literature there have been many attempts to distinguish the terms *religion* and

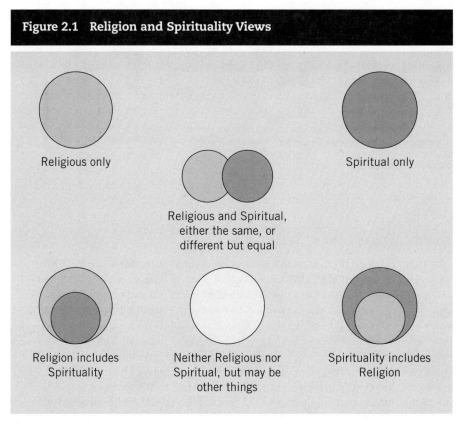

Figure 2.1 Religion and Spirituality Views

Religious only

Spiritual only

Religious and Spiritual,
either the same, or
different but equal

Religion includes
Spirituality

Neither Religious nor
Spiritual, but may be
other things

Spirituality includes
Religion

Source: Adapted from Canda & Furman, 2010.

spirituality, especially through identification of disciplinary differences (Zinnbauer et al., 1997). However, the term *spirituality* is especially complex and there is much overlap across perceived meanings.

What Is Soul?

Soul is related to spirituality, but it is a concept most people see as separate from that which is spiritual. In modern times, the idea of soul is clandestinely concealed in the word *psychotherapy*. The word derives from the ancient Greek *psyche* (breath, spirit, soul) and *therapeia* (healing/medical treatment). In Homer's *Odyssey*, the soul was depicted not as a present state but as a monument to the life once lived, a world of memories. Soul is conjectured today to be grounded in everyday life, the depth of a person or thing. It is mysterious but meaningful (Moore, 1993). Soul may be the middle ground between spirit and matter, a way of living with full consciousness and a reflective space between events in life, and our experience of them. Soul is mediator between body, mind, and spirit, and contains a heuristic element of discovery. Although some may believe that soul carries the most meaning after death, soul for those yet alive is chiefly about relationships and interrelationships in the material world. It is the interpreter of our sense receptors. Soul is invisible like the wind, but sometimes it can be perceived and heard.

In accord with Ken Wilber's (2000) idea of integral psychology, one perspective of soul would display elements containing the domain below but also transcending it. In integral psychology (described in Chapter 4), all domains include whatever is below, thus nothing is lost. Instead, everything is enlarged as individuals begin to function at higher levels. English poet and painter William Blake (1975), living nearly two centuries ago, rejected much religious dogma. He reportedly experienced visions of religious themes and advocated for the value of direct experience scripted in the following view of the soul: "Man has no body distinct from his soul; for that call'd body is a portion of soul discern'ed by the five senses, the chief inlets of soul in this age" (p. xvi). Thus, in Blake's view, knowledge for the soul comes through the physical senses of sight, sound, touch, taste, and smell. Emerson (1890) suggested, "We see the world piece by piece, as the sun, the moon, the animal, the tree; but the whole, of which these are shining parts, is the soul" (p. 165). His concept supports the inclusivity of the soul. Aldous Huxley, writing in *The Perennial Philosophy* (1945) based on the work of Gottfried Leibniz (1646–1716), submitted that the soul is

> *Something similar to, or even identical with, divine Reality; the ethic that places man's [sic] final end in the knowledge of the immanent and transcendent Ground of all being—the thing is* immemorial and universal. *Rudiments of the perennial philosophy may be found among the traditional lore of primitive peoples in every region of the world, and in its fully developed forms it has a place in every one of the higher religions.* (p. vii)

Clearly the question, What is the soul? has intrigued philosophers, poets, and others for centuries. Contemporary poet Mary Oliver (1995), in her poem *Maybe*, advises that "Nobody knows what the soul is. It comes and goes, like the wind over the water" (p. 15). The soul functions in a number of ways. It seeks to keep us rooted to the ground of our existence. It seeks to keep us connected to communities where we can thrive. Finally, it wants us to know the truth of who we are and what the world is about as we remain in relationship to it (Palmer, 2004). "It persistently calls us back. . . . to lives that are grounded, connected, and whole" (p. 34).

Meister Eckhart has said there is a place in the soul that is mystery alone.

> *There is something that transcends the created being of the soul, not in contact with created things, which are nothing. . . . It is akin to the nature of deity, it is one in itself, and has naught in common with anything. . . . It is a strange and desert place, and is rather nameless than possessed of a name, and is more unknown than it is known.* (Walshe, 1979, Sermon 144)

John O'Donohue (n.d.) adds that one's identity is not the same as his or her biography: "This [this part of the soul] is a place where you have never been wounded, a place of deep tranquility, of confidence, of seamlessness." It is a place of sheer beauty, a place of belonging and being seen. Whatever the soul really is, the concept of soul seems to carry an incontrovertible virtue. In popular literature, at least 73 text titles (as of March 2014) incorporate the word *soul*.

In Figure 2.2, the self/ego is posited as body, mind, emotion, soul, and spirit. The body is shown as the core attribute of self because stimuli from the world are perceived through the senses. The mind, which seeks to understand the position of the self, is listed next. Emotion, although not usually shown separately, is a powerful key to individual characteristics and priorities, even when individuals may not be fully aware of their emotions on a conscious level. Soul is the mediator between body/mind/emotion and spirit. The soul calls us to know and complete our life goals and tasks. The spirit, shown at the highest level, can connect outward with universal

Figure 2.2 Inner Relationships of Self (Ego)

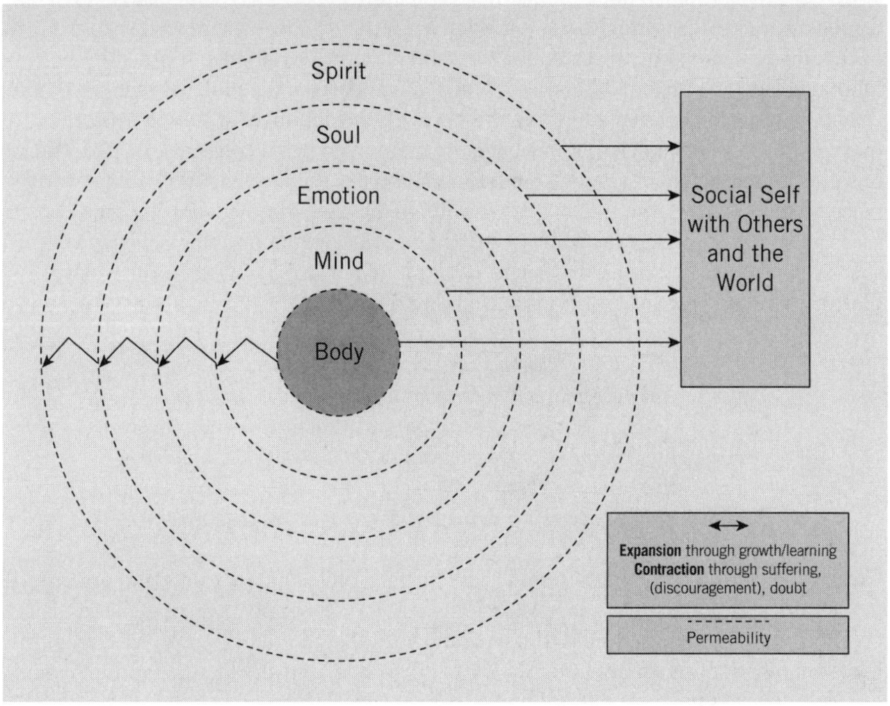

Spirit

Soul

Emotion

Mind

Body

Social Self
with Others
and the
World

←→
Expansion through growth/learning
Contraction through suffering,
(discouragement), doubt

- - - - - - - - -
Permeability

© Holly Nelson-Becker

beings, universal knowledge, or all life consistent with transpersonal theory, as described in Chapter 4.

Although Figure 2.2 is shown in two-dimensional space, it should be imagined three-dimensionally or even four-dimensionally, considering change across time. All of the components of self will, at times, contract or expand depending on life challenges met or openness to learning and growth. The bent arrows are intended to signify contraction or expansion. Each component also connects separately with others and the world in ways that either constrain, sustain, or stimulate the self to progress. The self/ego engages with the world at all component levels. Although lines are drawn to depict each component, these aspects are generally more integrative than can be shown. However, each aspect of the self shown in circular form does include the aspects shown as the smaller circles underneath.

WHO OR WHAT IS GOD?

This is not the easiest question to pose or to answer. In fact, many people including some older adults do not believe in the idea of a God or Sacred Source, a Prime Mover. With our human limitations, we cannot possibly stretch our minds far enough to comprehend who or what God may be. In fact, early cults and societies thought of her as a Goddess, the one who represents nurturance, fertility, earth, and the source of life. Early religions believed in a Goddess as the sole deity. The Greeks developed a mythology that included Aphrodite, Athena, Demeter, and Hera among other feminine forms. Hinduism continues to acknowledge many Goddesses, some as incarnations of certain deities. So God may be one entity to some people (monotheists) and many entities to others (polytheists). Descriptions of God include "There is no doubt that there exists a being, than which nothing greater can be conceived, and it exists both in the understanding and in reality," an argument known as the ontological argument by St. Anselm of Canterbury, created as a proof of God's existence (Dean, 1903). Voltaire has cited Timaeus of Locris, "God is a circle whose center is everywhere and circumference nowhere" (cited in Bowker, 2014, p. 3). Here, God is viewed as present in everything with the characteristic of no boundaries or limitations. Poet Les Murray has written that "God is in the world as a poet is in the poem" (Bowker, 2014, p. 4). How one experiences God and how one reflects about God lead to very different concepts of the nature of God among individuals. Neurobiological advances suggest that experiences of God might vary based on brain capacity or characteristics.

Humans have limited life in the world: They are born and eventually die (though, if fortunate, perhaps now at older ages). To use behavioral language, we might suggest that humans are contingent, but God is not. Exodus 3:14 states that God describes himself to Moses, "I am He who is, or I am who I am." Simply, God is. One aspect of God is *transcendence* or that which is beyond created order, functioning independently from the material universe. Another aspect is *immanence*, being fully present in the world and available to it, the *widthness* of God. Although these might seem to be mutually exclusive qualities, both are often ascribed to God, though transcendence often receives greater weight. This latter quality is similar to *animism*, a belief that a supernatural Spirit resides within all living things. The concept of the clockwork universe where God is the clockmaker who winds it up and then steps away is known as *Deism*. *Theism* shares the idea that a conscious being, present from eternity, caused all other things. The concept of God and the natural order as equivalent is *pantheism*, or God in all. *Panentheism* suggests that God is *within all creation* and there is room for mystery or for the unknown. The universe unfolds; what will happen is yet to be discovered.

What executes regularity in the universe? In the postmodern world of particle physics, the U.S. Department of Energy, Office of Science suggests that neutrinos are fundamental, abundant, elusive, oscillating, lightweight, diverse, mysterious, and even very mysterious (Biron, 2015). Perhaps that would also be a good description of God. A theoretical model of the composition of the universe suggests that 68% is dark energy, 27% dark matter, and 5% normal or visible matter (Moskowitz, 2011). Thus, most of what makes up the universe is completely unknown! If God exists, how then shall we know God? If we cannot know or understand God, then perhaps God reaches into the world to be known. These short paragraphs are certainly an inadequate description; however, this brief discussion may stimulate the reader to contemplate for himself or herself who or what God is or is not.

PROFESSIONAL DEFINITIONS OF RELIGION

For social work and other human service and practice-oriented disciplines, religion is generally defined as something other than spirituality. Although these two terms share core elements, religion is viewed as a subset of spirituality in health and mental health professions (Koenig, 2005; Koenig et al., 2001; Miller & Thoreson, 2003; Richards & Bergin 2005; Sessanna, Finnell, & Jezewski, 2007). However, in the fields of theology and religious studies, religion is viewed as the all-encompassing domain that expresses humanity's search for meaning through faith (see Browning, 1995; Paloutzian & Park,

2005; Wulff, 1997). For this text, the definitions common to health and mental health professions are preferred.

Religion generally refers to an organized faith community that shares particular beliefs, values, and traditions. Religious beliefs are transmitted over time and are often expressed in a code of behavior and rituals that open the way for divine connection and experience in the present (Nelson-Becker & Canda, 2008). Although religious faith practices may be modified to relate better to changing beliefs and contexts in modern life, there is usually a core substance that remains stable. This may be true across hundreds or thousands of years. Hinduism, for example, is an ancient faith tradition that dates as far back as 2000 BC (Hindu History, 2015). Although many religious leaders would likely prefer that adherents claim one religion, some individuals report that they follow two or more religious faith traditions or elements from such faiths as Catholicism and Buddhism (Canda & Furman, 2010; Thibault, 2009).

What sets the concept of religion apart? Religion is

- a recognition of divine power and presence;
- a set of beliefs;
- a community that shares these beliefs;
- a set of guidelines for living;
- a body of sacred texts or devotional literature;
- rituals or practices intended to bring members or co-religionists closer to ideal behavior;
- a growth and development orientation;
- a set of traditions that may include particular religious holidays or festivals, some of which may be adopted by secular culture (e.g., Christmas) as well as some culturally specific or local traditions (e.g., Diwali festival of lights);
- a story of beginnings (human origins) and eschatological endings; and
- a social justice stance that seeks to engage in the world in particular ways, sometimes against reigning political currents and sometimes in support of them, sometimes openly, and sometimes quietly through prayer or meditation.

Religion is usually valued in society because it promotes ethical behavior and participation in society in healthy ways. However, as in any group behavior, there is always potential for abuse and misunderstanding: Sometimes clergy, shamans, or other community religious leaders abuse the trust of followers. The sequelae of that betrayal are often deep and extensive, causing great pain and suffering, as well as a loss of innocence about the world and loss of assumptions that the world is a benevolent place.

Religion has a public and material aspect: Sociologist Berger (1974) identified domains of substantive, functional, and structural elements within religion. The substantive domain referred to beliefs or the creed of a religious polity. The functional domain suggests the purposes religion may serve for individuals and groups, for socialization needs, and for meeting material needs of the poor. Religious structures include physical objects such as a hymn book, communion cup, or Buddha statue as well as more intangible considerations such as the Sabbath and the ecumenical movement.

Religions and religious denominations receive tax relief from government (at least in the United States) and interface with other community structures. They often can be located in specific buildings or structures. Sometimes they have social service initiatives that provide housing, food, foster care, and older adult daycare. They have individuals who advocate for immigrants, the poor, and others whose voices are faint. Today, there are many faith-based organizations affiliated with and supported by religious denominations that through social justice approaches help to meet gaps in care for those in need all over the world.

Religion also has a private aspect. Individuals may consider themselves strongly or loosely affiliated with their chosen tradition. Some religious experiences are also spiritual ones. Spiritual experiences as detailed in James (1902/1961) have an ineffable quality. These lie beyond the power of language to adequately express and so can never be fully shared or described. However, as limited as language is to convey meaning, there is an understanding or insight that remains. When my daughter was baptized in our faith tradition (baptism by immersion at age 8), she reported later, "Something happened." The ineffable touched her. I never pressed her for a deeper description. Some aspects of life can just be what they are.

BACKGROUND OF SPIRITUALITY AND ITS RELEVANCE FOR AGING

Spirituality carries many meanings that diverge by age cohort, culture and ethnicity, and profession, among just a few variables that affect perception of this term; religion is more circumscribed in meaning and thus carries less misunderstanding or disagreement related to its connotation. Spirituality is regarded as an aspect of philosophical, religious, and existential questions (Nelson-Becker, 2006; Puchalski et al., 2009). Given the transdisciplinary context of this concept, common themes have been related to creating a sense of connectedness, life purpose, life meaning, and even transcendence of self (Ai, Tice, & Kelsey, 2009; Nelson-Becker & Canda, 2008). Far from stagnant or stable, spirituality may be seen as that creative refreshing element that moves us forward in life.

An end-of-life consensus working group conference, convened to identify spiritual care needs, suggested that spirituality is the way that people "seek and express meaning and purpose and the way they experience their connectedness to the moment, to self, to others, to nature, and to the significant or sacred" (Puchalski et. al., 2009, p. 887). Central to definitions of spirituality across monotheistic faiths is a sense of deep connection or interconnectedness, referring to a profound relation with a significant entity in life, that bestows all-encompassing purpose and meaning, whether religious or secular (Ai et al., 2009; Nelson-Becker & Canda, 2008). However, it is important to note that the nature of a significant entity or transcendent interconnection, sometimes called the sacred, varies broadly between individuals. As indicated above, the interpretation is affected by culture, ethnicity, and time.

Pargament and Mahoney (2005) suggested the individual meaning of sacred matters is essential for understanding older adult perceptions of religion and spirituality. A particularly significant aspect of the sacred is the "process through which aspects of life are perceived as having divine character and significance" (p. 183). Emile Durkheim (1915/2008), as well as many theologians since, have paradoxically related the idea of the sacred to both immanence and transcendence. *Immanence* of a sacred force implies it lies within the natural world of forest, rock, sky, and sea as well as within the immediacy inherent in difficulties and joys of daily life. *Transcendence* of god/spirit/

universal force implies it is above or beyond ordinary limits. It resides in the cosmic universe and is that which unites all living beings. In this light, deep connection, which is often viewed as the core of spirituality, can be seen as undergirding diverse individual perspectives (Nelson-Becker, 2003). For some individuals, the concept of what is spiritual could be stretched further to a philosophical secular context, such as in Confucianism or Daoism, as in the quote at the beginning of this chapter by Lao-Tzu, the 6th-century founder of Daoism and author of the Dao De Ching (Lao-Tzu & Mitchell, 2008). How individuals choose to ascribe meaning to their everyday and larger life experiences is often attributed to spirituality, though it could be attributed to humanism, existentialism, or another philosophical view.

When older adults face losses of physical health, ability, and of their ideal self, they enter a transformation process that involves those in their immediate social context. They have the opportunity to be changed: to share courage and grace or to encounter spiritual distress and despair. These issues are often highlighted in medical decision making. Sacrifice, as mentioned above, implies that giving up something, such as a former view of the self, and living fully into one's current reality can constitute a sacred act. Accordingly, exploration of spirituality with clients should include activities and practices associated with religious traditions and belief systems, but it also should include nourishing practices important to persons who do not engage in formal religious activities (Puchalski et al., 2009).

Spirituality has been identified as an essential component in care of those who are seriously ill and/or dying. For example, the biopsychosocial spiritual model of care for hospice developed by hospice pioneer Cicely Saunders, and in more recent times Sulmasy (2002), includes spirituality. This model suggests that an integrative approach to care can promote healing beyond the standard medical response to physical suffering alone. Research has found that a sense of meaning and purpose in life, supported by spirituality, tends to be related to lower death anxiety, death avoidance, and depression and greater subjective well-being (Ai & McCormick, 2009; Koenig et al., 2001). In a similar fashion, individual actions related to spirituality—which include investing in sacred matters, protecting and preserving sacred aspects of life, and drawing on sacred resources—are important means of coping with the challenges posed by serious illness and impending mortality. Although extensive efforts have been made to integrate spirituality into hospice and palliative care settings, spirituality also needs to be supported within the range of settings where people face life-limiting illness across the lifespan—such as their home environments—and among people with varying forms of spiritual and religious expression especially represented through culture (Chow & Nelson-Becker, 2011).

Defining Spirituality Across the Professions

The mental health and health professions of counseling, nursing, psychology, social work, medicine, and family therapy have all begun to address the importance of training practitioners to assist or properly refer clients who have religious and/ or spiritual concerns (cf. Barnum, 2011; Canda & Furman, 2010; Faiver, Ingersoll, O'Brien, & McNally, 2001; Frame, 2003; O'Brien, 2008; Paloutzian & Park, 2005; Puchalski et al., 2009; Spilka, Hood, Hunsberger, & Gorsuch, 2003; Van Hook, Hugen, & Aguilar, 2001). Nursing has produced films and other training materials related to discussion of spiritual issues with patients (McEwen, 2005). The Council on Social Work Education (CSWE) has responded by requiring content regarding spiritual and religious diversity to be included in accredited programs of study (Prest, Russel, & D'Souza, 1999). Though studies show that most social workers received no training on these issues through their university curricula, that is beginning to change (Canda & Furman, 2010). By 2004, of the 171 Master of Social Work programs that were accredited or in candidacy status, 57 of them offered, and 7 more planned to develop, a course with a spiritual or religious focus (Barker, 2007, p. 147).

Over time, each of the disciplines and mental health professions have had scholars who have considered the psychology of religion and spirituality, the sociology of religion and spirituality, the theology of religion and spirituality, and health-related aspects. Some of these have been grounded in a gerontological focus while others have not. Some have also developed competencies (ASERVIC, n.d.). The following are definitions from the literature on spirituality

- Spirituality is the search for significance in ways related to the sacred (Pargament, 1997)

- Spirituality is an interpretive act, created by people as they relate to others in their environment over time (Cowley, 1993)

- Spirituality is a sense of wholeness, connectedness, and openness to ultimate meaning (Shafranske & Gorsuch, 1984)

- Spirituality is an innate human quality, a life force as well as an experience of that life force (Faiver et al., 2001).

- Spirituality is that aspect of humanity that refers to the way individuals seek and express meaning and purpose by connecting to the moment, to ourselves, to nature, to significant experience, or to the sacred (Puchalski et al., 2009).

- Spirituality is the unique dynamic discovery of purpose, meaning, relationship, connectedness that is the essence of the human experience (conference workgroup discussion, 2009).

Definitions specifically related to aging:

- Spirituality is not just one compartment of life, but the deepest dimension of life (Fischer, 1998).

- Spirituality is the consciousness of a relationship with the Lord, and modification of one's attitude and behavior (Fahey & Lewis, 1991).

- Spirituality is also viewed as an inner path of development where the soul helps create those types of experiences (both positive and negative) that it requires to better understand its purpose over the life course (see Martin, 2010; Rohr, 2011).

- Spirituality is a process of lived transformation of self and community with what is understood within a given cultural context to be sacred (Rothberg, 2000, p.163).

Contemporary definitions of spirituality, as shown above, thus vary across and even within disciplines. In positive psychology, spirituality is defined, alongside religion, as "having coherent beliefs about the higher purpose and meaning of the universe: knowing where one fits within the larger scheme; having beliefs about the meaning of life that shape conduct and provide comfort" (Peterson & Seligman, 2004, p. 30). Likewise, from a sociologist's viewpoint, "spirituality consists of all the beliefs and activities by which individuals attempt to relate their lives to God or to a divine being or some other concept of a transcendent reality" (Wuthnow, 1998, p. viii). In social work, spirituality is seen as the private space connecting individuals to the Ultimate, nature, or whatever else is regarded as sacred. Regardless of the unique aspects of the definitions provided above, there are also many similarities evinced through the common concept of connections.

OTHER ASPECTS: EXISTENTIAL WELL-BEING, SPIRITUAL WELL-BEING, SPIRITUAL SUFFERING, AND SPIRITUAL CARE

In discussion of spirituality with clients, related concepts also require attention. Existential views are often featured instead of spiritual or religious views, particularly when these ideas gain a higher profile, for example, at times when death approaches. Further, spirituality is related to action when people care for themselves spiritually, when they suffer, or when they care for others in spiritual ways. These concepts are addressed below.

Existential Well-Being

Existentialism is a philosophical approach in which the primary task is to find what determines meaning in life. The existential tasks of life are also allied with a humanistic approach. (See Maslow and humanism in Chapter 4.) Existential well-being relates to spirituality in the search for meaning and purpose, though is distinct from it in that one often feels a disconnection from any type of transcendent power. This may involve an anguished process in which prior beliefs no longer seem valid, and one begins a journey to find one's own meaning in life. (See the writings of Albert Camus and Jean-Paul Sartre.) One of the major propositions of existentialist thought is that existence precedes essence. One must find his or her own meaning. Meaning is often conceived in a way that is personal and acknowledges that others may hold quite different meanings. Existentialist views also may be preferred by those who consider themselves to be humanists—holding ethical views about right treatment of others and working to translate these views into action, but without the assistance of any divine being or philosophy/theology. Some existentialists may hold atheistic (no belief in a divine being, deity, or transcendent power) or agnostic (those who question the existence of god and believe that the nature of reality cannot be known) beliefs. Existential well-being denotes finding a purpose to life.

Spiritual Well-Being

Spiritual well-being concerns our inner life and our relationship with the outside world. It includes our relationship with the environment, others, and with ourselves, but the focus is on maintaining or regaining healthy balance. Although it is a state of being, it requires many active adjustments to retain.

Historically, the term *spiritual well-being* was considered at the 1971 White House Conference on Aging for the first time. A White House aging conference had been held about every 10 years since 1951 to consider topics that could benefit older people. Papers about religion were included in both 1951 and 1961 conferences, but in 1971, there was concern about a publicly funded conference addressing religion

(Ellor, 2013). Still, interest in the topic remained. One of the conference planners and a gerontologist, Clark Tibbets, had participated in developing the idea of psychological well-being and so suggested spiritual well-being as a possible politically correct term. Ultimately this was used at the 1971 White House conference in a set of papers developed by sociologist David O. Moberg (1979). Although not defined by Moberg then, a definition was provided in 1975 at a meeting of 33 religious representatives of the National Interfaith Coalition on Aging (NICA). They defined spiritual well-being as "the affirmation of life in a relationship with God, self, community and environment that nurtures and celebrates wholeness" (National Interfaith Coalition on Aging, 1980, p. xiii). Then, as now, it did not provide clear guidance for operationalizing research.

A nursing diagnosis concerning readiness for "enhanced spiritual well-being" is defined as an "ability to experience and integrate meaning and purpose in life through a person's connectedness with self, others art, music, literature, nature, or a power greater than oneself" (North American Nursing Diagnosis Association [NANDA], 2005, p. 68). Elements of spiritual well-being may include

- an enhanced desire for hope;

- meaning and purpose to life;

- sense of peace or serenity;

- surrendering to love;

- forgiveness of self and requesting forgiveness of others;

- a satisfying philosophy of life;

- joy, courage, or heightened coping;

- prayer or meditation;

- connection with others, nature, a power greater than oneself;

- service to others;

- connections with or a desire to create art, music, or literature, particularly of a religious or spiritual nature;

- mystical experiences; or

- religious activities.

Spiritual Suffering, Spiritual Struggle, and Spiritual Concerns

The opposing dialectic for spiritual well-being is spiritual suffering. Spiritual suffering may have multiple causes and expressions. (See Table 2.2 Spiritual Concerns for examples of spiritual suffering and spiritual struggle.) Spiritual suffering includes existential questions of meaning, usually in the face of concerns about failing or having failed to live a meaningful life. Further, if one holds faith in a deity, questions about why one feels abandoned by God/the Universe/Transcendent Power can be prominent. Anger at this deity, particularly if life has not proceeded as one hoped or envisioned, can cause spiritual suffering. Conflicts about beliefs may cause suffering and struggle. Ideas once held to be true may no longer seem sufficient and, for those who are attached to early beliefs formed in childhood or younger ages, it can feel like a betrayal

Table 2.2 Spiritual Concerns

Spiritual Concern	Primary Condition	Illustration
Abandonment by God/others	Expresses low level of relatedness, lack of feeling loved	*God has abandoned me.* *People don't care about me.*
Anger toward God or others	Projects anger toward religious figures or clergy, inability to forgive	*Why would God allow this cancer to come back?* *Why did she steal from me?*
Challenged or conflicted beliefs	Demonstrates inner tensions, may have conflicts between religious beliefs and suggested medical treatments	*What I have been taught no longer works for me.* *My faith tradition would not support this type of care.*
Despair/desolation	Carries sense of helplessness, hopelessness about the future	*I have nothing to live for.*
Existential concerns	Poses questions about life meaning, what will happen after death, what is the purpose of suffering	*I feel useless.* *My life has no meaning.*
Guilt/shame	Reveals an act that caused pain to someone else or a time when dishonored by another, lack of self-worth	*I am not worthy.* *I'm so sorry I hurt him.*
Isolation	Shows feelings of loneliness	*Why don't people visit me?*
Lack of faith (when faith formerly held)	Exhibits change in faith/beliefs	*I am totally on my own and I don't know what to do with that.*
Loss/grief	Feels deep sorrow with deaths of friends/family and loss of good health/home	*I don't know how to go on without my sister.* *I wish I could still walk every day.*
Relationship with God/Doubt	Does not sense God's presence, or presence of the Ultimate	*Where is God now?* *Why can't I feel him/her?*
Religious or spiritual struggle	Displays deep level of discomfort with spiritual questions which are pervasive	*Why am I feeling this way?*
Specific religious concern	Unable to practice religious or spiritual rituals that had given meaning	*I can no longer even pray.*

to grow beyond them. Absence of faith or doubt may be a very specific result of experiencing a major life challenge. Loss and the resulting grief in coping with the loss can cause spiritual suffering or spiritual struggle. Spiritual struggle denotes the stresses individuals sometimes experience when expectations and relationships are challenged or broken. There is a dynamic quality to this term: An individual may be standing on an imaginary balance beam working through the struggle to move toward well-being on one side and away from suffering on the other.

Guilt about actions that have brought harm to others can be a recurring stressor in late life. For some, shame about facets of the self that were experienced, such as sexual violence and abuse from others as victim or toward them as perpetrator, may figure prominently in suffering. Suffering may not ease, especially when individuals feel unable to seek counseling or to make public a private pain. The need to give or receive forgiveness, but inability to fully do either, can be a cause of suffering. Finally, isolation from a religious tradition, either self-imposed or through actions such as shunning—in the Amish community members will refuse to speak to those whose actions are deemed unacceptable—can cause great distress. Shunning is an organizational tool to modify the behavior of those who fail to comply with standards or to discredit or disempower them. It may occur formally or informally in religious communities. There are a number of conditions such as emptiness; holding a depleted self; engaging in workaholism; cynicism; or carrying guilt, shame, or blame, that do not meet criteria for DSM-5 conditions (explained in Chapter 6), but do represent "maladies of the soul."

Because aging is a time of visible losses as well as gains that are visible or invisible, some aging persons experience the losses common at older ages quite vividly. They have difficulty detaching from aspects of identity or what they did that can no longer be retained (e.g., physical beauty, mobility, certain friendships). Despair and hopelessness may also be aspects of suffering that are spiritual in nature, especially when they become pervasive and prevent engagement with life.

Spiritual Care

Spiritual care for clients recognizes and supports the holistic need for healing. Spiritual care involves attention to the needs of the soul for compassion—both giving and receiving love, meaning/purpose, hope, faith, and reconciliation. It involves initiating an assessment to determine if spirituality and/or religion are important to a patient and if so, including these aspects in whatever manner is requested by the client, is ethical, and does not do harm to the practitioner. In social work, the term *spiritually sensitive practice* includes a reminder for practitioners to listen for spiritual cues. Many times, the spiritual discourse has been a hidden discourse and although it may be personally important to individuals, the value of it will not be revealed unless a patient is explicitly asked (Nelson-Becker, 2003; Puchalski et al., 2009). Chapter 6 discusses spiritual assessment.

Spiritual care may be legitimately offered and provided in many contexts, such as hospitals and outpatient health organizations. Chaplains, rabbis, ministers, imams, and lamas within a client's own tradition may be good referral resources for specific spiritual problems. However, at times the first responder—the counselor, social worker, nurse, or psychologist who is present—needs to listen to these concerns to the best of his or her ability, even if the area feels foreign and uncomfortable. This occurs specifically when the need for care is immediate and critical. Spiritual suffering is one of the worst forms of suffering and can prevent an individual from fully participating in other forms of healing and health maintenance or recovery protocols.

SPIRITUALITY, STANDARDS OF CARE, AND THE PROFESSIONS

Counseling

In counseling, as in other professions, there has been renewed interest in formal training for counselors around client concerns in religion and spirituality as well as attention to self-awareness in regard to spirituality. Spiritual issues were addressed by just over half of 48 programs accredited by the Council for the Accreditation of Counseling and Related Educational Programs (CACREP) in a survey by Kelly (1997). The current CACREP standards developed in 2009 have eliminated specific wording about religion and spirituality in favor of a more general approach to multicultural trends; the standard to address "counselor's roles in developing cultural self-awareness; . . . and other culturally supported behaviors that promote optimal wellness and growth for the human spirit, mind, or body" (cited in Gold, 2010, p. 28) remains. In a survey of 220 university counselors, Kellems, Hill, Crook-Lyon, and Freitas (2010) found that those with some training in religious and spiritual (R/S) issues felt more confident in working with R/S concerns in their clients.

The importance of expanding four general knowledge domains are suggested by Miller (1999): (1) knowledge of spirituality, (2) awareness of one's own spiritual views, (3) awareness of client spiritual views, and (4) spiritual interventions. However, Young, Cashwell, Wiggins-Frame, and Belaire (2002) advise that these are not always well-addressed in counseling programs due to lack of training by faculty, traditional skepticism about the subjective aspects of religion and spirituality within a scientific evidence-based paradigm, and negative personal experiences with religious institutions. The American Counseling Association (ACA) has specific competencies on religion and spirituality developed by a subgroup, The Association for Spiritual, Ethical, and Religious Values in Counseling (ASERVIC), that are used to complement existing competencies (see Table 2.3).

Nursing

The Code of Ethics for professional nurses recognizes the importance of spirituality and health (American Nurses Association, 2004). This is illustrated in Provision 1 of the code that indicates that the nurse should practice with compassion and respect the inherent dignity, worth, and uniqueness of each individual. Further, Standard 1.3 indicates "the measures nurses take to care for the patient enable the patient to live with as much physical, emotional, social, and spiritual well-being as possible." Nurses are cautioned in Standard 2.4 to be aware of professional boundaries and their limits. "The intimate nature of nursing care, the involvement of nurses in important and sometimes highly stressful life events, and the mutual dependence of colleagues working in close concert all present the potential for blurring of limits to professional relationships." In the nursing profession particularly, nurses can become especially close to their patients in ways that sometimes make care strenuous. "Maintaining authenticity and expressing oneself as an individual, while remaining within the bounds established by the purpose of the relationship can be especially difficult." The transdisciplinary nature of the work and attention to emergent issues are key aspects of nursing.

Table 2.3 Competencies for Addressing Spiritual and Religious Issues in Counseling

Preamble

The Competencies for Addressing Spiritual and Religious Issues in Counseling are guidelines that complement, not supersede, the values and standards espoused in the ACA Code of Ethics. Consistent with the ACA Code of Ethics (2005), the purpose of the ASERVIC Competencies is to "recognize diversity and embrace a cross-cultural approach in support of the worth, dignity, potential, and uniqueness of people within their social and cultural contexts" (p. 3). These Competencies are intended to be used in conjunction with counseling approaches that are evidence-based and that align with best practices in counseling.

This Preamble must accompany any publication or dissemination, in whole or in part, of the ASERVIC Competencies.

Culture and Worldview

1. The professional counselor can describe the similarities and differences between spirituality and religion, including the basic beliefs of various spiritual systems, major world religions, agnosticism, and atheism.

2. The professional counselor recognizes that the client's beliefs (or absence of beliefs) about spirituality and/or religion are central to his or her worldview and can influence psychosocial functioning.

Counselor Self-Awareness

3. The professional counselor actively explores his or her own attitudes, beliefs, and values about spirituality and/or religion.

4. The professional counselor continuously evaluates the influence of his or her own spiritual and/or religious beliefs and values on the client and the counseling process.

5. The professional counselor can identify the limits of his or her understanding of the client's spiritual and/or religious perspective and is acquainted with religious and spiritual resources and leaders who can be avenues for consultation and to whom the counselor can refer.

Human and Spiritual Development

6. The professional counselor can describe and apply various models of spiritual and/or religious development and their relationship to human development.

Communication

7. The professional counselor responds to client communications about spirituality and/or religion with acceptance and sensitivity.

8. The professional counselor uses spiritual and/or religious concepts that are consistent with the client's spiritual and/or religious perspectives and are acceptable to the client.

(Continued)

Table 2.3 (Continued)

9. The professional counselor can recognize spiritual and/or religious themes in client communication and is able to address these with the client when they are therapeutically relevant.

Assessment

10. During the intake and assessment processes, the professional counselor strives to understand a client's spiritual and/or religious perspective by gathering information from the client and/or other sources.

Diagnosis and Treatment

11. When making a diagnosis, the professional counselor recognizes that the client's spiritual and/or religious perspectives can a) enhance well-being; b) contribute to client problems; and/or c) exacerbate symptoms.

12. The professional counselor sets goals with the client that are consistent with

13. the client's spiritual and/or religious perspectives.

14. The professional counselor is able to a) modify therapeutic techniques to include a client's spiritual and/or religious perspectives, and b) utilize spiritual and/or religious practices as techniques when appropriate and acceptable to a client's viewpoint.

15. The professional counselor can therapeutically apply theory and current research supporting the inclusion of a client's spiritual and/or religious perspectives and practices.

Revised and Approved, 5/5/2009 ©ASERVIC 5/5/09

Note: The American Counseling Association (ACA) has endorsed *The Spiritual Competencies* (http://www.aservic.org/wp-content/uploads/2010/04/Spiritual-Competencies-Printer-friendly1.pdf).

Source: Permission granted by W. Bryce Hagedorn, PhD, LMHC, NCC, MAC, QCS (FL) President of the Association for Spiritual, Ethical, and Religious Values in Counseling (ASERVIC) Program Director of Counselor Education University of Central Florida College of Education & Human Performance, ED 322C Orlando, FL 32816-1250.

Psychology

In professional psychology, guidelines and principles for accreditation are developed by the American Psychological Association (APA). Standard 3.c in the 2005 document recognizes "cultural and individual diversity" for its value in understanding client identity and behavior. Shafranske and Malony (1990) discovered that only one-third of clinicians in their survey felt prepared to discuss religion and spirituality with clients, although most thought these areas were relevant to clinical work. Brawer, Handal, Fabricatore, Roberts, and Wajda-Johnson (2002) found that 77% of clinical training directors thought these should be addressed in supervision, although 17% indicated this content was covered in a systematic way and 16% said there was no coverage at all. Only 13% of programs offered a course at that time. A survey by Russell and Yarhouse (2006) found that fewer psychologists tended to believe in God (72%) than the general population (90%), and 51% endorsed the idea that religion was of little importance compared to 11% of the general population. Of psychologists responding to the survey,

64.7% reported no training in spiritual or religious matters while 21.9% indicated these were considered under multicultural diversity.

Two APA standards that include 2010 revisions address spirituality, but in a somewhat indirect and oblique manner (https://www.apa.org/ethics/code/index.aspx). Standard 2 includes an understanding of religion along with many other cultural factors that lead to competence and self-understanding of limits to competence. Standard 3 suggests that religion be listed in the factors that should not be a basis for discrimination. Accreditation standards for APA programs (updated 2009) include "Domain D: Cultural and Individual Differences and Diversity" that suggests students should be trained in multicultural diversity related to psychological phenomena (APA, 2013).

Social Work

The National Association of Social Workers *Code of Ethics* (2008) expresses six core values: service, social justice, dignity and worth of the person, importance of human relationships, integrity, and competence. Social workers are taught to interact with others in a kind and respectful way, mindful of both individual differences as well as cultural, ethnic, and religious diversity among other forms of diversity. In the Code, Standard 1.01 Commitment to Clients addresses the need to promote the well-being of clients. Standard 1.05c indicates that Cultural Competence and Social Diversity include religion. Standard 4.01 Competence asks social workers to remain proficient in their practice and performance of professional functions, including basing their practice on recognized knowledge.

Social workers understand that relationships among people are an important channel for change and engage clients as partners in the helping process. The goal for social work is to promote, restore, maintain, and enhance the well-being of individuals, families, communities, and organizations, thus keeping a dual emphasis on the individual and his or her environmental characteristics.

Chaplaincy

Chaplains generally hold an M. Div. degree, which is usually conferred after four years of graduate seminary study including the internship (McClung, Grossoehme, & Jacobson, 2006). Chaplains complete 1600 hours of closely supervised clinical pastoral education (CPE) plus post-CPE requirements to be eligible for certification. CPE involves training in community institutions, such as hospitals and long-term care institutions, using a combined experience and reflection strategy enhanced with process recording methods often used in nursing and social work. The Association of Professional Chaplains (APC), the largest single chaplaincy group, accepts members from many faith groups. APC Board Certified Chaplain (BCC) requirements include clinical pastoral education, three years of approved theological education, ordination and endorsement by a faith group, and one year experience as a chaplain. Set standards of practice should be successfully met during that year of work (see Table 2.4).

Hospitals directly hiring chaplains now often require board-certified chaplains or those eligible for board certification. Assisting patients and others to integrate body, mind, and spirit while addressing illnesses, trauma, and other life losses is one of the key foci of the chaplain's role (VandeCreek & Burton, 2002 in McClung et al., 2006). Chaplains assist patients in dealing with difficult emotions such as anger or grief; with more unstructured time available, they can also help families and serve as advocates. Chaplains may also offer support to staff.

Table 2.4	Selected Common Standards for Professional Chaplaincy

- Articulate a theology of spiritual care that is integrated with a theory of pastoral practice.

- Facilitate theological reflection in the practice of pastoral care.

- Formulate and utilize spiritual assessments in order to contribute to plans of care.

- Incorporate the spiritual and emotional dimensions of human development into the practice of pastoral care.

- Incorporate a working knowledge of ethics appropriate to the pastoral context.

- Articulate a conceptual understanding of group dynamics and organizational behavior.

- Provide pastoral care that respects diversity and differences including, but not limited to culture, gender, sexual orientation and spiritual/religious practices.

- Provide pastoral care to persons experiencing loss and grief.

Source: American Association of Professional Chaplains, 2005.

SUMMARY

This chapter has offered expansive views of the meaning of religion and spirituality with particular attention to use in the helping professions and their standards for inclusion in professional training and practice. Further, discussion of the related terms of existentialism, spiritual well-being, spiritual suffering, and spiritual care were addressed. The reader may refer to the Appendix: Older Adult Definitions for definitions of religion and spirituality from older adults themselves. The data described there represent 79 older adults interviewed about their personal definitions of religion and spirituality, which were their practical philosophies for living.

CASE STUDY: SPIRITUAL SUFFERING AND SPIRITUAL CRISIS

Chiyoko Yamagata was a 78-year-old widow who lived in a large urban center in the Midwest. Her mother had recently died, and in her mother's papers she discovered a diary her mother had kept during her time in an internment camp in California during World War II. The diary spoke about the difficult physical conditions of living in the large camp, which had only a very small space for privacy. Both of her parents worked on projects for the state, and this supposedly paid for the meager rations and their rent. As a very young child, Chiyoko only knew that she got to see her friends often at the large dining hall they all went to for meals. Nearly all of their possessions had been left behind and later apparently sold after their forced relocation. When they were released from camps, her parents received $25.00 to begin their new life. Later in the 1970s, they did receive more from the government. Torn relationships, however, were the most difficult. Mrs. Yamagata's mother had suffered greatly because, although her neighbors of 10 years had once been very friendly, when the family was asked to go a detention center, they would no longer speak to her and became very distant. As a result, her mother suffered a great deal of shame. To her surprise, Mrs. Yamagata learned that her family had been Buddhist and also practiced some Shinto rituals along with ancestor veneration. After the war, the family abandoned Buddhism and converted to Christianity in an attempt to enhance their reputation and community status. Mrs. Yamagata never knew about this part of her family heritage. In fact, as her family worked diligently to reintegrate into society, they had become westernized. She wondered whether her parents had suffered because of this change in religious affiliation. Mrs. Yamagata was a Nisei (second-generation Japanese), but she became angry when she learned that this part of her family history had been covered up. She had always felt a strong attraction to Buddhist belief, but her parents had forbidden her to investigate while they were alive. There were some things about the Christian faith that had always troubled her, and now she wondered what other significant aspects of her parent's lives had been compromised by this unjust imprisonment. The discovery of her mother's diary precipitated a spiritual crisis for Mrs. Yamagata. What was her true spiritual heritage and what did she really believe?

Questions to consider:

1. What might indicate that Chiyoko Yamagata is undergoing a spiritual crisis?

2. What questions would you ask her if she came to you as a client?

3. What would you recommend now? How can she heal from the pain of knowing more about her family's situation during World War II, something they had never discussed with her when she was younger? Are there aspects of her culture to which you might redirect her?

QUESTIONS FOR DISCUSSION

1. What is your own definition of religion? Of spirituality? Do you consider these the same or different? Discuss with a partner in class and then engage in full class discussion.

2. Why is it helpful to consider different approaches to using these terms? Why do you believe there is no uniformity of views?

3. What is the soul, in your view? Is the idea of soul relevant in modern times?

4. Looking at the professional standards related to inclusion of religion/spirituality in training programs, what is common and different across sets of standards? Were your expectations met about their inclusion or absence? What do you see in your own professional standards, if you are associated with any?

5. This question refers to material in the Appendix. What did you learn in reading through older adults' comments about religion and spirituality? Do you think their comments would be different from or similar to individuals from younger generations and cohorts?

MEDITATION: RELAXATION, ALSO KNOWN AS BODY SCAN

You may participate in this meditation or observe if you are in a group with others. Begin with the breath, consciously relaxing as you concentrate on breathing intentionally, letting concerns and worries float away, and clearing out negative thoughts. Bring attention to the toes on the right side, squeezing and releasing muscles. Move up to the calves, the thigh, and the hip, squeezing and releasing each muscle group sequentially. Do the same with the left side. Then move to the right hand, right forearm, and right shoulder. Do the same with the left side. Then squeeze and release the stomach, the chest, the neck, the chin, the eyes and ears. Pause and then check for any areas of tension and work at squeezing and releasing those areas again. Then squeeze and release the whole body. Rest a moment before returning to the group and present time awareness. You may use this meditation with older adults as well as students.

ASSIGNMENT: INTERVIEW AN OLDER ADULT

1. Reflect on or discuss your own definition of religion and spirituality with another individual. What theorists or theologians from class materials do you draw from in building these definitions, if any? What are your own experiences that inform your definition?

2. How might your definition be similar to or different from that of older persons that you know?

3. Briefly interview an older person from your internship about his or her views of religion, spirituality, and the importance of these in his or her life. Be prepared to hear all viewpoints: that religion/spirituality is important, mildly important, or not at all important. You might ask these questions or create your own:

   a. What keeps you going? Why? What helps you wake up each day?

   b. Do you have a religious or spiritual group? If not, what is your philosophy of living? (What constitutes a good life? What has your life meant/does your life mean to you now?)

   c. How does this viewpoint influence the way you live?

   d. Do you believe in God, an Ultimate Power, or other Higher Power? (Who is God for you?) If so, what terms do you prefer? If not, why not?

   e. In what ways do you sense God?

   f. Does your religious or spiritual view include a belief in afterlife, heaven, or hell? Please explain.

   g. What does your religious or spiritual view say about the role of the family and the role of older adults? What do you think about them?

   h. Do you attend religious services? If so, how often do you attend?

   i. Do you pray? If so, how does this affect you?

   j. Do you consider yourself more or less spiritual than when you were growing up? How has your spirituality changed since you got older? (What is your religious or spiritual trajectory?) Explain.

   k. How does your spiritual view help you? Is there anything about your view that causes you difficulty or pain?

   l. How does religion or spirituality influence how you see the experience of aging?

4. Afterward, write an essay discussing how the views of this person were similar to or different from your own views. How might the views of your interviewee affect how others in society viewed or treated him or her, particularly if he or she held a minority viewpoint? How might this interview inform your future work with older adults? Your essay should follow APA format and be 7–10 pages.

EXPLORING YOUR SPIRITUALITY: OBJECTS OF MEANING AND MEMORY

Sociologist Emile Durkheim wrote about distinctions between objects considered sacred or profane. The origins of the word *profane* mean *before or outside the temple*. Although now the word is usually taken to mean something disrespectful of religion or of what is regarded as sacred, the origin of the word in middle English (*pro + phanen*) implied everything had its place: either in daily or ordinary life or the life of the temple (extraordinary life). "The sanctity of a thing is due to the collective sentiment of which it is the object" (Durkheim, 1915/2008, p. 17).

We invest objects with meaning because of the context surrounding that particular object, although objects do also carry intrinsic value. At times in classes on spirituality I have invited students to bring in an object that was particularly meaningful for them or that represented hopes for their future. Sometimes students will bring in photos or objects given them by a grandparent. Sometimes lost objects or objects of shared meanings come to us in surprising ways, as happened to one student who unexpectedly received a treasured stopwatch after a grandparent committed suicide. Another student received a set of ballet shoes from the parents of her best friend after her death. Her best friend had been a skilled dancer, and these shoes remind and encourage her of what she needs to do in her own life. Sometimes the object does not endure, as a wildflower picked from a forest walk. Sometimes a stone selected from a beach or a mesa can represent sacred space and carry us back in memory to a moment of significance. (It is important to caution that some stones at certain sites are protected and should not be removed as they carry significance for anyone who visits there—e.g., standing stones in Scotland and England. Further, stones have their place in the natural world, may be connected, and should be asked if they can be taken.) As embodied beings, we live in a materialistic world and objects hold symbolic meaning for us beyond what they are.

1. Identify one or two objects that carry significant meaning for you. This meaning may include the typical function of the object (e.g., a paring knife used to cut up apples for a pie), but it usually will also include a memory of a place or relationship.

2. What is the story that this object conveys? How is the story related to the object itself?

3. Where is this object typically stored in the place that you live? Is it somewhere your eyes land often? Do you see it only on rare occasions to sustain its sense of worth or keep it private? Is it something that you approach with your senses of touch, hearing, and so forth?

4. What feelings does this object evoke in you? In what way is it connected to your present and your future? How does it endure? Has focus on this object changed it today for you?

5. In what way(s) do you consider this object sacred? In what way is it not sacred but profane (according to the original meaning), taking its place in ordinary life?

6. Journal about this exercise.

WEBSITES

Dan Buettner: How to Live to Be 100+

http://www.ted.com/talks/dan_buettner_how_to_live_to_be_100

Dan Buettner's work for the National Geographic on the aging experience. Note the spiritual and social aspects of life that support longevity.

Kepler's Tally of Planets

http://www.nytimes.com/interactive/science/space/keplers-tally-of-planets.html

How does this comparison chart change your concept of life on our planet, if it does? How could this relate to spirituality?

Hubble Frontier Field Abell 2744

http://www.nasa.gov/content/hubble-frontier-field-abell-2744

What do images from the Hubble telescope suggest about aging, meaning, and time?

RECOMMENDED READING

Goldman, C. (2009).*Who am I now that I am not who I was?* Minneapolis, MN: Nodin Press.

This site features interviews by a former NPR journalist with middle-aged and older women.

Keen, S. (1994). *Hymns to an unknown God: Awakening the spirit in everyday life.* New York, NY: Bantam.

A social commentator discusses everyday spirituality.

Ricard, M. (2010). *Why meditate: Working with thoughts and emotions*. New York, NY: Hay House.

A molecular geneticist turned Buddhist monk, Ricard brings a unique perspective to the practice of meditation. He teaches about meditation practice in simple, clear language.

Salzberg, S. (2010). *Real happiness—The power of meditation: A 28-day program*. New York, NY: Workman.

This excellent book for beginners by a Buddhist teacher comes with a CD.

Sarton, M. (1997). *At eighty-two: A journal*. New York, NY: Norton.

A careful observer shares reflections on a personal journey through aging.

CHAPTER THREE

VALUES AND ETHICS WITH OLDER ADULTS

Cultivating right effort helps us to give ourselves
energetically to each day, no matter how difficult, and to
avoid shrinking from life's challenges.

—Life and Teachings of the Buddha

What is a good man but a bad man's teacher?
What is a bad man but a good man's task?
If you don't understand this, you will get lost,
However intelligent you are.
It is the great secret.

—Lao-tzu

Be grateful for whoever comes, because each has been sent
as a guide from beyond.

—Rumi

The foundation of all ethical systems lies in commonly accepted principles of behavior. Values such as kindness, compassion, integrity, patience, generosity, responsibility, fairness, and forgiveness stand at the center of relationships. Virtue ethics, according to Rachels (1999), suggests that we should have a clear understanding of what constitutes a virtue, identify which character traits are virtues, and articulate why these traits are attractive. For professionals, it is also important to tackle the question of whether virtues are the same for everyone or vary between individuals and cultures. The latter seems likely. If people can agree on universal virtues, the expressions of these virtues will vary by culture and history. For instance, acceptable comportment for mourning in Western cultures historically involved donning black clothing, while Eastern cultures prescribed wearing white. Even today in the West, many people wear some black in funeral attire, though it may be mixed with more lively color. In this postmodern era, many conventions are overthrown. If a bride wears black to a wedding, this might necessitate greater explanation for older relatives and friends who might wonder at the message. Although young adults may want to free themselves from convention, to older people, convention can provide a sense of continuity and comfort.

Indeed, people often feel passionately about beliefs. Further, bias is often transmitted generationally when people fail to consider issues of class, race, and gender, and make instinctive and inaccurate assumptions. The work of ethics is about posing questions that may be uncomfortable in order to be mindful about the basis for belief. Being mindful involves looking for alternative possibilities for action that results in the greatest good and trying to achieve greater clarity about how to proceed. Clarity of thinking may come after first dwelling in the uncomfortable position of ambiguity and doubt. Ethics is, overall, a process that entails identification of basic virtues at play and determination about what should have priority for others and ourselves. Ethics should never be automatic, but rather a careful unfolding of considered action beyond dogma, defensiveness, and self-rationalization (Weston, 2011). Like much else in life that is worthwhile, ethics is effort: It is not something programmed, routine, or impulsive.

This chapter addresses the virtues, both ancient and modern, as compelling standards for ethical practice. The principles of ethical theory are described, followed by an ethical guide for practice with older adults. Boundary issues in clinical work with older people, especially in religious areas, are discussed. End-of-life ethics are presented. Finally, intergenerational ethical concerns and attention to preservation of global human rights of older people are given.

EMPATHY, COMPASSION, OR SYMPATHY

Love for self and other is a foundation of human agency and society. *Empathy*, *compassion*, and *sympathy* are three terms that signal different aspects of professional care. The origin of the word *empathy* is ancient. It is comprised of two Greek words, *em* (in) and *pathos* (feeling). In German, the word became *Einfühlung*, or feeling into. Later, the word *empathy* emerged in English. Empathy is the capacity to understand what another experiences by entering his or her frame of reference. Empathy involves a range of emotional states, includes concern for others, holds a desire to help, and may stretch to discerning or intuiting the other person's thoughts and feelings (e.g., feeling the pain of another). Empathy is relational and is an important characteristic of caring. It is the beginning level of caring for professionals.

Compassion is similar to empathy, but it may operate at a more advanced level by including natural wisdom. It involves feeling *with* others, especially when they suffer in some way. This form of empathy connects closely to suffering; it shifts beyond reactive sympathy or pity, desiring to manifest an open-hearted sense of goodwill and caring to help clients or others relieve and regulate suffering (Germer & Siegel, 2012; Ritchie, 2014). Compassion can be understood through three components: affective (feeling for), cognitive (understanding), and motivational (desiring to help; Germer & Siegel, 2012). The neuronal brain networks explored in neurocognitive science suggest that empathy activates the pain-related parts that are associated with emotions (Singer et al., 2004; Siegel, 2012). Beyond empathy, compassion often gives itself fully to the arena of action. Compassion carries healthy personal boundaries or acquires them, so the professional helper does not lose herself in the act of giving. It is sustainable; empathy can consume itself if unchecked.

Sympathy conveys the idea that people can understand and resonate with the suffering of others, but it remains an interlude apart. In sympathy, people give only a tiny part of themselves away—sometimes recognition is tinged with judgment or self-congratulation that one avoided the misfortune. *Apathy* would fall below the foundation of helping, a point where one neither cares nor completely fails to care. It is an ambiguous position; however, the failure to connect or relate to others, or lack of interest in doing so, can be problematic. Below apathy lies a group of pathological, destructive, or afflictive emotions that lead to harm in interrelationships. These latter emotions are incongruent with or out of proportion to events and too strong or relentless for the situation. They often signal mental projections or ties to unresolved personal history.

Imagine a hierarchy of care. Sympathy would stand on the beginning or first level of this theoretical hierarchy. Empathy, at the second level, is an important first step for those in the helping professions, although it does need management to avoid compassion fatigue or burn out. Compassion could be considered the larger umbrella over both at the top level of the hierarchy. All religious traditions foster compassionate responses in living. Below sympathy lies apathy. Below apathy sits a range of pathological or destructive emotions (see Figure 3.1 Emotional Hierarchy of Care).

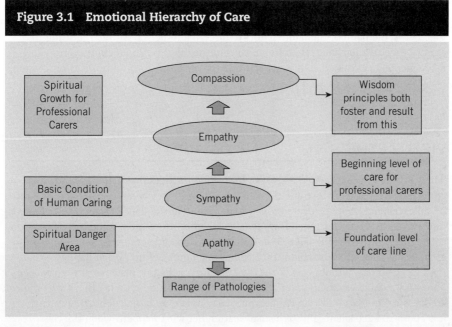

Figure 3.1   Emotional Hierarchy of Care

© Holly Nelson-Becker

Evidence-based practices are important; our work as professionals is grounded in disciplinary and interdisciplinary knowledge. A risk of applying scientific evidence unmindfully might too quickly place the individual client in a normative category in which a certain treatment may have high rates of effectiveness, but other factors could deter success. Holistic treatment for mental health suggests recognizing the importance of multilayered individual factors. The *invitation to categorize* is too often a default option. It can circumvent an ethic of care in which recognition of individual dignity and worth both humanize and vivify the interaction and thus make it more likely to succeed (Dybicz, 2012).

When mental health work either does not succeed or succeeds too well and professionals are overwhelmed, compassion fatigue may result. Does compassion wear out? Secondary traumatic stress (STS) is a better descriptive term that incorporates experiencing stress from hearing the trauma of clients. STS may have multiple causes, such as over-giving without replenishment. It is less the case compassion wears out as that layers of stressful events are deep enough or forceful enough that the natural restorative process and resilience displayed by mental health and health professionals are overburdened. There is too much to handle reasonably at the level of care needed. This is a good reason to have emotional "brakes" so that our actions are not overdetermined by unprocessed emotion. Other factors that cause STS include overload without the ability to adjust, have outlets, or decline work. There should be a healthy balance between accepting tasks given by an organization, stretching to meet deadlines, but also recognizing when the demands are unreasonable and can lead to unhealthy outcomes.

Mindfulness-based cognitive therapy allows individuals to find new space and fresh perspectives by rethinking the reasons for powerful feelings rather than returning to old well-rehearsed tracks that keep playing the same tune. When individuals can decelerate the rush of emotion that leads to ill-considered action, they begin to delink destructive emotions from thoughtless behavior. They catch themselves first. Then they can substitute reflection that results in better decisions. Mindfulness also helps individuals refrain from verbal attacks on others or their positions. People facing conflict can first try to understand the other's position. It is like holding two opposites together in the palm of the hand. Effort to discern another's position, repeating the essence of what they have said, often results in the other person feeling heard. When heard, people feel valued. There is a natural path open to give and receive compassion, a place of equanimity. A second effect is that the one who hears is deepened. Out of the exchange, both are changed.

VIRTUE ETHICS

The basics of ethical practice consist of following practices that will make our lives and the lives of others more enriched and satisfying. The virtues, traits that represent moral excellence, help us locate tools for attaining that standard of happiness. None of the virtues would matter much if we lived in isolation from each other, but our world is connected and the virtues call to attention how we should act in relationship. However, at times the search to be virtuous means that our values collide. What happens when we want to be honest, but honesty is not the kind approach? For instance, if we privilege honesty, we could say to an older client, "Your shirt has a stain on it." But if we privilege kindness, we might realize that appearance may not trouble the client and perhaps it is better to keep silent. This is a small matter, but what happens when the clash involves a larger issue? What if a Korean daughter tells us that she recently learned her mother has cancer, but she does not want the medical team to tell her mother? In Western culture, that secrecy would be abhorrent, but in Eastern cultures, the family is sometimes the decision maker and the parent may prefer this.

Ancient Virtues

Of all of the virtues, there are four master or core virtues identified by Plato for the ideal city: wisdom, courage, temperance (or self-restraint), and justice (Dahlsgaard, Peterson, & Seligman, 2005). Plato saw different virtues resident in social status. For instance, wisdom belonged to the governing elite, but the philosophers who were able to be the least self-interested (in his view) should rule. For the individual, Plato regarded wisdom as advancing through reason, courage through the *spirited* part, and self-restraint important to impose on what one desired. For both society and the individual, justice would result when each social class carried out its responsibilities. Wisdom is the "ancient dream of excellence," according to Baltes and the Berlin Max Planck Institute (1993, p. 585), who define it further as an "expert knowledge system about . . . the pragmatics of life" that involves expert judgment about uncertainty (p. 586). St Bernard, abbot of Clairvaux (1090–1153), said that what we reach for gives us knowledge, but what grabs us gives us wisdom. Courage is about taking action while threatened, although the threat may not be a physical one. Temperance involves living in a balanced, moderate way and achieving self-control. Justice is defined as social assistance to maintain equity in distribution of resources and equal consideration under the law of the state or nation.

Aristotle accepted Plato's list and added a few more: friendliness, generosity, wit, magnificence, truthfulness, and greatness of soul (Dahlsgaard et al., 2005; Peterson & Seligman, 2004). Aristotelian supplemental virtues largely disappear into the broader categories accepted by positive psychology. To the four master virtues of Plato, the positive psychology school would add two more: *humanity*, referring to altruistic or prosocial behavior, and *transcendence*, describing something sacred that points to what lies beyond the self and may constitute the response to the "search for significance" definition of spirituality elucidated by Pargament (1997; see Figure 3.2). Aristotle also articulated the worth of the *Golden Mean*. The Golden Mean was the desired amount of a virtue. For instance, courage taken to its greatest amount might be deemed recklessness, but at its least amount (or absence) it is viewed as cowardice. The Buddha likewise advocated a similar idea in his *Middle Way*, discussed in Chapter 5.

Six Core Virtues and Aging

Each of the six core virtues identified by the positive psychology school—wisdom, courage, temperance, justice, humanity, and transcendence—has particular relevance to aging (Petersen & Seligman, 2004). Aristotelian virtues may be implicit, but they are not explicitly included there. Although wisdom is not necessarily synonymous with age, aging does offer greater opportunity to achieve it with its longer time horizon. Courage is greatly needed by older people as they face the unknowns and ambiguities of aging. Temperance is a type of denial of self (such as in diet choices) that can result in better health that is good both individually and for society in reduced costs for social and health care. Justice involves the actions undertaken by society to protect the most vulnerable, a category that includes older people as well as children. In fact, statistics on elder mistreatment suggest that being an older adult leads to higher risk of abuse, especially for older women who are abused at a higher rate than males (National Center on Elder Abuse, 2014). This could be an artifact, however, of the

Figure 3.2 Development of a Modern Set of Virtues

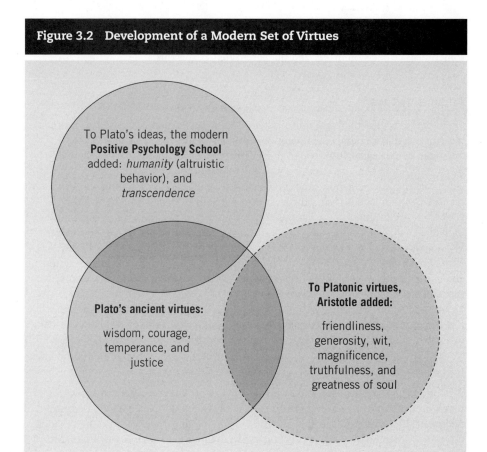

To Plato's ideas, the modern **Positive Psychology School** added: *humanity* (altruistic behavior), and *transcendence*

Plato's ancient virtues:

wisdom, courage, temperance, and justice

To Platonic virtues, Aristotle added:

friendliness, generosity, wit, magnificence, truthfulness, and greatness of soul

© Holly Nelson-Becker

issue that women have a longer life expectancy. Further, justice includes social policy provisions of care that should be balanced generationally. Humanity upholds the social interactions through which older adults are both benefitted and benefit others. Older people may have great impact on society through civic volunteerism. Finally, transcendence, the last of the six core virtues, describes the capacity of older people to go beyond the borders of their current lives and find meaning and purpose, even in the wake of suffering.

To what extent does a moral perspective inform an older person's identity? Patients with Alzheimer's disease (AD), amyotrophic lateral sclerosis (ALS), and frontotemporal dementia (FTD), three kinds of neurodegenerative diseases, were assessed for perceived identity change by spouses or parental caregivers who completed several measures (Strohminger & Nichols, 2015). moral injury—defined as antisocial behavior, apathy, reduced empathy, and reduced social inhibitions—suggested that an impaired moral system was primary in identity change; the study unsurprisingly implied a significant association with impaired caregiving relationships.

RELIGION AND ETHICS

Religion offers the benefits of tradition, history, and moral codes to guide behavior. This guidance carries authority and holds prescriptive ideas about how to live the best life possible. These ideas are transmuted and encoded in the larger cultural surround as rules for living. Because they are presented as divine laws, it would seem easy to follow these rules and then to be held harmless for having made good decisions. However, using the Bible as example, among some books, laws conflict. The Old Testament speaks about giving an *eye for an eye* (Lev. 24:19–21) in retributive justice, but the New Testament asks individuals to forgive up to seventy times seven, seen as a metaphorical number for beyond counting or always and forever (Matt. 18:21–22). The same question about how to achieve justice occasions two very different answers. Administer justice in the measure you have received harm, or let it go—*forgive*.

Out of the Old Testament in the Jewish and Christian traditions come the Ten Commandments, which are held as basic principles for conducting behavior. The Golden Rule, *Do unto others as you would have them do unto you* or *We must treat others as we wish others to treat us*, comprises an ethic of reciprocity that extends across cultures and religious faiths. This ethic is expressed by the parable of the long-handled spoon (source unknown). In this narrative, a rabbi visited hell and witnessed people seated at tables with plates piled with scrumptious food, yet they moaned with hunger. The people there had both arms splinted, so even though they had long-handled spoons, they could not bend their arms and bring the spoons to their mouths. They suffered. Then the rabbi traveled to heaven. The conditions were the same, with tables piled high with food before people who had arms bound in splints. Yet, here people were smiling and happy. The difference is that they fed each other with their long-handled spoons. Although the Golden Rule offers helpful guidance, it does not do all the work in decision making. We don't often know whether others want to be treated in the same way we do.

In completing advance directives, people will have different preferences for how they want to be treated in the face of life-threatening illness. Whether they want curative treatment, artificial hydration and nutrition, and a DNR (Do Not Resuscitate order) or whether they prefer a more natural death are important decisions, but not everyone receives the death they want (over some things we must, in the end, give up control). In another situation, when two people have competing needs that may dually require the voluntary assistance of the same caregiver, the questions Who is my neighbor? and To whom should my time best be given? are not easily resolved. Although religious faiths and sacred texts offer direction, they regularly require interpretation to apply to specific times and contexts. While literalists would hope that what is written is Truth, when the meaning is unpacked, it can be confusing or reach a different point than expected. And to those who say the words of God are fixed and unchangeable, even Abraham argued with God about the lowest number of righteous people that would save the city of Sodom. Words point to ideas but are always interpreted as signifiers, even more so given the variety of languages, cultures, and historical understandings. According to the story, God was moved and changed his or her mind about that number, reducing it (Genesis 18:16–33). Ultimately, religion offers guidance and is an external framework that suggests how we should act, though some might feel religion tells us specifically what we should do, and that sense of certainty can be comforting.

SPIRITUAL AND EXISTENTIALIST/HUMANIST ETHICS

Although religion offers concrete guidance through its many texts, writings, and interpretations (both oral and written) that emanate out of traditions, spirituality and existential/humanistic philosophies also contain within them guides for ethical behavior. Spirituality has been investigated for its role in workplace ethics and behavior (Biberman & Whitty, 2007). Business ethics is a type of applied ethics. Overall, ethics is usually viewed as a system or frame for decision making, while morality is a form of ethics or right behavior in action.

Kohlberg (1984) arranged ethical behavior in a type of moral hierarchy described as levels of *preconventional thought* (age 9 and up), *conventional thought* (adolescent and adult), and *postconventional thought* and *universal principles* (about 10–15% of adults). He thus ascribed ethical response to a developmental framework based on the cognitive work of Jean Piaget. Preconventional orientations were described by punishment and obedience or a growing understanding of accommodation to different ethical interpretations that would still result in equal exchange. In conventional orientations, individuals internalize standards. They are concerned with abiding by laws and how they are viewed by others. Postconventional reasoning is based on a more complex assessment of justice and individual rights. The greatest developmental capacity occurs with universal principles, when people develop their own set of moral guidelines, even if these go against conventions.

Kohlberg's (1984) framework was criticized for building on a small sample followed at 3-year intervals for 20 years. His sample included only boys who were directed to share their rationale for decisions in hypothetical cases. One of his most recognized cases was the story of Heinz, who must choose whether to steal a drug he cannot pay for to save his dying wife. Gilligan (1977) offered another perspective, suggesting that a sex bias existed in Kohlberg's data. Women, she asserted, approached ethical decision making from an ethic of care instead of an ethic of justice.

An example of an ethic of care includes a recent focus on listening to stories in which moral injury occurred. Moral injury involves a shattering of trust after a betrayal of core beliefs, for example, when civilians were accidentally targeted in war time and responsibility was not taken by military leaders. This betrayal was legitimized by someone in authority. A moral injury, then, is a serious transgression leading to internal conflict regarding a failure to uphold beliefs about the value of humanity (Litz et al., 2009). Some older adults who were involved in World War II may have felt forced into actions for which they carry great guilt. I have an older German friend who has spoken little about his experience in World War II when invited, except to suggest that he participated in actions of which he is not proud.

Although Litz and colleagues have written from the perspective of veterans, the idea of moral injury relates to many situations of betrayal, especially of religious, spiritual, and existential/humanistic beliefs. Shame, guilt, and self-condemnation can result. Abuse of many kinds as well as rape can result in symptoms of posttraumatic stress disorder (PTSD). Older adults, like younger generations, have been both perpetrators and victims. Sometimes there may be little need to open up such wounds. However, even layered with years, at other times these are important areas that call for a witness. In the hearing comes the healing. Gilligan (2014) suggests that her writing about "a different voice" was quite simply a human voice—not gendered but connected to emotion, mind, and body. This is listening that does not try to make sense of disconnection by searching for the right category of interpretive meaning. A zookeeper and his wife sheltered and subsequently saved 300 Jews in occupied 1939 Warsaw right in the closed zoo at the city center (Ackerman, 2007). When recognized after the war by Yad Vashem for being Righteous Among the Nations, they stated this was not heroism, just an act of humanity.

NONVIOLENCE AND INTERRELIGIOUS HARMONY

Principles of nonviolence and interreligious harmony are fundamental to peaceful human existence. There is a human need to give and receive compassion, kindness, and caring. Theistic approaches to those goals are linked to religions of Judaism, Christianity, Islam, Hinduism, Sikhism, and Zoroastrianism, among others. Nontheistic religions, such as Buddhism and Jainism, ground ethical practice in the idea of *karma*, that intentional acts have consequences. All religions are established on an understanding of life that cannot be empirically proven. Hence, debates between science and religion, operating on different planes, can never reach consensus. Theistic religions have an end goal of salvation; nontheistic religions teach an end goal of liberation. Humanistic approaches, such as existentialism, seek the highest understanding of what it is to be human and to care for each other.

Two dimensions comprise spirituality: *well-being*, inner psychological and emotional strength and balance, and *religion-based spirituality*, which includes beliefs, practices, and cultural context from a particular tradition (Dalai Lama & Norman, 2011). This suggests that spirituality contains both inner and outer components. Two ethical principles underlie and thus unite both religious and existential/humanistic/secular ethics: (1) a sense of shared humanity and experience, and (2) recognition of interdependence. The nature of humanity is to seek out the best of life for ourselves and others as well as to avoid suffering (Dalai Lama & Norman, 2011). The resolution of our common problems cannot come out of one perspective or dimension, but only when we consider all directions of an issue: what stands at the center of the four directions around us, what is above us, and below. This is one way of thinking about holism in accord with an American Indian approach of honoring the directions. When we narrow our thinking rather than expand it, we can easily subscribe to the outcome of hopelessness.

For long-term intergenerational harmony, there are three levels for thinking about ethical practice (Dalai Lama & Norman, 2011). One is an *ethic of restraint*. In medical ethics, this is voiced as do no harm, or nonmalfeasance. The second level is to better understand and develop our *internal ethics*: cultivating virtue and values. The third level is to operate on a level of *altruism*, working for the welfare of others which, in the end, is also our own. When we act with restraint, we act in ways that are honest and authentic, confirming trust. We remember or call together our reasons and motivations for treating each other well. We are mindful and self-aware. When we act to uphold virtue, we are generous when experiencing the mistakes of others. As with Aristotle, we live courageously, with patience, justice, and through mustering the highest level of wisdom we can access. We offer our support to others in their pain and share celebration in their joy. When we act altruistically, we act to the highest good we can discern, without harm to others. Although our positive emotions can guide us, the destructive ones such as anger, fear, and self-blame can cause projections and distorted perceptions if they are not tempered with accurate cognition. The roots of our uncomfortable emotions often lie within us, as much as we try to seek the source outside us. The value of greater emotional awareness is addressed in greater detail in Chapter 9.

In positive psychology, there is a concept of "whole-being" that involves holding or developing awareness of both high *positive* emotions and low *negative* emotions as well as the tensions between them. Both are quite often useful. The low emotions, if we allow ourselves to consider them, can be especially enlightening. Low emotions such as guilt can be important resources for guiding behavior. If we didn't experience guilt or similar low emotions, we would likely remain unaware that our beliefs and behavior were contradictory. A sense of guilt, for example, can help guide ethical behavior as an internal alarm system to warn us that our values and practice do not align (Kashdan & Biswas-Diener, 2014).

Acceptance of suffering is epitomized in Victor Frankl's (1984) response to injustice. Frankl, a professor of psychiatry and neurology at the University of Vienna prior to World War II, spent three years in concentration camps during the Holocaust. There he developed his ideas of logotherapy and the search for meaning. In a speech to the Toronto Youth Corps, Frankl suggested "If we take man [sic] as he is we make him worse, but if we take him as he should be, we make him capable of becoming what he can be" (Frankl, 1972). Frankl called this the most important maxim for psychotherapy in its encouragement of clients to search for their own points of meaning. Further, *acceptance* of suffering is different from *surrender* to suffering. In acceptance, we can achieve solidarity with others and gain strength, rather than become overwhelmed by difficulty. Nelson Mandela became president of South Africa at age 76. He served for 6 years subsequent to an uninterrupted 27-year imprisonment for anti-apartheid activism. His acceptance of injustice led to transformation and service at the height of his human capacity to give.

ETHICAL THEORY FOR PRACTICE IN BRIEF

A very brief consideration of ethical theory will demonstrate why two good people, thinking through the best course of action in the same situation, may reach completely different decisions. Normative ethics is the study of ethics that suggests how one ought to act (Reamer, 1995). Thus, it is prescriptive rather than descriptive, recommending what one should do, rather than exploring how people actually resolve difficult situations. Ethical theories stand as philosophy's attempt to assist people in seeing how values form a system of judgment. There are two main types of actions one may choose: *deontology* (best known in Emmanuel Kant's work) that seeks to honor the person, and *teleology* (represented by the writing of Jeremy Bentham and John Stuart Mill) that seeks the greatest good for all.

Deontology

Kantian Ethics. Consonant with deontological approaches to ethics, one acts because that action is good and right in itself, regardless of what may happen afterward. The actor is not responsible for consequences. This approach also honors the worth of persons. Martin Buber distinguished between people who interacted with others as an *It*, an object to their desires, versus a *Thou*, someone who had desires as valuable as one's own (Weston, 2011). He characterized these relations as *I-It* versus *I-Thou*; the latter is an encounter that acknowledges richness and depth in a way that transforms the interaction. Immanuel Kant, living in 18th-century Germany, was the chief proponent of thinking of other people as ends in themselves rather than a means to an end. His view is known as the *categorical imperative* or unconditional obligation. "Act only according to that maxim by which you can at the same time will that it should become a universal law" (Kant & Ellington, 1983, p. 30). In this view (simplified though it is here), rules, rights, and principles should never be violated; they are the highest good that has been recognized by society. In this line of thinking, the goals of an action never justify the means. The idea of right or wrong action as a process prevails.

Divine command. A second form of deontology is divine command. This view states that actions are right because they are performed as duty, such as refraining from work on the Sabbath might be in a Christian context. There is no implication that any particular good outcome will ensue, but rather that the action itself is correct and true. The action chosen follows best practice or morality as interpreted by religious standards; it is what God requires and commands.

Rawls's theory of justice. A further idea that can be helpful for mental health workers and is particularly salient for health care policy is John Rawls's theory (1971, 2001). This can also be considered a form of deontological thinking. He addresses the problem of the just distribution of goods in society and suggests that all people are in an original position of equality, guaranteed by the U.S. Constitution, blind to their own status in regard to advantages or disadvantages. In the condition of this "veil of ignorance," people are unaware of whether at some future time they may stand in greater need of, for example, health care resources, than others (Stallard, Decker, & Sellers, 2002). Two principles ensue from the need for social and economic redress for the least advantaged: these are the "difference principle" and "fair equality of opportunity" (Rawls, 1971). Rawls advocates that people should be guaranteed fair access to resources, though not necessarily equal access (Banerjee, 2005; Rawls, 2001). His difference principle would allow inequalities in the distribution of goods *only if* those inequalities benefit the members of society who are considered to be in the most deprived or worst positions. The difference principle is basically a principle about reciprocity, but even though Rawls's theory has had wide acclaim, it does not always support the needs of those who are poor, older, or disabled. Equality of access to goods is not always fair when it disadvantages those who simply have greater need. Greater redress is needed beyond minimal distribution of social primary goods. Rawls's view of reciprocity articulates that any extra societal expenditures should benefit others as well as ourselves, which does not always promote the first-place position of those who have greater need (Banerjee, 2005; Hartley, 2011). The difference principle is not the principle of redress as stated by Rawls in 1971, nor does he include physical and health care in his delineation of primary goods.

Teleology

The second major type of ethical approach is *teleology*, sometimes called *consequentialism*. In this form of reasoning, the rightness of any act is determined by the consequences of that act. Thus, individuals should anticipate possible outcomes of a variety of likely decisions and weigh their relative merits. Individuals acting under this concept emphasize what is good and what is desirable. The classic example of the deontological and teleological approaches is the good Italian Catholic priest living in Fascist Italy near the German border. Two young Jewish men come to his home and ask him for sanctuary, but the outcome could be very different depending on his ethical position. If he is a deontologist and he believes that telling the truth in all situations is the highest good, what will happen when two Nazi-uniformed soldiers knock at his door and ask if he is harboring any Jewish people? He would affirm that this is the case, though he might try not to answer the door. The Jewish men would be captured and possibly sent to their deaths. If he is a teleologist, even though he believes the principle of telling the truth should usually apply, knowing what he has heard about Nazism, he will answer "No" when he is asked if two Jewish men are living with him. He will lie (possibly risking damnation in his faith belief for lying) for the greater good of saving two lives. This example illustrates how a person of good intentions might reach two very different conclusions dependent on his or her reasoning.

Two separate schools structure teleological approaches: *egoism* and *utilitarianism*. In egoism, individuals make decisions that will maximize their own good and augment their self-interests, no matter what the effect on others could be. This would seldom be the approach advocated in any mental health profession. In utilitarianism, actions are deemed to be right when they promote the greatest good for all. Other possibilities within utilitarian approaches are what produces the greatest total amount of good or what produces the greatest good possible for the greatest number of people. Further, two subtypes of utilitarianism are *act utilitarianism* and *rule utilitarianism*. Act utilitarianism suggests that the goodness of the consequences for an action determine whether it is the right one for that particular case. Rule utilitarianism considers the precedent that would be established and the long-term consequences produced if the case is generalized to other situations in the future. However, in rule utilitarianism, the interests of minority groups could be jeopardized or might be weighted equally, not allowing redress for those more negatively affected. Affirmative action policies sought to correct this problem.

Another form of teleology is *situation ethics*. In situation ethics, the untangling of a dilemma occurs through posing the question, "What is the most loving thing to do?" Four principles are primary: (1) pragmatism—what causes the greatest love, (2) relativism—actions may apply to one situation and not another, (3) positivism— what is the most important choice, and (4) personalism—people are more important than the laws (Fletcher, 1997).

Casuistry is a type of case-based or applied ethics that is useful in reasoning for medical situations (Freeman & Francis, 2006). However, the meaning of the term is fluid and more likely to be negative than neutral. In casuistry, the circumstances of a case are essential in evaluation of the best way to proceed. Rather than being informed by theory, decisions are informed by other cases that can be reasoned to be similar. Figure 3.3 Thinking Ethics identifies these common principles in reasoning through ethical dilemmas.

Ethical decision making is complex, especially when two good choices—or perhaps two equally poor choices or more—are the ones visible. This is often decision making under duress. No one, for example, wants to be in the position of having to make a choice about an undesired transition to an institution providing a higher level of care, such as an assisted living or long-term care facility for an older person. Possibly, the decision at stake may concern an end-of-life scenario in which the determination is for aggressive or comfort care. An ethical decision-making framework is presented in Figure 3.4 that considers the views of the older person and significant others, specific values, the agent who will make the decision, and the expected outcomes of each alternative. A feedback loop for monitoring and evaluation of the decision selected is also represented.

VALUE DIMENSIONS FOR PRACTICE

For any professional mental health worker, respect and even moving beyond respect to *appreciation* for diverse forms of spiritual and religious expressions are important precursors of and outcomes from engagement. Mental health practice with older clients

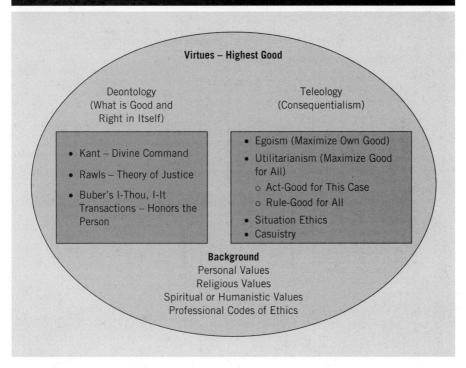

Figure 3.3 Thinking Ethics

Virtues – Highest Good

Deontology
(What is Good and
Right in Itself)

- Kant – Divine Command
- Rawls – Theory of Justice
- Buber's I-Thou, I-It
  Transactions – Honors the
  Person

Teleology
(Consequentialism)

- Egoism (Maximize Own Good)
- Utilitarianism (Maximize Good
  for All)
  o Act-Good for This Case
  o Rule-Good for All
- Situation Ethics
- Casuistry

Background
Personal Values
Religious Values
Spiritual or Humanistic Values
Professional Codes of Ethics

© Holly Nelson-Becker

can help practitioners achieve value clarity. Grappling with issues that arise underscores limits as well as strengths in working with religious and spiritual matters. A spiritually sensitive approach is one that welcomes all positions as a starting point for work. When a professional begins to sense that he or she is dismissive of a client's spiritual viewpoint or, conversely, begins to assume a client's firmly held viewpoint is pathological, he or she has an opportunity for self-learning and self-awareness.

Is it possible to be too supportive of unquestioned religious belief? If one's own views align too closely with those of a client, then some possibilities for growth or change may be overlooked. In addition, examples of different styles of engagement with clients around religion and spirituality might be attempts to control or channel spiritual/religious beliefs or practices out of concern or, at the other extreme, might be evidence of being so invested that one assumes a quasi-role of spiritual director, even if unprepared for that function. Sometimes professionals of religious faith in their zeal, energy, and honest convictions seek to proselytize, persuade, or convert others to their faith. Because these actions subvert the self-determination of individuals and their personal views, they are not acceptable as ethical practice. Strengths-based, positive psychological stances that affirm religious and spiritual views, but hold them gently and provisionally, can lead to clients flourishing even in otherwise difficult circumstances, such as in a long-term care facility. Respect, trustworthiness, client-centeredness, and inclusivity are some fundamental principles that aid ethical practice (Nelson-Becker, Canda, & Nakashima, 2015).

Figure 3.4 Doing Ethics

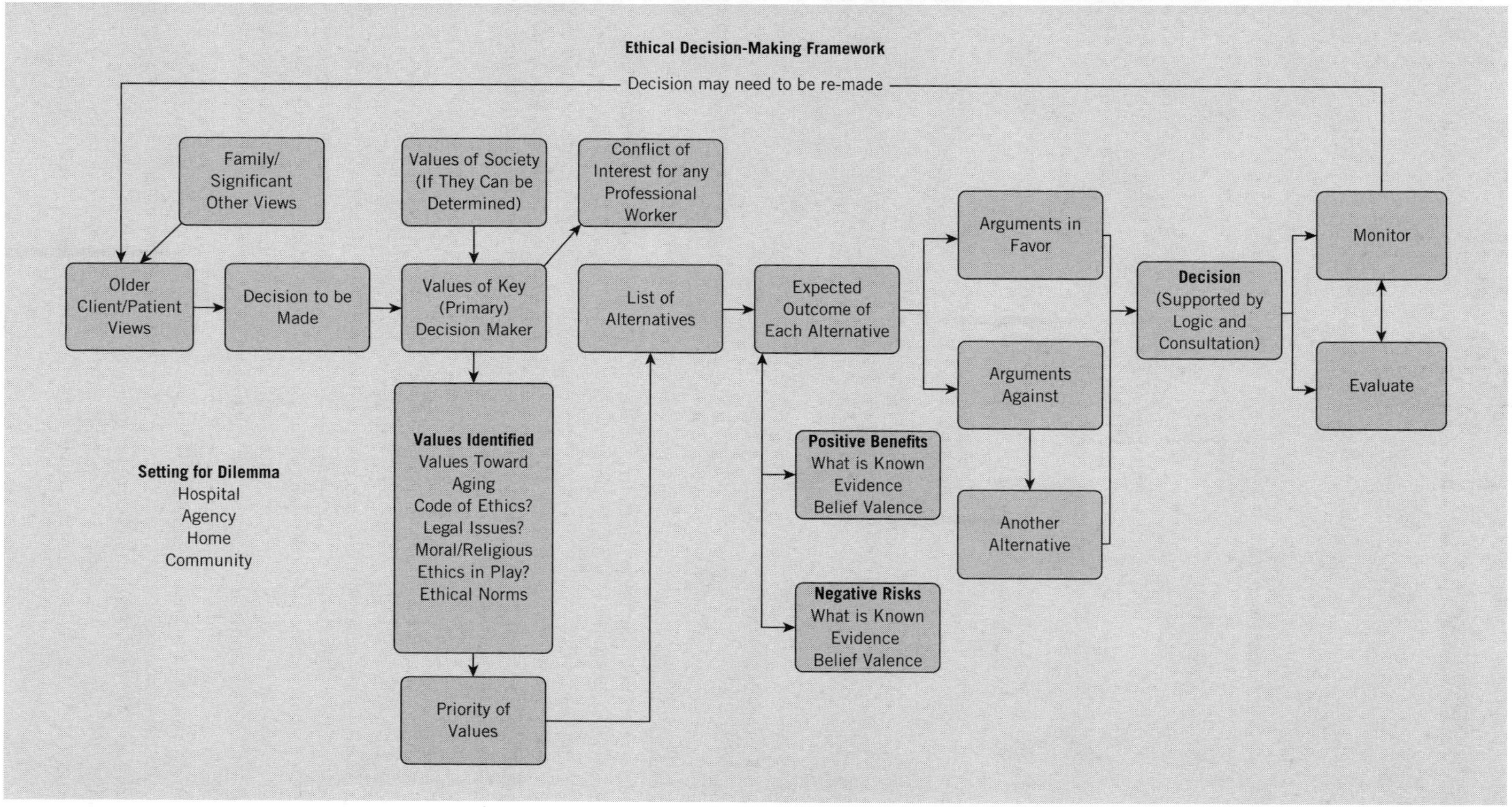

Ethical Decision-Making Framework

Setting for Dilemma
Hospital
Agency
Home
Community

© Holly Nelson-Becker

Respect

Respect is an operational value important both inside and outside religious and spiritual traditions. Although this may seem basic, it is also absent from many of our civic public spaces today. Its absence leads people to feel unheard and thus not valued or undervalued. Lack of respect for older people is evidenced through age bias, still unfortunately prevalent. Wherever older people's opinions are discounted because they are old, ageism is active. Respect considers the effect of such power differentials and seeks to redress them.

Trust

Trust concerns itself with the challenge of who to trust as well as the act of giving trust. It is an important part of all relationships and transactions. Trusting others, especially professionals, to keep confidences unless mandatory disclosure laws deem otherwise, is an important aspect of all mental health counseling. This is what clients should expect. Trust means relying on someone to fulfill whatever commitment the individual has made. Trust consists of faith in people's skills as well as their good intentions (Hawley, 2012). Clients trust the knowledge of professionals as well as their sincerity in both what they say and do, including saying nothing when that is appropriate (saying something could damage the trust others place). Overall, trust involves belief in competence and honesty and is a compliment, though it also carries expectations that the professional will meet the standard of trust others place in him or her. Distrusting others is a harm that can lead to a downward spiral and less social capital in personal relationships (Hawley, 2012). Reciprocal altruism is created when trust is maintained. The quality of the relationship undergirded by trust was the key feature in accomplishing treatment aims in one study (Rugkåsa, Canvin, Sinclair, Sulman, & Burns, 2014).

Client-Centeredness

Client-centeredness suggests that professionals must honor client aspirations, values, and dreams, even when they are very different from a professional's own views. This value privileges clients' viewpoints, unless they are acting in a manner that would be a danger to themselves or others and thus require immediate intervention for safety. Another term for this value is *person-centered care* or *relational care*, care that considers the nature of the interactions in a dyad or family. This value suggests that success is measured by assisting older persons to attain their own goals for health and life, rather than goals others might choose for them. Self-determination is highlighted here, especially in situations when caring family or professionals worry about older adult safety and pressure an older person to move to a residence offering greater care before that need is clear. Client-centeredness preserves older adults' dignity on their terms.

Inclusivity

Inclusivity concerns the ability to move from tolerance of a particular perspective to appreciation of what a particular religious or spiritual stance does in an older person's life. It may ground the older adult by providing a foundation and strength to cope with health concerns, for example. This value causes professionals to turn older people to what matters for them, rather than responding with dismissiveness. This position also welcomes and encourages a multitude of views that an older person may hold, finding ways to soften or take the edges off some views that could be seen as internally inconsistent. Further, an inclusive approach in clinical work can assist professionals and their clients to go beneath surface principles and access a deeper level of understanding.

BOUNDARIES IN ETHICAL PRACTICE

Spiritual assessment and intervention can be accomplished respectfully and noninvasively. Spiritual assessment should be included as a routine aspect of any assessment for older people, part of a biopsychosocial spiritual assessment. Failure to include what is a vital part of existence for some older people is an ethical lapse. Sensitive older adults will be alert to its absence and may believe that addressing it would not be welcomed by their professional carer. Some of my students who participate in agency internships report varying levels of engagement with spiritual assessment in practice. Some agencies do address it in some manner. Others, while having a question that focuses on religious or spiritual faith, may choose to ignore it. Chapter 6 discusses approaches to completion of a spiritual and religious assessment as a component of integrated care. This next section focuses on rationales for introducing assessment in this area and building appropriate boundaries.

Importance of Assessing Religious and Spiritual Needs

It is important to ask broad questions when conducting a religious and spiritual assessment. First, it is essential to learn whether these areas are important to the client and second, whether she or he would like them to be included in therapeutic work. If unasked, older clients will often not mention what could be a significant source of comfort or distress. Taking cues from the practitioner about what is perceived as a level of discomfort, they may hesitate to reveal the spiritual or religious beliefs that are fundamental and integral to their constructed self. If religion or spirituality (R/S) emerges as an area of interest or concern for the client, then the task for the practitioner becomes one of listening fully and holding in check assumptions and stereotypes. When client beliefs shift outside mainline norms, psychologists may be more likely to rate these beliefs as pathological, even though they see religion as beneficial overall (Post & Wade, 2009). Further, when a particular religious faith affiliation is disclosed by the older person, he or she may have developed a unique understanding and expression within that faith and so is not completely aligned with it in his or her personal perspective. The professional may misunderstand or assume characteristics about the relationship of a person to their chosen faith tradition.

Religious Conversion/Proselytizing and Related Concerns

A major concern mental health practitioners hold about initiating spiritual and religions conversations with older clients is they may be perceived as proselytizing or seeking to convert clients to a certain system of belief. It also may be a concern of some older adults and their families. Of course, some older clients will seek out Christian or faith-based counseling centers. Conversion to other belief systems happens outside of religion, and in fact mental health practitioners legitimately attempt to influence client thinking about, for example, their capacity for change and for becoming their best self. However, the issue of religious conversion is particularly important as it erodes self-determination and fails to protect important clinical boundaries. People who adhere to fundamentalist religious beliefs may worry about the condition of the soul of a client and seek to evangelize—share their faith—in situations where the client's goal is very different. In the past, people of good will who thought they held the best answers have blindly stepped across these boundaries. This remains a present concern.

Clients seek help at times when they are most vulnerable. Because of the power differential in the relationship, this puts them at risk for manipulation. Any assent to religious conversion during this time of vulnerability, from pressure by someone who carries a responsibility to be neutral and unbiased, is not help but coercion. This is a very important point to know and abide by in practice. Under this condition, any assent is not freely given as an act of faith. Autonomy and self-determination must be protected at all times, particularly where religious influence may be a risk. Outside of a clinical situation, if both individuals were to meet by chance at a religious event, the context would carry a different meaning, although a concern about dual relationships might then prevail.

Further, even though religious belief and practice have resulted in positive outcomes for many older people, this is not universally the case. The level of intimacy and level of credulity (and thus potential for undue influence) one may concede to religion or spiritual belief is such that religion cannot be prescribed the way one might suggest exercise, certain reading material, or other behavioral homework. Some people have been abused by those in positions of religious power. Older people without family have sometimes been victimized by clergy or other religious leaders who have encouraged the older person to make them an individual beneficiary in their will, separate from a gift to the faith denomination for a building project or program.

There can be other damaging effects of religion and religious interpretation. At times, religious leaders or others may instill fear (e.g., If you have sinned, you will not be able to go to heaven). They may also instill guilt about previous actions when the client was young, such as having had an abortion, releasing a child for adoption, or failure to follow religious rule or law (according to the particular faith). Instances where an older adult is LGBT-NC and has not disclosed his or her identity because of worry about nonacceptance can also lead to exclusion and fears about perceived marginalization within the religious community.

When Religious or Spiritual Issues Arise

When spiritual and religious issues emerge as a main concern, older clients can be referred to board-certified chaplains available from many faith traditions or to leaders in their own faith community. However, there are occasions when the need is so immediate and the pain so profound that psychologists, counselors, social workers, and other professionals should listen intently and promptly, no matter their own background or personal faith or nonfaith preference. Some practitioners may feel unprepared and assume that it is best for clients to work with someone from their own religious or spiritual group. However, practitioners do not need to match clients on their spiritual genetics. In fact, at times a person from a secular or humanistic background may serve as the best resource because she or he can approach the problem with a fresh mind free of assumptions. The key requirement is that the professional be prepared to use all of his or her training and skill to listen deeply to what the client may find extremely difficult to discuss or be conflicted about revealing.

Use of Prayer With Clients

Prayer can enter the therapeutic encounter in several modes. Prayer may be a part of a professional's personal spiritual practice. He or she may ask for guidance in his or her work or simply offer thanks for the opportunity to work with clients, among other possible emphases. Professionals may want to pray *on behalf of* clients, a form of intercessory prayer. Professionals may want to pray *with* clients, either being present in a supportive way or leading the prayer. How do these forms of prayer align with ethical clinical work?

Prayer for oneself is always appropriate, if desired. Therapists or professionals from any discipline should always have the freedom to make choices about what will best nourish them. In fact, they may want to create an implicit spiritual environment for themselves through prayer and meditation, among other activities. To dissociate them from a source of strength and assistance seems misguided. However, other forms of prayer initiated by professionals in their interactions with a client may be unethical. Any action that subverts individual authority to agree or disagree, especially prayer on behalf of someone who wouldn't agree if they knew this was being done, is unethical practice. Unethical practice regarding prayer includes conditions under which (1) the client has not provided informed consent for prayer and it is not part of the client's treatment plan; (2) it does not align with the client's belief system; (3) it represents imposition of the professional's own religious or spiritual perspective; or (4) it is done to emphasize the power differential or influence the therapeutic relationship (Snodgrass & Noronha, 2015).

Prayer on behalf of a client should only be done if the client is directly asked and agrees. Otherwise it constitutes a violation of individual agency and choice. A client seeking counseling from a pastoral counselor or at a Christian counseling agency is more likely to understand, appreciate, or even ask for this type of prayer. This type of client, more directly embedded in a religious or spiritual environment, might even assume this is being done privately. However, it would be best to make this discussion explicit as part of informed consent.

Prayer with a client brings up possible concerns. First, as much as it may open up space for change, support, or growth, it could also contravene client expectations. There are many forms of prayer, which will be discussed in Chapter 7. If one prays from the heart, one is not always in control of what direction that prayer may take and one could move into an area for which the client is ill-prepared. Second, there is a question of competency in religious matters. The client is working with the professional because of the authority invested in that person through education and experience. The sector of religion and spirituality has its own faith credentials, which may be formal or informal. However, the professional who carries the authority of her discipline will likely not carry equal authority or standing in the religion of her client. Whether common ground is reached in interreligious prayer is contingent on the interface between client and professional. Although prayer with a client could be helpful if a client agrees, it also may take the professional into an area outside her training and is thus a possible concern for competency. Of course, many would argue that the client-therapist bond does represent sacred space, and so prayer could create new energy, inspiration, and vision.

The last concern is whether the professional is able to maintain his or her own beliefs and stay true to them without pressure from a client. What if the client invited the professional to pray with him or her and the professional is neither religious nor spiritual? If the professional agrees to do something that violates his or her own beliefs, then could that not also diminish his or her own authenticity and sense of power? Depending on the background of the professional, she or he might consider standing/sitting in respectful silence while the client prays. Following the client's initiative, without engaging in behavior that would seem to cause harm to the professional's own belief system, seems like the optimal approach.

Shadow Sides of Religion and Spirituality

Religion and spirituality, besides offering capacity for strengths-based work and healing, also have the capacity to uncover darker sides, both in a client and a practitioner. Consequently, this area of work calls out for clinical supervision so that practitioners, both those with a religious and spiritual sensibility and those without, can be aware of and acknowledge potential biases. Biases are often based on experience, but experience changes with every situation, so it is valuable to bracket prior experience through cultural humility. Cultural humility involves a life-long orientation to self-reflection and self-evaluation around areas of difference that relate to religion, spirituality, race and ethnicity, class, and other anthropological factors that can be hidden to those holding membership in primary groups.

At times people compartmentalize the self, making a part of who they are off-bounds for discussion. This is sometimes done out of fear that this side of the self will not be respected. Integration of all aspects of a self is helpful for holistic balance and healing. *Spiritual bypass* is a term used for undue focus on religious or spiritual beliefs to the exclusion of painful necessary work, for instance in dealing with emotional residues (Clarke, Giordano, Cashwell, & Lewis, 2013). In this way, spirituality could become a shield rather than a light, preventing a client from seeing what he or she most needs to see. Some clients might choose to discuss their spirituality in a shallow way that could deflect serious work or "seek spiritual highs" at the expense of psychological archeology. Spiritual bypass is the language of denial and avoidance. It includes searching for and pointing out inconsistencies between priority values and actions on the part of the older person. However, another perspective is that serious and authentic work in the spiritual domain, often supported by external unseen forces such as the Transcendent Power, would ultimately uncover all depth counseling needs.

There are other shadow sides of religion. At times, leaders in religious organizations have been abusive. Sexual abuse has received greater acknowledgment in recent years. Although more rigorous standards of conduct have been put in place as prevention, some older adults will have suffered abuse years ago, when this was more hidden in the culture due to shame as well as guilt. Power differentials within religion can also cause older people to feel excluded and hurt when their needs are ignored or their capacities are not fully engaged. Other abusive areas include fasting that leads to a negative effect on the body or places one's health in danger or stopping medication due to concern that certain scriptural passages might forbid it. Religious faith leaders sometimes encourage alternative treatments that have little or no grounding in evidence-based practice. Some may be innocuous, but others could lead to harm. At times, people are scapegoated and criticized, leading to negative psychological effects, shunning, and other harmful effects. Finally, the distance between their ideals and their current standpoint may cause older people to feel rejected by or alienated from God.

END-OF-LIFE ETHICS

Most jurisdictions support the right of adults to forego life-sustaining treatment at the end of life, even treatment that would save their lives, as long as they are mentally competent to make such decisions (Beauchamp & Childress, 2013; Johnstone & Kanitsaki, 2009). In the Jain religion, people are permitted to practice *santhara*, a voluntarily cessation of nourishment and water, when they are nearing life's end or suffering greatly. Approval is needed from both a guru and family members. Rather than suicide, this is considered a practice of welcoming death consistent with *ahimsa* (nonviolence). However, some fear this radical renunciation of life could be a form of suicide imposed by external pressure—encouraged by those wanting to free themselves of the burden of care. Some court jurisdictions in India have been looking closely into this concern.

In the United States throughout the 1980s and 1990s, information about *advance directives*, decisions about desired medical treatment under many kinds of circumstances, began to be developed and disseminated (Jordens, Little, Kerridge, & McPhee, 2005). This movement grew after media-inundated cases such as those of Karen Ann Quinlan, Nancy Cruzan, and Terri Schiavo raised community fears. Though younger women, all were in persistent vegetative states, on life support equipment, and had family members who appealed to the courts for the right to allow their loved one to die. The hope was that most people would prepare advance directives; this would ease the burden for caregivers in knowing and implementing wishes. However, this goal has largely been unrealized (Perkins, 2007). Many people still find it difficult to discuss end-of-life wishes. Families, even caring for each other greatly, find this task difficult. In the course I teach on loss, grief, and dying well, some of my students who completed their own advance directives wanted to discuss their decisions with their parents but found parents did not want to listen. Often, because of social distance, professionals are better able to facilitate such conversations than clinicians can do even in their own families.

Advance care planning is now known as the process of hosting conversations around end-of-life wishes. This includes the following: (1) completing a power of attorney, especially a durable power of attorney document for health care; (2) considering how goals of care might change if interventions resulted in unforeseen outcomes or complications; and (3) establishing a specific plan of care using Physician Orders for Life Sustaining Treatment (POLST) guidelines, now available in many states, for addressing emergency medical care. POLST is a set of medical orders for those who are seriously ill and not an advance directive itself. It is important to note that the POLST form allows religious preferences to be honored. For instance, information available on www.polst.org suggests that Catholics may make decisions consistent with the *United States Conference of Catholic Bishops Ethical and Religious Directives for Catholic Health Care Services*, 5th ed. (2009), and POLST ensures that those decisions will be honored in emergencies. POLST recommendations to allow natural death (AND) are viewed differently from euthanasia or physician-assisted suicide (PAS). POLST recommendations address such areas as cardiopulmonary resuscitation (CPR); level of medical care desired in an emergent situation such as comfort only, limited treatment, or full treatment; and whether artificial nutrition or hydration should be provided.

The value of advance care planning is that it can be accomplished in less stressful conditions as one is prompted to contemplate carefully the best-case scenarios for one's dying. By best case, I am referring to situations in which one's wishes will be followed because first, they are known, and second, the decision maker is both willing and able to complete them. In advance care planning, the patient or client has the central role. This person has decisional capacity, can reason, understand, and make choices he or she prefers. The client or patient's proxy or surrogate decision maker (previously appointed) does not need to wing the decision making if the primary decision maker (the principal) is incapacitated, but he or she can make decisions confidently. The agent knows what the patient wants. Often, major problems arise when either the patient's wishes are not clearly known or family preferences collide. Even within families who have a long history together, preferences and thoughts about best practices around health care vary. There is typically a presumption of assimilation from the majority cultural view toward minority cultures and religions: Those with minority religious views should conform to national standards of behavior. This can make it especially difficult for adherents of some religious faiths, such as Jehovah's Witnesses, to have their wishes honored, especially concerning such faith issues as declining a needed blood transfusion (McCormick et al., 2012). More recently, language about "respecting patient choices" enables patients to refuse medically futile care.

There are many pitfalls to decision making that surround personal values, suggests Periyakoil (2015) in a *New York Times* opinion piece. The call of love sometimes leads decision makers to override a patient's decision to forego life sustaining treatment based on their own personal needs and desires. The call of duty—what it means to be a responsible spouse, son, or daughter—can lead decision makers to ignore visible suffering. The call of redemption is often heard by decision makers as a last opportunity to repair broken relationships by keeping loved ones alive. A final issue is financial incentives for greater care may lead to authorization of that care when a different form of comfort care would better meet client needs at the end of life. For instance, nursing care facilities treating patients with feeding tubes receive higher rates of reimbursement, but feeding tubes do not lead to higher quality of life in older adult patients (Arinzon, Peisakh, & Berner, 2008). Some families are reluctant to make decisions that reduce care because they feel guilty about not doing everything possible for their loved ones. Spoon feeding rather than tube feeding is one example of care that may lead to a higher quality of life. To assist families in relieving unnecessary guilt, some have suggested applying the term *intensive comfort feeding* or *intensive comfort care*. Mindless aggressive care is a common outcome for older people at the end of life due to overmedicalization, technological medical advances, and the cultural disposition toward saving lives. Religious and spiritual ethical values suggest the need to invoke thoughtful reflection on individual preferences at life's end.

END-OF-LIFE CASE

Mrs. Kim (name changed) was a 78-year-old Korean woman who lived in a nursing care facility in the United States, suffering from severe rheumatoid arthritis and the effects of a Cerebral Vascular Accident (CVA) with hemiparesis which had occurred eight years earlier. Due to severe rheumatoid arthritis, she had difficulty grasping objects, navigating around her room, and getting to the bathroom. Consequently, she was completely dependent on nurses for her daily needs. She had immigrated with her husband and children to the United States at the age of 50, but she had

(Continued)

(Continued)

not been able to master the English language. She could understand spoken English, but had difficulty herself in speaking, both because of lack of fluency and speech impairment.

Mrs. Kim's husband had died about 10 years earlier. While living in Korea, she had always expected her children to care for her at home in her older years, as had been the custom for earlier generations. Her daughter, Anne, also lived in the United States and had, indeed, cared for her mother in her home from the time of Mr. Kim's death until the previous year, when her own health problems made the care too large a burden. Mrs. Kim appreciated the care she received in Anne's home, but she understood and accepted her own admission into the nursing care facility.

During visits three to four times a week from Anne, they often spoke of possible future scenarios. Mrs. Kim had told Anne that she did not want to ever be kept alive by artificial means and that she entrusted her daughter to do "the right thing" if the time ever came. However, she had never signed any type of advanced directive (AD) as she had a distrust of official papers she could not read in her own language. Because Mrs. Kim's English was difficult to understand, she often asked her daughter to be present and act as her interpreter with the physician and other medical staff. She had a Buddhist background and also followed Confucian principles. Even though she did not actively practice these beliefs, she was angry at the Catholic religion for *taking* her son away from his Buddhist roots. This situation

is an illustration of the complexity of religious practice and spiritual beliefs— although she was a nonpracticing Buddhist, Confucian spirituality was still a powerful spiritual influence on her life, and she resented the intrusion of other spiritual beliefs into the lives of her children. Her daughter Anne could only provide limited help in navigating this spiritual terrain because, although she was familiar with some Buddhist rituals, she did not herself profess a religion nor have strong spiritual practices.

Over a two-week period, Mrs. Kim developed pneumonia that became increasingly severe. The staff did what they could to keep her comfortable and then sent her to the hospital for treatment. She lapsed into a coma and had difficulty breathing. The doctor was a fundamentalist Christian who believed strongly in the sacredness of life. He told Mrs. Kim's daughter he would place Mrs. Kim on life-support equipment, though the daughter tried to explain Mrs. Kim would not have wanted this. In addition, Mrs. Kim's son Andrew flew in from Korea and said he supported the doctor's position. Andrew was also a devout, conservative Catholic who rejected Buddhist principles. As the oldest child, he believed it was his duty alone to make the important decisions for his mother. This is how both he and his sister had been raised, and he felt certain their father would have wanted him to take this role.

Anne asked the hospital whether they could arrange for a Buddhist chaplain to visit her mother so he could chant for her but, at the time, they did not have any Buddhist chaplains affiliated with the hospital. Still, hospital administrators wanted to be sensitive to the request, so the Director of Chaplains searched for a Buddhist monk in the area who would be willing to visit. The director then learned that Mrs. Kim's son had requested the sacrament of the Anointing of the Sick for his mother from a Catholic priest.

1. What are the key religious and spiritual issues important to this case? What are the preferences for care that each person has?

2. Who needs to be heard in this situation? What is the complication of the role of filial piety?

3. Assume a therapist is involved in this case, either through the hospital or as a previous support to the patient or one of the family members. What can this professional suggest?

Case adapted from Nelson-Becker, H., Ai, L. A., Hopp, F., McCormick, T. R., Schlueter, J. O., & Camp, J. K. (2013). Spirituality and religion in end-of-life care: The challenge of interfaith and cross-generational matters in changing environments. *British Journal of Social Work*, 1–16. doi:10.1093/bjsw/bct110

INTERGENERATIONAL ETHICS

The material aspects of life have become the most sought-after riches in the modern world (Dalai Lama & Norman, 2011). Because of this, intentional development of spiritual and mental health, a virtually limitless growth potential, has been neglected. The amount of material goods we can acquire is limited; our spiritual and mental capacities are not. At some point in life, perhaps if we are lucky in older ages, external goods will be recognized for the illusion they are. If we have pursued personal and compassionate growth directed toward alleviating the suffering of self and others, this stance just might be enough to sustain happiness.

How did we get to the point of imbalance in resource use? The *Story of Stuff* website (http://storyofstuff.org/) makes available a video that describes the process of extraction of resources to production, to distribution, to consumption, to disposal—together called the materials economy. It is a linear system on a finite planet, largely controlled by corporations and, to a lesser extent, governments. Natural resource exploitation uses up water, mountains, trees, and so on. Further, although the United States holds about 4.4% of the world's population, we use about 30% of the world's natural resources (Worldometers Real Time World Statistics, 2014). "In this system, if you don't own or buy a lot of stuff, you don't have value" (Priggen & Fox, 2007). About 50 years ago, the current group of older adults practiced values like stewardship and resourcefulness, but in 1955 they were urged to change those patterns. "Our enormously productive economy demands that we make consumption our way of life, that we convert the buying and use of goods into rituals, that we seek our spiritual satisfactions, our ego satisfactions, in consumption" (Lebow, 1955, p. 3).

How much impact that had is uncertain, but people did move toward a greater focus on shopping, to the neglect of other important pursuits. The ability to shop with few limits also has global consequences as some people are exploited to meet capricious desires that, at the same time, exhaust limited natural resources. This has mighty implications for intergenerational justice, so that older people who may have financial means do not overuse societal economic benefits in a way that could leave younger generations with greater struggles. This question of intergenerational justice is one that is compelling for the usually younger therapists who work with older people as well as for society at large.

As generations age, they remain accountable for their attention or inattention to the environment as well as normative actions in society. Older people and previous generations have either exercised good stewardship over the land—as happened when Teddy Roosevelt doubled the number of national parks in the early 1900s and sought other land protections—or destroyed the land through such activities as hydraulic oil fracking that can contaminate ground water. The earth is not a renewable resource. How we care for it—with its abundant gifts that nurture, body, mind, and spirit—will matter to all generations that follow. At the end of our lives, will we measure our value by what we left undone, as well as by our accomplishments and who we became?

THE RIGHTS OF OLDER ADULTS

Intergenerational justice is a concern in modern times, but on a broad level, securing the rights of older people around the world is of equal significance. Older people are an easy target of abuse for many reasons, including frailty, cognitive diminishment, and the love they have for their children and others that places them at risk. Recognition of these dangers on a global level helps ensure attention and may lead to prevention. Although many forms of harm are materially oriented, ultimately they result in spiritual harms: the marginalization of the older person and loss of his or her dignity. There is a direct connection between the material world, how we view it, how we choose to live in it, and how that affects the lives of persons around us. Those harms as well as the benefits are spiritual indicators of the level of soul health.

Human Rights and the United Nations

Compassion suggests that aggression and hurtful behavior should be neutralized through an appropriate response consistent with justice and universal human rights, the kind ratified in the Universal Declaration of Human Rights by the United Nations (U.N.) General Assembly on December 19, 1949 through persistent efforts by then–First Lady Eleanor Roosevelt who acted as Chairperson of the Commission on Human Rights. Another version of these human rights had been introduced in 1941 during Franklin Roosevelt's State of the Union address under what came to be known as the Four Freedoms: freedom of speech, freedom of religion, freedom from fear, and freedom from want.

These were the basic aims of the U.S. government adopted by the Allied Forces during World War II in the face of atrocities and extreme abrogation of human rights perpetuated by the government of then-Nazi Germany. Freedom of religion was especially notable at a time when people who were Jewish and as well as other religious minorities often were marginalized—even in the United States. The Marshall Plan enacted by Secretary of State George Marshall in 1947 after the war gave about 13 billion dollars to 18 nations, including Germany, to rebuild war-devastated regions, remove trade barriers, and to modernize industry. While also seeking to thwart a concern about Soviet communism, the overall goal was to help Europe once again achieve prosperity through generosity.

1991 U.N. Principles for Older Persons

The first United Nations World Assembly on Aging occurred in 1982 when consideration was given to the human rights of older persons. In 1991, the U.N. approved a resolution on Principles for Older Persons that was designed as a normative ethical framework for aging. The need was especially apparent due to the increasing global longevity and accompanying concerns about the challenge rapid population aging represented. The overarching preamble suggested it was important to "add life to the years that were added to life." Five areas were addressed: independence, participation, care, self-fulfillment, and dignity (see Table 3.1). The areas supporting independence sought to assist in ensuring a basic platform for rights. The participation dimension sought to ensure inclusion and combat ageism. The dimension of care, while recognizing some of the needs of aging elders in terms of health, also suggested that older people should be included in the decision-making process. Self-fulfillment was important in suggesting growth continues throughout the aging experience. Finally, the dimension of dignity set a standard and thus a warning about potential abuse.

Table 3.1 U.N. Principles for Older Persons, 1991

Under *Independence* were the following key recommendations:

- Older persons should have access to adequate food, water, shelter, clothing and health care through the provision of income, family and community support and self-help.

- Older persons should have the opportunity to work or to have access to other income-generating opportunities.

- Older persons should be able to participate in determining when and at what pace withdrawal from the labour force takes place.

- Older persons should have access to appropriate educational and training programmes.

- Older persons should be able to live in environments that are safe and adaptable to personal preferences and changing capacities.

Participation included the following:

- Older persons should remain integrated in society, participate actively in the formulation and implementation of policies that directly affect their well-being and share their knowledge and skills with younger generations.

- Older persons should be able to seek and develop opportunities for service to the community and to serve as volunteers in positions appropriate to their interests and capabilities.

- Older persons should be able to form movements or associations of older persons.

(Continued)

Table 3.1 (Continued)

Care included the following:

- Older persons should benefit from family and community care and protection in accordance with each society's system of cultural values.

- Older persons should have access to health care to help them to maintain or regain the optimum level of physical, mental and emotional well-being and to prevent or delay the onset of illness.

- Older persons should have access to social and legal services to enhance their autonomy, protection and care.

- Older persons should be able to utilize appropriate levels of institutional care providing protection, rehabilitation and social and mental stimulation in a humane and secure environment.

- Older persons should be able to enjoy human rights and fundamental freedoms when residing in any shelter, care or treatment facility, including full respect for their dignity, beliefs, needs and privacy and for the right to make decisions about their care and the quality of their lives.

Self-fulfillment included the following:

- Older persons should be able to pursue opportunities for the full development of their potential.

- Older persons should have access to the educational, cultural, spiritual, and recreational resources of society.

Dignity included the following:

- Older persons should be able to live in dignity and security and be free of exploitation and physical or mental abuse.

- Older persons should be treated fairly regardless of age, gender, racial or ethnic background, disability or other status, and be valued independently of their economic contribution.

Taken from the U.N. Resolution 46/91 on the *Implementation of the International Plan of Action on Aging* and related activities, by UN General Assembly, © 1991 United Nations. (pp. 160–161). Reprinted with the permission of the United Nations.

MADRID INTERNATIONAL PLAN OF ACTION ON AGING, 2002 AND BEYOND

Robert Butler of the International Longevity Center at Columbia University emphasized the need for laws to protect older people and expand their roles in advance of the 2002 U.N. World Assembly in Madrid (Butler, 2002). The preamble to his points highlighted global assaults on dignity and worth, prejudice, and discrimination. One of the rationales he provided included the concept of reciprocity in considering that "older people were once young and the young will one day be old" (p. 153).

> *This Declaration comes at a time of misery and chaos for many older citizens of the world who have lost children and grandchildren in armed conflicts, who are often homeless and destitute, who suffer from malnutrition and ill health, and who live in societies that cannot provide them with the basic necessities of life. It comes at a time of global disharmony in the context of powerlessness and attendant rage, shaped in part by vast divides in education, wealth, and longevity as well as ideology and theology [emphasis added]. (p. 152)*

> **Source:** From Madrid International Plan of Action on Ageing by the Second World Assembly on Ageing © 2002 United Nations. Reprinted with the permission of the United Nations.

The International Plan of Action on Aging, approved by the U.N. at their 2002 Madrid conference, called for development of common understandings, policies, and practices *at all levels in all sectors*. The goal of this document was to encourage a view of aging as a time for empowerment and realization of potential as well as safeguarding a floor for security and dignity. It was intended as a practical tool for policy makers. Goals were built on themes from earlier U.N. conference and General Assembly meetings; these are

- the full realization of all human rights and fundamental freedoms of all older persons;

- the achievement of secure aging, which involves reaffirming the goal of eradicating poverty in old age and building on the United Nations Principles for Older Persons;

- empowerment of older persons to fully and effectively participate in the economic, political and social lives of their societies, including through income-generating and voluntary work;

- provision of opportunities for individual development, self-fulfillment, and well-being throughout life as well as in late life—for example, access to lifelong learning and participation in the community—while recognizing that older persons are not one homogenous group;

- ensuring the full enjoyment of economic, social and cultural rights, and civil and political rights of persons and the elimination of all forms of violence and discrimination against older persons;

- commitment to gender equality among older persons through, inter alia, elimination of gender-based discrimination;

- recognition of the crucial importance of families, intergenerational interdependence, solidarity and reciprocity for social development;

- provision of health care, support and social protection for older persons, including preventive and rehabilitative health care;

- facilitating partnership between all levels of government, civil society, the private sector and older persons themselves in translating the International Plan of Action into practical action;

- harnessing of scientific research and expertise and realizing the potential of technology to focus on, inter alia, the individual, social and health implications of aging, in particular in developing countries; and

- recognition of the situation of aging indigenous persons, their unique circumstances and the need to seek means to give them an effective voice in decisions directly affecting them. (United Nations, 2002)

Priorities addressed included older persons and development, enhancing health and well-being into older age, and ensuring environments that would be enabling and supportive instead of disparaging or abusive. More recently, the U.N. General Assembly (2015) has created a more expansive document, *Follow-up to the International Year of Older Persons: Second World Assembly on Aging,* that identifies and presents recommendations for action in six areas: poverty, health, gender equality, employment and decent work, inclusive cities, and environmental emergencies.

GENEROSITY, SPIRITUAL WEALTH, AND SERVICE

The concept of generosity is related to empathy, but it also moves to the more expansive level of compassion presented in Figure 3.1. When our thoughts, hearts, and actions reach out to others and we permit our concern to linger with them, that attention can shift us toward engagement with them in ways that can support their growth or change. Further, acknowledgment of all the planetary gifts that have been given freely—clean air to breathe, water to drink, food to eat, and beauty around us whenever we choose to notice—culminates in an understanding of both reciprocal generosity and spiritual wealth.

Spiritual wealth is not about ownership but about maintaining harmony and equilibrium with our environments, both built and natural. Spiritual wealth appears concomitantly with individual and collective attention and action to protect the earth and respecting the visions and values of others. There are many older people who may not possess *material* wealth, but they do possess a high level of empathy and charity that keeps them in strong relation with the world around them—even though technologically the world may advance at a different pace. However, there are also those older persons who remain in spiritual poverty, still seeking land, goods, or power, and harming those unlucky enough to interact with them. Nature is not a commodity to be monetized.

Earth is neither inert nor passive but alive and enriched by the life lived upon it. All creatures share mutual interdependent responsibility to care for the earth. Those who are old share in the responsibility to leave a legacy of joint nurture of earth with later generations, in whatever way they choose.

For many older adults, abundant living comes through service. The path to service is one of the traditional religious and spiritual vocations. Inviting older people to consider the kinds of situations and persons that can benefit from their time as volunteers can upend depression and loneliness. Helping them expand the range of possibility and then try out different forms of volunteerism with different organizations or groups—children, people with disabilities, homeless individuals, new immigrants, people with severe mental illness, abused persons or animals, people living in poverty—can be highly rewarding. Although younger older adults may have more financial and physical freedom to choose broadly, even older adults with disabilities or frailty can volunteer through various avenues, including telephone reassurance programs for other older people. Reconnecting older people to their own values is important ethical work.

SUMMARY

This chapter addressed many dimensions of values for practice. Historical and modern virtues were discussed as well as religious and spiritual/existential virtues. Traditional competing components of ethical theory were introduced, such as deontology and teleology and how these perspectives may lead to different practice decisions. Values important in clinical practice with older people were presented as well as important boundaries for ethical practice in religion. Religious conversion and prayer are areas where practitioners may falter, especially when personal values may seem more compelling that professional distance. End-of-life ethical considerations in decision making often become very complex with older people, so discussion of that was addressed in this chapter. Finally, macro considerations of intergenerational justice and global human rights in aging were given as cautionary notes for the present. These will be important issues long into the future as we work to create just societies.

QUESTIONS FOR DISCUSSION

1. Reflect on the discussion about virtues. What is your greatest virtue, the one easiest for you to display or the one in which you carry great skill? What is the virtue most difficult for you to attain or express? What virtues are easily recognizable in older adults? Which ones might be both related to and unrelated to the experience of aging?

2. What virtues are most important in getting along with other people? What virtues seem most important for societies to hold?

3. Which ethical theories seem most appealing to you? Why?

4. What professional ethical dilemmas have you faced? How did you proceed at the time? What might you do differently now?

5. Under what conditions might prayer be useful with older clients and when might it be unethical?

6. What examples of intergenerational injustice have you noted? What might be some solutions?

7. Why should clinicians be concerned about global elder injustice?

MEDITATION: CHANGING OF THE SEASONS

When the seasons begin to change, especially summer into fall and winter to spring, people at times experience that change in their bodies in negative ways. However, there is rhythm to all of life. It flows unceasingly from birth to death, and sometimes rebirth. As existentialist and writer Albert Camus recalls, "In the midst of winter, I found there was, within me, an invincible summer." You can begin this exercise anywhere in the life cycle.

Pause and pay attention to your breathing, breathing in and out slowly. Think of a flower, possibly your favorite flower. Imagine it in a place that you see every day. If it is winter, imagine your flower as just a seed lying in the cold earth. One day, you walk by and notice just a little stalk of light green or white poking its top just above the soil. You think about your flower and all of the joy it has brought you. You look forward to watching your flower grow, and it does. Each day, this stem grows a little taller and becomes a little more green. Soon a bud forms at the top, then a leaf starts to emerge. In late March or April, the bud begins to grow larger, then slowly opens over time. Now it is a full flower, in its early stage with the color gently emerging. As you walk by in May and June the flower grows richer in color and is soon at its peak. It has a lovely fragrance. In July and August, you begin to note an edge of brown on a petal. Soon, your flower begins to wilt. One by one the petals blow off. Now, in September and October, there is just a stalk. It, too, turns brown and then falls to the earth. Soon, the first snow of the season covers it. You can no longer see it, but you know it is there—and you think about the time when you will see its beauty one again. In the midst of winter, a thought of the summer. Come back from this meditation.

EXPLORING YOUR SPIRITUALITY: SPIRITUAL-ETHICAL WILL

While the spiritual-ethical will may be written at any point in life, it is particularly meaningful at older ages when it can provide a sense of completion and fulfillment. It is an integration of head and heart that shares a unique voice—yours. It may hold therapeutic value as writers select the most meaningful personal stories to share and consider the worth of their life as well as their relationships with those who will see this will.

1. Imagine that you are at a point in life where you are ready to share the distilled knowledge of your life's learning.

2. What family history is most important for your family or friends to know? What particular incidents meant a lot to you and why? What are the main life lessons you want to share from these experiences?

3. What are your spiritual and personal values?

4. Are there areas where you want to ask forgiveness of others? What would you say to them if they were present to hear? What would you want them to know about you now?

5. What are your hopes, dreams, and blessings for your children, grandchildren, or close friends? While you cannot control what will happen to them, what are your thoughts about best-case scenarios for their lives, wherein they still retain their own freedom and choice?

6. What are your wishes for advance directives at the end of your life at this point in time?

7. How do you want to be remembered by your family or friends?

EXPLORING YOUR SPIRITUALITY: VISION

How we see, observe, and witness what is around us is critical to formation of our own unique worldview. What we see and how we see is affected by many factors, including memory, mind frame, and focus among others. What have we become numb to? Sometimes what becomes too familiar to us also becomes invisible. We fail to see it freshly, so it is difficult for us to understand what may hinder us or hold potential encouragement for us. A story encapsulates this well: "My uncle would say to me, 'You ought to follow the example of the shunktokesha [wolf]. Even when he is surprised and runs for his life, he will pause to take one more look at you before he enters his final retreat. So you must take a second look at everything you see'" (Eastman as cited in Jacobs, 2008, p. 139). We find it difficult to know our experienced world unless we juxtapose it against other views. The more we allow ourselves to see, the more we can see. Nature often helps us. We may witness a leaf fluttering and spinning relentlessly to the earth in autumn. We may see a pair of birds frolicking in spring, or a bird dive bombing us when we walk close to his nest. Traveling overseas or just to a new and unknown place can be also helpful. In the unfamiliar customs and ways of being found in other cultures, we begin to better understand our own.

1. Think of yourself as a stranger stepping ashore and encountering this situation for the first time. What features do you particularly notice about it that seem to be key characteristics?

2. Compare this view to the one you held previously. What has changed?

3. Based on your new view or fresh mind, what might you want to do or say to alter a problem, possibly a client's situation, so that you can move toward problem resolution or enhance or mine untapped resources together?

4. Journal your response.

EXPLORING YOUR SPIRITUALITY: SCENT

Our five senses of sight, hearing, smell, taste, and touch are important as ways of interacting with the world. They are mediators of our embodied selves and their acuity and accuracy determines in part the way we understand what the world is. However, these senses are not equally aroused in our modern world. Media gives foremost attention to what we see (sight) and hear (sound) and so shapes what we know primarily through these two senses, though scent branding is an emerging method for businesses to connect with potential customers on an emotional level. In ancient times, frankincense and myrrh were highly valued and known as kingly commodities, but the power of smell seems to have lost its pungency today. Sweet grass, sage, cedar, and tobacco in the cultural stories of indigenous American Indian tribes represented traditional gifts given by the Creator. As those words are read you may be able to recall the fragrance of each. Scents can be calming like the scent of lavender, jasmine, or chamomile; they can delineate holy spaces as does burning incense. Measured amounts of incense mark time while burning and are evanescent, yet they may create lasting memories.

Smell takes us back to earlier experiences and enables us to recall them vividly. One of my students who was close to her grandmother was very sad when her grandmother died. Her younger cousin had trouble recalling their grandmother, so my student took her into the hall closet where they would breathe in her scent in the clothes still hanging there. Her aunt had kept the house, so they were able to do this for some time until the scent finally faded years later and the clothes were long gone. People who grieve may find it difficult to part with the clothes of their loved one: sometimes they wear a garment of the deceased relative so as to recapture their scent.

Think about the smell of fresh rain in the air, of newly mown grass, of a walk in the forest, a flower garden as well as a walk by a compost heap, rotting fish or other food, or a weeks-old unwashed body. My school at the University of Kansas stood alongside on Lilac lane. This was aptly named for in the spring we would be enfolded by the sweet smell of lilacs from trees lining the walkway from the building to class. The smell of baking bread or freshly made apple pie can make us think of home, security, all is well with the world, or that we are hungry. Recently, I stepped onto a Metra train, surprised that this particular car had only a few people while other cars were packed. I soon discovered the reason: someone on that car had not bathed in some time and it stank. Like others I'm sure, I exited that car and moved to one behind at the next stop, all the time chastising myself for that lack of generosity in failing to stay present to that unsavory odor. We are drawn to pleasing smells, and avoid bad ones. We might dismiss scent as a less valuable sense, but it aides us in largely unacknowledged ways. Older people can lose their olfactory sense and concomitant with that the sense of taste resulting in diminished appetite and weight loss. And for a few people, scent can be experienced as overwhelmingly strong and can sicken or cause allergies through heightened sensitivity.

1. What experiences have you had with scent, either pleasant or offensive? If pleasant, what do you recall and how did the scent make the experience enjoyable and memorable? What particular scents appeal to you? What fragrance or fragrances do you seek out? How? In a store available for purchase? In the natural world?

2. If offensive, from what did the odor emanate? What was the cause? What was your resulting reaction, both physical and emotional? Did you stay or were you able to leave? How did this experience shape you for future selected action—for example, did you avoid anything based on this experience?

3. Imagine a world with no scent. How would this world be diminished from the one you experience now? (Or, if you are one who has many scent allergies, how might this world be preferable?)

4. How might you choose to pay attention to scent—to notice scents in the future? In what way is scent connected to spiritual experience for you, if at all?

5. Journal about your responses.

WEBSITES

Aging with Dignity

https://agingwithdignity.org/five-wishes/about-five-wishes

This website presents the Five Wishes document, which can facilitate end-of-life conversations. It is fee-based, though nominally. Previously it was freely available.

Advance Care Planning, North Shore Hospital, North Shore University Health System

http://www.northshore.org/health-resources/screening-prevention/advance-care-plan/

This site provides very useful tools for developing an advance care plan including a downloadable guidebook.

Building a 7-Generation World

http://www.youtube.com/watch?v=OYJg7zuEhQw

This local TED talk by Susan Bosak discusses legacy and placing yourself within the seven-generation framework of aboriginal people.

Center for Practical Bioethics, Kansas City

http://www.practicalbioethics.org/download-caring-conversations

This site features Caring Conversation workbook guides in English/Spanish and for several kinds of populations with age diversity.

Good End of Life

http://www.goodendoflife.com/worksheets/GoodEOL_Worksheet2_Advocates.pdf

How to choose a good end of life decision maker is detailed.

Gray is Green

http://grayisgreen.org

This advocacy site has sections on healthy aging, families and grandkids, and taking action.

Let's Talk about Dying

http://www.ted.com/talks/peter_saul_let_s_talk_about_dying

This TED talk features the importance of preparing for end-of-life care needs and scenarios.

National Center on Elder Abuse

http://ncea.acl.gov/

Current information regarding research, training, best practices, news, and resources on elder abuse, neglect, and exploitation are provided here.

The Elder Justice Initiative

http://www.justice.gov/elderjustice/

This site is a resource for "victims of elder abuse and financial exploitation and their families; practitioners who serve them; law enforcement agencies and prosecutors; and researchers seeking to understand" and address this issue.

Strengthening Older People's Rights: Towards a UN Convention

http://social.un.org/ageing-working-group/documents/Coalition%20to%20Strengthen%20the%20Rights%20of%20Older%20People.pdf

A joint 2010 publication calling for a special U.N. convention to uphold the rights of older people was written collaboratively by nine age-focused international organizations.

The Global Alliance for the Rights of Older People

http://www.rightsofolderpeople.org

Established in 2011, the Global Alliance for the Rights of Older People was born out of the need to strengthen the rights and voice of older people globally. It is the result of a collaboration across nine international organizations.

The Oxford Martin School at the University of Oxford

http://www.oxfordmartin.ox.ac.uk/policy/

This is a "world-leading centre of pioneering research" that addresses global challenges. This website includes policies and ideas about achieving intergenerational justice. See specifically "What Is More Important Than Protecting the Interests of Future Generations?" (http://www.oxfordmartin.ox.ac.uk/opinion/view/260).

Prepare for Your Care

https://www.prepareforyourcare.org

This free online user-friendly resource helps older people especially make decisions about who should serve as a surrogate as well as describing care options.

UN General Assembly 2015 Report: Follow-up to the International Year of Older Persons:

Second World Assembly on Aging

https://documents-dds-ny.un.org/doc/UNDOC/
GEN/N13/402/51/PDF/N1340251
.pdf?OpenElement

This report addresses a post-2015 development agenda from an older person's perspective: poverty, health, gender equality, employment and decent work, inclusive cities, and environmental emergencies. The report also provides updated information on recent developments on aging from the regional commissions. The report concludes with recommendations for ensuring that no older person is left behind in the implementation of the agenda.

Who Gets Grandma's Yellow Pie Plate?

http://www.extension.umn.edu/family/personal-finance/who-gets-grandmas-yellow-pie-plate/

This website housed at University of Minnesota extension services is concerned with ethical property transfer from an older generation to a younger one. It suggests how to discuss this issue and different means of looking at fairness, for example, by worth or quantity or desirability. It includes information on a workbook to share with families and professional article references.

RECOMMENDED READING

Brother Emmanuel of Taizé, & Livingstone, D. (Trans.). (2011). *Love, imperfectly known: Beyond spontaneous representations of God.* New York, NY: Continuum International.

This erudite book written by a brother from the Christian community of Taizé, France, discusses images people hold of God from a psychodynamic perspective. His discussion involves the projections people carry, often of parental figures, which keep God from being truly known by them. This is a wonderful and insightful book that will take people deep into a fresh perspective on compassionate love and loving.

CHAPTER FOUR

RELIGION AND SPIRITUALITY IN THEORY

The theory of relativity [showed] that even such
fundamental concepts as space and time
could be changed and in fact must be changed on account
of new experience.

—Werner Heisenberg

Science is based on personal experience, or on the
experience of others, reliably reported.

—Werner Heisenberg

T his chapter discusses why theory is important to research and practice and how some of the great philosophical questions of life have entered into theory building. Pathological and positive theories about the aging experience both find place here. The theories and theoretical perspectives are generally presented in the order of their emergence, with an understanding that earlier theories and changes in the cultural milieu have affected the development of later theories. Key theories of social gerontology— disengagement, activity, continuity, and the life course perspective—are discussed in relation to spirituality. Freud and Jungian views of religion are identified, while the lack of room for spirituality in most behavioral approaches is also mentioned. The work of major developmental theorists Erikson, Tornstam, and Fowler related to religion and spirituality is described. Humanism and transpersonal psychology, deeply concerned with man's spiritual nature, are discussed. The chapter concludes with theories of positive aging, successful aging, and the strengths perspective.

WHY DOES THEORY MATTER?

Theory is more than a convention. It is a lens that helps one see particular aspects of a problem in relief, while relegating other aspects to the background. Students of the social and psychological sciences study theory because theories help them understand and conceptualize the precursors to and outcomes of problems. Theories help expand understanding of causes and, in the case of micro-to middle-range theories, guide or suggest helping activities that may improve conditions. An agent of change, in this case, a counselor, nurse, social worker, or other professional helper, can never thoroughly remove him - herself from all of the underlying assumptions that help weight the decision to choose one theory over another. However, greater self-awareness can help bring these assumptions to consciousness. In some cases theoretical assumptions of two different theories may collide, while in other cases, theories can and do support each other (e.g., cognitive theory and behavioral theory) thus serving to enhance each one when combined in some manner. Theory may serve several functions. First, theories are used to explain phenomena, to solve puzzles or mysteries beyond what is observed or witnessed. Second, theorizing is a process rather than an end product. Theories help us reach understanding. They assist us to challenge what we currently know and consider how we can expand our understanding of what is conceivable and achievable. Last, applied theories should be explicit, so that the assumptions and biases that are associated with the selected theory are known.

Theories are often referred to in a formal way: sets of propositions that lead to hypotheses that are testable. Another approach to use of theory is as a mechanism to understand reality. Theory applied in this chapter helps create a framework for knowledge about human behavior. However, theory is also not a hunch. It is based on the best scientific evidence available about rationale for behavior emitted under specific conditions that range from personality variables, broad societal traditions, culture, to other situational aspects of the environment. In gerontology, theories of aging are interdisciplinary or transdisciplinary, drawing on many academic specialties such as sociology, theology, philosophy, and psychology. Theories highlighted here will include theories common to social gerontology as well as theories about individual behavior and development, however all theories identified will be discussed in relation to spirituality and aging. It is important to recall that theories themselves are influenced by the predominant societal values that influence scientific inquiry and interpretation. So theory development is not often as pristine a process as sometimes thought. In the past, old age was often constructed from a pathological platform, but now as more people are living into older ages with greater health, an optimistic approach to aging has become a focus. There is wide understanding that while many people live with chronic illness, decline is only one feature of aging. This transition is valuable because it opens up more possibilities to explore in promoting a positive view of the aging process. Seeing possibility widens opportunities for growth and creativity, which are two key components of spirituality and aging.

SOCIAL GERONTOLOGY PERSPECTIVES AND THEORIES

Aging as Pathology

The "aging as pathology" perspective is included here to describe the thinking prevalent in the mid- to late 20th century that still has residual effects today. This was the first period when the normative life length began to extend to older ages, partly due to advances in medicine and health consciousness (Administration on Aging [AoA], 2009; Nelson-Becker, Chapin, & Fast, 2006). This new phase of life held some potential for growth and connection, but also potential for depression and despair according to many historical writers (Macnicol, 2010). On the one hand, older adults were valued for the wisdom or life knowledge they could share; but on the other, the many visible losses of aging and the consequent results when physical impairment led to unwanted housing relocation and losses of other freedoms, generated fear of this life stage. Autonomy and control, highly valued in our society, were often seen as reduced. Relinquishment of a driver's license remains the symbolic and practical precursor to restricted mobility and choice. Overall stereotypes of older adults endure (Hummert, 1990; McCann & Giles, 2002; Rupp, Vodanovich, & Crede, 2005).

Aging as pathology is witnessed through lingering societal stigma. Aging is viewed as a disease process that is not welcome. Robert Butler was the first director of the National Institute on Aging and the author of the book *Why Survive? Being Old in America* (1975), which sought to convince readers that more than survival was possible (cited in Achenbaum, 2014). Butler coined the term *ageism* to correspond to words like *racism* and *sexism* that devalued certain sectors of society. Up until recent time, a disparaging view was promoted in society through birthday cards that took on a dark tone using sarcastic or negative humor, through unsympathetic slang labels for older adults, and other visible stereotypes particularly present in the media.

Aside from adverse attitudes to aging, employment discrimination against older adults existed and continues to exist in places. Some organizations have been successfully sued for workplace discrimination against older workers. Finally, age discrimination has existed in the distribution of goods and services: there is concern in health care about older people using a particularly high volume and high dollar cost share of resources in the month before they die.

Some view ageism as originating from our internalized fear of aging and death. Ageism may have sociobiological and human capital roots in the lowered social status sometimes attributed to older people because they reach a point of absent economic productivity (Macnicol, 2010). A psychological explanation would add that we are hardwired to favor youth. The more positive potentials of the aging process such as a time in older adulthood to focus on spiritual growth and give back to society through intergenerational interaction are not considered in ageist attitudes. In the parlance of younger or middle-aged adults, rather than age-shaming, age claiming should be the social norm.

Social Gerontology: Theories From the Kansas City Studies

Common perspectives and theories about aging present opposing views of the aging experience. In most of these, spirituality is not formally considered, though it may be implicit. The first three theories of aging discussed below, disengagement, activity, and continuity, emerged from the Kansas City Studies of Adult Life begun in 1952 and directed by Robert Havighurst, William Henry, and Bernice Neugarten (Neugarten & Maddox, 2001). This Carnegie Corporation and NIMH–funded research was the first to focus on social and psychological changes that occurred as individuals moved from middle to older ages. The initial study was based on a probability sample of 750 people aged 40 to 70 and was cross-sectional. A second set of studies was conducted on 280 people aged 50 to 90 interviewed at multiple points over six years. From this work several theories emerged.

Disengagement. The disengagement theory (Cumming, 1963; Cumming & Henry, 1961) suggested that older adults enter a natural process to disengage socially and mentally as they transition from their working life. This was the first formal theory that sought to explain aging. Society and the older person were seen to mutually withdraw from each other, however the disengaged older adult would continue to enjoy a sense of psychological well-being and life satisfaction, now free of oppressive social norms. Gender role differences were prominent in disengagement as well because women were viewed as holding socioemotional roles (responsible for developing and maintaining social ties), in contrast to the instrumental roles of men, which were often allotted the practical tasks of financial support and home maintenance. Older people were assumed to enter a time of decline that emphasized greater inaction along with decreased social space, but also possibilities for life review. As other relationships changed, there was an implicit assumption that spiritual focus might grow, particularly if individuals became more introspective. Demographic patterns have changed markedly for older adults in the years since those studies (AoA, 2009). With longer periods of health post retirement, many older adults continue to remain involved in communities through second careers, volunteerism, and other forms of civic engagement (Morrow-Howell, Hinterlong, & Sherraden, 2001). Thus, the validity of the disengagement theory has not held up well over time. It has also been critiqued for reinforcing stereotypes about the aging experience.

Activity. Activity theory, in contrast to disengagement theory, promoted the need for older adults to remain invested in life through ongoing physical and social activity (Hooyman & Kiyak, 2008). Optimal aging was interpreted as resisting the narrowing of the social world and discovering substitutes for relationships lost through retirement or death. Reanalysis of the Kansas City studies data using different measures found a moderately positive correlation between life satisfaction and activity, lending some support to this theory (Neugarten & Maddox, 2001). This theory does not explicitly consider the spiritual domain, although it could be argued that there is room in activity theory for a spirituality of social involvement and building community assets. An activity theory perspective of spirituality would imply that older adults who identify as religious maintain their involvement in religious communities to the extent possible over time. Differences in sociocultural settings and interindividual variability suggest that there is no single pattern for optimal aging, but rather there are many.

Continuity. Continuity theory (Atchley, 1999; Havens, 1968) hypothesized that traits and ways of engaging the world developed by middle age would continue to be the preferred lifestyle in older ages. This theory went beyond activity theory by suggesting that not all older adults desire an active lifestyle. The internal structure of identity one developed in younger ages would be continued in later ages. This would be reinforced by the stable external structure of ongoing roles and relationships. The key idea of this theory is that people become more of what they were as they age into their futures. Continuity could be an adaptive strategy to manage changes of normal aging. When individuals reflect on their experience and ability, they can set new goals to maintain or extend their priorities in living. Certainly, in practice people often do continue behavior learned in earlier decades that worked well for them. However, this theory does not consider the many undesired adaptations required for some elders in the aging process, nor does it explicitly consider the developmental growth and change that can mark a spiritual path both through challenges as well as successes. A continuity theory of aging and spirituality would suggest that the spiritual disciplines integrated in daily life could continue to be a resource. Or, if one did not identify a personal need to develop or maintain a spiritual perspective in earlier years, the value of a nonreligious nonspiritual path would likely remain.

Life course perspective. Of all the social theories and perspectives of aging discussed above, the life course perspective is probably the most complex, taking into account social roles and age-related events (timing of marriage and birth) embedded in culture and historical norms (Bengston & Allen, 1993; Elder, 2001; Hooyman & Kiyak, 2008). Multiple interlocking trajectories are a distinguishing feature of the life course. Age, period, and cohort effects are the primary variables. The specific age of a person may designate the type of activities in which she or he participates. For instance, age 17 to 18 usually denotes high school graduation in U. S. culture and ages 14 to 45 specify the range of fertility. The historical period of time overlays additional effects, such as the deprivations of the Great Depression of the 1930s, which caused some older adults to carefully preserve resources. A cohort effect takes into account the values and priorities of each generation as it moves across time. While values established in World War II marked the Greatest Generation, the more controversial Vietnam War engendered strong feelings for Baby Boomers. The life course can be viewed as an interactive nonlinear process. It highlights the ways individuals refer to age-related explanations for behavior. Rather than a theory per se, it may be viewed as an approach to inquiry and a framework that guides problem identification and analysis.

The life course includes consideration of several levels of analysis. It can encourage examination of the impact of microsystem relationships for an individual, the mesosystem of family relationships, and macrosystems such as social policies and connections with social institutions or dominant paradigms. Ideas about what constitutes a particular lifetime (temporality), age as a basic element of life structure (chronology), and greater freedom from social control (individuality) may be considered (Elder, 2001). A spiritual view of the life course could extend it outside of time, chronology, and individuality. Many world religions view time lived on earth as one aspect of the soul that exists both before birth and after death. Age matters in earth time as the body begins to wear down and parts wear out, but age has less relevance to the soul self. The soul continues development according to the opportunities that present at different ages, but is less constrained by chronological age. The purpose of the soul according to some religions such as Buddhism, is not to attain the highest level of individual development possible, but instead through enlightenment to lose the sense of a separate self. So the self transcends the ego to achieve a state of unity with other enlightened beings or Bodhisatvas (Gethin, 1998).

The life course involves five principles: how the past shapes the future, timing of lives, linked lives, sociohistorical and geographical location, and personal control and agency (Elder, 2001). First, lifespan development encourages questions about how early life actions influence later life opportunities or *how the past shapes the future*. For example, an older adult who was not able to attend college or university may have limited income at later ages. Second, *timing of lives* encourages questions about the sequencing of a person's major life events. If an older woman stayed at home to care for an older parent, she may have never married or married at a later age, precluding the ability to bear children. Timing also refers to generational or cohort time and the broader events of historical time. Third, people are embedded in relationships and live *linked lives*. Because of this degree of interdependence, an event that might occur to one person in a family, for instance a severe car accident, could lead to major life changes for a spouse or parent who might have to change work patterns to offer care. Social ties affect us deeply.

Fourth, *sociohistorical and geographical location* matter in simple survival. The concept of lives in time and place identifies the historical impact of living during a particular time. A major event like the war in Afghanistan has different effects on cohorts, from the younger cohorts who may serve in the military forces to older cohorts who may lose a child who serves or pay increased taxes to fund the war effort. Some children in third-world nations never survive to older ages because of poverty, poor nutrition, and health challenges. Fifth, *personal control and agency* means individuals express their own choices and make decisions about how they want to proceed based on their personal values and priorities. If one could know all aspects of their relationships, their experiences, and the influences of their historical time and culture, it would still be difficult to predict the decisions made by others. The interconnection of these principles illustrates the richness of the life course perspective. This perspective challenges us to think about what happens across a life as an integrated system rather than what occurs in separate segments or windows of time. At older ages, one has the gift of this longer perspective that is never visible in early and midlife views.

THEORIES OF INDIVIDUAL BEHAVIOR

Not all theories offer room for religion and especially spirituality—with its focus on internal understandings—in their assumptive foundations. The idea of enlightenment or salvation that religion fosters recognizes the limits embedded in human nature. For this reason, there are three values common to religiously attuned philosophies that uphold transformation or self-transcendence. These include a sense of wholeness, community, and ultimacy (Forsyth, 2003). Wholeness includes knowing the self beyond what is apparent in everyday material reality, community fosters the idea of compassion and connection with others in contrast to alienation, and finally ultimacy refers to discovery of a personal ground of meaning or purpose.

Psychodynamic and Freudian Perspectives

Freud viewed religion as creating a cultural and moral boundary for adherents of a faith (Freud, 1927/1989). He believed civilization sought to control nature with technology and relationships through law, culture, and religion. He saw an inherent conflict between the individual who seeks gratification and society, which requires subjugation of instincts for participation in public life. These limits particularly included physical aggression and sexual pursuits. The superego internalizes prohibitions and values of parents and later society in Freud's estimation. Formation of a moral nature is thus an internalization of an outer process of socialization. In this perspective, religion acts as an agent of culture by suggesting that God forbids murder, stealing, dishonesty, and so on. These same sanctions also serve as the glue that promotes social cohesion rather than disruption.

The anxieties of adulthood cause individuals to project the need for a loving, protective father onto their image of God in Freudian views (Forsyth, 2003). However, the ambivalent feelings toward a natural father, reflected in relief and gratitude for God's love but dismay at the commandments of God, have origins in the oedipal developmental stage. Freud thus considered religious belief an illusion based on our wishes for protection. He saw belief in God as supporting helplessness rather than promoting independence and growth. The actual objective truth claims of religion, however, cannot be assessed in his view.

> *Just as they cannot be proved, so they cannot be refuted. The riddles of the universe reveal themselves only slowly to our investigation. But scientific work is the only road which can lead us to knowledge of reality outside ourselves. It is merely an illusion to expect anything from intuition and introspection.* (Freud, 1927/1989, p. 40)

For Freud, religious belief had a psychological motivation; it was an illusion that may or may not be true. He did not define it as delusion or an error of thinking because that proof was outside testable methods. Primarily, his theory sought to provide an analysis of religion and to suggest there was value in retaining it for the education of children and the needs of individuals and community. How does this apply to older adults? Because of the length of time older adults have lived with an internalization of social values, some may indeed rely on God in a passive form of coping. However, just as older adults have many views of God, some also have images of God that span a spectrum of belief (see Pargament, 1997).

Jungian Theory

While Carl Jung long had a close association with Freud, their relationship ruptured over their opposing views of the role of religion and spirituality in human development. Jung (1939, 1963) observed that religion, whether it contained a system of doctrine or not, involved the human quest for meaning and achieving wholeness. This quest was central in the developmental process and he advocated exploring dreams, art, and mythology, as well as learning religious views of clients. He wrote that the original meaning of the term *psyche* is "soul." Thus, *psychotherapy* means "healing of the soul." Balance and harmony were important in his view and, in concert with them, he developed the ideas of archetypes and the collective unconscious.

Archetypes are the primordial images often manifested in dreams and visions, such as the shadow, the anima, and the wise old man. Further, there are *archetypes of transformation*, which are symbols that carry manifold meanings and may also be paradoxical (Laszlo, 1993, p. 403). The archetype is largely unconscious content that changes as it moves into consciousness; the collective unconscious is the subconscious awareness that connects individuals to each other (Laszlo, 1993). Water is often the chief symbol of the unconscious, powerful in its image of fluidity. In recent history, the fall of the Berlin Wall in 1989 and the subsequent opening of many previously closed Eastern European national boundaries may represent this type of collective unconscious connection because these events happened rapidly in a place and era when communication was largely absent.

According to Jung, the task of the second half of life is to reconnect with unconscious beginnings and to recover the soul (Forsyth, 2003). Our connection with the unconscious occurs primarily through dreams, rituals, and other symbolic content. Symbols act as mediators that help bring the unconscious to consciousness and reconcile discord and suffering in a transcendent way. Principles of growth or individuation have religious qualities that can lead to wholeness or understanding of self. Jung favored the inner experience of religion and cautioned against the dogma present in organized religion.

Behavioral Theories

Behaviorism, based on observable interaction, considers the principles of learning through which behavior is shaped by antecedent conditions and consequences (Sharf, 2008). John Watson and B. F. Skinner were early adopters of behavioral principles. In a behavioral perspective, it is the actions of individuals that are the key to future change. For behaviorists, what is observable is known: ideas, thoughts, and other internal processes have little value. Actions may be reinforced or extinguished through the type of attention that is provided. Shaping and modeling are two key treatment methods. Other theories that have their roots in behaviorism include social learning and exchange theories developed by Albert Bandura (Robbins, Chatterjee, & Canda, 2006). Behavioral theories, although useful in understanding and shaping interactions, have little direct connection to spirituality because the concept of a reality beyond what is known through immediate sensory perceptions is discarded. However, they do offer learning in terms of the practices and rituals individuals select that may be spiritual or religious, such as meditation, prayer, or religious attendance. Connections with religious institutions may be understood through reinforcing or punishing mechanisms, but there is less space for understanding growth through development of ethical standards, for example, unless this is modeled by others.

DEVELOPMENTAL AND TRANSPERSONAL THEORISTS

Developmental theories share a belief that individuals can grow, adapt, change, and transform. The spiritual self, though not often explicitly mentioned in most of these theories, has the capacity to make choices for or against learning and growth, and it can reach toward new understanding or shirk away. Development has a biological basis, but it also can be acknowledged as containing psychological, emotional, social, and spiritual components. Each of these levels of development varies and it is *not expected* that an individual who may function at a point of advanced growth in one area is also at that same point in other areas of his or her life. Because specific individuals are closely associated with certain developmental orientations, this section is organized by the authors of major theories, even though the theories also build on each other.

Erikson's Lifespan Developmental Theory

Erikson formulated a developmental model that included seven separate stages of development across the lifespan (Erikson, 1950, 1982; Erikson & Erikson, 1997; Erikson, Erikson, & Kivnick, 1986). The task of each stage is to overcome a common life challenge, the resolution of which will lead to the next stage. These challenges take the form of basic strengths against core pathologies or antipathies, such as generativity versus stagnation (middle age). Each stage offers a syntonic or positive task (integrity in older age) followed by a dystonic, negative one (despair), with the goal of achieving a healthy balance between the two. While this stage-based theory is often presented in a linear time/sequential manner, there was also provision for a recursive process as people may move back and forth between tasks of each stage until they are ultimately resolved. These challenges can be viewed as "an epigenetic recapitulation on a higher developmental level" (Erikson, 1997, p. 50), rather than a failure to work through the basic struggle that each life stage presents. His use of the term *epigenetic* did not relate to genetic development but rather development that was *before* in time and *above* in space. It was understood that each stage relied and leaned on all previous learning, while maintaining the *invariable core* that served as the integration of past, present, and future orientations of the self. Furthermore, successful completion of each stage led to outcomes such as Wisdom, Care, and Love in adult stages and Hope in infancy. All of these represent spiritual values and virtues generally supported by religion (see Table 4.1).

The eighth stage of older age was identified as *integrity versus despair and/or disgust*. This period entails the task of reaching a fundamental acceptance of positive and negative experiences in life. A general goal is to feel at peace with who one has become, without regret or self-reproach. As one reviews events that unfolded over a lifetime and across the challenges of each stage, she or he is more likely to view life with satisfaction if some contribution was made toward improving the lives of self and others (connecting to the generativity stage of midlife). If an individual is not successful in achieving integrity, she will experience despair and fear of death. He may see life as one of lost opportunity, regret, and wish for a second chance. Successful mastery of this final life stage brings wisdom and the ability to recognize states of integrity in other people. In the epigenetic schema, each stage retains aspects of earlier phases, so this eighth stage also maintains a *grand generative* capability. Wisdom is expressed through reliance on basic trust formed in infancy even though hope may be challenged by losses. Living with *intensity of being* may assist older adults to achieve the gerotranscendence identified by Tornstam (1996, 1997, 2005). Erikson and Erikson (1997) suggest in an added chapter to the 1997 version of the *Life Cycle Completed* that one can move beyond a time-linked identity to a timeless one in older ages. At the beginning of life, one lives with what is given, the independent variables of life. By midlife one understands something about generosity to others, so one *is* what one has given away. The task of later life is to recognize death as a final gift, the opportunity to give back what one has become, an entity with increased consciousness (Erikson & Erikson, 1997). "Gerotranscen-*dance* [emphasis added] is . . . a regaining of lost skills, including play, activity, joy, and song, and above all, a major leap above and beyond the fear of death" (p. 127). This is a dance of magnificent proportions, a dance of life that connects beyond present frailty to beauty. This final task, though not explicitly identified as such by Erikson and Erikson, is a spiritual one.

Tornstam's Gerotranscendence

Tornstam (1996, 2005) suggested that gerotranscendence involved a paradigmatic shift in perspective from a materialistic and individual perspective to a cosmic and transcendent one. He indicated that development toward gerotranscendence might include the following eight elements: (1) an increasing sense of cosmic connection with the universe; (2) a redefinition of perceptions of time and space; (3) a redefinition of the meaning of life and death; (4) an increased connection to both living and future generations; (5) a decreasing interest in unnecessary social interaction; (6) a decreasing interest in materialism; (7) a decrease in concern about the self; and (8) an increase in meditation time (Tornstam, 2005). In contrast to Erikson and Erikson's (1997) earlier theory building, which suggested that the highest form of adult development involved integration of elements of the past, Tornstam (1982, 1996) held

Table 4.1   Erikson's Epigenetic Crisis Stages and Basic Virtues

Crisis (including adaptive strength)	Basic Virtue and Secondary Virtue (and related strengths)	Life Stage/ Relationships/Issues
1. **Trust** vs. Mistrust	**Hope and Drive** (faith, inner calm, grounding, basic feeling that everything will be okay, enabling exposure to risk, a trust in life and self and others, inner resolve, and strength in the face of uncertainty)	Infant/parent relationship, feeding and being comforted, teething, sleeping
2. **Autonomy** vs. Shame and Doubt	**Willpower and Self-Control** (self-determination, self-belief, self-reliance, having a voice, being one's own person, persistence, self-discipline, independence of thought, responsibility, judgment)	Toddler /parents, bodily functions, toilet training, muscular control, walking
3. **Initiative** vs. Guilt	**Purpose and Direction** (sense of purpose, decision making, working with and leading others, initiating projects and ideas, courage to instigate, ability to define personal direction and goals, able to take initiative and appropriate risks)	Preschool/family, exploration and discovery, imagination, adventure and play
4. **Industry** vs. Inferiority	**Competence and Method** (making things, producing results, applying skills and processes productively, feeling valued and capable of contributing, ability to apply method and process in pursuit of ideas or objectives, confidence to seek and respond to challenge and learning)	Schoolchild/school, teachers, friends, neighborhood / achievement, and accomplishment
5. **Identity** vs. Role Confusion	**Fidelity and Devotion** (self-confidence and self-esteem necessary to freely associate with people and ideas based on merit, loyalty, social and interpersonal integrity, personal standards and dignity, personal identity, seeing useful personal role(s) and purpose(s) in life)	Adolescent/peers, groups, influences, resolving identity and direction, becoming a grown-up
6. **Intimacy** vs. Isolation	**Love and Affiliation** (capacity to give and receive love—emotionally and physically, connectivity with others, social and interpersonal comfort, ability to form honest reciprocating relationships and friendships, reciprocity toward the good)	Young adult/lovers, friends, work connections, intimate relationships, work and social life
7. **Generativity** vs. Stagnation	**Care and Production** (giving unconditionally in support of children and/or for others, community, society, and the wider world, altruism, contributing for the greater good, making a positive difference, building a positive legacy, helping others through their own crisis stages)	Mid-adult/children, community. giving back, helping, contributing
8. **Integrity** vs. Despair	**Wisdom and Renunciation** (calmness, tolerance, appropriate emotional detachment—nonprojection, no regrets, peace of mind, nonjudgmental, spiritual or universal reconciliation, acceptance of inevitable death/ departure)	Late adult/society, the world, life meaning and purpose, life achievements, acceptance

Source: Adapted from Erikson, E. H. (1982). *The life cycle completed: A review.* New York, NY: W. W. Norton. Chart 1 on pp. 32–33 and Chart 2 on pp. 66–67.

that gerotranscendence reaches forward to include a reformulation of reality for the present and foreseeable future yet-to-be lived. Reminiscence then is not only useful in helping older adults maintain continuity, but could move toward a reorganization and reconstruction of identity leading to new understandings of existence, maturity, and wisdom (Tornstam, 1999).

Time perceptions change. Views of the past, present, and future are not so discreet but become better linked as older adults reflect on their relationship to previous and future generations. Sometimes this is a time period when people begin to search for their personal genealogical history. Ideas about life and death are redefined when one can longer ignore the approach of death (Nelson-Becker, 2006). Further, some people experience a need for reduced social interaction. Time spent in solitude is rich and expectant with opportunity to reflect and grow (Tornstam, 1997). The generativity of middle years is often more fully articulated as older adults thoughtfully consider the moral/ethical or physical/financial legacy they want to entrust to the generation that follows. The concepts surrounding gerotranscendence fit well with spiritual perceptions of the developmental process.

Fowler's Stages of Faith

Fowler (1981) developed a stage-based model that was unique in seeking to incorporate a faith development perspective. Thus all stages will be described here. This six-stage model conceptualizes stages that are linked to age development. The first stage is titled *intuitive-projective* faith and occurs between ages 3 and 7. At this time, children begin to develop an awareness of self and the constraints of society's rules/norms. They are exposed to the effects of the unmediated unconscious, but also revel in a rich imaginative process. The second stage is termed *mythic-literal* faith and is found primarily in school-age children. Symbols and rituals are important and justice and reciprocity are viewed as standard elements of the universe. Increasingly, individuals in this stage are able to take the perspective of others in their relational processes. Persons at this stage are *trapped in their own narrative* that seeks perfectionism and depends on a legalistic view of religion. The third stage is a *synthetic-conventional* faith that begins in adolescence. Fowler believed most adults remained at this stage. Here, individuals order their world through conformity to religious beliefs and do not critically reflect on their faith until contradictions with lived experience may thrust them into the next stage.

The fourth stage is *individuative-reflective* faith where individuals begin to question their identity and belief in a demythologizing process. This stage is primarily existential; disillusionment is the defining factor. If persons enter this stage, they do so generally in their mid-20s to early 40s. If they remain here, they may become bitter. Stage five is the stage of *Conjunctive* faith, where individuals reach a more expansive level and can witness and be present with paradox. They now know what is important to them and what they believe, but also understand that there may be other truths beyond their present one. The world is once again sacred and this new inclusiveness leads to a comprehensive view of justice. Thus, truth is not absolute but multidimensional and evolving. They understand that paradigms will be challenged, but may hope for an elusive ultimate truth that never arrives. The challenge of this stage is not just to live in wonder, but to also be able to integrate new understandings, make decisions, and live their truth. The final stage six is that of *universalizing* faith, where individuals glimpse a unitive view of life similar to that expressed in transpersonal theory. The need to promote the self diminishes as one works to enlarge understandings of community and

Table 4.2 Fowler's Stages of Faith

Stages	Age Frame	Key Features
1. Intuitive-Projective Faith	Children ages 3–7	Foundation of trust or mistrust
2. Mythic-Literal Faith	Children ages 7 to early adolescence	Literal interpretation and simple rules about what is fair, limited perspective-taking ability
3. Synthetic-Conventional Faith	Begins in adolescence, possibly present in adulthood	Beliefs and values not open to critical interpretation; personal worth judged by treatment from others
4. Individuative-Reflective Faith	Adulthood, if present	Distancing from previous values, "executive ego" allowing one to take responsibility for one's beliefs
5. Conjunctive Faith	Mid-adulthood, if present	An integrative stage moving beyond either/or categories, openness to discovery of a deeper self, awareness of social influences, and ability to embrace paradox
6. Universalizing Faith	Rare, probably appears in older ages	Inclusiveness of all being and universal values that are applied in living

Source: Adapted from Fowler (1981).

compassion. Their work in the world involves nonviolent strategies and respect for all beings. It is also possible that their radical views lead to both personal impatience and negative reactions from others who are puzzled or fearful of their approach. See Table 4.2 for Fowler's stages.

Fowler was criticized for basing his theory on a small number of nonrandom interviews. His view was that few people ever reach the final sixth stage. This sixth stage also presupposes time spent in the other earlier stages. He may not have had many older adults in his sample, but older life stages often allow the types of experiences that might enable one to reach this sixth stage of expanded understanding and enlarged choice. While Fowler's theory is one of the few that directly discusses faith development, it is also closely aligned with Piaget's cognitive developmental stages and Kohlberg's theory of moral development. The latter both advance stage models, though Fowler focuses more explicitly on religious and philosophical components. By suggesting that most adults do not go beyond a type of blind faith acceptance, he appears to devalue the ability of adults to reflect on and construct their own world view. A further question concerns his lack of evidence for suggesting which categories most represent the views of midstage and older adults. This theory makes religious faith the central concern that defines major life tasks.

HUMANISM

The humanistic movement was considered the Third Force of psychology behind the First and Second Forces of Freudianism and Behaviorism. Humanism emerged in the 1950s in response to existentialist influences pre–and post–World War II that indicated people were responsible to create their own meaning in a disordered world harboring no intrinsic meaning. While people enjoyed freedom to create their own purpose, this existential view also led to the anxiety of knowing there was nothing *out there* that fully explained life. Existence came before essence. Thus people were tasked with creating their own meaning (Sartre, 1958/2003). The humanistic approach emphasized individual strengths such as compassion, meaning, creativity, and freedom. Although existentialists would likely shun any explicit connection with spirituality, the search to understand more about the human condition and common human needs is relatable to the search to better understand one's spiritual self, defined as the highest ideals and virtues of what it means to be human.

This psychology focused on health carried several assumptions. These included a biologically based inner nature partly unique and partly common with others that could be discovered (Maslow, 1968). This nature was good or neutral rather than bad or evil, although evil could surface in violent actions when intrinsic needs and emotions were not fulfilled. However, if this inner nature were nurtured, then individuals would grow to be healthy and happy. The characteristics of healthy people are (1) an enhanced perception of reality; (2) increased acceptance of self, others, and nature; (3) increased naturalness and spontaneity; (4) increased ability to focus on problems; (5) increased detachment; (6) increased independence; (7) greater freshness of appreciation; (8) greater frequency of peak experiences; (9) increased identification with people; and (10) improved relationships, changes in values, and a deeper level of creativity (Maslow, 1968). These attributes are attainable by everyone if they are able to work through fears about knowing who they are and become more conscious of weaknesses as well as strengths. Healthy growth is a series of choices, where each successive choice validates the risk by adding more joy. Courage and fear stand at two opposite ends, competing forces in a change process. Maslow (1971) later expressed concern that his earlier writing was somewhat unbalanced in his emphasis on individual attainment, for he then believed that basic human needs could only be filled by and through associations with other people.

Maslow was one of the key figures of the humanistic psychological approach. While grounded in a framework that encouraged individuals to reach their full capacity, Maslow's work also pointed to transpersonal psychology, which he termed the *fourth force* (Maslow, 1968). He was disturbed by his profession's focus on abnormal or ill individuals and sought to develop a positive health psychology that he termed orthopsychology. He viewed humanism as a transitional philosophy to this way of thinking centered in the cosmos. Transpersonal psychology led to self-transcendence that moved beyond the needs and interests of self-actualization alone (Maslow, 1968).

Two key concepts thus emerged from humanism: *self-actualization* and *self-transcendence*. Self-actualization is the process by which one satisfies first priority needs and then is able to address increasingly complex needs. Self-transcendence is defined as moving beyond self-actualization and the boundaries of the self to join other beings and the ground of being in a state of unitive consciousness with that force known as God, the Divine, or by other names (Robbins et al., 2006). In this state, the self disappears and one is outside time and space. What may seem a routine act (attending a graduation ceremony in the hot sun) becomes an experience of joining with all of the great educators of history and all of those generations of scholars, intellectuals, and students who will come after to the generations yet unborn in one great procession slipping out of time. Dichotomies, polarities, and conflicts are resolved at this level of being into a greater state of wholeness. All of the regrets, guilt, and shame of the past may be fully accepted into one's present self. One transcends the ego.

Maslow's theory identified a hierarchy of needs as a triangle or pyramid shape where the first and broadest level included physiological needs for air, food, water, and shelter. We have witnessed this focus on basic needs in the aftermath of 2010 earthquakes in Haiti and Chile. The second level above (though not more important) included needs for safety and order, when one feels secure enough to venture beyond current boundaries. The third level consisted of needs of belongingness and love such as affection for family and friends. The fourth level consisted of esteem needs such as those of achievement, responsibility, reputation, and self-esteem. At this level, one begins to know one's own worth. The fifth level involved self-actualization needs, which Maslow (1970) later expanded beyond personal growth and fulfillment to include aesthetic sensibility, creativity, altruism, and justice as well as cognitive needs for knowledge and meaning. This category of needs went beyond the desire to acquire wealth and social standing and in fact, people at this level often had little interest in such pursuits.

The lower instinctual psychological needs were termed by Maslow the *deficiency* or *D-needs* (Hoffman, 1996). When meeting these needs had one's attention, one could not move on to consider higher-order needs without first satisfying these prerequisite needs. However, every need level is equally important. Moving up to satisfy higher order categories of needs is a type of unfolding process of natural emergence and growth, like that of a great English elm tree growing for a hundred years as it is nurtured by water, soil, and air from its origin as a small seed falling from a mother tree. Table 4.3 describes some of Maslow's suggested methods for moving out of the deficiency realm. Self-actualization was important in its emphasis on full humanness. This state is the highest point of human growth, which is a yearning for further growth in creativity, emotional spontaneity, wisdom, autonomy, and commitment, also known as *being-cognition and motivation.*

Maslow developed much of his theory through interviews with self-actualizing people; he found as many transcenders among businessman and managers as he did among priests, poets, and musicians. He also found paradoxes and destruction of his long-cherished beliefs. He delighted in new understandings such as the ability to appreciate nature for-itself and in-itself rather than for human purpose. There were three types of transpersonal experience in Maslow's (1970) schema: *peak*, *nadir*, and *plateau* experiences. In the *peak* experience, an individual may experience moments of deep insight, heightened perception and awareness through the senses, great compassion and connection with others, understanding of the immensity of the universe, and communion with an ultimate or sacred source of meaning. The *nadir* experience involves a powerful slide into illness, psychological crisis, or a brush with death that breaks open new understanding of self in relation to all. The *plateau* experience is one where happiness and joy suddenly enter into awareness in a relatively tranquil, relaxed, and blissful manner. This may have been one of the several meanings of the work by C. S. Lewis (1955), *Surprised by Joy.* Joy was also the name of C. S. Lewis's wife. Without doing anything to stimulate the encounter, one is enveloped in a serene state of being. The challenge of these mystical experiences of illumination or awakening is not to seek them or value them exclusively, but rather to integrate the new perspectives into daily life, so that wonder, significance, and beauty are always accessible (Maslow, 1970, 1971).

Maslow (1971) also seemed to share the societal bias against older people. He commented that "the aging body is less capable of tolerating a really shaking peak

Table 4.3   Reaching the Being-Realm

Reaching the Being-Realm by A. H. Maslow:

1. Get out of the deficiency-world by deliberately going into the being-realm. Seek out art galleries, libraries, museums, beautiful or grand trees, and the mountains or seashore.

2. Contemplate people who are admirable, beautiful, lovable, or respect worthy.

3. Step out into "clean air" on Mount Olympus. Step into the world of pure philosophy, pure mathematics.

4. Try narrowed-down absorption or close-up fascination with the small world, for instance, the ant hill, insects on the ground. Closely inspect flowers or blades of grass, grains of sand, or the earth. Watch intently without interfering.

5. Use the artist's or photographer's trick of seeing the object in itself. For instance, frame it and thereby cut it away from its surroundings, away from your preconceptions, expectations, and theories of how it *should* be. Enlarge the object. Or squint at it so you see only general outlines. Or, gaze at it from unexpected angles, such as upside down. Look at the object reflected in a mirror. Put it in unexpected backgrounds, in out-of-the-ordinary juxtapositions, or through unusual color filters. Gaze at it for a very long time. Gaze while free associating or daydreaming.

6. Be with babies or children for a long period of time. They are closer to the being-realm. Sometimes, you can experience the being-realm in the presence of animals like kittens, puppies, monkeys, or apes.

7. Contemplate your life from the historian's viewpoint—100 or even 1,000 years in the future.

8. Contemplate your life from the viewpoint of a nonhuman species, for example, as it might appear to ants.

9. Imagine that you have only one year left to live.

10. Contemplate your daily life as though being seen from a great distance, such as from a remote village in Africa.

11. Look at a familiar person or situation as though viewing it for the very first time, freshly.

12. Look at the same person or situation as though viewing it for the very last time, for instance, that the individual is going to die before you see him or her again.

13. Contemplate the situation through the eyes of the great and wise sages; Socrates, Spinoza, or Voltaire.

14. Try addressing yourself, or talking or writing, not to the people immediately around you but over their shoulders, that is, to history's great figures like Beethoven, William James, Immanuel Kant, Socrates, or Alfred Whitehead.

Source: Hoffman (1996). Permission granted by Ann R. Kaplan

experience. . . . maturing and aging means also some loss of first-time-ness, of novelty, of sheer unpreparedness and surprise" (p. 348). Further,

> *Older people, making their peace with death, are more apt to be profoundly touched, with sweet sadness and tears at the contrast between their own mortality and the eternal quality of what sets off the experience . . . e.g., "The surf will be here forever, but you will soon be gone. So hang on to it; appreciate it; be fully conscious of it. Be grateful for it. You are lucky." (pp. 348–349)*

While science sought to eliminate the bias of values, Maslow understood that little activity is value-free. Even research is based on values concerning what is important to investigate. He advocated a Daoistic approach to inquiry that included receptivity rather than force and asking rather than instructing in all humanistic encounters with clients. Some of his *B-values* included truth, goodness, beauty, aliveness, uniqueness, completion, playfulness, and simplicity, while his list of metapathologies included their opposites (Maslow, 1971). In *Religion, Values and Peak Experiences* (Maslow, 1970), he summarizes his view:

> *The great lesson from the true mystics, from the Zen monks, and now also from the Humanistic and Transpersonal psychologists—that the sacred is in the ordinary, that it is to be found in one's daily life, in one's neighbors, friends, and family, in one's back yard, and that travel may be a flight from confronting the sacred—this lesson can be easily lost. To be looking elsewhere for miracles is to me a sure sign of ignorance that everything is miraculous. (Preface)*

TRANSPERSONAL PSYCHOLOGY

Transpersonal theories are those that address the united elements of human behavior in our need for creativity, giving and receiving compassionate acts, finding meaning and purpose, and building community with other people, the planet, and the universe. The way to develop these aspects is to go inward and learn to understand and integrate all parts of ourselves, including the submerged or hidden shadow sides. Then, understanding ourselves and working toward our own self-actualization, we can also join to help others achieve their full capacity in kindness and love. The term *transpersonal* refers to experiences that move beyond the ego-bound limits of the person. Thus, these theories incorporate room to identify, critique, and share the spiritual experiences that are difficult to translate into words. Older adults in the years beyond the stress of parenting, earning a living, and contributing to their communities may have greater capacity to understand and experience the connections that mark a transpersonal sphere of living.

Existentialism

Existentialism was a school of thought that emerged in the wake of the destruction in Europe from World War II and consequent rapid societal changes. French existentialists Camus and Sartre wrote of the anxiety associated with finding meaning in a world devoid of inherent meaning (Camus, 1991; Sartre, 1958/2003). Because life is absurd—without ultimate meaning—one's task is to learn to be happy in the face of mortality. The task of every individual is to create meaning for themselves while coping with spiritual exhaustion and despair. Because of this, choice is one of the most powerful weapons one has against meaninglessness.

Logotherapy was a therapeutic approach to the anxiety of existence advocated by psychiatrist Victor Frankl (1992). He survived a Nazi concentration camp through persistence and his decision not to give up emotionally. His view asserts that the main motivation of people is to find their own reason for living, even in conditions of unbearable suffering. Life, he asserts, always has meaning, even in the worst conditions. In a coping study of older adults, this view was confirmed by one concentration camp survivor who explained that she had a friend in the camp and they looked after each other. That was the only reason she believed she made it out of the camps alive (Nelson-Becker, 2004a). Further, Frankl asserted that individuals always have the freedom to choose their response, even if they cannot change other conditions of their life. This concept of engagement in a search for meaning is consistent with many spiritual and religious approaches that seek to help older adults and others reconnect with sources of meaning and purpose.

Key Concepts in Transpersonal Theory

Many developmental theorists address *pre-egoic* and *egoic* developmental phases (Robbins et al., 2006). The *pre-egoic* phase is when biological processes and drives for nurture of all kinds are primary for the infant. The *egoic* phase begins to appear in childhood when a separate self is recognized apart from caregivers. At later ages, tasks of building healthy and intimate relationships are the focus. The *transegoic* phase added to the two other stages in transpersonal theory includes periods when the self is viewed as joined with others, rather than just connected with them. Often these states are referred to as cosmic consciousness or union with the sacred.

Sri Aurobindo writes of two forms of consciousness—outer ordinary reality and one inner concealed consciousness (Dalal, 2001). As one's inner consciousness opens, one is able to live increasingly in the inner being, which becomes more real as the outer world becomes more like the dream. This inner consciousness is "not the intellect, nor the ethical or thinking mind, but divinity within or Spirit" (Dalal, 2001, p. 25). It is aware of the intersections of both personal and universal forces that create spiritual light not unlike material light. This inner mind operates by perception and vision rather than by thought.

Behavioral manifestations of human consciousness are identified by Wilber (2000) as *functions* including perception, desire, will, and acts; *structures* that include body, mind, soul, and spirit, and *states of consciousness* that distinguish between normal waking, dreaming, sleeping and altered conditions such as nonordinary and meditative states. Reality is viewed as a Great Chain of Being or Nest of Being where each level of existence—matter/body, mind, soul, and spirit—encompasses all of the previous levels. While some traditions of the perennial philosophies indicate only 3 levels, others suggest as many as 7 or 12, up to 108. These levels are known as *holons* of consciousness, which are wholes that also form parts of other greater wholes, such as soil that forms the earth that forms part of the planetary system. Visually these form a series of concentric circles each enfolding the smaller circle with the edges overlapping like the spectrum in a rainbow. Wilber's (2001) integrative psychology suggests that through these four basic levels of body, mind, soul, and spirit (imagine a *y*-axis) flow at least 24 developmental lines (imagine an *x*-axis) that include such areas as self-identity, affect, cognition, altruism, communicative competence, kinesthetic skills, and empathy among others.

Further, Wilber identifies four quadrants: individual subjective (I), collective intersubjective (We), individual objective (It), and collective interobjective (Its). See Figure 4.1.

The upper left subjective individual quadrant and the lower left collective intersubjective quadrant are both interior focused and characterized by interpretive

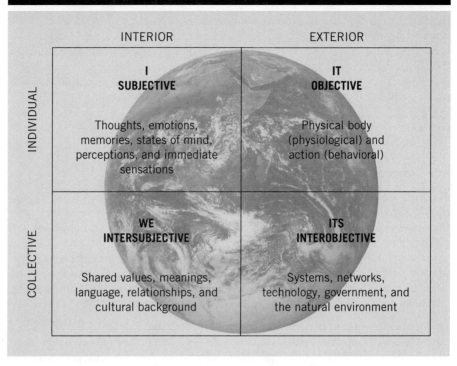

Figure 4.1   Ken Wilber's Four-Quadrant Model

	INTERIOR	EXTERIOR
INDIVIDUAL	**I** **SUBJECTIVE** Thoughts, emotions, memories, states of mind, perceptions, and immediate sensations	**IT** **OBJECTIVE** Physical body (physiological) and action (behavioral)
COLLECTIVE	**WE** **INTERSUBJECTIVE** Shared values, meanings, language, relationships, and cultural background	**ITS** **INTEROBJECTIVE** Systems, networks, technology, government, and the natural environment

Source: Adapted from Wilber, K. (2005). *Introduction to the Integral Approach and the AQAL Map.* Retrieved from http://www.kenwilber.com/Writings/PDF/IntroductiontotheIntegralApproach_GENERAL_2005_NN.pdf.

and hermeneutic approaches; the upper right individual objective quadrant and the lower right interobjective collective quadrant are both exterior paths characterized by empirical and positivistic thinking. The task of integral psychology is to integrate these four quadrants with the four levels of consciousness (Wilber, 2000, 2001). Premodernity was all-level, but not all-quadrant, while modernity was all-quadrant, but not all-level. A full-spectrum therapy works to pull away defensive layers so our deeper knowledge of who we are is revealed layer by layer, as in peeling an onion. Rather than being linear, development forms a spiral pattern. People can be at different stages of development in any of the developmental lines, such as social relations and cognitive capability. They can move downward as well as upward and may have peak experiences into higher transpersonal states of consciousness (Wilber, 2000). However, the general trend is to move toward growth and greater understanding of self in relation to others (Robbins et al., 2006). It may be the case that living to older ages provides more opportunity to grow along all of the developmental lines and to understand and live by four-quadrant reasoning, even if individuals have never heard this term.

THEORIES OF POSITIVE AGING, SUCCESSFUL AGING, AND STRENGTHS

Earlier decades of research focused on depression and depletion in the aging process, but many of the same investigators who championed such ideas as learned helplessness have more recently begun to focus on the contributions available through the gift of long life (Seligman & Cskiszentmihalyi, 2000; Saleebey, 2009). The compensation model (Baltes, 1993), the concept of successful aging (Rowe & Kahn, 1998), aging well (Valliant, 2002), and creative aging (Cohen, 2005) have all highlighted the opportunities available when people attain older age. This strengths-based focus relates well to connections between aging and spirituality where even crises may be appreciated for their potential to waken the spirit and nudge individuals toward new paths of growth.

Selective Optimization With Compensation

The Selective Optimization with Compensation (SOC) perspective suggests that older adults can continue activities that gave them pleasure by attending to deliberate modifications (Baltes, 1993). Rather than succumb to restrictions that may be inevitable in aging and release cherished goals, people adjust. Baltes provides an example of an aging concert pianist who still chooses to perform on stage. To compensate for memory and dexterity changes, she selects fewer musical compositions, optimizes them by more practice, and plays them at a slower pace. The SOC perspective applies to spirituality and aging by suggesting that an aging person is empowered through his/her choice to continue participation in a desired activity, though in an altered way. Agreeing to adaptation preserves a core interest that maintains vitality. This is not, however, just about letting go of former standards, but also about gaining new understanding and living in a deeper way. Though the pianist in the example above may play fewer pieces, she may cherish them and breathe with them differently, uncovering new dimensionality and possibility. This view aligns with positive views of the aging process in its suggestion that adaptation can help one retain joy in life.

Successful Aging

After several decades of concern about society-wide focus on the myths and pathology of aging, a new direction developed. The MacArthur Foundation funded dozens of researchers including physicians Rowe and Kahn (1998) to study aging in America. Rowe was chair of the interdisciplinary panel of scientists. The prevailing myth at the time was that presence of certain genes led to either physical vitality or acute and chronic illness, disease, and disability. However, Rowe and Kahn discovered that individuals have some control over their aging process through the lifestyle choices they make regarding nutrition, exercise, and mental stimulation. Questions addressed by that study included what does it mean to age successfully, what can each person do to achieve that state, and what changes in American society can facilitate that goal? Successful aging was defined in this landmark group of studies by three key characteristics: (1) low risk of disease and disease-related disability, (2) high mental and physical function, and (3) active engagement with life. In this paradigm, we see echoes of activity theory and continuity theory that were prevalent in earlier decades. A major portion of their book focuses on ways to avoid disease—prevention and early detection—as well as information about exercising and nutritional standards such as merits of specific vitamins. The roles of social support and connectedness are explored. Productivity, defined as any activity—paid or unpaid—that generates goods or services of economic value, is viewed as a goal for aging positively. Rowe and Kahn promote ways to maintain learning, keep work roles if desired, and develop leisure pursuits in this period of life, suggesting that functional losses are preventable.

By calling attention to positive aspects of aging, the MacArthur study demonstrated that cognitive decline was not normative. Further, it delineated that maintenance of social networks as a key predictor of psychosocial adjustment to the aging process. However, there have been a number of critiques of the concepts of successful aging (Crowther, Parker, Achenbaum, & Larimore, 2002). One of the main themes is that people who are disabled and unable to engage actively in life as defined by the study would be considered unsuccessful agers. Another concern is that spirituality is not addressed at all, yet is considered by developmental theorists as well as helping professionals to offer value in aging well that may be as powerful as social support to those older adults who find religion and spirituality important to any extent. Indeed, Crowther et al. (2002) argue that spirituality should be considered the fourth factor in successful aging due to many positive correlations between health, religion, and spirituality. While aging successfully helps to derail stigma surrounding the aging experience, the limits on who is included in the definition could cause some older adults to negatively appraise their capacity as they compare themselves to peers.

Harvard Study of Adult Development

The Harvard Study of Adult Development, like the MacArthur study, examined the psychosocial factors associated with successful aging (Valliant, 2002). Wisdom was another factor identified by Valliant as vital to healthy cognitive functioning in later life. His definition of wisdom was "the capacity and the willingness to step back from the immediacy of the moment—whether it is an affect, a judgment, or a conflict—in order to maintain perspective" (p. 251). Valliant saw the development of wisdom as something accessible to all socioeconomic classes, not only those older adults who were well-educated. Along with wisdom, generativity—or the concept of feeling a sense of responsibility for the next generation—was also viewed as a positive factor in aging well. More recently, Valliant (2008) has written about the value of bringing positive emotion to consciousness and restoring acknowledgement of the power of spirituality.

Generativity

The desire for generativity leads older adults to nurture relationships with relatives or friends younger than themselves. Through this form of caring, they evidence ongoing care and concern about the earth and its inhabitants. This also represents a major developmental challenge of mid-adulthood according to Erikson's schema where the seventh life stage consists of generativity versus stagnation/self-absorption (Erikson et al., 1986). Generativity reflects a spiritual value that reminds individuals that they are connected to others. They both affect and are affected by the external environment. People have the choice to make a contribution back to the world or to withdraw from it the resources they believe they require. Sometimes the latter choice also can leave a residue of ill will or destruction. The desire to offer a return or contribution to the world may be fulfilled through monetary donations to causes one supports; volunteering time to schools, humane societies, or many other civic organizations; or sharing ones thoughts and ideas in a formal way, such as through an ethical will.

The term *generativity* has meaning related to the word *generosity*. For the Blackfoot and Plains American Indians, gathering wealth was unimportant. Instead, the virtuous act was giving wealth away, which brought status and security to the giver (Hoffman, 1996). So generativity was actioned by giving wealth away, though wealth may have other than material dimensions. Generativity to later generations may be expressed through an ethical will. An ethical will is a Hebrew tradition in which one passes on a personal philosophy for living a good life (Reimer & Stampfer, 1991). In the Middle Ages, ethical wills were typically written in an informal personal style intended for teaching children. A modern example might be *The Last Lecture* by Randy Pausch (2008), who was a professor at Carnegie Mellon and dying of cancer when he was invited to give a Last Lecture, a common but distinguished lecture at his institution. Typically an academic exercise, Pausch chose to use that time to share his perspective about life and living. An ethical will may be written at any point in life. Participating in this exercise during life cycle changes, such as times of impending marriage or birth, may help a couple clarify values.

Positive Aging: Ongoing Growth in Aging in the Work of Gene Cohen

Like many other gerontologists, Cohen felt that the aging process had been devalued and the potentials obscured by a society-wide focus on illness and loss. At the same time losses occur in some areas, there is expansion in others. For instance, while older adults may have some short-term memory deficits, they make have strengthened their neural brain network in a way that leads them to find solutions to complex problems more rapidly (Nakamura, Kobayashi, Ohasi, & Ando, 1999). Using interviews and questionnaires with 3,000 older adults, Cohen investigated creativity and aging (Cohen, 2005). His research led him to postulate four phases visible in mid-life and beyond: reevaluation, liberation, summing up, and encore. These phases are not necessarily consecutive and may not be experienced by all older adults. The reevaluation phase (from the mid-30s to mid-60s) is a period of exploration and quest rather than a midlife crisis. Here, people ask themselves questions such as, "What am I doing with my life now and where do I want to go?" Neuroplasticity of the brain documented in recent work stimulates further development of intelligence and wisdom may emerge. The liberation phase (mid-50s to mid-70s) is a time of release from prior boundaries and continuing discovery. People seek novelty and feel free to speak their true thoughts. Retirement usually occurs during these ages and offers time for further experimentation. The summing up phase (late 60s into 90s) is one of review, resolution, and generativity. Individuals attend to what is yet undone; they are motivated to tell their stories for the next generation or even for themselves. The final encore phase (from the French, *again* or *still*) appears from the late 70s and may last to the end of life. During this phase one recognizes and comes to terms with major life themes while also building on those themes. This expresses a desire to remain vital even in oldest ages. These phases all come about through inner drives—*pushes*—or maturation and are assisted through brain development.

These phases generated by Cohen extend Erikson's developmental stages in a more flexible way. Rather than addressing a challenge, crisis, or conflict that must be overcome, they simply present an enriched view of the aging process, holding out a hopeful view of time considered from spiritual, emotional, and physical standpoints. While Cohen contends that what he offers here is novel, Erikson's last book, completed by his wife Joan, does address these themes though not as separate phases. The key contribution of Cohen's work is that the brain provides evidence of plasticity in older ages; this neuroplasticity then offers hope for development instead of deterioration so often posited by earlier decades of research.

Strengths Perspective

The strengths perspective was developed to assist adults who sought treatment at mental health centers (Saleebey, 2009). Now it has filtered into many settings and disciplines. Similar to resilience and solution-focused models, this perspective recognizes the inherent capacity of individuals to serve as experts on their own lives and to find the way out of difficulty when given support (Kivnick & Murray, 2001; Nelson-Becker et al., 2009). A strengths orientation is consistent with a spiritual view that people possess a self-righting potential that can be empowered through relationship. A strengths approach with older adults addresses five primary goals:

- All individuals have strengths at every stage of life and under all conditions. Discovering and building on strengths of older adults will facilitate hope, self-reliance, and personal satisfaction.

- Traditional diagnosis and assessment often make assumptions that limit rather than expand capacity. Acknowledging that older adults have the capacity to learn, grow, and change is fundamental.

- Developing a collaborative therapeutic relationship can motivate the older adult to achieve aspirations.

- Participating in decisions, making choices, and determining the direction of the helping process are primary roles for older adults.

- Identifying, uncovering, or co-constructing environmental resources and enlisting them is a useful joint task between older clients and professional helpers. (Nelson-Becker et al., 2009)

In a practice setting, the strengths approach would include an inventory of seven to eight domains chosen by the older adult. Examples of key areas might be daily living situation, religion and spirituality, social support health, finances, and leisure interests (see Table 4.4). A mental health professional would explore the uniqueness of an older adult: values, experiences, and interests. Next steps would include learning how the individual has coped with difficulty in the past, the strengths currently held, and visioning the kind of life desired for the future.

There are some elemental questions to ask an older adult that address strength components rather than focusing solely on problem-based language (Nelson-Becker et al., 2009):

- Who is important to you in your life? (Social support)

- What do you do in a typical day? (Normal activities)

- What makes life worth living for you? (Life satisfaction, meaning, spiritual foundations)

- What has worked well for you in the past? (Coping skill inventory)

- What is going well for you right now? (Present-oriented strengths)

- If things could be different, what would you wish for? (Visioning)

One of the major benefits of the strengths perspective is that it teaches both older clients and mental health professionals to focus on possibility and what is working well. This focus then ideally reaches acceptable solutions for problems in living, similar to a solution-focused model. Although it does not have the richness of theory, it does present a model that is easily learned and applied with older populations.

Table 4.4 Inventory of Strengths Example

Life Domains	Past: Personal/Social Resources *What have I used before? How did that work?*	Present: Current Status *What do I have going for me now?*	Future: Desires/ Aspirations *What do I want?*
1. Daily living situation			
2. Religion and spirituality			
3. Health/mental health			
(Continue until client has chosen 7 or 8 domains.)			

Source: Adapted from Fast & Chapin, 2000.

THEORY INTEGRATION

Although this chapter has not addressed all possible theoretical paradigms with relevance to religion or spirituality—hermeneutics, for example, remains absent—it has identified a number of central concepts. See Figure 4.2 for a summary of aging-related theories in the Theories Integration Chart.

A few of the theories are more limited in their view or consideration of holistic aging, such as Freud's theory of psychoanalysis and Skinner's behaviorism. Others reflect positive aging and the upper reaches of capacity, such as Tornstam's gerotranscendence model and Cohen's concept of creative aging. These theories are intermixed along the time continuum—the ones falling below the timeline are both limited and expansive, for example. Theories may disagree about both the relevance of religion and the structural position of spirituality in human lives, but they do provide guidance for mental health practitioners who want to understand how religious and spiritual values may intersect with life experience. An interesting theory for aging not addressed here is Carstensen's socioemotional selectivity theory (Lockenhoff & Carstensen, 2004). This theory discusses the nature of social relationships in aging. This theory may have indirect relevance to spirituality through its suggestions about how older adults pare their social networks to mine for the gold in maintaining a few deeply satisfying relationships, but it is less directly related to spirituality.

Figure 4.2 Theories Integration Chart

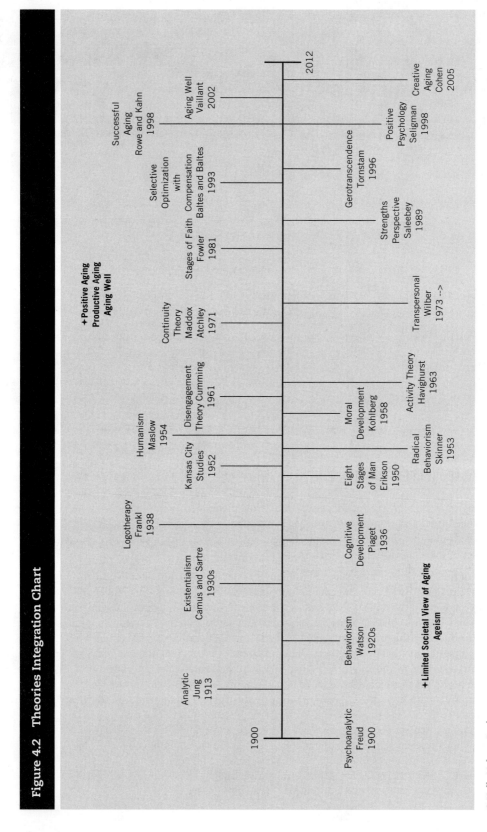

© Holly Nelson-Becker

SUMMARY

This chapter has addressed major theoretical perspectives and considered their relationship to aging, spirituality, and religion. Some aging-related theories define themselves explicitly as aligning with or distancing from religion, and in some cases but less often, spirituality. For other theories mentioned here, the focus lies implicitly in the ancient and modern virtues extolled and most sought. The search for the good, the beautiful, and the true ultimately represents a search for happiness, however one defines it. This search is more than symbolic; for some is more necessary than having food and drink at the ready. "Whatever is true, whatever is noble, whatever is right, whatever is pure, whatever is lovely, whatever is admirable—if anything is excellent or praiseworthy—think about such things" (Philippians 4:8, New International Version). Said another way, "Your worst enemy cannot harm you as much as your own unguarded thoughts" (attributed to the Buddha).

CASE STUDY: LETHA BAINBRIDGE

Reason for Referral

Letha Bainbridge is a 78-year-old woman who lives in First Light Nursing Care Facility and was referred for treatment for depression by the medical director. Her husband died from cancer six months earlier. Her fall two months after her husband's death left her with limited mobility. This, as well as worsening arthritis, has led to her nursing facility admission as she needs more care than could be provided in an assisted living facility, and her financial resources as a widow are limited. She has no children; however, she does have a sister who lives out of state.

History and Spiritual Themes

Letha agreed to meet with the social worker. As Letha shared her life story and circumstances, it was clear that spirituality was important to her. She recalled when she was a small child of three to four, she was often sent outside to play alone in her backyard. Although she was alone, she never felt lonely because of the beauty that surrounded her. Small animals such as squirrels and caterpillars seemed to have little fear of her and would come up close to her. She was entranced by the bright reds and pinks of tulips and roses in the garden. There was an old apple tree that, although it produced sour apples, had wonderfully shaped branches for climbing. She often felt a peace here in the garden that she did not always feel inside the house where her parents often traded verbal blows. Her parents seemed to have little time for her, but she had the space to experience and revel in nature, finding joy there. This was a peaceful time in her early spiritual understanding.

As she grew to be six, her mother began to take her along to a community church located in the neighborhood. She attended a Sunday school class where she formed an image of God as a grandfatherly figure with a white beard who loved her. She was happy with this idea of a God who accepted and loved her. But the pastor would often admonish the congregation, saying they were all sinners who needed to repent as God asked. She had difficulty understanding these two opposing views and felt confused. Letha also felt as though everyone disapproved of her because no one went out of his or her way to greet or welcome her. A year later, her parents divorced; she remained with her mother and sister. She thought that this was in some way her fault and her punishment for not being a better daughter. Her father seldom visited and her mother took little interest in her now as the mother began to date again.

One night, Letha was left with a family friend who babysat Letha and her younger sister. She was sexually abused, but there was no one she could tell as this man warned her he would find out and hurt anyone she told. The abuse continued over three years and her self-worth plummeted. At age 10, she tried to commit suicide by taking a bottle of prescription pills her mother had. Her mother found her and she was revived by paramedics, hospitalized, and entered out-patient counseling. This was the nadir or pit of her spiritual, emotional, and psychological life. Her mother finally paid attention to her now, and they began to talk for the first time. She told her mother and her counselor about the abuse, and her mother felt great regret. The man who abused her was arrested and the case went to trial. Letha testified and the family friend received 10 years of prison time. Sometimes, she wondered how a God who loved her could allow such abuse to happen to her.

In high school, Letha became involved with a teen religious group. Conservative in orientation, this group enveloped her with their friendship and became a point of connection for her. She also spoke with her school counselor about her abuse and was referred for counseling, which she followed for three sessions. Finding acceptance here in her religious group, Letha also did not think too much about her own beliefs, which were only a partial match with those of her religious peer group.

She worked for two years after high school in a village Woolworth's drug store to save money for college. She went to the University of Kansas, majoring in education. While there, she met the love of her life, Edwin Bainbridge. They married and celebrated 55 years of marriage before his death from cancer. He was a farmer, and though he enjoyed good social relationships with others in the community, he was never particularly good at managing the farm. After a couple of years at home, Letha became a grade school teacher to help the couple financially and found she was very good at it. She loved using her creativity to design lessons and other teachers looked to her often for guidance. She taught for 15 years and then her mother became very ill. Letha took care of her during evenings and weekends, but eventually felt she needed to leave her teaching career to care for her mother full time. With her husband's agreement, they moved Letha's mother into their home. The stress began to be intense and, although she had long ago forgiven her mother for her role in placing Letha in a bad situation, she also experienced some inner unresolved issues from her decision not to complete therapy many years before.

When her mother died a year later, Letha reentered therapy and also recognized that she missed her former religious connection. She joined her husband's Methodist faith community, which fit her own beliefs fairly well. He had attended only sporadically, but now they became enthusiastic members and supporters of their congregation, becoming leaders on church committees. This role was very satisfying for Letha as she formed friendships with people who she respected who also respected her. As she had in childhood, she renewed her interest in the natural world. She began to take long daily walks in the countryside, where she experienced a deep connection with nature and found herself observing and learning more about herself as she learned more about the outside world. The years leading into her older age had been very satisfying for her spiritually and it was a calm period in her life.

Current Concerns

Mrs. Bainbridge's transition to the nursing facility had been unexpected and difficult. Staff has noticed that she always seeks to make others feel good about themselves, but she seems to be unable to replenish her own joy. Letha's serenity and equanimity in her interactions with others were appreciated by staff and residents alike. However, when she thought she was alone, staff has observed her crying in her room on many occasions. When asked, she has refused to discuss her feelings.

Questions for Case Discussion

1. What kind of depression does Ms. Bainbridge appear to have?

2. Did she experience a spiritual crisis and, if so, what did it involve? What was the nature of her spiritual development? Identify any strengths she built from it.

3. In what ways did Ms. Bainbridge's spiritual views give her support or discomfort throughout her lifespan?

4. What would you suggest to her and to the staff now?

QUESTIONS FOR DISCUSSION

1. What are the reigning societal views about aging today? Do religion and spirituality promote positive or negative views of aging? Address each domain, religion and spirituality, separately.

2. In what way do theories of social gerontology—disengagement, activity, continuity, and the life course—relate to religious viewpoints? Spiritual viewpoints?

3. What was Freud's view of religion? Jung's view? Compare and contrast them.

4. Which developmental theorists address spiritual frameworks as part of or the whole of their theory? Do they believe everyone has the capacity to achieve the most advanced developmental levels? Why or why not? Is spiritual development explicitly addressed and, if so, how? Is it viewed as a linear or a recursive process? Explain.

5. What was Maslow's perspective of aging and spiritual needs?

6. How does transpersonal psychology address spiritual issues?

7. In what ways do theories of optimal aging relate to spirituality?

MEDITATION: THE TREE THAT WAS PLANTED THE DAY YOU WERE BORN

Believe me, you will find more lessons in the woods than in books.

Trees and stones will teach you what you cannot learn from masters.

—St. Bernaud de Clairvaux

Imagine that on the day you were born your parents planted a fruit tree or other important tree in your honor at or near your house. Now, after many years, you are returning to be in its presence again. What kind of fruit tree is this? An apple, cherry, pear, or walnut tree? Is it an oak, maple, or fragrant pine? Where was it planted? Was it in an open field, a corner of the yard, or elsewhere?

Now you are aware of your feelings as you see the tree again for the first time in many years. You might feel joy, excitement, or surprise to see how tall it is, whether it is straight or crooked. You note the tree's size, how it reaches up toward the sky. You approach the tree and circle around it viewing the color of the leaves, what it looks like from different angles. You touch its bark and are aware of how it feels, whether it is smooth or rough. Consider the fruit hanging from the branches. Is it abundant or skimpy? Pick a fruit and note its color, texture, and flavor. If it has only leaves or needles, pick one of those and assess its health. Consider what you like and do not like about it. Speak to your tree and hear it respond. Become your tree and consider how it feels. Thank it for being strong for you. Now, look at this tree with new eyes and know that it is perfect. Thank it for growing alongside you and mirroring your pain and joy, for teaching you and being a place of refuge, for the peace it gives you. Sit with your tree for a moment and absorb what it shares with you.

EXPLORING YOUR SPIRITUALITY: DEVELOPING A SPIRITUAL HISTORY

Think about your own spiritual development over time from your childhood to the present. Consider your relationship to spirituality and or religion and how it changed or has remained the same at different points. You may want to consider each five years or decade of your life, taking note of exceptional experiences. How does your journey represent a hero's or heroine's journey?

1. In narrative form, write about the highs and lows (peaks and nadirs) of your spiritual life. If you have maintained a stable relationship with spirituality or a small steady growth pattern, discuss that too. Give attention to quantity and quality of these experiences. Did you have any connection to religious faith communities or spiritual groups? Who were the spiritual mentors, role models, guides, or spiritual friends who have helped you on your path? What were significant points of deeper insight or understanding? Did you develop any spiritual symbols that carry meaning?

2. How would you depict your journey in nonnarrative form? Can you draw a graph, using the x-axis to represent increments of time and the y-axis to represent your baseline relationship to spirituality, highs and lows? Could you draw a picture or shape that would better symbolize your path? This would also be a good exercise to use with colored markers or pencils. Google the word *timeline* to find examples of, and software for, graphs you can create online.

3. History is often told according to literal interpretation, but that depends on the view of the interpreter. Now, retell your spiritual development story from a mythic point of view to a friend. Tell it in the third person, allowing metaphors and word images to bring it to new life. What is the difference between your history and your myth? What insights did you gain?

4. Journal about your experience.

EXPLORING YOUR SPIRITUALITY: DEFINING A PEAK EXPERIENCE

A peak experience, as described by Maslow (1971), is effortless and lifts you to a new level of feeling or knowing. Like a rainbow, "it comes and goes and it cannot be forgotten" (p. xvi). Simply, what ought to be, is, and the deep roots of human nature are glimpsed vividly. Try to apply this definition to your own experience.

1. Think about the most inspiring or moving experience you have had. This may be a moment of great happiness, unexpected creativity, or deep insight. Try to describe the experience then as it is to you now.

2. What were your emotions during and after the experience? What did you see, hear, think, or know? Did this experience occur in the flow of time or out of time? What role did connection and wholeness have, if any?

What was the nature of your embeddedness in the event
(e.g., being a part of the event or witnessing it as an outside observer watching a movie)? In what ways did this represent a departure from your ordinary life?

3. How are you different today because you had this experience? Did you tell anyone about it? If so how did their reaction—support or incredulity—affect your re-imagining of the event?

4. Have you had similar experiences since that peak experience? If yes, how were they the same or different? If no, why do you think this is so?

5. Sit with these questions a few minutes and then journal your response.

WEBSITES

This Chair Rocks: How Ageism Warps Our View of Long Life, with Ashton Applewhite https://www.youtube.com/watch?v=r_uoZC5pE08

This a 41-minute video highlights ageist views.

Human Values in Aging newsletter.

This monthly e-mail newsletter discusses issues of aging and provides brief quotes and web links. Join by e-mailing Rick Moody (AARP) at hrmoody@yahoo.com.

Positive Aging Newsletter

http://www.taosinstitute.net/positive-aging-newsletter

This website hosts the *Positive Aging* newsletter, which is written by Ken and Mary Gergen (developers of social construction theory). The newsletter is also available by joining the Listserv.

Positive Psychology

http://www.ppc.sas.upenn.edu/

The Positive Psychology website is hosted by University of Pennsylvania, Martin Seligman (also known for his work on learned helplessness and depression).

RECOMMENDED READING

Bentson, V. L., Silverstein, M., Putney, N. M., & Gans, D. (2009). *Handbook of theories of aging* (2nd ed.). New York, NY: Springer.

This comprehensive volume, much expanded and improved from the previous edition, draws on key gerontologists within many fields to develop the role of theory in subdomains of interest to gerontologists. Included chapters address meaning (Chapter 6), phenomenology (Chapter 20), and spirituality (Chapter 36).

Hargrave, T. D. (1994). *Families and forgiveness: Healing wounds in the intergenerational family*. New York, NY: Routledge.

Hargrave elucidates four stations on the journey of forgiveness. Useful for clinical work.

Huxley, A. (1945). *The perennial philosophy*. New York, NY: Harper & Row.

This text identifies commonalities in many religious traditions that can form a universal understanding of the ultimate purpose of human life.

CHAPTER FIVE

RELIGION AND OLDER ADULTS

If the doors of perception were cleansed, everything would
appear to man as it is: infinite.
For man has closed himself up, till he sees all things
through narrow chinks of his cavern.

—William Blake, *The Marriage of Heaven and Hell*

Christian, Jew, Muslim, shaman, Zoroastrian, stone,
ground, mountain, river, each has a secret way of being
with the mystery, unique and not to be judged.

—Rumi

To better understand the context in which older adults live, it is helpful to have background on the major religious faiths and belief systems to which they subscribe. Judaism, Christianity, and American Indigenous Religion/Spirituality are described first, as they represent the primary religions of Western culture. Islam, a monotheistic religion like the first two, is discussed next. Moving toward Asia, the ancient religion of Hinduism is described, followed by Buddhism, Confucianism, and Daoism. Of course, there are many other traditions that are not included here, simply for reasons of time and space. Within each of these traditions, the perspective on aging they promote is described. In many cases, there is no explicit writing by interpreters of the religion about views on aging, but aging-related propositions are found within religious text.

JUDAISM

The history of Judaism began with the land, a people, and the history they made. Referring to themselves as *the people of the book*, the Jewish people arose from a small group of nomads, of whom no one took any particular notice. Tracing their roots back to the exodus from Egypt, the Jewish people consistently made meaning of the events of their lives in relation to the God they knew. Judaism is a text-based religion, first drawing on the Torah, then the Hebrew Bible, and lastly rabbinic texts. The Hebrew Bible has been this religion's guide, authority, and inspiration. The Bible opens with the words, "In the beginning" (Genesis 1:1). "From beginning to end, the Jewish quest for meaning was rooted in their understanding of God" (Smith, 1958, p. 255). The history of the Jewish people revealed a loving and compassionate God who takes an interest in their lives.

A distinctive contribution of this religion was the belief in monotheism. Rather than a God who was amoral and uncaring, the god(s) of the Jews' contemporaries, God became personal. "Hear O Israel, the Lord Our God, the Lord is One" (Deuteronomy 6:4) is known as the Shema, the central part of morning and evening prayer. Jewish sacred texts are named the Tanakh, which includes the Torah (the law), the Prophets, and the Writings. This is similar to the Old Testament of Christianity with books in a different order, but because the Old Testament implies a new one, that term is not used. The Talmud is a collection of rabbinical commentaries that interpret, explain, and apply the Torah. The Midrash is a collection of early sermons and other material dating back to the 4th through 6th centuries.

In the story of the Jewish people, four themes seem prominent in their relationship with God: creation, liberation, revelation, and redemption. God is portrayed as an all-powerful entity who both creates and directs the universe. A good God has formed a good creation. God's covenantal relationship with the Jewish people symbolizes a God who protects all humanity, yet also requires a response from His people in return. Their future is intimately tied to God's plan. God's ongoing involvement with the Jews climaxed in freeing the Jewish people from oppression. "In exchange for God's protection and promise of prosperity in the Promised Land, the Israelites must be prepared to obey God's will, and follow God's commandments" (Kerner, 1991, p. 285).

The Jewish quest for understanding their role as a chosen people led them to see that creation has meaning because God created the world. God revealed Himself to them in deeds, so they know a God of righteousness and love. Even though people err, they are also God's beloved children. Created people have choices (at times choosing poorly) and those choices determine their destiny. Nothing happened by accident, and because God was the ruler of history, history provides ground for opportunity. God is central in a Jewish understanding of reality, with action taking precedence over belief. Obeying the commandments and Jewish law brings God's will into that everyday reality. Jews also are required to live out their responsibilities to their neighbors in the Mitzvah. The Mitzvah refers to the religious duty to perform acts of kindness. Concern for the marginalized in society became part of Jewish communal life. Ritual and ethical obligations were strongly connected, with the *vertical* (to God) and *horizontal* (to other human beings) obligations of the Jewish believer equally weighted.

Jewish relationship to society and culture changed in the 18th and 19th centuries. The Enlightenment period challenged the role of religion as the core of Jewish experience. The Jewish way of life was introduced to Western languages, philosophy, and sciences, which raised new questions about reality. The Jewish Emancipation, experienced in the 19th and early 20th centuries, meant political enfranchisement for the Jews, resulting in the collapse of traditional Jewish societies. With these new understandings came an awareness of the need for new expressions of the Jewish faith; among them were the Reform, Orthodox, and Conservative forms of Judaism. Judaism no longer was a unified faith.

Although most religious groups have faced a period of persecution, the Jews lived through (or didn't) an extreme form in the Holocaust (Shoah) of Nazi Germany against them. On a social level, this may have been, in part, due to their many financial successes and entrance into elite positions. In 1948, the United Nations established the state of Israel, partly for reasons of security. Holocaust victims still survive, though their number is diminishing.

For Jewish people, life is grounded in tradition. Ceremonies and rituals are utilized to script and direct responses to life events such as death. Celebrations of Sabbath, of coming of age in the Bar and Bat Mitzvahs, the Passover feast, and the Day of Atonement (Yom Kippur)—a day of intensive prayer and fasting—all serve to make everyday life holy.

Judaism and Aging

Traditional Jewish texts about aging and old age suggest Judaism values older people, seeing them as a repository of knowledge within the community (Sedley, 2012). The Torah proposes people rise in the presence of those who are old, and the biblical book of Leviticus commands people to honor older persons. The meaning of the term *old* is later defined by commentaries. Ecclesiastes and the Psalms are biblical books that acknowledge some of the physical concerns that may emerge with aging. Older people are deserving of respect and are viewed as leaders, as advisors, and guides for the community. Judaism sees old age as a continuation of the path a person has chosen through life; there is no sudden transition to old age. Though repentance is possible, preparation for old age begins while a person is young.

The rabbis in the Talmud (Avot [Ethics of the Fathers] 5:24) articulated what they saw as the stages in a person's life with an emphasis on study:

> *At five years old a person should study the Torah, at ten years for the Mishnah, at thirteen for the commandments, at fifteen for the Talmud, at eighteen for the bride chamber, at twenty for one's life pursuit, at thirty for authority, at forty for discernment, at fifty for counsel, at sixty to be an elder, at seventy for gray hairs, at eighty for special strength (Psalm 90:10), at ninety for decrepitude, and at a hundred a man is as one who has already died and has ceased from the affairs of this world.* (as cited in MacKinlay, 2010, p. 89)

It is suggested that "the more a person is aware of their mortality and their finitude, the more they will be able to make the most of every moment and build up the skills and mental attitudes that will give them a happy and meaningful old age" (Sedley, 2012, p. 3). Finally, old age is viewed as an opportunity to prepare for death, so that older adults can live life without fear.

Today, Jewish agencies support the well-being of older people. Before the development of the Jewish Family Service agencies (JFS), synagogues were the locus of providing services to Jewish families. Guiding the mission of JFS are the concepts of *Tikkum Olam*, the pursuit of social action and social justice, and honoring one's parents. Jewish values of sanctity of life, and respecting and caring for elders in the community, are paramount. "The fundamental role of JFS is to act as the 'heart and hands' to demonstrate that the Jewish community is a caring community that upholds the basic Jewish value of not 'forsaking' its elders" (Newstein & Frumer, 2006, p. 226). Helping people age in place, providing access to eldercare information, and enabling them to fulfill their potential as volunteers or workers, are three ways that the Jewish community fulfills this responsibility.

The Jewish community has a vested interest in developing programs that meet the evolving needs of their older adults. At the forefront of developing community-based programs is a focus on helping older adults age in place and remain connected to their community. With a goal of assisting older people to reach their full potential, a variety of programs ranging from housing, meal delivery, social services, skilled nursing care, adult day programs, and opportunities for socialization help older adults meet needs. JFS helps older adults cope with the challenges of aging by providing consultations, care planning, and counseling. The Sage-ing model developed by Rabbi Zalman Schachter Shalomi promotes the importance of passing wisdom to future generations, illustrating the reciprocity and ability of older generations to offer much in return.

CHRISTIANITY

At its core, Christianity is centered on the worship of one God, revealed in the life of Jesus Christ, who was born between 6 and 4 BCE (Before the Common Era) and lived to between 30–36 CE (Common Era). Christianity is one of the three great monotheistic religions alongside Judaism and Islam. Christianity begins with the portion of the Jewish community who had known Jesus, heard him preach, saw the results of his message, and came to believe that more than a prophet, he was the Son of God, the Messiah, the Anointed One, as he suggested. Smith (1958) conjectured that there must have been something about the life of Jesus that made those who knew him come to the conclusion he was divine. Three central questions about Jesus remain: what he did, what he said, and who he was.

The Gospels, as written by interpreters, reveal a man who went about doing good, healing, helping, and counseling. His miracles were not performed to convince people to believe in him, but to show them the power of a God who loves. These stories were not just recollections, but teaching about God's involvement with his people. His words were difficult to hear, simple but urgent, passionate but loving, direct, and countercultural. In his time, he was deeply misunderstood and this led to his death by those who were jealous of his appeal to the people. Everything he said focused on God's overpowering love for humanity, inviting people to receive this love, and share it with neighbors. The two central commands of the New Testament are thus to love God and to love one's neighbor as closely as one loves self. As a Jew, Jesus's heritage was founded in the knowledge of a God who loved and walked with His people. "God had been unswerving in loving kindness and stubborn love" (Smith, 1958, p. 307). Jesus was a witness to this loving God, not only teaching his followers about God's love, but also embodying that love in a total sharing of his being and life. Jesus expanded this teaching in showing disciples how to respond to this freely given love—to do likewise with their neighbor without counting the cost. Jesus's death by crucifixion was not the end of the story; the apostles' resurrection faith added another dimension. "For if Christ's life and death had convinced the disciples of God's love, his resurrection convinced them of his power, demonstrating that neither the worst men can do nor even the seemingly inexorable laws of nature can block God's work" (Smith, 1958, p. 312).

The spirit of Jesus lived on in his disciples, changing them into transformers of the world. Told to "Go and make disciples of all nations" (Matthew 28:19), the church and its members carried a witness of the living Christ who overcame death. A part of Christian belief centers on life after death, although the features of this are largely unknown and taken as a part of faith. As the fuller understanding of his mission became apparent, the followers of Jesus began to separate from the Jewish community and the synagogue by reaching out to Gentiles as well as Jews. Early on, Christians believed and affirmed that their God was a threefold unity of Father, Son, and Holy Spirit and that Christ gave a new meaning to the Old Law of sacrifice, *an eye for an eye*, and other records of God's dealing with people in the Hebrew Scriptures. Over the centuries, guided and energized by the Holy Spirit, Jesus's message of love was extended beyond the Jewish people to the world.

By the middle of the 16th century, Christianity had divided into three main branches that are still recognized today: Catholicism, Orthodoxy, and Protestantism. At the present time, the Catholic and Orthodox Churches differ on the role of the pope and are not in communion with each other, but similarities do exist between Catholic and Orthodox Christians. Both believe that the teaching of the apostles and the powers Christ gave them can be traced back to the earliest days of the church. Tradition plays an important role as well in both churches. The Jesus prayer, a Christian version of a mantra, is considered especially important in the Orthodox Church. It coalesces around the words, "Jesus Christ, Son of God, have mercy on me, a sinner," though it can be condensed into just a few words and has other versions.

Protestantism, which began as a reform movement in the Roman Catholic Church, led to a further split in the church. Arising as part of the Reformation movement in the16th century, Protestantism is a series of movements, each of which rejected the central authority of the papacy. Martin Luther, in his 95 theses, John Calvin, and others called for a purification of the church and a return to the authority of the Bible and to revelation rather than tradition as the source of spiritual authority. At the time of the Reformation, questionable practices had entered church doctrine such as paying for indulgences, which represented a release from, or forgiveness of, sin. At many points, faith communities needed to be called back to their mission and purpose.

There are many other differences across the denominations, which include among them Adventism, Anglicanism, Baptist churches, Reformed churches, Lutheranism, Methodism, Pentecostalism, and many affiliated, nondenominational, and independent churches. Protestantism tended to privilege such ideals as industry, frugality, calling, discipline, and responsibility. These values aligned strongly with groups who immigrated to the United States in the 18th and 19th centuries. These religious groups also advocated for the separation of church and state and religious freedom. In many Protestant faiths, women have been ordained to ministry since the last half of the 20th century, but each denomination has distinct beliefs and practices. Broadly speaking, the differences with the Catholic Church centered on beliefs about (1) the nature of God's interactions with persons and (2) the centrality of the Bible over tradition. "Protestantism is more than just a collection of different churches. It is also a way of being Christian that is rooted in a personal relationship with God through Jesus Christ" (Brown, 2014, para. 9).

Jesus's teachings impart a way of life for his believers and ethical considerations for how to live that life. Serving as ethical guidelines are the Ten Commandments, which were given to the Jewish people. These commandments refer to the believer's relationship with God and with one another. Other teachings that assist in helping one respond as a Christian are the six precepts (laws of the church) for Catholics, the Beatitudes (Jesus's teachings on hope and the blessings of life), and the parables or teaching stories Jesus told (Schineller, 2000). Guidelines for what unites all Christians address how Christians are to live their life, the beliefs of their religion, and their relationship to God and neighbor. They suggest that God is deeply loving, present in the universe, and people are to live in community with each other. These statements capture the core and essence of Christianity: to know and love God, and to love one's neighbor as oneself.

Christianity and Aging

To understand Christianity and aging, one must look both at the individual and the community. Christian spirituality is about being in right relationship with God and living out the sense of the sacred in relationship with others in the faith community and the wider human community (Downey, 1997). Christians believe that the covenantal relationship (based in love rather than law) that God has with the community is not determined by issues such as age, race, and financial status. A covenant indicates that this relationship is based in love rather than law. As God has been faithful to humanity in love, so Christians are tasked to be faithful in loving service to each other.

The Bible holds the view that old age is a blessing from God. Old age is also a symbol of loss and limitation. Too often aging is looked at as something to avoid rather than a source of wisdom to be embraced. Neither of these views is complete, yet both offer an insight on aging and complement each other. Besides providing spiritual support, most Christian churches also provide pastoral outreach for those in need. Visits are made to those in homes and hospitals who can no longer attend church, so that they remain connected. Practically, Christian religious services are often held in nursing care facilities and other places where older people may live. At the present time across Christian churches, older people tend to attend religious services more frequently than other age groups (Pew Forum on Religion & Public Life, 2007).

In Christian and Jewish scripture are examples of people who lived long lives and remained faithful to God's teachings. Sarah and Abraham are said to have had their first child Isaac in old age after encountering many problems. Methuselah reportedly lived 969 years, although this story is likely allegorical. The story of Job considers why God allows suffering. Job had received many gifts from God and yet in his old age suffered much loss. His friends first sought to console him, then blamed him for disappointing God as he must have sinned. Job himself began to question God, who then asked where he was at the creation of the world, suggesting Job cannot know God's purposes. It is a question Job could not answer. Ultimately, Job's faith endured and all of Job's possessions and more were restored; he lived on to have more beautiful and highly cherished children.

Christian spirituality involves the whole person, holding each one in the dignity that comes with being human and a child of God. Christian aging offers the individual the opportunity of reflection, and an invitation to empty oneself of all that no longer matters. What lessons do older adults still need to learn? How are they sources of wisdom for the community? What values and ambitions should older people relinquish because they no longer serve their needs? These are questions that aging Christians might engage. The losses that come with aging—physical, social, financial—can also serve as reminders that all life is fragile. In seeing things as they really are, older people let go of illusions and false securities and live in the present. The fundamental imperative of love is applied to all ages. Love "seeks to promote the good in a person's life and to ensure that she be treated in a way that befits her worth" (Wolterstorff, 2011, p. 93). Older adults remain vital partners in the work of building the kingdom of God on earth, witnessing with their lives, and serving as a prophetic voice for the community.

AMERICAN INDIAN RELIGION/SPIRITUALITY

There is little agreement on what single term to use in referring to indigenous American peoples. The southwestern part of the United States uses the term *American Indian*, as does the national museum by that name in Washington, D. C. The northeastern region of the United States has applied the term *Native American*, while indigenous tribes in Canada are usually called *First Nations*. When a particular tribe name is known, that specificity is usually the preferred approach of clients (Weaver, 2013).

As America became colonized, the early settlers thought the indigenous people had no *real* religion and at first paid little attention to their rituals and beliefs. Submission to authority and domination of colonial power were at the crux of the colonial encounter between American Indians and European Americans (Lomawaim, 1999). Christian missionaries tried to impose their beliefs and also European culture on these indigenous peoples. The Federal Indian Religion Ban of 1883, dispersed through the Rules for Indian Courts, had been advocated by Christian missionaries for more than a decade earlier (McGaa, 2004). Through this Act, wholly insensitive by modern standards, indigenous beliefs were suppressed. With the ever-westward movement of the settlers, the American Indians were soon stripped of their land but not their culture or their spirit. For them, spirituality and ordinary life are fully interconnected. In fact, the word *religion* implies a separation of spheres of daily life, a segmentation between sacred and secular that was not present for American Indians. Everything, in their view, carries spirit.

According to the most recent statistics from the Bureau of Indian Affairs, there are 566 federally recognized American Indian tribes and Alaska Natives in the United States (Who We Are: Bureau of Indian Affairs, n.d.). Besides indicating the rich diversity of this population, each tribe has its own rituals, which must be understood and honored. "Indian traditions are not alike across tribes or geography, [but] nonetheless, a universal trademark in Indian tradition comes from the potency of the nuclear and extended families" (Stemmler, 2009, p. 108).

Most tribes experienced a history of oppression from European Americans, including the spread of disease for which they had no immunity, walking the Trail of Tears following the Indian Removal Act of 1830, and being sequestered on reservations. Removal of children at young ages, first to mission schools and then to boarding schools where speaking in native languages and engaging in other aspects of culture were fiercely prohibited, left many broken hearts within families. Religion, too, went underground for a time.

American Indian religions have prehistoric roots, with indigenous Americans migrating to North America more than 12,000 years ago. "There is no single Native American Religion. Having no church buildings, and no church hierarchy or organizational structure, they are more strongly tied to nature and its rhythms" (Hartz, 2014, para. 7). With no written set of beliefs or creed, American Indians relied on an oral tradition to pass on beliefs to generations who followed. Tribe members were taught by example and lessons were internalized as members grew to adulthood.

The World Council of Indigenous People calls American Indians and other indigenous peoples the Fourth World, in contrast to the First World (industrialized nations), the Second World (socialist nations), and the Third World (developing nations). The Fourth World believes the people belong to the land, while the other three worlds live as though the land belongs to the people (Beversluis, 2000). A Dunwamish Chief (as cited in Beversluis, 2000) stated, "Every part of the earth is sacred to my people. Every shining pine needle, every sandy shore, every mist in the dark woods, every clearing and humming insect is holy in the memory and experience of my people" (p. 43).

Analysis of the indigenous American belief system has shown a richness and depth to their beliefs. Historically, one can find some basic concepts common across most American Indian religions: (1) there is a Great Spirit/Creator that underlies all of creation; (2) all life forms interact with each other and contain spirit within them, thus use of animals for food, and so forth, has limitations; (3) individuals are called to walk in balance and harmony with the universe and the spirit world, referred to as "walking in the sacred way;" (4) values, beliefs, moral, ethics, and tradition are passed on orally, and ritual is important for cultural bonding; (5) shamans have ties to higher powers that are used for the healing and spiritual good of the community; (6) humor is part of the sacred way, so that we are reminded of our foolishness; and (7) thankfulness to the Creator undergirds spirituality (Beversluis, 2000 Hartz, 2014;). Some tribes believed in a deity or deities and others simply in mystic energies. The Iroquois called the supernatural force "the Orenda," or inherent power residing in all persons and objects (Woodhead, 1992). Algonquin tribes called it "Manitou;" the Osage people called the Great Spirit "Wakan."

There is no segmentation of life into either secular or religious for the indigenous American. Culture and religion are one, and work is viewed as prayer. Living with a constant awareness of the spirit world that surrounds them and the knowledge of earth as home, everything has a sacred dimension. Life is not just a spiritual journey, but is also marked with ritual and celebration. These rituals can be seen in naming ceremonies, in coming-of-age ceremonies for both boys and girls, in rites of passage from childhood to adulthood, ceremonies marking marriage, as well as maturing and death rituals. Special ceremonies include the vision quest for contemplation in nature, the usually communal sweat lodge for cleansing and refreshment, peace pipe ceremonies of petition toward the four directions using spontaneous prayers from the heart, and the Plains Indians Sun Dance, banned from the 1880s until the 1950s. The Sun Dance was conducted to thank the Great Spirit as a tribe and to fulfil vows if a favor or request had been granted. Although at one time the Sun Dance was exclusionary, for enrolled tribal members only, some traditional holy men have dissented from that view (McGaa, 2004). Tobacco and peyote may be included in ritual, and peyote has been used as a substitution for vision quest (Woodhead, 1992).

Legalization of peyote occurred through legitimization of the Native American Church, chartered in 1918 in Oklahoma and later in many other states.

Healing for Indigenous Americans

"Therapists [of all types] should listen carefully, ask questions, and assume nothing when gathering information about American Indian clients" (McGoldrick, Giordano, & Garcia-Preto, 2005, p. 53). It is important to be culturally cognizant in working with this population. For instance, a lowering of eyes generally signals respect rather than shyness. Understanding the value of traditional practices helps build cultural empathy. Wellness and healing from an American Indian perspective considers the communal context, seeking balance in mental, spiritual, and physical aspects of living. American Indian spirituality has a sense of connectedness to the spiritual elements found in all living things, exemplified by the Red Path (the path to wholeness and harmony with nature, the right path in life) or the medicine wheel. All of the cosmos (not just humans) is considered imbued with spirituality including rocks, rivers, trees, and all plant life.

The medicine wheel was used in healing rituals for nearly every illness. It was referred to as *Wakan-Tanka* (the "Great Everything" or "Universe" in the Sioux language) and also represented personal space. The medicine wheel focused on balancing all things. This was essential in healing illness, where spiritual imbalance was considered the source of all sickness. The wheel symbolizes the circle of life, the life giving essence of the sun, and contains within it the four cardinal directions and four primary colors. The center represents beauty and balance or the self. The medicine wheel also may signify sacred space, protection, a place to honor nature and to attune with earth energy. Historically, using the medicine wheel, tribes came to peace with each other when they realized that responses such as anger were something over which individuals inwardly held control and could make choices.

Similar to the medicine wheel, the sacred hoop is divided into quarters and symbolizes the vastness of the universe. It was described in a vision by Black Elk, an American Indian Oglala Lakota traditional healer whose stories were told in a book by John Neihardt (1932/1979). In Black Elk's vision, the six powers included the west (black), the north (white), the east (red), the south (yellow), sky power (blue) and earth power (green). Each direction is associated with certain traits or strengths. The sacred hoop concept has been a part of recent initiatives by American Indian university students to handle loneliness through connection with local, though not related, American Indian grandparents with whom they have shared familiar rituals. Awareness of great beauty is also denoted and finds expression within many tribes. From the Dineh (Navajo) tradition the Beauty Way song, also known as the Blessing Way, has emerged. "With beauty before me . . . , beauty behind me . . . , beauty above me . . . , beauty around me, may I walk. In old age wandering on a trail of beauty, lively may I walk. . . . It is finished in beauty." When perception of this great beauty enfolding humanity is disrupted, the reminder call to recognition restores. For many people, this beauty is unmistakably present in natural settings.

Common American Indian healing practices include the pow wow; music such as drumming, singing, and flute; smudging; story telling; the pipe ceremony; and use of herbs (Rybak & Decker-Fitts, 2009). Each of these rituals links the hearer and participant in a spiritual experience of connection and belonging. The ritual of story telling used an oral tradition to connect the tribe with their past. This story telling helps join the person with their identity, path toward healing, and offers faith and hope to the individual. Much like what a retreatant would experience in the second week of the Ignatian exercise learning about the life of Jesus, or simply learning his or her own family stories, one discovers connection and understanding. The past becomes a source of knowledge, which helps both emotionally and spiritually. Therefore, it is important for the counselor, social worker, mental health professional, or chaplain to know the acculturation level of a client/patient and to understand the importance of their cultural traditions for them. A client history needs to be assessed both individually and collectively to understand issues such as generational grief, anger, and trauma issues to name only a few. Even if seemingly unimportant in the moment, a gradual reconnection to these roots can be very meaningful to an older American Indian or others.

American Indians and Aging

There is great respect for tribal elders in American Indian cultures. Elders are not solely identified by chronological age, but through the wisdom they carry and leadership they exercise in families, clans, and/or communities (Drywater-Whitekiller, 2006). Family is the foundation of the Indian community, even when it occurs across many miles and beyond state lines. Even locally, alongside parents, children are often raised by aunts and uncles who are not actually blood relatives, but care for the community as a whole. Recognizing that the preservation of Indian tradition is through elders of this population, the value of elders must be viewed as greater than their contribution to the immediate family.

In American Indian communities, rates of elder abuse and neglect, where known, are high, partially due to historical trauma and cumulative stress (Cribbs, Byers, & Moxley, 2009). Because elders are seen as the heart of the Indian community, it is the community's responsibility to ensure their well-being. Those who live to old age are models and wisdom figures and are needed to give advice and pass on tribal lore, culture, and sacred history to the children of the tribe in what is, at times, an unstable environment. This is especially important because the health disparities regarding alcoholism, diabetes, and suicide are much higher for American Indians (Indian Health Service, 2006), and there have been barriers to sharing cultural identity with younger people. It is the elders who teach the language and traditions, and their teaching assists young adults to "walk in the two worlds" (respondent cited in Drywater-Whitekiller, 2006) of bicultural identity.

Because many American Indian tribes do not have resources to provide long-term care for the elderly population, long-term care is a growing problem that needs to be addressed. The report *Policy Recommendations for Native Elders*, prepared for the National Congress of American Indians 2005 Midyear Conference, surveyed 171 tribal nations regarding elder needs (Ludtke, 2005). This report focused on issues ranging from health care, funding issues, chronic disease management, and access to services, to increased availability of home/community-based long-term care services in rural areas. Issues such as these need continued monitoring to ensure that basic health care needs are met with an aim to enhance the quality of life and well-being of American Indian elders.

ISLAM

Islam is a monotheistic religion, similar to Judaism and Christianity, and emerging after both. The term *Islam* is often interpreted as "submission to God's will in the service of bringing harmony and peace" (Esposito, 2011; Gordon, 2002). Besides belief in the

Prophet Muhammad, Muslims believe in prophets of the Hebrew Bible, such as Noah, Abraham, and Moses, and in prophets of the New Testament such as Jesus. Muslims refer to Jews and Christians as *people of the book* because of the common lineage from Abraham across the three religions (Esposito, 2011). They also accord with other monotheistic religions in holding belief in a cosmology of heaven and hell, angels, and a Day of Judgment, Resurrection, or Reckoning that results in a final assessment of humanity. Beings known as *jinn* (the origin of the term *genie*) are unique to Islam, and predate it, being incorporated from Arab culture. The jinn inhabit the unseen world, can be physical, and are good or evil.

Muslims believe the Prophet Muhammad (b. 570 CE, d. 632 CE) received revelations recorded in the Qur'an from the Angel Gabriel to correct human errors in the scriptures of Judaism and Christianity (Esposito, 2011). It is thus not a new religion, but one that represents the original revelations of God. The Qur'an is viewed as the direct word of God; oral recitation and chanting of the Qur'an remains a source of inspiration to believers. Whether fully understood or not, Muslims of any nationality memorize and recite the Qur'an in Arabic as well as praying in Arabic. The Hadith complements the Qur'an by detailing the life of Muhammad, how he thought and acted. The Imam is the religious leader of the community and interprets legal and doctrinal considerations. Sufism, the mystical dimension of Islam, is concerned with the search for inner spirituality and closeness to God, but is also integral to the faith.

The Five Pillars

The Five Pillars of Islam, or obligations of the faith, form the framework of Muslim life (Esposito, 2011; Gordon, 2002; Lewis, 2009; Nadir & Dziegielewski, 2001; Smith, 1994b). These include the testimony of faith, prayer, giving *zakat* (support of the needy), fasting during the month of Ramadan, and the pilgrimage to Mecca that occurs, if possible physically and financially, once in a lifetime.

1.The testimony of faith. The first pillar is called the Declaration of Faith. A Muslim is one who bears witness. This declaration is known as the *Shahada* (witness, testimony). Allah is the Arabic name for God, just as Yahweh is the Hebrew name for God used in the Old Testament. To become a Muslim, one need only make this simple proclamation, "There is no God but God, and Muhammad is his messenger" (Gordon, 2002). The first part of this proclamation affirms Islam's absolute monotheism, the uncompromising belief in the oneness or unity of God; the association of anything else with God is idolatry and an unforgivable sin.

2. Prayer. The second pillar of Islam is prayer (*salat*). Muslims pray (or, perhaps more correctly, worship) five times throughout the day: at daybreak, noon, midafternoon, sunset, and evening. Although the times for prayer and the ritual actions were not specified in the Qur'an, Muhammad established them in his *hadiths* (sayings). In many Muslim countries, reminders to pray, or calls to prayer, echo out across the rooftops from a minaret or tower. Prayers make use of the 99 names of God, each representing a distinct quality believed to be fully held by God, although the quality may be partially held by humans. Women generally pray at home but have separate areas designated for them when they pray in the mosque. A source of fresh water is required for ritual cleansing that precedes prayer.

Reminders throughout the day help keep believers mindful of God in the midst of work and family with all their attractions and distractions. It strengthens the conscience, reaffirms total dependence on God, and puts worldly concerns within the perspective of death, the last judgment, and the afterlife. These prayers are accompanied by a sequence of movements: standing, bowing, kneeling, touching the ground with one's forehead, and sitting.

3. Giving zakat (support of the needy). The third pillar of Islam is called the *zakat*, which means "purification." Like prayer, which is both an individual and communal responsibility, zakat expresses a Muslim's worship of and thanksgiving to God by supporting the poor. An annual contribution of 2.5% of an individual's wealth and assets is required, not merely a percentage of annual income. In Islam, the true owner of things is not man but God, and people receive assets as a trust from God. Therefore, zakat is not viewed as charity; it is an obligation for those who received riches from God to respond to the needs of less fortunate members of the community. The Qur'an, as well as Islamic law, stipulate that alms are to be used to support the poor, orphans, and widows; to free slaves and debtors; and to support those working in God's cause (e.g., construction of mosques, religious schools, and hospitals). Zakat, developed 1,400 years ago, functions as a form of social security in a Muslim society.

4. Fasting the month of Ramadan. The fourth pillar of Islam, the fast of Ramadan, occurs once yearly during the month of Ramadan, the ninth month of the Islamic calendar and the month in which Muhammad received the first revelation of the Qur'an. During this month-long fast, Muslims whose health permits must abstain from dawn to sunset from food, drink, smoking, and sexual activity. Fasting is a practice common to many religions, sometimes undertaken as penance or for release from undue focus on needs and desires. The Ramadan fast is intended to stimulate reflection on human weakness and dependence upon God, focus on spiritual goals, and identification with and response to the less fortunate. At dusk, the fast is broken with a light meal, the *iftar*, referred to as breakfast. Families and friends share a late evening meal together, often including special foods served only at this time of the year. Many go to the mosque for the evening prayer, followed by special prayers recited only during Ramadan. Children and older adults are exempted from the fast.

5. The pilgrimage to Mecca. The fifth pillar is the pilgrimage, or *Hajj*, to Mecca in Saudi Arabia. Mecca is the site of the birthplace of the Prophet Muhammad and the revelations written in the Qur'an. At least once in his or her lifetime, every adult Muslim who is physically and financially able is required to make the sacrifice of time, possessions, status, and normal comforts necessary to make this pilgrimage, becoming a pilgrim totally at God's service. The pilgrimage season follows Ramadan. Every year more than two million believers, representing a tremendous diversity of cultures and languages, travel from all over the world to the city of Mecca to form one community who live their faith. In addition to the Hajj, there are the lesser pilgrimages called the *umrah* (visitation) that involve visiting holy sites at other times of the year. Male pilgrims wear distinctive simple clothes which hide distinctions of class, status, and culture so that all stand equal before God.

The rites of the Hajj include circling the Kaaba seven times and going seven times between the hillocks of Safa and Marwa, as Hagar did during her search for water. Then the pilgrims stand together in Arafa and ask God for what they wish and for His forgiveness, in what is often thought of as a preview of the Day of Judgment. The end of the Hajj is marked by a festival, Eid Al-Adha, which is celebrated with prayers. This and Eid al-Fitr, a feast-day commemorating the end of Ramadan, are the two annual festivals of the Muslim calendar.

Islam and Aging

In the Islamic world, domestic life, such as marriage, is regulated strictly. Family members are strongly interconnected in a system of largely patriarchal authority. One rarely finds nursing care facilities solely for older Muslim people because care is usually provided in the home. Caregiving for parents in later life is considered a blessing and an opportunity to grow spiritually (Ibrahim, 2002). Muslims pray for their parents, but they also are to act with limitless compassion, remembering the time when they were cared for as children. Mothers are especially revered because they have held the primary tasks of childrearing. When Muslim parents reach elderhood, they are treated with respect, kindness, and selflessness. Children, parents, grandparents, and sometimes great-grandparents may all live together or visit together often.

Serving parents is a duty second to prayer and worship of God, and parents have a right to expect it (Al-heeti, 2007; Ibrahim, 2002). It is considered disgraceful to express impatience when those who are old become difficult. Treatment of aging parents is discussed in the Qur'an:

> Your Lord has commanded that you worship none but Him, and that you be kind to your parents. If one of them or both of them reach old age with you, do not say to them a word of disrespect, or scold them, but say a generous word to them. And act humbly to them in mercy, and say, "My Lord, have mercy on them, since they cared for me when I was small." (Qur'an, 17:23–24)

Older Muslims are seen as an ongoing part of the community. Their children are expected to care for them at home just as they were cared for as youth (Al-Heeti, 2007; MacKinlay, 2010). The sayings of the prophet Mohammed, also known as hadith, suggest that the first people for whom children should concern themselves are their parents. Further, this deeply held conviction is so strong that some see sending elderly Muslim parents to a nursing home as a form of elder abuse. Practically, there is also a concern about fulfilling requirements of dietary law about not eating pork, for example. Gender sensibilities also suggest discomfort if intimate care is provided by someone from a different gender in an institutional setting (Al-Heeti, 2007). Further, there is little provision for Islamic religious worship, celebration of holidays such as Ramadan, or other religiocultural social connections in residential care. There is no stage of life given to renunciation and reflection similar to Hinduism. It is expected that older adults will continue to contribute to society as long as they are able to do so, given that aging is often a time of increasing dependence prior to death.

As Muslims move toward death, they should lay on their side if possible (Rassool, 2000). After death a Muslim is washed, usually by a family member and someone of the same sex, wrapped in a clean white cloth tied at the head and feet, and buried with a brief standing prayer, preferably the same day or within 24 hours. The body is not embalmed nor cremated. When the body is buried, the head should face toward Mecca in a grave with no casket unless there is a specific reason for it. Mourners each fill the grave with three handfuls of soil. Women are cautioned not to tear clothing, a traditional sign of grief in some cultures, or to engage in loud weeping. Most graves are plain and unadorned.

One of the concerns in modern Islamic society, especially in immigrant communities, is the problem of lack of respect (Khirfan, 2012). Older Muslims believe that younger people will outgrow this as they age, and this is often the case. However, they fuel a power imbalance by using the skills of children or grandchildren to translate what they need to know because many have not learned the language of the host country. Difficulties include social isolation and inability to drive, so reliance on family to bring them to religious functions and social events is common. However, this dependence results in a diminishment of traditional respect.

Supporting Spirituality in Aging Muslims

In hospitals, counseling and pastoral visits are provided to patients and families through community imams and hospital volunteers. In order to better respond to the needs of Muslim patients, educational training for hospital staff might focus on preferred interactional styles, especially related to gender and dietary (*halal* or lawful) obligations (Esposito, 2011; MacKinlay, 2010). For instance, some Muslims do not shake hands with non-Muslims because of beliefs about ritual impurity. They are expected to abstain from pork and also from animals not slaughtered according to prescriptions of law. Muslims are expected to perform ablutions, washing hands, face, feet, and rinsing mouth and nose prior to prayer. When older people cannot do this because of illness, they would want to be assisted. Caring for those who are ill or elderly is a service within Muslim communities, and in the past special societies took on these responsibilities, especially for those who were poor (Gaspar, 2007).

Gaspar (2007) also suggests that Muslims must "make a commitment to share suffering. As we nourish their spirits, offer comfort, friendship and consolation, we must bring a sense of wholeness and connection to the Muslim community, repairing and healing our world" (para. 12). In her appeal, she summons echoes of both the Catholic option for the poor (sharing suffering) and Judaism in mention of repairing the world, similar to the Hebrew expression Tikkun Olam, mentioned above. However, somewhat different from mainline Catholic and Jewish worship, music is not a part of worship. Still, in an older Islamic community, use of the tambourine, drum, and devotional Arabic singing would provide linkage to what is familiar.

HINDUISM

Hinduism accepts many contradictions and polarities within it, and is thus one of the most open, tolerant, and universal of religious systems. Although Hindu practice has many commonalities among believers, it is not a unified system, but contains within its concepts wide diversity in interpretation. This religion affirms that there are many paths to God. One Hindu author explains that Hinduism, although monotheistic, believes that God manifests in many forms (Chakravarti, 1991). It is more than 5,000 years old, with prehistoric roots (Klostermaier, 1999). Unlike many of the other world religions, it has no individual founder. Hinduism draws on the Vedas, which date from c. 1500–800 BCE, a set of orally transmitted Sanskrit texts that represent the authoritative scriptures of the tradition (Melton, 2009). The Vedas represent texts which are heard or directly revealed versus what is remembered. They consist of four volumes that contain hymns, incantations, and rituals.

The Upanishads, probably written a bit later, also provide many of the teachings that have come to be known universally in Hinduism. The word *Upanishad* means "sitting close to" and is reminiscent of the oral tradition and tie between a teacher and his or her students. Fundamental teachings such as *samsara* (reincarnation), *moksha* (nirvana), *atman* (soul), and *karma* (actions resulting in both good and bad outcomes) are contained within the Upanishads. They provide a spiritual vision for self-realization, especially in the disciplines of meditation and yoga. The Bhagavad Gita, part of the Mahabharata, dates from the 5th to 2nd century BCE and narrates the story of prince

Arjuna and his guide Lord Kṛiṣhṇa. Conflicted about his duty to fight with relatives, Arjuna is exhorted by his charioteer, Kṛiṣhṇa, to fulfill his Kṣatriya (warrior) duty and proceed with the just war. Set in a battlefield, it has been interpreted as an allegory of ethical struggles in human life. It comprised a call to selfless action that inspired many leaders including Mahatma Gandhi. It further sought to harmonize various strands of Hindu thought.

Hindus thus share beliefs in reincarnation, nirvana, and karma, and engage in common practices like various forms of yoga (Smith, 1994c). Hinduism has a set of beliefs that invest in the concepts of Gods and Goddesses. Although there is one supreme God, there are three primary expressions of God in Hindu teaching: Brahma, Vishnu, and Shiva. Brahma is the Creator God. This concept is not equivalent to the idea of God in the monotheistic religions, but a god who transcends all limits and dualities, a god who creates new realities. Both immanent and transcendent, Brahma is the source of all things, an interpenetrating reality. Vishnu is the Protector and embodiment of mercy, maintaining the social order with peace and compassion. Vishnu does not sleep, is often depicted on a coiled serpent, and has had many reincarnations. Maheswar, or Shiva, both creates and destroys: his goal is to destroy the universe in order to recreate it. This includes the destruction of illusions. These three beings work together in tandem for common goals: Brahma creates the universe, Vishnu protects and defends it, and then Shiva destroys it and recreates in a new cycle. Shiva was married to Parvati, also known as the female force Shakti, which is creative, cosmic energy. There are 108 names for Parvati due to the same number of reincarnations.

There are four aims of Hinduism, three of which are for those in the world (the *pavritti*) and the fourth one for those who renounce the world (the *nivritti*). The first three aims are: (1) *dharma*—behavior involving personal duties, virtues, justice, and the right ways of living; (2) *artha*—economic success, career-related aspirations, and financial security; and (3) *kama*—desire or longing to find sensual, sexual, and mental enjoyment. The fourth aim is *moksha*—liberation from samsara, the cycles of karma involved in reincarnation and eternity. This involves self-actualization. Dharma refers to the universal law that governs everything and is applied to all aspects of life. Essentially, karma in one lifetime determines how someone will be reborn, to a higher or lower level of life including as an animal. Through pure acts of self-sacrifice, one can escape samsara (reincarnation) and achieve enlightenment.

The ultimate goal of life is moksha, or self-realization, and merger with the ultimate reality or God/Brahman. This concept of moksha, freedom, essentially means the more one lives in awareness, the less the possibility that behavior is determined by any past experience or personality. This consciousness signals a freedom so unfettered that nothing can determine it. In a way, it is similar to the Christian concept of offering the other cheek when struck on the first one. Although one interpretation may suggest a nonviolent response, a broader reading suggests a response not determined by anger or any other emotion. It is an unexpected response, contingent only on what the actor views as the need or highest response in the moment. In the face of this type of freedom, behavior is not predictable. People may be observed to act against what others might think would be their own interest. This is spiritual freedom.

Practice of yoga leads to realization of the Divine or Ultimate Source; it is one of many paths to this outcome. Rather than just a fitness routine that concentrates on asanas or poses, it is a spiritual path: a way of thinking, a way of conducting oneself, and a philosophical and practical way of living. It involves an integration of individual and universal consciousness and consists of four styles or types: *bhakti yoga* (through devotion and/or love), *jnana yoga* (through knowledge), *karma yoga* (through work), and *raja yoga* (through meditative exercises; Littleton, 1996; Melton, 2009; Smith, 1994c). These four forms of yoga appeal to different types of persons and thus are different pathways to God. *Bhakti yoga* is the love experienced by the worshipper toward the God who is personally known. It often involves recitation of a mantra, a sound, syllable, or word chosen for its sacred power, and concerns itself with devotion and service. *Jnana yoga* appeals to more reflective individuals who appreciate philosophical concepts and logical demonstrations of thought. Practitioners of jnana yoga seek true knowledge by setting aside false identities and exploring their true nature. Disciplines of study, ethical training, and meditation are the methods employed. They achieve the realization that levels of self are finite and the eternal self lies beyond finite qualities of size, gender, or emotions. Individuals more centered on emotion than thought learn to experience God in work and their own actions in the world. *Karma yoga* suggests that any activity, no matter how small, can be a spiritual practice if dedicated to God. Although desire motivates action, it can also bring disappointment and pain, keeping one in the cycle of rebirth (samsara). *Raja yoga* is considered by many individuals to be the highest path to God. It aims at controlling thought and the vagaries of thought through meditation. It leads to quiet detachment, mastery of the senses, and transcendence.

Beyond beliefs, Hinduism inspires an intense identification with the presence of the sacred in many forms. Temples, shrines, and holy places are sites of pilgrimage from which individuals may bring water or soil as symbols with which to integrate their homes. Festivals are times for worship (pujas). Religious ritual incorporates many regulations that are related to hygienic practice such as a daily bath. A householder who is Hindu is to rise before sunrise and to speak the name of a deity of his choice (Klostermaier, 1999). The first thing she or he holds should be a favorable object and he or she should touch the earth as a first favorable action. His or her aim for the day should be to increase right action and wealth. Morning prayer is observed by many and is followed by morning, noon, and evening worship. Many people who are Hindu have a room or a corner of a room reserved for placement of images and for worship (Klostermaier, 1999). Additionally, the sacred is acknowledged in nature, a practice dating back to the pagan origins of Hinduism. The river Ganges is considered holy and is the site of many life beginning and ending purification rituals.

Social relationships are also important; however, they have been defined in part by social status. The caste system was a social hierarchy that dates back to 2000 BCE. It was strongly identified with Hinduism, but has been interpreted with greater or lesser flexibility at different times. The caste was assigned through birth and within each caste there are stratifications (Littleton, 1996). The *Brahmins* were the intellectual and spiritual leaders, the priestly class. The *Kshatriyas* were the protectors of society, the politicians, police, and military. The *Vaisyas* were the artisan, farming, or merchant class. The *Shudra*s were the maintenance workers or hard laborers. In the lowest stratification of *Shudras*, those who did the bottommost form of menial duties were known as *untouchables*. Within castes there was equality, opportunity, and social insurance. It was assumed that over lifetimes people would move up through the different castes. Privileges were defined in proportion to responsibility. Positive discrimination or affirmative action policies, known as reservation, offer special advantage in education and work in the public sector to undo years of discrimination. The Indian constitution today prohibits discrimination on the basis of the caste system in India.

Hinduism and Aging

Older people are highly respected for their experience and wisdom. They take pride in acknowledging their age and are fully embedded in reciprocal caregiving within families. Interdependence and interconnectedness form part of dharma. Thus, families are usually consulted in mental health or health issues. Sacredness is embedded in daily life to the extent that people seek to live in harmony both individually and corporally with the design of the universe. Meditation, rituals, and use of herbs and oils as in Ayurvedic treatment may form part of a holistic approach (Hodge, 2004). Deference is often given from women to men within a marriage for decision making. As with some other cultures, direct eye contact with elders and others may be seen as disrespectful. For certain purposes, such as asking for permission to marry, the supplicants will make appointments with and touch the feet of all older family members.

The Hindu religion has a belief system regarding the four stages of life (Ashramas) that commence at about age 8 and continue throughout life (Klostermaier, 1999; Littleton, 1996; Mehrotra & Wagner, 2009). Each stage requires certain conduct and modes of response. Women's responsibilities are often connected to those of the dominant man in their lives and his current stage of Ashrama, whether he is a father, husband, or son. A woman is seen as dependent and protected by the man, so her task is to maintain domestic religious life. This model for aging (developed primarily for males) thus provides ethical expectations that change at different stages. There are four general stages: student, householder, retirement, and renunciation.

- The student stage begins between ages 8 and 12, lasting for about 12 years. The goal for the student is to be receptive to learning from the teacher and to acquire skills and knowledge necessary for the current and following stages of life. Most time is spent in study after an initiation ceremony. The goal is to be able to live an effective life.

- The householder stage begins with marriage. The householder is engaged with responsibilities and pleasures of developing a vocation, raising a family, and contributing to the community. During this phase, dharma (law of righteousness) is observed. Hindu writing suggests that the householder stage supports people at all of the other stages of life. This stage is the height of power and achievement.

- The retirement stage may begin when a grandchild is born (or when the first gray hair is sighted). The individual moves from household duties to a more contemplative life in gradual phases. Previously the individual and/or spouse were known as forest dwellers, seeking out forest solitude for self-discovery (Smith, 1994c). While previously the individual needed to specialize and devote energy to immediate tasks, now the individual has time to ponder the deeper questions about life's purposes, to find meaning amidst mystery. The goal is to overcome the senses and dwell with the reality of the natural world, to conceive a philosophy and then make that philosophy a way of living.

- In the renunciation stage, the last phase of life, one neither loves nor hates any object or person, but is indifferent to all. One seeks to become united with the supreme reality or Brahman through liberation from all possessions (moksha). Through such practices as noninjury to animals, detaching the senses from pleasurable pursuits, and performance of rituals detailed in the Vedas, this state of unification may be attained prior to death. This stage is viewed as the state of serenity, similar to Baltes's (1993) concept of wisdom. Geography previously mattered in the retirement stage (elders would leave the household and retire to live in the forest or other remote areas) since people needed to relocate to gain new understanding and to be seen differently; now they are so inner directed that location no longer is important. They are able to clearly differentiate between finite self and true or infinite self.

Final rites at death are universal and most deceased individuals are cremated within hours after the body is washed, a shroud covers it, and flowers are amassed upon it (Klostermaier, 1999). The eldest son lights the pyre at the cremation grounds and Vedic hymns are recited. Safe passage is requested into the next realm. Ritual cleansing and purification is done afterward. Ceremonies continue for one year at prescribed intervals.

Common to most Hindu practice is the belief that outward life and suffering are mere illusion, *maya*, and recognition of this will lead to release from suffering. Thus, in later ages individuals have the capacity to take a larger perspective. One of the most sacred symbols is repetition of the syllable *om* (Littleton, 1996). This represents the wholeness of the universe and the vibratory sound of the universal soul, Brahman. Meditation on the sound *om* is reported to result in enlightenment and immortality. *Ahimsa*, one of the highest ethical precepts for Hinduism (as well as Buddhism) is the pledge of noninjury to life. The practice of vegetarianism originates in ahimsa. Together, these practices represent spiritual disciplines that enhance life.

BUDDHISM

Discussion of Buddhist beliefs often begins with telling the story of the central figure of Buddhism, the Buddha, which sets a context for Buddhist principles (Melton, 2009; Seager, 2009). There are many different forms of Buddhist practice, yet they all follow the same essential principles from the life of the Enlightened One (or Buddha), Siddhartha Gautama. Born a prince around 563 BCE at Lumbini near the kingdom of Shakya, India, his mother died at his birth. Before the birth she dreamed that he would be a great leader if he remained in the palace. If he declined this course, he would become a Buddha. According to traditional accounts, Gautama grew up in the court and was shielded from contact with the world, the people he would someday rule. He married at 17 and fathered a child in a happy marriage, but was restricted to life in the palace by his father. His life was enriched in a number of ways and his family hoped he would be satisfied. However, the contours of his life changed dramatically in 529 BCE after a series of excursions outside the palace that took place with the help of his charioteer (Melton, 2009). There he saw people living in poverty and illness, and he was devastated. He also saw a monk, holding the bowl of a beggar but radiating peace. He departed from the palace, abandoned his worldly existence, and began to seek a way to end the cycle of suffering and rebirth.

Gautama spent the next six years visiting Indian religious groups and experimenting with religious practices such as asceticism and meditation. He finally concluded that keeping a malnourished body would not welcome an awakened mind. His companions who had supported his self-neglect abandoned him. His search ended in 523 BCE while he was in meditation and contemplation at the foot of a Bodhi tree located at Sarnath and considered a sacred Buddhist shrine (Melton, 2009). He reportedly accepted gifts of milk-rice and fresh grass on his birthday with a cushion to sit on. As this meditation began, Gautama reportedly sat in serenity. He understood how the darkness of the mind comes about and how it can be destroyed. Delusions were ended and he achieved full clarity. He attained *Bodhi*, or enlightenment, and as a result became known as *Gautama the Buddha* or the *Enlightened One*. After his enlightenment, Buddha began to preach and teach, and disciples were drawn to him. A movement began to grow in northwest India. The Buddha died due to dysentery about 480 BCE at age 80 (Seager, 2009).

The essence of Buddhism is found in the teachings of the Buddha. These teachings outline the Dharma, that is, the laws of nature and true living. The Dharma is both profound and simple. Buddhists share a belief in the Buddha's Dharma, which centers upon the *four noble truths* and the *noble eightfold path*. The four noble truths are: (1) all existence involves suffering; (2) the cause of suffering is desire: craving for pleasure, prosperity, and ongoing life; (3) there is a path leading to freedom from suffering; and (4) the eightfold path leads to cessation of desire and suffering.

The noble eightfold path is pictured in the eight-spoke wheel, a symbol second only to the seated Buddha as a sign of Buddhist faith. The path consists of the following:

- right understanding,

- right purpose,

- right speech,

- right conduct,

- right livelihood,

- right effort,

- right attention or mindfulness, and

- right concentration.

The enlightenment of Buddha was by his own efforts, and followers are also taught that their path to enlightenment is their own responsibility. The Buddha taught the value of the middle way, the path that avoids extremes. In his own life, he had known both great luxury and great asceticism. Buddhism is essentially non-theistic and denies the existence of a self. It borrowed heavily from Hinduism and the Vedic tradition. A basic belief is that people are good in their nature. Good karma is achieved for the layperson who gives food and alms to monks and nuns. Karma is the law of moral causation that suggests people can earn merit through good deeds and demerits through current or past malicious deeds. People are thought to have experienced thousands of lifetimes and that to attain human birth is both rare and precious. There are no dietary restrictions, but many Buddhists may be vegetarian out of respect for animals.

The basic scriptures of Buddhism are the *Tripitaka* (Pali Canon) or Three Baskets. They include the *Vinaya*, the *Sutras*, and the *Abhidhamma*. The *Vinaya* are rules for the monks and information about Buddha's life; they address about 250 rules for monks and 300 rules for nuns. The *Sutras* are oral teachings of the Buddha and his disciples, originally written on palm leaves sewn together. They are concise statements that are often intended for memorization by students. Commentaries exist to explain them. The *Abhidhamma* is composed of seven philosophical discourses of Gautama or his disciples. Other scriptures have been added to the Tripitaka by different Buddhist sects.

Buddhism developed out of Hinduism and thus included elements of Hindu principles, although many ideas were revised, including transmigration of the soul, or reincarnation. After the Buddha's death, the First Council was held, which successfully organized the Buddhist movement and encouraged its spread. Another significant leader, Asoka, was remorseful about his acts of conquest as ruler of the Indian empire. He became a monk and was responsible for spreading Buddhism throughout India and other countries. Buddhism was protected by a Greek king, Menander, who followed shortly after Asoka's dissemination of the religion.

Two primary schools of Buddhism developed, *Theravada* (Hinayana) and *Mahayana*. *Theravada* formed around the writing of Sariputra, an early disciple of Buddha. His interpretation of Buddhism focused on the role of the monk and the monastic way of life as leading to nirvana, a stillness of mind after desire has been extinguished. *Vispassana* and Insight Meditation have emerged from this school. *Mahayana* had a more universal approach and accepted the role of non-monks in the faith. A key goal was the ultimate salvation of all living beings. *Zen* Buddhism developed out of Mahayana Buddhism and emphasized understanding the Buddha-nature and the expression of this in ordinary life, especially for the benefit of others. Thus, it de-emphasized knowledge of sutras and doctrine while preferring direct understanding through zazen and interaction with teachers. *Pure Land Buddhism*, also a form of Mahayana Buddhism, advocates chanting the name of Amitabha Buddha with total concentration, trusting that one will be reborn in the Pure Land where it is much easier to become enlightened. A third school is the *Vajrayana* or Tibetan Buddhism. This dates from the 8th century and is rich with ritual. The Dalai Lama is affiliated with this school.

Buddhism and Aging

Recognition of impermanence is a key principle in Buddhism. Changes abound in the aging process and change is a central feature of most Buddhist practice. People grow old and die, but every breath can offer something new. Nothing lasts, and acceptance rather than resistance offers new ways of seeing what is. In aging, people let go of some dreams in favor of constructing new ones. Further, if people choose to downsize or have it imposed on them, they also let go of household stuff and connected memories (Ekerdt & Sergeant, 2006). Mindfulness meditation practice is about letting go, paying attention to changes in the body, and what is happening in the present moment. Mindfulness involves giving attention without judgment and doing reflection throughout the course of a day.

Ahimsa is an expression that translates as do no harm (Esposito, Fasching, & Lewis, 2012). Nonviolence, as demonstrated by the life of Mohandas Gandhi, is a key principle of Buddhism. Externally, to hurt another is to hurt oneself because of the interconnections of all beings. Thich Nhat Hanh (1995) referred to this sense of oneness as "interbeing." Internally, this suggests that rather than fight the negative aspects of aging, a better path is the way of acceptance. Violence against the self through negative thoughts toward our bodies or diminishing energy can increase suffering. Respecting the process of aging is thus important, because it decreases the tendency to hurt ourselves. Respecting aging also helps older people note the positive aspects of growing older, such as increased or deeper connections with successive generations. Further, although older people may not think or problem solve as quickly as younger people, they take mental shortcuts that result in access to expert knowledge (Baltes, 1993). This is a more integrative problem-solving approach than what younger adults typically employ. Reframing experience and demonstrating courage in facing life challenges are key processes of approaching change that accord with Buddhist principles.

Buddhist practice includes acknowledgment of aging and illness in its writings, and these concepts often intersect with other Eastern philosophies, such as the need for filial piety and intergenerational responsibility found in Confucianism (Nakasone, 2008). Buddhist teaching (dharma) sets the dilemma between having long life and holding fear of death. Yet, there are compensations. Dron-me (as cited in Lecso, 1989) writes, "I gave not a single thought to death or the advent of old age. The noise of the friends and relatives who surrounded me constantly held my attention and turned my face from everything else" (p. 59). Further, if one makes good use of education at early ages, then this continues in later years. "Youth is the time to learn and to become familiar with the teachings. Then as one grows old . . . it is easy to dwell within practice" (Dron-me, in Lecso, 1989, p. 64). Finally, the value of spiritual practice is reinforced through the following poem by Nagarjuna,

> *However, if one practices the spiritual path the mind abides in joy, regardless of one's age. Then when death falls one is like a child gleefully returning to his home. Even Buddha did not speak of a more profound method than this.* (p. 65)

One of the comforting messages of Buddhism is that attention to ongoing development lessens the perception of problems in old age. Problems will be understood and accepted in context within the greater blessing inherent in longevity. Buddhism, in sum, teaches the values of holism and balance.

CONFUCIANISM

The goal of Confucian practice is to realize one's authentic nature. It is both a philosophy and a religion, as attested by Huston Smith (1994a) in his writings on religions and by others (Taylor, 2004). Smith suggests that although Confucianism is primarily a social teaching about an ethical approach to living, it does contain a transcendent dimension in its discussion of the compartmentalization of the world into heaven and earth. Heaven was the place of the ancestors and earth was home to humans, but death was merely a connecting transition between the two coexisting phases. Although Confucius shifted attention from heaven to the earth part of the equation in his lifetime, he did not remove heaven. The Will (Mandate) of Heaven was what first required respect and was an ultimate source of authority (Smith, 1994a; Taylor, 2004). The ruling house was not viewed as divine. When unbearable conditions led to revolution, if the government checked the revolution, the emperor retained his mandate to rule, but if he was overthrown, it was evident that Heaven ordained a new dynasty (Thompson, 1989). Emphasizing the value of prayer, Confucius suggested, "He who offends the gods has no one to pray to" (Smith, 1994a, p. 117). There were many gods in early Chinese society: Ti, the Supreme God, as well as the God of Wind, God of the Sun, God of the Moon, and so on. (Thompson, 1989). Further, deceased ancestors were enjoined through ritual to confer blessings. There was mutual dependence between the dead and the living to the extent that elaborate formalized funeral rites and periods of mourning were instructed through ancient texts and sustained through public opinion and law.

Confucianism takes its name after Confucius (551 BCE–479 BCE), a westernized form of the phrase K'ung Fu-tsu, which means Master K'ung (Taylor, 2004). He advocated peace and equity reforms by Chinese leaders for the nation's administration. Although his own career was not so notable, from his teaching came a class of scholars who ruled China. In the Han dynasty (206 BCE–220 CE), his work became the foundation for the state religion, but he was also a transmitter of earlier writings. The Confucian ethic has been thoroughly intertwined with Chinese values, to the extent they are difficult to distinguish. It has also been adopted in Japan and Korea.

Confucius and his disciple Mencius maintained that because of biological limits, humans encounter the inevitable fate inherent in birth: aging, disease, and the end of physical life. However, possessing conscience, humans should act beyond self-interest. The Doctrine of the Mean still practiced upholds a preference for negotiation and mediation over legal threats to remedy behavior (Thompson, 1989). This appointment, or Way of Heaven, meant that biological destiny differed from individual nature. Someone following the ordinances of heaven would fulfill their moral calling and this could be accomplished only through right action. It has been proposed that Confucianism addressed five parts: ideas about destiny, a model for thinking, ethics for ordinary citizens, ethics for scholars, and self-cultivation (Hwang, 2001).

The self/ego was not constructed solely through self-effort, but through social interaction. In this way, it corresponds to some of the theories of human behavior such as social exchange and social interactionism as well as Cooley's looking-glass self, where self-image is shaped by how we see others seeing us. The self was also situated to pursue a lifetime of learning. "While you do not know life, how can you know about death?" (Legge, 1893, ch. 11). Three ideas are paramount in Confucian thinking (1) the interaction between heaven and earth leads to endless capacity for creation; (2) the nature of the universe is cyclical change and when things are at their worst, they mend; and (3) all things in the universe have a vital essence (Hwang, 2001). "Heaven exists within humans. As humans bring out their internal virtue, they bring to light the Way of Heaven" (The Analects, Liu, 1989/1992 as cited in Hwang, 2001, p. 184). This suggests that although primary focus was on what humans should do for right interaction, following this prescriptive method could bring heaven and earth a wee bit closer.

The foundation of benevolence underlay an ethical system that established and maintained social order. This was also known as *jen*, conscientiousness and sympathy or empathy (Taylor, 2004). The Chinese character *jen* (humanity) is created from the two characters that represent *human being* and *two*. Thus *jen* represents ideal human behavior between two people. Benevolence, righteousness, and propriety (*ren–yi–li* in Chinese) are viewed as methods of countering innate biological desire (Hoobler & Hoobler, 1993). Benevolence concerns displaying affection for those in close relationships. Righteousness is interpreted as respect for those who are superior. Propriety suggests that people should love others according to who people are, and respect for superiors according to their rank gives society stable structure. Social relationships were assessed according to level of closeness and level of status. The term *li* was known as *seamlessly proper conduct* in all social circumstances (Toropov & Buckles, 2011, p. 161) and originally had a religious connotation, which was later lost. Fulfilling *ren-yi-li* was the Way of Humanity that would allow one to fulfill one's heavenly destiny. Through practicing these methods, one could achieve the virtues of wisdom, benevolence, and courage. Here benevolence was seen as both a method and a goal. The code of *li* was elaborate, first applying only to nobles (similar to the idea of the French *noblesse oblige*), and later to commoners and most of Chinese society (Thompson, 1989).

According to Mencius, the later disciple of Confucius, there were five basic relationship types and preferred values. "Between father and son, there should be affection; between sovereign and subordinate, righteousness; between husband and wife, attention to their separate functions; between elder brother and younger, a proper order; and between friends, friendship" (Mencius, n.d., ch. 10:8). Relationships between father and son, and rulers and those they rule, were primary before others. All relationships were arranged according to a vertical hierarchical dimension, suggesting prescribed roles of kindness, gentleness, righteous, and benevolence to be practiced by those holding higher social status, and filial duty (for the son), obedience, submission, deference, and loyalty to be exercised by the various lower status-holding individuals. Kindness is also specifically mentioned as a role of elders with deference to be given by those younger than the elders are. Benevolence (also known as perfect virtue) was about loving all men, but when asked if someone was perfectly virtuous, Confucius would respond by saying, "How can we know?" (Hwang, 2001, p. 190). He understood this task was so complex that few were able to achieve it.

What are the key writings of Confucianism? Texts incorporating the work of Confucius and Mencius as well as commentaries by others include the four books: *Analects* (teachings of Confucius compiled after his death), the *Great Learning*, the *Doctrine of the Mean*, and the *Book of Mencius*. The *I Ching* (Book of Changes) was a much older text of divination/prophecy that informed the work of Confucius along with four other classics (the Book of History, the Book of Poetry, the Book of Rites, and Spring and Autumn Annals). Together with the *I Ching*, these are known as the *Five Classics* (Hoobler & Hoobler, 1993; Taylor, 2004).

Education, for Confucianism, was about ethical practice, learning by doing, rather than theoretical reasoning. Experiencing shame, for example, the potential outcome when words differ from actions, was useful for learning although certainly not a preferred approach. The role of scholars differed from ordinary people in that they should benefit the world through the Way of Humanity (their actions) rather than seek material prosperity. Scholars were given higher standards to reach in their ethical attention and practice. Further, those in positions of power should be sensitive to the needs of the group. If anyone in a position of authority acted in wrong ways, the person in an inferior position could legitimately correct them. This may be why rulers never fully embraced Confucianism, according to references I consulted.

Confucianism and Aging

Aging and the respect accorded to older people are fully embedded in this philosophical and religious approach to life. Mencius maintained that developing the virtue of benevolence begins in service to parents. "There has never been a benevolent person who neglected his parents. . . . Of services, which is the greatest? The service of parents is the greatest. There are many services, but the service of parents is the root of all others" (The Analects, Li Lau as cited in Hwang, 2001). Further, the Hsiâo King, or Book of Filial Piety, states, "Our bodies, to every hair and shred of skin, are received from our parents. We must not presume to injure or to wound them. This is the beginning of filial piety" (Dawson, 1915). The ideograph or Chinese character for filiality (Hsiâo) is a representation for old, supported by a pictograph for a son underneath (Thompson, 1989). Practicing filial piety was thus considered the ethical way to interact with parents and of utmost importance in maintaining good relationships in society. Overall, Confucius in his writing largely expounds standards of conduct based on the idea that one could learn from everyone, no matter their station or standing.

However, for women in Asian society, this has led to support for unequal treatment. The three obediences require that women first submit to their fathers, then their husbands, and finally to their oldest son (Shim & Nelson-Becker, 2009; Taylor, 2004). A positive interpretation would be that this also afforded women the opportunity to be cared for by society at different phases of life, but abuse has sometimes been the outcome. Because the status of women in earlier times meant that it was quite difficult to function independently, they could also be easily victimized. Further, the wife of the oldest son, as daughter-in-law, was expected to serve her in-laws food for their lifetimes. If the daughter-in-law was given a gift, she should offer it to her mother-in-law. If it was returned to her, she was to consider it a gift given for the first time (Thompson, 1989). A young couple would seldom establish their own home independent of one set of parents (Hoobler & Hoobler, 1993). Confucian philosophy did offer support for gentle opposition if persons were not well-treated, however if these entreaties were not heard and he or she were punished, they should not complain (Hwang, 2001; Taylor, 2004).

Ritual has been an important feature of life to older people. One performs ritual not for its own sake, but to enter into relationship with the object of ritual. Evidence of this is present in the veneration of ancestors that occurs, especially on certain feast days. For someone who practices Confucianism, the inner feelings generated from participation in ritual are of highest import and are a symbol of connections to the world as well as social cohesion. Considered repositories for the spirit, the ancestral shrine was typically within a room in a home and consisted of an altar on which sat tablets inscribed with the name of a deceased family member (Taylor, 2004). The eldest son would perform daily devotions at the altar, including reports on recent events (Hoobler & Hoobler, 1993). Five generations would be so venerated, with a newly deceased family member supplanting the oldest one. There is an expected reciprocity, with blessings and guidance to come from deceased relatives.

The Analects report the developmental path as Confucius viewed it. At age 15 he began to study ancient texts in a serious manner. By age 30 he believed he had formed his character and knew his position in the world. At age 40 he no longer held doubts. This was important in a context where at the time there were many warring political entities with differing administrative and moral views. At age 50 he was said to report he knew the will of Heaven, the correct way to govern.

> The Master said, *At fifteen, I had my mind bent on learning. At thirty, I stood firm. At forty, I had no doubts. At fifty, I knew the decrees of Heaven. At sixty, my ear was an obedient organ for the reception of truth. At seventy, I could follow what my heart desired, without transgressing what was right.* (The Analects by Confucius, n.d., Part 2)

Veneration of the elders perhaps has been imbued in no nation to the extent it has in East Asian Confucian-infused countries. Through social practice that honored aging, older adults could expect treatment that grew kinder as they aged. Adult children might be expected to live near parents and fill every expressed need. In modern Asian countries, families under economic stress who have fewer children to care for aging parents, at times abandon the deep injunctions of Confucian principles and filial responsibility. Sometimes this action is initiated by children, but also sometimes by parents who choose to remove the responsibility from their burdened children by entering nursing care facilities.

DAOISM

Faith in natural processes, noncontrol, and noninterference, is an overarching principle in Daoistic philosophy. The ideal lifestyle presented in Daoism (also called Taoism) would be that of a farmer who lives in simple harmony with the natural cycles of the land. Natural features such as rivers, mountain, and caves are considered sacred spaces. *Ch'i* is the vital matter or energy that flows through everything and is both immanent and transcendent (Oldstone-Moore, 2003). Daoism is both a philosophy and a religion; it is addressed to both human nature and the proper functioning of society (Bowker, 1997; Oldstone-Moore, 2003; Thompson, 1989; Zhao, 2010). The Dao is also known as "the way" or "path." The Dao is that nameless and formless power that sourced all things, out of which they came into being (Oldstone-Moore, 2003). Daoist texts suggest a transformation of character within, out of which an ideal society will develop. This contrasts with Confucianism, which suggests respecting and obeying identified common values will result in the ideal society.

Much of Daoistic thought is expressed in the *Tao Te Ching* (*The Book of the Way*, or *The Book of the Way and How it Manifests Itself in the World*), of which there are several translations. Another Daoist text is titled *Master Chuang* (*Chuang Tzu*). The *Chuang-Tzu* is addressed to individuals, rather than rulers, and named for its author, who wrote in the 4th century BCE (Oldstone-Moore, 2003.) One version of the *Daode jing* (*Tao Te Ching*) I like the best is the translation by Stephen Mitchell (1988) for its crispness of language, large-heartedness, beauty, and wisdom. Further, he expresses gender fluidity in his use of the pronouns *he* and *she* where "the master" is written. I have used some of the sayings from the *Tao Te Ching* as beginning chapter quotes in this text. The *Chuang-Tzu* is addressed to individuals rather than rulers and named for its author writing in the 4th century BCE (Oldstone-Moore, 2003). Like other religions, Daoism had ordained priests and hermits who would remove themselves from society (Thompson, 1989). It is considered to be the original native religion of China. It has a liturgical tradition based on ritual texts as well as techniques to advance a goal of attaining transcendent immortality.

Little is concretely known about Lao-Tzu, the author of the *Tao Te Ching*. He was likely older than Confucius (551 BCE–479 BCE). He may have been a keeper of archives or librarian in one of the small kingdoms that proliferated at the time (Ai, 2006; Chung, 2000; Oldstone-Moore, 2003). It is reported that the guardian of the gate asked Lao-Tzu to write down some of his wisdom before he left the border of China (Thompson, 1989). Mostly what we know about him is through his book, a manual in the art of living. To hold the sense of connection and care he holds for others suggests he was not a recluse. One of the principles he advocated was *wei wu wei*, translated as "doing not doing." Far from a passive approach, the goal was to be fully and seamlessly engaged in whatever one is doing: the dancer is not different from the dance. "Open yourself to the Tao, then trust your natural responses. Everything will fall into place" (Mitchell, 1988, p. 23). This is a soft and supple, almost intuitive approach to life. Evil is not something to resist but a condition of disharmony with the way of the universe. "What is a good man, but a bad man's teacher? What is a bad man, but a good man's job? If you don't understand this, you will get lost" (Mitchell, 1988, p. 27).

The Dao is considered to be the ultimate principle: it serves as the foundation of the universe and encompasses all. The Dao recognizes inevitable change that comes with life. In this way, it speaks well to the condition of older adults who encounter many changes as they age into the end of their years. It also considers the forces of yin and yang which represent the two complementary energies involved in all process (Chung, 2000). Yin is often defined as female energy and yang as male energy, although that is a simplistic approach. Men often express a softer side and women a stronger side, for example, in childbirth. People exhibit different yin/yang components of themselves, their identity, depending on the situation. Yin energy, for example, may represent negativity (absence), passivity, and darkness while yang energy represents the positivity (presence), activity, and light. A symbol that represents this is often the circle with an

Figure 5.1   Yin-Yang Symbol

Source: Used from Wikimedia commons.

s-shaped line drawn within its boundaries, one side white and one shaded black (see Figure 5.1). Contained within each section is a small circle representing the contrasting white or black shade. Both yin and yang are creative manifestations. Together these complementary parts form the whole. They balance polarities and become each other. Yin-yang principles, although not discussed above under Confucianism, are also accepted in Confucian concepts. Achieving balance between both aspects is the goal.

Two principles stand out in Daoism. The first was the outer elixir *(wai-tan)* that, like the search for the philosopher's stone, embodied the search for the elixir of immortality. It is possible that the idea of alchemy began in China and spread to the West (Thompson, 1989). This elixir, when drunk, led to longevity; it was also able to transmute base metals into gold, a symbol for an incorruptible life. The political state was anxious to prevent counterfeiting of money and sought to execute those involved in this practice, so all formulas went underground and were written in obscure almost indecipherable language. The *nei-tan* was the inner elixir that refined the spiritual self or soul to liberate it from the physical body. Although this could be accomplished through death, religious Daoists believed it could be accomplished in present life. *Ch'i gung* or *qigong* refers to disciplined practices that strengthen or balance Ch'i. Four categories of Ch'i gung involve sitting, lying down, standing, and moving. In the last category, T'ai-chi ch'uan, a slow-motion ballet, was seen as a way to conserve the life force energy which could be depleted.

The Dao is like the old story of the farmer whose beautiful stallion ran away. "Bad luck," commented his neighbor. "We'll see," replied the farmer. The next day the stallion returned with three wild mares. "Good luck," observed the neighbor. "We'll see," answered the farmer. The next day the farmer's young son rode one of the mares, fell, and broke his leg severely. "Bad luck," voiced his neighbor. "We'll see," replied the farmer. The following day soldiers came for conscriptions for the state, but the farmer's son had to be left behind. "Good luck," commented the neighbor. "We'll see," said the farmer. . . . The Dao contains and honors paradox as suggested by this tale. There is unity in opposites. It exemplifies the idea that change brings both good and bad results, and perhaps one should not hold on too tightly to either aspect, but learn to embrace both. Above all, the Dao accepts the mystery and not-knowingness of life. "When you look for it, there is nothing to see. When you listen for it, there is nothing to hear. When you use it, it is inexhaustible" (Mitchell, 1988, p. 35). The Dao, in itself, is the one stable force on which one may depend.

Rather than inaction, the Dao actually teaches effortlessness, like water flowing. True inaction is the most efficient action possible. Inaction here does not exactly refer to doing nothing, but knowing when to do nothing and when to act. Living in this natural manner is considered a high spiritual path that evokes mystery, adventure, unpredictability, and adaptability. Like Confucianism, submission and right action are taught, but here the path reveals itself or unfolds, rather than being understood from the beginning in the form of directives expressed in Confucian ideas. Like Buddhism, Daoism promotes relinquishment of unnecessary desires and a search for simplicity. There are thus a number of natural connections between these three religious/philosophical approaches of Daoism, Confucianism, and Buddhism that facilitate compatibility. Thus one may find when working with clients that they have beliefs incorporating parts of each of the three traditions.

Daoism and Aging

One important concern with older Chinese individuals is possible hesitancy to seek mental health services (Chan, Chan, & Chan, 2014). There remains a stigma around help-seeking in the Chinese culture; symptoms of depression or anxiety are often somatized into health issues for which they can more readily seek aid. When older Chinese people do find assistance, their symptoms are thus often more severe. Daoist terms may better represent their experience. "The word yu ('not flowing, entangled, or clogged'), . . . shares common characteristics with depression" (p. 63). Daoist principles point to pursing equilibrium and letting go rather than avoidance of pain and suffering. An integrative approach to treatment such as found in inclusion of Tai Chi, Qigong, and traditional Chinese medicine, helps to positively impact aspects of body and mind. *Chi* or *Qi* is a term for the energy that underlies everything. It is found in many energy treatments or exercise forms such as Reiki, Akido, and Qigong mentioned above.

Daoism does not teach anything about a relationship with god or a deity, nor about the afterlife (Ai, 2006). The practice of Dao fully concerns the here and now. However, in healing practices, each person is recognized as having their own system or patterns of energy interchange which engage their surroundings in unique ways. Thus individual attention and treatment is preferred to group intervention in working with fluctuating mental health problems. In Daoism, older people are presented as wise. "The ancient masters were profound and subtle. Their wisdom was unfathomable. They were careful. . . . alert . . . courteous . . . fluid . . . shapeable, . . . receptive . . . and clear" (Mitchell, 1988, p. 15). This implies that older people may hold wisdom about which they may not be fully aware that can manifest in their personal choices. To maintain health, older people are invited to practice self-care and participate in energy management such as Tai Chi exercise alongside traditional medical care (Ai, 2006). One often sees older Asian people practice this form of exercise in public parks. It is one culturally important method of nourishing physical, mental, and spiritual energy to obtain flexibility, strength, compassion, integrity, longevity, and healing from a lifetime of challenges.

Overall, the principles of the Dao teach older people an approach to managing whatever comes their way with a calm spirit. It is a wisdom beyond wisdom. "If you realize you have enough, you are truly rich. If you stay in the center and embrace death with your whole heart, you will endure forever" (Mitchell, 1988, p. 33). If older people can live in a manner that maintains equilibrium in the face of either joy or sorrow, the promise is that that their resilience will keep them in the center of their experience of life.

INTEGRATION OF RELIGIOUS PHILOSOPHIES AND AGING

There are many paths to God and spirit. Each tradition offers a unique way of experiencing what is sacred and, to a greater and lesser extent, of applying that to ordinary life. The human quest for self-transcendence has appeared throughout history in the search for what has been called "the sacred" (Mircea Eliade), "the Holy" (Rudolph Otto), or "ultimate reality" (Paul Tillich). Variables used to describe a culture largely shape the preferred pathway to what is holy: through private or public forms of worship, through rituals rooted in particular ways of interacting that may be partially related to geographical space, and through degree of openness or closedness to encounters with different ways of seeing what is spiritual and/or religious. Individual preferences, too, define needs for practices that appeal more to introverts or extravert propensities. Needs for familiarity versus novelty also factor into the balance. Within any faith or philosophical tradition there is likely room for many personal interpretations, but some traditions can only stretch to a certain point before either breaking or holding their ground in very public ways. That may be the time when some people exit their tradition or turn to another one for a closer fit to their needs.

Older people have in large part felt that their early religious tradition or another latterly adopted one has answered deep needs and answers them still. In Table 5.1 Common Aging-Related Principles Across Religious Faiths, I have suggested some of the concepts important in gerontology and how, in my threshold-only view, different traditions address these aspects. There is always room here for further expansion of such a table by those more deeply rooted in each tradition. Models of aging refer to older people held up by the tradition as exemplars, people whose behavior is worthy of emulation. Harmony and balance are attributes that some religious traditions hold as being key virtues. *Karma* refers to the concept that one's present actions influence what will happen to the person in the future, particularly in a reincarnated form. The value of releasing attachments, letting go or surrender, has been discussed much in Eastern traditions, but is usually the opposite of what is sought in Western households, material acquisition and sometimes experiencing. The private component of a religious or faith tradition refers to private prayer or mystical approaches to aging. The other items are largely self-explanatory.

One of the benefits of a religious/philosophical tradition, including humanism, is the set of values that it champions. Although there are differences across religions, in some of the fundamentals, there is great similarity. Table 5.2 identifies a common value in how one is to interact with others. The table identifies the tradition, the exact text supplied by the faith tradition, and the source of the value. Although some concepts are phrased positively ("Do") and others negatively ("Do not"), the correspondence of a parallel idea is striking. Perhaps after all, the foundational differences across religious faiths (although not how they are interpreted) are not all that prodigious.

Table 5.1 Common Aging-Related Principles Across Religious Faiths

Common Aging-Related Features	Christianity	Judaism	American Indian Religion	Buddhism	Hinduism	Islam	Confucianism	Daoism
Respect for older people	Yes	Yes	Yes	Yes	Yes	Yes	Yes, filial piety, ti	Yes
Hospitality: Welcoming the stranger	Yes	Yes	Yes	Yes	Yes	Yes, "Guests are more precious than your father"	Not explicit	Not explicit
Golden Rule (may be worded negatively)	Yes	Yes	Yes	Yes	Yes	Yes	Yes	Yes
Models of aging in historic lives	Yes, Methusaleh, Abraham, Sarai	Yes, some same as Christianity	Yes, but less well known outside the tradition; Black Elk, etc., across tribes	Yes, Dalai Lama	Yes, Gandhi	Not explicit. Muhammad died at 62, not considered an aging model	Yes, Confucius	No
Harmony or balance	Not specific	Not specific	Yes, care for earth, but different language	Yes	? Accepts many beliefs	Yes*, but in social justice perspective	Yes, strongly	Yes, strongly
Meaning in suffering	Yes	Yes	?	Yes	?	Yes, Divine plan evident in suffering	Not addressed	Not addressed
Belief in afterlife	Yes	Yes, some sects	No death, only a change of worlds	Yes, reincarnation	Yes	Yes	Yes	Yes
Belief in karma	No	No	No	Yes	Yes	No	No	No
Value in releasing attachments	Yes	?	Yes, e.g., potlatch ceremony	Yes	Yes	No	No	Yes

(Continued)

Table 5.1 (Continued)

Common Aging-Related Features	Christianity	Judaism	American Indian Religion	Buddhism	Hinduism	Islam	Confucianism	Daoism
Concern about the earth, sacredness of creation	Yes, more recent	Yes	Yes, ancient	Yes	Yes	If you kill one person, you kill humanity	Yes	Yes, strongly
Devotional practice: Group & individual	Yes, both	Yes, both	Yes, both	Yes	Yes, both, Puja	Yes, both. Prayer is second pillar, group prayer more valued	Yes, veneration of ancestors	Yes
Concern for generations to follow	Yes	Yes, ethical will	Yes, to the 7th generation	Yes, you might be that generation	Yes, fulfill role given at birth	Yes, water plants for travelers	Yes, emphasis is on right relationships	Yes
Forgiveness	Yes, "70 × 7"	Yes, repent, forgive, reconcile with God, less humans	Yes, apology is gateway to open a door	Yes, strongly	Yes, ksanti	Yes, immediate, revenge not allowed	Yes, less so. Virtue in nonresentment, reciprocity only	Yes, Tao te Ching, ch. 62
Compassionate action	Yes, servant role	Yes, Tikkun Olan	Yes, follow wisdom keepers, grandmothers	Yes, tonglen	Yes, Seva, selfless service	Yes, service to humanity	Ren-humaneness	Through Wu-wei, "3 treasures" includes compassion
Has individual component?	Mysticism, prayer	Kabbalism, prayer	Vision quest, prayer	Meditation	Chant, prayer	Sufism, prayer	No	Yes

© Holly Nelson-Becker

* In Sura 102 balance refers to keeping balance between the fear of God and love of God, remaining humble, being devoted but avoiding extremism. Sura 17, Verse 35 suggests that the Children of Israel need to "weigh with an even balance what is good." This chapter calls for respect for parents and calls for patience and control in the face of the persecutions the Muslim community will face.

Table 5.2 Values Common to All Faiths

Religion	Text	Source
Judaism	Love your neighbor as yourself.	Hebrew Scriptures, Leviticus 19:18
Christianity	Do unto others as you would have them do unto you.	The Bible, Luke 6:31
American Indian	Respect for all life is the foundation.	The Great Law of Peace
Islam	No one of you is a believer until you desire for another that which you desire for yourself.	Muhammad, The Sunnah (from the Hadith)
Hinduism	This is the sum of duty: Do naught unto others which would cause you pain if done to you.	Mahabharata 5:1517
Buddhism	Hurt not others in ways you yourself would find hurtful.	Udana-Varga 5:18
Confucianism	Do not do to others what you would not want them to do to you.	Analects 15:23
Daoism	I am good to the man who is good to me: Likewise, I am also good to the bad man.	Tao Te Ching
Humanist	Always act so as to elicit the best in others and thereby yourself.	Ethical Culture

© Holly Nelson-Becker

Adapted from Arizona Interfaith Movement Calendar of Religious Holy Days for 2014.

From comparing these religious and philosophical views discussed here and placing their beliefs and practices consecutively (though in greatly condensed form), it is hopefully clear that no one tradition can be considered better or more advanced than another. Rather, each spoke to the historical and geographical context from which it emerged and was nurtured over time by culture. Of course, within any tradition there can be vastly different interpretations that in some cases may lead to abusive behavior. Sometimes the behavior advocated leads to a diminishment of self rather than expansion of all a person can become. It is also important to note that although some faith traditions and religious philosophical traditions do seek commonalities and work together on common causes of interest (e.g., United Council of Churches in the Christian traditions), there are points which they consider essential that are not similar or negotiable at all. Perhaps ultimately, there is something positive about this richness and diversity of traditions as they speak to different kinds of people in their common needs. Compassion may be one of the enduring key commonalities across faiths and respectful communication is needed to solve the world's problems (Lama, 2010). As the Buddhists have suggested, when one begins to walk the path up a mountain, there are usually several to choose from and the paths can look quite different at different points—entangled in trees, heading over rocks, reaching clearings. Yet, as each path gets closer to the summit, the perspectives all begin to converge. Traditions serve as a guide and older adults, to a large extent as suggested by demographic assertions in Chapter 1, have taken advantage of this guidance.

SUMMARY

This chapter clarifies fundamental beliefs in eight common world religious faith/philosophical traditions: Judaism, Christianity, American Indian Religion/Spirituality, Islam, Hinduism, Buddhism, Confucianism, and Daoism. It also made connections from each tradition to the aging experience. In sum, this information can only serve as backdrop to a deeper individual exploration with each client of their own beliefs and their degree of closeness or distance from the traditions, if any, they have adopted.

QUESTIONS FOR DISCUSSION

1. In the past, there was a strong focus on what separates different religions and belief systems. However, in this chapter, you will find many convergences. What are some of the convergences or similarities between belief systems that are new to you?

2. What human needs do you think led to the founding of each of these systems? Which ones had a natural leader or founder who shepherded the development of the religion or thought system and which did not?

3. Choose two of the religions or belief systems and discuss how they approach aging.

4. Which religion or philosophy do you find personally most appealing and why? How might this help you in your work with older clients?

ASSIGNMENT: FRAMING THE LANDSCAPE OF RELIGIOUS RITUAL

It is a privilege to be permitted to observe or participate in a religious or spiritual ceremony, event, or ritual to which one is otherwise a stranger. There may be times when it is especially helpful to do this to better understand a client's life space. If the service or ceremony occurs after a client's death, it can be particularly meaningful for friends and relatives when a helping professional attends, although professionals may have different views about the wisdom of this action. Another reason to attend such a gathering may simply be to expand knowledge of a particular religious or cultural tradition. Employing an anthropological lens of inquiry can help one see what is present. Below are some ideas about what to observe.

1. Before you attend, think about how you learned about the group and the time and place of its gathering. How easy or difficult was it for you in obtaining permission to attend?

2. When you enter the place where the ceremony/ritual is to be held, what do you observe about the meeting place and level of context it provides for the ceremony? Questions to consider include the following:

a. What is the nature of the physical building and the space? What is the shape, size, or other remarkable characteristics? What kind of decorations are present? What kind of lighting is present and how does this affect mood? Is the space simple or elaborate? How do you feel in this space and why?

b. What kind of seating is available for participants? Can anyone sit anywhere or do there seem to be designated seats for some? Is seating in rows, a circle, or other format? Are people expected to stand? If so when? How does the seating/standing/kneeling or alternation of these activities affect you?

c. What kind of literature is available? Is there a program about the order of service, about the faith tradition, or does it seem to serve another purpose?

d. What are the sacred objects that you note in this space? What kind of musical instruments are present, sacred texts, statuary, songbooks, or other items?

e. What type of apparel do people wear? Is it formal or informal dress? Does the apparel seem to reflect the particular cultural home of this faith? Do spiritual leaders have different robes or apparel from other participants?

3. What activities are performed?

    a. Describe whether there is speaking, reading, singing, chanting, dancing, praying, kneeling, praying, testimonies, and stories? Is the language easy to understand or is it stylized (or in a foreign language)? As an observer, in what can you participate?

    b. Does the group participate together or individually? Are there some activities that the spiritual leaders alone perform? Are men and women separated? Families and children? Are participants grouped in certain ways? What is the nature of interaction, if any?

    c. Who seems to be here? Are older people present? What is the level of their participation? How do they seem to be acknowledged and included? Other age or cultural/ethnic groups?

4. What are your reflections?

    a. To what extent were you welcomed to this ritual? What was the message given through any talk or the activities in which people shared? Were any groups disparaged or admired? Does this group seem to have any current challenges? How do they seem to see their role?

    b. What did the purpose of this gathering seem to be? Was it reverence, worship, healing, teaching, learning, fundraising, or another goal?

    c. How did others seem to react? Were they energized or subdued, peaceful or angry, inspired or satisfied? What were the verbal or nonverbal cues?

    d. If you visited with another person, discuss your observations with that person. What is your feeling? Did you experience any sacred moment? Would you return? If so, under what conditions?

    e. How might your visit have affected this group, if at all?

5. Journal about this experience and your learning from it.

ASSIGNMENT: SACRED SPACES EXERCISE

Respond to the following questions in a short six- or seven-page essay. These questions relate to development of an understanding of those aspects of life that one would call sacred. The objective of this assignment is to understand the capacity of the environment for healing and self-care and how your own understanding has changed over time. Use APA style and include a title page. A prerequisite for doing this assignment is first defining for yourself what the word *sacred* may mean. For some, traditional religious sites such as churches, synagogues, and mosques carry great meaning. Others find sacred those places they invest with particular meaning, inscribed there because of something that happened. Historic battlefields and war memorials may constitute holy, sacred ground. There are natural places in and on the land that also seem to carry spiritual power. Some of these are ancient sites that hold great importance for many who visit, and other sites are largely unknown places that carry meaning for the few fortunate to experience them.

1. Think about the places you visited that were or became sacred to you. Were they natural sites or manmade or a combination of both? Identify several that were particularly meaningful. In what decades of your life did you visit or come to know them? How did or does your own aging change what you would call sacred—if it does?

2. What about them was sacred? Why do you think your attention was drawn to these particular places? What happened there? What did you feel, see, hear, or experience there?

3. What did you come to know that was new or important? In other words, what new

understanding or what change did you come away from this sacred space carrying with you? If you have actually gone to or been in this place more than one time, what have you learned or gained on subsequent visits?

4. What is the meaning to you of this place in present day and time? Why has it remained important, if it has, or why was the meaning associated only with that time, if it was?

5. Are there places in your life today that you would call sacred? If so, what are they? What need or purpose do they fulfill? How often do you visit them or try to visit? How do you visit (e.g., in person, in imagination)?

6. If you wanted to plan a sacred space, what would go into it? What would it look like? How would each of the senses—sight, hearing, smell, touch, taste—connect to it? Where would it be located? Who would have access to it? Individuals? Communities?

7. How can sacred spaces be important to older people who are no longer able to travel there? Try asking an older individual about his or her sacred space.

MEDITATION: PRESENT MOMENT AWARENESS

This practice helps our minds rest and reset in present-moment attention. In beginning this practice, it is important to keep the mind in present time instead of letting it drift to problems in the past or concerns about what might occur in the future. The point of this practice is to resist focus on any object or specific content and to rest in awareness. What will likely happen is that memories will appear and thoughts will emerge. Rather than worry about this, just observe them and let them go as a leaf floating down a river or a cloud passing by in the sky. As you practice, you will likely find short sequences when your mind observes images but doesn't get involved in them. You will begin to see your thoughts as mental constructions rather than the reality external to you. As in cognitive distortions identified in cognitive behavioral therapy (CBT), this meditation helps individuals resist falling into common ruts or tracks well-worn in their thinking patterns. Instead, they become aware of what it is like to be without entanglements, misrepresentations, and biases that can often alter perceptions of what is. When you experience this freedom, you can see freshly what is present. Sit, and experience the moment.

EXPLORING YOUR SPIRITUALITY: RHYTHM AND MOVEMENT

Rhythm is the secret key to balance and belonging.
                    —O'Donohue (2004, p. 84)

Our rhythms can be long as in a program at university, or short, as in our daily routine. Knowing (attunement to) and falling into sync with the rhythms of our lives is valuable. This is true when we get the amount of sleep we need in accord with our optimal biorhythm and diurnal cycle as well as when we get adequate nutrition. But there is another type of rhythm which is being aligned with our destiny. What is your unique "calling" in the world? Is it to be a good friend, to care for animals, to foster hope and change in clients? Although we may think at times that other people could replace us, no one brings the exact gifts and talents that each of us have. Some people take long years to discover them, some after going in seemingly opposite alternative directions. We fall out of rhythm when we agree to be mediocre, rather than to give our best effort. This rhythm that each of us carries is linked to the ancient rounds of the earth: rotation, the rhythm of changing seasons, and ocean tides. Consider your own life rhythms.

Some life rhythms unfold across years as old habits and ways of thinking taught by others re-emerge. Some rhythms form the boundaries of our daily life and help keep us organized. Other life rhythms are ones we consciously set in place. As important as the rhythm, is the still point found within it. William Butler Yeats submitted, "Except for the point, the still point, there would be no dance, and there is only the dance" (O'Donnell, 1994). Within the broader opus of our lives, lie untold millions of still points—the captured present moment where we lift our heads up and notice.

1. What rhythms mark your life now?

2. How do you know when you are in rhythm with your life purpose and goals? If you have not yet experienced this, just imagine how you would know.

3. When you are in rhythm, what and/or who helps you stay there? In what way are you (would you be) balanced?

4. How does the momentum of the rhythm, which may itself change, bring you just what you need to move into new territory with ease, grace, and courage? What new rhythms, if any, do you want to strive for. What new rhythms can you listen for?

5. Write about your thoughts.

EXPLORING YOUR SPIRITUALITY: PILGRIMAGE

Exterior pilgrimage is a metaphor for the journey within.

—Martin Gray

The pilgrimage is a process by which we change what we think and transform who we are. Prayer is the pilgrim's walking stick.

—Marianne Williamson

Why focus on pilgrimage? Isn't the term *pilgrimage* a rather dusty description of how one achieves a defined destination, a phenomenon common to former centuries? The concept of pilgrimage has lasted through the ages. The term comes from the Latin *per agrum*, which means "through the field/country," suggestive of leaping fences and crossing natural boundaries to arrive at completion. Finding one's path and being on a journey are more modern symbols that recognize the spiritual goals of discovery, living into meaning and purpose along life's course. Although this may be an intentional search for some, many people might feel as though they step on and off this path, not fully understanding that the obstacles, ordeals, and blessings with which the way is bestrewn are all part of something larger.

In pilgrimage, one takes an intentional journey to a place of meaning. One may know or sense what the meaning is, or go with anticipation and expectations of something to be found, not fully knowing what that is. The journey encapsulates a departure, arrival, and return or in Joseph Campbell's language of hero-making: separation, initiation, and return. The goal of sacred journey is achieving wholeness through this circular process. A person plans

for this journey out of a sense of something that may be missing or yet gained, whether that be enlightenment, salvation (as in ancient times), or just being open to what may emerge. Although the place of pilgrimage may be formal and well-known to other pilgrims, it can be a place of solely personal meaning as well. An older person might make a pilgrimage to her natal home or other long-yearned-for place. Although the pilgrimage is often about receiving transformational energy, it also includes what we offer back to the earth through our presence. The act of giving and the act of receiving together form a whole.

There are several ancient pilgrimage routes that are either sustained or being reclaimed in modern times. One such ancient pilgrimage is the Hajj to Mecca, a sacred site in the Islamic faith that all Muslims are invited to experience if they are financially and physically able to do so in their lifetime. This pilgrimage is so important that it has prescribed prayers and tasks and is known as one of the five pillars of faith in Islam. The Kaaba that originally stood at the center of the mosque was believed to have been built by Adam, the first man, at God's request, and it was said to be rebuilt by Abraham and his son Ishmael. This pilgrimage is a sacred way to demonstrate love for Allah and respect for the prophet Muhammad. Another pilgrimage is to Jerusalem, a holy site for Jews, Christians, and Muslims. The River Ganges represents a sacred site for Hindu people. Many hold the belief that those who die in Varanasi on the Ganga are freed from the cycle of death and rebirth. There are numerous places of pilgrimage worldwide and across faith traditions.

The Camino de Santiago (The Way of Saint James) de Compostela that ends in Spain is another pilgrimage site. There is an archetypal story surrounding relics of the Christian Saint James found there and pilgrims or *pelegrinos* walked in ancient time to receive an indulgence (or assistance in receiving purification in Catholic theology). A pilgrim's passport/credential may be stamped at locations along the way and verification results in the award of a compostela, or certificate of accomplishment at the journey's end. Routes begin in France, Germany, Italy as well as in the Pyrenees. The scallop seashell is a symbol of the journey, often worn by pilgrims, as the lines within it recall all of the various routes by which one can arrive at the goal, meeting at a central point. On the Camino, the strangers one meets as well as one's fellow travelers become a community with which much can be shared as these individuals continue meeting along the way.

When I walked the Camino with my partner and a friend in 2009, we learned from and gained much satisfaction in the relationships with these strangers who became friends. Meeting them again coincidentally in separate groupings at the end of the journey near the Santiago Cathedral without intentionally planning to meet was a highpoint. But the Camino is also a microcosm of a larger journey. One of the early companions of St. Ignatius of Loyola remarked that *The road is our home* (cited in Martin, 2010, p. 394).

1. Think about a time or times when you intentionally took a journey. Why did you do so? How did you prepare? What did you expect to achieve? Were your expectations fulfilled or not?

2. In what way is a pilgrimage different from a journey? If you have taken a type of pilgrimage (whether formal or not such as to the sight of a former home or school), describe it.

3. How has the road been your home? How have your physical travels and your larger psychosocialspiritual travels changed you? What parts have been expected and also unexpected as you have aged and are aging?

4. Did your ideas and operationalization of your vocational path transform over time? Is it transforming now as your training and education proceed? If so, how?

WEBSITES

Arab Culture and Civilization: Islam

http://acc.teachmideast.org/main_menu.php?module_id=2

This website provides basic information about Islam including material from a text by John Esposito, who has devoted his career to disseminating information about Islam in an academic community.

Association of Religious Data Archives

http://www.thearda.com/rcms2010/

This particular site, part of a larger trove of data on religions, contains a data source on U.S. religious congregations and membership. Reports can be generated by any county to look at distributions.

Beyond Coping: The Buddha's Teachings on Aging, Illness, Death, and Separation: A Study Guide by Thanissaro Bhikkhu (1999).

http://www.accesstoinsight.org/lib/study/beyondcoping/index.html

This website features writings from the Pali canon Buddhist text on aging, illness, death, and separation and coping with problems of aging.

The Blessing Way: Navajo Nation

https://www.youtube.com/watch?v=ajC94N0KJSw

The Beauty Way or Blessing Way song from the Navajo tradition: This rich visual repast shares the words of this song on a walk through nature.

Confucian Classics

http://www.chinaknowledge.de/Literature/Classics/jingbu.html

This site provides information on the teaching of Confucius and Chinese history.

Contemplative Care: A Film by Bobby Sheehan

http://zencare.org/contemplative-care-film

This is a 15-minute file about caregiving in the Zen tradition.

The Harmony Project

http://www.theharmonyproject.org/index2.html

"What joins us is greater than what separates us." This site contains information about 14 religious faiths.

Ignatian Spirituality

http://www.ignatianspirituality.com/

Associated with Loyola Press, Ignatian Spirituality is an in-depth website that offers Jesuit devotions, prayer, educational material, and connections to Jesuit communities, both online and in person.

Internet Sacred Text Archive: Confucianism and Traditional Chinese Beliefs

http:// http://sacred-texts.com/cfu/

This archive contains the Confucian canon of writings, including the Five Classics and Four Books.

Jewish Sacred Aging

http://www.jewishsacredaging.com

This site appears to principally showcase the work of Reform Rabbi Richard Address, who has written and presented on aging and spirituality.

New York Zen Center for Contemplative Care

http://zencare.org/

This website offers an archive of talks. It also features training opportunities in New York area.

Parliament of the World's Religions

http://parliamentofreligions.org/

Featuring the most recent parliament met in 2015 in Salt Lake City, Utah, this website hosts articles, videos, and webinars with relevance to interfaith interests.

The Pluralism Project

http://www.pluralism.org

This project from Harvard University looks at the changing face of the religious landscape in America.

Places of Peace and Power

https://sacredsites.com/martin_gray/biography.html

This site includes an 11-minute video on the importance of sacred sites.

Quaker Aging Resources

http://www.quakeragingresources.org/

These resources offer many apt topics for living a meaningful life at older ages.

The Tao of Longevity by Drew Leder

http://www.secondjourney.org/itin/09_Fall/Leder_09Fall.htm

This is an essay that offers interesting thoughts about growing older according to a Daoist perspective.

RECOMMENDED READING

Baldridge, D. (2004). Double jeopardy: Advocating for Indian elders. *Generations, 28*(1), 75–78.

Interesting ideas on advocating for older indigenous Americans.

Cooper, D. E. (2012). *Convergence with nature: A Daoist perspective*. Totnes, UK: Green Books.

This book explores human connections with nature, including ethical concerns.

Cribbs, J. M. (2009). Serving older Native Americans: Challenges facing gerontological social work in Indian country. *Journal of Ethnic and Cultural Diversity in Social Work, 18*(4), 261–275.

Practical strategies for inclusion, outreach, and capacity-building with older American Indians.

Harding, J. S. (2012). *Studying Buddhism in practice*. London: Routledge.

This text is a compilation of interesting field notes by anthropological and other scholars about their work and learning about Buddhist practice.

Richmond, L. (2012). *Aging as a spiritual practice: A contemplative guide to growing older and wiser.* New York, NY: Gotham Books.

This book provides an overview of spirituality and aging.

Weibel-Orlando, J. (n.d.). *Chapter 13. Grandparenting styles: The contemporary American Indian experience.* Retrieved from http://faculty.usfsp.edu/jsokolov/webbook/weibel.pdf

This chapter details the many different kinds of parenting American Indian grandparents do.

PART TWO

PRACTICE DIMENSIONS OF SPIRITUALITY AND RELIGION IN AGING

CHAPTER SIX

SPIRITUALITY AND RELIGION IN CLINICAL ASSESSMENT

You should not lose your self-sufficient state of mind. This
does not mean a closed mind, but actually an empty mind
and a ready mind. If your mind is empty, it is always ready
for anything; it is open to everything. In the beginner's
mind there are many possibilities;
in the expert's mind there are few.

—Shunryu Suzuki, *Roshi*

Let us get down to bedrock facts.
The beginning of every act of knowing,
and therefore the starting-point of every science,
must be in our own personal experience.

—Max Planck

Older adults typically value the importance of religion and spirituality. These can serve extrinsically as a mechanism for social support or intrinsically as a personal resource for expanded understanding and coping with life challenges. Even if these domains offer nothing of value to the older adult, this too is helpful information and assists a practitioner to avoid assumptions and errors in solutions they might suggest in the intervention phase of treatment or helping. As a consequence, it is very important to include questions about these two areas of religion and spirituality in any overall mental health assessment. If they are included as part of the original assessment, then their inclusion will be normalized if this becomes an area of later focus. The first quote by Suzuki above relates to this: It is important in assessment to bring an open mind or stance to one's clinical work. Although expertise in any area is of value, the leaps it takes to solutions also can leave out consideration of unexpected pathways. The quote by physicist Planck suggests that even factual knowledge flows out of individual experiences. Because individual experience is the beginning of knowledge, asking the right questions helps uncover meaning and suggests areas of potential intervention.

The first section of this chapter will discuss the need for religion and spirituality in any client assessment. Next, general aspects of religion and aging will be identified, including potential harmful effects of religion as well as spiritual needs. How the helping professions and other nonprofit organizations with therapeutic goals regard inclusion of religion in clinical assessment protocols will be described. A second section of the chapter will address professional assessment practice, including the principle of bringing an open curiosity to one's work. Concerns of both professionals and clients in dialoguing about this topic will be identified. The place of religious and spiritual problems according to the *Diagnostic and Statistical Manual of Mental Disorders* (DSM-5) will be addressed. The third section will identify and critique clinical assessment tools and rapid assessment instruments related to multiple aspects of religion and spirituality.

WHAT'S IMPORTANT ABOUT RELIGION AND ASSESSMENT?

Why Include Religion and Spirituality in Assessment?

How do we know these areas are important to older adults? Sixty-five percent of American adults aged 65 and older believe religion is "very important," with another 20% stating it is "somewhat important" (Pew Research Center, 2014c). Another 65% of this same age group report daily prayer; 13% participate in weekly prayer. According to the 2014 Pew Religious Landscape Survey, 85% of American adults over age 69 reported affiliation with a Christian religious faith, and an additional 4% with a world religion or a non-Christian religion such as Judaism, Islam, or Buddhism (Pew Research Center, 2014a). An additional 11% over age 69 reported no affiliation. Of Baby Boomers between age 50 and 68, 78% endorsed a religious faith. Those numbers decline across following generations down to 56% of Millennials age 18 to 24 who report holding a religious affiliation. By contrast, those endorsing no affiliation represent 36% of Millennials, the highest of any age group (Pew Research Center, 2014a).

Gallup polls from 2001, 2004, 2007, and 2014 asked all adults about their belief in God. The most recent poll asked this several ways, including "Do you believe in God or a universal spirit?" Interestingly, 89% reported either belief in God (79%)

or were unsure (10%), which is the same as the response for belief (89%) when the only response choices were yes or no (Gallup, 2014a). A 2014 Gallup poll suggests that 62% of adults aged 65 or older believe that religion can answer today's problems, the highest of any age group (Gallup, 2014b). There is also a current phenomenon in many Western religious denominations of a *graying* pattern of the membership: Higher numbers of older adults enter the doors of local churches than of middle-aged and younger adults. This suggests that in comparison to other younger age cohorts, religion remains important to current age groups of older adults.

It is important to include religion and spirituality in assessments with older adults. These are matters about which many feel strongly, and they can also be a component of solutions for difficult life problems or a pathway to positive aging. In addition, because of a traditional separation of church and state, many older adults would not typically discuss their religious or spiritual preferences because they assume that the clinician might not want to know about it. Thus including a spiritual assessment in a formal way, whether within a larger assessment process or at another time, validates any related concerns and normalizes religion and spirituality as central components of life.

Religion and Aging

As health and mobility decline in older ages, formal religious participation tends to decrease, but private spiritual expressions—use of prayer, the Bible, and religious radio/ TV—tend to increase (Levin, 2001). Not all older adults who may want to attend religious or spiritual ceremonies are able to do so. Partly this occurs because some older adults may have increasing physical disability that makes it more difficult to attend religious services: to walk further distances or climb steps in an older facility (even with some retrofitted with elevators), to hear clearly with inadequate speaker systems in echoing spaces, and to participate in small conversational groups with several individuals speaking at once. When older adults give up their driver's license, attendance may also decrease if they are reluctant to ask others to transport them to their church/synagogue/mosque or other religious meeting places. In many areas, public transportation is not pervasive enough to be an available resource, especially on Sundays, if that is when a religious or spiritual group meets. Relocation to smaller housing or new geographic areas, for example to live closer to children, may also disrupt formal religious ties. But disruption of formal connections to a particular religion, if it occurs, may not lesson the value of religion to an older person who was previously involved in such a community.

On the other hand, it is equally important to know that older adults do not tend to become more religious as they age (Schmall & Pratt, 1996). Sometimes a life-changing transformation occurs along the life course, either leading to greater interest and/or commitment to religiousness or spirituality (such as often happens with a near-death experience) or to less or no interest, if one believes life questions cannot be adequately answered by religious faith or tradition. Many older adults express their religious and/or spiritual values in a manner consistent with the way they did when they were younger (Pargament, Van Haitsma, & Ensing, 1995). This also means that there is a significant group of older adults for whom religion and spirituality carry little or no interest (Nelson-Becker, 2005a). They may have formed their values from the pragmatics of everyday living or from mentors or other models in the community when they were in their teens or younger. Clinicians should thus be prepared for any type of response when conducting a spiritual assessment for an agency or private practice.

Negative Effects of Religion

There are some individuals who have been wounded or felt anger from perceptions of religious rigidity occasionally shown in cases of lack of tolerance or compassion by religious organizations. One research participant told me that his mother was asked to pay or contribute money to join a religious community. She was unable to do so and, seeing her pain, afterward he had no use for any religion. Another research participant in a different study told me that he attended a funeral where the minister told the congregation that his childhood friend would "go to hell" because she was never baptized a Christian, yet when an individual who had problems with alcohol, "a rounder" (someone who made the rounds of bars) died, that person was eulogized as "going to Heaven" because he had been baptized a church member. This respondent globalized this experience to include all religions and never again attended a church.

A further harmful aspect of religion revealed to a greater extent in recent years is spiritual abuse: Religious leaders have used their power to sexually abuse parishioners, congregants, or other members. Most religious institutions now exercise greater caution and oversight, particularly where children are involved in youth activities. But the residue of years of hidden abuse is still being uncovered and it sometimes emerges at later ages. There is an aspect of deep betrayal to this type of abuse that makes it particularly repellent.

Although these represent individual viewpoints, it is helpful to understand that people base their beliefs on their experiences and perceptions, which can and do result in a whole range of emotional and intellectual responses. Clinicians should be prepared to hear stories of injury as they also hear stories of strength and support from religious and spiritual beliefs. Learning about forms of harm related to religion is valuable in both understanding clients and helping them recover and heal.

Spiritual Needs

Spiritual needs pertain to the universal desire to locate meaning and purpose in life. These needs are considered spiritual because they transcend physical/social needs and are answered in unique ways by each individual according to their interests and abilities. Among many types of spiritual needs, there are three commonly expressed by older adults: the need to create meaning and purpose, the need to become empowered through connection to a Higher Power/Transcendent Force or Nature, and the need to give and receive support (MacKinlay, 2006a; Nelson-Becker, Nakashima, & Canda, 2007). In addition to these basic spiritual needs are ones identified by Lemmer (2005) that include forgiveness and self-transcendence, that is, taking a broader perspective of one's life. Fourteen needs are identified by Koenig (1994). These tend to be more religiously focused and presume religious affiliation. Besides meaning and hope which he combines together and transcendence, they include a need for support in coping with loss, continuity (based on continuity theory which was dominant at the time the Koenig's 1994 book was written), need for validation and support of religious behaviors, need to engage in religious behaviors, need for dignity and a sense of worthiness, need to express anger and doubt, need to feel God is on their side, need to love and serve others, need to be thankful, need to forgive and be forgiven, and the need to prepare for death and dying.

A meta-analysis of 22 qualitative and quantitative studies from the medical literature identifying patient needs reported that in each study, from three to eight need categories were developed, including love/belonging/respect, religious/divine, positivity/gratitude/hope, meaning and purpose, morality/ethics, appreciation of beauty, and finally resolution/death (Galek, Flannelly, Vane, & Galek, 2005). At a minimum level, older adults have a need to make sense of their life, but not all will express the same needs. Some needs will be fully met in the context of particular life circumstances. Others will go unrecognized.

Older adults who are ill may have unmet emotional needs regarding fear, loneliness, sadness, or hopelessness (Clark, 2003). Pastoral care professionals further identify needs to love and be loved and to believe the client will not be forgotten. When emotional and spiritual needs are not met by professionals, clients may become disillusioned about the services provided and discontinue them. Research has shown that patients and physicians both consider apologies important when medical errors have been made (Gallagher, Waterman, Ebers, Fraser, & Levinson, 2003).

Although the list of what may be a need versus what may be a chosen interest is open to revision, it is worth considering what may be essential life practices, either for daily support, future growth, or reconciliation. Needs for meaning, empowerment, and connection are foundational to live life fully. Entering a later stage of the life course often compels one to consider what one has contributed to life or the meaning in one's life. This often includes looking beyond the immediate situation and refraining from defining oneself according to immediate circumstances alone. For example, one woman residing in a nursing care facility while she worked at recovery from a cardiovascular accident (CVA) or stroke was overheard to describe herself as "no good to anyone." Although she was depressed about the amount of staff and medical personnel time she required, she was also a beloved grandmother to five grandchildren. Her life did indeed have meaning that she later was able to acknowledge.

Many older persons need to find empowerment through their sense of connection to a Sacred Higher Power. A 66-year-old client had coped relatively well with Parkinson's disease and bipolar illness, but when she received a diagnosis of cancer in her nasal passage, her coping mechanisms were overwhelmed. A devout Catholic, she was very angry at God but she felt her faith did not allow her to be angry, resulting in internal conflict that she was unable to resolve alone. The counselor helped her expand her view of God and, with her permission, contacted her chaplain for a visit. At times a social worker or other practitioner will be with a client at a point of immediate need and could do triage work around their idea of who God is—if this concept causes suffering. The boundaries of this discussion are fairly open depending on what the client wants and what the professional feels able and has competency to discuss. All work should be done within the context of direction given by the client and his or her needs. Counselors, social workers, or nurses who are not comfortable in this area and not ready to explore it should always refer the client.

If the idea of a benevolent universal force holds no meaning, then sometimes there is something else that provides such benefit. A research participant who survived the Holocaust remarked that she no longer had any use for a God who failed to intervene in any manner when millions from her same cultural heritage were sent to a torturous existence in concentration camps and even death. "Where was God then?" was her anguished comment (Nelson-Becker, 1999). Yet she did feel the need for connection in her life and eventually found it—after two failed marriages—in time spent in the natural world. Her connection to the ultimate then, was through nature, walking in the forests or parks, or looking at one of the Great Lakes, of which she could see a tiny corner outside her upper story window. "What I see out my window is a view of eternity," was her response to me.

Continuing old affiliations or making new ones help maintain connections to community and continue to facilitate contributions. In older ages, adults who have chronic illness or reduced capacity typically receive many forms of social services such as meals on wheels, housekeeping, or transportation; they need to know that they can still make significant contributions to others, whether through sharing wisdom-based stories or imparting knowledge gained as a by-product of lifelong vocational pursuits. They value the support they both receive and provide to others. Sometimes this support is found in religious communities and sometimes it is found in connections within families, particularly between grandparents and grandchildren. Connection is equally important for those who are cognitively impaired or have dementia.

Professional and Organizational
Stances on Religion and Spirituality in Assessment

There is increasing recognition and development of formal standards of care that suggest the spiritual component of life be included in formal caregiving. The Joint Commission on Accreditation of Healthcare Organizations (The Joint Commission, 2003) and National Association of Social Workers (2005) both revised their accreditation standards for hospitals and social service organizations respectively to require the inclusion of spiritual assessment questions. The Joint Commission (2003) has affirmed that patients' "psychosocial, cultural and spiritual values affect how they respond to their care" (R1–8).

In regard to palliative care, national guidelines were developed by the National Consensus Project for Quality Palliative Care in 2004 (National Quality Forum, 2006). These clinical guidelines relate to care delivered in a range of treatment settings such as long-term care, critical care, and oncology, where palliative care is incorporated into daily practice routines. Of eight domains of care, the fifth domain is categorized as spiritual, religious, and existential aspects of care.

Social work is one example of a profession that has expanded its biopsychosocial model for assessment of the person in environment to a biopsychosocial spiritual model. This also subsumes other important domains such as the affective and cognitive components. Affective areas include positive and negative emotional reactions and stances while cognition refers to the active appraisal and choices one makes. Spiritual aspects of the model consider how one relates one's life to ultimate and universal themes. The Council on Social Work Education (2008), in its 2008 revision of 2001 standards, further specified how religion should be included in curriculum. First, these standards include religion as part of a core competency. Religion is included as an aspect of engaging diversity and difference in practice. Secondly, spiritual development is listed as one among many variables to consider in applying knowledge about human behavior and the social environment.

The counseling profession has incorporated the value of spirituality as an important area of human development integrated with personal growth (Corey, Corey, & Callanan, 2003; Steen, Engels, & Thweatt, 2006). Medical students now receive training on addressing religion in their coursework and clinical experiences. The American College of Physicians has developed guidelines for communicating with patients about spirituality. The nursing profession mentions respect for spiritual beliefs in the International Council of Nurses Code (2012) and added a nursing diagnosis for spiritual distress as early as 1978.

The American Psychological Association guidelines encourage respect for individual value differences. Richards and Bergin (2005) suggest three primary reasons why spiritual assessment should be conducted by psychologists and others: spiritual assessment provides a greater understanding of client worldviews, provides the background to determine level of health/unhealthiness regarding religious/spiritual orientation, and helps one visualize how religious/spiritual beliefs and communities may function as possible resources. Whether spiritual interventions should be a part of therapy, and whether unresolved spiritual doubts or needs should be a focus of work, can also be answered through this type of assessment.

Some form of spiritual assessment is thus now suggested and even encouraged by professional disciplines. It is mandated across a variety of publicly accountable settings. These include hospitals, home care organizations, long-term care facilities, hospice organizations, and behavioral health care organizations such as those providing substance abuse and addiction services. Organizations that have chaplain services readily available such as hospitals and hospices have been some of the leaders in adopting and implementing religious or spiritual assessment protocols.

MENTAL HEALTH ASSESSMENT

It is helpful for mental health practitioners to remember that the area of religion and spirituality has been underdeveloped in the mental health disciplines. Partly this has occurred because of stigma and assumptions by professionals about religious intolerance from fundamentalist-directed religious traditions. Another reason has been the fear that opening up this topic might be misunderstood as some form of religious proselytization by the practitioner, a concern that a client could think that even asking such questions would imply affirmation of religion or spiritual practice. Further, most mental health workers tend to be less religious than their clients (Richards & Bergin, 2005). Thus, they are less comfortable asking questions about an area where they do not feel fully competent. However, as with any specific area of mental health practice, practitioners and others will learn from their clients as they explore the client's relationship to these areas. Expertise is built when further knowledge is sought through exploration of research, religious texts and analysis, and discussions with religious or spiritual leaders and experts in the community. When formal assessment instruments are used, it is important to consider the underlying assumptions in the purpose for which the instrument was developed.

Being Curious

Asking questions is of fundamental importance. Although some areas require greater sensitivity in approach and the establishment of a prior therapeutic alliance, no area should be beyond the scope of inquiry, as long as it is acceptable to the client. Learning how to ask good questions that open up important areas of exploration is a skill. The value of first establishing a therapeutic alliance cannot be underestimated. In the national collaborative research project to treat depression where two psychotherapeutic approaches were matched with psychopharmacology, client ratings of therapeutic alliance better predicted improvement than the type of therapy (Duncan, Miller, & Sparks, 2004). Among all factors that predict positive client change, 60% relate to common factors (the therapeutic alliance), 30% to allegiance factors, and 8% to therapeutic approach or technique (Duncan, Miller, Wampold, & Hubble, 2010). Working with clients to build connections helps provide clients with a sense of safety as well as confidence in the therapist's ability to offer their presence and their expertise.

Being able to pose good questions means first opening oneself up to all kinds of *wondering* aloud. Questions help us explore and develop the hypotheses that can be instrumental in awakening understanding and problem resolution. As Rilke (1954) suggests, "Try to love the questions themselves . . . Live the questions now" (pp. 34–35). Sometimes, courage is required. Not all questions are easy to ask. I worked once on an assessment team in a county mental health hospital, treating a client who came in for depression after his three children drowned in a black bottom pool. His level of despair seemed to be inconsolable, so I asked him eventually, "Do you in any way feel responsible for their deaths?" Yes, in fact, he had told them to go outside, forgetting the gate to the pool was open, and catching a phone call that left the children unattended too long. Asking that question cut through a weeklong obstruction and the resident psychiatrist gave me a high five after the client had left the room. Not all questions are easy to ask, but there are many that should be asked. Would we have gotten to the heart of this client's despair if we had waited for him to share the cause? Possibly, but not until more time had passed and his distress had increased.

Formulating good questions is important, but not all questions can be easily or quickly answered. The question "Why?" is often unanswerable, but "How, what, and who?" are approachable. Perhaps one of the most difficult questions is the one posed by a client when exploring personal meaning or contribution, "What is the meaning of my life?" This helps one review, define, and assess life mistakes and accomplishments. Another difficult area may be the end of life, where an older adult may ask "Is there anything after this life? If so, where will I go?" or "Is this it? Is this all there is?" Professionals will not know all the answers to these forms of questions, nor are they expected to know them. However, being open to travel with the client to these uncomfortable places is of great assistance. Helping clients learn to pose meaningful questions, questions that help them understand a problem from a different vantage point, can help teach them how to enter places rich with potential learning that they may not have known how to access alone.

The area of question formulation is one where mental health professionals can bring a *beginner's mind* mentioned in the chapter quote as well as the sum of their prior experiences and expertise. Asking good questions is a fundamental skill. What are good questions? They are ones that take a client into new places or help them uncover new layers of life and understanding. Asking questions is a skill, one that older clients and professionals both may have suppressed. The ability to be reflective about one's life and the experience of living in society and culture may be acquired, but is not often taught well in universities or in the formal educational system in lower grades. Finally, asking for feedback and acting on it (Feedback-Informed Treatment [FIT]; Duncan et al., 2010) creates a culture of feedback that better helps address client needs.

Maslow was one who believed that the horticulture method of uncovering growth and supporting change was better than the sculpting or molding model (Hoffman, 1996). In that way he advocated that rather than trying to change a rose into a lily, a practitioner should try to create the best rose possible. This philosophical approach was similar to Carl Roger's invitation to offer warmth/empathy, genuineness/authenticity, and unconditional positive regard in a person-centered therapy approach (Rogers, 1961). This implies a Daoistic acceptance of where people are and an appreciation of the sacred and unique qualities of each one. This humanistic style is centered on core respect and openness to learning with the client what it means to actualize the best possibility of his or her own healthy and effective self.

Spiritual assessment tools are increasingly being developed and entering the literature (see, e.g., Fetzer Institute, 1999 and Hill & Hood, 1999). Some of these are protocols that have clinical value and some are scales or instruments that provide greater awareness of specific spiritual or religious directions or concerns. These will be discussed in detail later in this chapter. Spiritual assessment tools can assist in expanding the religious and spiritual assessment conversation.

Older Client and Therapist

Concerns in Discussing Religion/Spirituality

Older adult clients, too, may fear talking about religion and spirituality with professional helpers. They may believe that a professional has no interest in this part of their lives—whether of deep personal importance or not—and so they compartmentalize and metaphorically move it off of the table as an area of potential problems or potential resources. They also may fear that the professional will fail to understand and honor their beliefs, so they do not want to risk harming a nascent therapeutic relationship. This is an area that an older adult will be hesitant to bring up unless the practitioner specifically asks questions about it. Many of my clients were surprised when I first began including questions about spiritual/religious beliefs and coping strategies as early as the late 1980s. Many also told me that had I not asked, they never would have told me about religious or spiritual preferences and concerns. Therefore, it is the role of the professional to include questions that determine the relative importance or unimportance of these areas both in the initial assessment and as a potential area for inclusion in therapy.

One reason professionals may hesitate to ask questions in these areas is also because of concern or anticipation of what the response may be. As Neils Bohr once stated, "The world is not only stranger than we thought, it is stranger than we could think" (Polkinghorne, 2002, p. 86). Gravitational waves, the ripples or distortions in the fabric of space-time that were postulated by Einstein and discovered through a set of coincidences in September of 2015, can now be heard (Overbye, 2016). The Laser Interferometer Gravitational-Wave Observatory (LIGO), stretching from Louisiana to Washington state, had failed to detect any waves between 2002 and 2010. Ongoing funding by the National Science Foundation was threatened, but the waves were heard for the first time just two days after an enhanced system came online in 2015 after a multi-year closure. People, too, sometimes have experiences outside of their ability to understand.

Many professionals likely use the test of reasonableness when their clients share their experiences. "Is this reasonable? Could this have happened?" may be questions they ask themselves. For instance, bereaved individuals may report seeing visions of their deceased loved one or believing that some form of communication has occurred through a butterfly that hovers, an uncommon bird that lingers, or another animal that wanders into one's life frame. In a 2014 *New York Times* opinion article, "Stricken by Grief, Finding Solace in a Robin," writer Tom Crider relates that although he feared readers would think him childishly sentimental, "I couldn't help thinking that the robin was Gretchen [his deceased daughter], or some form of her spirit, saying, 'Hi, Dad.'" He concluded that the experience "felt real and somehow healing." Some of my students have also spoken of animal sightings where the animal seemed to connect with them after a loss. A few professionals may find it difficult to suspend their disbelief and honor the client's version of events, yet doing so can affirm an attempt to recreate meaning.

There is always a tendency—and correctly so—for trained professionals to look for indications of broader mental health problems that may meet criteria for a DSM-5 equivalent diagnosis, the standard for biological and mental health based assessment usually needed for reimbursement. Clinicians are often asked to focus on a diagnosis and at the same time to meet the client where they are. Before reaching for the DSM, it is important to understand the client's larger context and background. In treatment of older clients who have had a serious and persistent mental illness (SPMI) diagnosis in the past, particularly one such as schizophrenia where visual or auditory hallucinations may have been documented, it is important to rule out experiences as being a current manifestation of a mental illness that could respond to psychopharmacological or psychotherapeutic treatment. Thus, a further question to ask themselves may be, "Why do you think this is so?" or "Why may this be the case?" This type of question still looks for evidence, but opens up the standard to include many forms of personal experience and helps older adults and their helpers to look for other types of personal validation or affirmation of their experiences, some of which may rest beyond quantification or further empirical testing. Triangulation of the data is a useful process in research to validate results using different forms of data collection such as self-report, observation, information given by third parties, quick assessment instruments, or documents. It also can have value in a clinical context as the therapist helps individuals to explore or process their concerns, questions, strengths, or difficulties.

DSM-5 Standards

The DSM-5 has several goals: the two primary ones are to provide consistency in diagnoses and diagnoses that will reliably guide treatment decisions. A third goal is for the information to be evidence based, although research and clinical practice sometimes result in conflicting outcomes. Fourth, because International Classification of Disease (ICD) codes from the World Health Organization are used by both medical doctors and psychiatrists, a further goal was to harmonize DSM-5 codes with ICD-11, the most current ICD code. The fifth goal seeks to provide greater dimensionality: "Because the previous DSM approach considered each diagnosis as categorically separate from health and from other diagnoses, it did not capture the widespread sharing of symptoms and risk factors across many disorders that is apparent in studies of comorbidity" (American Psychiatric Association, 2013, p. 12). Further, "the various disorders are clustered according to internalizing and externalizing factors" (p. 13). Last, of particular interest in work with older adults and to the professional practice, "the DSM-5 seeks to enhance Development and Lifespan considerations to place the various diagnoses in the context of life markers and socio-cultural conditions" (p. 13).

The category Religious or Spiritual Problem continues from the DSM-IV-TR to the DSM-5, with the same code number, V62.89, and similar language: "Examples include distressing experiences that involve loss or questioning of faith, problems associated with conversion to a new faith, or questioning of spiritual values that may not necessarily be related to an organized church or religious institution" (American Psychiatric Association, 2013, p. 725). Instead of treating a religious or spiritual problem itself as pathology, this code suggests that religion and/or spirituality can affect or nuance underlying pathology. A section that follows in the DSM-5 on Cultural Formulation also includes religion and spirituality listed after language and before "family structures, life-cycle stages, ceremonial rituals, and customs, as well as moral and legal systems" (p. 749). This parallels the social work paradigm that suggests religion should be considered under culture and diversity.

The inclusion of this V code category was important because it recognized that individuals might experience periods of spiritual crisis or spiritual emergence that could lead to chaos and feelings of being overwhelmed. Psychiatrists David Lukoff (Lukoff, Lu, & Turner, 1989) and Stanislav Grof (Grof & Grof, 1989) were some of the early proponents of the need for this designation. A form of spiritual emergence may occur at any age as it is not contingent on other developmental milestones, so older adults too may experience this as well as other forms of religious and spiritual problems.

What was notable here was that this problem was depathologized and separated from other mental health problems. It is common for people with schizophrenia to have delusions of a religious or spiritual nature when they are flagrantly hallucinating. I have had clients who believed they were God when they failed to remain compliant with psychotropic medications and subsequently entered the county mental health hospital for court-ordered treatment. This and other types of hallucinations where religious images or rituals take on unusual meanings can be symptoms of mental health problems. However, the use of the V code was intended to move practitioners away from adding to stigmatization of clients. In older adults, guilt, lack of forgiving others or feeling forgiven, concern about disparities between religious beliefs and use of medical treatment, loss of faith, and questions about life meaning can be a few of the manifestations of this type of problem. Further, if an older adult has held membership in a religious minority group that has not achieved validation in the larger society, this, too can be a source of embarrassment or discomfort.

Older adults from minority cultures may practice religious rituals not generally accepted in the American cultures. Such customs as ancestor worship or seeing a shaman may signal religious or spiritual health within cultural in-groups, but may be misperceived or misunderstood by a majority culture. Careful cultural assessment is critical. People who have Jehovah's Witness, Amish, or Seventh Day Adventist backgrounds would not always show obvious differences in physical appearance, yet may have beliefs that bring them outside of mainstream traditions when they interface with the larger majority culture. Although generally, this may not reach the level of identification as a problem, at times the discrepancy between personal religious beliefs and public principles may be large enough to cause distress. For instance, blood transfusions or other invasive medical treatments may be declined based on the intersection of religious and medical beliefs.

Overall, development of a spiritually sensitive practice requires a strengths-based approach that includes listening to the profound and diverse questions clients express and demonstrating openness to hear all expressions of grief, longing, confusion, and joy that emanate from the human experience. It also comprises learning the religious and/or spiritual history of the client. Spiritually sensitive practice involves the ability to recognize and respond to these expressions with clients, but it does not impose a viewpoint that is contrary to the perspective of the client. It is a hearing of the heart: an ability to hear the pain and the hope in the stories clients tell and an ability to highlight for clients important themes or subtexts of which they may not be fully aware.

THE CLINICAL ASSESSMENT PROCESS WITH SPIRITUALITY

Professionals may ask questions about religion and spirituality with their clients formally as part of an assessment process or informally as they become more familiar with clients and development of the therapeutic relationship becomes a bond that supports further discussion. Assessment should occur throughout the period of clinical work with clients, as there are often layers of concerns and problems that may feel too overwhelming for clients to fully disclose at the beginning. In this text, the term *spiritual assessment* is used as a general process of learning more about the client. In the medical field, spiritual screening refers to a triage process that determines the need for immediate referral, possibly to a chaplain, for spiritual distress. A spiritual history refers to the detailed interview with a client, usually with a structured set of questions that form part of a comprehensive assessment, where the professional seeks to understand needs and resources. Spiritual assessment in medicine, as in mental health, refers to the more extensive process of active listening and application of an interpretive framework to enhance understanding. One outcome may be a spiritual care plan. In some medical settings, professionals only have a brief moment to interview clients before a quick discharge. In this case, a couple of preliminary questions (provided below) may be posed about the importance of religion or spirituality and whether the client has spiritual concerns he or she would like to have addressed.

Ongoing assessment allows a practitioner to keep his or her questioning stance open, rather than to foreclose possible areas of treatment prematurely. Once the problem that brought the client in for treatment is addressed, there may be other areas that emerge. A phenomenon familiar to many therapists is that 10 minutes before a session is ready to end, a client may bring up an emotionally charged area that needs to be the focus of further work. Most therapists who receive clients from insurance panels are generally limited to 6 to 12 sessions of brief treatment, but with older adults, there may be more flexibility in treatment duration.

Best practice suggests that it is always advisable to give clients the tools they need to deal with problems in living. Teaching clients how to work through problems is much better than solving problems for them because when one problem is resolved, others may easily fly in to take their place as the sorcerer's apprentice learned when his broomstick multiplied beyond his control as he sought the easiest solution to carry water to clean a floor. However, it is not only knowing the practical steps of working through problems that is important, such as partializing the problem, developing alternative approaches, practicing the approaches, and so forth that matters. Just as important is helping a client develop confidence in his or her own ability and the hope that a resolution may be found. Ultimately, there are a number of objectives that may be reached through the spiritual assessment process:

- Open the theme of religion and spirituality as one of many possible areas of exploration.

- Create an environment in which a client may share spiritual and religious beliefs and values if she or he chooses.

- Invite questions about how the client defines spirituality and its role in his or her life.

- Assess for spiritual struggle, spiritual distress, or spiritual suffering.

- Assess for spiritual strengths (hope, meaning, community).

- Build the therapeutic relationship.

- Identify spiritual goals for treatment, if appropriate and desired.

There are two forms of formal assessment of religion and spirituality. The first form is a clinical assessment tool that helps uncover areas of need for further work. It identifies areas of concern that may not be openly apparent to the client and/or practitioner and does so with an open-ended narrative approach. The second form consists of rapid assessment instruments or other instruments, indexes, or scales with closed-ended questions. These are typically scales normed with older adults that can be used to compare individual scores with groups or with their own past rankings. Comparison with their own prior scores allows a within-subject evaluation that can denote change. Differences in scores provide a change score that can help both a client and clinician denote improvement or stagnation on a mutually agreed goal. Further, scores on tests designed to measure different components of religion may be correlated with other variables. Both forms of assessment will be addressed here. Research is also underway to look at psychoneurological mechanisms related to the brain and behavior, for instance what parts of the brain may be affected by prayer, but this research lies outside of the purpose of this chapter and will not be addressed here.

Early Historical Inquiries About Religion

In early clinical work, if religion was addressed at all, it was usually included as a question about religious affiliation, such as, "Are you a member of any religious organization?" Later questions extended this inquiry to ask how often individuals attended church or synagogue, and more recently included the mosque, temples, sangha, and other types of religious meeting places. To some this was a measure of just how religious a person was. We understand now that a person can be religious to varying degrees and have different purposes for affiliation with religious and spiritual groups. For instance, some people attend a religious group for the positive socialization aspects or to maintain social standing; they are "extrinsically religious," as Gordon Allport (1950) would have said. Sometimes a person participates to reinforce moral codes for children or grandchildren or to take part in supporting the community—a number of Habitat for Humanity house building projects are led by religious as well as civic organizations. Not everyone attends a religious group to develop a closer relationship with the Ultimate. In fact, some people fear it.

Also in our modern society, there are many activities or situations that interfere with frequent church or other religious group attendance, such as health, travel, and family responsibilities. A grandparent who wants to watch a grandchild's soccer game may need to forgo church to do it, as school matches are as likely to be held Sunday morning, a traditional day and time for worship, as on other days. Some older adults hold post-retirement jobs that require Sunday morning shifts, such as retail stores like Walmart or Target.

Other questions that have been added to the attendance questions of "What religious or denominational group?" and "How often?" are questions about the importance of religion and/or spirituality: "On a scale of 1–4, with 4 representing Very Important and 1 representing Not at all Important, how would you place yourself regarding the importance of religion?" Given the definitional differences of religion and spirituality addressed in Chapter 2, the same question should also be asked regarding spirituality. "Do you pray?" and "How often?" or "Under what conditions?" are other standard questions often asked by sociologists and psychologists (Wulff, 1997). In fact, this question about use of prayer was first applied by Galton in 1872 to study the effects of prayer on the personal lives of clergy and royalty around him, whether it was correlated with longer or healthier lives. (It wasn't correlated in his results.)

In 1914 and again replicated in 1933, Leuba studied the beliefs of American scientists regarding whether they believed in God and their view about mortality. The probability of belief declined related to categorization as a greater scientist over a lesser one and the greater the level of disciplinary knowledge one held (Wulff, 1997). A little later, in the 1930s, Thurstone, a psychologist from the University of Chicago, developed scales to measure attitude toward the church and attitude toward God. In factor-analyzing these scales, it appeared that religiousness operated as a unidimensional concept. However, more recent research also shows evidence for the multidimensionality stance where low intercorrelations were found among different measures of religion (Wulff, 1997). It is important to understand that no single measure can capture the richness of the concept and different instruments may be useful at discriminating among factors of particular interest. Thus a clinician needs to be able to judge the usefulness of choosing a particular scale, after adequate psychometric statistics about its reliability and validity have been established.

CLINICAL ASSESSMENT PROTOCOLS

The first of the two major assessment forms, the clinical protocol, is concerned with whether religion and/or spirituality are important to any extent and how religion and/or spirituality functions in a person's life. An essential starting point in spiritually sensitive practice is to create a supportive and collaborative space for older adults to freely reflect on their religious and spiritual views and experiences according to their own overarching beliefs and interests. Spiritual assessment is an exploratory process that, rather than compel one view or another, encourages reflection on the memories and experiences that provide coherence for an older adult. The assessment process, too, forms a part of this relationship building process. Spiritual assessment can help the social worker or other mental health practitioner to determine whether the client would like to explore spirituality further by incorporating it into treatment in some way, perhaps through receiving counseling from the social worker about particular matters or through referrals to other sources where the practitioner determines that the need is beyond his or her level of expertise.

It is important to note that spiritual assessment may not be the best term for this process with clients themselves. Some individuals may prefer to talk about this process as a discussion about quality of life matters. Others may prefer not to include it in formal treatment; perhaps to acknowledge it, but to leave this sometimes intimate topic outside the circle of problem identification and solution finding. For some, this component of life may be a second consideration after the primary crisis is ended.

Spiritual Screening Tools

Spiritual screening is a precise term that has particular relevance where several professionals may be working with a client or patient. Spiritual screening is a quick beginning assessment—a type of triage—that can be completed by a nurse, social worker, physician or chaplain on a medical team. As the term *screening* suggests, this is prelude to either further and deeper work with spiritual and or religious concerns, some limited discussion, or setting the topic aside. The screening will end the discussion if the client or patient has no further interest. All clinical and mental health professionals should be prepared to conduct spiritual screenings. However, if another team member is available who holds specific expertise in spirituality, such as a board-certified chaplain, that person could take responsibility for the in-depth assessment. In a mental health clinic, there is likely no professional available with specific formal religious or spiritual expertise. Although all professional staff should acquire some level of comfort with spiritual screening, referrals can always be made to outside chaplains or spiritual leaders if the issue at hand is beyond the expertise of the clinician. However, the risk is that the matter would be abandoned as a lower priority if not addressed early.

Before embarking on a detailed spiritual assessment, the professional should ask four opening questions. These preliminary or screening questions can be included as part of a longer mental health or case management assessment, or they may stand alone.

1. What helps you to experience a deep sense of meaning, purpose, hope, or guidance for values in your life? (Indirect approach)

2. Is spirituality, religion, or faith important in your life? (Direct approach) If so, please give examples. If not, please explain why they are not important or, if you prefer, we do not need to discuss this. (You can skip to Option 2 in question 4 below.)

3. If important to you, what terms for referring to spirituality, religion, or faith do you prefer? (Searching for clarity and understanding)

4. Would you like to incorporate spirituality, religion, or faith in our work together? Please explain. (Inviting conversation)

Option 2: (If the client is not comfortable with the terms *spirituality*, *religion*, and *faith*) Would you like to incorporate ways of experiencing meaning, purpose, or life satisfaction that you mentioned earlier? Please explain. (Taken from Nelson-Becker et al., 2015)

Another preliminary tool was developed by Puchalski and named the FICA, for "Faith and Belief, Importance, Community, and Address in Care" (Puchalski & Romer, 2000). Although this tool was developed explicitly for physicians, it does have value for many other professionals. The questions begin, "Do you consider yourself spiritual or religious?" or "Do you have spiritual beliefs that help you cope with stress?" If the patient responds, "No," the physician might ask about what gives meaning to life. Questions about the importance of faith or belief and whether a client is a member of a spiritual or religious community are included. The last question asks how the patient would like the provider to address these issues in the health care process. Both of these models present a way to evaluate whether a conversation with a professional around spirituality and religion is welcomed or whether it is not.

The HOPE assessment format (Anandarajah & Hight, 2001) is another brief tool that, like the FICA tool, can be used in screening (see Table 6.1). This form asks about sources of meaning, organizational and personal spirituality, and what these might mean in a medical or end-of-life setting. The HOPE tool is an especially easy mnemonic device as the word *hope* is often associated with religious and spiritual beliefs.

Ortiz and Langer (2002) have also developed a short protocol for conducting spiritual assessments with older adults, and Ai, Tice, Peterson, and Bu (2005) have developed a spiritual support scale with a medical focus.

Table 6.1   The HOPE Questions for a Formal Spiritual Assessment in a Medical Interview

H: Sources of hope, meaning, comfort, strength, peace, love and connection
O: Organized religion
P: Personal spirituality and practices
E: Effects on medical care and end-of-life issues

Source: Anandarajah and Hight (2001), pp. 81–89.

Domains of Spirituality Tool

A comprehensive clinical assessment tool that can be quite detailed in assessing spiritual needs in older adults is one developed by Nelson-Becker et al. (2015). This tool (Table 6.2) presents 11 domains of spirituality, with 3 to 6 assessment questions for each domain. The domains presented relate particularly to older adults:

Table 6.2 Domains of Spirituality		
Domains	**Definitions**	**Relevant Questions**
1 Spiritual Affiliation	The formal religious or nonreligious spiritual groups with which the client closely identifies his or her orientation.	• Do you belong to any spiritual/religious group(s)? • What does membership in this group(s) signify to you? • Do you express your spirituality outside of participation in religious or spiritual support groups?
2 Spiritual Beliefs	Perspectives and ideas related to existential issues, the divine, nature, meaning, or purpose in life.	• What religious or spiritual beliefs give you comfort or hope? Describe. • What religious or spiritual beliefs upset you? Describe. • Do you believe in God, a Transcendent Power, or Sacred Source of meaning? • Describe your vision of who God or this Sacred or Higher Power is? • How would your beliefs influence your medical decisions if you became very ill? Would your beliefs interfere with or enhance your medical care in any way? • Do you believe in an afterlife? What does this mean for you now?
3 Spiritual Behavior	The spiritual practices or actions engaged in daily lives or special occasions such as prayer, meditation, or worship (including both private and public, and organizational and non-organizational).	• What religious or spiritual behaviors do you engage in? • How often do you engage in these religious or spiritual behaviors? • Do you engage in these privately, with family, or spiritual groups? • What about these behaviors do you find nourishing or undermining?
4 Emotional Qualities of Spirituality	Feelings associated with spiritual beliefs and/or experiences/activities (both positive and negative).	• Have you recently experienced an emotion such as anger, sadness, guilt, joy, love, or relief in the context of religious or spiritual experiences? • What significance, if any, did this have for you? • What feelings did you have in response (to a specific experience)?
5 Values	Moral principles and ethical guidelines derived from spiritual beliefs.	• What are the guiding moral principles and values in your life? • How do these principles guide the way you live?
6 Spiritual Experiences	Private or shared profound transcendent experiences shaping sacred meanings including both ordinary or altered states of consciousness.	• Have you had any spiritual experiences that communicate special meaning to you? If so, please describe. • Do you experience a connection with spiritual forces such as God, angels, spirits, or deceased loved ones?

Domains	Definitions	Relevant Questions
7 Spiritual History	Developmental trajectory of spiritual beliefs, values, practices and experiences. Includes both gradual change and pivotal points involving crisis or life enhancement.	• Were you raised in a spiritual or religious tradition? Do you now practice in the tradition in which you were raised? Describe early experiences and parental involvement. • In what decades of your life were you involved in spiritual practices? Would you rate your involvement as low, medium, or high for each? Were there any change points? • What events in your life were especially significant in shaping your spirituality? • Who encouraged your spiritual or religious practices? • Describe any spiritual breakthroughs that are relevant to you now.
8 Therapeutic Change Factors	Unique spiritually-focused individual strengths and environmental resources available for healing, growth, and improvement of well-being.	• What might be an object or image that symbolizes/ represents your spiritual strengths? • Could you tell me a story of how it helped you to cope with difficulties in the recent past? • How may this particular spiritual strength help your current problems? • What spiritually-based strategies, rituals, or actions have helped you to cope with times of difficulty or to experience healing or growth?
9 Social Support	Assistance and support offered by other individuals and groups that promotes client coping and spiritual well-being.	• When you have religious/spiritual concerns and problems, who do you talk to? • In the past, what types of supports have you received from these people that you have just described?
10 Spiritual Well-Being	Client's subjective sense of happiness and satisfaction related to his or her spirituality.	• How worthwhile do you find living your current life? Can you tell me more about it? How does this relate to your spirituality? • How does your spirituality help you to find meaning in your life? • How strongly do you feel connected to God/higher Power/Spiritual/Universe?
11 Extrinsic/ Intrinsic Spiritual Focus	Extrinsic focus: client's spiritual identity and orientation tied to a certain group membership and conformity; Intrinsic focus: client's spiritual identity and orientation that may or may not be tied to a group membership, but is more flexible and relatively self-determined.	• Do you find the teachings and values of your spiritual groups similar or different from your own? Please explain. • How integrated are your spiritual practices with your daily life apart from spiritual group participation?

Nelson-Becker, H., Canda, E. R., & Nakashima, M. (2015). Spirituality in professional helping interventions. In B. Berkman & D. Kaplan (Eds.), *The Oxford handbook of social work in health and aging* (2nd ed., pp.73–84). Boston, MA: Oxford Press.

(1) spiritual affiliation, (2) spiritual beliefs, (3) spiritual behavior, (4) emotional qualities of spirituality, (5) values, (6) spiritual experiences, (7) spiritual history, (8) therapeutic change factors, (9) social support, (10) spiritual well-being, and (11) intrinsic/extrinsic spiritual focus.

Spiritual affiliation refers to formal/informal membership in any religious or spiritual groups. *Spiritual belief* describes the overarching worldview as well as particular beliefs that provide meaning and purpose. This considers the cognitive content of a spiritual perspective such as belief in the nature of an ultimate or transcendent power. *Spiritual behavior* incorporates common behavior older adults might express such as prayer, church attendance, and religion or spiritual-specific rituals such as lighting a candle or certain styles of meditation. Devotional practices such as reading holy or sacred texts would also be included. *Emotional qualities of the spiritual* include remembrance of powerful emotions such as joy, awe, and despair that can be motivating factors or need repair. *Spiritual values* refer to the personal ethical foundation one has adopted that provides guidance for living. *Spiritual experiences* relate to personal or shared experiences that convey a sense of special meaning about life. Transpersonal experiences and ones that may be altered states of consciousness would also be examples. *Spiritual history* explores the developmental pathway an older person has traveled over time. Often, discussion of pits and peaks as well as mentors and guides might be included here. Therapeutic change factors consist of the individual strengths one might carry that can be called on for assistance in healing pain or sorrow. It can also include larger environmental resources. *Social support* details the nature of the social environment that supports or hinders spiritual expression. *Spiritual well-being* relates to an older adult's subjective sense of contentment or satisfaction. This also connects to a term identified by the National Interfaith Coalition on Aging in 1975. *Extrinsic/intrinsic spiritual focus* considers the preferred style of an individual in interacting with the spiritual dimension. This focus style was first described by Allport, a psychologist who did extensive work within this area in the 1950s and has also been identified as valuable in assessment by Canda and Furman (1999).

This assessment tool is designed to be thorough and relate specifically to the life of an older adult, although it might also have value to younger individuals. Questions are created to identify areas that may be of particular assistance to clients. It is likely that not all of the domains would be discussed in depth at one time. The domains themselves could be described to clients and then the ones that may be of particular interest or compelling need can be expanded through the questions presented within each category. For instance, under values, one might ask a client if they want to discuss their guiding moral principles and how these are integrated in daily life. Of course, the questions do not need to be strictly followed and the creativity of the therapist or practitioner may amplify a domain in other ways. For example, Nelson-Becker et al. (2007) use clinical case vignettes to describe and identify domains.

Fitchett's 7×7 Model for Spiritual Assessment

From his experience as a health care chaplain, Fitchett (1993) has identified a number of dimensions that may be considered in assessment. His 14 dimensions fall under two broad categories, labeled "Holistic Dimensions" and the "Spiritual Dimension" (see Table 6.3). The spiritual dimensions he further breaks out are included under the holistic dimensions. While most of his dimensions are self-explanatory, a few are not. His holistic dimension labeled *societal* considers any structural issues that may cause oppression. Under the spiritual dimension, his term *community* includes

Table 6.3 Fitchett's 7 x 7 Model for Spiritual Assessment	
Holistic Dimensions	**The Spiritual Dimension (Expanded)**
Medical	Beliefs and Meaning
Psychological	Vocation and Consequences
Psychosocial	Experience and Emotion
Family Systems	Courage and Growth
Ethnic and Cultural	Ritual and Practice
Societal Issues	Community
Spiritual Dimension	Authority and Guidance

Used by permission from CSS Publishing Co., Inc., 5450 N. Dixie Highway, Lima Ohio, 45807.

the descriptions of the types of communities in which one has formal or informal membership and the roles one plays in those communities. His *authority and guidance* term reflects assessment about whether the client trusts the practitioner enough to disclose thoughts and feelings, has enough personal authority or self-esteem to be able to make necessary changes, and has other sources of authority in his or her life. What is helpful about this general assessment model is the way it integrates spiritual dimensions into a larger framework.

Other Clinical Assessment Tools:
God Images, Spiritual Histories, EcoMaps, Lifemaps

There are other types of clinical assessment tools that can assist practitioners to better understand the spiritual lives of their clients, and also help their clients explore their own spiritual lives in a deeper way. Because these tools are both assessment and also therapeutic intervention, they will be listed in this chapter, but readers should appreciate they also have utility for practice. Older adults who are interested in these deeper assessment tools will find accommodation in them for personal development history, layers of family complexity, and environmental resources.

God images. The concepts that older adults hold about who God is are foundational in shaping both religious and everyday beliefs and behavior. Pargament (1997) suggested that older people form ideas about God that are expressed through the coping strategies they choose. They either rely on themselves for coping rather than on God (self-directing), they leave decisions up to God (deferring), or they are active partners with God in finding solutions to problems (collaborative). In the first style, God exists, but more or less absents himself/herself from the action and just listens. Older people who follow this style evince a greater sense of personal reliance. In the second style, people choose to wait for God to take control or make things clear. They may tend to reflect doctrinal orthodoxy and extrinsic religiousness (e.g., using religion for social support purposes). In the last style, people pray for assistance and involve God in their plans. They are more likely to express intrinsic religiosity (have a relationship with

God, apart from religious ties) and may have higher self-esteem. Images of God and the association of these images, particularly God as benevolent, with health were tested by Krause, Emmons, and Ironson (2015). They found that over half of the effect on hope of spiritual support, defined partly by sharing religious experiences and knowing God better, operated through God images and sense of gratefulness to God. They suggested that church associations shape images of God and in turn strengthen health. Overall, internal working models of God—such as God as partner, punisher, or guide—can have an effect on how people process stressful conditions.

Spiritual history/spiritual lifemap. This form of assessment can be visually or orally based. Here, a client might draw two axes; the x-axis would detail personal historical time from birth to the age one is currently. The y-axis could represent the high and low spiritual points, such as might develop from a job loss or a death of a significant friend or relative. Special friends and spiritual guides might also be included. As an older person begins to think through the events and feelings they experienced in a spiritual dimension, more thoughts and memories usually surface. This offers a pictorial representation of influences of the past, present, and a potential course for the future.

Spiritual genogram. A spiritual genogram is similar to the family genogram developed by McGoldrick, Gerson, and Shellenberger (1999) and updated by Hodge (2005). It offers a spiritual template across three or more generations in a family, illustrating religious and spiritual affiliations, spiritual breaks, spiritual experiences, and changes in religious orientation. The number and thickness of lines (as with the genogram) can be used to illustrate closeness or distance to/from spiritual relatives/ mentors or nonspiritual relatives and/or family friends. Breaks or cut-offs may be shown by a line perpendicular and cutting through the relationship line. Family names are placed in circles modeled after a hierarchical organizational chart to show generational positioning; key information which may include birth/death dates may be reported.

Spiritual ecomap. A spiritual ecomap is used to show an older adult all of the religious/ spiritual influences in his or her present life. The client who is the focus would be in the center circle and other people and organizations would be drawn in close or distant proximity to the center with bold lines (strong) or dotted lines (weak) to show the nature of the relationships. Organizations that have a strong and present influence (including religious TV or radio) would be shown within the surrounding circles. Circles are labeled and formal and informal support systems would probably be incorporated. This tool, in contrast to the other two, is oriented to the now rather than the past or future.

RAPID ASSESSMENT INSTRUMENT PROTOCOLS

One of the controversies in assessment is whether it is better to use a general clinical assessment approach as detailed above, or whether a specific instrument that has adequate psychometric validation for reliability and validity is the best approach. Some spiritual experiences do not lend themselves well to systems of measurement. In those cases especially, a clinical protocol designed to explore the nature of the problem offers the potential for more qualitative richness. Use of specific measures does make sense when we understand the nature of the problem clearly and it is a particular one for which a measure does exist. In this case, the individual's score can be used as indicator for them of how they compare to others or to themselves when the instrument is repeatedly given over time. Furthermore, it is possible that rapid assessment tools may be contextually sensitive and culturally specific. The Fetzer Institute (1999) is one group that has developed measures designed to relate specifically to older adults and health, supported by the National Institute on Aging, which is part of the National Institutes of Health. By grounding the work in health research, it appeals to a wide audience but also risks accompanying limitations of assumptions about the nature of religion, spirituality, and health relationships. Still, the focus on looking at independent areas of religion and spirituality has been helpful. The Fetzer report includes 12 papers that each gives background and a sample instrument. Detailed below are the primary dimensions.

The daily spiritual experiences scale seeks to capture the ordinary experiences of elders rather than experiences of a transpersonal or extraordinary nature. It was developed for use with a primary Judeo-Christian population and uses the word *God* in its terminology. Nine key dimensions include less common aspects such as sense of awe and sense of gratitude. Since publication, this scale has been the subject of further research both in the United States and overseas. *Private religious practices* (developed by Levin in Fetzer, 1999) looks at four individual level behavioral strategies. These include such items as reading the Bible and watching religious TV.

Meaning and religious/spiritual coping consist of two subscales. The meaning subscale draws on the work of Victor Frankl, the Jewish psychiatrist who survived the Holocaust and takes a nonreligious approach. The religious/spiritual coping subscale devised by Pargament looks at positive and negative coping as well as three styles of coping related to relationship with God: deferring, collaborative, and self-directing.

Values describe a subscale that looks at the goals of values and the process for reaching them. This results in a range of values that are rated. Idler, the author of this scale, acknowledges that there is little direct correlation with health other than in a lesser proclivity toward seeking pleasurable sensations.

Beliefs in this scale are those related to health outcomes and those primarily related to a Judeo-Christian or Muslim background such as belief in life after death and a personal relationship with God. *Forgiveness* identifies forgiveness of self, God, and others as well as feeling forgiveness from others. *Religious or spiritual history* (developed by George in Fetzer, 1999) suggests items that look for significant religious/spiritual associations or experiences by age, period of change in religious views, and separate ratings of amount of religious involvement by decade.

Religious preference or affiliation provides a categorical list of a number of possible world religion affiliations though it is not exhaustive. It does suggest that it is preferable to ask for the specific religious/spiritual affiliation one holds. It is often difficult to fit religious group membership into prescribed categories. For example, my own denomination is not independently listed, but subsumed under another theologically dissimilar group. Some consideration of a specific time frame (the present may be best) is also useful as people change religious affiliations through different life stages. *Organizational religiousness* considers attendance and nature of religious behaviors such as worship experience. *Religious support* describes a subscale measuring associations with coreligionists in terms of emotional support received and given and anticipated.

Commitment seeks to define the level of translating beliefs into action through a three-item measure. "I try to carry my religious beliefs over into all my other dealings in life." Also asked is the amount of average monthly contribution, though differences in SES could presumably make this difficult to compare, and how many hours are spent on activities for religious/spiritual purposes.

Though there is acknowledgement that many of the items in the Fetzer instruments pertain to a Judeo-Christian theology, there is an attempt in a few subscales to make some items relevant to those who practice world religions. However, the effect is not consistent, making this series of instruments most useful for the older adult who practices a Judeo-Christian faith.

Olson and Kane (2000) conducted a broader review of ways to measure or assess spirituality in older adults, though this takes less of a clinical focus. In addition, social work has developed spiritual assessment tools to assist practitioners (Bullis, 1996; Canda & Furman, 1999; Hodge, 2005; Nelson-Becker, 2005b), as have medicine and nursing (Anandarajah & Hight, 2001; Fitchett, 1993; Koenig, 2002; Puchalski & Romer, 2000; Sulmasy, 2002). Many of these were developed for wider use than a specific population and would have varying applicability to older adults specifically. For instance, the Spiritual Support Scale (SSS) was developed by Nelson-Becker (2005b) according to a Rasch analysis protocol where some items were hypothesized to be easier for older adults to endorse and others more difficult. This tool had factors of religious, social service and death acceptance as well as an alpha reliability of .86. See Table 6.4 for the list of items.

Table 6.4	Spiritual Strategies Scale (SSS) How often have you used the following? (Circle your response.)				
	Never	Rarely	Sometimes	Often	Always
1. Praying	1	2	3	4	5
2. Talking to friends about problems	1	2	3	4	5
3. Providing service to others	1	2	3	4	5
4. Meditating	1	2	3	4	5
5. Developing a personal discipline of some kind (fasting, studying)	1	2	3	4	5
6. Participating in a religious ritual or ceremony	1	2	3	4	5
7. Looking for meaning in your night dreams	1	2	3	4	5
8. Writing a spiritual journal	1	2	3	4	5
9. Reading spiritual, devotional, or religious writings	1	2	3	4	5
10. Forgiving yourself	1	2	3	4	5
11. Forgiving others	1	2	3	4	5
12. Looking to God/Power for meaning in life	1	2	3	4	5

	Never	Rarely	Sometimes	Often	Always
13. Accepting death	1	2	3	4	5
14. Participating in a religious fellowship or community	1	2	3	4	5
15. Assessing your life	1	2	3	4	5
16. Leaving something for the next generation	1	2	3	4	5
17. Watching religious TV programs	1	2	3	4	5
18. Participating in support groups	1	2	3	4	5
19. Finding peace in nature	1	2	3	4	5
20. Experiencing the spiritual in the arts (art, music)	1	2	3	4	5
21. Finding hope	1	2	3	4	5

Source: Adapted with permission from Nelson-Becker, H. (2005b).

Another great resource for rapid assessment instruments is *Measures of Religiosity* (Hill & Hood, 1999). This compilation includes 17 chapters or categories of religious measurement each including scales of religious attitudes, spirituality and mysticism, God concepts, and scales of death as well as categories similar to the Fetzer distribution and more. As with most scales in this area, many are not applicable to world religions and have not all been equally validated on groups outside of university students. Their use with older adults would thus need to proceed with some caution. Further, whether the purpose is clinical or research-based will determine instrument selection.

SPIRITUAL DISTRESS ASSESSMENT

Spiritual distress may become evident when completing some of the tools detailed above. However, there is a newer spiritual distress tool that offers strong clinical utility, the Spiritual Distress Assessment Tool (SDAT) which has been tested with older hospitalized adults (Martin, Jobin, Büla, Rochat, Monod, & Spencer, 2010; Monod, Martin, Spencer, Rochat, & Büla, 2012). In studies of this instrument, 65% of older hospitalized patients reported some spiritual distress, with 22% having serious spiritual distress on at least one item. This tool has been shown to be acceptable to both patients and clinicians with good outcomes. It is also parsimonious, containing only five areas of spiritual need: (1) To what degree does the *Need for Life Balance* remain unmet? (2) To what degree does the *Need for Connection* remain unmet? (3) To what degree does the *Values Acknowledgement* remain unmet? (4) To what degree does the *Need to Maintain Control* remain unmet? And finally, (5) To what degree does the *Need to Maintain Identity* remain unmet? Each question has three to five patient interview subquestions. Spiritual dimensions assessed include meaning, transcendence, values (two dimensions), and psychosocial identity. All of these have a four-item response set. Spiritual distress, when it is apparent, is often one area of great and immediate need.

SUMMARY

This chapter provided evidence for the value of including assessment of religion and spirituality directly in any general assessment of older adults. More so than other cohorts, older persons tend to have lived lives affected by a strong religious patina. Although religion has been helpful for many people, it is also important to recognize that for some it has been painful and has even caused suffering. Thus, a mental health practitioner should not assume that exploring contexts of religion and or spirituality will always be immediately welcome. However, in cases where religious structures or organizations have been the source of pain, then that is also helpful information to learn. In these cases, if the client is willing, healing work can be accomplished.

Older adults as well as all individuals have spiritual needs that often go unexpressed.

Spiritual needs are different from psychological and emotional needs and deserve their own place in the panoply of assessment questions. Professional helping disciplines are becoming more aware of the need for spiritual assessment and are beginning to incorporate that into professional standards.

Screening tools, clinical assessment protocols for older adults, and rapid assessment instruments focusing on particular areas of religion and/or spirituality are in a developmental stage. Thus, greater assistance is now available for those wanting to make religion and spiritual assessment a part of their therapeutic work with older adults. Several screening tools and assessment instruments have been reviewed in this chapter.

QUESTIONS FOR DISCUSSION

1. Discuss your views on spiritual needs of older adults. Which seem most salient or important? With which needs listed in this chapter do you agree? Which may not be universal common needs? Are there other spiritual needs common to older adults that you can identify from your own experiences?

2. Consider the standards that relate to spiritual assessment from your own profession. If your professional discipline has a code of behavior, take a look at it and see what parts of the code might endorse completion of a spiritual assessment either explicitly or implicitly. If you are already familiar with your own profession's stance on inclusion of religion/spirituality, then you may want to look at the standards of another related discipline to note differences and similarities.

3. What is important to know in order to develop and ask questions that are helpful to both you and your client? In what way is asking questions an art? In what way is it a science?

4. Compare some of the assessment instruments described in this chapter. Discuss the pros and cons of each and under what conditions they might be most useful.

5. Look at the Domains of Spirituality Questionnaire. Read through the domains and questions first. Then divide up into pairs with a partner. Ask each other questions that you both agree on. What questions are most comfortable for you to ask? Which ones are most uncomfortable for you? Why? What did you learn when you asked the question? How did that learning change your understanding?

MEDITATION: FOCUSED ATTENTION

Use a candle that is lit or another object that you can place in your visual field. In this exercise, the candle or object serves as anchor or attention holder. Relax your mind and maintain focus on your object. Try to imagine it as heavy and bright to help you focus your attention. Pay attention to your mind as you look at it, so that you do not fall asleep, become distracted, or become too relaxed. When you tire and find yourself losing attention, just return your attention to the object. If you have paper and pencil, draw a short line on the paper each time your attention wanders. Do not criticize yourself when this happens. Try this for three minutes. When you finish, breathe deeply in and out to relax yourself fully. When you can learn to focus in a sustained manner, you can engage the whole force of your mind.

EXPLORING YOUR SPIRITUALITY: DISCERNMENT

St. Ignatius of Loyola considered that discernment formed a key aspect of the spiritual journey in everyday life. However, without the help of friends, a spiritual director, or others who live life in an intentional manner, it is often difficult to see the larger connections and meaning in one's own life. This is because our own subjectivity can blind us to important realizations or insights. Further, sometimes it's hard to envision whether an act will lead to good outcomes for all or negative outcomes for some.

Discernment is the process to determine the value and meaning of an experience. The etymology is from the Latin *cernere*, to separate, sift, distinguish, or resolve. *Discernere* adds the ideas of sever, separate, and part. It involves moving past perception and into evaluation. The term *judgment* is often used, but judgment can imply measurement. This form of measurement often relates to the self: whether one is better than or less than others. Such an action can stop us cold and obstruct the opportunity to move further in our own development or judgment. If we perceive ourselves as *better than*, there is little incentive to move forward. If we perceive ourselves as *less than*, we may give up, thinking to ourselves, "What's the

point?" It is when we see ourselves as living on our growing edge, looking at the opportunity to learn in failure as well as success, that we can fully explore what is available to us in discernment.

1. Discernment is first being able to see deeply what is there. When did you fail to see something that was important for you to know? How did you become aware later of this missing knowledge? Did you suffer because of this failure to *see* or distinguish?

2. Have you ever judged someone in a way that limited his or her ability to engage with you? What was the result of that judgment?

3. What action can you take to help you understand difficult situations better? How can you learn to hold two different points of view in your hand and consider them both from the standpoint of the person who expresses each view?

4. Do you think catching yourself in thoughts of judgment will change you? How? In what way can this create greater peace within you or your community?

5. Journal about your thoughts.

EXPLORING YOUR SPIRITUALITY: EMOTIONAL MINDFULNESS

In order to better understand spiritual expressions of others, it is helpful to explore your own understanding. In previous chapters we have explored intention and paying attention; sensory elements of spirituality through vision, scent, and rhythm; and developing internal resources of breath and centering. Assessment involves developing skill at observation. Skill at observation is best acquired when one also has the courage to look inward at one's own internal construction of emotions.

1. There are times when you will experience very negative emotional distress from clients. It is helpful to be able to look back at a difficult experience you have had using emotional mindfulness. Emotional mindfulness involves learning how to feel your emotions rather than just describe them. Choose a challenging experience and think about it with emotional mindfulness. How did you feel? Do this with kindness to yourself.

2. Emotional literacy concerns being able to talk about your emotions. Expand your emotional vocabulary by thinking about the feelings you experienced in this difficult time and trying out different words to describe your feelings. As you use different words, such as sadness or anxiety, notice how you may feel different physically. When emotions remain unnamed, they are often more scary. Naming your own emotions will help you to recognize the emotions that arise in your client when you touch on topics during assessment and later in working on goals together.

3. A further step you can take when you are ready is to contextualize your own negative experience in a new way. Make the story larger than you. Did you know or hear of others who went through a similar experience? How did your experience help you connect to others who were suffering? Can you reframe this challenging experience given your new understandings of it?

4. Write about this exercise in your journal.

EXPLORING YOUR SPIRITUALITY: COMPOSITION OF THE PLACE

This exercise invites you to develop an imaginary or imaginal place that you can return to for personal healing and restoration. This place may be any place you desire. It may be a meditation room, a walled garden, a bench by a waterfall, a park where children play, or a retreat space such as a cabin in woods near a lake or by the ocean. In previous exercises, you have been asked to explore deeply a particular sense, such as vision or smell. The purpose was to pay attention and in giving attention to the sensation, to expand and deepen it. There are many things that distract us in the world and our attention is often snatched and diverted into situations about which we may care little, so there is value in learning to focus more clearly and heighten our awareness. In this exercise, you are invited to imagine the scene of your choice very thoroughly and intensely, as if you were there and the scene were unfolding before you.

1. Think of a place where you will be at peace. Landscape it or furnish it with appealing colors and objects. Some of these objects may carry symbolic meaning for you, or invite spiritual connection. The objects might be traditional, such as a cross or a candle, or may hold meaning for you personally, such as a stone, a photo, or a painting or drawing of your creation.

2. What are the ambient sounds? Are there birds singing, frogs croaking, or music playing? If music is playing, what is the genre of this music? Or is silence your preference?

3. What are the textures in this place? How does it feel to your touch as you reach for objects, flowers, stones? Is there wind wafting through? What is the temperature? What is the larger "feel" of being present here?

4. What are the scents within this place? Do you smell pine needles, new rain, roses, or other flowers?

5. Walk in this place you have imagined. Are you barefoot or are you shod in shoes of some kind? How does it feel to walk in your place? How does it look from the side, the back the front? Other vantage points?

6. What kind of safety or spiritual freedom do you experience in this space? If safety, from what? If spiritual freedom, from what or for what?

7. Fix this place in your imagination and return to it at various times of day when the lighting has changed or in different seasons. Also know that you can alter it by bringing in or removing objects as you desire. Understand that this place can be a place of restoration and healing for you now and in the future. How are you different after visiting it, if you are?

8. Journal about your experience and/or discuss with a peer.

Note: This practice of composition of the place is an ancient spiritual practice written about by St. Ignatius of Loyola. It is also often used with *Dwelling in the Word* in some Christian traditions. In this practice, one vividly imagines oneself present in a scene from a specific scripture, such as a place where Jesus spoke to the people, by calling on all of one's senses. Any sacred writing from any religious tradition that suggests a scene could be used. Or it can be a nonreligious formulation as suggested above.

One of my students shared her sacred space very vividly:

> There is a cabin in the woods by a lake. And in this one plot of land there is a large tree just a little way up from the shore. A swing is attached to that tree and it is there that I often like to sit listening to the water lap gently on the shore. Down by the lake, which is dark and still, a handmade pier reaches out and holds onto a small boat, roped around the dock's wooden post. Looking up from the lake, a cabin can be seen. Though it is made of wood, as not to be an outsider amongst the other trees, the cabin has huge windows that reveal soft warm lights from inside. Right beyond the panes of glass is the kitchen, filled with the potential of gatherings and conversations fueled by homemade food and drink. But the other, almost hidden room, that is tucked around the corner, is the library. This room is walled with books that require a modest ladder to reach. This is my room. This is my cabin. This is my place that allows for solitude, reading, cooking and gathering with those that I love . . . it provides me great comfort in times of stress. (personal communication from Lauren Dowden, MSW)

WEBSITE

Living Without Religion

http://livingwithoutreligion.org/

This website is an option for those who are having trouble or do not identify with a religion. This informational website gives those individuals an opportunity to connect with others who may feel the same way about religion as they do. Living in a country that has a strong emphasis on religion may be isolating for those who do not. It may be more difficult to find websites or places to connect where there is no emphasis on religion. This website provides the user the opportunity to do so. Showing the older individual that he or she is not alone and that his or her views are fully acceptable may pave the way for a stronger relationship.

RECOMMENDED READING

Kane, R. L., & Kane, R. A. (2000). *Assessing older persons: Measures, meaning, and practical applications.* New York, NY: Oxford University Press.

This book has a well-written chapter on spiritual assessment by Olson and Kane.

Paloutzian, R. F., & Park, C. (2013). *Handbook of the psychology of religion and spirituality.* New York, NY: Guilford Press.

This edited work offers a chapter on measurement and assessment as well as major sections on development, psychology subdisciplines, construction and expression of religion, and spirituality and applied areas.

Pargament, K. (2008). *Spiritually integrated psychotherapy.* New York, NY: Guilford Press.

This book offers a range of material on working with clients coping with spiritual distress and the search for the sacred. It is written by a well-regarded psychologist.

Pargament, K. I. (2013). *APA handbook of psychology, religion, and spirituality.* Washington, DC: American Psychological Association.

This comprehensive edited two-volume text has a number of chapters of interest on measurement of religion and spirituality. It includes sections on why and how people are religious and spiritual, specific populations, major orientations to change, theory research and practice related to depression and anxiety, and specific contexts.

Richards, P. S., & Bergin, A. E. (2005). *A spiritual strategy for counseling and psychotherapy* (pp. 29–48). Washington, DC: American Psychological Association.

This book offers background in theory and philosophy of religion and psychological approaches. It offers material on religious and spiritual assessment that is useful.

CHAPTER SEVEN

RELIGIOUS AND SPIRITUAL INTERVENTIONS WITH CLIENTS

The ultimate creative principle is consciousness. There are different levels of consciousness. What we call innermost subtle consciousness is always there. All of our other [kinds of] consciousness—sense consciousness and so on—arise in dependence on this mind of clear light.

—The Dalai Lama

Zero Circle (excerpt)
Be helpless, dumbfounded,
Unable to say yes or no.
Then a stretcher will come from grace to gather us up.

—Rumi (translated by Coleman Barks)

This chapter addresses spiritual approaches in therapeutic practice with older people. Application of traditional therapies can accomplish much in psychotherapy. However, as the Rumi poem "Zero Circle" suggests, sometimes intuition or inspiration from unknown external sources is what puts us on our feet again. This chapter commences by sharing an overall macro-level philosophical approach to practice and therapeutic listening and continues by discussing several mid-range therapeutic areas of care and concern, such as use of hope, faith, forgiveness, narrative therapy, and ritual. It closes by addressing micro-level individual care strategies that can address religious and spiritual needs primarily through emphasis on the arts.

SECTION 1: PHILOSOPHICAL APPROACHES TO THERAPY WITH OLDER PEOPLE

Deep Listening: An Empathetic Frame for Intervention

In psychotherapeutic approaches, the act of knowing is related to empathy. When we embrace our natural empathy, we can better appreciate the experience of our client. This flows out of deep listening: listening attentively with the entirety of the therapist's past knowledge, experience, and intuition available. Empathy involves the ability to feel with, to touch the inner nature of the other person's being, as suggested in Chapter 3. Empathy is relational. One does not impose one's frame of reference as projection nor assimilate the other's viewpoint as one's own (Puhakka, 2000). The need for clear boundaries entails watchfulness. The other person is respected and connection is created, as much with nonverbal as verbal communication. This is accomplished from a condition of openness rather than a desire to possess and/or control. There is often a residual response in both people. Sometimes this is subtle, sometimes profound, but in most cases where a shift has happened, there is change. Transformation. The therapeutic alliance between client and therapist is built on validating the client, learning and addressing client expectations, the therapist's perceived credibility, as well as his or her ability to sense accurately the obstacles to treatment and to change, and asking for client feedback (Ardito & Rabellino, 2011; Roth & Fonagy, 2006; Miller, Duncan, Brown, Sorrell, & Chalk, 2006). Far more than using one approach or another, these are the common factors that seem to affect measures of alliance and treatment success. These factors form the basis for deep listening, which is necessary but not sufficient for growth.

When clients or therapists/helpers have an emotional block, empathy may not be the outcome. Instead, anger, sadness, or anxiety may emerge that reflect the therapist's or client's need for attention to self. However, if empathy is extended to the client and received by him or her, then the client feels heard. Unadulterated empathy is almost irresistible in that it is rare. Empathy without agenda, but empathy with boundaries. It is also a measure of true acceptance. In this way, empathy can be considered a spiritual technology.

Sometimes, two people enter a space of shared awareness. Buber (1923/1958) referred to this as creating "I-Thou associations" versus "I-It associations." I-Thou occurs in relationships when both people treat each other as subjects rather than subject to object. I-Thou relating is a form of intersubjectivity where knowing leads to mutual respect. By contrast, formation of subject-to-object I-It relations leads people to distance themselves from each other, from poverty and pain, and is a kind of social injustice. It is about holding a voluntary blindness to knowledge. The gates are shut, the walls are up, and the curtains of full awareness are closed. What should be known cannot be known.

Thich Nhat Hanh (2002) calls this intersubjective response *interbeing*, a word that refers to the connection between all living and nonliving, human and nonhuman things. This may extend beyond Western mindsets that would stretch to find and form connections between living beings of all genres alone, besides trying to do this with nonhuman things. Yet the concept is important. Hanh advocates engagement in 14 mindfulness trainings, which are practices for living. These are

- openness,

- nonattachment to viewpoints,

- freedom of thought,

- awareness of suffering,

- simple healthy living,

- dealing with anger,

- dwelling happily in the present moment,

- community and communication,

- truthful and loving speech,

- protecting the sangha (spiritual friends or community),

- right livelihood,

- reverence for life,

- generosity, and

- right conduct.

Interbeing happens when an individual bravely first looks deeply into his or her *true mind;* she will discover compassion and nourishment for the self there. However, the act of facing one's true self is not to be taken lightly. Many people fear this meeting and avoid it all of their lives, even when opportunities masking as problems slide into their path.

How we know something to be true forms a type of tacit knowledge. Because it goes deeper than language, it is not something we teach or often speak of. Active ways of knowing can solidify over time into programmed actions that keep us from the flexibility and permeability we so greatly need to be able to respond deftly and with imagination to events and circumstances. People often move circularly in habitual or rule-bound approaches. However, tacit knowledge can also be the mental shortcut that saves energy for doing difficult intellectual work.

In complete awareness and compassion, there is no object, but the subjectivity and multidimensionality of everything is recognized. There is no side hidden from view. The viewer no longer sees from a particular location and toward a particular direction, but apprehends comprehensively (Puhakka, 2000). This is one of the gifts that mindfulness meditation and other spiritual practices can give: heightened awareness. Heightened awareness keeps the therapist fully present with the client, doing the hard work of giving his or her full attention. At its best, this builds and sustains the therapeutic alliance.

As suggested in Chapter 3, compassion constitutes a more integrated level of care beyond empathy. What are sticking points to compassion? Where are the places our attention to compassion stops or shatters? Compassion fade can occur when we observe too many places in need of compassion on a grander scale. Västfjäll, Slovic, Mayorga, and Peters (2014) note a decrease in affect and behavior when our attention is overwhelmed by too many calls for compassionate response. The number of needs can influence sense of personal responsibility, elicit compassion fatigue, and thus a type of psychic numbing. Just as it is important to understand what builds compassion, it is also useful to understand what can diminish it.

Section 2 addresses a number of mid-range technologies or interventions. Identified here are hope, faith, forgiveness, the value and meaning of home, narrative, and ritual. Hope and faith provide motivation for clients to step into the future. Forgiveness is a powerful tool that liberates the one who forgives. These spiritual practices also align with religious values and practices. Everyone needs to have an experience of home, of being at peace and at place in the world, whether that is an actual geographical space or a metaphorical sense of well-being. Finally, ritual—whether formal, informal, or spontaneous—can create meaning beyond lexicons and thus transcends language. There are other areas, such as persistence, self-understanding, adaptability, and authenticity, that could be addressed and perhaps should be in a separate manuscript. However, those selected and discussed below provide a critical foundation.

SECTION 2: MID-RANGE INTERVENTIONS OF CARE

Hope

Hope is an often neglected though important aspect of the helping relationship. Hope is a belief that goals will be attained. Jerome Frank, professor of psychiatry at Johns Hopkins, and Julia Frank, professor of psychiatry at George Washington University, wrote about the need for hope in their 1993 book *Persuasion and Healing*, suggesting that when clients came in feeling hopeless and discouraged, one of the implicit therapeutic strategies should be to hold hope for them until the client could begin to rebuild his or her own. Hope is valuable because it helps a client see how his or her life can change, be enriched, or be lived differently. A motivational interviewing process was developed by Prochaska, DiClemente, Norcross, and Fowler (1992) and Miller and Rollnick (2002, 2013) who recognized that clients went through several stages before meaningful change could be reached. This behavioral process is a means of facilitating hope in a tangible way. Often this was applied to addiction behavior such as substance abuse, but it can generalize to other kinds of needs as well, especially in building support for changes in health behavior over which older people have control.

Motivational interviewing (MI) is a direct approach to hope facilitation. It features nonjudgmental and nonconfrontational interviewing. First, clients enter a stage of *pre-contemplation* where, although they may not be convinced of the need for change or see the risk or negative effect of maintaining current behavior, they retain some understanding of the problem or issue (Miller, 2014). The therapist works with them to encourage self-exploration and affirm that the decision to change or not *is their own*. Second, clients enter *contemplation*, a time when they consider change but remain ambivalent. A therapist would help clients assess the benefits and potential losses of participating in change. Third, clients would begin *preparation* for change. They would *test the waters* by making initial small steps and building support for their anticipated change with the therapist and their social network. Fourth, clients take *action* by practicing and evaluating new behavior over three to six months. A therapist would help clients imagine potential barriers and devise strategies to surmount them. Fifth, clients seek *maintenance* of the behavior for six months to five years. At this time, they craft ongoing support and develop internal or external rewards that positively reinforce the new behavior. They may also prepare for potential *relapse* and identify how they might proceed if this occurs. If they relapse, ideally they would seek support again and go through this process a second time or more.

The basic process is described above. What Miller (2014) actually found is that clients of therapists with *high empathy* (defined as listening closely and reflecting back meaning in a targeted and skill-based way) achieved the best outcomes. Principally, the therapist (1) makes the argument for change together with the client; (2) evokes the client's motivation to change; (3) listens with empathy; (4) minimizes resistance by not opposing or confronting it—instead, flowing with it; and (5) fosters hope and optimism. What is particularly surprising is that when an empathetic counselor provided one brief session for problem drinkers, that was sufficient for clients to change on their own. The spiritual aspects of this type of approach are salient. The therapist sees the client as his or her best self and shares that vision, honors client wisdom, and offers acceptance through nondependency. Rather than providing support for the client to improve in a one-way unequal and power-differentiated knowledge exchange, the therapist recognizes that the only power to change resides in the client. What the therapist can do is call it forth, a task that honors the wisdom resident in the person. The therapist also assists in reducing the person's discrepancy between the present self and his ideal self through acceptance. Acceptance is very, very powerful. This approach is also consistent with a second behavioral approach: Acceptance and Commitment Therapy (ACT). This latter approach encourages people to accept both their positive and less affirming thoughts and to simply be present with them (Hayes, Strosahl, & Wilson, 2012). Next, individuals should clarify their values and, finally, act on them with cognitive flexibility, which should result in more vibrant living. At present, although there is only modest research support for ACT therapy, the American Psychological Association does support it.

Hope can be viewed as containing two components: pathways and agency (Snyder et al., 2000). Pathways correspond to an individual's ability to discover realistic and achievable means for attaining a goal, while agency denotes an individual's perceived capacity to attain that goal. Hope can affect the caregiving experience because hopeful people will place themselves in situations where they can be successful, and they also hold positive thoughts of their capacity to accomplish what they wish to achieve. In family caregiving for an ill older person, hope facilitates improved adaptation to pattern adjustments in family functions (McCubbin, 1999). One qualitative analysis revealed that caregivers felt especially hopeful when they were able to reminisce, share stories, and write about their experiences (Duggleby, Williams, Holtslander, Cunningham, & Wright, 2012).

The energy of hope is light and playful, allowing for creativity to emerge in relationships. Some individuals have identified sudden mystical experiences that produced immediate and complete change (James, 1902/1961; Miller, 2014; A. Greeley, personal communication, 1997). These experiences are often hard to describe in words, as they lie beyond language expression. People relate that these experiences are positive and transient, and cause complete acceptance, a sense of unity, transcendence, and awe that is lasting. These individuals feel apprehended by God, the Sacred Source, the Great Mystery, or the Cosmos. For those who have such experiences, hope is undimmable. As Eliade (1987) alludes, in mystical experiences people open a door to a worldview from which they can never return—nor do they wish to do so.

Some older clients when young were delivered rules against developing too much hope. "Don't get your hopes up. Be realistic!" were comments I often heard reflected back in counseling older adults. However, that injunction serves to keep people from acting differently and from doing what is needed to move into novel ways of thinking and being. Choosing not to hope leads to despair; despair sweeps joy from life. Choosing to be hopeful has a positive effect that self-impels and inspires. Further, acting *as if* one is hopeful begins to unbundle despair and creates that hope that is sought.

How hope is expressed in older ages. In my study of older adult coping with difficult life events (Nelson-Becker, 2003, 2005a) hope emerged at a number of points to encourage the spirit. One study participant advised that having hope that the Second World War would soon end was easier for her than for her parents. Another participant spoke of "hoping for the best" for her family; she held a best-case scenario vision of how life could unfold for each member. Similarly, a participant who suffered ill health commented, "For myself, I don't know how much of a future I have, but for my son and his family, yes. For my other relatives, I hope they all will have a wonderful future." Hope was noted for both long-term and short-term conditions. "I won't say anything against anyone because I have faults—a lot of them. I hope people like me in spite of my faults." For this participant, the hope of maintaining strong social connections with people who accepted her was paramount.

A definition of hope was given in question form. One participant asked, "Is hope the same as prayer? If someone is sick and you hope they get well, would that be a prayer?" One participant recognized hope as a sometimes unconscious process that lay below the surface of life, "You always have to hope. Nothing is hopeless." Another study participant asserted, "Sometimes you have no idea of outcomes, only hope [for the best ones]. The inner leafing (development) of various ideas is rather stunning in a lot of ways if you are hopeful about it. I've learned not to expect, but I do hope. At my age, I'm still hopeful." All of these older persons relied on their sense of hope to affect events around them as well as their own lives.

Some situations, however, are recognized as holding little hope. One participant detailed a situation where she resided that she saw as hopeless. Although she wanted to help and had, in fact, tried to help, she was frustrated by the outcome.

> When the opportunity arises I try to help, unless it's something I think is hopeless. For example, this is a senior building. There are a lot of people in here who are a little vermischt [mixed up]. There's a little lady in her 80s who's intelligent but a little forgetful. We all are. I visited her apartment. She has cockroaches all over. That makes me ill. If I saw cockroaches, I'd be on the phone calling . . . to get the exterminator out. She told me that I was seeing things. So I tried to get her to call the exterminator . . . I couldn't help her because I would anger her.

Another study participant spoke of an experience of disappointed hope in marriage.

> I was so I in love with him. I gave up my church, my family, everything for him. It didn't work out like I hoped. Then they let me come home after marriage. I had been away two years. It was wonderful when I came back. I was happy to be home and with my family again. I got a job and started working and settled into it. I was glad to be free. I was so dominated by him. I was glad to be able to do what I wanted, when I wanted.

For this participant, although her personal hope in the social institution of marriage was not realized, her hope for the future changed to appreciation of freedom and gratefulness for family who took her back from a failed marriage in a time when that return was stigmatized. Snyder et al.'s (2000) definition of hope as both pathways and agency is confirmed through these research participant comments above.

Faith

Faith must be distinguished from belief. Sometimes the word *belief* is used in a context that implies religion. An example is the question, "Are you a believer?" Faith can also be a synonym for religion, but in the larger sense it refers to trust. Beliefs can be helpful because they provide structure to our conception of the world, and we tend to assume they describe the nature of reality. However, beliefs are often formed from tradition and what we are told by others at early ages and beyond, so they are just as often incorrect as true. Newtonian physics dominated scientific thought until it was proven incomplete by quantum physics. Smaller truths become subsumed in larger ones. As people grow, they often naturally shed beliefs that don't seem to work and acquire others. This may be more difficult for some people who are fearful of living with the tension of uncertainty. Beliefs also prescribe what we can see and understand. If we believe people are generally kind and good, then we tend to interact with them that way and bring out these qualities in them. Our beliefs, then, can be self-reinforcing. Beliefs are useful, but they can be constraining unless we are free to develop beliefs that are functional.

Faith expands us. Faith is about holding trust in the universe or in other people. Elaine Pagels (2003) writes in *Beyond Belief: The Secret Gospel of Thomas*, "the Greek term for faith is the same one often interpreted simply as belief, since faith often includes belief, *but* [emphasis added] it involves much more: the trust that enables us to commit ourselves to what we hope and love" (pp. 183–184). We hold faith in those things we believe to be true. Faith challenges us to allow new truths to unfold before us. When we can live in trust and confidence that the universe will unfold ultimately in a manner conducive to our growth, we live *confides* (with faith), even in the midst of doubts or darkness. Faith does not necessarily carry a religious sensibility; instead, it is evidence of what is not seen but can be known, such as the moon appearing nightly and the earth turning on its diurnal course.

Pagels (2003), a Princeton professor who had been away from church for decades, found herself after a sports run in the vestibule of the Church of Heavenly Rest listening to the choir. She had just learned her young son had a fatal disease. Perhaps startlingly due to her years-long absence from faith expressions, she recounted thinking, "Here is a family that knows how to face death" (p. 3). She wrote that in the presence of that worship, her "defenses fell away, exposing storms of grief and hope. . . . In that church I gathered new energy, and resolved, over and over, to face whatever awaited us" (p. 5).

This is the power of faith for some people in modern times: It strengthens resilience and resolve across the lifespan, but especially for those who manage the burden of cumulative grief in older ages. A therapist can explore the value of faith for a client through exploratory questions to discern faith's role. If this is accepted as a useful goal, the client and therapist might work together to strengthen faith by looking for stepping stones of faith in the past, places where the stone held firm and stable in a river of turmoil. That faith, or an altered one, may be constructed for current need.

Forgiveness

Contemporary society offers many disruptions to internal (and external) peace. Violence on a macro-level results in wars flaming throughout the world. Violence on an interpersonal or personal level damages ability to move forward in life goals. Learning to forgive others (interpersonal forgiveness) as well as ourselves (intrapersonal forgiveness) is part of many faith traditions. Forgiveness is one pathway to peace. Forgiveness is valuable because it can serve as resolution for painful emotions of loss and grief. It involves a process, or shift, out of feelings of ill will (usually because of a perceived wrong) into a neutral, or even a constructive state. Forgiveness involves releasing any right to reparation from injury. There is an expanding literature within research on forgiveness that shows its multidimensionality (Lawler-Row, 2010; McCullough, Root, & Cohen, 2006; Pronk, Karremans, Overbeek, Vermulst, & Wigboldus, 2010; Worthington, 2005). The psychological literature has a somewhat different emphasis than the theological literature which, in the case of Christianity, emphasizes this as a Christian virtue. Judaism, Christianity, Islam, and Hinduism all explicitly discuss forgiveness (McCullough, Pargament, & Thoresen, 2000). Buddhism contains the concept of forgiveness under compassion and good-natured tolerance or patience toward lack of competence. Although reconciliation is related to forgiveness, forgiveness may not result in reconciliation.

Incentive for offering forgiveness, however, can be found beyond traditional religious norms through improved health and stress relief (Lawler-Row, 2010). Pronk et al. (2010) suggested in an empirical study that strength of executive functioning in the brain predicts ability to forgive. McCullough et al. (2006) highlighted clinical findings that suggested those asked to search for and write about the benefits of experiencing a transgression as victim, were better able to forgive than those who focused on the trauma or neutral effects. The Fetzer Institute, The Science for Greater Good center, and the Templeton Foundation have all supported research on forgiveness in recent years. Forgiveness should be freely given and never coerced. For survivors of trauma, encouragement to forgive too soon can result in further victimization.

A Holocaust example of forgiveness. Are some acts beyond forgiveness? At the time of writing of this chapter (2015), a trial was completed in Lüneburg, Germany for then frail, but mentally alert, 94-year-old Oskar Gröning, who was a Nazi soldier and bookkeeper at Auschwitz. At first he admitted moral complicity, but he stopped short of an apology. "Even if I was not directly involved with these murders," his statement read, "I did, through my activities, contribute to the functioning of the Auschwitz camp. I'm aware of this." Records indicate he tried to transfer out of the camp three times before his request was acccpted. Later in the trial, he held that the evil of the Holocaust was so great only God could pardon him. Finally, he did apologize, saying, "I am truly sorry," though he was criticized for not asking forgiveness of his victims. He attributed his participation to psychological repression or being raised in a culture of obedience. Family members of those murdered participated in the trial and testified the apology was not enough. One former judge involved in bringing the case to trial, Thomas Walther, commented, "We accuse because of time, which heals no wounds but instead burns them deeper into our souls" (Smale, 2015).

Eva Kor, who was a prisoner in Auschwitz, supported an alternative view. In the film *Forgiving Dr. Mengele,* she related how she and her twin, both survivors, were subjected at age 10 to so-called medical experiments designed to likely kill them. At age 71, she chose to meet with a German doctor who had worked alongside Mengele, but who had been found not guilty of war crimes. He continued to suffer from depression and nightmares. Ms. Kor decided to forgive him and wrote him a letter saying so. On the 50th anniversary of the liberation of Auschwitz, she flew to Germany and publicly read a letter sent to her by city officials of Munich acknowledging corporate guilt. Her response to write the letter was unpopular. In fact, she was called a traitor by a few. "In my own name, I forgive all Nazis." She continued later, "I felt as though an incredibly heavy weight of suffering had been lifted. I never thought I could be so strong."

Because she offered forgiveness, she felt she was able to free herself from victim status. She did make a distinction between forgiving and forgetting, saying she would not forget, but she deserved to free herself from the heavy burden of hate. Many other survivors were horrified by her action and failed to understand. At age 81, Eva Kor placed a kiss on the cheek of Oskar Gröning as his trial began, offering him forgiveness. He was so overwhelmed he reportedly fainted. She suggested that better than a trial and prison, if acquitted, he could use his remaining life to teach.

Forgiveness is most often a retrospective process by which individuals come to recognize common humanity in the failures and poor decisions made by others. In releasing them from serving as objects of their own entrenched bitterness, those who forgive release themselves. Forgiveness is not the same as forgetting or failing to acknowledge the abuse or evil, which in itself could be abuse in another form. Forgiveness, when offered, is often part of a larger healing process.

Intergenerational trauma: An American Indian example of forgiveness. Another minority group for whom forgiveness is a factor is American Indians who, as an indigenous people, were recipients of great injustice. Exploitation included having their children removed to distant schools where native language and culture were effectively discouraged and physical, sexual, and other forms of violence were unrestrained. This is one unfortunate example of effects when children are wrested from parents and families are then fragmented. Boarding schools, in the misguided goal of assimilation, were begun in 1860 with the philosophy of "kill the Indian, save the man" (American Indian Relief Council, n.d.). It was not until the Indian Child Welfare Act of 1978 passed that parents were finally given the right to prevent placement in schools off of the reservation.

This history of intergenerational trauma may have exacerbated health problems now in older American Indians. A movement has arisen to counter these painful negative influences through focus on wellness. In 2009, the White Bison movement led a 40-day *Journey For Forgiveness* (https://www.youtube.com/watch?v=vZwF9NnQbWM). Public comments by older American Indians acknowledged they were raised with few signs of affection. One man said it wasn't until he was age 50 that he received a hug from his mother and was told she loved him. Several tasks were recommended to older people: recognize, acknowledge, forgive, and change. The first task was to move out of denial and remember (or see) what occurred. Second, it was important to receive validation of their experience from society. Third, elders of the community directed survivors to forgive the unforgiveable in order to unleash a great healing; and finally, people needed to find the courage to change. Forgiveness was said to have four levels: basic forgiveness, forgiving others, forgiving self, and forgiving the unforgiveable.

The White Bison and Wellbriety movement has employed the power of culture to assist in drug and alcohol recovery. The White Bison philosophy includes four Laws of Change: (1) change is from within; (2) in order for development to occur, it must be preceded by a vision; (3) a great learning must take place; and (4) you must create a healing forest, an environment of care (White Bison, n.d.). Supportive statements include recognition that healing occurs through spirituality, culture, and interconnectedness (White Bison, n.d.). Forgiveness does not deny the need for justice; acts of restorative justice are still possible within the lifetimes of perpetrator and victim.

Process of forgiveness. The above examples feature forgiveness in response to societal-level crime. But forgiveness can also be a daily act. Forgiveness can lower blood pressure and reduce stress. Everett Worthington's mother was murdered, and forgiveness research became his main pursuit as a clinical psychologist. Worthington (2003) suggests five steps that he calls the pyramid model of forgiveness, or REACH. In his conceptualization,

1. R represents *Recall.* It is helpful to recall the events and the resulting pain objectively.

2. E represents *Empathize.* An invitation is extended to understand what happened from the point of view of the person who committed the wrong act.

3. A represents the *Altruistic gift* of forgiveness. The participant is invited to recall a time when he or she caused someone else to suffer but was forgiven. This gift of forgiveness can be offered similarly to the person who committed wrongdoing.

4. C represents *Commit* to forgive publicly. The participant is invited to write a letter of forgiveness (whether sent or not), write in a journal, tell a friend about the experience, or, if possible and safe, tell the person who wronged him or her.

5. H represents *Holding onto* forgiveness. Forgiving is not the same as forgetting the unjust act and uncomfortable emotions can still surface. However, forgiving is a choice, a decision.

Worthington (2003) views the need for forgiveness as an injustice gap. This is the space between what happened and the ideal resolution. When the offender acknowledges what occurred, the gap narrows, making forgiveness easier. The person offended can tell a new story about the loss (possibly rationalizing something in the life of the offender), stop judging, or simply accept what happened. All of these acts work to reduce the gap. However, sometimes the offender does nothing to decrease the space or he or she dies, leaving no room for reconciliation. In these cases the injustice gap is wide and harder to close. Worthington (2003) suggests that two forms of forgiveness are decisional forgiveness (choosing this action) and emotional forgiveness, which is the deeper act that expands the heart.

Another process of forgiveness is delineated by Malcolm and Ramsey (2006), who suggest that first there needs to be a will to forgive. They allude to Christian theology, in which the cross is a symbol promising space for something new out of forgiveness. Importantly, forgiveness does not try to erase the fact that an offense took place. Instead forgiveness is a process of decreasing feelings of anger and revenge and increasing feelings of goodwill if possible. Ultimately, it is a process of finding space beyond the rightness or wrongness of what transpired. This takes time and reflection. Understanding how forgiveness is perceived by particular cultural contexts also needs to be explored where applicable. Forgiveness is a sensitive area in clinical work. Although fruitful to explore, it is important for the client to understand he or she is not being asked to forgive, only invited to consider the situation and to discern whether forgiveness may be able to play any role in healing.

The Value and Meaning of Home

Home serves as a metaphor for being comfortable in the world and finding one's place. An important aspect of adjustment throughout the life course is feeling at home in changing environments. Many older adults fortunate to survive to older ages are living with chronic illness that results in fluctuating ambiguity at their end-of-life time (Bern-Klug, Gessert, & Forbes, 2001; Federal Interagency Forum on Aging-Related Statistics, 2012). Both older and younger persons seek health care services when unexpected health events occur or chronic illnesses become acute. Further, preparation for and attention to dying in a way congruent with one's beliefs is fundamental, and often individual values are overlooked or ignored as professionals seek to manage deteriorating health conditions. Social, psychological, and importantly, spiritual needs have received less attention at these times. However, for many persons faced with serious illness, religious and/or spiritual beliefs have been the center of maintaining continuity of self and a sense of belonging.

Geographic continuity, commonly referred to as aging in place, is the standard for good care. *Aging in place* is a term that has been most frequently applied to the preferences of older adults to live and die at home. Research suggests that most older adults specify home as the preferred place for care at any time of life (Golant, 2003; Higginson & Sen-Gupta, 2000; Tang, Liu, Lai, & McCorkle, 2005). Home may mean individual residence, assisted living, memory care, or a nursing care facility. As individuals require increasing levels of care, they may work to adjust and to feel *at home* in new environments. The meaning of home can be invested anywhere one feels connected and at ease; however, many older people resist calling places of care *home*. This resistance can fuel a sense of alienation, discouragement, and disease. There are challenges to aging in place due to the complexity of illness and end-of life issues. One of these challenges is the preference of dying persons to make decisions in a manner that will not burden family members (McPherson, Wilson, & Murray, 2007). Moreover, although hospitals are seldom considered "home," many people experience repeated hospitalizations at the end of life, and some people will die in hospital settings. Spirituality is viewed as an important dimension in maintaining quality of living and quality of dying within habituated spaces (Dhar, Chaturvedi, & Nandan, 2013; World Health Organization, 1995).

Spaces are transformed into places through emotional attachment and familiarity. In her memoir written with a grand-nephew (*My Life in France*), American chef Julia Child wrote of leaving her beloved French home in 1992 after the deaths of her husband and friends. She called France her "spiritual homeland" and acknowledged that it had become part of her and she it, remaining thus until she died in 2004. Places are containers for expression of the spiritual self. In fact, some of the difficulty in leaving home relates to the *temporal depth* that was created through repeated patterns of use, increasingly differentiated awareness, and layers of emotional awareness (Rowles & Bernard, 2013). Place became a reservoir of experience as identity was reinforced there. However, wherever one lives, if one makes the choice to dwell, then it can become a place of centering for daily life and a place of belonging (Whyte, 1997). Adjustment to transitions in residence, though stressful, is a skill that can be acquired.

Traditionally many persons [were] born and die[d] in their family home. Ideally community members surround[ed] these primary life experiences with good wishes, prayers, meals and other homemaking sustenance. In addition to the life framing events of birth and death, one's home is the site of cultural transmission through daily rituals such as meals, relaxation, reading, planning, conversation and more. The home can be a treasured site for extraordinary holiday rituals and special events such as parties. Home is the place to which one returns after venturing out daily to school or work. Regardless of the level of harmony it offers, the home is the center of the universe for most humans. That is, from an archetypal point of view one's home represents a sacred center, from which an individual or family group creates the universe that immediately defines their lives (Eliade, 1958).

—Sarah Hanson,
Loyola MSW graduate, 2015.
Used with permission.

Posing a question to older adults about their particular meaning of home can help them recapture key moments of difficulty, distress, and also joy and belonging. Exploring their life through the places they have lived is one way of moving through time together. Exploring their understanding of home can help build resilience for future relocations, desired and undesired. Home also carries meaning through our excursions out of it. We make pilgrimages to our workplaces, to school, and to other places of community gathering such as places for religious worship or places that carry an innate sense of the holy due to ancient travels, the land itself, or who may have been laid to rest there, such as burial grounds. A pilgrimage implies carrying a sense of purpose, a reason for the travel, which sometimes may also bring its share of travails. Too many times people leave home on a daily basis with a type of thoughtlessness that overlooks connection to place and the emergent power that resonates across time. It is through remembering that this power of place can be reengaged. Being or feeling at home are key cornerstones to living lives of tranquility.

The Power of Narrative in Aging

Narrative explores embodied human action and experience, thus corresponding well to the search to understand the spiritual self. People inhabit their stories; older people encompass longer and often thoroughly interesting lived stories with many interconnecting streams. In organizing memory and emotion while a story is unspooled, the inner world is reformulated and re-learned. Thus, narrative begets integration, harmony, and enriched meaning (de Medeiros, 2014; Lieblich, McAdams, & Josselson, 2004; McAdams, 1997; McAdams & McLean, 2013). There is a co-construction of meaning when life stories are told and two persons are positioned within the conversation. These retrospective accounts comprise both facts and interpretation to arrive at narrative truth. The narrative truth can be informed by memory and imagination: memory recalls it and imagination augments the story so that it is not locked in to a single interpretation. Lives are re-storied to affirm identity in the midst of life challenges and suffering. Master narratives of aging (those that reinforce larger society norms) sometimes constrict a story, such as the idea of aging as decline. Overall, narrative identity is shaped and reshaped as older adults return to Eriksonian questions of "Who am I? What is the meaning of my life?" as the arc of their life stories reaches greater coherence at advanced age.

The form of the story can include a number of components (Polkinghorne, 1988). First, the *chronology* of the story suggests how it moves through time. It also points to the end of the story, which the narrator alone knows. Second, the story is marked by its uniqueness or *particularity*. Others will not have experienced it—at least not from the same point of view. Third, the story contains *multiple expressions*. Usually there are plots and subplots containing their own tension and dialogue so that the story may not cohere in parts. Finally, there is a *setting* for the story that includes cultural background and other spatial locations.

Stories help unveil the richly layered and largely hidden facets of meaning. The meaning of home was discussed above; it has roots in the academic environmental gerontology literature, but the client may avoid discussing the meaning of home when that home has to change due to worsening illness or greater need for assistance. Still, being and feeling at home are key foundations of peace. Students in my Loss, Grief, and Dying Well class have, over the years, identified multiple relocations as one of the most difficult losses in childhood and adolescence. This continues to resonate for older people. The example below suggests one way that larger myths, legends, and classical tales can inform personal stories.

Using archetypal stories. The German tale of Hansel and Gretel by the brothers Grimm tells of a wicked stepmother who takes the two children out of the house and deep into the forest, hoping to lose them there because the household is starving (and maybe she also doesn't like what they represent—competition for her husband's affection). The first time left in the forest, Gretel gathered white stones which she placed at intervals and the children were able to find their way home. The second time, she is only able to distribute bread crumbs, which unfortunately are found and eaten by birds and forest creatures. The lost children find the house of a witch who imprisons them and tries to entice them into the oven, but they outwit her after many days and find their way home, this time to a home with only their father (who always loved them) still alive. After all of their difficulties, they come back changed and know the value of home in a richer way. Without such travails, they would never have understood the multidimensional nature of what home really is. Although there is an outer journey, there is also a parallel inner one. Home is a metaphor for soul (Rohr, 2011). The inner journey moves across both time and space. Ironically, it is in leaving home that we can find it.

A more modern story is the classic chronicle of Dorothy and the Wizard of Oz, set in Kansas, which is prone to tornadoes. Dorothy and her dog Toto are gathered up in the cyclone's center and find themselves in the strange Land of Oz. The heroine's journey, on one level, is to return home to Auntie Em and Uncle Henry's farm. Traveling along the yellow brick road to find the Wizard (who Dorothy believes can help her achieve her aim), she meets a scarecrow browsing for a brain, a lion craving courage, and a tin man hunting a heart. All are invited to find Oz. In the end, they discover that the wizard, too, has flaws and does not have the power to send Dorothy home. However, the power is within her in the form of her red shoes, which she only has to strike together three times and say, "There is no place like home" in order to return there. The scarecrow, lion, and tin man also have inside what they seek. Each of these unlikely companions could only find what they sought by starting out on the road and remaining open to the unknown and difficult experiences that would challenge them. There is a deconstruction of self and belief that evolve in this process. In the end, they each find what is *home* for them. This story has endured because it, like the tale of Hansel and Gretel, and many other fairy tales narrate a deeper truth that what we need lies inside us. To bring it out, we need the help of life circumstances and paradoxically, trouble. The protagonists of these stories walk through the circumstances of their lives to find their true freedom. In stories clients can find parallels and motivation for their own lives and any changes they hope to begin.

Religious stories, classic myths, and fairy tales, both ancient and modern, resonate with us because they urge us to find that point of belonging that is our true home and encourage self-appreciation of the marvelous beings we are. Clarissa Pinkola Estes shares similar stories in her book, *Women Who Run with the Wolves* (1992), advocating a deeper reading for classic fairy tales and the unfolding archetypes women can use to better understand and live their lives. Sometimes men and women need to hear stories told several times to get their true meaning—many are not in the mind frame where they can hear the deeper nuances the first time. We do not necessarily restore self through these narratives, but begin to see the unfolding of new aspects of selfhood. Clients can be asked to identify the ancient stories that have resonated for them in their lives. Further exploration with the therapist may reveal aspects of the story that provide particular meaning when applied to an individual's life circumstance. This process can help them feel less alone as well as supply ideas about maneuvering around obstacles. Ultimately they are the hero or heroine of their own story—as it's been given to them and as they continue to create the endings.

Telling spiritual stories. Spiritual stories have great power to sustain a vision for our lives. Stories from indigenous peoples such as American Indians and Australian Aborigines have been passed from generation to generation. They share the history of the people and thereby confer a sense of value and destiny, often in the midst of messages from the dominant culture that taught otherwise. As Kay Olan, a storyteller from the Mohawk-Wolf Clan of the Mohawk nation in upstate New York suggested, stories bring us together (Global Spirit, n.d.). We live as part of each other's stories, but in reflection we are able to see more and go to profound places. An invitation to share our story is empowering—in the storytelling we have the possibility to see our story in new ways and experience the Ah ha! moment of insight. Olan proposes that when we enter each other's stories, especially in times of distress, we should ask, "If you can't hold the intention for your future, can you allow me to hold it?" This single act can be therapeutic at any age. Even someone at age 90 has a future, although the length of that future is unknown, as it is unknown for us all.

When a story is told, it becomes more real and the possibilities for knowing, learning, and healing become more authentic as well. We are typically taught to see differences, but it is what we share in common that attracts us to each other in respect and hope for all we can achieve. In a well-crafted narrative, everyone can find a point of reference. Everyone can learn something and connect to similar events in his or her own life. In good therapeutic moments, both the therapist and the older person share life-affirming connection. Further, in telling stories, the backgrounds of our lives are backlit, so that a new way of seeing sharpens forgotten edges or smooths long-held, though possibly fabricated, frictions. Stories help us understand who we are and thus facilitate our understanding of others.

Religious communities build common stories through sacred texts, charismatic leaders, and a shared sense of community across localities. In sacred text, paradoxes and ambiguities are present, analogous to confusion present in our own evolving and unfinished stories. Subcommunities formed in parishes, synagogues, mosques, or sanghas portray the identity markers for their groups, even as they alter them in the act of their living. In the Hebrew Testament writings are stories of Moses, a man with a speech impediment chosen by God to lead his people out of bondage in Egypt. There must have been other people who might have appeared to be better choices, but Moses was selected for capacities known to God that would sustain his people as they wandered both literally and figuratively in a desert. The story of Job quivers with age-old questions of why suffering is allowed. Prince Arjuna in the Bhagavad Gita showed great compassion toward his adversaries and bore injustice with stoicism. All of these stories are layered with meanings. Some of these are clear, but some must be teased out by the storyteller. The stories retold from sacred text seek to recover a fuller history of religion as it is encountered, practiced, and lived. The mediators of these stories—such as priests, rabbis, teachers, imams, and sages—connect these ancient accounts to modern contexts of meaning.

Spiritual reminiscence. Spiritual reminiscence is a particular form of connection to life history and life dreams. Reminiscence itself has been linked to three purposes: *identity maintenance* where the past affirms present sense of self, *life review* (promoted by Butler) which reintegrates self after a life challenge, and *social reminiscence* which facilitates movement into an elder role (Coleman & O'Hanlon, 2004). Spiritual reminiscence can serve other purposes which include creation of meaning and legacy, and contemplation of hope, despair, vulnerability, and strength.

As Kenyon (2003) has implied, and as alluded to in the section above on spiritual stories, there can be something sacred about both telling and hearing stories that moves the storyteller onto new ground or into new space. Telling stories facilitates new understanding and thus, lives can be *re-storied*. Reminiscence acknowledges plasticity and cognitive reserve that enables reckoning with gains and losses over the lifespan, while embedded in a single historical cohort and cultural frame unique to the person. Remembering the past for a purpose can yield outcomes such as psychosocial spiritual health and emotion regulation, but may also highlight unresolved conflicts that heighten anxiety. However, in its most practical form, reminiscence accesses minor memories and helps a client understand how these may form part of the self-schema and serve as a gateway for self-acceptance or self-change.

Webster, Bohlmeijer, and Westerhof (2010) suggest three types of reminiscence with varying intensity levels. This framework differs from Coleman and O'Hanlon (2004) in its prioritization of method over purpose. These methods are *simple reminiscence* (such as occurs in autobiographical storytelling), *life review* (evaluative integration of positive and negative history), and *life review therapy*, which seeks to build a new coherent strength-based story particularly in light of depression or anxiety. Spiritual stories are the stories told that are most intimately linked to what we believe to be true about ourselves; as a result, they are often not easy to share publicly or to work with therapeutically.

Regret can surface as a part of spiritual reminiscence. Regret is often discussed in terms of behavioral economics and decision making, but it can emerge at a more profound level. At older ages, regret can merge with guilt about decisions made or not selected, leaving outcomes that were less than desired. Some older people ruminate excessively about perceived losses and what might have been. Research suggests that those who can accept past opportunity compromise and decisions about life paths not taken are better able to adapt to loss, especially in bereavement, than people who live with the pain of those regrets throughout the life course (Brassen, Gamer, Peters, Gluth, & Büchel, 2012; Torges, Stewart, & Nolen-Hoeksema, 2008). Regret resolution is affected by perceptions about the enormity of the issue, emotional resources, and configuration (breadth and depth) of social networks, as well as level of personal control over the issue. Regret ties older people to the past and prevents them from engaging fully in the present or future planning. Thus, cognitive behavioral therapy to identify, challenge, and change intransigent beliefs and integrate spiritual beliefs and practices into treatment is one helpful modality (Rosmarin, Auerbach, Bigda-Peyton, Björgvinsson, & Levendusky, 2011). Successful disengagement from regret, as with forgiveness, can free older people to engage effectively with what is available to them in their immediate environment and increase life satisfaction.

Narrative therapeutic work with older people is beautifully aligned with a common aspect of growing older. One way to engage with younger generations is to tell stories, and older people generally enjoy this. At the same time they tell their stories, the stories can, if desired by clients, be turned back for therapeutic exploration and benefit.

Ritual

Ritual has an important place in assisting people to move through change in noncognitive ways. Religion has long valued the importance of ritual and many religions have room for different ritual elements in sacred space. Bells or a shofar calling congregants to prayer, singing bowls to meditation, water used for ritual washing or baptism (Christian initiation rite), lighted candles, and burning incense are but a few common ritual elements. Although some aspects of ritual are notably visible, others are invisible and represent inner transformation and revitalization. Some religious traditions (Catholic or Episcopal) employ many rituals and some, such as the Quakers, employ very few. Rituals require honesty, purity of intent, and encourage intimacy. Rituals can also move outside of religious frameworks to embrace spiritual areas (a house altar with meaningful nonreligious objects such as a seashell, a piece of driftwood, a stone, or a picture), or everyday experiences which can convey meaning beyond the action such as a kiss hello or goodbye or sipping a cup of tea.

Why employ ritual and how does this relate to therapeutic practice? Four *effective features* that characterize psychotherapies were suggested by Frank and Frank (1993): (1) a confiding and emotionally stimulating relationship with a healing person or person who has similar characteristics, even if largely unacknowledged; (2) a healing venue; (3) a conceptual framework or rationale (myth) that delivers an explanation for client symptoms and provides a system (ritual) for treating them; and (4) a procedure (ritual) that requires active participation by both therapist and client, which both accept as a method for restoring patient health. As discussed above, when a client comes into our setting expressing hopelessness, we can hold hope for them (ritually or metaphorically) until they receive or rebuild it back. Safety and confidentiality form the boundaries of this setting. In these ways, ritual offers a largely unacknowledged potential for breaking through demoralization and contributing to spiritual healing.

Life stages, or *rites de passage*, associated with rituals have three primary phases (van Gennep, 1960). These include separation, transition, and incorporation/aggregation. Van Gennep (1960) suggests that rites of separation are conspicuous in funeral ceremonies, while rites of incorporation are present at marriage ceremonies. Rites of transition (also known as liminal rites) may be planned to celebrate engagements or adoptions. Initiations into adulthood commonly occur in Bar or Bat Mitzvahs (at the age of 12 or 13) in the Jewish tradition. At older ages, rites of transition can occur as people transition into elderhood or the stage of the crone (a term previously defined as a withered old woman, but now reframed and reacquired as a wise person). A man can be referred to as a *patriarch*; either gender may be known as a *sage*. These rites can have a regenerative effect; in systems thinking a structure may gradually wind down to entropy if no new energy is brought in. The same also serves for individuals. Even those who successfully make solitary lives are those who do so because they connect either to the spiritual or natural world.

As with Eliade and Trask's (1965) designations, both the sacred—in this case either what is religious or what is deemed sacred or outside of ordinary life—and the profane or secular (Durkheim, 1965) define the boundaries of transitional stages. In the new condition or stage, an individual engages in rites which assimilate him or her into the group and ordinary routines. The change may be difficult to absorb such as a death, and the rite of passage is intended to moderate and decrease the sense of disorder as well as highlight a change in social status. These rites or rituals in their incorporative traits also have implications for those who might be otherwise alienated from society such as widows or widowers. One of the goals of ritual can be restoration, helping bring a person in crisis back to equilibrium. I present one framework for designing ritual in Table 7.1. Other models have been discussed by Rando (1993, pp. 318–331) and Canda and Furman (2010, p. 344–347).

Literally, a door is a boundary between society and the inner world in a house, or between the everyday and sacred worlds in a temple or synagogue. Thus, crossing a

Table 7.1 Guidance for Therapeutic Ritual Design

1. Assist the client to consider the why, where, who, and how elements for this ritual. Why will it be performed? Where will it be conducted? Who should be invited? How will it develop? Assess the client's background characteristics, relevant history, level of support, and any areas of loss that the ritual may be intended to mend or restore. What is the client's history with rituals and other ceremonies? What is the client's expectation or hope?

2. Think about the goals for the ritual. What are the immediate and ultimate goals? Are they celebratory, transformational, or healing? Will the ritual address:

   a. transitions—major life transitions such as marriage, adoption, entry into elderhood, or death.

   b. continuity—reinforcing bonds and stability of relationships during times of change, for example., when a young family member leaves for the university a special meal may be designed with an opportunity for each member to share objects of meaning with the one departing and wisdom thoughts, or when a grandparent transitions into an assisted living or long-term care facility, family members can facilitate a goodbye and hello ceremony.

3. Specify the types of thoughts and feelings that will be symbolically expressed: love, regret, forgiveness, endings and openings, for example. This can guide the activities to be planned.

4. Consider whether the client prefers to engage in a familiar ancient ceremony and participate deeply or to creatively craft a new or modern ritual.

5. Engage the client's spiritual or religious support system or family system if desired. It can help if there are witnesses—especially if the sorrow is a community sorrow.

6. Co-consider sensory elements:

(Continued)

Table 7.1 (Continued)

- What elements will affect sense of smell?
- What colors and visual elements will be present?
- What music or sound will be made or listened to?
- What will be tasted or sipped?
- What or who will be physically touched and in what way?
- What symbols will be present? Examples might include candles, a stone, another natural object, a small statue, a painting, or a photograph.

Also consider whether some aspect could be offensive to anyone who attends, cause allergies, or be harmful in another way.

7. What can be prepared in advance or constructed by hand?

8. Co-create procedures:

- Who will be invited and what will be their role? Who will preside or lead?
- What symbolic acts will occur? Examples include reading personal writing, sharing a handshake or hug, reading poetry or sacred text, planting a tree, releasing balloons, or passing a talking stick.
- What will be open and impromptu and what will be determined?
- What will the location, tone, and preferred timing for the ritual be?
- Ensure privacy, if desired, and safety of setting.
- Establish the beginning and ending, or how to know when ritual is complete.

9. Implement the ritual and evaluate both the process and result.

10. Identify whether further ritual work or something else might be needed to complete the healing process.

11. Celebrate what has been achieved!

Source: Adapted from Rando, T. (1993). *Treatment of complicated mourning.* Champaign, IL: Research Press.

threshold can hold many forms of meaning, among which is a passage or transitional stage. In former times, a man would sometimes carry his bride over the threshold, an act with symbolic meaning. In earlier societies and cultures, it was only the main door of the house that had this quality of consecration, and so a corpse that was waked in a parlor of a home would usually be carried in and out by a side door to prevent contamination (Van Gennep, 1960). It is helpful to note that we have many everyday rituals, such as the washing of hands, a rite of separation from previous tasks before the sharing of a meal. It is both a health practice and a symbolic one. Sharing food represents a rite of incorporation and act of communion. Generally rituals are behaviors which advance in a pattern. They often include elements such as convention (tradition), repetition, and condensation or compression of longer ceremonies. The symbolic, noncognitive aspects trump language. Learning to open all senses and attend to input from each one can heighten sensitivity to meaning. Thus, ritual is both a traditional and modern approach to healing that is appreciated by many older people.

The mid-range activities discussed above are useful in addressing values for positive aging practices. They touch on some community-building activities, such as story sharing and ritual. The next section, in contrast, identifies and addresses religious and spiritual activities individual older adults could consider as options for expanding their spiritual repertoire. The boundaries between the larger perspective and the smaller one are, however, somewhat malleable.

SECTION 3: MICRO-LEVEL INDIVIDUAL SPIRITUAL CARE ACTIVITIES

Religious and Spiritual Practices

All of the foundational information above represents spiritual concepts that can be used in therapeutic approaches. Religious and spiritual practices can be helpful to identify for younger practitioners who may emerge with little exposure to religious and spiritual matters from secular households. Again, because *religion* is the preferred term for many older adults, religious practices will be identified first. Although spiritual practices are included here for what approaches a more complete listing (though the universe of possible spiritual practices is wide indeed), they are less likely to be exercised as first choices by current cohorts of older people.

Religious practices include any common and customary behaviors that are associated with a particular religion or many religions. Thus, there is a range of religious behaviors that are more or less affixed to faiths and are the province of the penitent, congregant, parishioner, synagogue or mosque member, gurdwara (Sikh community), or sangha (Buddhist). Although some religious acts may be performed by priests or spiritual leaders and on a single occasion, such as entrance into the faith, others may be performed by the people or community of believers. Some common practices include:

1. *Affiliation* with a religious community (formal through membership rites or informal through attendance). Being there.

2. *Prayer* (both private and public forms, spontaneous or set, use of prayer beads or rosary). Prayers may be prayed for oneself or others (intercessory prayers). A common form is the ACTS prayer consisting of adoration, confession, thanksgiving, and supplication. When one is witness to immediate need, a quick thought prayer can be sent directly to the person or situation. There are thousands of formats and kinds with no one form being better than another. Imagine that a single sincere prayer joins thousands of other prayers in a prayer band that circles the earth.

3. *Meditation* (in the religious sense meditation could be similar to centering prayer or contemplation in the Benedictine practice of Lectio Divina—lection, meditation, oration, and contemplation). Centering prayer is similar to meditation in some Christian traditions.

4. *Fasting* in any form (e.g., from food, alcohol, or repetitive actions for religious purpose).

5. *Worship* of God (either individual or corporate). Expressions of reverence, awe, or honor toward a deity.

6. *Singing, playing instruments, chanting, or listening* to sacred music, hymns, or drumming. Being enfolded by the music.

7. *Reading, reciting, or study* (usually *of* religious texts or material or *about* religious matters in this classification). Reading wisdom literature is included here.

8. *Service* (done with a community or from religious motivation, though this also can be a spiritual or humanistic practice).

9. *Simplicity* (a focus on paring away excess to live in a more focused manner).

10. *Celebration* (holy days in a religious year such as Sukkot [Jewish festival of the harvest], Ramadan [Islamic month of fasting], Diwali [Hindu festival of lights], Christmas [Christian festival of Christ's birth], and Vesak [Buddha's birthday]).

11. *Retreats* with other believers or *pilgrimage* to holy sites. These are places that often have a tradition or history, build community, and may represent or quicken nonordinary experience.

Spiritual practices are those practices one performs to move into sacred space whether this space is visible, invisible, or has other spiritual characteristics. A spiritual practice may be repeated often and is usually undertaken as a discipline to enhance spiritual development. Because spiritual practices are often, though not necessarily solitary, it is helpful for practitioners to have guides, teachers, or groups for both support and direction/consultation. The line between what is spiritual and what is secular is sometimes blurred, but intent defines the border. The range of spiritual practices is very wide, but a sampling follows:

1. *Mindfulness and meditation* (many forms such as Vipassana [insight], Zazen, Lovingkindness [Tonglen or Metta] meditation, Chakra meditation, Sound meditation, Transcendental meditation, Mantra meditation, Yoga meditation, Taoist meditation, Qigong meditation).

2. *Exercise* such as done through walking meditation. Exercise, besides engaging the mind, offers the most important benefit to older adult health.

3. *Surrounding oneself with nature* and noticing what is present, listening to natural sounds.

4. *Engaging in the arts:* creating, composing, or appreciating music, drawing, painting, writing.

5. *Involving oneself in team sport with goals of enjoyment and encouraging community.* As one ages, the team sports may be less physical and more cerebral, such as mahjong, chess, or bridge.

6. *Movement practices such as t'ai chi, aikido, or yoga* to the extent the body allows.

7. *Contemplation* using curiosity to pose questions and to learn, accessing knowledge from one's guides/mentors.

8. *Reading poetry, philosophy, and books that offer spiritual support.*

9. *Investing in relationships:* sustaining family members and friends and nurturing intimacy and trust.

10. *Cultural acts* such as learning a Japanese or Korean tea ceremony, taking the role of student/receptacle for an older teacher wishing to entrust a legacy of knowledge.

11. *Acts of service* (out of humanistic concern).

The next micro-level helping activities section expands selected activities and practices above to provide more detail. The readers should realize that this section provides only a small window on what is a vast and growing literature (both academic and popular) of possible spiritually related practices adaptable for older people and others. Rather than expand each of the areas identified above, just a few will receive further elaboration in sections below.

Prayer

One aspect of prayer is a response to experienced difficulties in most faith traditions where belief in a god or gods is ascribed. Prayer can be a spontaneous request for assistance, a response to beauty, offered in gratitude, given in examen (as in the Ignatian tradition discussed in Chapter 9), spoken in public mourning or private grief. A prayer attributed to American theologian and ethicist Reinhold Niebuhr (1892–1971), known as the Serenity Prayer, addresses cognitive dissonance and anguish. This prayer has been adopted by Alcoholics Anonymous and other 12-step programs.

SERENITY PRAYER

God grant me the serenity

to accept the things I cannot change;

courage to change the things I can;

and wisdom to know the difference.

Living one day at a time;

enjoying one moment at a time;

accepting hardships as the pathway to

peace.

Similarly, a Buddhist Indian scholar of the 8th century, Shantideva, advised as follows.

If there's a remedy when trouble strikes,

What reason is there for dejection?

And if there is no help for it,

What use is there in being glum?

(as cited in Padmakara Translation Group, 2008, p. 130)

These two frames provide a positive psychological interpretation of hardship according to two different belief systems. Prayer, besides reaching for God and benevolent universal forces, offers a way to engage with difficult events and situations and attain peace. In times of national mourning when little sense can be made from events, prayer is offered as a powerful force for healing. Although there are many well-known prayers from many traditions, perhaps no prayer is as powerful as one recited extemporaneously from the heart. Therapists may want to invite clients to discuss whether and how prayer has been of benefit previously and reinforce client use where it has been helpful.

Writing Therapy and Use of Restorative Language

How professionals and others use language as we interact with older people is significant in shaping their cosmological views. Language can be expended to either disparage or elevate the spirit. As discussed in Chapter 4, there are many narratives about aging that see it as a time of suffering, physical imperfection, and inadequacy. The DSM-5 language and philosophy incontrovertibly identify constellations of symptoms that comprise such problems as major depression or dementia. However, though both have biological markers, they remain elusive. In depression, there seem to be different etiological pathways and varying pathophysiological mechanisms in patients (Krishnan & Nestler, 2010). In dementia, though much research is addressing pieces of the causal puzzle, only autopsies can still signal the level of physical impairment through the signature fibrillary plaques and tangles. However, in some cases, brain scans are able to detect changes as does neuropsychological testing.

Problems are defined through use of language; language may also serve as resolution to the problem. Clients can be encouraged and empowered to find their own language, their own metaphors, for the uniqueness of their situation that addresses their capacities for and experience of renewal, reengagement, and hope. Writing through their experience encourages older people to adopt language that can lead them into successes rather than failure. Writing memoirs or doing life review work can reconstruct experience and facilitate sharing to offer transformative power not just to the subject of the experience alone, but to all. Writing poetry is a particularly robust way to engage spiritual sensibility.

An exercise by Neimeyer, Torres, and Smith (2011) invites the participant to write an imaginative experience by choosing a specified number of items from three columns of Figures/Voices, Situations/Settings, and Objects. They term this a *virtual dream*. A virtual dream is one over which the participant may have some conscious control, different from a night dream (see Table 7.2 Chart of Elements for a Virtual Dream Exercise). I have adapted the list. Alternatively, one can choose any item or setting as was done in the narrative that follows. An example is provided in Table 7.3 Example of a Virtual Dream: The Dark Room/The Room of Illumination. Questions follow to include the reader/audience in addressing his or her own experience.

WRITING EXERCISE

Neimeyer et al. (2011) suggest that every element of the virtual dream is potentially a *keyugak* (Inuit word for "helping spirit"), which can help us become aware of some part of our total self or life experience. For example, a virtual dream about the loss of a key might reveal that we have within us something mysterious that requires unlocking or self-understanding. For a spiritual perspective, use of religious and spiritual figures or people such as angels, holy men and women, or saints might be helpful. Religious objects or symbols such as a cross, a menorah, sacred text, chalice, incense, joss stick, prayer shawl, rosary, statues, icons, prayer flag, prayer beads, totem, mandala, minaret, the color green (associated with life in Islam), etc. may be added.

Choose up to two elements from each column in Table 7.2 (Figures/Voices, Situation/Setting, or Object) and begin to write a story about them. Or, you can use your own elements. Many of the possible elements appearing below are archetypal or imaginative, facilitating the access of deep material. Choose elements that can facilitate feeling/understanding/working with a recent loss. Writing should be free flow without too much thought, resulting in a paragraph or a page of material within 10 minutes.

1. What are the images that seem to jump out for you? Reflect on your writing.

2. After this short period of writing, if you are with a group, turn to the person or persons next to you and discuss.

Table 7.2 Chart of Elements for a Virtual Dream Exercise

Figures/Voices	Situations/Settings	Objects
Celestial music	A field of lavender	A broken toy
A medieval bard or troubadour	A musty library	A Celtic cross
A wise woman	A mint-scented kitchen	A rusty sword
A white owl	A subterranean lake	A burning fire
A childhood friend	A promise	A full moon
A priest, rabbi, or imam	A hidden village	A rose
A talking unicorn	A tree-lined path	A torch
A bright angel	A stormy night	A wooden coffin
A tinkling faery	A gothic cathedral	An open door
A wise man	A prayer of petition	A treasure chest
A black stallion	An iridescent stairway	A lever lock
A physician	A lingering illness	A beautiful dream
A wandering monk	A dark forest	An ancient book

(Continued)

A shaman	An aquifer or well	Fragrant herbs
A mentor	A high mountain	A family crest
A nurse	A treehouse	A Buddha statue
A professor	A physical disability	A plain gold ring
An enemy	A secret garden	A stone wall
A quiet whisper	A starry sky	A swift arrow
A chaplain	A foggy window	An empty cradle
A grumpy wizard	A failing memory	A towering skyscraper
A cry for help	A dark cavern	A lotus flower
An attentive social worker	A wide promontory	A paintbrush
A puppy	A stormy sea	A skeleton key
A concentrating counselor	A message from the past	A half-empty bottle
One's future self	A chronic sorrow	An open heart
The whimsical women of Wednesday	A glistening beach	A genie's lamp
An urgent inner voice	A wheat field	A broken mirror
A soldier	A painful secret	Two roads diverging in a green wood
A melodious harp	A distant horizon	An unfinished story
A mysterious stranger	A clearing in a valley	A standing stone
An adversary	A lengthy journey	A hand-written note
A peacemaker	A stone-laid labyrinth	A double-end rainbow

Source: Adapted from Neimeyer, Torres, and Smith (2011).

Author Joan Didion (2006), after losing both her husband and her daughter within a short time, attempted to sort through her grief experience and depression in a narrative manner, calling on her readers to be witnesses to her unfolding work of trying to understand what had happened. She also acknowledges the assistance the reader as audience will indirectly provide her in this process.

> *The way I write is who I am, or have become, yet this is a case in which I wish I had instead of words and their rhythms a cutting room, equipped with an Avid, a digital editing system on which I could touch a key and collapse the sequence of time, show you simultaneously all the frames of memory that come to me*

Table 7.3 Example of a Virtual Dream: The Dark Room/The Room of Illumination

I was told I needed to open an emotional door. When I began to visualize this door, at first I couldn't touch it. It was a little above me and to the right. I envisioned it as being full of scary stuff. I put my hand on the handle and turned. This time that was enough. Later I approached this door again. This time I turned the handle and pulled the door with trepidation. I realized that it was positioned as a trap door. I expected lots of stuff to fall out and drip over me, like nasty smelling liquid, or boxes of junk. To my surprise, nothing happened. I waited. Still nothing. I began to realize I had been envisioning this door in the wrong way. It wasn't a trap door, it was an actual regular-size door, a door I needed to walk through. Ok, got it. That's a bit scary. I wondered, what was behind this door?

This morning I thought I would try again. I put my hand on the doorknob and turned it, full of courage. When it opened, I could see a small light in the back of the room to the upper right. This light backlit what was in the room. I saw that there were many suitcases. Some of them were in a very old style, as if from the last century or the early part of the 20th century. Some had straps around them. They were brown in color. There was a small blue child's suitcase. Also my current suitcase was there, that I carried on flights to Kansas for 9 years and still use on trips to AZ and England. I checked around me and saw that the inside of the door had a doorknob, too, so if the door closed behind me—as doors sometimes do, I could find my way out. I also realized that I could always imagine my way out, using a wand like Harry Potter's or some other imagined device. My fear dissipated and my curiosity led me forward.

I knew I had to open these suitcases and I began to realize this room was a heritage room that contained all of the bad stuff in my ancestry. Which suitcase to open? My attention was drawn to one of the scuffed brown suitcases with straps around it. I opened it and the memories of my mother drifted out. I saw the abuse she witnessed in her family, how this shaped her, and the many questions she carried. I was able to forgive her—saw her confusion and her attempts in a household of limits to do what was right and good. Then my attention went to the little suitcase and I saw that it was mine from my childhood. I opened it and a lot of pain fell out. I saw the time I set the table when I was about 4 and accidentally dropped and broke an everyday ceramic plate. This caused a great anger to well up in my mother and she beat me repeatedly—my brother later told me that my parents were worried about me and called a doctor to visit me at home as I lay in my bed. They made house calls then. Besides being badly hurt with bruises, I was broken in spirit. I gave up a part of myself. Other memories slid out as well. . . .

Then the room began to lighten, as if daylight were dawning. I began to see that this room had windows. It was not only a room of darkness, but there were good things here too. I saw my father's family, his parents (my grandparents) and all of the good things they did for their community. Family lore says that my grandfather attended farm auctions/foreclosures during the Great Depression and walked potential bidders past a hanging noose. My dad relayed that no one ever bid on a farm at one of these auctions. My grandfather did many kind acts in his life and I carry that legacy too, from him and my grandmother. I began to see this room in a very different *light*. It was not something to fear but something I could return to when I wanted to learn more. From the opened suitcases, I let the bad stuff fall through the floor and into a recycling well. It had disappeared. So this wasn't a room of dark stuff, but a room of cleansing and healing. I was now ready to leave with a deeper understanding. I opened the door and walked out, knowing I could return here again.

How can you envision your own pain? What shape is it? What does it look like? What does it sound like? Can you touch it? Take a point at the top of your head and let your own healing power come in and go through your arm to your hand and finger. Touch your pain with the healing energy only you can provide for yourself. Can you see it explode, dissolve, melt away, shatter, or sizzle as a fire going out—or some other way? If there is any residue left, let it flow down into a recycling well located in the ground a few feet in front of you where the material will be cleansed and sent back wherever it belongs.

© Holly Nelson-Becker

now, let you pick the takes, the marginally different expressions, the variant readings of the same lines. . . . This is a case in which I need whatever it is I think or believe to be penetrable, if only for myself. (Didion, 2006, pp.7–8)

In this way, the problem of grief (and resulting depression) is externalized and the aid of an audience is enlisted to help one understand what is difficult to process. Thus although language can be disempowering and stigmatizing, writing narrative can also provide the doorway out into understanding the intricacies and power resident in subjective experience.

Visual Spirituality: Invitation to Use Photography

More than just sharing photographs of images that return positive memories (of value in itself), the process of photography can add a second layer of meaning if done with intention. Photography includes selection of objects, events, people, or places that enrich life through remembrance and recall of how that item, person, or place summarizes meaning. These resulting photos serve as synecdoches for the spiritual. For instance, a photo of a seascape or a forest can recall the peace found in nature. When I conducted interviews with hospice participants, I would invite them to share what brought them meaning. Often they would show me photographs of family members, religious texts or objects, artwork, or locales that held special significance and served as symbolic representations. In particular, environmental spaces are often places where God or the spiritual was visible. After a subject is chosen for photographing and the image is shared with a therapist, family, or others, an inter-view—a viewing together—can prompt spiritual narratives. These acquire meaning through the manner in which the subject/object of the photography is included and becomes a marker for spiritual experience. The narrative retelling of the story can add a second layer of meaning and dimensionality, even power, as the story is recast for a new audience.

Williams (2010), as part of the Spiritual Narratives in Everyday Life Project, completed individual photo elicitation interviews using photos taken by individual participants as a means of sharing their enchantment and constructing space for God. Though not all photos depicted something invested with spiritual content, others did, even by some individuals who indicated they were not religious or spiritual. Interviewees made space for God not in time set apart or settings that were always explicitly religious, but in time that was often also occupied by other activities. Williams suggests that the spiritual often emerges in unexpected places and in time synchronous with other (often family) activity. In his project, individuals were given disposable cameras to use for capturing sacred space/objects, the camera was handed back, and then the project staff developed the photos which were shared with participants at the time of the second interview. This same process could be done with older people or the counselor could assist with the camerawork. The immaterial is materialized and a deep discussion and healing conversation can ensue.

Visual Spirituality in Art: Acknowledging Beauty

Paying attention to the aesthetics of life has the potential to lift one into new levels of appreciation; this can access the spiritual domain. Art gives dimension to life. Reading art involves voicing what is seen, including assessing color, pattern, texture, distance, and shape. Considering style, feeling tone, theme, or idea, what might the artist have wanted to say, and how do you experience it from your own social location? What *is* it that you see and how do you make sense of it? How are separate items or images in the picture or other medium related to each other? Questions can include description, analysis, interpretation, and judgment. Perhaps most important is how the viewer appropriates the experience for his or her own life.

One of the possible loss experiences in which I ask students to participate and reflect includes visiting an art museum, selecting a work on loss or grief, and writing about it with some professional assistance, either from a docent or online research. I was surprised when two students separately chose the same work, Picasso's *The Old Guitarist* (1903). Other artistic works students have explicated included Picasso's *The Weeping Woman I* (1937), *The Picture of Dorian Gray* (Albright, 1943–44), as well as an *ofrenda* (altar) dedicated to a friend's father in the Día de Los Muertos exhibit at the National Museum of Mexican Art (Chicago). The essays are always different and bring in the writer's world and perspective on their own life experience. This could also be done with a group of older adults.

Other important avenues of both healing and integrating the self can be found beyond reflection on art to its creation. This can be simple as coloring a mandala. Mandalas represent the universe or wheel of life in Buddhist traditions. Coloring in pre-imaged mindfulness art books as well as free form creations with paper and pencil, forming clay, or working with other media are other possible practices.

John Keats's (1819) verbal depiction in his Ode to a Grecian Urn suggests, "Beauty is truth, truth beauty—that is all ye know on earth, and all ye need to know" (lines 49–50). There is something about being in the presence of beauty (in many forms) that can nearly take one's breath away and assist in reorientation. For many individuals, thinking about or being involved in nature can facilitate spiritual reflection. In constricted space, watching birds, flowers grow, or other life force outside the window can expand the space virtually. We should not underestimate the power and potential of people in their ordinary lives to seek and find what is spiritual and meaningful.

Music and Spirituality With Older Adults

Music contains healing and restorative properties (Darnley-Smith & Patey, 2003). Music can facilitate exploration and expression of emotions, responses to personal experience, and assist movement toward goals through focused attention on the words captured within the music. Music has been successfully used to treat widely varying mental health problems such as depression, posttraumatic stress disorder, anxiety, and grief (Darnley-Smith & Patey, 2003; Horne-Thompson & Grocke, 2008). Clients can be invited to share music that has helped them heal in the past, locate music they find meaningful, or listen to music that returns them to a time from which they may still carry a sense of incompleteness or regret. This last selection could then be used to explore ways to restore a sense of peace in present time.

One important method that can lift the spirit is through entering a song, either alone or in a group. There are many ways that people can join together and experience community in the present moment. With dementia, someone who may no longer speak may vocalize a sound or series of sounds. One way to communicate is to mirror back to them the sounds they emit. One counselor reported that when she engaged in song play with a person on a Memory Care unit, this felt like the most authentic experience they had shared together. Singing together draws on mirror neurons in the brain that allows the patient/client to incorporate the abilities of the other person as it facilitates connection (Sacks, 2007).

With a group, it is helpful when people can form a circle so that they can see each other's faces. A warm-up can be done through raising the arms and just letting any sound out as the arms drop to the side, followed by another sound as the arms are raised. As people participate, they may find that their voices begin to harmonize. Second, people can take their arm and pretend to fling a Frisbee or disk to the far corner of the room, letting a sound follow their aim and throw. Third, they can hold their hand as if they were holding a paintbrush. Centering it on an imaginary point in a circle, they can move it in spirals outward and then back inward. As they begin to move out from the center, the voice can follow the motion by rising and falling in register with the spiral, then growing louder with the larger circles. As they follow the spiral back to its center point with the imaginary brush, the voice can diminish and grow softer.

After this series of vocal warm-ups, people can stair step their voices up together as if following a scale with four notes. It is often helpful if someone motions this movement with their hand, guiding the group. This is a way of walking the voice by connecting from note to note (or chords) one step at a time. People who are more adventurous can actively harmonize as they keep in stride with and listen to the rest of the group members. Finally, the group can sing common tunes together in rounds, with a short delay in the start of each subgroup. Some familiar tunes which share similar melodies are *Three Blind Mice*, *Frère Jacques*, and *Row, Row, Row Your Boat*. When people sing in unison or in harmony, it is hard to simultaneously think about all the tasks ahead or to worry. They are completely present and available to the group.

It is wise to begin with favorite and familiar tunes for persons with dementia. Adding simple motions can help them carry the song, and adding people (and voices) can strengthen the sound where someone's voice may falter. Listening to music is always good, but being able to sing along or play an instrument (rhythm or otherwise) can enhance the experience. Often memories of times when the music was previously enjoyed will ripple forth and these memories can be encouraged. This can build a shared moment when conversation becomes difficult. Song can be a gift of presence. See Chapter 10 on dementia for more commentary on spirituality and music.

Movement and Spirituality: Kinesthetics

There are many aspects of embodied action and performance that can access spiritual components of the mind, heart, and spirit. Dance can be one avenue of giving oneself to a spiritual pursuit. The Sufi mystical practice of whirling or spinning by dervishes is a means of abandoning ego to reach God. With left hand pointed up to the sky and the right hand toward the earth, receipt of God's blessing is then extended to the world through the performer. Walking meditation is a pursuit that can be done anywhere; one grounds to the earth and opens the senses. Yoga actually predated Hinduism. Though commonly practiced within the Hindu religion, yoga is independent of any particular religion and can be practiced for spiritual or nonreligious nonspiritual reasons. This text is about older people and some may wonder at including movement practice due to assumptions about what it means for the body to grow old. In many Asian cultures, older people are the ones who perform fan dances, yoga, tai chi, and other group exercise in public parks. Arise early and find a park in Beijing or Seoul. You will likely walk by a number of different groups of older people moving in unison.

A labyrinth walk offers potential for spiritual enlightenment. The labyrinth is an ancient practice developed from sacred geometry of the circle and the spiral. The symbolism of this exercise transcends any particular religion or spirituality. In fact the origins of the labyrinth were likely pagan, though today many labyrinths can be found near or in churches (Chartres, France) and public spaces (the city of Edinburgh, Scotland), and sometimes near health rehabilitation sites. There are several forms for the labyrinth (classical, Chartres, contemporary, concentric, Cretan, Reims, and Roman, among others) and it can be walked in many different ways. One can walk alone, with others, reflectively, quickly, and so on. There is no right way to walk it. Commonly one follows a twisting path to the center where one pauses and then returns, retracing steps.

This discussion of religious and spiritual practices offers only a beginning consideration of the many avenues to personal healing that can be successfully encouraged with older people. Although any practices should be vetted and directed by client need and interest, engagement of all types of therapeutic approaches can result in holistic restoration of body, mind, and soul. I close this chapter with these words—an urgent call to recover the self by feminist writer May Sarton.

Now I become myself. It's taken

Time, many years and places;

I have been dissolved and shaken,

Worn other people's faces,

Run madly, as if Time were there,

Terribly old, crying a warning,

Hurry, you will be dead before—

SUMMARY

A spiritual view of life suggests that no one escapes life's difficulties; many older people leave behind them a trail of false steps and starts among the sure ones. However, it is through the courage to live through those difficult moments that people can become their most authentic self. This also happens when therapists also demonstrate the courage to help clients face and heal their most vulnerable parts.

There are several levels to consider in working with clients around spiritual themes. This chapter identified philosophical approaches to psychotherapy and mid-range interventions of hope, faith, forgiveness, the value and meaning of home, the power of narrative in aging, and the use of ritual. The concept of home is something we seek throughout our lives and carries a spiritual resonance as we find it or make it in many new settings across the lifespan. The third section identified micro-level religious and spiritual helping strategies. A few of the practices highlighted were use of prayer by clients; writing or journaling; and visual, music, and movement therapy. All of these ideas can have place in spiritual work with older clients.

QUESTIONS FOR DISCUSSION

1. What philosophical, spiritual, or religious approaches can therapists make use of in addressing religious and spiritual themes of concern or interest to clients?

2. Why can hope be useful for older adults? Is it realistic to think that older people still have much to hope for? How might hope be brought into therapeutic work and on what does it center?

3. How is forgiveness an important topic in therapy with some older adults? In what way is forgiveness related to religion or spirituality? Can it also be used in more humanistic-centered ways? If so, how?

4. How might you use narrative therapy with clients? What classical stories, religious stories, myths, apocryphal legends, or other well-known tales can shed light on individual identity transformation at older age for particular clients you have worked or are working with?

5. What specific micro-level strategies can be useful in working with the religious or spiritual self in aging?

6. This chapter focuses mostly on inclusion of spirituality and religion with older people in salutary ways. However, at times religion or spirituality has been a source of suffering or struggle. Should therapists ignore asking about these in their work with clients? How would you invite and open discussion in these areas if desired by the client?

MEDITATION: BRINGING YOURSELF TOGETHER

We live in a time of many distractions. These distractions cause us to lose focus and diminish our energy and our power. Sometimes a part of this weakening is from the attachments we reasonably form, but then do not know how to disengage from. Close your eyes and breathe in and out slowly and deeply from your belly once or twice. Think about the places you have visited over the past month, the past year. Which places were significant for you in some way? Is it possible that you left a part of yourself, your mind or your thoughts, in that place? *Call yourself back from all of the places you have been to be fully present and alive in this moment.* This means mentally gathering up parts of yourself that have been strewn over time and across space. Visualize these pieces falling back into you and integrating with your innate self. When you are ready to come out of the meditation and open your eyes, feel the new strength that you hold. This is your Self, completely present.

EXPLORING YOUR SPIRITUALITY: THE LABYRINTH

Note: An example of a walking meditation is provided in Chapter 10. A walking meditation may be done in a rural setting, a garden, or any other outdoor location.

Labyrinths are ancient walking path designs that take one on a journey and back to the beginning. The labyrinth is said to have diverse spiritual origins in Celtic, pagan, and ancient Greek cultures. The labyrinth has been adopted by Christianity and can be found in many churches; probably the most famous labyrinth lies at the Chartres Cathedral in France. The labyrinth holds power for meditation and spiritual transformation. Its symbolism includes many aspects of journey and pilgrimage. Some see it as an allegorical way to the heart of God or the center of the Universe. As one enters the path of a labyrinth, one is subject to its twists and turns and blockages. In a sense it is an act of faith that one will successfully arrive at the center. One surrenders to the direction of the path, at times nearer the center and times further away, all the time moving forward. At the center, one can pause for a moment of meditation, but there is also a path outward. Although a person might just step away, the act of the return is as meaningful as the entrance. There are many labyrinthine patterns, Cretan (classical), Roman, Chartres, and others, and many ways to walk them. However, if one walks with some preparation, intent, or expectation, that openness may lead to new understandings. If a family or group walks together, it is likely they will have dissimilar experiences.

I recently came upon an old grass-overgrown Chartres-style labyrinth while on a silent retreat with my university. As I began to walk, a gentle drizzle also commenced. I was flooded from all of my senses—smell, sight, sounds of nature, my feet touching the path—and also with thoughts from every direction about the paradoxes of life from the macrocosm of the universe to the microcosm around me. I journaled about it afterward, although it was not easy to capture all of the ideas that saturated me along with the rain. I walked it twice and each time was different in terms of pace and thought streams. It was powerful and meaningful.

1. Do you have any experience with walking a labyrinth? If so, what was the context of that walk, who were you with, if anyone, and where was it located?

2. Is there any labyrinth near you that you can ask to walk or freely enter? If so, and you can arrange to walk it, create an intent that can be on a spectrum from being outside on a nice day to something you want to ask or experience. There are also small-sized labyrinths that may be traced with a finger

3. Walk this labyrinth or trace it.

4. Journal about your experience. Share this with someone else, if you want to.

EXPLORING YOUR SPIRITUALITY: BUILDING INTENTIONAL SPIRITUAL PLACES

In our world it is easy to stay perpetually distracted. It is much harder to return to our own center and to dwell in the present moment, as Thich Nhat Hanh (2012) would say. When we experience calm, we are more likely to find solutions to our concerns. Further, the built environment holds the power to support us or to drain our energy. That is why it is helpful to be aware or learn awareness about how we are affected by colors, sights, and sounds. Where we place things can also matter: the positions things hold in relation to each other can make a difference in resulting feelings. When a place is cluttered, that can exacerbate anxiety. In fact a few people experience sensory defensiveness, heightened awareness to senses that can lead to avoidance, anxiety, hypervigilance, or other reactions and may require this awareness more than most. Feng shui is one process that helps facilitate good energy (chi) in the places we live. Short verses we create, called *gathas* in Buddhist thought, can be posted around us and call us back to mindful thought.

Setting apart a small space where you can sit helps facilitate mindfulness, especially if it is a place primarily used for this purpose. In this way you make it sacred. When you go there, you are primed to dwell in your center and with repetition will get to this point more quickly. Meditation like this is not for thinking, but for resting (though not sleeping). This space can help us break through

our perceptions and see things as they are in a clearer manner. Hanh (2012) suggests that most of us do not have a room for breathing. We have no house altars on which we may pose sacred images (pictures of Christ, the Buddha, or family members), a candle, a stone, or other meaningful objects. The use of such an altar may not mean we worship these things, just that we offer our respect to them. This room we create should be a place protected from anger, a place of peace. Use of a bell can invite calm, and in a household, anyone can be the bell master when things become chaotic or confusing. The bell can call us back to our breathing; three breaths can call us back to ourselves.

If there is tension in a household, Hanh (2012) suggests we offer the cake in the refrigerator. It doesn't matter if there is a real cake, but tea or coffee, or anything good to eat in the refrigerator, may be brought out and served. As people share in the drinks or food, healing can begin.

1. Think about your ideal place for breathing. What objects would it contain? Who else might be involved in creating this place with you? How and when might you use it?

2. How can having and using this place change you?

3. Journal about your thoughts.

WEBSITES

Centering Prayer

http://www.centeringprayer.com/

Fr. Thomas Keating provides information about centering prayer on this website.

Dreams and Elder Initiations

http://www.secondjourney.org/
itin/2011Fall/11Fall_Moody.htm

This site includes thoughts by Harry Rick Moody, long with AARP, and a visionary in spirituality and aging.

International Forgiveness Institute

http://internationalforgiveness.com/

Founded by Robert Enright, this site offers different kinds of information for those wanting to learn about forgiveness.

Greater Good: The Science of a Meaningful Life

http://greatergood.berkeley.edu/

This is a very richly endowed site that looks at core themes of gratitude, altruism, compassion, empathy, forgiveness, mindfulness, and happiness. With a commitment to both practice and science, this offers many materials on living a meaningful life. Among them is a free online course on the science of happiness.

Late Works

http://www.newyorker.com/magazine/2006/08/07/late-works

This is a piece by John Updike on aging artists.

National Center for Creative Aging

http://www.creativeaging.org/about-ncca-0

The National Center for Creative Aging showcases the vibrant relationship between creative expression and aging. Under the Programs and People tab can be found nearly 40 page-length stories of older adults who are have successfully interwoven the arts into their own life and the lives of others. The Research Center for Arts and Culture under the Resources tab contains many terrific downloadable reports. Browse the site.

Path to Forgiveness

http://www.evworthington-forgiveness.com/diy-workbooks/

This site features three 80-page workbooks on becoming a more forgiving person, forgiving oneself and breaking free from the past, and on humility—becoming a more humble person. This site also has links to a number of related journal articles by Worthington. His homepage at http://www.evworthington-forgiveness.com/ is worth exploring.

The Power of Forgiveness

http://www.thepoweroforgiveness.com/understanding/index.html

With support from the Fetzer Institute and the Templeton Foundation, this site has a number of free resources available from quite a number of authors and researchers, including information on Buddhism and forgiveness.

The Positive Aging Newsletter

http://www.taosinstitute.net/positive-aging-newsletter

This newsletter is edited by Kenneth and Mary Gergen. Kenneth Gergen has made especially strong contributions to the aging literature, especially social constructionism, over many years. The newsletter is published several times a year and is a great resource of spiritual clinical work.

SorryWatch

http://www.sorrywatch.com/about-sorrywatch/

This site analyzes apologies in the news, history, and culture. It suggests which are better than others and why this is so. In this sense it is a teaching site. It also has links to information about different types of apologies and, importantly, a process for apologizing.

Spiritual Competency Resource Center

http://www.spiritualcompetency.com/

This center by David Lukoff offers culturally and ethically sensitive applications of spirituality in mental health. The center offers a free course on forgiveness (*Forgiveness III: Psychological Research on*

Forgiveness) and other material on self-compassion, including work of Neff and Germer.

Wellbriety Journey to Forgiveness

https://www.youtube.com/watch?v=vZwF9NnQbWM

This 2011 well-done hour-plus film (also available for free) teaches about historical intergenerational trauma. Heart-felt statements are given by older people about their experience and results of those experiences, including how their religion was discouraged through the abuse. This also recognizes unresolved grief, using the culture to heal, and the inherent strengths and blessings of a people.

Writing Our Way Out of Trouble: Sue Reynolds at TEDxStouffville

http://www.youtube.com/watch?v=kvb2QV0xMUs

Sue Reynolds discusses writing for therapeutic benefit.

RECOMMENDED READING

Chase, S. (2011). *Nature as spiritual practice.* Grand Rapids, MI: Wm. B. Eerdmans.

This excellent book enlivens our awareness of how we respond to nature and how it evidences a Creator. It also includes discussion of closing the loop or sacred circle by giving back.

Foster, R. J. (1978). *Celebration of discipline: The path to spiritual growth.* San Francisco, CA: Harper & Row.

This book explains the spiritual disciplines from a Christian perspective. This might enhance knowledge of both practitioner and client.

Foster, R. J. (1992). *Prayer: Finding the heart's true home.* San Francisco, CA: Harper.

Many forms of prayer and their application are explored in this focused book.

Hamma, R. M. (2004). *In times of grieving: Prayers of comfort & consolation.* Notre Dame, IN: Ave Maria Press

This short book offers specific prayers for many different situations of distress including grief.

Lee, M. Y., Ng, S., Leung, P., & Chan, C. L. (2009). *Integrative body-mind-spirit social work: An empirically based approach to assessment and treatment.* New York, NY: Oxford University Press.

This comprehensive text covers new ground in discussion of integrative practice. It elucidates a foundational philosophy of care and treatment while also offering many suggestions for practice.

McGaa, E. (2004). *Nature's way: Native wisdom for living in balance with the earth.* New York, NY: HarperCollins.

Using paradigms reflective of different animals (eagle, bear, lion, wolf, orca, owl, etc.), this writer, speaking from within an American Indian tradition, addresses some individual but mostly larger macro-level concerns about honoring and restoring our environments.

Nelson, J. (2009). *Psychology, religion, and spirituality.* New York: London: Springer.

This text offers a very detailed look at conceptual, historical, and empirical aspects of prayer in Chapter 13. It also discusses differences in contemplative and centering prayer as well as prayer and the true self. It offers equally detailed instruction on different forms of meditation.

Nepo, M. (2012). *Seven thousand ways to listen: Staying close to what is sacred.* New York, NY: Atria.

This book offers many worthwhile suggestions on how to engage in spiritual conversations.

CHAPTER EIGHT

SPIRITUALITY, RELIGION, AND HEALTH

The begging bowl of the Buddha represents . . . the ultimate
theological root of the belief not just in the right to beg, but
in openness to the gifts of all beings as an expression of
the interdependence of all beings. . . . The Christian spirit is
one of compassion, of responsibility and of commitment. It
cannot be indifferent to suffering.

—Merton (2008, pp. 30–36)

When you realize where you come from,
You naturally become tolerant,
Disinterested, amused, kindhearted as a grandmother,
Dignified as a king.
Immersed in the wonder of the Tao,
You can deal with whatever life brings you,
And when death comes, you are ready.

—Lao-tzu

In this chapter, health, failing health, suffering, biological aging, and diminishment are addressed from a religious and spiritual perspective. Four religious traditions discussed in Chapter 5—Judaism, Christianity, Islam, and indigenous American Indian religion— and their approaches to healing are explored in more depth. Differences between fast and slow medicine are explained. Research on religion related to older people is briefly surveyed. Caregiving is a significant component of many relationships in aging, and its spiritual opportunities for building and strengthening relationships are examined.

DEFINITIONS OF HEALTH

As people age, physical health becomes increasingly a matter of conscious concern. This occurs particularly where attention begins to linger over less reliable body part functioning. But as the World Health Organization (WHO, 1946) makes clear in its definition of health, more than mere physical well-being is involved: "It is a complete state of physical, mental and social well-being, and not merely the absence of disease or infirmity" (p. 100). This definition has not since been amended. In their groundbreaking McArthur study on health and aging, Rowe and Kahn (1998) similarly define healthy aging as low risk of disease and disease-related disability, high mental and physical functioning, and active engagement with life. But what is missing in both definitions is the idea that health exists on a continuum and that many people live satisfying lives in spite of chronic illness. That they do so can in many cases be attributed to their drawing on spiritual or religious resources.

Several other definitions of the concept of health have been formulated. Health is considered "a dynamic state of well-being . . . which satisfies the demands of life commensurate with age, culture, and personal responsibility" (Bircher, 2005, p. 336); others see it as a condition free of disease and disability and "a basic and universal human right" denoting a justice element (Saracci, 1997, p. 1410). The Aboriginal Health and Medical Research Council (AHMRC) of New South Wales, Australia suggests that individuals who achieve their multidimensional health potential are able to engender the well-being of their communities (AHMRC, n.d.). This suggests regard for an aspirational aspect of health that lies in interrelatedness with a larger group. Where people are members of caring communities, health is more easily realized. Another view suggests that balanced, integrated energy systems regulate health and this is generated through such practices as traditional Chinese medicine (TCM), Ayurvedic medicine, acupuncture, and many other mind-body integrative systems (Lee, Ng, Leung, & Chan, 2009; Saylor, 2004). When health is considered more broadly than physical well-being, the range of protocols and practices that can result in good and poor health outcomes becomes more extensive and includes the complexity of all dimensions of life. An inclusive approach that considers the intersections of these different dimensions is one conceptualization of spiritual health. Another more narrow definition might look at only questions of meaning and suffering.

Spiritual health has not yet been adequately defined in the literature. This is first, because it is difficult to operationalize, and second, because it is still emerging out of a period of obscurity and marginalization of religion and spirituality. Even the social factors related to health have received greater attention and now been more widely incorporated into research studies. Spiritual health minimally refers to possessing a sense of inner peace and equanimity. But it usually implies more than that, including having a sense of purpose or meaning, living in alignment with one's own values and ethics, and allowing others to have their values (not being distressed or distraught with that) even if they are different. It includes compassion and care for others, self-compassion, and forgiveness for self and others.

An idea related to spiritual health is the concept of medical spirituality. Medical spirituality observes the effects of spirituality on physical health and relief of suffering. Bessinger and Kuhne (2002) suggest it should be an interdisciplinary venture that has a goal of integrating the complexity of spirituality with medicine, the precursors of illness as well as the consequences. Medical spirituality should be "evidence-based, non-sectarian, and theologically neutral" (p. 1385). Ethical boundaries should be observed, principally a nonsectarian approach in general medical care supplemented by faith-specific approaches, when invited by the patient or client.

AGING AND THE BODY: FAILING HEALTH

Many people today are growing old in good health. However, as people age, chronic diseases become more likely, especially heart disease, cancer, effects of stroke, diabetes, and arthritis. But aging brings other common problems as well, among which are the following:

- *Loss of flexibility.* With age, muscles lose cartilage density and bones lose calcium. Tendons become less elastic and the body loses efficiency and fluidity of movement. Sometimes people experience stiffness when they move or resistance to their intended action.

- *Weariness and slowing down.* Weariness can take at least two forms. It may include feeling sleepy and having difficulty staying awake through the day, often due to either interrupted sleep or medication side effects. Weariness can also mean experiencing fatigue/weakness and the need to move more slowly. Fatigue constitutes the inability to perform a task after multiple repetitions when the body wears out, or fatigue may involve difficulty initiating a task at all.

- *Balance and gait.* As people age, they may experience more difficulty locating themselves in space. They can become dizzy. Sensitivity and reaction time of the inner ear apparatus become less accurate, leading to balance problems. The peripheral nerves (nerves that conduct signals to muscles) conduct more slowly and reflexes are slower. Length of stride and sureness of foot placement may also vary, leading to a shuffling effect.

- *Decreased reserve capacity.* People require more time to recover from illness and other physical strains. They no longer bounce back as quickly and completely from temporary physical setbacks.

Still, despite these assaults, on a global measure of physical health (On a scale of 1–5, with 5 being excellent health, how would you rank your health today?), most older people rate their health as 4-very good or 5-excellent (Idler, Hudson, & Leventhal, 1999). They consistently rate their own health higher than their physicians would. They report better health than peers, even if physician ratings might not concur. A biographical explanation of health (Woodward, 2008) accounts for health status based on life story, history, and holism. Thus health is not determined by physical conditions alone, but by linkages with mental and spiritual outlooks as well. Older people with a positive outlook on their lives, who are at peace within themselves and with their friends and family, may be better able to manage health problems. Achieving harmony of body, mind, and spirit can mean that one facet of the triad may be somewhat out of balance without causing severe injury to the system.

Activities of Daily Living, Instrumental
Activities of Daily Living, and Health

In the aging experience, there are common health assessment tools that determine need for outside assistance. Activities of daily living (ADLs) and instrumental activities of daily living (IADLs) are two ways that functional capacity is assessed (Katz, 1983). ADLs are considered primary activities of living; the six basic ones are bathing or showering, dressing, ability to feed oneself, mobility (whether on one's own or with assistance, such as use of a cane or wheelchair), ability to use a toilet on one's own, and continence. In order to live independently, more complex skills, IADLs, are required. The term *IADL activities* is behavioral language for how one interacts with the environment. These are commonly assessed as ability to manage finances, using public transit or driving, shopping, preparing meals, ability to use the telephone or other communication devices, managing medications, and doing light housework such as laundry. ADLs and IADLs are particularly important in determining whether an older person has the capacity to live independently or requires assistance in certain areas.

Health for older people can be recognized in three key ways: absence of disease, resilience when illness appears, and ability to function in daily life. Absence of disease or illness becomes less likely as people grow older, although it is possible. They are, at the oldest ages, more likely to have had an illness and to have recovered from it. Longevity itself signifies older adults have been sufficiently hardy to live past middle age and early old age. Thus, it is likely that they bear innate physical resilience which can come from both a good gene pool and decisions throughout life to care for their bodies in refraining from smoking or limiting use of alcohol. However, this is not always the case, as some centenarians gleefully suggest that they eat and drink what they please. Ability to function is the most important marker of health in aging. Although care facilities and assisted living facilities exist (sometimes conjoined with independent living in a continuing care retirement community [CCRC]), they are not yet appealing enough to see older people eagerly stream into them when they reach the age of 65 unless other physical conditions warrant necessary consideration of alternative housing options.

Most older people prefer to live independently or with friends and family. Would there be a way to fashion congregate housing for older people so that it would become a more attractive option? Possibly, but discussing the financial means to do so, if not the environmental means, would be beyond the scope of this book. In a compassionate society, there may be ways to create spiritual as well as functional communities for older persons beyond CCRCs that offer weekend religious services and limited activities. This is an exercise for the creative imagination as it lies beyond almost anything present today. The Green House model from the Eden Alternative Project of Dr. Bill Thomas may approach this, with its small housing units (often 20 or fewer) where caregivers knock before entering, as they would in respecting the boundaries of a single-family home. There, where person-centered care is provided, a *Shabazz* ("royal falcon," in Persian) provides both physical care and nurturing, a sort of cross between an aide and a pastoral care minister.

Diminishment

The physical decline evident in aging is sometimes referred to as "diminishment." This contrasts with the time when the health of the body did not call attention to itself and was largely taken for granted. Diminishment includes periods where energy is not sustained, as well as decreasing energy levels. Fatigue sets in and can limit ability to meet life goals. Hearing may be less acute, and vision less sharp. Twinges of pain may accompany small movements. One consolation is that this is considered a normal aging experience. Although the mind likes to think of itself as young and vibrant, the body suggests otherwise. Diminishment is a universal aspect of the effect of time passing.

How can one make peace with these changes? Although some may assume that as the body shows signs of wear and tear, the spirit can still take a larger perspective of life and living, this is not always true. Certain individuals have transcended imprisonment or reduced living spaces, such as Nelson Mandela or Aung San Suu Kyi, to become an enlarged self who holds a focused sense of mission. Some people do seem to grow more spiritual with time and move toward transcendence, as suggested by Tornstam's model discussed in Chapter 4. Yet aging/physical diminishment and spiritual growth do not necessarily stand in inverse relationship. Many people find it hard to transcend physical limitation. Instead, perhaps an integration of one's current physical condition with other life goals can lead to acceptance which is the more spiritual way. Simone de Beauvoir, in her book *The Coming of Age* (1972), in fact suggested that coming to terms with aging occurred only through commitment to a cause that would continue beyond one's own lifetime. Victor Hugo avers, "Fire is seen in the eyes of the young, but it is light that we see in the old man's eyes" (de Beauvoir, p. 206). Ignoring infirmity, illness, or disability will not necessarily improve it (and could make it worse if treatments are evaded). But instead, saying to oneself, "This is what is and the condition under which I have life now," can lead to acceptance which may alter life goals slightly but also make accessible new ideas and understanding.

A holistic approach includes more than acceptance, however. Assessment and then activities based on that assessment are useful. One tool to assess frailty is the Study of Osteoporotic Fractures (SOF) Frailty Tool (Ensrud et al., 2009). This tool assesses level of frailty through three simple measures: a weight loss of 5% in the past year, the inability to rise from a chair five times without the use of arms, and a negative response to the question, "Do you feel full of energy?" Another similar measure is the FRAIL scale (van Kan, Rolland, & Morley, 2008) based on five domains: fatigue, resistance (ability to climb a single flight of stairs), ambulation (ability to walk about one block), illnesses (more than five), and loss of weight of more than 5%. Affirmation of two or more suggests a condition of pre-frailty while three or more suggests a state of frailty.

Fast Medicine and Slow Medicine

Medicine has many facets. Traditional or conventional medicine offers both benefits and risks. Traditional *fast* medicine, medicine governed by third-party insurers, pressures practitioners to spend little time with patients and to prescribe rounds of medicine based on standard protocols and expensive surgeries. The task to preserve *quality* of life is sometimes nearly lost amid rounds of ever more invasive treatment, difficult-to-manage medication side effects, and financial incentives to treat. Two examples will illustrate the problems: insertion of a peg feeding tube in end-stage dementia and starting dialysis for people with multiple health problems over age 75. First, with use of a feeding tube, mortality in the year after placement was 64% at a median of 56 days (Merel, Demers, & Vig, 2014). There is increased social isolation (patients are more likely to be left alone) and risk of complications. Hand feeding would be one option that would also foster interconnection, but it takes time. Second, with hemodialysis, 61% of older patients regretted their decision and had substantial symptom burden that affected health-related quality of life (Davison & Jhangri, 2010). Although there was an intervention that could be prescribed for those over age 75 needing hemodialysis and many physicians recommended it, the outcome did not preserve life quality.

A fee-for-service health system can have perverse outcomes, such as financial incentives to offer certain treatments to patients. Treating less invasively or not treating at all can result in more satisfying outcomes. *Slow medicine* refers to a more integrative approach to treatment, one that encourages medical practitioners to ask questions that lead to deeper awareness of individual patient needs. This approach can help patients recover optimal health for their conditions. This includes attention to environment, human contact, and shared decision making. It is a more methodical and thoughtful approach to treatment that is watchful for unintended consequences and includes palliative medicine practice when that is appropriate. Slow-medicine practice, with its alignment with holistic treatment, reflects a spiritual approach. Sweet (2012), in her book about practice of medicine in a county hospital that treated marginalized groups, suggested that we should consider healing like tending a garden. This more measured approach fosters quiet spaces, healthy food, humor, and Hildegard of Bingen's "tincture of time" in a low-tech, high touch healing place. Some hospitals are now being redesigned with greater attention to environment in order to foster healing similar to the hospices of the Middle Ages, though more advanced and modern.

HISTORICAL VIEWS ON RELIGION AND HEALTH

Before Hippocrates (c. 460–377 BCE), health was considered to be a gift from the gods or divinely bestowed. In ancient Mesopotamia and Egypt, the origins of disease were thought to lie in supernatural powers as well as malevolent humans, violation of taboos, and other reasons unknown, but often attributed to displeasure or capriciousness of the gods. Cure was sought through amulet, chants, and herbs, forms of folk medicine still present in many cultures. Asclepius was the god of healing in Greece and pilgrims would come to his temple seeking help after purification and a small sacrifice (Ferngren, 2012). Healing came in the form of incubation which involved spending the night at the temple where the pilgrim might be healed through a dream in which Asclepius appeared to cure or advise. Apparently enough healings ensued, found in archeological evidence of earthen models of limbs, eyes, ears, and so on, that the practice continued. Even now in modern times, some churches, especially in Central and South America, feature rooms of walls of small metal legs, arms, crutches, and other symbolic tokens left by those happily healed.

Hippocrates instituted the valuable idea of natural observation and examination of the body through such practices as palpitation and auscultation (listening to internal sounds through a stethoscope); at this juncture, medicine moved toward science and craft (Breitenfeld, Jurasic, & Breitenfeld, 2014). He purportedly wrote a text called *The Sacred Disease* that expressed an argument against assigning control of disease (probably epilepsy) to the divine, thus rendering it without cure. Instead he advocated active investigation and treatment of the natural causes of disease. The Greeks thought health signified equilibrium or harmony among all physical elements such as body fluids and matter. Disease was a disruption of this equilibrium. At the time, the four humors— blood, phlegm, yellow bile, and black bile—were considered the basic components of the body. Bringing them into proportionate balance and thus restoring harmony were the necessary antecedents of health.

During the Middle Ages in Europe, monastic hospitals arose combining care of the body with cure for the soul. According to the Oxford Latin dictionary, the separate meanings of *cure* and *care* both came from the Latin word *curare*, which means "to take care of." The original meanings of the noun were *care, concern, responsibility*, and especially *spiritual care*. Charity was one of the doctrines of Christianity. Benedictine monks and nuns, particularly the Sisters of Charity, formed hospitals not only for their members but also for the community, in fulfillment of their mission (Risse, 1999). These hospitals were designed with a footprint similar to churches and cathedrals. The rhythms of life in these hospitals echoed those of religious life, with beds in sight of an altar and religious ceremonies as part of treatment. Some of the expectations for patients in those times included confession to purify the soul and avoid damnation. In the Middle Ages it was thought that the infirmity of the body was due to the condition of the soul. Physical illness was thus a sign that the body was not in harmony; some spiritual wrong had been committed, such as pride, envy, gluttony, lust, anger, greed, or sloth. Illness was viewed as punishment for sin. Echoes of this perspective persist today. Residents were well-treated, however. Medicine was not professionalized, but herbs (some out of the Arab world, which was quite advanced in the sciences at this time) were often used, as well as fresh food, and opportunities for frequent bathing were available. During this period religion and medicine were clearly interwoven, perhaps not always to the patient's benefit.

In ancient times there was general acceptance of the complementary nature of both religious healing and healing through the hands of physicians. However, as medicine advanced in the late 19th and early 20th centuries, many doctors chose to rely on science and eschew religion. These two areas became mostly separate spheres of influence, in line with increasing secularization within the larger society itself.

This brief mention of historical renderings of religion and health suggests the tension apparent today. Medicine representing scientific empiricism, and religion representing belief and transcendence, do not always accept the terrain of the other when it comes to maintaining or restoring health. That may generally not be an issue, except where personal beliefs are devalued, rendering support of holistic health and complementary and alternative medicine practices at risk. A holistic health model accepts the influence of body, mind, and spirit on achieving wellness. This model recognizes the power of the mind and spirit to influence healing processes. One pragmatic example is that some hospitals have been designed or retrofitted to include noise reduction, interfaith or meditation chapels, fountains of water or some type of water feature, benches located in common spaces to invite conversation, flower gardens, peaceful spaces, attention to lighting and availability of natural light, and art for visual beauty and reflection.

FROM HOLISTIC HISTORICAL RENDERINGS TO MODERN CULTURAL HEALTH CONSIDERATIONS

Health cures in some ages were a second priority, especially in times of decimation from plague and other perils. In those ages, there was little time to practice holistic treatments other than application of prayer. One recent concern in the framing of individual health in the larger context of epidemiology is the nature of the cultural environment (Aronowitz, Deener, Keene, Schnittker, & Tach, 2015). Minority cultures may accept practices that test the boundaries of the dominant culture's social as well as medical suitability standards. A majority culture may consider its health practices valid while labeling health practices of other groups not legitimate or healthy. This occurred, for instance, with the use of peyote (a substance found in certain desert cacti having hallucinogenic properties) in the Native American church. For a time, usage was prohibited by law until the American Indian Religious Freedom Act Amendment in 1996 affirmed its use in bona fide traditional ceremonial purposes. This is one example of a cultural difference that led to competing views. Cultural and religious interpretations of illness can lead to requests for reduced treatment or different kinds of treatment than medicine would typically recommend (McCormick et al., 2012). One example of this occurs with those professing to be Jehovah's Witnesses who decline blood transfusions.

The subjective illness experience is different from the actual process of the disease (Kleinman, 2013). Kleinman suggests that in privileging the story of the illness itself, professionals have separated "meaning from economic, emotional, and relational contexts and lived experiences of suffering" (p. 1376). The process of illness narrative construction itself is dependent on personal and cultural experiences that may affect healing (Mattingly & Garro, 2000). Some health practices are legitimized as the preferred approach for everyone, when instead they may represent majority views. Evidence can bolster grounds for medical recommendations, except when available evidence falls short of answering important health questions because many cures are still unknown. This can lead to a devaluation of certain cultural views rather than respect for their traditions. Alternative medicine and spiritual practices are frequently marginalized, although mindfulness practices are beginning to gain greater research support.

Closing the gap in physical health disparities of minority groups remains a challenge, particularly where certain culturally consonant health practices may be important spiritually and religion or spirituality is integrated into cultural views. By contrast, some health practices advocated for spiritual reasons such as vegetarian-preferred diets and limits on smoking and alcohol common among the Seventh-Day Adventists, Latter Day Saints (Mormons), Hindus, and other religious groups are broadly supported in the larger culture and their health benefits undergirded by evidence-based research. Another value of religious traditions is that they can provide guidance and support to believers that can assist in alleviating the guilt of families who must sometimes make difficult end-of-life decisions for loved ones in health-related contexts.

SUFFERING

To live involves suffering. Expectations of our ideal life cannot always be met, especially the more specifically this ideal is conceived. Sometimes people hold dreams they cannot accomplish. To live a longer life can involve greater suffering, for one has more chances of interactions or events with negative outcomes to occur, especially negative health events or deaths of significant others. Lack of motivation and obstacles to learning, such as from a traumatic childhood event, can create or recreate adverse circumstances that may lead to alcohol dependence, any other addiction, or self-destructive actions. However, a measure apart from longevity alone might suggest that with long life, people learn how to relax expectations, to give greater weight to momentary joy, and otherwise to experience life more deeply. Thus the weight of misfortunes that ensue is made more bearable. Developmentally it is important for people to be able to form attachments, but also to detach, to engage and to relinquish—a subtle process of giving and receiving that mirrors the heartbeat and the respiratory process which are life-sustaining. At the far end of the continuum of life and death, toward the death phase, palliative care and hospice as well as other institutional settings may become places of divestment, where patients learn to let go in a supportive environment. Alongside divesting, what remains may be richly savored: appetizing food, pleasant views, conversations with friends, crafting a legacy, or involvement in life completion tasks.

Spiritual suffering may include questions about God's presence or absence. *Theodicy* refers to the question of why a God/Universal Being/Sacred Source who is good would allow evil to exist. Evil can be applied to many actions, but illness may also be addressed as an unexpected evil. This question is often raised in relation to disclosure of a terminal diagnosis or a sudden and cataclysmic loss. In antiquity, illness was frequently moralized as being sent to sinners as retribution for sin. Thus religion did not always invite a compassionate response to suffering but rather reinforced a sense of shame. However, in the Middle Ages religious groups interpreted their duty as caring for the sick while also offering the person who was ill a period of introspection. Even today, echoes of the connection between sin and suffering still continue. This question of theodicy is largely unanswerable for believers other than from a stance of faith. What is the outcome? Does life-threatening illness emerge from natural human and environmental limits that give patients and other persons a chance to reflect, learn, and cope through prayer and use of social networks? Any purpose or meaning ascribed to the illness can only be assessed individually by the sufferer who has sole jurisdiction over its value. Mental health practitioners and others particularly need to listen to these faith-formed and existential inquiries that cannot be dismissed, but may eventually lead to personal insights and growth.

Physical pain is defined as actual tissue injury or localized bodily discomfort, but it can also include perceptions of that discomfort that sensory neurons convey to the brain. That is why some forms of pain can be alleviated through relaxation responses, meditation, exercise, or other active management. However, suffering is also multidimensional; physical pain understandably grabs attention, but emotional, psychological, cultural, spiritual, and socioeconomic forms may manifest. Emotional pain may emerge from depression and its constellation of features such as low self-worth and listlessness. Psychological pain can come out of trauma, failure to meet life goals, and negative self-attributions. Cultural forms of pain may come through lack of acceptance when norms are violated. Spiritual pain appears when questions of meaning and life purpose or the failure to sense God's presence overwhelm. Socioeconomic forms of pain include the effects of joblessness or marginalization due to issues of race or class that land atop health vulnerabilities. None of these are absent in aging. Dame Cicely Saunders, founder of hospice, perceived the need to identify and address total pain (Clark, 1999; Saunders, 2001).

Older adults suffer when friends and family members die and they edge ever nearer to being the last of their cohort alive. This is another of the many nonphysical forms of suffering. To outlive friends is a longevity success, but paradoxically also a failure when few close friends can be companions to their end.

Not all pain leads to suffering and not all suffering is related to personal pain. However, pain can heighten fear, decrease hope, and interfere with disease management compliance. Uncontrolled pain reduces resilience. Physical pain can be secondary to disease, an effect of treatment, or temporary such as from a headache. Studies of hospice patients have suggested that some hospice patients who do experience minimal distress from physical symptoms still suffer physically and nonphysically (Abraham, Kutner, & Beaty, 2006). In a sample of patients suffering from advanced cancer, qualitative interviews suggested that 50.5% of those who suffered identified causes of suffering from psychological, existential, and social issues (Wilson et al., 2007). However, nearly half of the larger sample did not perceive themselves to be suffering. Other dimensions of pain include length and intensity. Physical pain can be acute, related to a specific event, or chronic, defined as more than three months (Ars & Montero, 2004). An analgesic plan can be developed beyond the use of drugs to resolve more than physical injury. Although we seldom hear the word *analgesic* apart from administration of drugs, using different language can sometimes foster creativity in development of treatment for all forms of suffering. When the specificity needed for prescription of drugs is considered—dosage, form of administration, frequency, and so on—it might be helpful to apply these same kinds of specificity with other treatment considered for spiritual pain— such as what, when, who—with attention to the preferences of the patient and discussion of his or her total pain outlook.

Toward the end of life, effective pain relief permits consciousness that provides the element of time. This time differs from ordinary time in its greater scope of awareness. A period of pain-free living can facilitate the healing of relationships even as they end. Fragmented relationships can reintegrate, leaving the dying person with a sense of wholeness. If patients desire, they may express spiritual pain, desolation, or longing. Formal caregivers, family, and friends may not be able to resolve these issues, but their presence and openness to hear difficult non-normative things can bring a type of resolution, saying in effect, "We love you and you matter." The patient's wishes for solitude should also be honored. Some dying people need privacy and space for inner work. This is not a rejection of significant others, but just the dying person's preferred path. Some dying persons may, for example, wish to hold a hand at their death, while others will send family away. Buddhists fear that being touched will either bring them back as they are dying, or keep their soul from leaving.

At times it is the professionals who suffer. They witness the suffering of those for whom they care; they report that emotional and spiritual forms of suffering may be intrinsic to dying for a few. Patients can be burdened by intense sense of loss and impending loss, death anxiety, existential fear, abandonment or loneliness, fear of dependency, concern about familial coping and the financial future, or other future for loved ones (Beng et al., 2015; Halifax, 2008; Hanks, 2010). Professionals may feel uneasy at being unable to relieve suffering as they have been trained to do, and thus feel ineffective. At a minimum, medicine as well as other professions ought to recognize all forms of suffering, even when treatment of some forms is outside of competency. A doctor who would be fully a physician and not a technician should also be a knower of souls, not least his own (Kass, 1980). Validating the suffering that their patients feel, being present and offering support instead of alienation and distance, can assist in transforming the experience of suffering to one of acceptance for the patient, the patient's family, and even the professional.

VIEWS OF HEALTH FROM RELIGIOUS PERSPECTIVES

Judaism and Healing

In the Jewish tradition, all healing represents a demonstration of God's miraculous power. Jewish perspectives on health and healing include the relevance of rituals and sacred texts for modern quandaries, the value of community, and participation in daily life (Levin & Prince, 2011). Even when the possibility of medical cure is small, many Jewish people will prefer continuation of medical treatment (Mackler, 2007). The Torah, Talmud, and Midrash each provide prescriptions for health and healing (Levin & Prince, 2011). In Judaism it is understood that there is a moral duty to heal those in need (Cohn-Sherbok, 2012). Preservation of life as well as healing are thus fundamental traditional values. A traditional prayer for the sick asks God to grant both healing of the body and healing of the soul, suggesting that health is not determined by the body alone, but by the complex interplay of body and spirit. Maimonides, from the 12th century, is one of many Jewish figures who developed expectations for the role of the healer, including the duty of the physician to restore health so individuals could be in salubrious relationships with God.

In Judaism, people are invited to fulfill their responsibilities even if a positive outcome is not assured. The Talmud and rabbinic sources suggest that human life is of such great value that it is permissible to ignore Sabbath proscriptions and other rules to save it (Cohn-Sherbok, 2012). Every instant of life is viewed as possessing infinite value. Both physical and mental pain should be addressed if possible, even when infractions of religious law might be needed to do so. Visiting the sick (*bikkur holim*) is especially valued. The Talmud (B. Nedarim 39b–40a) affirms that those who visit the sick relieve their burden and those who fail to visit increase it. Even through adversity, resilience has been a trait of the Jewish people, exemplified in the return of the exiled people to a Jewish state in both antiquity and modern times (Israel). "Blessed are you Adonai, source of our health and strength" proclaims one common prayer (Address, 2012, p. 28). Judaism evinces a reverence for life that persists, thus authority is given in the Torah for people to heal and not stand idly by (Levin & Meador, 2012). In early Jewish medical practice there was a tradition of using magical spells, incantations, and exorcism of demons; remnants of this philosophical view may still persist. However, healing today is viewed as a partnership between physician and God, and treatment is based on medical evidence.

Illness and suffering are addressed in the Torah and the Tanach, which stands for Torah (5 Books of Moses), N'vi'im (prophets), and Ketuvim (writings). Although illness may be a form of divine punishment, God is also a healer, as recognized in Exodus (15:26) and Deuteronomy (28:21–68). The book of Job sought to separate illness from sin, but the question of why bad things happen to those who are good has continued through the ages. This question is unanswerable, but the task for Jewish people is to assist God in repairing the world (*tikkun olam*) as they also work to repair the individual soul (*tikkun hanefesh*). The Shekinah, an indwelling presence and a source of nurture and support, has in modern times assumed the feminine aspects of God and is one of many symbols of recovery for Jewish women in particular (Spiegel, 1996). The Jewish *halakha* (law) is a way of working toward one's own healing through understanding models in Biblical heroes, liturgy in the observance of Jewish holidays and rituals, and mystic approaches that include transformation and redemption (Bronstein, 1999).

A Talmud text describing Johanan, a 3rd-century scholar, has this to say about the value of community in healing:

> *Hiyya b. Abba fell ill and R. Johanan went in to visit him. He (R. Johanan) said to him: "Are your sufferings welcome/beloved to you?" He replied: "Neither they nor their reward." He said to him: "Give me your hand." He gave him his hand and he (R. Johanan) raised (healed) him.*

> *R. Johanan once fell ill and R. Hanina went in to visit him. He (R. Hanina) said to him: "Are your sufferings welcome/beloved to you?" He replied: "Neither they nor their reward." He said to him: "Give me your hand." He gave him his hand and he raised him. Why could not R. Johanan raise himself? They replied: "The prisoner cannot free himself from jail."* (Levin & Meador, 2012, p. 104)

Along with acknowledgement of the healing power resident in community, *responsa* (questions) can be asked of Jewish authorities who then look to Jewish traditions to find knowledge that can apply to current circumstance (Address, 2012). This seems similar to Islamic *fatwas* that also search out religious guidance for modern situations. Hope in Judaism, as in Christianity, centers on what can properly be hoped for, even in the case of a life-limiting illness. Causes for hope may exist in visiting with family and passing on stories to the next generation or just having and knowing one's ability to cope with whatever comes. Participation in holidays and festivals such as Yom Kippur (with its prayers for forgiveness) and Sukkot (abundance/harvest) provide present meaning and continuity through health and illness.

Jesus and Healing in Christianity

Early Judea formed the geographic boundaries of the life of Jesus and comprised a culture where harmful worldviews about disease were prominent: disease was often regarded as punishment for sin, the sin of ancestors' actions, chastening discipline from God, or a test of loyalty to God, among other beliefs. The residue of some of these viewpoints still may prevail in the minds of some these centuries later. Jesus taught that in the ideal society or Kingdom of God, disease had no place. So Jesus sought to cure all manner of disability as well as to preach the gospel to the poor. He also did this simply because he was a compassionate being.

There are a number of instances of healing provided in the New Testament of the Bible. For older people affiliated with a Christian faith, these can be particularly compelling examples that bring hope. The gospel of Mark is generally viewed as the first written of the three synoptic gospels: these are scripted narratives from the life of Jesus which have many overlapping and synchronous accounts. The book of John also details Jesus's life through different structures. These books were written a few decades or longer after his death, most likely by people who were not his followers during his lifetime, and he is cited in Greek, which was not his native language. The differences in these texts demonstrate that his words and actions were not perfectly preserved. Despite the uncertainty generated by this disconcerting confluence of factors, the concept of the historical Jesus and the Jesus of faith has not weakened in its capacity to inspire and teach.

Mark provides several references to spiritual and physical healing from its very first chapter; these suggest the importance of these acts in the faith (Canda, Ketchell, Dybicz, Pyles, & Nelson-Becker, 2006). Jesus healed the man with the "unclean spirit" (Mark 1:23–26), leaving the scribes amazed at Jesus's innate power and authority. Next in the narrative, he healed Simon's (one of the 12 apostles) mother-in-law of fever (Mark 1:30–31). Her immediate response after this healing was to serve Jesus and the apostles. At sundown, people from the city arrived, and he healed many who were ill with diseases as well as cast demons out (Mark 1:32–34). Jesus healed a leper and a man who was paralyzed (Mark 1:40–42, 2:3–12). He touched the leper, a consequence that typically brought defilement and automatic exclusion from society because of the fear of contagion. This healing ministry was not an addendum or an afterthought to his mission and message; instead, it was a central aspect that is recurrent throughout the gospels.

The examples given in the Christian gospels constitute three modes of healing: physical, mental, and spiritual. Narratives of physical healing are described above. The stories told in Mark of the unclean spirit and casting out demons are examples of restoring mental health. A man possessed of so many demons that restraint by chains could not hold him regained his "right mind" after the demons departed at the word of Jesus. Spiritual healing is related to—and perhaps in the larger perspective indistinguishable from—the other two forms, but it connotes the atonement aspect of his ministry. The atonement or "at-one-ment" refers to holistic relationships of being in the world: this is humanity's place, or in another rendering as a physicist might say, humanity has an ecological niche in the universe. We are part of an entire interconnected system of life and being.

In the Christian story, Christ came into the world to reconcile humanity to God and that reconciliation emerges from breaking down separateness from the world and promoting health holistically. Sensed separation is created through many decisions that have privileged the self over others. Christ's role was to restore people to wholeness by (a) creating the doorway to redemption by his crucifixion and resurrection (orthodox model) or (b) demonstrating God's love and unity by removing race, class, and all other distinctions. The latter perspective is a postmodern model—the option for the poor in Catholic social teaching suggests preference should be given to the well-being of the poor and the powerless. To say it in another, non-Christian but complementary way, we are an intrinsic part of creation, the unbroken wholeness accepted in Buddhism and evidenced in particle physics.

Healing disability was not the only objective of Jesus's life and ministry, but his compassion led him to care for the immediate needs people had. His philosophy of kindness is also shown in the Beatitudes—statements of blessing—for the poor in spirit, those who mourn, the merciful, and others who had spiritual needs (Matthew 5:3–11). The second goal Jesus held for others was transformation, to see beauty within the everyday self and become light to/for the world. For some people, this could be possible in spite of brokenness. For others, expressing one's personal light could only be achieved if healing were accomplished. In those situations, people who experienced healing also stood as witnesses to the power and presence of the Holy Spirit. This Christian context for healing can serve as a powerful source of aspiration, promise, and action for those of the Christian faith as well as others who have encountered this viewpoint in culture. Dearmer (1909) asks,

> What might not happen if we could bring our sick to holy places of rest and prayer, to centres of pilgrimage where religion and science were at their best, to churches of deathless beauty, hallowed by worship and by sacraments, by past associations and the present efficacy of united faith? . . . We ought to be able to give much better if those glorious churches which they have bequeathed to us should ever recover their large original intention of ministering to both the spirit and the body. (p. 285)

It is commonly accepted that the ministry of Jesus was one of preaching, teaching, and healing. Jesus is today sometimes referred to as the Great Physician. Healings were documented in early sources and they appear to have been relatively common both within Judaism and the Hellenistic world (Borg, 1987). Further, even the adversaries of Jesus did not question the healing power he exerted. Nearly one-fifth of the gospels detail Jesus's acts of healing (Kelsey, 1987; 1995). In fact, his healing ministry was presented as evidence that Jesus was the Messiah (the anointed one, or Christ), "Go and tell John what you hear and see: the blind receive their sight, the lame walk, the lepers are cleansed, the deaf hear, the dead are brought to life" (Matthew 11:4–5).

Jesus most commonly healed through words or touch. In a few cases he used saliva, alone or mixed with mud. Although the gospels do not specifically note that Jesus used oil for healing, his disciples apparently did, as noted in Mark 6:13, "They cast out many demons, and anointed with oil many who were sick and cured them." Healing sometimes occurred when individuals touched Jesus or his clothes, and sometimes the faith of the individuals seemed to be a factor in the healing. On several occasions, healing occurred after Jesus first felt compassion for people. Second, he actively cured them of their condition. In fact, the reason he most often healed is because he cared so deeply. He loved people and so he healed them. Healing was a natural result of the person he was, both divine and human. Table 8.1 provides Biblical New Testament examples of Jesus's healing acts across all of the synoptic gospels and the book of John.

Table 8.1 The Biblical New Testament Record of Healing: A Closer Look

No.	Healing	Matthew	Mark	Luke	John	Method
1.	Man with unclean spirit		1:23	4:33		Exorcism, word
2.	Peter's mother-in-law	8:14	1:30	4:38		Touch, word, prayer of friends
3.	Multitudes	8:16	1:32	4:40		Touch, word, faith of friends
4.	Many demons		1:39			Preaching, exorcism
5.	A leper	8:2	1:40	5:12		Word, touch, leper's faith and Christ's compassion
6.	Many sick of the palsy	9:2	2:3	5:17		Word, faith of friends
7.	Man's withered hand	12:9	3:1	6:6		Word, obedient faith
8.	Multitudes	12:15	3:10			Exorcism, response to faith
9.	Gerasene demoniac	8:28	5:1	8:26		Word, exorcism
10.	Jairus's daughter	9:18	5:22	8:41		Word, touch, faith of father
11.	Woman with issue of blood	9:20	5:25	8:43		Touching His garment in faith
12.	A few sick folk	13:58	6:5			Touch (hindered by unbelief)
13.	Multitudes	14:34	6:55			Touch of His garment, friend's faith
14.	Syrophoenician's daughter	15:22	7:24			Response to mother's prayer, faith
15.	Deaf and dumb man		7:32			Word, touch, friend's prayer
16.	Blind man (gradual healing)		8:22			Word, touch, friend's prayer
17.	Child with evil spirit	17:14	9:14	9:38		Word, touch, faith of father
18.	Blind Bartimaeus	20:30	10:46	18:35		Word, touch, compassion, faith
19.	Centurion's servant	8:5		7:2		Response to master's prayer, faith
20.	Two blind men	9:27				Word, touch, men's faith
21.	Dumb demoniac	9:32				Exorcism
22.	Blind and dumb demoniac	12:22		11:14		Exorcism
23.	Multitudes	4:23		6:17		Teaching, preaching, healing
24.	Multitudes	9:35				Teaching, preaching, healing

No.	Healing	Matthew	Mark	Luke	John	Method
25.	Multitudes	11:4		7:21		Proof of John the Baptist In prison
26.	Multitudes	14:14		9:11	6:2	Compassion, response to need
27.	Great multitudes	15:30				Faith of friends
28.	Great multitudes	19:2				
29.	Blind and lame in temple	21:14				
30.	Widow's son			7:11		Word, compassion
31.	Mary Magdalene and others			8:2		Exorcism
32.	Woman bound by Satan			13:10		Word, touch
33.	Man with dropsy			14:1		Touch
34.	Ten lepers			17:11		Word, faith of the men
35.	Malchus's ear			22:49		Touch
36.	Multitudes			5:15		
37.	Various persons			13:32		Exorcism, and not stated
38.	Nobleman's son				4:46	Word, father's faith
39.	Impotent man				5:2	Word, man's faith
40.	Man born blind				9:1	Word, touch
41.	Lazarus				11:1	Word

Source: Dearmer, P. (1909), pp.150–152).

Notes: There are 41 instances of healing by Jesus in the gospels (books of Matthew, Mark, Luke, and John); none are addressed in all synoptic gospels (books using common source material and thus sharing similar narrative accounts) plus the book of John, but 11 are recorded in 3 of the 4 gospels.

Five parallel passages are found in Matthew 12:24 and Luke 11:15.

Muhammad and Islam

The Prophet Muhammad's view of health, sickness, and death is followed by a high proportion of practicing Muslims and may be inferred from the following verse in the Holy Qur'an: "The Lord of the worlds; it is He who heals me when I am sick, and He who would cause me to die and live again" (Qur'an 26:80, cited in Awofeso, 2005). In Islamic approaches to medicine, harmony and balance prevail in a holistic understanding of the interdependence between body and spirit. All of life is considered a sacred experience. The crescent has served as the symbol for medical care in the Middle East through the Red Crescent Society established during the Turkish Ottoman empire in reaction to deaths from disease, numbers that were greater than war casualties after the Crimean War of 1868.

Patience, perseverance, and thankfulness help one align oneself to be receptive to physical and spiritual well-being (Rassool, 2000). The evil eye (the bestowal of a hex) may be given credence by some because it is mentioned in the Qur'an as a source of poor health (Inhorn & Serour, 2011). Disease, suffering, and death are viewed as a test from Allah. Illness is one of the means by which one grows in understanding of Allah. Thus, it may be considered an agent of purification and balance. Treatment for illness should be sought and is not in conflict with the religion. In fact one hadith (saying of Muhammad) suggests that all illnesses have a remedy and it is the duty of the faithful to seek it. Prayer is a means for maintaining well-being in both sickness and health. The patient has an obligation to pray for recovery as well as a better life in the next world. "The prayer of the sick person will never be rejected, until he recovers" (hadith of Muhammad as cited in Rassool, 2000, p. 1480). Medications should also be used, unless they derive from alcohol or pork products. Although the role of the doctor is valued especially in diagnosis, cure is deemed under the province of God's will, especially for older Muslims. The Arabic term *inshallah* (God willing) refers to submission to the desires of God for the future. This is not resignation nor a passive approach but evidence of desire to align projects and plans with those of the divine source.

Three approaches to health are developed in the Qur'an: legal issues, guidance, and direct healing. Legally, health behaviors that promote well-being in an ethical code are prescribed (moderation in food intake) and behaviors that would harm it are prohibited (tobacco and alcohol consumption). Guidance is given on how to conduct one's daily life through nourishment of the soul and integration of thoughts and actions. A very high standard of physical cleanliness is suggested. In an institution, older women may prefer to use a bathroom than a bedpan, for example. Direct healing can come through meditation on the Qur'an. More traditional Muslims may believe in the value of a shaykh, or spiritual doctor/healer, for recovery and spiritual development.

A few aspects of the faith have direct impact on end-of-life concerns. Life support for a person in a vegetative condition is not supported, assisted suicide and euthanasia are not supported, and autopsy is not permitted unless legally required (Rassool, 2000). Medical opinions by clerics (fatwas) can be issued privately or publically and show great diversity, though many practices such as dialysis are viewed as halal (religiously acceptable). Overall Islam teaches an ethic of caring and Muslim nurses and physicians are asked to treat all persons equally, not just those who are Muslim. Knowledge is highly valued and people are asked to obtain knowledge and expertise to enhance the lives of all beings. When death seems imminent, Muslims prefer to die in their home over an institutional death (Assous, 2013).

Muslims who carry strong religious values are less likely to seek counseling because of a preference for having their religious perspective addressed, worries that their religious values will not be respected, and language communication difficulties for some immigrant Muslims (Ahmed & Amer, 2012; Keshavarzi & Haque, 2013). Even Muslim psychologists generally practice more out of their psychological training rather than their religious one. Practically, Muslims generally prefer care by a Muslim physician of the same gender. Issues such as being asked to undress for a clinical examination, cross-gender touching, and requests to remove a headscarf or wear a revealing gown can all cause discomfort. Rather than offering a handshake, a hand placed over the heart in greeting may be most acceptable to older devout Muslims. If a health care professional visits the home of an older Muslim, he/she should knock and wait longer than he/she may think necessary for a response in order for females to make themselves presentable in their preferred dress. He/she may remove shoes before entering the home as a sign of respect. Honor and pride may complicate interactions with older men; interactions with older women are usually formal.

American Indian Tradition and Healing

As with the Abrahamic traditions described above, there is diversity within American Indian tribes in terms of specific approaches to healing, but overall the approach is syncretic: many practices have been combined either consecutively or congruently. Spirituality is generally integrated into the rhythms of daily life, leaving many American Indian tribes without even a specific word for religion in native language (Garrett, Brubaker, Torres-Rivera, West-Olatunji, & Conwill, 2008). Outcomes of colonialism and oppression in terms of high rates of alcoholism and abuse have tended to separate some American Indians from traditional spiritual and religious grounding, as have past governmental policies.

Ritual and ceremony are important for lifting people into extraordinary periods of deep awareness in the context of community. Some common ceremonies that include integration of physical and mental health components include: the blessing way ceremony, pipe ceremony, pow wow, sweat lodge, sun dance, talking circles, and vision quest, each of which can connect participants to therapeutic space within the land or within themselves. Connection to the land is often seen as sacred and strengthens the potential for healing to occur (Goodkind, Gorman, Hess, Parker, & Hough, 2015). Conversely, separation from the land or natural elements promotes alienation. One research participant in a qualitative study of Dineh people by Goodkind et al. (2015) reported she found entering a church after an accident suffocating, but participating in a ceremony with a medicine man led to her healing. Presence in the natural environment was often mentioned as an antecedent to healing through empowering connections to identity, history, community, and the sacred.

Gone (2010), of a northern plains tribe, laments the dearth of comparative studies of traditional health practices and the lack of explicit details in much of the literature. However, he acknowledges that many traditional people would eschew publication of such knowledge. Further, he suggests that traditional healing practices have continued to evolve and some past practices would not be conducted in contemporary times. Soul wound psychotherapy by psychologist Duran (2006), of American Indian ancestry, offers an unconventional healing discourse that shifts out of psychology and into spirituality. Interestingly, one example of deconstruction, decolonization, and reconstruction in clinical work with someone who abused alcohol included referencing Jesus's spiritual deal-making in healing encounters from the Christian story (Duran, 2006). In this blended context for healing, therapy was seen as ceremony and harmonious relationships were sought. Any therapist guiding this soul healing work for others also needed to be engaged in his or her own soul healing.

The Cherokee practice of *Ayeli* described by Garrett et al. (2008) also facilitates community healing. In this model, four spiritual forces representing fundamental facets of life correspond to the four directions of north, east, south, and west. Interactions among them contribute to harmony and balance. East corresponds to belonging (spirit); south symbolizes mastery of self and linkages with the natural environment; west symbolizes independence, determination, and physical awareness (body); and north symbolizes generosity and wisdom (mind). These four directions form a circle representing the self. Other concentric circles correspond to outward relationships moving from family, to tribe, to society. Vision is another principle underlying all circles. People are invited to come to the center of a circle to give their symbolic giftedness (present time) and to receive a portion of what they envision (future time). The concept of a symbolic medicine bag emanating from ancestral legends suggests participants take away spiritual gifts they can draw on when needed. Medicine comes out of every memory, person, place, and event (Garrett, Garrett, & Brotherton, 2001). Medicine can emerge from failure as well as success. As with any technique that resides with a certain group or culture, it should be implemented respectfully for its universal virtues with absence of intent to misrepresent or misappropriate.

Religion and the Body

In *The Therapeutic Importance of Religion,* Dearmer (1909) presciently addresses a number of ideas concerning the power of cognition and belief to have a restorative effect on the body.

> *The main contention of this book has been that the forces of religion, its faith, and hope, and love, its prayer and peace, its rites and sacraments, have a powerful influence for good on the spirit of man [sic] and through the spirit on the body, that therefore these religious influences have or can have, a valuable effect on the maintenance of that inward balance and vitality we call health.* (p. 330)

Holistic health includes many perspectives on what it means to be healthy. For some, it refers to the absence of illness. It can signal a return to health after illness, or a measure of health despite presence of illness. Health can indicate presence of capacity or reserve beyond energy expended. Health can be regarded as spiritual quiescence, social integration and support, or psychosocial well-being. Finally, health can be expressed by vitality and present-centeredness as well as behaviors that create a healthy life. In terms of medicine, joint use of traditional as well as complementary and alternative therapies is often referred to as *integrative medicine.*

RESEARCH ON THE INTERSECTIONS BETWEEN RELIGION AND HEALTH

Since 1995 there has been an explosion of quantitative and qualitative research in the area of religion, spirituality, and health (George, Kinghorn, Koenig, Gammon, & Blazer, 2013; Koenig, 2012, 2015; Koenig, King, & Carson, 2012), with more than 3,000 studies in quantitative methods alone, plus many more conceptual, theoretical, and review articles. Further, many studies now include measures of religion and/or spirituality (R/S) in clinical practice domains as part of demographic components or interventions, providing evidence of mental health and health outcomes. Research in R/S includes studies with randomization, large samples, longitudinal designs, clinical trials, and rigorous analysis with appropriate tests. In short, these studies are now becoming as rigorous as those conducted in any field, a prior point of criticism. Religious research now meets higher standards, is more carefully designed with attention to randomized controlled trials or control variables, and restricts confounding variables—permitting differences among different groups of people (women, race and ethnic groups, geographical areas, ages, etc.) to be assessed.

Some points to consider about the relationships between religion and health include: (1) the causal nature of the interaction: whether religious behavior affects health, health status affects religious participation, or a third factor affects them both; (2) how religion is practiced varies greatly within a tradition, so it is helpful to hold what is known about a religious faith and its effects on health provisionally; (3) status within a religious organization and degree of inclusion and exclusion can affect perceived benefits or sense of well-being; and (4) the status of the religion within the larger environment and its general level of acceptance may affect a client's willingness to discuss it. Whether a tradition is a widely practiced religion, such as Catholicism, versus a religion viewed as new-age or cult can affect legitimization of religious behaviors. Knowing something about a religious tradition may mean little in terms of individual practices. For instance, prayers may be public or private, spontaneous or set. There are some health models which suggest that those who are strongly affiliated with religion experience greater sense of well-being and a protective effect in terms of engaging in less risky behavior through social support, positive role models, encouragement to participate in altruistic behavior, and positive moral teaching/guidance (Koenig, 2012).

Although religion is generally positively perceived in regard to health outcomes, religious beliefs may affect health behavior in nonsalubrious ways. Religious beliefs may interfere with blood transfusions or contraceptive use, or result in judgment that discourages people from seeking health care, including parents who may withhold it from their children. Sometimes religious authorities may allude to religious doctrines in a manner that implies people should stay in abusive relationships, for example. Further, actual religious and spiritual abuse can occur when people are forced to do things they would otherwise refuse to do. Religious transgressions or sin can cause spiritual anguish as individuals compare their own behavior to the ideal behavior sanctioned by their faith. When layered onto a physical illness, spiritual care can be very complex and lead to ethical dilemmas.

The pressure on health care systems globally due to increased population aging suggests the need from policy, economic, and mental health perspectives to consider methods for integrating many types of care into treatment. This should include religious and spiritual forms often favored by older people. In the United States, the Department of Health and Human Services (DHHS) and its program Healthy People 2020 (DHHS, 2010) have developed goals to sustain a high quality of life and to pay attention to social determinants of health through prevention and management of health risks. Certain ethnic groups, such as African Americans and Latinos, are known to have stronger links to religious organizations. These, in turn, have the potential to encourage healthy behaviors and health screenings. Complementary and alternative medicine is gaining more currency through the beginning of funded studies on therapies such as tai chi, meditation, and prayer particularly with older adults. Finally, religion and spirituality are known to be a familiar coping style for many older adults, as mentioned in Chapter 1 and shown by my research (Nelson-Becker, 2005).

Research Indications for the
Role of Religion in Aging and Health Care

What do we know about religion, health, and aging? One study of public and private religiosity in 274 women over age 55 in Tennessee stratified by race used Pargament's coping scale of self-directed coping, deferring authority to God, or collaborative coping (Ark, Hull, Husaini, & Craun, 2006). Findings indicated that self-directed coping without assistance from God led to more physician and ER visits as well as inpatient hospital days in Caucasians. By contrast, deferring authority to God led to more inpatient days though fewer physician visits. Collaborating with God was not related to health visits. In African Americans, however, self-directed coping led to fewer health visits of any kind, deferring led to fewer inpatient days, and collaboration with

God was consistent with more inpatient days, demonstrating an inverse relationship. Generally, across all aspects, lower health service use occurred in those who endorsed more religiosity.

A random sample of 14,500 community-dwelling older adults in Europe showed that daily prayer was more frequent in those with worse self-rated health or mental health (Hank & Schaan, 2008). This may indicate that religious coping can be a signal of distress. Religious beliefs can also affect health directly. It is known that in religious groups that practice moderation of food, alcohol use, and sexual behavior, there appear to be positive health outcomes (e.g., Seventh-Day Adventists).

Research reports that people prefer to have their physicians ask them about their religious and spiritual practices even if they (the patients) are not religious (see Balboni et al., 2007). Published studies suggest about 75% of patients surveyed would like spirituality included in care, about 40% would like physicians to ask about their religion, and another 50% prefer that their physician prays with them (Daaleman & Nease, 1994; King & Bushwick, 1994). Among surrogate decision makers whose family member was in an intensive care unit (ICU), 78% described religion as fairly or very important to them, yet religion was discussed in fewer than 17% of goals of care conferences (Ernecoff, Curlin, Buddadhumaruk, & White, 2015). Seemingly, religious statements were largely ignored by physicians, who changed the topic to a more practical medical matter. If this signals discomfort in addressing this topic when it seems to be valued by patients, then other health care and mental health professionals may need to alter this balance. The long range goal, however, is to teach physicians how to respond.

Other research suggests that although many physicians agree that spirituality should be included in medical care, few feel confident, competent enough, or have time enough to do it (Monti & Beitman, 2010). There is also controversy about exactly how spirituality, religion, and health care should be connected and who can do that, especially if medical staff is atheist or agnostic. Sloan and Bagiella (2002) have raised concerns that patients could be led to think that insufficient faith could lead to poor health. Chaplains are a clear choice to engage discussion of spirituality and religion as strengths or struggles, but not all hospitals have them available on staff, nor do they have the time to meet with everyone admitted. Some have advocated that medical professionals routinely take religious and spiritual histories and certainly conduct spiritual triage to determine the level of importance a patient lends to spiritual and religious domains as well as most importantly, spiritual distress (Koenig, 2012; Puchalski & Ferrell, 2010).

Clinical Implications for Including Religion in Care

Why should religion be considered in health and mental health care? Religion has an effect on health through behavioral, psychological, and social pathways (Koenig, 2012). Many clients do report religious and spiritual needs related to health and mental health and those needs may be unmet, particularly in an older adult client who may be less connected to a faith community, though not a faith tradition. Religious and spiritual struggle can adversely affect health outcomes (Balboni et al., 2007). Religious coping also affects whether people hold on to hope and strive for the measure of wellness they may achieve, or whether they succumb to despair. Religious beliefs may affect medical decisions and compliance with suggested treatment regimens. Further, spiritual and religious beliefs of the practitioner may affect whether and how the S/R preferences of the client are honored. Health care standards in place through the Joint Commission on Accreditation of Hospital Organizations require religious and spiritual values and beliefs to be regarded and appreciated for the significance clients ascribe to them (The Joint Commission, 2003).

At times certain beliefs clients hold may be outside social norms and stretch the credulity of professionals. This is only important where it intersects with client behavior. The starting position has to be one of respect, but a second response may be to gently explore and confront these beliefs. If there is a question of harm to the client or others, then the confrontation requires urgent action. If a client is hospitalized, spiritual care should be included in the plans for discharge where important to any extent.

CAREGIVING

Most care for family members is done informally by relatives, who may experience emotional, spiritual, and physical fatigue and sense of burden. Sixty percent of caregivers are female and the average age of caregivers is 49, though many caregivers of older people are themselves old (National Alliance for Caregiving [NAC], 2015). Older caregivers are more likely not to have outside paid help and nearly half of care recipients continue to live in their own home (48%) or in the caregiver's home (35%; NAC, 2015). Further, 59% need help with any ADL. Seventy-five percent of caregivers spend more than 21 hours caregiving per week, while 23% provide 41 or more hours. Caregivers may be likely to provide caregiving at home when religious beliefs are prevalent (Choi, Tirrito, & Mills, 2008). In Judaism, one question posed by the Talmud is who should pay costs for care? A modern reading suggests that although dignity is preserved when the older care recipient is able to pay financially, younger family members *pay* through the time they spend in caregiving. An older reading suggested that respect and honor for older family members was preserved when children paid financial costs for parental needs (Address, 2012). Further, if the burden of caregiving becomes too great, it is acceptable in the tradition to provide care by proxy, or institutional care. In Islam, family caregiving is the norm and family members who place a loved one in care may face stigma.

Findings from a small qualitative study demonstrated that common concerns of caregivers were decline in caregiver health, role conflict, lack of preparation and educational support, and the importance of faith (Bialon & Coke, 2012). Family members who chose to provide care demonstrated a strong commitment based on moral and religious views, ability to embrace a caregiver identity, affection for the care recipient, and an awakened sense of compassion (Piercy, 2007). Coping was strengthened through acceptance of the situation and making small adjustments, support of other family, using some formal care, and viewing caregiving as a growth-inducing opportunity. Those with weaker commitments to caregiving expressed ambivalence about the role of caregiving (Piercy, 2007), suggesting that those who sustained this role largely found in it meaning and purpose. Other studies have found that caregivers find ways to cope by remembering past life experiences together, taking time to nourish the self, using religious and spiritual faith, viewing caregiving as a meaningful activity, using prayer, and seeking information needed (Bull, 2014; Morano & King, 2005).

Caregivers who receive religious support may experience less depression and less anger and view their caregiving as an expression of love (Marquez-Gonzalez, Lopez, Romero-Moreno, & Losada, 2012; Morano & King, 2005; Stuckey, 2001). Often there is much unrecognized and unaddressed loss, especially in early stages of an illness. Failure to address the losses of caregiving—both losses of their previous relationship to the loved one and losses of plans, projects, and time—can lead to symptoms of complicated bereavement. Mental and physical health consequences can be severe. Applying a grief framework, then, can help validate the experience of caregiving. Encouraging caregivers to find humor in their caregiving and to allow opportunities for the care recipient to share something of what they are still able to give can help sustain the relationship.

Caregiving Stress and Aging

Psychological stress experienced by caregivers may affect the rate of aging (Koenig et al., 2012). Telomeres protect the end of chromosomes from deterioration or fusion with other chromosomes. When cells divide, the telomere is not fully replicated each time. With each cell division the telomere thus becomes shorter, and when shortened a certain amount, the cell will die. One study comparing high- and low-stress female caregivers of healthy and ill children found that high-stress mothers experienced shorter telomere lengths that represented 9 to 17 years of additional aging (Epel et al., 2004). Similarly, a 2007 study of 41 caregivers of persons with dementia found shorter telomere lengths compared to a control group (Damjanovic et al., 2007). It is possible that spiritual and religious practices may lead to reduced stress and thus, less shortening of telomeres, but research has yet to determine that.

Spirituality in Caregiving Methods

A valuable book by Richards (2010), aptly titled, *Caresharing: A Reciprocal Approach to Caregiving and Care Receiving in the Complexities of Aging, Illness, or Disability*, suggests that this special relationship is not one of dependency, but interdependence. This recognition helps shift the balance to a relationship where both parties are viewed to offer benefits, with one neither over benefitting or under benefitting. Learning to receive help can be hard for caregivers, but asking for assistance can also offer blessing to others. Sometimes caregivers may feel others have failed them. At those times it may help to depersonalize the situation, be flexible and forgiving, look for the deeper meaning, and simply ask family and friends to help.

In caring for others, we need to respond to what is vibrant and alive in them. If this is not obvious, it's important to ask and cultivate these aspects, including searching for novel communication methods when the old ones no longer seem sufficient. This includes seeing and acknowledging the essence of the individual, past their frailty, disability, or pain. They may continue to be able to offer prayer for others, despite physical limits. I remember entering the room of a woman in a nursing care facility and being so touched by her kind presence. She was dying, yet there was a tangible solidity in her room. Something about her being-ness was palpable. I saw her a second time, surrounded by family, yet she invited me in and we visited a brief time with family present. Her extended and extensive family were not there because they had to be there, but because she offered something to them even in her dying time. Of course not all relationships are sweet like this, and sometimes a caregiver continues to suffer as ancient wounds are reopened. Allowing roles to evolve and regain functionality are two important aspects stressed by Richards (2010). Further, she suggests that it is sometimes best to break the family rules and learn to release any accompanying guilt for a greater good—as long as respect for the care receiver is maintained.

To keep the spirit of both the care recipient and caregiver alive, Richards (2010) offers four ideas: (1) see the whole person, (2) affirm the care partner's value, (3) build on what the care partner can still do, and (4) meet the care partner's needs at their level. It is helpful for caregivers to realize this may change hour to hour, especially in the case of cognitive impairment or dementia. In sundowning, a syndrome common in some forms of dementia, the person with dementia may grow more agitated and confused toward the end of the day. However, beyond potential burden, caregiving offers benefits of growth and fulfilment in valuing and responding to basic human needs.

PRAYERS, RITUALS, AND SYMBOLS

Prayers

Spoken or unspoken prayer provides a way for believers to feel close to God, the Divine, or Sacred Source. Prayers may be spontaneously offered or sourced from sacred texts which are memorized or read. They often are a resource for emotion-focused coping and many people believe that entering into prayer can produce positive outcomes. Religious traditions have conventional prayers that offer comfort. Prayers requesting peace or healing (prayers of supplication) are often recited. What follows are well-known prayers in each faith.

- Judaism uses the Shema: "Hear O Israel, the Lord is our God, the Lord is One" (*Shema Israel, Adonai eloheinu, Adonai ehad*; Deuteronomy 6:4). This serves as a declaration of monotheism and is central to the Jewish faith.

- In the Christian tradition, the Lord's Prayer, beginning, "Our Father in heaven, hallowed [holy] be your name" (Matthew 6: 9–13) is what Jesus taught his followers to pray. Psalm 23, "The Lord is my shepherd, I shall not want," is often used for comfort in times of difficulty or stress.

- In Islam, after washing (ritual ablution) as far as possible for one who is frail, one practices Salaat. The ritual prayer begins, "God is the most great. I bear witness that there are not gods but God" (*Allaahu Akbar* [4×] *Ashhadu an la ilaaha illa-Lah* [2×]). The Shahada is the Muslim profession of faith, expressing the two simple, fundamental beliefs that make one a Muslim: There is no god but God and Muhammad is the prophet of Allah. The first statement is a clear affirmation of monotheism; the second proclaims Muhammad as God's messenger.

- In Hinduism or Buddhism, a mantra or sacred chant (such as Om or Aum) may be repeated and facilitates deep meditation.

Rituals

Rituals are practical expressions of a faith. Jewish ritual or law (*halakha*, the path one walks) directs daily life as well as religious life. It addresses concerns from how to dress and what to wear, to what to eat, to how to help the poor. Eating kosher foods, foods approved according to the law, is one aspect. Observance of halakha shows gratitude to God and brings a sense of the sacred into everyday life, solidifying Jewish identity.

In Christianity, the sacrament of Communion (also known as the Lord's Supper or Eucharist) involves eating a wafer or small piece of bread and drinking from a communion cup (either communal or individual) to remember Christ, receive forgiveness, and participate in the body of fellow church members/believers. In times of illness, ordained ministers, priests, or elders of a faith community may practice the sacrament of administration to the sick, anointing of the sick, or laying on of hands as briefly mentioned earlier. This is often conducted by two ministers (or sometimes one priest) who anoint the ill person with consecrated (usually olive) oil, place their hands on top of the head (at the 7th chakra in the Hindu tradition), and then offer a prayer or prayers. This is done according to James 5:15: "Is anyone among you sick? Let them call the elders of the church to pray over them and anoint them with oil in the name of the Lord." Both of these ritual experiences might comfort a patient, although the second one is used particularly for unwell persons.

An American Indian sacramental or ritual tradition might include drumming, use of herbs, and other rituals where possible with frail older persons. Sweat lodges are particularly used for purification and healing. In small buildings often built of saplings with animal hides or blankets as covering, hot rocks are placed in a shallow hole dug in the middle of the ground. Water is thrown over the rocks to produce steam, which is symbolically cleansing.

In Islam, prayers are given five times a day—dawn, noon, mid-afternoon, sunset, and at night—bowing and kneeling on a prayer rug facing Mecca. Parts of the Qur'an are recited. After thanking God for blessings, prayers of supplication (request) may be offered for healing or any other thing. As written above, prayers are spoken after ritual washing.

Hinduism has many rituals of worship, some which take place in a temple and are directed to a god or goddess and some which take place in the home. People who are Hindu greet each other by placing their hands together (a *mudra*) before the heart and bowing their head slightly, saying, "Namaste." In this way, a person who is Hindu offers respect to the soul within (*atman*) and also to God who is within the heart (*Paramatman*). A *puja* is a religious ritual that some perform every morning after bathing and dressing, but prior to eating or drinking. It usually involves bowing, making a sacred offering, and chanting. Participating in puja relates humans to the divine.

Symbols

Religious traditions have symbols that evoke the tradition. Many times these are objects of the faith. Symbols of Judaism might include a prayer shawl (*tallit*) or *kippah* placed on the head or a star of David (six-pointed star). A Christian might like to wear a cross, use a rosary in prayer, or have an image of Jesus nearby. The seashell is a symbol of baptism and pilgrimage. An American Indian might use eagle feathers, animal totems, a sacred pipe, or a large number of other symbols, depending on tribal connection. The sun symbol may, in particular, represent healing energy to certain American Indian tribes. Rather than a visual symbol (as visual symbols are not mentioned in the Qur'an), a Muslim might prefer listening to devotional music. Although the star and crescent together is sometimes used as a symbol of Islam, this is a symbol from the earlier Ottoman empire. Geometric shapes are often appreciated in Islam; images of living creatures are prohibited. A person who is Hindu might use a lotus or a banyan tree, among others. A Buddhist might use prayer beads, have a statue of the Buddha or a wheel of dharma, or color a mandala, sometimes using sand. There are some symbols that are used by many faith and spiritual traditions: these include water and candles/light.

HOPE, MEANING/PURPOSE, AND MENTAL HEALTH

Hope is an important part of mental health work with older adults as it provides motivation for people to keep living intentionally and for immediate discomfort to ease. Koenig (2015) and his team found 40 high-quality studies examining hope, religion, and spirituality. About 73% of those reported significant positive relationships with hope. Of 45 studies of meaning and purpose prior to 2010, 93% had significant positive findings with religion and spirituality. Overall, population studies that have controlled for confounding factors have found associations among religion, spirituality, and positive mental health. However, not all religious behaviors promote health (George et al., 2013). Some religious beliefs promote judgment, control, or views of the Sacred Source/God as punishing and thus have a negative effect on health/mental health.

Guilt and loss of hope are sometimes connected with depression in an inverse relationship to religious beliefs. Studies indicate that those with no religious affiliation are at greater risk for depression and people involved in faith traditions seem to be at reduced risk (George et al., 2013). Stories of religious and spiritual figures may serve to acknowledge and validate emotional pain. In situations that are incomprehensible, R/S may help provide a buffer. Although religion or spirituality should never be prescribed, it will be important to see how related behaviors could be included or modified for clinical settings. Sociologically, religious participation is declining while private religious or spiritual behavior is increasing. This is also true for older adults, not necessarily because they are becoming disaffected with religion, but as they age it may become physically more difficult for them to attend and remain active. However, religious leaders in many traditions also command less authority among believers than in prior generations (George et al., 2013), leaving older people with more freedom to make decisions in moderate and liberal denominations at least.

SUMMARY

This chapter discussed the nature of health and spiritual health, biological aging, and diminishment. Historical views on the intersections of religion and health were explored as well as the nature of suffering. Views of healing within four religious/spiritual traditions were elaborated: Judaism, Christianity, Islam, and American Indian. A few of the intersections on religion and health in research, particularly related to older adults, were presented. Caregiving is a major component of relationships at older ages, from younger family members to older family members and from older adults to other older people. Thus, spiritual resources for caregiving were identified here. So that the reader might begin to develop greater familiarity with what might bring comfort, prayers, rituals, and symbols common to some religious traditions were reviewed. Overall, this chapter discussed health from a broad spiritual view with very specific examples of what may be used as spiritual or religious supports in healing.

CASE STUDY: HEALTH AND SPIRITUALITY

Daniel Thompson was a 76-year-old Caucasian man who presented to an academic medical center for difficulty breathing and fluid in his lungs. He was treated by an academic medical team, which included an attending physician, resident physician, and two medical student interns. He had a medical history significant for Stage IV lung cancer, heart failure, and diabetes and was currently receiving weekly chemotherapy for Stage IV lung cancer. There were a number of consulting services involved in his care, including oncology and cardiology. The social worker was consulted for information regarding hospice and palliative care.

Daniel's wife, Carla, was very involved in his care and was at his bedside daily; they did not have any children and lived independently in their home. Their social network consisted of family and friends from their church. Daniel identified himself as Catholic, though he declined a visit from his minister. He read scripture daily, found comfort in prayer, and found strength from his faith in God. He did not attend church regularly due to medical problems. However, he had attended regularly in the past.

During this hospitalization, Daniel learned that his cancer had spread to his bones. He was given a prognosis of two months by his oncologist. He reported feeling concerned about the ultimate value of chemotherapy and continuing treatment, stating, "I have no hope for a cure." Until this hospitalization, he had been receiving weekly chemotherapy. After learning the cancer had spread, he reported this treatment had made him feel toxic and synthetic: He explained that he felt less

human and more distant from life due to all of the chemicals that were being introduced into his body as part of treatment. He made significant note of his inability to interact and be social due to side effects. During the hospitalization, he told the social worker that his decision to obtain chemotherapy signified a lack of faith in God to cure him, for which he felt guilty. He explained that he now had made the choice to put his faith in medicine. He declined the social worker's invitation to speak with the chaplain, insisting the chaplain would see him as unworthy due to his lack of faith in God and his decision to obtain treatment. He indicated he felt safe speaking with the social worker about spiritual matters and wanted to continue receiving her support.

Questions for Case Discussion

1. How do you imagine the social worker was able to establish a relationship with this patient?

2. What is Mr. Thompson's background in and attitude toward religion?

3. How should the social worker proceed?

4. Should the social worker involve or consult with the chaplain? If so, how? How might nurses working with this patient also benefit from this information?

QUESTIONS FOR DISCUSSION

1. What is your definition of health? Spiritual health?

2. What role does suffering play in health, if any? How do religious views foster health or elicit harm in older patients?

3. What features of *slow medicine* have found acceptance in medical health care today?

4. How do activities of daily living, instrumental activities of daily living, and diminishment serve as measures or fail to serve as adequate measures in older adult health?

5. What are specific references to healing in the Abrahamic traditions of Islam, Judaism, or Christianity? How do any of the North American Indian traditions approach healing?

6. What does research on religion and health tell us? What are the implications of this research for aging?

7. In what ways can religion and religious views assist caregivers? Spirituality and spiritual views? How might religious and spiritual beliefs or views and practices be used in caregiving?

MEDITATION: TASTE

The raisin meditation is one that has been written about by Jon Kabat Zinn (2005). Do not do this if you have any allergy to raisins. An orange or nut might be a good substitution. It is an excellent meditation to do in a class or group and discuss afterward as people have different sensations and ideas to contribute.

First, place the raisin in your hand. Examine it carefully as though this was the first time you had seen it. Become aware of its shape, texture, color, and size. Is it hard and dried out or soft? Bring it to your nose and sniff it. Anticipate for a moment that you will taste it soon and wonder what that may be like. How does the raisin feel in your hand? Is it heavy or light?

Place the raisin in your mouth. Be aware of how your tongue encounters it. Is it hard to keep from chewing and swallowing it right away? Bite into it gently, feeling it squish. Chew it slowly. Describe the taste and texture of it. Think of it growing on a vine as a grape and all it went through to be picked, sorted, washed, transported on a truck or train, and sold in a market to reach you today. What other thoughts about it emerge? Finish chewing it and swallow. Discuss this experience with your group.

EXPLORING YOUR SPIRITUALITY: TOUCH

Although the sensation of touch begins with a physical process, it can take us beyond the material world into cognition, emotion, and spirit. To touch is to believe as did Thomas when he touched the wounds of the risen Christ, that Jesus returned to life after his death. Then Thomas believed a mystery of the faith. He knew by touch what his mind could not process. Metaphorically, the Buddha touched the world when he went beyond the palace walls to witness the difficult life circumstances of many of the poor. He was forever changed and began his search for enlightenment. Some religious and/or spiritual traditions involve the sensation of touch, such as Anointing of the Sick (Catholicism) or Reiki which is an energy modality for healing now commonly performed in some hospitals with people recovering from illness or surgery.

There are times when we are afraid of being touched or when touch feels bad—dishonest, exploitive, or abusive. People are hit and hurt by bad touch. However, touch can also comfort and soothe, such as kissing a child lightly in the spot where they have a scrape or giving and receiving a hug from a friend long unseen. Both of these kinds of touch can produce emotion at opposite ends of an emotional spectrum. Touch matters throughout the life course. Newly born infants who are not touched experience failure to thrive. Older people often experience sensory deprivation when spouses die and they seldom receive hugs or other forms of touch. Buddhist lamas suggest that when people are actively dying they may not wished to be touched as this may keep them longer in the physical world. Scientifically we know things we touch feel solid, but this is an illusion. Quantum mechanics showed us that objects are made of rapidly cycling subatomic particles, quarks with flavors like up and down, charm and strange. ("Flavors" are the attributes given to quarks that have no direct link to how they behave.) Yet touch does provide a sense of texture and form, as when a blind person reads the face of another with his fingers.

1. Imagine a world where no one touched each other and no object could be touched. What might this be like? What would be lost and what would be gained?

2. Think about what it feels like to touch a cotton ball, a muddy tire track, a child's cheek, a rose petal, a wooden board sticking out of a dump, a piece of wood that will be carved by an artisan, and wet sand under your bare feet as you walk along a shore?

3. What are your personal boundaries? Try walking toward someone and notice how close you can get to him or her before you or the other person becomes uncomfortable. What does this tell you about yourself and that person and the space between you? Does this sense ever change? Under what conditions?

4. Are there times when you prefer not to be touched? In some religious and cultural traditions such as Jewish Orthodoxy, men and women who are not married are forbidden to touch. What are the cultural sanctions about touching in your own culture, if any?

5. When do you welcome touch? From whom do you like to be touched?

6. Hold your hands upward as if you were going to clap them. Now move your right hand toward your left hand, holding the left hand stable until it is about an inch away. Then move the right hand out again and back and different rates of speed. What do you feel in your left palm, if anything? Keep practicing and see what, if anything, you can sense.

7. Journal about your experiences with touch, both touch that enfolds you positively and touch that does not.

EXPLORING YOUR SPIRITUALITY: TASTE AND SAVORING

As with our other sensory perceptions, taste is an important way for us to explore our world and expand our spiritual senses. People respond to objective tastes with diverse responses. A spicy dish is sought by some, but eschewed by those who find that their mouths burn uncomfortably at first awareness. Bitterness, sweetness, sourness, or saltiness can be perceived with varying intensity. There may be several reasons for this that include genetic predisposition, memory and meaning, and cultural acclimatization. Individual nerve fibers have mixed sensitivity to tastes, thus enabling some individuals to experience taste in a more robust manner. Supertasters express this genetic variation in taste perception and may even find careers in testing new food combinations. The memory of a strong taste may take us back to a moment when a similar taste was experienced. When I was a child, my grandmother who I dearly loved, made us sandwiches out of cow tongue for the eight hour ride home. The texture was so displeasing to me, that I could not eat it. Her love for me did not induce me to eat this particular food. Certain cultural culinary traditions such as found in South Asian (Indian) or Thai foods include foods spiced with curry or red chili power that result in an especially pungent flavor. Exposure over time may facilitate adjustment. Gustatory adaptation may occur if an individual exposes himself to spicy food at longer intervals.

Tastes can also be involved with rituals. The tastes of special dishes at a Thanksgiving or Christmas meal can last a long while in memory. Certain sacraments such as the Lord's supper/Holy communion/Eucharist involve the preparation and tasting of bread and wine in memory of the last meal of Jesus with his disciples and is a reconnection to a covenantal relationship. Passover marks the deliverance of the Jewish people from slavery in Egypt and includes a meal with bitter herbs, unleavened bread, and wine or grape juice. Islamic dietary law (Halal) identifies certain foods that should not be eaten, similar to Kosher (Kashur in Hebrew) law for people who are Jewish. People who are Mormon or Community of Christ are urged to follow practices that limit "hot drinks," often interpreted as caffeine, as well as abstain from tobacco and wine. Seventh-Day Adventists also suggest members should avoid wine, tobacco, and meat. Following these laws where given is a practice of obedience, holiness, and often may result in good health. Seventh-Day Adventists who were studied in Loma Linda, CA comprise one of the "blue zones" where people have been found to have the greatest longevity.

Taste is often connected to smell. Each of these senses can enhance or diminish the other. Both are further receptive avenues for experience. In positive psychology, the word *savor* has achieved prominence in suggestions of how to process experience. This stands in contrast to rushing through experience. Savoring also suggests enjoyment, no matter how little or great the amount of time given to the task. How we think about tastes can change. Brussel sprouts as prepared by my mother—boiled—was my least favorite of all vegetables. It was absolutely last. However, I recently tasted a Brussels sprouts dish prepared by my niece that changed my thinking and my experience of Brussels sprouts. The difference? She had broiled it in the oven lightly oiled, then salted. The result? A very tasty dish.

1. Consider something that you have tasted that was objectionable or repugnant. Why did you find it this way? Have you ever tried a similar item a second time? Did your experience of this item change?

2. What have you tasted that was ambrosia—like food for the Gods? In what way have you

sought this out again? Was your experience similar or different from that first time?

3. How does taste enhance your life? Is it a major or minor aspect of your life satisfaction?

4. How do your experiences with taste help you to savor life? What especially do you savor?

5. Journal about your experience.

WEBSITES

Center for Spirituality, Theology, and Health

http://www.spiritualityandhealth.duke.edu/index.php/publications/crossroads

Crossroads is an e-mail newsletter published by Duke Center for Spirituality and Health that updates recent research developments in health and spirituality as well as presentations and grant applications calls.

Spirituality in Patient Care

http://www.spiritualityandhealth.duke.edu/index.php/cme-videos

Five videos are available free on sign-in from the Center for Spirituality, Theology, and Health. This five-part educational series is designed to train health professionals to integrate spirituality into patient care as part of the practice of *whole person* medicine. Health professionals, regardless of specialty, are encouraged to watch all five videos (even though the first three videos are designed for physicians).

The Green House Project

http://www.thegreenhouseproject.org/about/visionmission

The Green House Project, initiated by Dr. Bill Thomas, provides room for addressing spiritual aspects in a care environment. Although it has become a brand, it began from an organic, community-based vision.

Inner Health Studio

http://www.innerhealthstudio.com/relaxation-scripts.html

This Inner Health Studio resource offers coping skills information on stress and anxiety in the form of guided meditations, relaxation audio clips, and podcasts. In particular, it offers free meditation scripts that would be ideal for caregivers to use with a client or for themselves. There are scripts for Visualizations, Relaxation for Anxiety, Guided Meditation, and Sleep Relaxation, each with numerous sublistings. Mindfulness and meditation are helpful entry points for clients who may not identify with a specific religious or spiritual tradition but are seeking a supportive outlet. The scripts are provided in detail so a caregiver could read it to a loved one verbatim. For a more tech-savvy caregiver, there is a podcast option that provides a new meditation each week for free.

Merck Manual

http://www.merckmanuals.com/home/older_peoples_health_issues

This site is a subsection on the Merck Manual website titled *Older People's Health Issues*. The website illuminates numerous issues beneficial for providers to explore. This free site breaks down seven topics: provision of care to older adults, elder mistreatment, health care coverage for older people, the aging body, social issues affecting older people, aging and drugs, the older driver, and falls. Each of the subtopics has a handful of articles that list statistics and provide an in-depth discussion.

Family Caregiver Alliance, National Center on Caregiving

https://caregiver.org/

National Center on Caregiving offers many resources to support caregivers through its mission to improve the quality of life for caregivers.

New York Zen Center for Contemplative Care

http://zencare.org/

The Center provides many resources including an archive of lectures.

RECOMMENDED READING

Byock, I. (2012). *The best care possible: A physician's quest to transform care through the end of life*. New York, NY: Avery/Penguin.

An excellent book about holistic care at the end of life.

Gawande, A. (2014). *Being mortal: Medicine and what matters in the end*. Toronto, ON: Doubleday/Random House.

This is an excellent book addressing many important matters in health care. This is a valuable resource on several levels, including a spiritual and cultural view. Gawande, a physician, provides interesting background on expected changes in health status in aging from assessment of Activities of Daily Living (ADLs) to appropriate housing for older people to assist them when frailty emerges, including the history of assisted living and Bill Thomas's Green House movement. He then moves into discussing difficult end-of-life scenarios and the reluctance of physicians to engage in meaningful discussions about what clients want at the end of life. He flavors his writing with some interesting cases, including his own father's difficult and declining health to ultimate death. Finally, a spiritual ritual on the River Ganges to assist his father's passing that included some health preventative measures still does not preclude him from contracting the parasite that causes giardia.

Sweet, V. (2012). *God's hotel: A doctor, a hospital, and a pilgrimage to the heart of medicine*. New York, NY: Riverhead books.

Using her part-time work as a physician at Laguna Honda hospital in San Francisco as backdrop, Sweet weaves a story of the conflicts between modern efficient medicine and curing through the caring given in a hospital that becomes a community. Laguna Honda is described as one of the last of the hospital almshouses that cared for the poor, the homeless, and those with no other resources. She also has studied the history of medicine, with particular interest in the medicinal writings of Hildegard of Bingen, who was also a great mystic. Further, during her writing of this book she walks the ancient pilgrimage of Santiago de Compostela in northern Spain, doing parts of it in successive years. She includes some of her reflections from this walk in the book as she champions the benefits of slow medicine.

CHAPTER NINE

SPIRITUALITY IN EMOTION, DEPRESSION, AND ANXIETY

If we had a keen vision and feeling of all ordinary human
life, it would be like hearing the grass grow and the
squirrel's heartbeat, and we should die of that roar
which lies on the other side of silence.

—George Eliot, *Middlemarch*

I stand
And suddenly understand
That you, Deep Night,
Surround me and play with me,
And I am stunned.
Your breath comes over me.
And from a vast, distant solemnity
Your smile enters me.

—Rainer Maria Rilke, "The Vast Night"

This chapter begins with discussion of the power of emotions. The concept of modern maladies of the soul is introduced. Standard types of depression and their etiology are identified as well as other depression-like states such as demoralization, desolation and the dark night of the soul, and despair. Research studies and clinical interventions are provided. Eudemonia, the opposite pole of depression, is briefly described. Anxiety and anxiety interventions conclude this chapter.

EMOTIONS AND THEIR MEANING

Studies have reported that emotional well-being and threats to that well-being are distinct from psychological well-being (Keyes, 2013). Positive and negative affect and life satisfaction are the common features of emotion as measured by population studies. Thus, understanding the emotional makeup of an individual is important in assisting him or her to function at the highest capacity.

Generally, the value of the emotions for self-teaching has been underaddressed. In Western culture, individuals tend to be reticent to recognize and to own some of their emotions, especially the "darker" emotions, such as anger, fear, depression, and despair. Partly, this is due to the discomfort we have with witnessing emotional expression in others, particularly strong emotions such as anger or sorrow. When we are uncomfortable with our own strong emotions, how can we sit with strong emotions emanating from our clients?

We each have an individually tailored spectrum of emotional range. This range includes visible emotions that we easily share with others and that elicit approval through their politically correct expression. However, another part of our spectrum descends below the visible to the politically incorrect emotions that we feel but are afraid to identify, discuss, and heal. This fear may stem from two aspects. First, we fear that if we share our feelings, they will move beyond our ability to control. They may be raw and unmediated. Second, other people may not understand or accept them and judge us in an unflattering manner. Although we know we need to address them in clients, we may touch on them as little as possible within ourselves, or hold open space primarily for the acceptable and attractive feelings of joy, love, playfulness, and the neutral feeling of calm. This gradually restricts our emotional range and can limit our ability to tune in to client feelings and *resonate* with them. The mirroring we can do for clients through quickly sensing the feelings that may lie just outside their conscious attention and gently reflecting them builds a sense of safety. Thus, if we have incapacity in our own attention to personal emotional repertoires, this will constrict effectiveness with our clients.

Alongside emotional range, everyone has a unique emotional profile consisting of the emotions that present themselves most fluently in everyday life. Emotions tend to filter the knowledge available, so that people can only interpret events consistent with the emotion experienced. Thus, emotions flavor our perceptions of reality. Emotions are notable for several factors: signaling, rapid onset, and our own lack of recognition of their presence (Dalai Lama & Ekman, 2008). Other people tend to be aware of our felt emotions (sometimes more than we are ourselves) through the body language that expresses them. Signaling occurs through our facial expressions or visible muscle tightening, aspects that are usually not distinguished by the thoughts we think. Emotions often develop rapidly in response to what we perceive. In fact, people with bipolar illness sometimes suffer from too-rapid cycling between emotional extremes. Finally, many of us live largely unaware of our emotional state. We seldom take the measure of our emotions as we do our body temperature.

A recent term related to the goal of mental health functioning used in positive psychology is *flourishing*. Moving toward the aim of flourishing, older adults can experience moderate and even elevated mental health, successfully adjusting to assaults on well-being. However, lack of attention to emotional setbacks and concerns can cause older adults to linger in a languishing form of mental health at the other end of the continuum that encapsulates symptoms of depressed mood and anxiety.

EMOTION AND THE SACRED

Spirituality and religion, standing as universal capacities within culture, can shape the origins and expressions of emotion. These two capacities also provide context for that expression. In the face of great beauty, sometimes the most appropriate response may be tears. Those tears can signify joy, a sense of being overwhelmed, and gratitude in addition to sadness and grief. The structure of the brain also influences emotional expression. The limbic system is the emotional center of the brain and includes the fear-producing amygdala. This stands in reciprocal relationship to the rationality of the frontal lobes (Newberg & Waldman, 2009). The limbic and frontal lobes are connected by the anterior cingulate, thus joining emotion with cognition. This network is thought to be involved in the development of positive emotions over negative ones and of increased skills in social awareness, particularly heightened through meditation practice. However, efficient functioning can be interrupted by stress and unregulated emotional expression, as evidenced in giving into the impulse toward sudden explosive anger.

Emotion has been categorized into three scaffolded factors: affective traits, moods, and emotions (Emmons, 2005; Rosenberg, 1998). Affective traits form the highest level and represent stable predispositions that influence the threshold for emotional experience. For instance, if a person has a tendency to feel happy and optimistic, she or he may experience this at a lower level of stimulation than another person. Moods fall under affective traits in the emotion hierarchy. They are largely unconscious and fluctuate over a day or days, yet still can exert a broad effect on consciousness. Under mood variability stand emotions. Emotions, in contrast to moods, are usually intense brief responses to a meaningful event that result from cognitive appraisal of that event. Therefore, they often engender action of some kind. The broaden-and-build theory of positive emotions submits that discrete positive emotions have the capacity to broaden momentary thought-action repertoires by strengthening personal resources cognitively, socially, and physically (Fredrickson, 2001). In contrast to negative emotions that may narrow choices to adapt to threatening situations, for example, the positive emotions carry both long-term and indirect adaptive benefits that can broaden the scope of awareness and create a wider array of possibilities. A key benefit is fostering resiliency and an upward spiral effect that encourages new solutions to adversity (Fredrickson, 2001, 2013). This type of broaden-and-build work with older adults, focusing on development of positive emotions and emotional well-being, could result in spillover to areas of current life challenge.

Basic emotions are commonly identified on the happy-sad spectrum, the anger spectrum, or the anxiety-fear spectrum. These are usually addressed in abnormal psychology or psychopathology classes. The ability to regulate emotions across contexts is adaptive. Findings from a study of bereaved widows and widowers demonstrated that those with complicated grief showed less emotionally expressive flexibility and poorer regulation of emotion (Gupta & Bonanno, 2011). There are other types of emotions that, until recently, were not generally included in studies of emotion, and still often are not. These include such complex emotions as emptiness and the depleted self, apathy, despair, boredom, loneliness, cynicism, guilt, and shame. Shame may be experienced as unworthiness or humiliation that are two of the deepest cuts to the heart. Shame is the sense of being insufficient or inadequate as a person. Guilt suggests a need to either ask forgiveness or to forgive the self. Cynicism is a way of observing the world wherein trust is sidelined and to its most extreme, the possibility for joy is absent or diminished. Loneliness is a felt sense of separation; it is often experienced by older adults when they move away from friendship networks and familiar locales as well as at other times when social networks weaken due to deaths. Boredom can be viewed from several angles. It can be seen as a failure of imagination or a feeling of being restricted from what one prefers to do. Despair will be discussed in more detail below because it is related to depressed mood. Although it may be related to depression also, apathy is a feeling that nothing matters. Worse, it can signal withdrawal from vital engagement with life and with former areas of interest. It may entail viewing a challenge as beyond one's influence—or what Martin Seligman (1975) used to refer to as "learned helplessness"—engendering little effort to respond. Instead, one estimates any effort as unlikely to succeed. Life grows increasing constricted.

When working with older people, it is helpful to consider results of environmental press: too much assistance can render them incapable of working to their ability, and too little can cause them to give up and abandon hope of success at whatever task is at hand. Emptiness and ego depletion are seen to impair the ability to reflect, so important in the approach toward healing. Self-depletion involves an impaired ability for self-regulation (Baumeister, Bratslavsky, Muraven, & Tice, 1998). Although these aspects of emotional impairment may escape typical assessment protocols, some of them can be intensely significant for older adults.

In 1997, I audited a course with Herbert Anderson at Catholic Theological Union in Chicago titled "Modern Maladies of the Soul." It addressed these important emotions often consigned to the substrata of consciousness. Despair, shame, guilt, or cynicism may be the emotions that older adults most need to address for healing and reinvestment in their encore life. Emptiness and depletion, apathy, boredom, and loneliness, too, are worth inviting into the room of therapeutic work.

Modern Maladies of the Soul

What are maladies of the soul in our current age and how do we recover or tend the soul? The terms disease and illness are well-worn today. In a disease, symptoms often develop after the disease has begun while an illness is coequal with symptom manifestations. In order to work with the concept of being ill, some people distance themselves consciously by remembering the illness—even the most compromising one—is not all of who they are. Although compartmentalization can be a fault, sometimes it permits a person to hold something unacceptable at a distance for a time until it can be healed (in one form or another—maybe not physically) and accepted as part of the holistic self. Other terms implying illness or absence of wellness are expressions like disorder, affliction, injury, and disfigurement. The concept of a malady can be broader than illness or disease to include any condition that involves suffering adversity or risk of suffering adversity. It is something normally avoided though at times people may have a reason not to avoid pain, disability or death, for instance, to save the life of another. Although maladies are intrinsically bad, they can be good on an instrumental level if something helpful is achieved through them. Finally, although the source of the malady may have once have been outside the self, such as black lung disease of a coal miner, it is now contained within the body or psyche of the person. The value of the term *malady* is that it de-medicalizes and de-pathologizes human suffering. It is also a cross-cultural indicator of vulnerability: The specific features and causes of what constitutes a malady may differ from one culture to another, but all cultures can subscribe to the idea of entering a state of suffering.

The soul is tended or recovered when therapists focus on building positive emotions in an authentic manner. Positive emotions also emerge from spiritual and religious experience alongside feelings of shame, hurt, and despair. A few of these are wonder, awe, gratitude, savoring, and forgiveness, along with faith, hope, compassion/love, and peace, which are traditionally taught across major world religions. Meaning systems can influence both positive and negative feelings expression especially within faith or spiritual communities. Although these positive emotions are quite valuable to address, they are not extensively addressed in this text except for brief treatment in Chapter 7. Both the generation and regulation of emotion can be modulated by belief (Emmons, 2005). For example, Pentecostalism and the charismatic movement within Christianity promote speaking in tongues (languages) and prophecy. This worship style facilitates demonstration of intense positive emotion, while the contemplative tradition facilitates quietude, such as in Quaker meetings or Taize worship, the latter form leading to a silent 10-minute meditation and often a feeling of deep peace. Beliefs about a punishing or loving God also entwine with religious emotional expression. Positive spiritual expressions of emotion may be found in a walk through a natural place such as a beach, nature preserve, or a park.

The 99 Names of God

In Islam, there are 99 names of God (99 Names of God, 2014). These names have been included in Table 9.1. The descriptors have been revealed in the Qur'an and describe different attributes of God. The pronunciations of these names are quite lovely, so the Arabic names are included along with their meaning. Different attributes may evoke different sensibilities as the names are spoken. Hebrew also has many names for God (Yahweh or YHWH) including El, Elohim, Eloah, Adonai, El-Shaddai, Hashem, and others. These, too, tend to highlight different attributes for God or suggest that the name cannot be spoken. The Kabbalah, a mystical branch of Judaism, suggests there are 72 names for God. Although for many people of faith or no faith one name for God may be enough, for others, the rich descriptions resident within names can expand thinking about who God may be and can be a useful exercise for older people holding a religious tradition. Each name touches on a different quality, and individuals may have significant emotional responses to certain names over others.

Spirituality and Emotion

To extend conceptualization of emotional range, Figure 9.1 suggests different emotions persons may experience in relation to the spiritual path. The three primary emotions are spiritual freedom, spiritual discovery, and spiritual suffering. Spiritual freedom depicts emotions such as poised freedom (or equipoise or surrender), centered energy, and feelings of happiness/bliss or flow. Beyond these, such feelings as vital, self-accepting, and light-hearted follow. Although depicted in a type of hierarchy, this is not intended to be a meaningful organization. Instead, the purpose of this figure is to draw out subtle aspects of emotion that may lie below awareness. The second area, spiritual discovery, shows amazement, confusion, and fear as one moves further along the pathway.

Table 9.1   The 99 Names of God in Islam

Pronunciation	Arabic	Translation	Pronunciation	Arabic	Translation
1. Allah	الله	God	28. Al Haqq	الحق	The Truth, The Real
2. Ar Rahman	الرحمن	The All Merciful	29. Al Wakil	الوكيل	The Trustee, The Dependable
3. Ar Rahim	الرحيم	The Most Merciful	30. Al Qawiyy	القوي	The Strong
4. Al Malik	الملك	The King, The Sovereign	31. Al Matin	المتين	The Firm, The Steadfast
5. Al Quddus	القدوس	The Most Holy	32. Al Wali	الولي	The Protecting Friend, Patron, Helper
6. As Salam	السلام	Peace and Blessing			
7. Al Mu'min	المؤمن	The Guarantor			
8. Al Muhaymin	المهيمن	The Guardian, The Preserver	33. Al Hamid	الحميد	The All Praiseworthy
9. Al 'Aziz	العزيز	The Almighty, The Self-Sufficient	34. Al Muhsi	المحصي	The Accounter, The Numberer of All
10. Al Jabbar	الجبار	The Powerful, The Irresistible	35. Al Mubdi'	المبدئ	The Producer, Originator, Initiator of All
11. Al Mutakabbir	المتكبر	The Tremendous	36. Al Mu'id	المعيد	The Reinstater Who Brings Back All
12. Al Khaliq	الخالق	The Creator			
13. Al Bari'	البارئ	The Maker	37. Al Muhyi	المحيي	The Giver of Life
14. Al Musawwir	المصور	The Fashioner of Forms	38. Al Mumit	المميت	The Bringer of Death, The Destroyer
15. Al Ghaffar	الغفار	The Ever Forgiving			
16. Al Qahhar	القهار	The All Compelling Subduer	39. Al Hayy	الحي	The Ever Living
17. Al Wahhab	الوهاب	The Bestower	40. Al Qayyum	القيوم	The Self-Subsisting Sustainer of All
18. Ar Razzaq	الرزاق	The Ever Providing			
19. Al Fattah	الفتاح	The Opener, The Victory Giver	41. Al Wajid	الواجد	The Perceiver, The Finder, The Unfailing
20. Al Alim	العليم	The All Knowing, The Omniscient	42. Al Majid	الماجد	The Illustrious, The Magnificent
21. Al Qabid	القابض	The Restrainer, The Straightener	43. Al Wahid	الواحد	The One, The All Inclusive, The Indivisible
22. Al Basit	الباسط	The Expander, The Munificent	44. As Samad	الصمد	The Long, The Impregnable, The Everlasting
23. Al Khafid	الخافض	The Abaser			
24. Ar Rafi'	الرافع	The Exalter	45. Al Qadir	القادر	The All Able
25. Al Mu'izz	المعز	The Giver of Honor	46. Al Muqtadir	المقتدر	The All Determiner, The Dominant
26. Al Ba'ith	الباعث	The Raiser of the Dead	47. Al Muqaddim	المقدم	The Expediter, He Who Brings Forward
27. Ash Shahid	الشهيد	The Witness			

Pronunciation	Arabic	Translation	Pronunciation	Arabic	Translation
48. Al Mu'akhkhir	رخؤملا	The Delayer, He Who Puts Far Away	77. Al Wali	يلاولا	The Patron
49. Al Awwal	لولأا	The First	78. Al Muta'al	يلاعتملا	The Self-Exalted
50. Al Akhir	رخٓلأا	The Last	79. Al Barr	ربلا	The Most Kind and Righteous
51. Az Zahir	رهاظلا	The Manifest, The All Victorious	80. At Tawwab	باوتلا	The Ever Returning, Ever Relenting
52. Al Muzil	لذملا	The Giver of Dishonor	81. Al Muntaqim	مقتنملا	The Avenger
53. Al Sami'	عيمسلا	The All Hearing	82. Al 'Afuww	وفعلا	The Pardoner, The Effacer of Sins
54. Al Basir	ريصبلا	The All Seeing	83. Ar Ra'uf	فوؤرلا	The Compassionate, The All Pitying
55. Al Hakam	مكحلا	The Judge, The Arbitrator	84. Malik al Mulk	كلملا كلام	The Owner of All Sovereignty
56. Al 'Adl	لدعلا	The Utterly Just	85. Dhu al Jalal wa al Ikram	ذو للاجلا و ماركلاا و	The Lord of Majesty and Generosity
57. Al Latif	فيطللا	The Subtly Kind	86. Al Muqsit	طسقملا	The Equitable, The Requiter
58. Al Khabir	ريبخلا	The All Aware			
59. Al Halim	ميلحلا	The Forbearing, The Indulgent	87. Al Jami'	عماجلا	The Gatherer, The Unifier
60. Al 'Azim	ميظعلا	The Magnificent, The Infinite	88. Al Ghani	ينغلا	The All Rich, The Independent
61. Al Ghafur	روفغلا	The All Forgiving	89. Al Mughni	ينغملا	The Enricher, The Emancipator
62. Ash Shakur	روكشلا	The Grateful			
63. Al 'Ali	يلعلا	The Sublimely Exalted	90. Al Mani'	عناملا	The Withholder, The Shielder, The Defender
64. Al Kabir	ريبكلا	The Great			
65. Al Hafiz	ظيفحلا	The Preserver	91. Ad Dharr	راضلا	The Distresser
66. Al Muqit	تيقملا	The Nourisher	92. An Nafi'	عفانلا	The Propitious, The Benefactor
67. Al Hasib	بيسحلا	The Reckoner			
68. Al Jalil	ليلجلا	The Majestic	93. An Nur	رونلا	The Light
69. Al Karim	ميركلا	The Bountiful, The Generous	94. Al Hadi	يداهلا	The Guide
70. Ar Raqib	بيقرلا	The Watchful	95. Al Badi	عيدبلا	Incomparable, The Originator
71. Al Mujib	بيجملا	The Responsive, The Answerer	96. Al Baqi	يقابلا	The Ever Enduring and Immutable
72. Al Wasi'	عساولا	The Vast, The All Encompassing	97. Al Warith	ثراولا	The Heir, The Inheritor of All
73. Al Hakim	ميكحلا	The Wise			
74. Al Wadud	دودولا	The Loving, The Kind One	98. Ar Rashid	ديشرلا	The Guide, Infallible Teacher, Knower
75. Al Majid	ديجملا	The All Glorious	99. As Sabur	روبصلا	The Patient, The Timeless
76. Al Batin	نطابلا	The Hidden, The All Encompassing			

Figure 9.1 Spiritual Emotions Chart

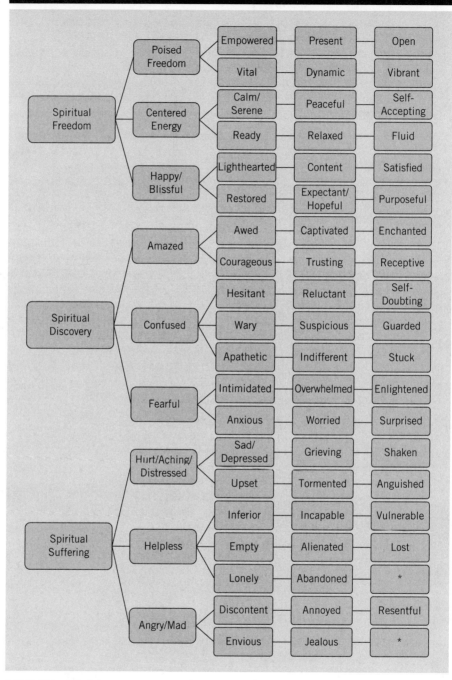

© Holly Nelson-Becker

In a discovery process, anything may be found. At times new ideas challenge cherished beliefs and this can be sensed as painful or liberating, for example. After *overwhelmed*, I have added *enlightened*, to show that feelings can shift and turn. The last area denotes spiritual suffering and includes hurt/distressed, helpless, and angry/mad. Related descriptors include grieving, alienated, and resentful among others. Although spiritual suffering is not a DSM-5 diagnosis at this time (nor should it be), it can be a source of significant anguish. Asterisks are left in open boxes for important emotional states that are absent; these can be completed by the reader.

Depression is experienced by many older adults and so will be discussed extensively here. There are several ways to conceptualize and understand the clinical features of depression. Eliciting causes and symptomology is important for treatment and so will be examined first in this section. However, beyond the typical mental health criteria now expressed in the DSM-5 and the ICD-11, lays a second type of interpretation of the social construction of depression: the despair that is expressed as "the dark night of the soul." The distinction between clinical depression and the dark night aspect is important. Depression is a mood disorder, a constellation of psychological symptoms. The dark night is a time of spiritual anguish and opportunity; it is an interval where having control or feeling in control is absent. It can result in transformation through the shedding of certain aspects of selfhood that no longer seem important or real. Finally, the term *despair* suggests an absolute state of detachment from the self. Thus, the typical indicators of key forms of depression, major depressive disorder and persistent depressive disorder (dysthymia), will be elucidated first. These will be followed by discussion of the origin and expression of the "dark night" concept and the features of despair.

INDICATORS AND ETIOLOGY OF DEPRESSION

Depression and other mood disorders are an ongoing concern in older adults (Blazer, 2002). Although older people tend to report life satisfaction generally, they do tend to be at risk for depressive feelings (Zarit & Zarit, 2011). To some extent, depression may parallel other losses such as death of a life partner, loneliness, increasing physical debilitation, and health concerns. Age-related physical changes such as hearing loss, vision changes, and/or other sensory difficulties that influence perception, decreased energy, and minor physical pains can affect how older people feel about their lives. For example in 2010, 46% of older men and 31% of older women reported difficulty hearing (Federal Interagency Forum on Aging-Related Statistics, 2012). As older adults move through the life course and continue to survive, their supportive network of siblings and friends begins to diminish. In my research with older people (Nelson-Becker, 2004b), several participants lamented this unforeseen circumstance of outliving valued support. A study by Tay and Diener (2011) confirmed that having someone available in an emergency and feeling respected by others, conferred by social networks, greatly enhance a sense of well-being, sometimes over material assets. Further, psychosocial resources also best predict well-being. But before we turn to what enhances well-being, it is important to explore the common emotional state of depression.

DEPRESSION TYPES

Several categories of depression are recognized by psychiatry and psychology and especially manifest in the DSM-5. The disorders recognized by this group, although based as much as possible on evidence, are formed out of a consensus of experts in the field. Ongoing controversy about categories and new areas of inclusion suggest that this process does not always result in a clear delineation of some mental illness syndromes. Classifying a set of symptoms as a mental illness, though it may be stigmatizing, is important for third-party payments under most insurance carriers in the United States. The key terms addressed in this section are major depression, melancholia, endogenous and exogenous depression, minor depression, persistent depressive disorder/dysthymia, demoralization, and the dark night of the soul. Each of these has its own criteria and sequelae, and they involve a mix of modern understandings and more classical historical terms. The formal DSM syndromes are major depressive disorder and persistent depressive disorder (dysthymia). Further, depression sometimes co-occurs with certain medical illnesses and carries its own category of Depressive Disorder Due to Another Medical Condition.

Major Depressive Disorder

Major depressive disorder (MDD) in the DSM-5 includes presentations of two or more of the following symptoms for two weeks or more: feelings of worthlessness or guilt, reduced concentration or decision making, fatigue, psychomotor agitation or retardation, insomnia or hypersomnia, significant increase or decrease in weight or appetite, and recurring thoughts of death or suicidal ideation (American Psychiatric Association, 2013). A key aspect of this disorder is that feelings of sadness and other changes occur suddenly and cause significant impairment. MDD is not often found to occur in older people for the first time. Generally, people with MDD at earlier ages either recover or may be less likely to survive due to health problems or suicide (Zarit & Zarit, 2011).

Melancholia

Melancholia or *melancholy* is a term for depression reported since the time of Hippocrates: It was referred to as the "black bile," one of the four humors. Hippocrates wrote that grief and fear that endure could cause melancholia. The experience of melancholy is part of the suffering that defines the human condition. Elements of sadness, sorrow, depression, discouragement, and hopelessness are experienced by most people and thus form part of the range of feeling in response to life events. However, when these feelings endure and are severe in strength, then they may form part of a disorder that can be addressed through psychopharmacology and psychotherapy. A NIMH three-state collaborative depression study demonstrated that combined treatment using medication and some form of cognitive or interpersonal therapeutic approach tends to have the most favorable outcomes (Gibbons et al., 2002).

Melancholia, as a disorder subtype in the DSM, described changes in psychomotor function such as agitation or retardation, worsening mood in the morning and early morning awakening, weight loss and excessive guilt. Further, loss of pleasure in activities and lack of reaction to pleasant occurrences were also features of this subtype. Biological indicators include dexamethasone nonsuppression (cortisone metabolism denoting increased stress) and reduced rapid eye movement (REM), which meant reduced time spent in deep restorative sleep (American Psychiatric Association, 1994; Coryell, 2007). Thus, older people who had symptoms of despondency and decreased or non-interaction with others may have some of the physical or vegetative signs of this form of depression as well. "Melancholia responded better than other kinds of depression to two treatments: tricyclic antidepressants (the first generation of the drugs) and electroconvulsive therapy (E.C.T., better known as shock therapy)"

(Greenberg, 2013, para. 7). A melancholy often emerges in the aging process. Different from depression, it denotes a minor key or a certain tonality. It can offer time for reflection, out of which wisdom may come. It can encourage a slower pace and the opportunity to serve as mentor to younger people. "You can live from your soul rather than your self—less certain of the truth of things but more in touch with intuition and emotion" (Moore, 2004, p. 294). Melancholy is not about cognitive processes but recognition of time passing.

Endogenous Versus Exogenous Depression

Other ways of conceptualizing depression include endogenous and exogenous forms. These are older terms but ones still in use. *Endogenous depression* refers to depression with either a biochemical origin or due to a personality disorder (Coryell, 2007). It tends to be a less exact term as it may refer to either major depressive symptoms or persistent depression/dysthymia. *Exogenous depression* generally refers to a depression that results from some life event or situation, such as a major loss event or death of a significant other. There are some terms related to exogenous depression like *chronic sorrow* (loss of an expected future), such as with a severely disabled child; *nonfinite losses* whose results endure, such as inability to bear children; and *ambiguous losses*, one form of which occurs when a significant other is present physically but mentally absent, such as in later stages of dementia (Winokuer & Harris, 2012).

Minor Depression

Minor depression, also known as subsyndromal or subthreshold depression, includes clinically significant symptoms of depression that are less severe, not fully meeting the criteria for major depression. This type of depression is often unrecognized and untreated. However, minor depression can still respond to antidepressant medication. Like major depression, minor depression leads to functional impairment, poorer self-rated health, and/or less social support. It is correlated with being female and unmarried (Blazer, 2003).

Persistent Depressive Disorder (Dysthymia)

A longer-term form of depression common in aging manifests as the following: depression without sadness that results in depleted energy, withdrawal, or apathy. Persistent depressive disorder formerly known as dysthymia in DSM-IV-TR (American Psychiatric Association, 2000) is a longer lasting, but less severe, form of depression that extends two years or more, according to DSM-5 criteria. Depression often co-occurs or is comorbid with other kinds of illnesses, such as heart disease, stroke (CVA), diabetes, and hip fractures. The Centers for Disease Control and Prevention (CDC, 2013) estimates that 80% of older adults have one chronic health concern and 50% have more than two, suggesting that clinicians should consider evidence for depressed mood in persons with a chronic health condition. Depressive symptoms also may appear in older adults with dementia of the Alzheimer's type (AD). Vascular depression is associated with difficulty in recognition memory, verbal fluency, and executive cognitive functioning. Vascular depression is less likely to have psychotic symptoms, be associated with genetic history, and presents with greater functional impairment and anhedonia—the absence of pleasure or the ability to experience it—than nonvascular-related forms of depression (Blazer, 2003).

DEPRESSION AS CULTURAL MARKER

It also may be useful to ask whether depression is a universal construct or mainly descriptive of Western culture (Zimmerman, 1995). The question of whether cultural variance predisposes recognition of the psychobiological components of depression is worthy of further consideration, although it may be the case that people are predisposed globally to positive emotions as these are more adaptive in response to life challenge. Individualism also may be a predictor of well-being over collectivist societies as people have greater choice in setting the course of their lives (Diener, Oishi, & Ryan, 2013). The literature reports that in collectively organized nations, people do tend to pay closer attention to interpersonally related emotions such as guilt, gratitude, and jealousy than in individually oriented nations where people are more attuned to emotions more common with independence (Diener et al., 2013).

EPIDEMIOLOGY

Rates of major depression for older people living in the community range between 1% and 5% generally and somewhat higher, between 12% and 20%, for those being seen in outpatient medical clinics (Zarit & Zarit, 2011). The latter reinforces understanding of the comorbid nature of depression with illness. In institutionalized settings, rates may extend from 4% to 16%, spiking as high as 44% for certain populations of hospitalized patients, and another 16% are those who have symptoms of depression although they do not meet criteria for MDD (Hybels, Blazer, Pieper, Landerman, & Steffens, 2009; Zarit & Zarit, 2011). Most people who suffer from MDD have had episodes earlier in life rather than a late life onset. At older ages, physical disability due to general medical conditions and cognitive impairment or psychiatric conditions may co-occur with a depressive state. Depression without sadness and a depletion syndrome that includes lack of energy and/or withdrawal/apathy may be additional subtypes that trouble some older adults outside of a formal diagnosis (Jeste, Blazer, & First, 2005). Overall, depression is generally underdiagnosed in older adults with chronic illness and those who reside in institutionalized care. Environmental mastery moderates the impact of health and functioning on depression in residential care (Knight, Davison, McCabe, & Mellor, 2011), suggesting that older adults who are able to function in a way that best expresses their identity experience less depression.

Older adults over age 75 are more likely to experience symptoms of depression, but overall, depressive symptoms tend to decrease with age, particularly in comparison to middle age (Zarit & Zarit, 2011). Adults over age 85 are at the highest risk. Women experience depressive symptoms at rates that are twice the rate for men (Zarit & Zarit, 2011). Reasons given for the relatively lower rates include: people with MDD may be less likely to survive to older ages through negative effects on health overall or suicidal outcomes; the presentation of depression may change in older ages; and older people may be less likely to complain of problems in mood, though expressing physical discomfort may be more acceptable.

EUDAIMONIA

It can be helpful to contrast these passages identifying and describing different forms of depression with the inverse emotions of eudaimonia and hedonia. Which is the more worthy goal for life? *Eudaimonia* is seen to facilitate maximization of capacity in all life domains while *hedonia* is often referenced in the literature as pertaining to maximization of pleasure (Keyes, 2013). Hedonia comes out of the Epicurean perspective and suggests expansion of pleasant feelings while diminishing unpleasant ones; it relates to one's experience in the moment and reflection on the experience. Eudaimonia emerged out of an Aristotelian view and describes goal-centered striving toward full functioning and realization of innate potential. The latter would be more consistent with a spiritual view that generally takes a larger perspective, while recognizing the need to understand how moment-to-moment experience contributes to development. However, hedonia, the power to motivate positively, and eudaimonia, the power to act positively, together constitute human flourishing (Fredrickson, 2013). By contrast, depressive and anxious states perpetuate languishing, the failure to feel one's best and achieve one's best. Can someone experiencing depressed states achieve eudaimonia? With assessment of need for medication and/or counseling, self-selected activities of interest can provide further motivation for individuals to act on behavior that might bring them to a eudaimonic state. When people act as if they are feeling happy, that feeling can become real. People who flourish tend to experience a bigger boost from small actions than those who are depressed (Fredrickson, 2013).

OTHER DEPRESSION-LIKE STATES: DEMORALIZATION, DESOLATION AND THE DARK NIGHT OF THE SOUL, AND DESPAIR

Demoralization

Clients with depression often articulate their hopelessness and feelings of helplessness, as I learned when working with patients in a county psychiatric hospital. These clients spoke about meaninglessness, low self-esteem, and a felt sense of being ineffective in their life pursuits. Clark and Kissane (2002) discuss this as an existential stance. In their view demoralization included such feelings as disheartenment (mild loss of confidence) to despondency (beginning to give up) to despair (losing hope) to demoralization (having given up). They distinguished this syndrome from depression because clients can smile in the moment while retaining a sense of pointlessness. Clients who are depressed emote a sad affect that includes a gloomy or flat countenance. Helplessness and hopelessness are chief characteristics of this type of depression. However, demoralization also may be the first step on the continuum to despair as suggested by Frank and Frank (1993). Patients had in fact, come for treatment. Although they suffered, they had not completely lost hope. That is how demoralization will be used here, as a concern, but not complete engulfment.

Immigration itself can be one example of a stressor that leads to feelings of helplessness and hopelessness due to low social support, new cultural expectations, and lower socioeconomic status than in the country of origin (Briggs & Macleod, 2006). This is especially a risk for older people who immigrated at older ages to be with family, yet who found it more difficult to learn the customs and language of the host culture. Feelings of resulting isolation or narrowed boundaries generated by living apart from but within a host culture can lead to sadness and yearning for the earlier time of comparative social freedom in one's natal land. Although this clearly may have some elements of an exogenous (externally caused) depression, it could also have entirely internal causes. Assessment would be needed to distinguish differences. Depending on severity, it could first be addressed with a therapeutic approach over medication, unless the client was also expressing suicidal thoughts.

A second example of demoralization can be present in individuals who fail to see any potential for improvement in some of the given factors of their life. In a way, this can represent a failure of imagination or just a deep inability to see potential. One illustration of this is situations of domestic or intimate partner violence where the partners have aged together, but the abuse level has not diminished (Shim & Nelson-Becker, 2009). In fact, at older ages, sometimes abused partners are the ones who serve as caregivers to the perpetrator. This can leave a mix of difficult feelings to untangle. Yet another example concerns people who age with mental illness, such as schizophrenia. The difficulty of managing symptoms and medication regimes may or may not improve with time, leaving older patients with life-long frustrations and hopelessness about being able to achieve once-held dreams of even simple pleasures such as living independently.

Desolation and the Dark Night of the Soul

The dark night of the soul is qualitatively different than the types of depression discussed above and can cause significant distress for people in mid- to late-life periods. *The dark night of the soul* was a term that originated in the Early Middle Ages—5th to 10th centuries—and carried within it a description of an uncertain relationship with God. The Early Middle Ages in Europe itself was a time of decreasing systemization in agriculture resulting in lower crop yields, decreasing population, increasing localism due to disruptions in trade and manufacturing, and overall decreasing infrastructure that led to less availability of schools and military security. The "dark night" presents an interesting correlation with a time in history that surely must have tested the resolve of individuals living then. Today, the concept of the dark night of the soul has garnered other meanings including a deep sense of alienation that can also describe a humanist or existential condition *sans a priori* considerations of God or a divine being.

For people who believe in a deity, the dark night is engendered by the fear that God is absent and His or Her presence can no longer be sensed. It is a time when perceptions of God are obscured. The Spanish word *oscura* has the root meaning "dark." This obscurity or dark night is a common experience of spiritual leaders, especially mystics. Mystics are those of every faith tradition and none who seek or experience a subjective encounter with ultimate reality or that which is deemed to be divine. Many of the mystic writers, such as Julian of Norwich (1342–1416), Teresa of Avila (1515–1582), John of the Cross (1542–1591), and more recently Thomas Merton (1915–1968), wrote about this period as being one of longing, suffering, and waiting through a very real sense of distance from spirit. Teresa was plagued by doubts and fears about her experiences in prayer for roughly 20 years, during which her religious community was concerned she had been overtaken by evil forces (May, 2004). She was attached to the beliefs of her community and thus was concerned that they might be right. Finally, she was able to rely on her own authenticity and trust her perceptions after a powerful spiritual experience and validation by a Franciscan friar who deeply understood her.

John of the Cross, a member of a Carmelite order of monks, wrote a series of poems about the Ascent of Mount Carmel; the fourth section he titled the *Dark Night of the Soul.* Darkness represents the difficulties the soul encounters in detachment from the world and reaching union with the Creator. There are several steps in this journey, related in successive stanzas, which detail the distressing experiences people endure as they grow in spiritual maturity. The poem is divided into two books that describe two phases of the dark night. The first phase is purification of the senses. The second and more intense of the two phases is purification of the spirit, which is the less common of the two. About this he writes, "[It] pertains to those who are already proficient, occurring at the time when God desires to bring them to the state of union with God.

And this latter night is a more obscure and dark and terrible purgation" (Saint John of the Cross, ca. 1500, para. 4).

In Chapter IX, three signs of the presence of the dark night are detailed. The first one is especially relevant here:

> *The first is whether, when a soul finds no pleasure or consolation in the things of God, it also fails to find it in anything created; . . . for, as God sets the soul in this dark night to the end that He may quench and purge its sensual desire, He allows it not to find attraction or sweetness in anything whatsoever.* (Saint John of the Cross, 2010, p. 33)

Others take a more nuanced view of the dark. Dionysius the Areopagite, writing earlier in the 6th century suggested, "The simple, absolute and immutable mysteries of divine Truth are hidden in the super-luminous darkness of that silence which revealeth in secret. For this darkness, though of deepest obscurity, is yet radiantly clear" (Pruter, 1985, p. 23).

The dark night refers to a sense of alienation and absence. Although this felt absence is often related to perception of God and lack of connection, it can also include a sense of alienation from one's own patterns of living. One experiences life as routinized and lifeless in the sense that vitality may be absent. A different interpretation of the night includes its restorative power. In the nighttime we sleep and quietly prepare for the day, a rebirth. Babies in utero presumably grow in the darkness. In a life, we figuratively die and are re-born each morning when we wake. There is transformative power in the night and it is to this that Dionysius the Areopagite may refer above. We are shaped by our nights as much as we are shaped by our days. Although we may think of the night as stagnant, there is always activity and motion within its boundaries as the night creatures who search for food at dusk suggest. Things must first fall apart before they can be put together. In the falling apart, we are forced to look at unsavory things and clean out the rubble resting there. The night time can be an initiation into spiritual maturity. The dark can be a time for growth just as the light.

Moore (2004) suggests that psychology seeks to bring problems into the light and to help make life manageable; however, darkness can deepen us, making us "more complex, more interesting, less one-dimensional" (p. 81). He theorizes that darkness gives individuals substance in the eyes of others. That is certainly a positive view, and maybe overly so; however, all lives do consist of darkness as well as light, and some darkness is self-created. Rather than rejecting our dark parts, engaging, welcoming, and learning to understand our shadow sides can lead to personal transformation in a paradoxical way. Although periods of darkness expose our vulnerability, they also can open space for a shift: greater caution and greater observance of sounds and sights of the night, which may carry their own teaching.

Distinguishing Depression and Desolation

Many people in the press of daily life do not often reflect on nor know their interior self. Aufauvre (2003) suggests that what some individuals label depression may be nothing more than weariness or overwork. Further, spiritual desolation may only be disappointment at failure to achieve perfection or the envisioned life. However, the vision itself may be formed unconsciously as a defense against childhood abuse or neglect. Depressed mood can involve concerns about self-image and how people think others see them in a mirror-within-mirror effect. The problem itself may be confusing and difficult to delineate or describe. Normal problem-solving skills are hard to engage. Lack of energy can obscure the ability to see deeply without professional help. People who experience spiritual desolation move into periods of spiritual poverty. Generally, they are fully aware of what they lack, but do not have awareness of how to change the situation. Perhaps a part of the learning is that they must wait in powerlessness. There is little that they can do to extricate themselves. However, the presence of a community, even if it is only one additional person, can bring the glimmer of healing. In the Biblical story of the prophet Job, suffering engulfed him, but not because of his own deeds. His response was to wait patiently, to sit with friends—even though they did not understand—and eventually, much that was lost was restored.

Despair

Individuals who experience spiritual desolation unquestionably enter dark waters, but usually there is an end. They emerge. Despair is perhaps the worst case scenario of demoralization, depression, and desolation. In despair, one fails to see possibility. There is a complete sense of hopelessness. Although something may be done to change the situation or the person, the perception is that nothing can be done. Despair is thus the endpoint to depression, demoralization, and desolation. No environment seems safe or welcoming. Despair may be masked as grief, apathy, or cynicism. A person who privileges biological causes for depression may seek medication through a physician or psychiatrist. A person who privileges psychosocial causes of depression will blame a relationship or himself or herself and see a psychotherapist. A person who privileges spiritual causes may believe she or he is being punished by God and seek the advice of a minister or chaplain. A person in despair will see no relief and seek out no help. This person is at risk for suicide. Restoration of the soul for one in despair begins with noticing and naming. It continues with validation from someone else that something is wrong. Sharing a professional viewpoint can be critically helpful here. The professional can be the mediator of a gentle hope achieved through a joint imagination of how things could be different. And ultimately, through waiting together—and medication, if appropriate—feelings change.

RESEARCH RELATED TO DEPRESSION AND RELIGION

Studies on depression and its relationship to religion have tended to focus more on religion—which is generally easier to study empirically as it is more often bounded—than spirituality. Koenig et al. (2012) reported a positive correlation between religiousness and optimism or hope. Feelings of low self-esteem are more likely found in those without any religious commitment (Dein, 2006). Of 70 studies looking at the correlation of religion and depression, 42 found less depression present with greater expression of religiousness (Dein, 2006). A sample of 2,800 adults found a curvilinear relationship with depression: Those who self-reported no religion and those who were very religious tended to experience more symptoms of depression (Schnittker, 2001). It is possible that individuals who are rigidly religious, for example, overly dependent on rules, ideas of guilt, and/or what constitutes sin, may be more likely to experience depression, although there are few studies specifically on this or religious fundamentalism and its relationship to depression.

Less depression was found in 232 male and female religious individuals residing in Benedictine monasteries who rated high on attachment to God and maintaining close friendships. Greater intimacy in friendships but less attachment to God led to increased stress that had a greater depression risk (Bishop, 2008). Third, lower friendship closeness and less secure attachment to God diminished the effect of stress on depression. This appears to support the concept of spiritual resiliency as a benefit of connection to religious community suggested by Ramsey and Blieszner (1999).

Attachment and Depression

Attachment is relevant in this chapter on depression as it addresses the emotional set points older adults carry that, according to Bowlby's (1969) theory of attachment, are related to early developmental experience and apply to later relational frameworks. Bowlby indicated that young children with secure attachment had an affectional bond that provided them a sense of safety in times of stress and gave them a secure base from which to explore and grow mentally (Granqvist, Mikulincer, & Shaver, 2010). This also led children to be able to regulate their own emotional tones and any distress they might feel in the broader context of security. However, this not only applies to childhood, but affects relationships all through life. Securely attached adults are more likely to demonstrate compassionate and prosocial behavior as opposed to those who show avoidant (emotionally distancing) or anxious (worry-filled) behavior. These are other developmental patterns that were shown by Ainsworth (1968) to develop in infancy and persist. Further, other attachment styles have been suggested that include a dismissing style that aligns with negative views of others, a fearful style correlating with negative views of self and others, and a preoccupied style with a negative view of self and positive view of others (Diehl, Elnick, Bourbeau, & Labouvie-Vief, 1998).

These cognitive schemas also apply to older adult attachment to God, the mental representations they carry regarding God that drives their understanding of who God is (Kirkpatrick, 2005; Pickard & Nelson-Becker, 2011). This is especially relevant because it affects the rationalizations people create for suffering—for instance, punishment from God or God accompanying one in one's suffering. Understanding attachment style can assist practitioners in knowing how to approach older adults whose views of God contribute to their anger and discouragement.

INTERVENTIONS

Clinical Considerations

Although many older adults do seek health care from primary care clinics rather than from a mental health provider, depression is underrecognized and undertreated (Barg et al., 2006). Those at greatest risk for depression are both homebound older people and older patients seen in primary care facilities (Choi & McDougall, 2007). When discussing symptoms of depression, older people may use the adjectives *lonely, lack of interest, down, sad,* and *not talkative* to describe their experience. These terms were reported by respondents in the Barg et al. (2006) study more than other more commonly recognized symptoms. These words were self-generated and not chosen from a list, giving the word *lonely* more salience. What is especially interesting about Barg and coauthors' study is that they captured participant comments about loneliness and depression in three ways: loneliness is a natural component of aging; lonely people carry responsibility for feeling lonely through withdrawal from friends; and loneliness can lead into depressed feelings. Thus, loneliness may be a signal that further assessment is needed to prevent depression.

Another study considered whether religion and spirituality might serve as a moderating effect between loneliness and depression (Han & Richardson, 2010). Findings suggested that the relationship between loneliness and depression was weaker among older people who identified as more spiritual. A representative national Canadian study indicated that people who had greater religious service attendance were less depressed, but those who identified as more religious or spiritual experienced more depression (Baetz, Griffen, Bowen, Koenig, & Marcoux, 2004). This highlights the complexity of the relationships among religion, spirituality, and depression.

Bowland, Edmond, and Fallot (2012) tested a spirituallyfocused intervention with groups of trauma survivors. The 11-week intervention resulted in lower depression and anxiety scores at posttest. A study of 66 older adult patients previously treated for depression and anxiety reported that 83% found it important to discuss spirituality and religion in counseling (Stanley et al., 2011). Benefits endorsed included increased support, acceptance, and comfort. The only disadvantage identified was a concern about mismatch in religious or spiritual orientation between the patient and counselor.

Overall, high touch and high tech modalities both offer great promise in depression. High touch strategies include the conversation that is delivered with such programs as Meals on Wheels. People do not need to be physically touched (although they might benefit); touching also includes reaching out in conversation and other engagement. Simple conversational interchanges in public places like grocery and department stores offer relief from loneliness and ultimately, depression. This type of "touching" recognizes the worth of persons and thus can be a spiritual expression of community. Although older adults are often touch deprived, care must also be taken by professionals to maintain necessary boundaries. High tech modalities, such as e-mail, Facebook, and telemedicine, are and will increasingly become important ways for older people to connect with their physicians and provide feedback about antidepressant effects. High tech also is now beginning to be used for in-home monitoring by physically distant family and physicians. Further, video-based therapies such as cognitive behavioral therapy are becoming available through online platforms. Spiritual and religious communities also might begin to reach out to older people in these formats.

Psychotherapeutic Approaches: CBT, IPT, and Behavior Therapy

After assessment by a physician for possible medication needs, psychotherapy may also be beneficial (Curran & Wattis, 2008). Effective psychotherapeutic treatments for both depression and anxiety include cognitive behavioral therapy (CBT), interpersonal therapy (IPT), and behavioral therapy. CBT involves looking at maladaptive thinking patterns, substituting distorted thinking with more adaptive thoughts. To assess this, a mental health practitioner may look at the antecedent conditions that lead to the unreasonable or distorted thought as well as the consequences of that thinking that allow the problem to persist. The goal is to break the cycle of irrational thoughts and reframe the problem. This process can include identifying unhealthy religious or spiritual themes such as acceptance of abuse as God's will. Beck and Alford (2009) suggest that depression is a result of cognitive schemas that do not function well for that individual. IPT assists clients to understand their relational patterns and establish more effective interactions. Behavioral therapy looks at the ABCs (antecedents, behavior, consequences) of behavior. As with irrational thoughts, a therapist would first conduct an assessment of what happens before, during, and after a problematic behavior. Along with altering thoughts, older clients would be encouraged to engage in pleasant events such as those enumerated on the Pleasant Events Schedule (Lewinsohn & Libet, 1972). This schedule lists 320 items that clients are asked to rate according to past frequency and level of enjoyment experienced (a copy may be found at http://www.healthnetsolutions.com/dsp/PleasantEventsSchedule.pdf). Examples of spiritual activities include reading the scriptures or other sacred texts, going to church functions, talking about philosophy or religion, seeing beautiful scenery, "feeling the presence of the Lord in my life" (as mentioned by older clients), saying prayers, and meditating or doing yoga.

Integrating religion and or spirituality into treatment with older people is preferred by the majority, but of course should always be invited rather compelled (Stanley et al., 2011). Religious beliefs should generally not be challenged unless they cause harm to the older person. Assessment of the client's underlying concern should occur first if a client asks a therapist about his or her faith. For instance, one older client asked a person of color about her religious faith affiliation. The true question here was, "Can you understand me and will I be safe with you?" Self-disclosure on the part of the therapist should only be done rarely, with caution, and when there is a possibility of sincere benefit for the client. Some forms of religious coping, such as deferral of decisions to God—rather than a view that entails collaboration with God—can result in exacerbation of psychiatric problems. Integration of religious beliefs and religious or sacred texts suggested by the client into CBT procedures can be perceived as quite helpful and support the therapeutic alliance. Guided imagery used to sense the presence of a higher being can increase hope and optimism (Paukert et al., 2009). Attending religious services, volunteering, as well as use of prayer or other well-accepted religious or spiritual rituals can also successfully diminish depressed mood. However, the purpose of the prayer may distinguish its psychotherapeutic benefit. Used passively and as a tool for avoidance it may not have the impact as it would if used for reflection and growth.

Other Forms of Treatment: Transcranial Magnetic Imaging and Electroconvulsive Therapy

Other kinds of treatment are available for those that do not respond to medication and/or psychotherapy. The combination of both of the latter is considered the gold standard for treatment of depression over medication alone. The following forms of treatment should only be used cautiously with older people because of greater biological vulnerability. Transcranial magnetic imaging (TMI), also known as transcranial magnetic stimulation, has shown some promise in people who do not respond well to other treatments. Electroconvulsive therapy (ECT) has also been used successfully with people who do not respond well to more conventional therapy, though memory loss can be a side effect, making this a more complicated form of therapy for older people. These treatments are biologically based rather than spiritually based, but the complexity of depression suggests that several forms of treatment may be useful. I have witnessed people respond favorably to ECT and when they did, the capacity to experience joy was unbounded. However, the effects may not endure.

SPIRITUAL INTERVENTIONS AND DEPRESSION/DESOLATION

A growing acquaintance with our emotions instead of the more common denial can stimulate deeper self-understanding. Often this is resisted because these emotions and their causes may stem from great pain. It is hard to hold onto emotions that keep us vulnerable to our necessary learning. We would rather close the door—and lock it. But there is a time for opening doors and having the courage to look at what is there. Often this can best be accomplished through accompaniment by a social worker, counselor, therapist, or spiritual director. Getting in touch and staying in touch with feelings can lead to renewed investment in our lives and in the world. Our passion shifts and then we have the ability to change the world, or at least our part of it. When individuals fail to consider their emotions, emotions can go underground and work subterraneously. Addiction, for instance, thrives on denial.

St. Ignatius of Loyola (1491–1556) taught that *spiritual desolation* was the experience of the soul in heaviness or darkness (Ignatius of Loyola, 1951; O'Brien, 2011). Doubts, unhealthy desires, self-focus, fear and anxiety, timidity, hiding, and alienation lead to being without hope, love, or faith. One feels separated from the Creator, or Source of all things. *Spiritual consolation,* by contrast, is a condition of feeling afire with the Creator's love in a way that leads to praise, love, and service for God and others. This consolation is fueled by a sense of gratitude for graces received such as companionship, guidance, and mercy that can lead to eudaimonia, discussed above. Through prayer and meditation one becomes more sensitive to the motions of the soul or spirit. These interior movements include emotions, dislikes, attractions, dreams, and possibilities. Ignatius termed the process of considering interiority the *discernment of spirits.* In the language of his time and religious culture, he spoke of good and evil spirits. Discernment involves the process of observing the origins of these spirits and their possible outcomes. Good and evil spirits can connect to both the good and evil within a person as well as the larger movements in society toward good—altruistic acts of mentoring, assisting at a homeless shelter, caregiving for an older person, and so forth—or evil—participating in groups that support a drug culture, violent means of redress, or denial of the Shoah (Holocaust) of World War II. Although discernment may seem like it should be obvious, because of our complicated lives and blindness, it can take practice and deep listening to achieve.

The nature of the spiritual life includes periods of both consolation and desolation. Ignatius of Loyola (1951) suggested that one tool in fortifying oneself against desolation is in times of consolation to "consider how he or she will act in future desolation, and store up new strength for that time" (SE 323). In desolation, Ignatius suggested that one consider "that with the sufficient grace already available he or she can do much to resist all hostile forces, drawing strength from our Creator and Lord" (SE 324). Using spiritual language, in times of desolation Ignatius asked people to consider prior experiences of joy and anticipate the time that joy would return as well as to act to bring that time closer. Further, in desolate periods, one should not make a change because one is under the guidance of the evil spirit and "thus we can never find the way to a right decision" (SE318). Regardless of belief in a Higher Power or Universal Spirit, this counsel offers timeless truth that where we focus our thoughts may help pull us out of certain depressions, and the warning that changes made when we lack focus and direction can be like striking out in a canoe without oars or a map of the terrain.

In his "Principle and Foundation" paragraph 23 (see Table 9.2), Ignatius provides what he sees as the essence of a life of faith. Similar to the third noble truth about Dukkha (suffering) in Buddhism that suggests cessation of striving is possible, he advised that we are to make ourselves indifferent to all things. "We ought to use these things to the extent that they help us toward our end, and free ourselves from them to the extent that they hinder us from it." The key here that shares a core truth applicable to many religious faiths and meaning systems is that people can experience *freedom from* attachment to unhealthy practices and ideas. This freedom from leads to *freedom for,* which encapsulates the endeavor to reach one's best self or highest state of being. Rather than scattered, one is focused. Rather than stuck, one is engaged in dynamic process, a poised freedom. This freedom signals a readiness to respond to spiritual leanings and whispers.

Table 9.2   Ignatian Spirituality
St. Ignatius Loyola—First Principle and Foundation
Spiritual Exercises, 23rd paragraph.
Human beings are created to praise, reverence, and serve God our Lord, and by means of doing this to save their souls.
The other things on the face of the earth are created for the human beings, to help them in the pursuit of the end for which they are created.
From this it follows that we ought to use these things to the extent that they help us toward our end, and free ourselves from them to the extent that they hinder us from it.
To attain this it is necessary to make ourselves indifferent to all created things, in regard to everything which is left to our free will and is not forbidden. Consequently, on our own part we ought not to seek health rather than poverty, honor rather than dishonor, a long life rather than a short one, and so on in all other matters.
Rather, we ought to desire and choose only that which is more conducive to the end for which we are created. (p. 32)

Source: From Ganss, G. E. (1992). *The spiritual exercises of Saint Ignatius.* A translation and commentary. St. Louis, MO: The Institute of Jesuit Sources. Permission granted by the Institute of Jesuit Sources, Chestnut Hill, MA, 2016.

ANXIETY

There are a number of anxiety disorders that older adults may experience, including specific phobias, such as of blood or spiders. Other types listed in the DSM-5 include social anxiety disorder (social phobia), panic disorder, and generalized anxiety disorder (GAD; American Psychiatric Association, 2013). A further distinction is substance or medication-induced anxiety disorder. Trauma and stressor-related disorders—for example, adjustment disorder with depressed or anxious mood—are under a different DSM category, as is hoarding, which falls under Obsessive-Compulsive and Related Disorders. Hoarding will not be addressed here, though it does especially occur in older populations. One particularly important feature of the DSM-5 is that it now takes into account considerations of typical and atypical behavior within discrete cultures. Further, anxiety often coexists with depression symptoms.

Fear is seen as the emotional response to a perceived aversive situation or threat, while anxiety is a response to a perceived *future* threat (American Psychiatric Association, 2013). Anxiety is most associated with vigilance and muscle tension; fear often leads to a fight or flight response. The content of the thoughts that lead to the experience of anxiety are important to assess. A diagnosis of anxiety is reached when the fear is out of proportion to what might be a normative experience. Anxiety may develop in childhood and persist. In social phobia, individuals avoid social interactions out of fear of being uncomfortable, embarrassed, humiliated, or offending others. As older people tend to be more socially isolated generally, a social phobia could exacerbate isolation. Panic disorders arise rapidly and arouse physical symptoms such as sweating or a pounding heart and cognitive symptoms such as racing thoughts. Sometimes these occur due to expected stressful situations such as being in an enclosed space and sometimes the situation is not expected to cause panic, but does. Persons with a generalized anxiety disorder (GAD) experience excessive worry about different aspects of their lives, such as performance in certain expected tasks (American Psychiatric Association, 2013). Some symptoms include feeling restless, on edge, or having difficulty concentrating or sleeping. GAD often results in a level of anxiety that is unremitting; the older person is seldom able to relax. These are the DSM-5 considerations of what constitutes a major disorder.

At older ages, features of anxiety can be masked or underestimated due to illness and medication complications. Chronic stress can affect immune functions. Further, older people may not report anxiety symptoms out of concern they will be labeled or should be able to manage them alone. Situational factors may cause anxiety that spills over into daily life. For example, if an older person has been mugged, he may become oversensitive to the environment and scan frequently. People who had a tendency to worry in younger ages may discover that this predicts an ongoing anxious temperament in later life especially as a response to stress. Studies indicate that brain scans of patients with OCD show decreased activity in specific brain structures after treatment (Rabins, 2005; Zarit & Zarit, 2011). Persistent, excessive, and life-changing behaviors are a sign that anxiety has reached a threshold where treatment is needed.

A Pervasive Fear or a Rational Response

Although the above features of anxiety are not untrue, a few people suggest we are living in an age of anxiety or fear (May, 1950; Smith, 2012), partly due to the advocacy of rationalist balance over dynamic interactions that provide opening for new kinds of ideas. Certainly two world wars in the last century as well as ongoing wars and conflicts suggest an inherent dis-ease (lack of ease). In 2010, use of the anxiety drug Xanax topped use of all other medications for mental health (Smith, 2012). The rates of anxiety disorders, of which there are several types, are as high as or even surpass those of depression (Zarit & Zarit, 2011). Although anxiety rates are higher in younger than older people, they often co-occur with symptoms of depression and have been found at a 9.5% prevalence in older adults (Zarit & Zarit, 2011).

Individuals worry more about the growth of financial assets than they do their own personal growth. In a sense, people fear some of the wrong things; their fear may not be enlarged enough to serve as a call to action, to master anxiety by achieving inner confidence that is transformative and results in a serenity marking greater ability to trust. A healthy level of anxiety or eustress may provide the necessary motivation to try a new activity or develop a new skill. As with the hero's journey à la Joseph Campbell, anxiety presages a call to action and adventure. However, this form of anxiety must be viewed as manageable, or an individual will be frozen in his or her fear.

Three kinds of anxiety are named by Gerzon (1997): natural anxiety that nudges us to growth and preparation for changes such as retirement, toxic or neurotic anxiety that serves to shut us down, and sacred anxiety that asks us to face the mystery of life and death. Toxic and sacred anxiety both result from situations beyond control, but while toxic anxiety leads to inaction or counterproductive behavior, sacred anxiety leads to self-reflection and spiritual growth. Natural anxiety is usually brief, toxic anxiety is chronic, and sacred anxiety, while continuous, rarely comes to conscious awareness. Alleviation of natural anxiety comes through responsible action. In toxic anxiety any relief is temporary, but the anxiety wins our attention. With sacred anxiety, relief comes through deeper awareness and living in harmony with the universe as well as becoming more aware of the sacred dimensions to life.

Tillich (1952) spoke about existential anxiety as having the courage to be despite our fears. He calls the anxiety of death the permanent horizon against which the contingent unpredictability of life continues on. Death is inescapable and so represents the outcome toward which all individuals advance. However, most people, once they are old enough to stand the inevitability of death, would rather ignore the prospect of that death. Rather than face it and structure their lives to achieve those goals that would bring them the highest satisfaction or seem to them the most worthy, they choose to live for lesser goals that bring them momentary satisfaction on a pleasure spectrum. Chasing momentary joy, while sometimes rational, at other times expends resources that are then forever gone—the most unreplenishable of which is time.

The threats of finitude, emptiness, and loss of meaning loom large in aging. Time is diminishing and that alone can precipitate an existential angst. The anxiety about existence and what, if anything, lies beyond nonexistence is irreducible in Tillichian terms. Although fear, which usually has a specific object, can be met with courage, the unknown offers no specific answer. An additional threat is that to deal with doubt, people sometimes surrender their freedom to ask questions of life and instead accept answers that have been imposed by others. "Meaning is saved, but the self is sacrificed" (Tillich, 1952, p. 49). Spiritual anxiety is the result. However, Tillich also affirms that all anxiety may be healed. He views the self as an "infinitely significant microcosm" that can mirror love for the universe (p. 120). Even loneliness is not absolute because all that the universe contains lies within an individual. This is an ultimately hopeful view, but one that is only shared when an individual can agree to its assumptions. Love is present in the universe, but not everyone is equally adept at perceiving it. That is clear from the problems mental health practitioners seek to transform in collaborative encounters with their clients. In practice, people who are members of one of the monotheistic religions generally have a subject-object relationship with God per Tillich (1952). Writing from a Christian perspective, Tillich views the role of the church as mediator of transcendent courage, a courage which can supersede this limited type of theism and connect to the God beyond. It is absolute faith that leads to self-affirmation through linkage with this ground of all being. Participation in something that lies beyond the self confirms self-affirmation, and thus meaning in existence. This becomes, then, one answer to the anxiety experienced in existence itself.

ANXIETY INTERVENTIONS

As with depression, beyond mediation possibilities, CBT assists clients in identifying their fears and choosing alternative ways to manage them. This particularly helps decrease catastrophic thinking that is often prevalent in GAD. Cognitive restructuring therapy (CT) teaches clients to substitute a more realistic thought for an obsessive one. Reassuring statements can be substituted for distressing ones. Thought stopping techniques sometimes include physical actions such as lightly snapping a rubber band against the wrist. Behavioral therapy has also been shown effective (Zarit & Zarit, 2011). Systematic desensitization, a type of exposure therapy, is a process that involves first identifying the hierarchy of fear or anxiety (the triggers) and second teaching clients to respond with incompatible behavior, such as participating in a relaxation exercise. Third, counterconditioning connects the incompatible relaxation response with the anxiety-producing stimulus at increasing dosages until it is fully resolved. This has been used successfully with people who have a fear of flying and are finally able to tolerate a flight.

Positive self-talk can be learned along with any of the above approaches. Positive self-talk would involve developing a patois with a client that would serve as successful response to anxiety:

- This is only anxiety—it will not hurt me.

- I have survived this before.

- I am healthy.

- These feelings will pass.

- I can manage this.

All of the above tools constitute active approaches that can be taught in coping and controlling anxious thoughts and behavior.

Spiritual Anxiety Interventions

The presence of natural anxiety alludes to a normalizing function. Most people experience anxiety for brief periods and those who do not may be subject to an unrealistic presentation of self. A key approach to this anxiety pervading all existence lies in acceptance of full consciousness. Awareness of ourselves and who we are is an antidote to anxiety (May, 1953). Further, we learn to be comfortable in the ambiguity of not knowing who we are becoming.

Counterproductive or toxic anxiety results in incessant inner chatter that feels out of control. Searching for the positive intention underneath the concern (reframing) changes the scenario to one of control and appreciation. If an older person angrily asserts, "My daughter wants me to move into an assisted living community because she doesn't trust me to call her if I fall," the therapist can help reframe the concern as one of fear and caring, a normal form of anxiety. A solution may be sought in the midpoint between a daughter not knowing about the welfare of her parent and the parent moving prematurely. This has a parallel in the middle way of the Buddhist path. Deeply embedded subconscious thoughts can be brought to the surface. The goal is to replace old habits of thought or patterns of thought with a more conscious response. Letting go of old tapes (habitual thoughts) can lead to a "beginner's mind" that permits novel solutions previously hidden to reveal themselves.

Another manifestation of anxiety is in the addictions which it fuels (Gerzon, 1997). Addiction can offer temporary relief from pain, but it is not a healthy nor balanced approach. Pursuing an addiction keeps one in a comfort zone; excuses may include a familial predisposition voiced to highlight inevitability and support resistance to change. Partnership, acceptance, compassion, and evocation of the client's own motivation for change are primary elements that elicit the spirit of motivational interviewing (MI; Miller & Rollnick, 2013). Compassion is a recently recognized element that clarifies the client's reasons are honored above those of the therapist.

Motivational interviewing that assists people to move through anxiety and support therapeutic change can be effective with older people (Cummings, Cooper, & Cassie, 2009). Although more directive than a person-centered Rogerian approach of warmth/ genuineness, unconditional positive regard, and empathy, valuable attributes include its non-judgmental and non-adversarial nature. MI supports change through engagement of clients, open discussion of resistance and potential barriers, and participation in change talk. Behavior change goals are small, important to the client, specific, realistic, and oriented in the present and/or future (Cummings et al., 2009). An underlying principle is that the client holds within what he or she needs for change. A motivational therapy approach has seven stages, introduced in Chapter 7: (1) precontemplation— resistance to change; (2) contemplation—considering change; (3) preparation—getting ready to make a change, including planning for it; (4) action—implementing the plan; (5) maintenance—sustaining change until it is well-integrated; (6) relapse/recycling/obstacles; and (7) termination (Miller & Rollnick, 2013). In their collaborative style, these approaches can make space for spiritual and holistic goals. Because they have planful elements, they can greatly reduce anxiety and return a sense of control back to the client.

Interpersonal neurobiology (IPNB) suggests that people have potential for transformation through processing emotions, thoughts, and behaviors (Siegel, 2006). Siegel posits that life experiences shape the neurological pathways in our brain and these can be altered through therapeutic intervention, especially in *presence* which includes openness and embracing uncertainty, *attunement* which includes regard for the signals others send, and *resonance* (feeling felt) and giving trust. In his view, well-being is achieved through balancing differentiated areas of the brain and then linking them, arriving at integration. This is accomplished through focusing attention in mindful ways without judgment, often improving empathy, compassion, and interpersonal sensitivity (Siegel, 2006).

Meditation is a very powerful way of gaining self-acceptance and reducing anxiety. A number of exercises are included in this text, so specific meditation examples and process steps will not be elucidated here. However, in any of its many renditions, it is one of the most potent antidotes to anxiety. Learning how to restore oneself through nature, service, solitude, prayer, fasting, honoring Sabbath or sanctuary interludes, as well as engaging or building friendship networks can reduce anxious temperaments. Spiritual disciplines present paths through the small anxiety of daily concerns and the larger anxiety of meaninglessness.

SUMMARY

This chapter elucidated key mental health problems of depression and anxiety in older people out of a more nuanced framework than the DSM-5. It includes both standard identifications and treatments of these concerns with a spiritual viewpoint. The spiritual viewpoints concerning maladies of the soul and the dark night of the soul may not apply to all older adults, but discussion of them can be the opening needed for a few individuals. Improved understanding of these terms can lead to a stronger alliance and better engagement, with the potential to resolve longstanding concerns.

CASE STUDY: DEPRESSION AND SPIRITUALITY

Mr. Harrison, an 82-year-old man, sought treatment for the first time at the suggestion of his son, William. William began noticing that his father had been experiencing "depression symptoms" since the death of his wife one month prior. At the time of the referral, William described his father as being fixated on signs of her presence, not eating, lethargic, irritable, and nonconversational. A previous restaurateur, Mr. Harrison took joy in entertaining and eating. Since his wife's death, he had not been taking pleasure in food or company, resulting in significant health problems and weight loss. He had been admitted to the hospital twice for heart palpitations in the weeks since her death.

Mr. Harrison presented for treatment as well-kept, eloquent, and had significant insight into his symptoms and feelings. He was educated and an engineer, having attended Harvard where he met his wife of nearly 60 years. He described their relationship as "magical" and stated that they were perfect for one another. He went on to state that he could not imagine a life without her. When Mr. Harrison presented for consultation, he described himself as "sad" since his wife's death and expressed ambivalence about seeking treatment and getting better. He did not complain about specific symptoms or desire to get well. He went on to explain that life was not worth living without her. He denied suicidal intent. He was easily engaged in conversation, though tangential at times. He often perseverated on signs of his wife's presence and focused on his hall clock, which had stopped working at precisely 3:00 p.m., the hour his wife had passed.

Two weeks after beginning treatment, Mr. Harrison was admitted to the hospital for chronic pain and heart palpitations. He became delirious and died shortly thereafter. William explained that he believed his father "died of a broken heart."

Assessments included Patient Health Questionnaire (PHQ-9) and Beck Anxiety Inventory (BAI).

Questions for Case Discussion

1. What are the indications that Mr. Harrison may have had depression? What form of depression do you think he had?

2. What type of relationships did Mr. Harrison appear to have with different family members, past and current? How did these help or hinder assessment of depression?

3. What other questions might you want to ask?

4. What might be your plan if you were the counselor working with this client?

QUESTIONS FOR DISCUSSION

1. How are emotions involved in religion or spirituality?

2. Peruse the Spiritual Emotions chart (Figure 9.1). Which emotions have you or your clients experienced in regard to the spiritual path? Which ones are you surprised to see here, if any?

3. Look at the Table for the 99 Names of God (Table 9.1). What images or emotions arise with some of the names. Which ones attract you? Are there any that are surprising?

4. How can depression be experienced in spiritual terms and how might it relate to spirituality and/or religion? What does the DSM-5 consider in determining symptoms of depression and anxiety?

5. In what way are boundaries between diagnoses porous? What considerations are absent in the DSM? "The historical aspiration of achieving diagnostic homogeneity by progressive subtyping within disorder categories no longer is sensible" (DSM-5, under Dimensional Approach to Diagnosis) .What does this imply? How can use of the DSM-5 manual be helpful for diagnosis? What are some cautions about its use?

6. How is anxiety experienced? What are different types of explanatory factors?

7. What story from the Hebrew scriptures or Talmud, the Bible, the Qur'an, other sacred text or myth might be useful to use for someone experiencing some form of mood or anxiety disorder?

8. Discuss other helping activities mentioned in this chapter or ones with which you have experience, highlighting the spiritual components of each.

MEDITATION: SELF-COMPASSION WITH MOVEMENT

Stand in a quiet place and center on your desire to open body and spirit to creation/nature, God, or the Universe.

First posture: Create a cup or bowl with your hands. Hold this in front of you. Imagine your bowl catching the tears of creation or God/the Universe. Be aware of tears for creation, for any sorrow you carry, and for the rest of the human family. Be aware of tears for you, specifically. Bring your cupped hands over your head and empty the bowl of creation/nature's or God's tears over yourself. Let these tears anoint you and bring you healing.

Second posture: Create a large circle with your arms in front of you as if hugging someone. Imagine Creation/God/the Universe embracing you and healing your wounds. Bring your arms inward to hug yourself.

Third posture: Bring hands together and crossing over your heart. Let them rest there. As you do this, give yourself kindness, caring, and understanding for what you have experienced.

Fourth posture: Bring your hands together in a prayer pose at the heart level, palms touching and fingers pointed up with thumbs close to the chest. Bow slightly and offer the phrase, *Namaste.* Namaste is a Hindu phrase meaning, *I bow to you* and is a form of deep respect. It also can mean *I honor the God within you.* It is a form of hello and good-bye.

Adapted from Community of Christ *Yearning for God* (n.d.). Retrieved from https://cofcspiritualformationcenter.files.wordpress.com/2015/02/yearningforgod.pdf

EXPLORING YOUR SPIRITUALITY: REGRET

Regret is a common feeling in the aging process, but it keeps us tethered to the past. We experience ambiguity about regret that we do not know how to resolve. We all have things we have done that we wished we hadn't, or things that we have failed to do that we wish we had. Regret is the emotion we experience if we think we would be happier if we had done something differently. Agency (the ability to choose) and imagination (making a different choice and spooling forward how we think things would change for the present) are two components of regret.

At many ages, we have experienced trifling remorse of "shopping regrets," items that we wished we had purchased, but declined to because of cost or other aspects that caused lack of commitment. However the regret discussed here is of greater consequence than shopping. Chittister (2008) calls regret "the sand trap of the soul" (p. 3). Kathy Schulz, in a TED talk of the same name, suggests, "Don't regret regret." We make the best decision we can make

at the time, given what we know. There is general societal attitude that we should live free of regrets. "What's done is done." Schulz suggests that first we deny what has occurred; second we experience *bewilderment* or puzzlement, wondering how we could have done that thing that we did; next we punish ourselves; and finally we perseverate about our action—often endlessly. She suggests that the best use of regret is to remind us that we can do better.

Moore (1998) suggests that remorse extends the idea of regret through its connection to conscience. The origin of the word *regret* means to "lament" or "weep," but *remorse* means to "disturb" or "bite back." Rather than keeping us tied to the past as does regret, remorse may launch us into our future through an altered attitude. Remorse can be useful by helping individuals move beyond guilt and encouraging them to live more from soul than ego. How can that happen? This exercise will explore this idea.

1. Identify a regret that stayed with you. Think about the features of this regret. Who was involved? What happened? Was there an outcome you hoped for at the time? What was the outcome that occurred? What was the level of discrepancy? Did you change at all through the experience?

2. Some aspects of what we regret are not controllable. Was there an element of what happened that was outside of your control?

Was anyone else hurt by your action? Is there any restorative work possible now?

3. At what point in your life did this regret occur? What was your developmental stage? How has time interceded to soften the edges of your regret? Has regret become remorse?

4. What have you learned from reflecting on past regret? Please journal about this.

EXPLORING YOUR SPIRITUALITY: FIGHTING FEAR

Fear is a feeling (transitory) or an emotion (of greater duration) that circumscribes our actions. Fear can be a felt sense of insecurity, a lack of self-confidence, or an overwhelming concern about what others may think, say, or do, in relation to ourselves. Fears and concerns are often legitimate. They may be based on prior negative behavior directed to us or our anxieties about what could happen to hurt us in some way. Often, people experience fear when they think about their own dying. At times fear can motivate us to protect ourselves or others, but mostly it holds us back from expressing who we really are or from learning through new experiences and adventures.

In the Hebrew Bible, many of the prophets suggested the people should overcome their fear. In the Christian Bible, Jesus, the countercultural rabbi, tells his disciples, "Do not be afraid." This was spoken after his disciples cowered in a boat seeing Jesus walk on water toward them with thoughts he must be a spirit. It was said by an angel in Luke at the birth of Jesus, "Do not be afraid. I bring you good news that will cause great joy for all the people." Fear is described frequently enough that we can understand it to be common to the human condition. The point seems to be that fear limits us, usually in ways that are unhelpful. How can we address the fear inside us?

1. Consider something that makes you feel afraid. After you identify this situation, get in touch with your feelings about it. Do your thoughts race? Does your heart beat faster? What are you experiencing?

2. Now, in your mind, walk around that thing that you fear. How does it look when you move closer to it? Is there any part of it you can touch?

3. How would you like your fear to change? What might you do to begin to move this fear so that you are not stuck within it? Can time change it? Are there other situations toward which you once held fear that resolved successfully? How did that come about? Can any of this tacit knowledge you hold apply here? How?

4. Imagine yourself in the same situation that you identified above, but holding no fear. What do you see differently now? What may have happened to bring you to this point of no-fear or fearlessness?

5. How can you manifest this fearlessness in your life? What will be the benefits? How will this bring you closer to being who you really are more fully?

6. Journal about your experience.

EXPLORING YOUR SPIRITUALITY: GRATITUDE

There are many unheralded aspects of our life that bring us joy, knowledge, increased skill, or simply the opportunity to continue being/living. As Buddhist monk and writer Thich Nhat Hanh has observed, we take much of our life for granted, not fully attending to it. Even such an unpretentious act as eating an orange can be an opportunity for reverence and thanksgiving. As we notice its color and shape, smell its fragrance, feel the texture of the skin as we peel it, and taste the sweetness of the juice we begin to appreciate that orange. Not only can we appreciate the elements of both our immediate micro- and larger macro-world contexts, but we can also include ancestors and associates in our act of appreciation. It has been said that as a civilization we stand on the shoulders of the giants before us. It is because of their skill and inventiveness that we have the tools we need to do what we are called to do in life. Practicing gratitude allows us to go deeper into our lives and those objects or people for whom we give thanks.

1. Take a moment and consider in what way you have benefited from the work of others. Begin with your family. How have your parents and grandparents supported you? Or if they have not or have only partially offered you support, were there friends or others who gave you their support and encouragement?

2. Who are the nameless individuals (those who probably have names though you don't know them) who have created or developed a tool or product that makes your life easier or more comfortable? Write down the objects for which you are thankful. Take a moment to thank them and the person who created them.

3. Try to imagine what your life would be like without each of these objects, books, or other product that has enriched your life. Do this with each item listed in Number 2 above.

4. It is helpful to recognize that even when we think we are alone, we are connected to others by all they have done for us. Who or what has specifically helped you to do something that is important to you and gives your life meaning today? If you know them or how to reach them, you may want to thank that person in person or through an email, phone call, or letter.

5. Can you look for ways to keep your gratitude moving? There is value in keeping this energy flowing so it does not get stuck. What acts of kindness can you generate from your presence in the moment or in thoughtful participation in life?

6. Write about your experience doing this exercise.

WEBSITES

Association for Anxiety and Depression

http://www.adaa.org/

This website has a number of resources including a section on older adults under the subsection "Living and Thriving."

Listening to Shame

http://www.ted.com/talks/brene_brown_listening_to_shame

This is a TED Talk by vulnerability researcher Brené Brown.

National Alliance on Mental Illness

http://www.nami.org/

This is an information and advocacy grassroots organization.

NIMH: Older Adults and Depression

http://www.nimh.nih.gov/health/publications/older-adults-and-depression/index.shtml

This includes many publications that can be provided to clients to teach them about depression.

The Power of Vulnerability

http://www.ted.com/talks/brene_brown_on_vulnerability

This is a TED Talk by vulnerability researcher Brené Brown.

The Psychology of Your Future Self

http://www.ted.com/talks/dan_gilbert_you_are_always_changing

This is a TED Talk by Harvard psychologist Daniel Gilbert about the end of history illusion. We can remember more easily than we can imagine. We are transient beings and that includes our tastes.

RECOMMENDED READING

Greenspan, M. (2003). *Healing through the dark emotions: The wisdom of grief, fear, and despair*. Boston, MA: Shambhala.

This text discusses paths to healing through emotional suffering.

May, G. G. (2004). *The dark night of the soul: A psychiatrist explores the connection between darkness and spiritual growth*. New York, NY: HarperCollins.

This text discusses how living through the dark side of life can lead to spiritual growth.

Miller, M., & Reynolds, C. F. (2012). *Depression and anxiety in later life: What everyone needs to know*. Baltimore, MD: The Johns Hopkins University Press.

This is a very accessible and well-organized book pitched to older adults as well as professionals.

Tillich. P. (1952). *The courage to be*. New Haven, CT: Yale University Press.

This wonderful little book poses questions that still resound in the postmodern era. This is a classic text from a famed theologian that discusses anxiety and its antidote.

Tillich, P. (1963). *The eternal now*. New York, NY: Scribner.

This sermon from a book of sermons by Paul Tillich contains very interesting and mental health–relevant topics (see http://www.thespiritwiki.com/index.php/Eternal_Now). "The Spirit can give you the courage that says yes to life in spite of the destructiveness you have experienced around you and within you. . . . One can compare the Spiritual Presence with the air we breathe, surrounding us, nearest to us, and working life within us. . . . Life is great and holy, deep and abundant, ecstatic and sober, limited and distorted by time, fulfilled by eternity." This book provides much insight for both Christians and nonreligious individuals interested in understanding emotions and spirituality.

CHAPTER TEN

MEMORY, DEMENTIA, AND SPIRITUAL CARE

The secret of health for both mind and body is not to mourn for the past, not to worry about the future, or not to anticipate troubles, but to live in the present moment wisely and earnestly.

—The Buddha

If you as an individual no longer found an identity from your thoughts, then you would break free of time and enter the sweetness and clarity of the timeless.

—Bernie Prior

This chapter describes normal memory, memory loss, and common forms of dementia as well as living with dementia for caregivers. It distinguishes delirium and dementia from depression, which are frequent areas of confusion. It addresses prevalence of dementia and concerns regarding disclosure of this diagnosis. Then it presents a less biological and more spiritual way of thinking about and working with persons with dementia, including Kitwood's person-centered care. Need-driven dementia-comprised behavior, Algase's model, is discussed, along with a behavioral approach to treatment that honors individual desires. Literature on spirituality and dementia caregiving is provided, followed by religious and spiritual practice principles and arts-based spiritual care.

MEMORY AND GROWING OLDER

Some forms of memory loss are temporary and common in the aging process. A woman phones her best friend to ask to borrow a recipe and forgets why she called. "Could that be Alzheimer's?" she wonders. A man searches the house for 20 minutes before he finds his car keys, laid absentmindedly on a table in the spare room. He asks his wife, "Am I becoming senile?" It is not uncommon for people to encounter memory changes as they age, and it is important to distinguish malleability of memory from the memory loss that can be a precursor to more serious forms of cognitive impairment or dementia.

The spirituality of memory loss is related to the vulnerability that people experience with changes in memory of any kind: whether mild and sporadic or intense and significant. Individuals experiencing memory lapse begin to understand what they once considered foundational and instinctive is, instead, a fragile ability. When involuntary memory—memory as automatic response to inner questions or sometimes unwanted intrusive ones—is no longer trustworthy, what implications does this have for the identity of the self? If we no longer remember who we are and know that we cannot remember, can we acknowledge to others that they carry the gift of holding our memories for us? Does this become easier for an older person who lived his or her life in very public ways enfolded by community than an older person who built a more private life? Embarrassment at this presumed failure of mind, especially when known by friends and acquaintances, may be too overwhelming to dismiss and can plunge the affected individual into a depressed state. Does the person who is diagnosed with mild cognitive impairment or beginning of dementia find any comfort in thinking they will continue to dwell in the memory of God?

The Hardware of Memory

The process of encoding a memory includes several interrelated steps, so at several points in this process, deficits can become apparent (Baltes, 1993; Tröster, 1998; Zarit & Zarit, 2011). The first step involves the act of sensory input. Sensory input itself is quite quick—a matter of milliseconds. If the senses record information without errors or distortion, then the rest of the process may follow unimpeded. Perception of stimuli via sensory channels occurs through (1) information registration; (2) information encoding (identifying, classifying, and sorting data); and (3) information consolidation (integrating and embedding the data in a framework). Information storage involves the final placement of information (Tröster, 1998). Information retrieval involves a nearly automatic process that combines contextual retrieval cues and memory trace with a slower intentional process of memory reconstruction. Here, retrieval cues interact with memory storage so that an image or representation of desired information can filter to the foreground.

Short-term memory consists of sensory memory, primary memory, and working memory (Tröster, 1998; Zarit & Zarit, 2011). *Short-term memory* involves remembering information for five to seven minutes at most. *Sensory memory* is the brief holding period that co-occurs with an afterimage. *Primary memory* is the amount of information that can be absorbed at a given time. One of the reasons persons may enjoy photos so much is that more is recorded in a photo than can be fully attended to in the moment. With a photo, the moment is captured and retained to be revisited, remembered, and further appreciated. *Working memory* refers to the processing and storing of the information received in primary memory. In a mental status exam, repeating digits as given by an examiner is an example of primary memory (e.g., 1, 10, 8, 32); repeating those digits backwards (32, 8, 10, 1) would be an example of working memory (Zarit & Zarit, 2011).

Long-term memory consists of information that has moved from working memory into a storage system from which it can be recovered when needed. Essentially this type of encoded memory is accessible throughout a lifetime. The three types of long-term memory are episodic, semantic, and procedural memory (Tröster, 1998; Zarit & Zarit, 2011). *Episodic memory* refers to memory of specific events that occur. *Semantic memory* involves the memory of language, the use of words to convey meaning. *Procedural memory* involves the important everyday ADL-related functions of how to use utensils for eating or how to button a shirt and dress oneself. As persons age, the largest change tends to be within episodic memory, the recall of specific events or circumstances (Zarit & Zarit, 2011). Other facets of memory retrieval include *free recall* (recalling memories with no cueing), *cued recall* (recalling memory with appearance of partial information or some form of categorization), and *recognition* (discriminating between similar items). A *source memory* involves remembering the context when a memory was encoded. That is why remembering details of a context can assist in retrieval of a memory, and memories can come unbidden in discussions with psychotherapists. *Prospective memory* concerns recalling plans for the future (Siegler, Poon, Madden, & Dilworth-Anderson, 2004). Different neural networks seem to mediate varying types of memory.

What happens when memory does not operate as desired? *Forgetting* involves a loss of information once captured or an obstruction of recall, for example, in memory decay or interference. *Anterograde amnesia* involves an inability to register new memories for later recall at a point after trauma occurred, such as brain damage occurring from an auto accident. Memories moving into the future could not be encoded in this situation. *Retrograde amnesia* consists of an inability to recall events *prior* to the trauma, even if these had previously been recalled. Further, in the various types of dementias, memory is biologically wrested away as portions of the brain begin to shrink. When language degrades, difficulties are termed *aphasia*, which is ancient Greek for "speechlessness." Although memory may be intact, someone with aphasia has difficulty in language reception—comprehension—or expression. There are several forms of this including difficulty with word finding and naming or neologisms (making up new words). *Agnosia* involves difficulty with recognition, for instance remembering faces, which is related to sensory input processing more than actual memory loss. *Apraxia* is difficulty with movement related to brain damage, but not necessarily memory. *Executive functioning* such as apparent in planning, organizing, sequencing, and making abstractions also may be impaired.

Everyday Memory

Everyday memory is important to each of us. Our own storage and retrieval system may vary depending on what was salient to us at the time. As our lives unfurl farther, there is more to remember, and sometimes we let certain events deteriorate into a poorly defined panorama—or maybe failed to embed them well in the first place. This is apparent when we meet people who knew us long ago, for instance at a high school or university reunion, and we may not remember a common experience that was significant to them and seems to be congruent with the range of our history and self-interpretation. They encoded it, but we did not. This is one way we are truly part of each other's stories and hold memory for each other. Parents often may serve this function; they are a memory retrieval system for times that we shared together and before, but they hold a different version from their adult vantage point. When a parent's memory begins to falter, that can leave gaps in the memories of their children. At the very time an adult child recognizes he or she needs to begin caretaking the parent, the loss is not only the time spent giving care—of whatever nature that may be: financial, household, or personal—but the loss of communal memory and fixed concepts about who the parent had always been.

Everyday memory offers the basis for reflection and reflective work. It is in reflection that we can hold our experiences aloft and consider them from four dimensions: height, width, depth, and time. Memories are one of the evident sources for transformation. Although occurring in one moment, they form part of a dynamic process that we revisit and learn from again with benefit of new experience and knowledge that is more than factual.

After publishing a memoir, writer and former restaurant critic Frank Bruni confessed a growing recognition that his memory of events differed from those of a sibling. Significant events were absent from his memory and thus not part of the repertoire he consulted for his writing:

> *What was missing and forgotten was less often crucial or even trivial details of events than the events themselves, gone in their entirety. . . . I remember, as if it were a movie clip I played just yesterday, the hospital room in which my mother died and the entire hour leading up to her death. But I couldn't remember a single theme or sentence from the eulogy I delivered until my older brother, Mark, sent me an electronic copy of it. I couldn't believe he'd kept one. I didn't, and have no memory why.* (Bruni, 2009/2011)

Validation of this startling aspect of memory comes from literature about eye-witness accounts of accidents or crimes (Sauer, Brewer, Zweck, & Weber, 2010). In memoir writing, there is controversy about sharing life stories, with some individuals stating that writers should fasten to the facts as a journalist should, but others suggest they approach their narration with an aesthetic sensibility that becomes the artistic truth of an event (Arbesman, 2012; Kupfer, 1996; Rasmussen, 2014). The latter group contends that listeners or readers should not have to slog through uninteresting details and further, because of individual receptivity to experience, what is salient for one person would not matter to another. To build a consistent narrative structure, for instance, time may need to be compressed or blurring of details about minor characters may need to occur (Kupfer, 1996). All of this suggests that memory remains malleable.

Given this plasticity of memory in normal aging, we should wonder to what extent we are our memories and what happens to the self when memory is destroyed. These are the questions that the interface between the spirituality of memory and the identity of the person give us. As well as the intersections of memory and normal aging, it is important for mental health practitioners to understand the physiological types of memory impairment as detailed below.

TYPES OF DEMENTIA AND BEHAVIORAL INDICATORS

There are several types of memory loss and dementias; people who want to learn more about spirituality and memory need to be familiar with them, especially because the psychosocial and spiritual needs of each also differ. Certain types of memory loss are temporary and reversible, especially those that co-occur with some diseases or treatments. Memory loss can also be stable and unremitting, for instance from a traumatic brain injury. Finally, it can be the beginning of a course of progressive decline as in Alzheimer's disease (AD) and other related dementias. *Dementia* remains the more generalized term used in public discourse; there are many subtypes discussed in the DSM-5, the most common of which is AD, also known as major neurocognitive disorder. Please see Table 10.1 for a comparison of different forms of dementia and their features. It is helpful to remember that the DSM-5 is a construction agreed to by many experts, but not all, and it is intended to be a practical reference rather than a definitive guide. Dementia is a diagnosis of absence as well as symptom presence; when other diagnoses are ruled out, dementia is the remainder.

Varieties of dementia have distinct biomarkers and irregularities in brain structure and functioning due to contrasting etiologies. However, validated and reliable biomarker tests remain in a developmental phase. The DSM-5 provides guidelines for diagnosing dementia-related illnesses in several categories: delirium, major or mild neurocognitive disorder (NCD), vascular NCD, NCD with Lewy bodies, NCD due to Parkinson's disease, frontotemporal NCD, NCD due to traumatic brain injury, NCD due to HIV infection, substance/medication-induced NCD, NCD due to Huntington's disease and a few other subtypes (American Psychiatric Association, 2013). Research is addressing strategies to incontrovertibly and accessibly diagnose different forms of dementia, but at present, autopsy continues to be the means of cost-effectively and definitively assessing the disease. A combination of computed tomography (CT) with positron emission tomography (PET) has also made advances in dementia diagnosis because these can demonstrate structural changes in the brain (Berti, Pupi, & Mosconi, 2011).

Although other mental and health conditions may feature cognitive and memory problems, in NCD a change from prior functioning is presented. Major neurocognitive disorder is thus identifiable through significant cognitive decline assessed by individuals themselves or significant others, testing results that affirm poor cognitive performance, and interference with independent completion of instrumental activities of daily living (IADLs), such as managing money and using the phone, described in Chapter 8. Medications can improve symptoms marginally for some people by increasing neurotransmitters in the brain with individual variation in results, but currently no medication is effective in reducing or halting progression of the disease (Alzheimer's Association, 2015). Research is underway to evaluate new drug formulations as well as nonpharmacological treatments such as exercise, mental stimulation, and other psychosocial activities. A recent theory suggests that AD may be the body's defense against inflammation and possibly autoimmune disorders (Lobjanidze, Akiashili, Beridze, & Janelidze, 2015). AD is more than occasional forgetfulness: Episodes when individuals no longer recall how to do something they have always done, or when they seem to forget something they have always known, like names of children or grandchildren, serve as tentative gauges.

Mild cognitive impairment (MCI) is assessed through minor changes in thinking that do not affect the person's ability to engage in daily activities. Although MCI may progress to advanced or major cognitive impairment (Major NCD, in the DSM-5), it does not always do so. It may remain stable or return to a normal condition. MCI can resolve if it is a result of medication side effects. Another interesting aspect of dementia is that it appears to be correlated with education. More education is associated with decreased risk for dementia. In one study, controlling for socioeconomic factors, health, and lifestyle reduced but did not remove the effect (McDowell, Xi, Lindsay, & Tierney, 2007). Education may account for a greater cognitive reserve in some aging adults.

Table 10.1 Comparison of Types of Dementias and Their Attributes

Alzheimer's disease (AD)	This is the most common form of dementia, experienced by 60% to 80% of all persons with dementia. Although most of these solely represent AD, some have mixed etiologies and thus are known as "mixed dementias." Onset is gradual (insidious) and progresses slowly. The hallmark signs of AD are progressive accumulation of the protein beta-amyloid (*plaques*) outside neurons in the brain and twisted strands of the protein tau (*tangles*) inside neurons. As a result of these changes, neurons are damaged and later perish. *Behavioral Signs:* Memory loss—the difficulty recalling names, events, or conversations—is an early signifier. Sometimes depression is also featured. At later stages, communication is impaired; confusion, disorientation (visual-spatial problems), poor judgement, and behavior changes occur. Toward the end-stage, persons with dementia experience difficulty walking, swallowing, and speaking.
Vascular dementia	Vascular dementia accounts solely for only about 10% of all dementias. However, of those with AD, it is a common additional form in older adults. Previously it was known as multi-infarct dementia (positing the result of a series of small infarcts, or strokes) or post-stroke dementia. Sudden onset and stepwise progression are distinguishing features. *Behavioral Signs:* Instead of memory loss, the first symptoms tend to be impaired ability to make decisions, make plans, or organize details. Attention deficits, psychomotor impairment, depression, and anxiety are characteristics. Working and procedural memory are troublesome.
Dementia with Lewy bodies (DLB)	Lewy bodies are abnormal aggregations (clumps) of the protein alpha-synuclein that accumulate in neurons. When they develop in a part of the brain called the cortex, dementia can occur. This protein similarly aggregates in the brains of people with Parkinson's disease (PD). *Behavioral Signs:* People with DLB and PD both are known to have Lewy bodies, but it manifests as cognitive impairment in DLB and motor impairment in PD.
Parkinson's disease (PD) dementia	In PD, the alpha-synuclein protein accumulates deep in the brain. It is supposed that these aggregations lead to a loss of the nerve cells that generate dopamine. The incidence of PD is about 10% of those with AD. *Behavioral Signs:* Due to the accumulation of Lewy bodies, PD often leads to dementia. People with PD frequently have a masked facial expression and may exhibit hallucinations in later stages.
Frontotemporal lobar degeneration (FTLD)	Dementias that fall under this category include behavioral-variant FTLD, primary progressive aphasia (affecting speech production, comprehension, reading or writing), Pick's disease, corticobasal degeneration, and progressive supranuclear palsy. As named, this illness affects nerve cells in the front and temporal (side) of the brain leading to atrophy. This form most often affects younger adults, beginning between ages 40 and 60 to 65. It begins gradually (insidious onset) but with a harmful effect.

	Behavioral Signs: Early changes occur in personality, behavior (hyperactive or apathetic, impulsive, emotional blunting, loss of empathy) and difficulty with language such as problems with naming, expression, word meaning, compulsive eating, and repetitive actions. Unlike the case with AD, memory often remains intact. Later in the disease course, there is loss of speech, motor skills, and muscle movement.
Mixed dementias	In mixed dementia, people manifest signs of dementia typical of more than one type, usually AD and one other. The most common pattern is AD and vascular dementia. *Behavioral Signs:* Mixed
Creuzfeldt-Jacob disease	In this type, a misfolded protein causes other proteins to misfold. One form may be hereditary. Another variant form is thought to be caused by consumption of cattle with mad cow disease. *Behavioral Signs:* Rare and rapidly fatal, this causes memory impairment, coordination difficulties, and other behavioral problems.
Normal pressure hydrocephalus	This is caused by impaired reabsorption of cerebrospinal fluid and resulting accumulation of fluid in the brain, causing pressure. Less than 5% of dementia cases are due to this. *Behavioral Signs:* These include memory loss, difficulty wakening, and poor urinary control.
Traumatic brain injury (TBI)	Dementia symptoms for TBI may appear in people who have sustained moderate head trauma (unconscious for 30 minutes or more) from accidents or in sports such as boxing and football. Minor injuries can cause neurodegeneration. *Behavioral Signs:* History of loss of consciousness, posttraumatic amnesia, disorientation or confusion, neurological signs such as seizures, and problems in visual field.

Source: Adapted from Alzheimer's Association (2015) and Zarit and Zarit (2011).

Common General Symptoms

What do people observe that can be indicators of dementia? Cognitive changes are the first sign, and alterations in behavior could follow:

- *Memory loss*—for example, a person forgets appointments repeatedly or cannot recall recent events.

- *Difficulty communicating or finding words*—a person struggles to find words to express meaning and will talk around his or her idea to avoid showing they cannot find the word.

- *Difficulty with complex tasks*—when there are many steps to a task, a person shows confusion or attempts to complete steps in a sequence that is not effective.

- *Difficulty with planning and organizing*—a person is unable to follow through on agreed plans.

- *Difficulty with coordination and motor functions*—a person may have difficulty doing personal hygiene tasks.

- *Problems with disorientation*, such as getting lost—a person who is driving may be unable to find the way home and may not even realize he or she is lost.

Psychological changes include the following: personality changes; inability to reason; inappropriate behavior, such as taking off clothes in a public place as it may feel too warm; paranoia; agitation; or hallucinations. Often these changes are negatively perceived by others, but when assumptions about normative behavior are removed, the reason for disturbing behavior can often be discovered and addressed. Further, this iteration of the person can have aspects that are more relatable. Some adult children identify occasions when parents who once exhibited passive-aggressive, bullying, or narcissistic behavior lose those edges and become *delightfully* demented. This process enables direct and enjoyable interactions. The parents become more gentle and kind.

Person-Centered Care: Elbert C. Cole's Story

Elbert C. Cole was the founder of Shepherd Centers of America, a multi-faith organization that engaged older adults as volunteers. He readily agreed to speak to a university social work and aging class I taught in the early 2000s in Kansas City. I gave him a number of suggestions for his guest lecture, which I thought would primarily focus on spirituality and aging, his area of expertise. However, he asked if he could speak about the needs of caregivers instead. He told the class that quality caregiving seeks to lift the care receiver to his or her highest functional capacity. The caregiver should resist apologizing or feeling ashamed of the care receiver and should think of the care receiver as a partner in the process. Finally, he shared his view that caregiving is a family and a community responsibility, opportunity, and privilege.

Cole's wife Virginia had dementia before her death. On initial diagnosis, she implied she should commit suicide, but he told her firmly that was not the way to handle a problem. They forged a contract, with her task to enjoy life and his to manage it. There were many difficulties he encountered in giving her care and maintaining a presentation for her that included preservation of her dignity. He described the hours it would take for him to dress her in hosiery and other clothing, combing her hair into her preferred bun, and applying makeup so her appearance would reflect her former interest in looking fashionably attired. He often felt clumsy and awkward. When he accepted speaking engagements, he traveled with her as long as he was able to, but using public restrooms was one of the most difficult tasks. This was prior to establishment of family restrooms. At first, he would stand near the women's restroom and ask someone to assist her in washing her hands and directing her out. Later, he would wait until the women's restroom was empty and take her in there, but he received many angry looks. Finally, he brought her with him into the men's room. None of these options worked out particularly well.

He began to look for moments to win at tasks and avoid passing on a sense of failure. He gave up the need for precision, but gave his wife small tasks to do, such as holding the second stocking while the first was put on. His focus was to foster a sense of interdependence and reciprocity. He would give Virginia the first opportunity to do a task but would assist when he could see she could not do something or her safety was threatened. "Her job was to watch the young mother walking her children, smile at strangers. Sometimes I thought she was more of a person than I was." He found benefit in snuggling with her at night and having a partner when they went out to eat. Rather than exclude her, he included her in his life and practiced the principles of person-centered care.

DELIRIUM, DEPRESSION, THYROID, VITAMIN DEFICIENCIES, ALCOHOLISM, AND OTHER TEMPORARY CAUSES OF DEMENTIA

It is important for any mental health clinician to know that a number of treatable illnesses can appear to be forms of dementia. These reversible forms of cognitive impairment are sometimes referenced as pseudodementias. One study reported that about 7.3% of 233 patients with cognitive impairment seen at an outpatient geriatric clinic had a potentially treatable condition (Muangpaisan, Petcharat, & Srinonprasert, 2012). Depression appears to be the most common reason for dementia symptoms. However, people who have depressed mood with dementia will often see their dementia symptoms improve in early stages if the depression is treated. Vitamin B-12 deficiencies, chronic hypothyroidism, alcoholism, and exposure to heavy metals also may lead to dementia. Although some of these are successfully treatable, not all of them are (Zarit & Zarit, 2011).

Delirium is another syndrome that can be confusing for the mental health clinician as well as the patient. Surprisingly, symptoms of delirium are not well-known nor well-identified by all health care professionals. A client who had just been discharged from a hospital was referred to me for counseling. When I went to assess her, her conversation made no sense at all. She was delusional and I found her swatting at imaginary large black bugs crawling over her. She was clearly not a candidate for counseling. When I looked at her chart, it was noted that she had a urinary tract infection. This is one of several common causes for delirium, as is hospitalization itself. It is thought that hospitalization in an unfamiliar environment may sometimes precipitate delirium. I alerted the staff and when I returned to check on her in a few days, there was no need for counseling. She was alert, oriented, and happy with her life.

Delirium is noted by a marked and rapid change in intellectual functioning. DSM-5 criteria include a disturbance in attention and reduced orientation to the environment. It often occurs in a very short time frame. Changes may include delusions or hallucinations, mood changes, and other impaired perceptions. It is important for all clinicians to recognize this possibility because it is eminently treatable if caught early, but if not, symptoms can result in permanent harm to the brain and higher risk of mortality. Available research, as well as continuing education unit (CEU) seminars, are aimed at helping professionals distinguish delirium, depression, and dementia (Dudley, O'Brien, Barnett, McGuckin, & Britton, 2002; Fick, Steis, Waller, & Inouye, 2013; Irving, Fick, & Foreman, 2006).

PREVALENCE OF DEMENTIA

According to census bureau data from 2010, it is estimated that approximately 11% of the population has AD (Hebert, Weuve, Scherr, & Evans, 2013). That is equivalent to one in nine people. The estimated population number in 2015 was 5.3 million people. Of that number, approximately 200,000 are younger than 65 and have the early-onset variety. Further, it is estimated that about one-third of individuals older than age 85 likely have AD (Alzheimer's Association, 2015). However, in the community AD is most likely underdiagnosed. Estimates suggest up to nearly half of the oldest-old community-dwelling adults are unaware they have the condition and have not been assessed for it (Alzheimer's Association, 2015).

Women are more likely to be diagnosed with AD than are men, at a ratio of 16% to 11% (Alzheimer's Association, 2015). Previously, the most widely accepted hypothesis was that because women live longer than men and the risk of AD increases with age, women are more likely to be affected. However, it is possible that genetic variation or lifestyle factors also may account for this difference. By race, AD is more prevalent in people who are African American or Hispanic, although by sheer numbers more European Americans have the disease (Potter et al., 2009). A possible rationale is that health conditions more prominent in these groups increase risk factors for AD.

DISCLOSURE OF AD AND RELATED DEMENTIA: A COUNSELING CONCERN

Having no knowledge of the presence of AD has the capacity to affect relationships with family members and with physicians as well as management of symptoms. There is a general consensus in bioethics that persons with dementia, and in fact all who suffer from illness, should be told their diagnosis. If not told out of supposed kindness, they are robbed of an opportunity to adjust and prepare for the eventual decline that will come, including the opportunity to complete advance directives. About 45% of patients with AD or their proxy have reported being told about their disease according to Alzheimer's Association data (2015). This is much lower than reported for other illnesses. Reasons given for failure to disclose include uncertainty of the diagnosis, lack of time, communication problems, and fear of causing distress. However, there are benefits to disclosure even though treatments are still being developed. A few of these benefits are improved decision making and planning for the future, coping, access to services, ensuring safety in the environment, and provision of social support (Alzheimer's Association, 2015).

Even if the diagnosis is shared, sometimes this information is not well assimilated. In one study, memory care clinic patients and their primary or nonprimary caregivers were asked to write their diagnosis on paper shortly after hearing it once the physician had left the room (Barrett, Orange, Keller, Damgaard, & Swerdlow, 2006). Of 37 patients with AD, 26 did not know their diagnosis, 6 of their 37 primary caregivers incorrectly reported it, and 5 patients were able to correctly give their diagnosis in cases the caregiver was unable to do so.

Formerly, physicians and others were reluctant to share a diagnosis out of concern for causing anguish or removing hope, especially if the diagnosis could be devastating. Now disclosure is considered a best practice standard based on ethical principles of truth telling and autonomy. Such news can be shocking, however, and persons with dementia and their significant others have difficulty absorbing and understanding it. What can facilitate comprehension? A method used to reduce confusion is *ask-tell-ask*. The professional can first ask the client and family what they understand about their illness. Based on the information given, the professional emphasizes certain points and eliminates misunderstandings. Finally, the professional follows this interchange by asking again what was understood. This serves as a way of reinforcing important messages and placing power in the hands of the client who is the subject rather than the object of the communication. On later losing capacity for meaningful expressive language, palliation for pain may become difficult and the voice of the person with dementia may be silent on end-of-life preferences. Advance directives enable those with power of attorney not to guess, *but to know preferences*. Acting on those preferences, rather than their own, they can safeguard interests of their grantor/patient.

ANOTHER PERSPECTIVE ON DEMENTIA

It is essential in knowledge development to understand how the scientific and medical communities consider dementia and specifically Alzheimer's disease. The basics of any mental health work with sufferers of these illnesses include professional knowledge about dementia, its medical varieties (which, because of individual variation, are not unlike James's many *varieties* of religious experience), and something about behavioral signs and symptoms. First, knowing something about these ideas, one can consider more closely the social constructions around these terms, including the emotional current the word *dementia* carries (Basting, 2009; Zeilig, 2014).

Critical gerontology invites us to question social understandings and social norms around dementia (Gordon, 2014; Zeilig, 2014). In fact, at present the social model of understanding and managing dementia has as much, if not more, to offer than a medical model providing few alternatives for treatment once the illness is diagnosed. Metaphors surrounding dementia also shape beliefs, which in turn shape action and interrelations. Metaphors provide practitioners with a way of processing knowledge. For example, dementia is often joined with words like *time bomb* or *an epidemic*, though technically, rates of dementia do not exceed what would normally be expected in populations of large numbers of older people. Risk is one aspect for older people, but reaching for earlier diagnoses to be made as some medical and policy professionals call for, with no psychopharmacological treatment and implications for loss of work and insurance, are even more concerning to some (Gordon, 2014). Persons with dementia are said to be *ravaged* by the disease and become *shells* of who they were. Both of these common constructions (as well as others you can think of, dear reader) make the hurdle higher for professionals and family members to continue to witness inner vitality and fluidly engage with persons with dementia. Is there a spiritual purpose in dementia? Where theologians have failed to work that out, it is a question I cannot adequately answer. However, there is a spirituality present in persons with dementia and also in the process of interrelating with them as experimental as that process usually is. Sadly, after a diagnosis is known, professionals may not create response opportunities or seek information about the person with dementia's background that would enhance communication. They are sometimes prematurely dismissive. However, understanding past behavior often is the gateway to the meaning in the metaphors they live daily.

The term *dementia* derives from the Latin *dementia*, madness, which also means "out of mind." That is a very strong metaphor—and also untrue in early stages. The idea of dementia risks cloaking the person who has it such that he or she is no longer seen as a whole person but one who is, in fact, his or her illness (Charmaz, 1991). Both the individual with the diagnosis and family/friends may see the person as impaired, so the individual's feelings are confirmed by others in their context. It is important for the mental health professional to be aware of this and to focus on the person as a whole person, not ignoring the diagnosis but not identifying the person as the diagnosis.

The biological nuances of dementia see deficit; the psychosocial spiritual nuances see presence rather than absence, but that presence is only marginally similar to what was once the personality. In dementia, personality shifts into something novel. So something is lost, but something also remains even if on a different plane. The language we use sets a condition of distance between the one who has dementia—and everyone else. What is the result of this distance-inducing language, where we, out of our fears, want to clearly affirm that we are not like those we assist? Identity is one of those markers of self that people tightly grasp—even those who seek personal growth and, dare we sigh the sacred word sotto voce, *change*. Who would seek to be different from who they are on the profoundest level? Maybe no one. Perhaps the core self still remains though shuttered by an errant APOE-4 gene. As one religious sister at a retreat where I stayed to begin this chapter articulated, "People with dementia still have the God-spark in them."

SPIRITUALITY AND THE SELF

Practice experience suggests that people with mild cognitive impairment or an early stage of dementia tend to minimize their disability and desire above all to maintain a sense of normality. Even greater than the stigma that can accrue to older adults and aging itself, the onset of dementia throws a support network into disarray and confuses acquaintances. Further, once the diagnosis is made, people are on the lookout for any small errors in thinking, and even if motivated by good intentions, subtly take control of decision making. Kitwood (1997) defined personhood as "a standing or status bestowed upon human beings by others, in the context of relationship and social being" (p. 8). He adroitly observed that the full expression of personhood in people with dementia was inhibited by environments and unenlightened staff practices, which he named "malignant social psychology." In this perspective, persons with dementia are first intimidated, then labeled, out-paced, banished, and finally, objectified, ignored, and disparaged. This belies the potential for social, emotional, and spiritual growth that can manifest in persons with dementia and their carers. This philosophical approach, introduced briefly earlier in the chapter, has come to be known as *person-centered care*.

Kitwood (1998) suggested that persons with dementia themselves move from "rage, paranoia, and depression" into a strangely persistent "trustful serenity" (p. 23). That sounds similar to the classic Kubler-Ross stage theory of reactions to dying, that Kubler-Ross herself suggested was malleable in the sequence or phase encountered. Kitwood, after outlining three excellent emblematic teaching cases, suggests that our interactions either "maintain personhood" or "undermine it" (p. 27). A caregiver can plan celebrations, for example, that both care receiver and care provider can enjoy and thus equalize the power between them: Ego edges are unguarded and selfhood expands. The person's identity can be valued in the midst of uncertainty, which may be the bioethical response problem. "In some mystical traditions, this [expansion] is the meaning of spirituality," avers Kitwood (p. 27). Identity is fluid, malleable, and yet still meaningful.

Sabat (2006), moving forward from Kitwood's views, suggests that the signification of dementia includes excess disability. This disability emerges not from the physical indicators of the illness, but from epiphenomena, or the way the person with the illness is addressed or fails to be addressed by others. The social positioning of the person with dementia often occurs through inattention of caregivers when they excuse behavior by explaining to others what illness the person in their care has. Positions ascribed by others can "define, strengthen, or weaken a person's moral and personal attributes" (p. 289), and dementia can result in malignant positioning. Once a person carries the dementia diagnosis, others no longer support his or her personhood (Scholl & Sabat, 2008). Diminishment begins long before the skill level or language of a person with dementia fades away. Old friends may no longer visit because they fear the person will fail to recognize them. Their prospective discomfort removes any opportunity to engage. All potential for growth occurs in the minute interactions of life, but longstanding friends dismiss the potential for any joyful exchange with the person they profess was their friend. In this manner, they preemptively consign their friend to a status of absent or missing. Yet as many loved ones of those with dementia attest, lucid moments often appear long into later stages of the disease. Although great difficulty in communication transpires, the person is still present.

There are three aspects of selfhood explained by Sabat, as cited in Swinton (2012). The first of these is the sense of self-in-the-present, or *Self 1*. This aspect of self remains throughout the experience of dementia. The second type of self, *Self 2*, is the self who is aware of itself, the attributes of the self, and the beliefs about those attributes experienced by the self. For instance, the level of education one received and one's level of satisfaction with that, or details of one's biography and how that is interpreted or valued, would characterize Self 2. *Self 3* consists of the social forms of self displayed to different people or in different situations. This representation of selfhood is dependent on an audience to maintain through the status it affords. Is there an actor with no stage or spectators? Is there a teacher without a student? Keeping a positive self-image in this mode is contingent on the feedback others fling out. The spiritual task of a community then is to help uphold membership status of the person with dementia in their midst, shifting to accommodate change, and likewise learning and growing in those actions. A faith community may provide this backdrop, but any community may open itself to this spiritual role. What are the narratives of both the person with dementia and the community as they find a nexus in this new space?

As the brain deteriorates and cells are slashed in the process, perhaps the essential nature of the person is uncovered. Some writers who themselves suffer from early-stage dementia suggest this hopeful reading of their life, as alluded to in quotes Killick (2006) shares. Rather than assume nonsense, a more productive task is to embark on an expedition to understand the behavior. Helping persons with dementia manage behavior in a person-centered manner both acknowledges need and supports them holistically. Facilitation of ADL behavior through the gaps of missing knowledge or in-the-moment opportunities for creations through dance or song are other possibilities of both honoring the person and living in his or her world. This form of engagement constitutes a model of low control—few sedatives—and high creativity or expression, which rather than bringing chaos, allows persons with dementia to live at their highest capability and relieves caregivers of the self-perception, if not denied, that they are tyrants and jailors. Accommodation for disruptive behavior is made in this model through thoughtful response rather than restrictive domination.

Further, the spiritual expressions of persons with dementia in early stages include reaching toward what is transcendent and retaining their integrity by reflection on what has had value in their past and retains value in their present. The familiarity and reassurance of religious practices and faith communities may continue to provide a space of acceptance and support for both family carer and person with dementia (Swinton, 2012). A life history approach is generally a useful therapeutic tool for most older people, but as persons with dementia move forward from their past into a new future autographed with spiritual growth and biological decline, the *what* of their identity transforms. It is then that the arts can bear the weight of what identity may mean.

Research addressing how persons with early stage dementia consider the self and then subsequently shift their perspective to still-meaningful engagement, accomplishment, or *is-ness* refutes the culturally prevalent text of irrelevancy and requisite warehousing (Beard, 2004; Cohen-Mansfield, Golander, & Arnheim, 2000; Cotrell & Hooker, 2005; MacRae, 2010; Sabat & Collins, 1999). Instead, although the public self changes, the *essence* of the self remains the same. However, as with Cooley's looking glass self and symbolic interaction theory sequelae, when treated by others as diminutive versions of their former selves, their voices are squelched, making them much dimmer than they could be. Interestingly, in MacRae's (2010) small qualitative study, respondents did not mention the early-stage AD that initiated them into the study as part of their identities. Continuity and coherence in how they continued to live and what they enjoyed, even if somewhat altered, mattered. AD was not the "master narrative" that subjugated the rest (Beard, 2004). These aspects are what mental health practitioners can listen to and support. Narrative therapy can assist clients in highlighting such continuities (see Young, 2010) and becomes a collaborative act.

Embodiment and Dementia

Another approach to examining the self in dementia consists of using the lens of embodiment (Kontos & Martin, 2013). In what ways is the physical body not only the dwelling for illness and for holding all the hopelessness of the biomedical model, but also the key to the revitalization of the self? The body's senses are how one knows and is known. Embodiment allows the person with dementia to experience appropriate pleasure through participation in the sensory qualities of religious ritual—and at times find inappropriate pleasure in behavior marked by unwanted sexual overtures. The boundaries between private space and public space in settings where care is provided are thin for the persons with dementia. Kontos and Martin (2013) detail a Dutch innovation in design for dementia care environments where "residents can meet as if they were on a public street, and streetlights and benches placed in the shopping area reinforce the impression of a public square" (p. 295). Many memory care units display boxes with photos of the resident near their rooms and meaningful artifacts such as trophies or awards. All of this reinforces history, memory, connection, and selfhood.

Elderspeak: A Barrier in Working With Persons With Dementia

Elderspeak is a communication style that is common in intergenerational interactions between staff and residents, especially in long-term care (LTC) settings (Williams, Kemper, & Hummert, 2003). Although some caregivers suggest that use of familiar terms such as *mama* may be reassuring to persons with dementia, others see this as infantilizing. Overly simplistic vocabulary, slower speech rate, elevated pitch and volume, use of the plural *we* in an inaccurate way ("Are we ready to go to the dining room?"), and unprofessional terms of endearment are other means of recognizing this linguistic form. Analyzing 80 staff-patient interactions on videotape, one study determined that use of elderspeak language led to a significant increase in patient resistance to care (Williams, Herman, Gajewski, & Wilson 2009). In working with persons with dementia, it is useful to provide uncomplicated and simple directions in short step-by-step sentences, but elderspeak dishonors the older person.

UNDERSTANDING NEED-DRIVEN, DEMENTIA-COMPROMISED BEHAVIOR

In Algase et al.'s (1996) model, need-driven dementia-compromised behavior (NDB) is affected by both *fixed* (unchangeable) and *proximal* (modifiable) factors. Interactions between staff and patients comprise one of the significant areas where attention and training can be given to heighten attention toward decreasing challenging behaviors. Dupuis, Wiersma, and Loiselle (2012) interviewed LTC staff in several areas about their interactions and concluded that many workers perceived patients through lenses of pathology, intentionality of action/reaction, perceived threat, social inappropriateness, and other ideas damaging to personhood as signposted in Kitwood's writing. "Opportunities to understand meaning in behaviors were often overlooked and not taken" (Dupuis et al., 2012, p. 169). Body movements of patients were not seen as reflecting past experience, but pathology. Dupuis et al. (2012) cite Fazio, Seman, and Stansell (1999) to ask what it would mean for responsive behavior if staff reinterpreted short-term memory loss, for example, as spontaneity. Reflection *in* action and *on* action (Schön, 1983) leads to more equal engagement, where both care receivers and care providers can benefit.

In a Japanese study using the Jiro Kawakita (KJ) qualitative method, experienced workers from a number of facilities were gathered to determine best practices in working with persons with dementia and teaching other staff to work with them (Fukui, Okada, Nishimoto, & Nelson-Becker, 2010). To address the common routine of the repeated appeal to go home, workers agreed on the following five steps: (1) Listen to the voice and go with the flow of behavior; (2) Learn about the inner experience; (3) Learn about the contextual experience of "here and now" situations; (4) Reflect on the care environment; and finally, (5) Find the keyword. In the case of persons with dementia and their repeated appeal to return home, the keyword was *najimi*, which means "familiar environment." The key to addressing behavior is to connect with past experience or feelings to create familiarity rather than unease. In its responsive discovery sequence, this process attunes to the spiritual context of learning the essence of what remains meaningful for the person with dementia. This can upend nonproductive relationships and change behavior distressing to staff, while respecting the person.

A Norwegian study of spiritual needs of persons with dementia conducted focus groups with 31 nurses and care workers (Ødbehr, Kvigne, Hauge, & Danbolt, 2014). Three themes emerged from comments: the need for serenity and inner peace, the need for confirmation, and the need to express faith and beliefs. To combat restlessness in a patient, one nurse played a religious CD found in a patient's drawer. As it played, tears began to stream down the patient's face, which she took as a sign of connection. Staff felt that residents wanted to be affirmed for who they once were to maintain self-worth and coherence. They appraised that patients had not completely lost touch with their identities. Singing familiar hymns and saying memorized prayers, such as the Christian Lord's Prayer, brought comfort. The most common fear expressed was being alone, but not dying. Especially notable was that nurses felt uncomfortable about open discussion of religious questions. They occasionally participated with residents in religious faith expressions, but primarily looked to a priest to meet this need. Although memory loss might affect retrieval of sources of meaning and meaning creation, study participants thought these needs were still present and thus unmet.

A Behavioral Approach

In mid-phases of dementia, using a behavioral approach to detect the underlying rationales for behavior can be combined with a spiritual view of personhood described above. Ultimately, it helps both the staff and the patient achieve a balance in needs and desires. Staff in nursing homes change frequently and often are not trained in addressing difficult behavior compassionately. In LTC consultations, it can be useful to write behavioral prescriptions or plans directly in record notes to assist staff to work effectively with challenging behavior. One common format is to invite staff to do the following:

1. Identify the target behavior.

2. Consider the antecedents of that behavior.

3. Creatively think about and apply ways to change the context of the behavior in terms of what mattered to the client (e.g., what rewards, such as special food, would be appreciated).

4. One problem in nursing care facilities with overscheduled staff time is that some patients are ignored unless they scream or become aggressive. So catch the patient doing something right. Enter his or her room—sometimes on a two-hour schedule, if needed—to check in and briefly chat.

5. If the patient presses the call light repeatedly, yells repeatedly, or throws something, suggest that you can't talk then (because of the poor behavior), but will check on him or her later.

6. Reinforce that staff must respond to call lights to check for an emergency, but if there is none, staff are free to leave and return later. This encourages more civil behavior and allows staff to come to know the patient in a better circumstance. In the best scenario, they might even find that they enjoyed each other.

Learning what encourages difficult behavior (antecedents or triggers), consequences that may reinforce the behavior, and then related factors such as time of day or who is present can assist caregivers to understand the behavior. In behavioral theory, this is known as learning the ABC's of behavior where A represents the antecedents, B is the behavior, and C is the consequence that can reinforce or reduce the behavior. Is the behavior too intense? Is it safe? Is it dangerous? Who has the problem? Is the behavior disturbing to the person with dementia or to others? These are helpful questions to consider.

Reframing the meaning of the behavior to the caregiver connects the behavior to the history of the person with dementia. Rather than confront resistance, resistance can thus be followed and explored. Exploring reasons for behavior and resolving them is a spiritual process because it respects what clients need and want and helps mediate both patient and staff concerns. Antecedents as well as responses to the behavior can be modified in a person-centered way. For instance, Asako Fujibayashi would get agitated around dinner time, wandering in and out of the dining room. Staff learned she had been a waitress, so they invited her to sit in a corner and fold cloth napkins before dinner. It didn't matter as much whether this was done usefully or not (though it could be a benefit); it gave Ms. Fujibayashi something to do with her hands that was familiar (*najimi*) and calmed her.

When a person with dementia no longer remembers faces, it is as if everyone who approaches is a stranger. Similar to the beginning theme of the film *Groundhog Day*, each day is new again, with little transfer of knowledge. Approaching the individual from the front, reintroducing oneself, using eye contact, and explaining what one will do with simple instructions are methods of gaining trust and respecting the person. This also may include returning to give care later if the person refuses at the time. Rather than struggling to bring a person with dementia into a reality long vanished, it is far more successful to step into the reality of that individual. This is in-the-moment stuff and can be fun. Curiosity should guide the exchange, rather than assigning an unwarranted judgment or label. Because of faulty sensory input, a person with dementia may believe, for example, that someone is in the house when no one is there. Behaviors are not always voluntary, so reasoning with a person with dementia is often ineffective, only resulting in frustration for the caregiver. Rather than correction, reassurance may be better received—and also ultimately lead to the preferred behavior. Making eye contact unless culturally incorrect, looking directly at the person, and speaking slowly in short sentences all make comprehension easier. A person with dementia can be cued to be successful by inviting behavior that is within capacity and taking a moment to think about the person beyond the disease.

Noncognitive methods of communication are especially useful at mid-stages of dementia. Offering positive and friendly facial expressions, using gentle touch such as holding a hand, and providing symbols that may carry religious or cultural meaning, such as a cross for Christianity, or a symbol of the Buddha can each provide opportunities for connection. Islam as a faith has historically had no image or symbol, though the color green is sometimes associated with it. A person with dementia in mid-stages will react more to the tone of voice or a facial expression than they will to words themselves. The ritual of prayer is useful across many religious faiths. It can calm and connect a person to his or her emotional center. Prayer can consist of familiar prayers or short extemporaneous ones that are easily understood. A picture of Jesus, the Buddha, or Kuan Yin (Goddess of Compassion) may evoke strong feelings. Religious symbols convey meaning, even if the meaning arises outside of conscious thought streams.

Caregivers should not lie to the person with dementia, but instead they should try to discern the underlying feeling and respond to that or redirect the person. If a person with dementia asks about his or her parent (a common repetitive question), rather than responding that the parent is dead and risking re-grief, the caregiver may realize that the person with dementia misses that parent. If time is available, he or she can sit down and ask the person with dementia to describe the parent and what the relationship was like. If a person with dementia insists he or she wants to go home and home is not possible, the caregiver can talk about the wonderful hotel room (as a metaphor) prepared for the patient here, or that they have two homes, or whatever creative response comes to mind. A word about telling untruths: A caregiver should be cautious about saying something they know to be completely untrue. Having to lie does something to the inner integrity of the caregiver and over time, can lead to exhaustion, unhappiness, and depletion. The spiritual way suggests that even if it takes extra time and imagination, the truth as far as it is known should be preserved.

LITERATURE RELATED TO SPIRITUAL ASPECTS OF DEMENTIA AND DEMENTIA CARE PRACTICE

Out of the nun studies consisting of cognitive tests and measures both early and late in life, and autopsies of the brains of women of religious orders, some interesting results have emerged (Riley, Snowdon, Desrosiers, & Markesbery, 2005; Snowdon, 2001). Linguistic ability in the form of lower idea density and lower vocabulary in young adulthood was associated with cognitive impairment at later ages. This implies that greater education and cognitive effort is associated with less dementia. Because of commonalities related to homogenous lifestyle factors in the nuns, it was easier to compare circumstances of stability and deterioration across the wider group. Even when some women had dementia, the religious community lovingly cared for and continued to make place for them.

The American Geriatric Society guidelines for mild cognitive impairment suggest *not* prescribing use of cholinesterase inhibitors routinely. Many families ask for them in hopes that they will prevent progression to dementia, but one study advised that although these medications raise hopes for treatment, they are ineffective in prevention and have gastrointestinal side effects (Russ, 2014). Kaufman, Anaki, Binns, and Freedman (2007) discovered a correlation between high levels of spirituality among dementia patients and lower morbidity and mortality. Using partial correlation statistical analysis, they demonstrated that higher levels of religious and spiritual activities predicted slower cognitive decline in patients with dementia ($n = 70$, $r = -0.315$, p < .05). In addition, these practices contributed to longer survival. Where biomedical care in early stages and cognitive care in later stages are not effective, spiritual care may maintain human connection.

There is an expanding literature on spiritual care for persons with dementia (Jewel, 2011; MacKinlay, 2006b; Swinton, 2012). Spiritual needs are met even without direct awareness by care facility staff when they facilitate connections between persons with dementia and nature; attending chapel, church, mosque, synagogue, or other faith-based activity; quiet time; and other multisensory activities (Bursell & Mayers, 2010). Although staff in the same study identified spiritual care as everyone's role, not just the province of the chaplain, ascertaining those needs and having the time to meet them were reported as burdensome (Bursell & Mayers, 2010).

A study of nursing home residents at mild, moderate, and advanced stages of dementia indicated they were able to express what mattered to them spiritually and/or religiously, both in the past and in their present (Power & Watson, 2011). Family and staff members emphasized the presence of emotional awareness and emotional memory even in residents perceived as noncommunicative. They described both breakthroughs as well as subtle signs of responsiveness in dementia-impaired residents. However, nursing homes tended to rank the importance of spiritual care low.

A review of literature on spiritual coping in early-stage AD yielded six studies across disciplines (Beuscher & Beck, 2008). Overall, the effects of AD were noted to create disconnections that were repaired through spiritual coping strategies to find meaning. A small convenience sample of 15 Christian persons with dementia suggested that this group encountered difficulty with what had been long-term religious practices such as church attendance, understanding sermons, and reading the Bible (Beuscher & Grando, 2009). However, spiritual practices such as prayer remained valuable as well as symbolic gestures such as folding the hands in prayer before meals. In a separate caregiver study, an eight-week phone-based intervention employed use of a *mantra* or *mantram* ("holy name"; Bormann et al., 2009). This involved repetition of a sacred word designed to relieve stress in caregivers of older VA clients with dementia (Bormann et al., 2009). There was no control group, but measures showed a decrease in distress.

A small but rich phenomenological study of six persons with dementia reported concerns over loss of a sense of self, such as feeling like a parcel that was passed person to person (Dalby, Sperlinger, & Boddington, 2011). Five themes reflected the experience of spirituality in dementia: (1) faith; (2) searching for meaning; (3) "I'm not as I was," expressing changes and losses in the self; (4) trying to stay intact cognitively; and (5) finding pathways to spiritual connection and expression. Participants suggested their "spiritual work" was ongoing and life purpose included "to develop the soul," as well as opportunity to learn and express compassion. Spiritual life was not viewed apart from daily life. Participant thoughts on dying were not sad. However, some felt increasing isolation. Finding acceptance, keeping hopeful, and recollecting (remembering) the self were coping strategies. Connections with support systems and spiritual communities remained important as well as the opportunity to be engaged in opportunities to help others.

One rigorous study triangulated interview and observational data between eight individuals with early-stage dementia, their significant others, and professional staff (Tracy, Sandee, & Phyllis, 2011). Creating or participating in a relational context of care built on knowledge of individual backgrounds and preferences led dementia-affected individuals to feel cared-for in moments held sacred. Small acts discharged by family, friends, and staff were not time-consuming and fostered personhood. Staff were surprised to note that clients unexpectedly reciprocated caring words. The meaning of symbols such as a palm leaf given at Eastertime were understood even when words failed. Regrettably, spiritual care provision seemed to be prioritized for the cognitively well rather than persons with dementia in nursing care facilities. The authors suggested that what is holy dwells within the ordinary features of life.

Other studies of spiritual and religious coping and the preferences of persons with dementia have enlarged understanding (Katsuno, 2003; Snyder, 2003). English literary author Terry Pratchett (2015), diagnosed with posterior cortical atrophy or PCA, a rare form of AD, identified the loneliness he experienced with the diagnosis and how he was avoided out of embarrassment when he "came out" with the disease. In his case, there was also public confusion and lack of validation by others: "We have extreme problems handling the physical world, but we can come pretty close to talking our way out of it so you don't notice." He felt he had two diseases: the disease itself and the knowledge that he had it. "Alzheimer's is me unwinding, losing trust in myself."

An arts-based program was conducted with 11 persons with dementia in a study by Byrne and MacKinlay (2012) that included their own critical review. Audio recordings were supplemented with reflection journals by facilitators, and facial expression charts were ticked by facilitator respondents who had some difficulty understanding the ultimate goals of their project. Doing artwork often was privileged by facilitators over uncovering themes and looking for meaning; research questions concerning how participants felt about doing the artwork and what they saw in their work were often ignored by facilitators. Breadth of responses were favored over depth, and linkages to meaning often were not reached. The researchers concluded that this person-centered style of relating and accompanying persons with dementia in their art making required greater openness and diligence by facilitators to connect the experience with meaning making (Byrne & MacKinlay, 2012). This highlighted the need for special attention and training to achieve desired outcomes.

RELIGIOUS AND SPIRITUAL PRACTICE PRINCIPLES FOR THE PERSON WITH DEMENTIA

> *The rabbit snare exists because of the rabbit. Once you've gotten the rabbit, you can forget the snare. The point of a word is the idea or meaning. Once you've gotten the idea or meaning, you can forget the word. How can I find a man who has forgotten words so we can have a few words together?*—
> Chuang Tzu (3rd century BCE)

This writing attributed to the Daoist philosopher Chuang Tzu was likely not intended to describe dementia. However, in learning to communicate beyond the use of words, meaning can unfold. In fact, in situations involving moderate and later stages of dementia, words thwart intention. The person with dementia forgets the words to use to describe something, and the words they do recall in later stages often are used wrongly, obstructing meaning. This creates a great deal of confusion and frustration in caregivers who previously relied on language as the primary vehicle for communication. However, once the caregiver and the person with dementia can move past the words into other communication formats such as singing, the outcome is often more rewarding. Some persons with dementia have learned American Sign Language in preparation for the time when they no longer have the memory for words.

Time

Time is a commodity we use, lose, spend, and save. Metaphorically we invest time and run out of it. We waste it. We speak of borrowing time, and ask how much of it we have left. So much of our lives is measured by our sense of time passing too quickly! In working with persons with dementia, we can alter our typical sense of time so that we can move into a shared space that operates on a slower schedule. Rather than feeling a sense of accomplishment only if we do something together, we can practice being with another person, which sometimes is all that is needed. There is a subtle communication that can unfold when we simply sit together, even if the past has disappeared and the future is not a factor. Darcy Harris (Winokuer & Harris, 2012) gives an example of a nursing intern who was in the room of a woman she had previously connected well with who lay dying. She was worried her supervisor would walk by, so she busied herself cleaning utensils that would not be used and filling a pitcher of fresh water that would not be sipped. The woman lying in bed opened her eyes and invited the student not to do something, but just to sit with her. That was what she most needed at that time. This may also be true of persons with dementia; someone willing to sit with them can bring a calming presence.

Another aspect of accompanying the person with dementia includes having the opportunity to hold their names and their stories for them, stories of their identity and accomplishments, or history of what was important to them (Swinton, 2012). As with many intentional models of spiritual companioning, there is little need in later stages of dementia to direct, but much need to continue the story by caring for these persons. This includes stilling anxiety about being pressed for time and the fear of wasting it when the typical feedback loop in the form of words or facial cues is absent.

Let Them Teach Us Who They Are

Persons with mild cognitive loss may struggle to retain their former identity. Risks for depression include a sense of loneliness and isolation if support systems draw back, and sometimes boredom. What friends may fail to realize is that people in early stages of the illness still retain enough identity that they can engage, and there can be a freshness to the relationship as old inhibitions disappear in an ego-lessened state. They continue to have humor and wisdom to offer in relationships, and they often are able to get at the essence of things. If bored, such persons can still participate in areas of their former interest, but in modified fashion. For instance, if they have enjoyed cooking, now they can do so with recipes that are written out and someone nearby to supervise.

Most of all, it is important that knowledge about how to live with the illness be shared and passed on, especially by those who contend with it. Strategies to live as fully as possible are sometimes quite ingenious and personalized. Persons with AD do not want to face stigma because of it, but at the same time they do want people to understand their sometimes unusual actions. "The end stage is our future. But not today," assessed one individual (Kleinfield, 2016, para. 3). There is still a need to find purpose and make a contribution. "If I have to measure up to what I was before I became this, I can't. But if you let that go, then you are still becoming something. And it's not necessarily a diminution of yourself" (Kleinfield, 2016, para. 1). People are still becoming, no matter in what condition they find themselves.

In early to middle stages of dementia immediate memory recedes. It is helpful to release expectations that previous lifelong habits will predict future behavior. If a visitor steps out for a moment and returns, they may be re-greeted with the same enthusiasm given to someone absent for a long time. These are not occasions for a mental health worker or staff to give explanation with overtones of inadequacy of the person with dementia ("Well, I was just here; don't you remember?"), but to enjoy the spontaneity of the greeting along with the person with dementia. Rather than carry deeply our knowledge of who this person with dementia has been, we can allow them to change and teach us who they are now. This practice also encourages us to surrender our hypercognitive training in favor of opening to a more intuitive response style. Further, our adjusted expectations can also limit what we notice and act on. If we set our expectation level too low, we may miss opportunities for connection and play that appear only briefly. Our presence—whether we consider ourselves spiritual, religious or neither—is a blessing, or a gift.

In mid-to late stages, communication is typically a challenge. A particularly compelling approach is to set aside the theory that is effective for most mental health work and begin a discovery process of dwelling in the moment. Holding no agenda except to offer the comfort of the relationship in an experimental manner can lead to a satisfying communion. This involves trusting the moment, which is especially hard for most Western practitioners, especially those who are early in their careers. Another aspect of working with someone in late stages may be learning to be comfortable in carrying a one-sided conversation. A physician spoke about sitting by the bedside of a generally nonresponsive woman to chart after her examination because billing allowed for increments of 15 minutes (Wyatt, 2012). The clatter of a tray outside the room and the patient's reaction alerted her that her patient was responsive. The physician began to talk with her about a photo by her bedside and then noticed her crying. She felt she had made a soul-level connection.

Ritual

Elements of ritual have been discussed in Chapters 7 and 8. However, in working with persons with dementia the effects of ritual can be particularly striking. De Sousa (2011) suggests that spiritual capacity is not connected to cognitive capacity. He and others have commended the value of multisensory components in religious services for those who are religious such as visual symbols, incense, chants, prayers, and singing. Ritual connects to instinctual sensibilities. Because many older adults were grounded in a faith tradition, ritual links them back to long-term memory and even what lies beyond memory in the bones. Staff has frequently noticed a mini-awakening that occurs when people participate in a religious service of some kind. The service does not always need to represent their same tradition. In the gathering, patients/clients can come alive again. (Perhaps they have something to teach us about elemental multifaith connection.) Consistent with the idea that working with persons with dementia can lead to the unexpected however, some persons with dementia who may have been members of a faith community may show little interest in participating in a religious service of any kind.

Religious and Spiritual Texts

Familiar religious texts out of every faith provide the ability to give comfort and reassurance. Favorite spiritual poetry or other sayings can give strength and courage to those clients who are nonreligious. When people are early in their diagnosis they may even want to express their feelings in writing. This can help them manage difficult feelings and could also serve as a legacy for significant others.

In Jewish and Christian traditions there are a number of biblical psalms that can help express what is inexpressible, including lament. Psalm 88 was discussed in detail by one caregiver for a person with dementia (Barclay, 2012). She identified how this psalm expressed her experience and sense of social exclusion even from her religious community. She grieved over the lack of holistic care that might have considered the person with dementia and his or her significant other a unit and strengthened their relational bond. She suggested a broader scope was needed to satisfy the concept of welcoming the stranger. The psalm taught her to wait patiently, accompanied in the darkness by God, even if her community did not want to hear her story of loss. Psalm 71 in verse 9 urges, "Do not cast me off in old age; do not forsake me when my strength is spent." It finishes by attesting to God's ongoing presence and the possibility of restoration in verse 20, "You who have made me see . . . will revive me again." Religious texts of comfort are available throughout world religious traditions; people who are members of these faiths can discover meaningful texts and share them with counselors and practitioners.

ARTS-BASED INTERVENTIONS

The arts of writing, performance, and music have great potential to clarify feelings at early stages of dementia. At later stages, use of the arts can revitalize, maintain connection, or simply reclaim an opportunity for joy. The creative arts enlist other parts of the brain that may be affected differently by the disease.

Story-Telling Workshops

Caregivers often experience diminishment of joy through the caregiving tasks that keep them on call 24 hours a day. With early diagnosis, there is a window of time during which the relationship between caregiver and care recipient can be enhanced. The care receiver is able to participate in decisions, can learn ways to cope with the disease, and find meaning (Molyneaux, Butchard, Simpson, & Murray, 2012). To support the sacred nature of relationship and couple strengths, one strategy is to engage in reminiscent story telling (Dowden, personal communication, November 20, 2014). A *master storyteller* works with the group to mine stories for key words and images. In the session, for example, participants might write briefly about their memories of the day they received their diagnosis. The master storyteller helps them think about what the doctor said to them, their subsequent emotions, and how others responded. Both the patient and carer then write a 50-word story about the diagnosis. These stories become part of their larger story and provide an opportunity for sharing. If the patient can no longer write, others can scribe. Couples are able to recognize their history of resilience and prepare for future change.

Improvisation

One method to enhance interaction comes from a presentation that considered the use of improvisational theatre techniques as providing an unconditional welcoming moment (Angelica, Gordon, & Koepke, 2015). With only the present moment, the presenters suggest enhancing caregiver competence through learning how to say *yes* to people with dementia and searching for the gifts in the interaction. For instance, although behavior may be noncongruent and difficult to understand, it is not random but emerges out of past behaviors. Investigating the signs and symbols for needs is similar to a semiotic communication system such as flags that signal at sea. Caregivers can mirror the ADL action they wish the person with dementia to participate in, such as putting on shoes or brushing their teeth. Directives can be phrased in positive language rather than begin in the dismissive language of "Don't . . ." Persons with dementia continue to have an emotional memory, and although they may not remember sequences of actions, they will remember how a caregiver made them feel.

In improvisational work, one goal is to make the partner look good. When a person with dementia makes a statement, caregivers can either *block the offer* or *advance the offer*. They block the offer when they deny the reality of what was said. They advance the offer when they extend some part of the interaction in a positive way. For example, if a person sees a couple sitting on a park bench and says to the woman, "What a beautiful shirt," the person with dementia might respond, "I sewed it myself." The caregiver nearby might respond factually, "No, that was a gift from your daughter" (blocking the offer). Or, he or she might add, "She always enjoys wearing that shirt" (advancing the offer). If the offer made by the person with dementia is blocked often enough, he or she may become frustrated and angry, yet be unable to express those feelings. The caregiver can try to affirm and validate, replying with the next logical response that comes to mind. As in behavioral therapy, it is important to cue the person with dementia to be successful and provide response opportunities. If the person with dementia thinks that the caregiver is someone else, although this can be painful, she can also choose to play the role she has been handed (Glazner, 2014; Killick & Craig, 2012). If the person with dementia believes the caregiver is a company CEO or a famous actor, she can play that part. Or, maybe the president is coming to dinner. Offering affirmation can lead to a healing moment. Key steps to creating this new style of discourse include the following:

1. Understand the environment and the possibilities of the situation; release any plan to command unfolding events.

2. Accept the reality of the situation; search for ways to say "Yes."

3. Affirm the partner; creatively participate to make them look good and feel good.

4. Reach acceptance; enjoy the experience in gratitude for having made a connection.

Improvisation, by teaching caregivers how to imaginatively engage, offers one solution to the isolation those with dementia often experience. Because it offers a counter-story to one of marginalization and opens a door to true sharing, it can be classified as a spiritual approach.

Music

Dan Cohen's volunteer work in nursing care homes with the simple tool of an iPod programmed with a patient's favorite music is revolutionizing care. The website about the film *Alive Inside* (http://www.aliveinside.us/#land) suggests that the film showcases an "exploration of music's capacity to reawaken our souls." As Oliver Sacks in the film denotes, music can activate more parts of the brain than other stimuli. In the film, one older gentleman, Henry Dreyer, who kept his head down and was minimally responsive, became animated when headphones with music from his favorite performer, Cab Calloway, were placed over his ears. He not only sang along, exhibiting an animated, happy facial expression, but he also began to answer questions that an interviewer asked. In a sense, he reacquired his identity through the music he loved. This is not just a temporary effect; it seems to last through a day. Rather than isolating residents, the music became a social experience. Music connects people back to their memories, which are then shared. This is the name conferred on the program, *Music and Memories.*

Even with such a stunning and visible response, Mr. Cohen described his difficulty in locating nursing care facilities who would agree to participate in the program. The use of personalized music was outside of their standard care. It is not reimbursable as medications are. In 2006 he heard a radio program that mentioned how ubiquitous iPods were. He phoned his local nursing home (Mr. Cohen was a social worker, but he did not work with older adults) and asked if he could personalize music for residents. The response was immediate and stunning; it seemed to transform moods. At first he was not linked to people with dementia, but when he began to include them, the difference in their status was profound. One woman lying nearly comatose in bed drawn up in a fetal position began moving to the music. Music seems to serve as a "back door" to an intact emotional system. Expectation and suggestion can also activate and enhance the auditory cortex (Sacks, 2007). As the person with dementia listens to music, the spirit appears to open. In this way, caregivers are able to move beyond the diagnosis to tap into the soul.

A second way that music can be included to engage persons with dementia is through one-to-one singing (Chatterton, Baker, & Morgan, 2010). Singing to a resident encouraged him or her to participate in ADLs and was found to reduce agitation. Singing offered mutuality in the interchange. The authors, music therapists, tentatively suggested that the singing is more important than who the singer is. Anecdotally, others propose that following a person with dementia who may do no more than sing "La, la, la" becomes a kind of interactive game that is enjoyable for both individuals. In earlier stages, persons with dementia may be able to sing their thoughts and responses, when it is difficult to use their normal speaking voice. As a society we are good at measuring disability and deficits, less good at learning how to draw out strengths and capacities. The cultural centrality of the importance of *remembering* can obstruct the capacity of caregivers and significant others to initiate play and relational engagement. Memory itself may reside as much between people as within one of them. Anne Basting's (2009) Timeslips story-telling programs have shown that imagination and creativity still dwell in persons with dementia. It is the task of the rest of us to offer them opportunities to reflect (when possible), engage, and enjoy their lives.

SUMMARY

In order to fully understand the abiding spirituality of a person with dementia and to honor relationships, it is helpful to first understand the process of memory in normal adulthood. There are many types of dementia and this chapter identified different types and basic symptoms. A behavioral approach to working with people with dementia honors their humanity, eliminates need for chemical restraints, and constitutes a first level approach. As cognition falters, a spiritual view continues to address social ways of relating and suggests arts-based methods of creating joy through microinteractions.

QUESTIONS FOR DISCUSSION

1. Generally, what is your understanding of how memory works? If memory is absent, what is the essence of a person?

2. What was your understanding of dementia before you read this chapter? How has your understanding shifted?

3. What is the prevalent view of dementia in our society today? What experiences have you had, if any, with persons with dementia? Did they support or challenge that view?

4. What is a spiritual view of persons with dementia?

5. What practices honor the spirituality of a person with dementia? If you were introduced to a person with dementia, how would you approach that person? How might stage of the disease make a difference? How might reflecting on this individual as a spiritual person make a difference?

MEDITATION: WALKING

Walking meditation is an active form of engaging with the environment. It differs from sitting meditation in that in this practice, one opens all of one's senses: seeing (vision), taste (gustatory), hearing (auditory), feeling (touch/sensibility), and smelling (olfactory). Through focus, one connects to the earth and heightens awareness of the body as well. This is best done outside or in a large space.

What do you see?

What do you taste?

What do you hear?

What do you feel/touch?

What do you smell?

Go through each of your senses and *catalogue* your responses.

As you walk, first notice your body. Pay attention to how it feels as you walk. Become aware of the sensation in the soles of your feet, your ankles, your knees. What do you notice as you take each step? What do you notice as your body moves forward? Where are your arms? How are you carrying your head?

Pay attention to your breath. As you breathe in, you may imagine yourself connected through the top of your head to the universe through an uncountable number of multicolored threads that represent all of your sensations. If you choose, breathe these in through your body, out through your feet and also in through your feet from the earth and up toward your head and beyond. This becomes a circular process of giving and receiving from the environment. As you take each step, you can imprint your gratitude and love on the earth.

Look for something new, something you have never seen before. Look for this one thing that calls to you, makes itself known to you. Prepare to bring this back in form or mentally to the group (if you are with one) and talk about it. Why did this particularly draw your attention?

EXPLORING YOUR SPIRITUALITY: SOUND

Sound enters our lives in many ways during the day. The sound of traffic signals congestion on the streets, a child's cries disturbs us, while music can touch our soul. Birdsong can lift us; a song that played in our teen years can take us quickly back to that time. The sound of wind can evoke freshness, a sense of cleansing after a storm. Words spoken can help us or hinder us. The universe of sounds reaches us through vibrations that we decode nearly automatically—unless our sense of hearing is absent or impaired—but even then people sometimes can sense the vibration of sound.

Music takes us to places where words alone do not. Sacred music consists of Sufi chants, Gregorian chants, Jewish cantillation, and many other rich musical and chant traditions. Hymns are often associated with Western religious faiths and date back to before the time of Homer. Homerian hymns in the 7th century BCE celebrated Greek mythical gods. Hebrew and Christian hymns in ancient times used the harp, lyre, and lute as suggested in Psalms in Biblical text. They range from simple melodies to complex structures. Overtone singing or throat singing is seen in Tibetan monks and in sacred harp or shape note singing from the American South. At university graduation this year, as one graduate's name was called, someone in the audience performed ululation, a high pitched vocalization with a trill. Contemporary Christian music and many other forms are designed to access the sacred through praise and prayer. Poems, too, can be lyrical. The sacred can be perceived in any music that touches the heart.

Sound also has a rich capacity for healing. In medieval times, bells called the community together in celebration or in mourning. Drums unite us, and if used in a musical group of any kind, keep instruments connected rhythmically. Some people participate in drumming circles, where everyone has a drum and their drumming or other percussive instruments fall together into rhythm. Certain instruments can call us to reverie, such as a flute or violin. A Tibetan singing bowl often emits several notes when struck. It is said that specific notes align with certain energy centers of the body. In hospice work, harpists will often play music intuitively for dying patients and their families. In grief work, we may suggest that adolescent grievers or others bring in music that is meaningful to them and listen together in counseling session.

Sound stimulates memory and can reduce anxiety. It can preserve or restore the self, as shown by programs that create individual iPods with favorite music for older people who seem generally nonresponsive to many stimuli. Sound is a form of self-expression for those who can no longer speak, and it can connect to emotions when words fail. The effects of listening can linger past the sound itself and alter moods, providing determination and resolve. Above all, music is a source of beauty. Beauty is needed in our lives for no other sake but its own.

1. Watch and listen to the "Prophecy Song" by Joanne Shenandoah, who is a member of the Wolf clan, Oneida Nation (https://www .youtube.com/watch?v=-A2_a-mGtlI). How do you experience this music?

2. Watch the online video "The Unexpected Joy of a Copenhagen Metro Commute" (http://www.onbeing.org/blog/the- unexpected-joy-of-a-copenhagen-metro- commute-video/6459). What reactions do you note? How does the older woman respond? Watch the *Washington Post* experiment, "Stopping for Joshua Bell," when he played his violin at a busy Washington, D.C. metro stop (https://www.youtube.com/ watch?v=hnOPu0_YWhw). What happened?

3. What is the role of sound in your life? If it is enriching, how does it do so? What sounds do you listen for each day?

4. What sounds annoy you?

5. What sounds do you create now or have you created in the past? Have you played an instrument or sung alone or with a group? If you enjoy making music either alone or with friends, what about it appeals to you? Why?

6. How does sound enter your body? What does sound mean to you?

7. Does sound engage your emotions? If so, how? Have you ever been healed by sound?

8. Who are your favorite musicians? How do you experience their music? If you create music, what do you experience from this act?

9. Journal your responses to any of the above.

EXPLORING YOUR SPIRITUALITY: TONGLEN PRACTICE TO INCREASE COMPASSION

Tonglen practice is a way of connecting with your suffering and the suffering of others and helping to heal it. The word *tonglen* means "exchanging the self for others or sending and receiving." This is a

Buddhist practice in altruism that has particularly been presented in the writing of Pema Chodron (1997). This practice is about awakening compassion through opening the heart and feeling the pain that other people feel. It is about recognizing the imperfect nature that others project through their selfishness, arrogance, stubbornness, and so on that subsequently allows us to recognize these less than desirable qualities in our own personalities.

1. To begin, follow your breath by breathing in and breathing out in a relaxed manner.

2. In meditation one typically lets go of thinking and keeps returning to clear space, but in this practice, permit your thoughts to wander regarding your own experiences of suffering. Focus on one that arouses strong feeling. Explore the details that cause you dismay. Once you have connected with this painful experience, breathe it in and allow it to fill you. When you breathe out, let the feeling dissipate. When you breathe in, locate the feeling again. Keep up this pattern with your coordinated in and out breaths.

3. Form an image of other people who suffer from the same condition or situation that you do. Follow your thoughts to wherever they range. Breathe in their suffering and connect it to your own. Imagine that through your breath you are alleviating the pain of these people by taking it into yourself.

As you breathe out let the feeling dissipate as completely as you can. Return to it; re-gather the feeling, as you breathe in. Continue.

4. Begin to pay attention to other feelings that emerge alongside the pain. You may be able to sense the possibility for peace. You can send this peace to them on the out-breath. Breathe in pain; breathe out a sense of well-being for others who suffer.

This is the basic practice. If this exercise begins to become abstract, reconnect with your own vulnerability. If you begin to feel overwhelmed by the pain of others, return to your breath, allowing images to dissipate. This can be done as a quick and immediate response to what you see or to a thought, or as part of a longer meditation.

Respond to the following questions:

1. After trying this exercise, what was the most difficult part of it for you, the area of greatest resistance?

2. How well did you connect with your own areas of suffering? With the suffering of others who you know or don't know?

3. How would you evaluate this exercise? What were the results for you? In what way did you experience an expansion of compassion? If you did not, why do you think this is so?

4. Journal about your response.

WEBSITES

Alzheimer's Association

http://www.alz.org

This is the go-to source on everything related to Alzheimer's disease by the national association.

Alzheimer's.gov

http://alzheimers.gov/

This user-friendly site explains what AD is and how it progresses. It provides information about the limited available treatment and clinical trials, challenges of care provision, and information on how to locate counseling and other resources.

Administration for Community Living

http://www.aoa.gov/

This is the principal site for the Administration on Aging of the U.S. Department on Health and Human Services. It offers a number of websites with resources for different aging needs including brain health and information for caregivers.

Meet Me at MOMA

http://www.moma.org/meetme/index

This program offers one example of working with art and making it accessible to those with dementia.

Memory cafes

http://www.alzheimerscafe.com/public.html
.alzheimersatoz.com/Welcome.html

The memory café is a platform to share ideas and resources for persons with dementia and their caregivers as well as offer opportunities for participation in activities. This toolkit is a quick information guide about beginning a memory café: http://www.thirdageservices.com/Memory%20 Cafe%20Tool%20Kit.pdf

Podcast: The Spiritual Terrain of Memory

http://www.onbeing.org/program/alan-dienstag-alzheimers-and-the-spiritual-terrain-of-memory/64

This is an interview with psychologist Alan Dienstag on his creative work with early Alzheimer's clients.

Singing for the Brain

http://www.nhs.uk/Video/Pages/singing-for-the-brain.aspx

This video from NHS UK provides information about the value of singing and recapturing connection.

RECOMMENDED READING: INFORMATION FOR PROFESSIONALS

Jewell, A. (Ed.). (2011). *Spirituality and personhood in dementia*. Philadelphia, PA: Jessica Kingsley.

This is a compendium of writing from a wide variety of perspectives on spirituality and dementia, including caregiver and professional views.

Shamy, E. (2003). *A guide to the spiritual dimension of care for people with Alzheimer's disease and related dementias: More than body, brain, and breath*. London: Jessica Kingsley.

This author writes about Alzheimer's from the perspective of a clergywoman and a caregiver, bringing many insights useful for pastoral care.

Killick, J. (2012). *Playfulness and dementia*. Philadelphia, PA: Jessica Kingsley.

With many ideas for the use of humor, this short book offers illustrations of how couples experiencing dementia can keep each other laughing when the meaning of words diminishes.

McFadden, S. H., & McFadden, J. T. (2011). *Aging together: Dementia, friendship, and flourishing communities*. Baltimore, MD: The Johns Hopkins University Press.

This book addresses ways to nurture relationships with friends and others who have dementia, with particular attention to the resources of faith communities.

Morgan, R. L., & Thibault, J. M. (2009). *No act of love is ever wasted: The spirituality of caring for persons with dementia*. Nashville, TN: Upper Room Books.

Suggesting hopeful ways for working with dementia, these authors also identify the transformational power in ongoing love given by family and paid staff caregivers in memory care units.

Swinton, J. (2012). *Dementia: Living in the memories of God*. Grand Rapids, MI: William B. Eerdmans.

Swinton writes that his book is both a challenge to current medical thinking and a challenge for theology in their considerations of dementia.

RECOMMENDED READING: MEMOIRS ON DEMENTIA

These are just a few selections on what is becoming a sizeable area of published writing.

Angelica, J. C. (2014). *Where two worlds touch: A spiritual journey through Alzheimer's disease*. Boston, MA: Skinner House Books.

Angelica, who has a divinity degree and brings a spiritual sensitivity, suggests we should lean into dementia and learn because persons with dementia have much to teach.

Bryden, C. (2012). *Who will I be when I die*. London: Jessica Kingsley.

Christine Bryden received a diagnosis of early dementia at age 46. At the time she held a position as first assistant secretary in the Department of Prime Minister and Cabinet in Australia and had been awarded a medal for outstanding service in science and technology. This book details her struggle with the illness and her advocacy for others as well as her search for meaning in her Christian path.

Burkholder, G. H. (2012). *Relentless goodbye: Grief and love in the shadow of dementia*. Harrisonburg, VA: Herald Press.

This account of a spouse dealing with a person with Lewy body dementia shares spiritual struggles and her journey into the reality of caregiving.

Goldman, C. (2002). *The gifts of caregiving: Stories of hardship, hope and healing*. Minneapolis, MN: Fairview Press.

A former correspondent for NPR, Goldman interviews a number of well-known figures about their experiences of caregiving.

Graboys, T. B., & Zheutlin, P. (2008). *Life in the balance: A physician's memoir of life, love, and loss with Parkinson's disease and dementia*. New York, NY: Union Square Press.

A Boston cardiologist details his view of his progressive illness. He sees this as a continuing contribution he can make to caring for the world by sharing his story.

Shouse, D. (2013). *Love in the land of dementia: Finding hope in the caregiver's journey*. Las Vegas, NV: Central Recovery Press.

The author details what she learned in interactions with her mother's increasing debilitation from dementia.

Walker, J. M. (2012). *The geography of memory: A pilgrimage through Alzheimer's*. New York, NY: Center Street Press.

An English professor writes of trying to manage her memories and her mother's deteriorating behavior long distance as she also chronicles tensions with her sister, who lives in proximity to her mother.

CHAPTER ELEVEN

SPIRITUALITY AT THE END OF LIFE

To feel the full force of your mortality and to open your
heart entirely to it, is to allow to grow in you that
all-encompassing, fearless compassion that fuels the lives
of all those who wish truly to be of help to others.

—Sir Thomas Moore
(in Sogyal Rinpoche, *Glimpse After Glimpse*, p. 21)

This chapter provides a foundation for understanding spiritual issues at the end of life. It includes sections on the nature of dying and a historical context for spirituality in palliative care, and it details findings from a study of older adults in hospice care. Modern palliative and hospice care movements are discussed. The National Consensus Project guidelines that include spiritual standards of care are identified. A spiritual care model is introduced, and some common spiritual care practices at the end of life are discussed. In addition, the importance of communication as an end-of-life skill is highlighted.

THE NATURE OF DYING

In the 21st century, very little about death is familiar. Extended dying has moved largely from the home into long-term care or medical institutions. Although funeral customs still may include a formal religious service, the most prominent feature of death is that it has been kept apart from life. The Chinese make use of the yin-yang symbol to describe seemingly opposite forces, such as dark and light, female and male, as referred to in Chapter 5. *Yin* often refers to the slower, softer, feminine nighttime side, while *yang* refers to the faster, more solid, daylight, masculine side. These forces, although separate and discrete, are also interconnected. In this circle split by a line in the shape of an *S*, each side contains a smaller circle that represents the opposite quality. Everything has both yin and yang forces inside a greater whole. These forces are balanced in a dynamic equilibrium and transform each other. In a continuum from birth to death, life may be viewed as the minimum form of death. Death is in our future and sometimes our thoughts, but it is only manifested in minor aspects, such as the little deaths one experiences through losses of many kinds. When someone is vital and active, it is difficult to visualize that death will come, but no one yet—except perhaps for a few great religious leaders and sages—has successfully conquered death. And from the state of absolute death, no one has returned to enlighten the living about its nature, unless by intuitive or spiritual methods, which usually do not lend themselves to empirical test. However, consistent with the yin-yang symbol, death too, is a minimum form of life. Unless one believes a being enters a state of nothingness at death, which some traditions do teach, there is something. Nuland (1993) has written on the physical processes of death, but few have written about the process of death preparation, even though many might consider life itself to be preparation for death. Buddhist traditions do offer a perspective about the contiguous experiences of living and dying and what one may do to prepare for death in that tradition (Sogyal Rinpoche, 1992).

When I visited Seoul, Korea in 2007, I toured a meeting at the Jogye Jung Senior Welfare Center of Seoul, a large multifaceted agency run by the Jogye Buddhist order that serves the needs of older adults in the community. One of the many culturally specific activities offered there is a class on death preparation. Sessions range from practical items, such as care for the body, to more philosophical issues. If it is true that the way we die, how we approach our death—because we can do little about the actual circumstances of our death—is important, then it might be valuable to offer such classes in senior centers. However, culturally in the United States at least, there is such discomfort with death generally, that a class of this nature might not have many students, unless they came from immigrant cultures. Although death acceptance is high among older adults (Cicirelli, 2002; De Raedt & Van Der Speeten, 2008), there is a difference between accepting death and actively working to prepare for it.

Much of the work of death preparation is spiritual. It is not primarily an intellectual or emotional task, though each of these does play a role. The Dalai Lama (2002) suggests that death preparation is about learning to be comfortable with one's future death by contemplating it as a part of life. He views this as useful even for those who do not believe there is an afterlife. If we begin to think of this life as impermanent, it is easier to sacrifice short-term goals for long-term ones and to develop the self-discipline that can help us and others. Death preparation is not about seeking death out; it is about becoming comfortable with the idea of dying.

There are many anecdotal reports of barrier crossings at death through dreams, visions, or voices of deceased relatives or friends (Aylor, 2008). Those who are dying will sometimes report hearing or seeing loved ones no longer living. And the crossing occurs in reciprocal directions. One client reported visiting with her deceased husband in the back garden, talking to him and feeling his presence. Yet another told me, prefacing her remark in the tentative language of "You probably will think I'm crazy," she saw her deceased husband's face smiling at her when she awoke. Many of these experiences are reported during hypnogogic (falling asleep) or hypnopompic (waking up) states. These appear to be times when thought processes are more open and individuals experience greater sensitivity and a relaxation of ego boundaries. The purpose of the experiences generally seem to be about bringing comfort and peace to the ones who remain, especially so they may be consoled in their grief and can reinvest in life. Sometimes, though, individuals also report experiences they believe were given to help them prepare for their own death. One nurse told me of a hospice patient who shared this dream. "I was in a room with no windows and no doors. I felt ready to panic. I wanted to get out and there was no way. Then an angel came. Together, we found the door." What was striking about this account is the timing of it. Two days later, the client died. The key concern for professional helpers is how the client or patient relates to the supernatural experience. If it is shared, then it may be useful to help the patient process this and explore potential meanings.

The Problem of Death

We are ever conscious of our mortality. Becker (1973) contends that the idea of death haunts humans and follows them more pervasively than any other fear. People hope that what they create in society will have lasting value that makes what they do sacred and heroic. The mythic hero of literature would go into the spirit world and return alive. Christianity similarly featured a hero/healer in the person of Jesus who possessed supernatural power, conquered death, and thus won out over other ancient cults. As people age, they must deal with the paradoxical condition of a symbolic self that confers infinite worth, but a body that grows increasingly frail. We seek to be free of anxiety about death, but it is life itself that arouses this anxiety.

Maslow (1963) reported we had a fear of actualizing our peak possibilities. He wrote that evasion of the full intensity of life was a Jonah syndrome, a fear of being torn apart by the experience of living fully. This is also related to fear of success and how it will change daily life as well as the feeling of emptiness success may lead to. "What will I strive for when I am successful?" is a question with which anxious people may grapple. Heidegger (as cited in Becker, 1973) delineated a difference about the anxiety *of* being-in-the-world and also fear *about* being-in-the-world. The former describes fear of life and all the vitality, joy, and sorrow that life brings, while the latter expression speaks of death, the ending of existence and possibility.

We have an inner symbolic self that bestows freedom but a finite body that limits that freedom, so we repress possibility, in Kierkegaard's view (as cited in Becker, 1973). But for everyday existence, to be able to function the fear must go underground or people would be paralyzed in inaction. In heroic terms,

Man [sic] breaks through the bounds of merely cultural heroism, he destroys the character lie that had him perform as a hero in the everyday social scheme of things; and by doing so he opens himself up to infinity, to the possibility of cosmic heroism, to the very service of God. . . . He links his secret inner self, his authentic talent, his deepest feelings of uniqueness, his inner yearning for absolute significance, to the very ground of creation. (Becker, 1973, p. 91)

The cultural self is gone, but the mystery of the inner self remains. "This invisible mystery at the heart of every creature now attains cosmic significance by affirming its connection with the invisible mystery at the heart of creation. This is the meaning of faith" (Becker, 1973, p. 91). The anxiety of forging life meaning is not gone, but it can be used in achieving a life task of growth into greater understanding, a multidimensional understanding, of reality in the face of death. Kierkegaard's worst assumption about human nature is that individuals "tranquilize themselves with the trivial" so they can live without thought to the bigger questions of life. It is in having the courage to face the bigger questions that we can live abundantly, in greater consciousness and vitality (Becker, 1973).

If an individual is well-practiced in living life moment to moment, he or she notices the liveliness that emerges from the freshness of each new instant. This is similar to a candle that is lit in the evening and burns on into the morning. The flame is continuous, but the evening flame is not precisely the same as the one ablaze in the morning that consumes different molecules of air and candle wax. Each flicker of the flame is new but so quick and close in time that we cannot perceive difference. This practice of living each moment fully can continue into the dying time as well. Moving toward death, time is sweetened by the poignancy of impending loss. The dying time is dense—or sometimes vacuous dependent on perception—but ultimately is a portal into a different dimension. Of what that dimension consists, no one can say with certainty. Religion sends us one way, spirituality another, humanism another yet—and some would say there is only ending. Within that ending can be completion, culmination, termination, cessation of life force, expiration, but definitely conclusion of physical existence.

SPIRITUALITY AT THE END OF LIFE: HISTORICAL CONTEXT

Through the 19th and into the 20th century, death was integrated with daily life in Western cultures. It often gave advance warning, was close, familiar, tame, and public; individuals often were pictured as knowing when they were about to die (Aries, 1981; Corr, Nabe, & Corr, 2006). Individuals who died from illnesses usually died at home. There was acceptance of death as destiny. Medicine did not benefit from the technology we now have and many children did not survive childhood due to the prevalence of disease and poor hygiene practices. Women often died in childbirth. Wakes were held at home and friends and neighbors came to the home to pay their respects to the person who was deceased and the family of the deceased. Religious rituals or funerals were designed and conducted according to the established ceremonies of the faith tradition that presided over the occasion. Prior to the custom of embalming in the mid-to late 19th century, flowers served to help mask odors of decay at funerals. Elaborate rituals of mourning (dependent on the culture) often designated behavior such as wearing a black band around a sleeve or black hat for men and black clothing for widows as well as the appropriate length of time these should be worn. Communities would recognize a death by the tolling of a bell, one year for each year of life of the deceased.

In the Middle Ages, the cemetery was a type of public square, a forum for meeting, and sometimes a marketplace (Aries, 1981). Even in modern times, families sometimes gather at the cemetery to mark the death anniversary, having celebratory fests and feasts. Death was important and it mattered. Even so, the idea that existence would continue beyond death was supported by evidence in the form of burial offerings from the Middle Paleolithic period. Ancient, as well as many modern, religions taught that life would continue.

After the black death of the 1400s, religious leaders identified a need to create a roadmap for dying. The *ars moriendi* were treatises on the art of dying well; they offered advice on how to die while handling struggles between good and evil according to 15th-century concepts of Christianity and culture. Some chapters discussed the temptations that would beset the dying person, such as lack of faith, despair, spiritual pride, and so forth. This was offset by consolations for each temptation, such as humility for pride. Other chapters outlined questions to ask the dying person, the importance of imitating the life of Christ, and directions for family and others on deathbed rules of conduct as well as what prayer should be spoken. Death was viewed as a transcendent battleground where demons and angels struggled for control of a soul. Hallmarks of the good death were showing faith, courage, and acceptance.

As health care became more professionalized and medicalized in the early 20th century, the place of death was removed from the home to the hospital (Aries, 1981; Becker, 1973). Death disappeared. Even in the hospital, death was viewed as a failure. "In a cult of cure, people did not die; they coded" (Hallenbeck, 2003, p. 4). Death was seen as the ultimate failure of medicine—people who were dying were still given aggressive treatment: They were not acknowledged as dying and given compassionate care toward that goal. Instead, physicians and other health care professionals were taught to keep a prognosis of death from the dying person and sometimes from the family. This led to a culture of denial of death that was awkward, unhealthy, and inauthentic. This culture of death denial brought death outside the normal processes of living and has made it more difficult for health care professionals and families to host honest and open discussions to prepare for dying today. Many families need help to plan for the future without this significant person in their lives as well as to honor immediate wishes of the dying individual regarding funerals, memorial services, or other preferred rituals and burial practices. We are still recovering from this cultural shift.

Cicely Saunders and the Hospice Movement

Since the founding of the first North American hospice programs in Connecticut, New York, and Montreal in 1975, palliative care and hospice programs have grown rapidly in recent years. The modern hospice model of care was developed and actualized in London in 1967 with the establishment of St. Christopher's Hospice by Dame Cicely Saunders. However, her preparation for this work began long before. One of the unique characteristics of Dr. Saunders was her education. She had trained in nursing, social work—she was an almoner in a hospital—and then medicine. The juxtaposition of her formal and informal training likely led to her advocacy of a holistic approach in care for the dying. She also valued spirituality personally and had a practice of engaging in prayer and religious reading: She attended the Church of England but was also comfortable interacting with Catholicism and its traditions. St. Christopher was the patron saint for travelers and it was not by coincidence that she borrowed this name to denote safe passage for the journey into death.

The hospice, this restorative place where travelers could rest, was congruent with a Medieval monastic tradition of providing care for pilgrims who journeyed to the

Holy Land. From the 11th century onward, hospices also cared for those who were ill, wounded, or dying. Sometimes these places were affiliated with monasteries or convents. Illness or death posed a threat to communities because people needed care and could not produce goods for their own support and survival. Further, there was sometimes a concern about contagion and superstitions prevailed. The genius of Dame Saunders was to integrate modern thought on pain relief for cancer patients, holistic symptom management, and bereavement counseling with this ancient tradition of spiritual and physical care.

She observed the role of the physician and witnessed the gaps in care in the early years of the British National Health Service, established in the late 1940s. In 1958 she wrote,

> It appears to me that many patients feel deserted by the doctors in the end. Ideally the doctor should remain the center of a team who work together to relieve when they cannot heal, to keep the patient's own struggle within his compass, and to bring hope and consolation to his end. (Clark, 2005, p. 7)

In a hospital where she worked in 1948, Dame Saunders met a dying Jewish émigré from Poland, David Tasma, with whom she discussed the possibility of opening a home to provide peace to people who were dying. He willed her 500 pounds and told her he would serve metaphorically as a window in that home of which they had spoken to observe and to help if he could. He was one of the influences on her expanding vision. A few years later she worked at a hospice operated by a religious order for the poor, and began to formulate her ideas of hiring a medical director, keeping clinical records, and developing missions of both teaching and research. She wrote of feeling "led by the Holy Spirit" to this work and termed it a personal spiritual odyssey. She held an image of care that would provide for a "freedom of the spirit and personal meaning" (Saunders, 1999, p. 2).Her goal in founding St. Christopher's was "help the dying to live until they die and their families to live on" (Saunders, 1983). Her persistence and dedication to the idea that dying individuals should not be treated in the same manner as those who are chronically ill has led to the conceptualization, development, and expansion of the modern hospice worldwide. Early hospices were inpatient units and were thus seen intentionally as sanctuaries from hospitals.

The hospice model was brought to the United States in 1974 by Florence Wald, Dean of Nursing at Yale, who had previously invited Dame Saunders to lecture at Yale. Later Wald took a sabbatical to work at St. Christopher's hospice in London under Saunders. Together with two pediatricians and a chaplain, Wald founded the first hospice in Connecticut. In 1978, a task force of the Department of Health, Education, and Welfare, determined that hospice was worthy of federal support. The funding of 26 successful demonstration hospice programs led to hospice coverage as a permanent Medicare benefit in 1986. The rapid growth in recent decades in the United States has arisen partly due to a favorable policy climate and also in response to growth in the population living with debilitating and life-threatening illness.

Elisabeth Kübler-Ross's Contribution to Improvement of Dying

In 1969, Elisabeth Kübler-Ross, a Swiss physician, published her book *On Death and Dying*, which established five nonlinear stages of grief. Like Saunders, Kübler-Ross had a multidisciplinary as well as a research background. She was a triplet who became a physician against her father's wishes. In her family position as a triplet, she struggled with achieving a sense of individual identity.

Kübler-Ross credits four theology students at the University of Chicago who came to her with a class project on life crises for the focus with which she is known. They had chosen to explore death. She volunteered to work with them to ask dying patients what dying was like and what fears and needs they might have. However, when Kübler-Ross asked to interview dying patients in a hospital, she was told there were none. In her professional work in hospitals in the United States, she often sat with dying patients. She noted that there was a professional denial that caused patients to feel awkward in discussing their dying experience, so she began to advocate for those dying. In her late life, she experienced a series of strokes that affected her ability to communicate. Sadly, she reported on her website that she felt like an airplane that had left the gate but was still awaiting clearance to take off. She wished she could either return to the gate or depart and soar, but dying itself was not in her control.

Kübler-Ross's stage theory was developed at a time when there had been little focus on the dying experience. Her observations led to a system of categorization that was helpful to both formal and informal caregivers (see Table 11.1). Her now classic stages of grief within dying identified denial, anger, bargaining, depression, and acceptance and helped to normalize the range of intense emotions that a patient might experience (Kübler-Ross, 1969). *Denial* was the almost necessary first step of rejection of the immanency of personal death. She believed that although denial might not be useful in the long term, it did at least serve a protective function in the short term as it gave individuals an opportunity to handle the surprise and fear inherent in response to the diagnosis. *Anger* could be directed to God or a transcendent power for allowing this illness to occur and was also a measure of the attachment people had to love and life. In a sense, anger could serve as a bridge across the unknown sea, the journey to death, in its ability to see and feel the contours of the pain from impending loss. *Bargaining* was a process of asking for more time (usually of God) and negotiating how one might be willing to live differently if extra time were granted. It involved building a series of "What if?" scenarios. *Depression* occurred when the reality of the loss fully settled in the soul. It involved a grappling with the reality of the situation. *Acceptance* described reaching a type of peace with a terminal diagnosis. Anticipating some of the emotions they might feel, while not preventing changes, did at least provide dying patients an awareness that they could move effectively through different states. It affirmed dying as a dynamic process.

Stage theories are useful because they help separate out the elements of a common experience so that we can understand it more clearly. For instance, there are theories about the lifespan that include stages, such as Erikson's eight stages of the life cycle, Levinson's seasons of a man's life, or even Valliant's four levels of defense in the aging experience (Robbins, Chatterjee, & Canda, 2006). Many of these theories imply that age and time determine the developmental sequence. The term *ontogenetic* refers to the idea that development is a function of age. However, stage theories are sometimes taken to imply that the order of development is static and unchangeable. The role of the environment is often not considered and yet at the end of life, the timing and place of dying, especially whether one had chosen it or not, can hold especially powerful meaning.

Once an individual is able to anticipate his or her death, for example, with the diagnosis of a terminal illness, there are many factors beyond individual disposition and personality that may affect how one experiences the dying process. Whether one is able to die with hospice support, at home, or in a facility without a hospice option may affect which of the Kübler-Ross stages of loss in death/dying one experiences as well as availability of social support from family and friends. Although death is a certainty,

Table 11.1   Kübler-Ross's Stages in Grieving/Dying

Characteristics of the Loss	Typical Stage Order	Explanation of Stage/Phase
Loss or news is sudden; first awareness.	Stage 1	**Shock/Denial**. Denotes a sense of numbness about the news of a terminal illness or death in which a person at first seems to reject the idea with expressions such as, "This can't happen to me!" or "I don't believe this is real."
Thoughts of impending loss affected by relationship role, strength of relationships or attachments, & social support	Stage 2	**Anger.** Denotes the emotional state that follows initial numbness after a growing awareness of the truth of the diagnosis is processed. The focus of the anger is often toward a transcendent power, health professionals, or the dying person herself. "Why is God allowing this to happen?" or "Why is God abandoning me?" are common responses. "That doctor didn't do his or her job!" may be another.
Perception of malleability, ability to influence outcome, belief one can affect God's will or fate.	Stage 3	**Bargaining.** Denotes a condition where a person tries to negotiate according to his or her belief system with a sacred source, transcendent power, others, or oneself. "I promise I'll treat my spouse/children/grandchildren better if I can just get well." "If I can live until my grandson gets married, I'll be happy." Or, "If I get well, I'll give more money to find a cure for cancer."
Loss affected by prior mental health states & emotional vulnerability, unfinished business.	Stage 4	**Depression**. Denotes the emotional state where a person recognizes he or she will not be able to successfully change the situation through anger or bargaining. Death is now real and the individual struggles with the anticipatory losses and changes that alter the meaning of life. People often become despondent or withdrawn or just very sad. Clinical symptoms of depression may appear. Reality of situation is understood.
Loss leads to living well with what one has. Continuum from acquiescence to appreciation and awe	Stage 5	**Testing/Acceptance**. Denotes a condition where people seek realistic solutions for their remaining life and enter into a type of peace with impending death. They typically are not hopeless nor resigned, nor do they waste time fighting what appears inevitable. Instead, they come to terms with death and experience it in the way they choose.

Source: Based on the grief cycle model and adapted from Kübler-Ross, E. (1969). *On death and dying*. New York, NY: Simon & Schuster. Interpretation (explanation) by Holly Nelson-Becker.

how one approaches death is not. Individuals who have prepared for death before it is a glimmer on the horizon, may not pass through denial, anger, or bargaining. However, stage theories are useful when individuals have not done preparatory work, nor prepared their families/significant others. Furthermore, not all dying individuals experience all of the stages or do so in equal time segments. Kübler-Ross's stages represent a constellation of feelings that the dying individual and his or her family may experience in phases, in an iterative manner, or singly. It is also important to note that research has not always supported this model (Corr et al., 2006). A too-close adherence to expectations of the model diminishes openness to hear and receive the unique experience of individuals through their sacred narratives. However, the work of Kübler-Ross in death and dying extended beyond her theoretical model. She also taught that dying people are still living and often have "unfinished business" that requires attention. Second, caregivers need to include the patient in interactions and listen actively to what can best help. Finally, people who are terminally ill can be our teachers and help us understand better how to live our own lives in dynamic and resilient ways.

OLDER ADULTS IN HOSPICE CARE

Dying well is about living fully and consciously in whatever way one chooses until the moment of death. When an older adult first enters hospice care, the constraints of illness have already influenced choices he or she has made about living. Achieving quality of life within these constraints remains a vital concern to both the dying individual and those in his or her environment. Although the physical parameters of life contract, the capacity to integrate one's life experiences may expand (Nelson-Becker, 2006). What are the resources that enhance resilience at the end of life? In a mixed methods study conducted with 30 older adults recommended by staff in four hospices—one with an in-patient facility—participants had a median age of 78 and a range of 63 to 96 (Nelson-Becker, 2006). Just under two-thirds of the sample was female, and 87% had incomes that suggested it was easy or very easy to pay for their needs. See Table 11.2 Examples of Resilience at End of Life Interview Questions, for a selection of qualitative questions.

Several major themes emerged. Many of these research participants experienced a *redefinition of self*, but one that was generally ego-syntonic and integrated with what had developed as their major life interests over time. For example, with illness, physical appearance often changes. If an individual based self-esteem on beauty or possessions they had acquired, unless they changed this idea, they would suffer. "It's like starting over, with everything. Got money? Doesn't matter. You got brains? Doesn't matter" (Participant #004). Respondents were not their illness, not their disease. One woman called her cancer "the invader." "It's like a houseguest you don't want" (Participant #018). A man assessed,

> *I couldn't do the simplest thing and I was angry. I began to think about how I am going to die rather than if [emphasis added]. I know from last week to this week how much I've lost. I've accepted everything that came along and incorporated it in my living. But my illness is not who I am. "Don't make a religion of your illness," is my advice.* (Participant #104)

In reaching a reintegration and new self-definitions, two pathways emerged: one was *religion or spirituality*; the second path *was uncertainty, doubt, and ambiguity of place and time*. Those who turned toward religion articulated the following:

- *Religion is more important as the end nears. I envision death as a kind of anesthesia. You don't know what's going on, you don't wake from it* (Participant #003).

- *Sometimes you reach a point where you say, "I can't do it anymore. God, you take over!"* (Participant #011).

- *I feel His presence—I know He is here right now* (Participant #002).

Table 11.2	Examples of Resilience at End of Life Interview Questions	
Question	**Probe(s)**
What inspires you to keep going?	• What do you value most in living your life?
What does living with this illness mean to you?	• What kinds of changes have you made because of the illness?
	• Has this illness served any purpose in your life?
How do you feel about your future?	• What lies ahead of you?
	• What will that be like?
What helps you handle difficult things?	• What resources, relationships, activities, or objects have helped you in the past or are helping you now?

- *Every morning I ask the Lord to help me accept what is my lot of the day and to keep my spirits as high as possible* (Participant #001).

Others did not employ a spiritual frame. They especially used this interstitial hospice stage to raise questions. Time seemed more fluid, less rigid and systematic to them now. The power of place was also altered as individuals began to release their connection to immediate environments, but still savored their social networks. Respondents spoke about entering a liminal period when everything they had known to be true was now altered. As a researcher, I was privileged to be able to hear profound questions. If religious/spiritual philosophies did not provide a sense of peace, they were on a quest to learn the meaning of their life in a context where the landscape seemed foreign and unfamiliar. For most, this questing time signaled a phase of ongoing spiritual growth.

- *I believe there must be something out there, but I'm an agnostic* (Participant #101).

- *The hardest thing for me is what's going to happen a minute after, a month after, a year after. Will I know any of this is going on or won't I? The uncertainty is the most difficult thing to deal with* (Participant #018).

Independence also mattered. Doing what they could still do for themselves as long as they could do it was important. More than one respondent spoke about the emotional impact of relinquishing a driver's license and the value of having friends trust them to know when the time was right to do that. The ability to continue to dress and do self-care as long as that was possible was also valued, and a distaste for social overbenefitting in relationship exchanges was expressed. "I've always been a caregiver and I can't give anybody care now. I'm being cared for—the role is reversed. I don't like it, but I try to give back what I can" (Participant #002).

Social relationships were particularly compelling. Although they may have always mattered, there was a sweetness and a healing quality evident in the ways people spoke about their social contacts. One woman said that she planned to remain alive until her grandson, a student, could come and visit her one last time. Physicians who listened and took time to look patients in the eyes, even when they were busy, also made a difference in supporting patient resilience.

- *I don't have a lot of really close friends, but those that I do have are just, they're like treasures to me* (Participant #018).

- *Neighbors bought groceries and cooked meals. When I eat other people's food, for some reason it's more appealing* (Participant #014).

- *I've heard from people I haven't heard from in years; it wasn't that they heard I was sick but just that they were thinking of me. That's the most gratifying thing I can think of* (Participant #101).

Finally, this group of patients all described an *ongoing social investment in life*. Even though they were leaving, they still cared about the world they were leaving behind. One respondent who had no heirs said she planned to leave a financial legacy to Greenpeace to help create better conditions in the world for others. Another man mused that as long as he lived he would continue to read the *New York Times* because what happened in the world still mattered to him.

Ultimately it is important to know the kinds of actions and supports that foster a high quality of life in dying (Reynolds, Henderson, Schuylman, & Hanson, 2002; Williams, 2006). It was clear that research respondents went through a period of self-redefinition in this life phase. Relying on religion/spirituality or entering a period of searching seemed to be common processes to all, who as referred patients may have been more self-reflective than some. Though they seemed to be in the process of reaching new understandings, none expressed radically different circumstances where they may have rejected how they had spent their lives. Instead, what mattered before still mattered. If they were pastime gardeners, they still enjoyed the flowers and plantings outside. If they had enjoyed exercise, they still exercised with restrictions. Patients in this study of mostly Caucasian respondents, consistent with cultures most represented in hospice in the United States, valued ability to remain independent. However, that independence also included discovery of increased value and meaning in everyday social interactions. Even in this difficult life phase, they expressed concern and care for the status of the world they would leave and in small and large ways sought to contribute to the overall good in society (see Figure 11.1).

The case study in Table 11.3 offers an opportunity to consider how you might address an end-of-life situation where religious and spiritual issues feature prominently.

Table 11.3   End-of-Life Case Study

Kate was a social worker newly assigned to a hospital palliative care unit. Mr. Johnson, one of her patients, was a 70-year-old retired farmer with stomach cancer. As a widower, his main concern was how his sons were handling the recent downturn in his condition. He began to consider his own death and worry about what would happen to him "on the other side." Now as never before, he wondered whether there was some divine power out there that could assist him, or was each person on his or her own to make meaning in life? He had never had much use for religion, and Sundays were usually days he needed to be outside tending to the fields and the cattle like any other day. He wondered if he'd gotten it wrong. He has asked to speak with Kate about his life.

1. Kate has a strong religious faith herself and is unsure how to handle the situation. What should she do or say when she meets with Mr. Johnson?

2. What boundaries should she be concerned about, if any? As her supervisor, what might you suggest to help her work with Mr. Johnson?

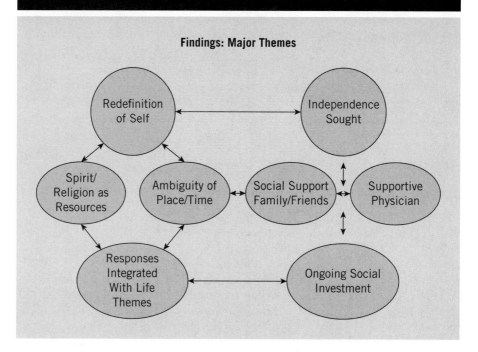

Figure 11.1   Older Adults at Life's End: Major Themes, N = 30

Findings: Major Themes

Redefinition of Self

Independence Sought

Spirit/ Religion as Resources

Ambiguity of Place/Time

Social Support Family/Friends

Supportive Physician

Responses Integrated With Life Themes

Ongoing Social Investment

MODERN PALLIATIVE AND HOSPICE CARE

Palliative Care

The root of the word *palliative* is *palliare*, meaning "to cloak" or "to shield." Palliative care differs from standard medical care because it focuses on reducing the severity of disease symptoms, rather than striving to delay, halt, or reverse progression of the disease or provide a cure. However, treatment to effect cure is not excluded. Death is seen as failure, so the term is sometimes diminished or rejected by the very institution that is often the ending place for a life. Palliative care is medical care typically provided by an interdisciplinary team, including the professions of medicine, nursing, social work, chaplaincy, counseling, nursing assistants, and related health care professions. Volunteers from the community are a significant part of hospice programs, which are one form of palliative care offered today.

Palliative care programs seek relief of suffering and support the best possible quality of life for patients facing serious life-threatening illness as well as for their families (National Consensus Project for Quality Palliative Care, 2009). The goal of palliative care is to identify and address the physical, psychological, spiritual, and practical burdens of illness while maintaining a patient's dignity. Dying is viewed as a natural process, so the goal is neither to hasten nor postpone death. In fact, those who receive palliative care may not necessarily have a terminal diagnosis. Palliative care is applicable early in the disease process and patients may continue to receive curative treatment alongside palliation. A first order concern is management of pain. The World Health Organization (WHO) defined palliative care as an active approach to the total care of patients that includes pain control, control of other symptoms, and addressing psychological, social, and spiritual problems (WHO, 1990). Principles of palliative care have been specified:

1. Provides relief from pain and other distressing symptoms

2. Affirms life and regards dying as a normal process

3. Intends neither to hasten nor postpone death

4. Integrates the psychological and spiritual aspects of patient care

5. Offers a support system to help patients live as actively as possible until death

6. Offers a support system to help the family cope during the patient's illness and during their own bereavement

7. Uses a team approach to address the needs of patients and their families, including bereavement counseling, if indicated

8. Will enhance quality of life and also may positively influence the course of illness

9. Is applicable early in the course of illness in conjunction with other therapies that are intended to prolong life, such as chemotherapy or radiation therapy, and includes those investigations needed to better understand and manage distressing clinical complications (WHO, 2002)

Notable features of palliative care are that it offers support to families as well as patients, seeks to enhance quality of life, and helps patients live as fully as possible until their deaths. Some individuals who receive palliative care are not on a dying trajectory. Many hospitals now have palliative care units, but training continues for staff and education is provided for potential users to assist in awareness of this option and to increase referrals. Chemotherapy, radiation, and surgery often form the first round of treatment for cancer, for example, but if repeatedly unsuccessful, the patient and family may opt for the comfort measures of managed pain and holistic care.

Hospice

In 2014, approximately 1.6 to 1.7 million individuals were served by hospice (National Hospice and Palliative Care Organization [NHPCO], 2015). It is estimated that about 38.8% of all deaths in the United States occurred under the care of a hospice program in 2007; this percentage was not yet determined at the time the 2015 NHPCO report was published. The median length of service treatment was 17.4 days in 2014, down from 20.0 days in 2007 (NHPCO, 2015, 2008). This reflects relatively late referrals to hospice, sometimes due to physician or family reluctance to admit that there is limited chance of a cure. The majority of hospice patients receive care in the place they call home (58.9%), although this includes nursing homes and residential facilities separate from private homes (see Table 11.4 Location of Death).

Hospice patients age 75 to 84 represented 26% of all hospice patients, down from 30% in 2007, while those 85 plus represented 41.1%, up from 36.6% in 2007 (NHPCO, 2008, 2015). Thus, a significant number of dying individuals using hospice services are older adults. Gender was relatively evenly matched at 54% female and 46% male, but ethnicity showed a significant disparity with 76% of users being Caucasian/White (NHPCO, 2015). Cancer diagnoses in hospice today account for 36.3% of patients, although at its beginning in the 1970s, most hospice deaths were due to cancer.

The majority of deaths apart from cancer are due to terminal chronic diseases, such as dementia (14.8 % of patients) and heart disease (14.7%). It is worth noting that as people have begun to live to older ages, the numbers of people dying of chronic disease requiring sustained care and leading to end-of-life confusion for caregivers, has also increased. There are approximately 6,100 hospice programs in the United States today, up from 4,700 in 2007 (NHPCO, 2015). Less than 20% of hospices are part of a hospital program; most are freestanding or independent.

Hospice is funded by a Medicare benefit that was first enacted in 1982 (National Association for Home Care & Hospice, n.d.). Admission criteria consist of the following: the patient is certified as terminal (a life expectancy of six or fewer months if the illness runs its course), the patient wants hospice care, and the patient has a physician who is willing to provide medical care and consultation. Certification or recertification for hospice is based upon a physician's clinical judgment. It is recognized that there are barriers to predicting the timing of death with accuracy. Throughout the process of determining the best fit within the medical treatment model, clear communication between care provider and patient as well as support for patient autonomy are important goals. The Patient Self-Determination Act (PSDA) of 1990 further solidified the need for advance care planning and patient inclusion in this type of planning.

Palliative and Hospice Care Intersections

The relationship between palliative care and hospice care can be viewed along a continuum, with palliative care sliding into hospice care when curative treatment is surrendered (see Figure 11.2). Palliative care extends hospice principles to a wider population, and no specific type of treatment is excluded. Goals of care, which may change, are kept in the forefront of physician-patient conversations. Hospice care focuses on caring instead of curing. After a family member in hospice has died, funded bereavement care continues for up to a year for significant others. Although many patients and families are reluctant to stop curative treatments, studies have reported that many patients live longer with better life quality in hospice and palliative care than those who die under traditional medical treatment (Gozalo & Miller, 2007; Mukamel et al., 2012; Temel et al., 2010).

Table 11.4 Location of Death 2006		
Location of Death	2014	2007
Patient's place of residence	58.9%	70.1%
Private residence	35.7%	42.1%
Nursing facility	14.5%	22.8%
Residential facility	8.7%	5.5%
Hospice inpatient facility	31.8%	19.2%
Acute care hospital	9.5%	10.5%

Table compiled from NHPCO Facts & Figures: Hospice Care in America (NHPCO Organization). Released October 2008 (Retrieved March 24, 2009 from http://www.nhpco.org/files/public/Statistics_Research/NHPCO_facts-and-figures_2008.pdf) and NHPCO Facts & Figures: Hospice Care in America 2015 edition (NHPCO Organization). Retrieved January 3, 2016 from http://www.nhpco.org/sites/default/files/public/Statistics_Research/2015_Facts_Figures.pdf

Figure 11.2   Hospice and Palliative Care at the End of Life

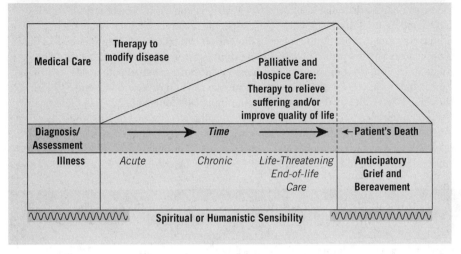

© Holly Nelson-Becker. Adapted from Figure 2: The Role of Hospice Palliative Care during Illness from Canadian Hospice Palliative Care Association. (2013). *A Model to Guide Hospice Palliative Care.* Ottawa, ON: Author, p. 7.

Figure 11.2 suggests the fluid nature of palliative care and hospice. Aggressive or curative medical treatment is separated from palliative care hospice, although the line is thin because palliative care does not preclude any treatment. The medical story unfolds above a foundational context that reflects a spiritual or humanistic sensibility. This spiritual sensibility is the particular spiritual DNA expressed by any individual. Anticipatory grief is experienced before the death event and bereavement occurs afterward.

NATIONAL CONSENSUS PROJECT GUIDELINES

The National Consensus Project for Quality Palliative Care (NCP) was developed with the support of five leading palliative care organizations: American Academy of Hospice and Palliative Medicine, the Center to Advance Palliative Care, Hospice and Palliative Nurses Association, Last Acts Partnership (no longer in operation) and the National Hospice and Palliative Care Organization. The plan was to establish clinical guidelines for practice of palliative care in a range of settings from specialized treatment teams to long-term care, oncology, and other units where this type of care might typically be given. Goals of this project were to facilitate ongoing improvement of care, create uniform definitions of care, establish national goals for access to care, and foster performance measures and quality improvement initiatives. These quality improvement components would represent evidence-based measures that could be linked to reimbursement. The national standards developed out of NCP were first published in 2004 and included the following eight domains.

> Domain 1: Structure and Processes of Care
>
> Domain 2: Physical Aspects of Care
>
> Domain 3: Psychological and Psychiatric Aspects of Care
>
> Domain 4: Social Aspects of Care
>
> Domain 5: Spiritual, Religious, and Existential Aspects of Care
>
> Domain 6: Cultural Aspects of Care

Domain 7: Care of the Imminently Dying Patient

Domain 8: Ethical and Legal Aspects of Care.

These standards are available at http://www.nationalconsensusproject.org/Guidelines_ Download2.aspx. This document provides specific recommendations about each domain of care. Previously, the spiritual dimension had received less emphasis than the biopsychosocial dimensions of care. In one study, spiritual and religious beliefs were found to be important in coping with illness by 88% of a group of patients with terminal cancer, but only 26% felt their needs were met by medical professionals, and 51% felt their needs were met by their religious community (Balboni et al., 2007). A Consensus Project conference to improve spiritual care in palliative care met in 2008 to further elucidate the guidelines for spiritual care as a dimension of palliative care (Puchalski et al., 2009). A 2013 revision has added greater specification and guidelines for the spiritual, religious, and existential. Domain 5 is listed below, in Table 11.5.

Table 11.5 National Consensus Project Guideline/ National Quality Preferred Practice for Spiritual Domain

National Consensus Project Guidelines

Domain 5: Spiritual, Religious, and Existential Aspects of Care

Guideline 5.1 The interdisciplinary team assesses and addresses spiritual, religious, and existential dimensions of care.

Criteria—Spirituality is recognized as a fundamental aspect of compassionate, patient and family-centered care that honors the dignity of all persons.

- Spirituality is defined as "the aspect of humanity that refers to the way individuals seek and express meaning and purpose and the way they experience their connectedness to the moment, to self, to others, to nature, and/or to the significant or sacred." It is the responsibility of all IDT [interdisciplinary team] members to recognize spiritual distress and attend to the patient's and the family's spiritual needs, within their scope of practice.

- The interdisciplinary palliative care team, in all settings, includes spiritual care professionals; ideally a board certified professional chaplain, with skill and expertise to assess and address spiritual and existential frequently confronted by pediatric and adult patients with life-threatening or serious illnesses and their families.

- Communication with the patient and family is respectful of their religious and spiritual beliefs, rituals, and practices. Palliative care team members do not impose their individual spiritual, religious, existential beliefs or practices on patients, families, or colleagues.

Guideline 5.2 A spiritual assessment process, including a spiritual screening, history questions, and a full spiritual assessment as indicated, is performed. This assessment identifies religious or spiritual/existential background, preferences, and related beliefs, rituals, and practices of the patient and family; as well as symptoms, such as spiritual distress and/or pain, guilt, resentment, despair and hopelessness.

Criteria

- The IDT regularly explores spiritual and existential concerns and documents these spiritual themes in order to communicate them to the team. This exploration includes, but is not limited to: life review, assessment of hopes, values, and fears, meaning, purpose, beliefs about afterlife, spiritual or religious practices, cultural norms, beliefs that influence understanding of illness, coping, guilt, forgiveness and life completion tasks. Whenever possible, a standardized instrument should be used.

- The IDT periodically reevaluates the impact of spiritual/existential interventions and documents patient and family preferences.

- The patient's spiritual resources of strength are supported and documented in the patient record.

- Spiritual/existential care needs, goals, and concerns identified by patients, family members, the palliative care team, or spiritual care professionals are addressed according to established protocols and documented in the interdisciplinary care plan, and emphasized during transitions of care, and/or in discharge plans. Support is offered for issues of life closure, as well as other spiritual issues, in a manner consistent with the patient's and the family's cultural, spiritual, and religious values.

- Referral to an appropriate community-based professional with specialized knowledge or skills, in spiritual and existential issues (e.g. to a pastoral counselor or spiritual director) is made when desired by the patient and/or family. Spiritual care professionals are recognized as specialists who provide spiritual counseling.

Guideline 5.3 The palliative care service facilitates religious, spiritual, and cultural rituals or practices as desired by patient and family, especially at and after the time of death.

Criteria

- Professional and institutional use of religion/spiritual symbols and language are sensitive to cultural and religious diversity.

- The patient and family are supported in their desires to display and use their own religious/spiritual and/or cultural symbols.

- Chaplaincy and other palliative care professionals facilitate contact with spiritual/religious communities, groups, or individuals, as desired by the patient and/or family. Palliative care programs create procedures to facilitate patients' access to clergy, religious, spiritual and culturally-based leaders, and/or healers in their own religious, spiritual, or cultural traditions.

- Palliative professionals acknowledge their own spirituality as part of their professional role. Opportunities are provided to engage staff in self-care and self-reflection of their beliefs and values as they work with seriously ill and dying patients. Core expectations of the team include respect of spirituality and beliefs of all colleagues and the creation of a healing environment in the workplace.

- Non-chaplain palliative care providers obtain training in basic spiritual screening and spiritual care skills.

- The palliative care team ensures post-death follow-up after the patient's death (e.g. phone calls, attendance at wake or funeral, or scheduled visit) to offer support, identify any additional needs that require community referral, and help the family during bereavement.

Clinical Implications

Spiritual, religious, and existential issues are a fundamental aspect of quality of life for patients with serious or life-threatening illness and their families. All team members are accountable for attending to spiritual care in a respectful fashion. In order to provide an optimal and inclusive healing environment, each palliative care tem member needs to be aware of his or her own spirituality and how it may differ from fellow team members and those of the patients and families they serve.

Source: NCP Clinical Practice Guidelines (3rd ed.), 2013, pp. 26–27. Permission given by Dr. Betty Ferrell, Chairperson of the NCP (National Consensus Project).

A SPIRITUAL CARE MODEL

A model of spiritual care within palliative care upholds the dignity of all persons and the responsibility of professionals to be a compassionate presence. The biopsychosocial spiritual model of care considers all individuals to have a spiritual history whether it unfolds within a religious tradition or through humanistic philosophies and life experiences. Thus, some form of spiritual assessment is critical to understanding whether and how spirituality and religion should be integrated in care.

The patient-centered model of care places the patient as the expert on what he or she needs and the way in which those needs can best be met. Similarly, a spiritual care model includes a patient-centered aspect. In this model the medical provider and care team become consultants to the patient rather than the sole decision makers. Values and beliefs of the patient are honored and supported unless they are unhealthy or would cause harm to others. Similar to healing in pre-scientific civilizations, modern science also considers healing to include restoring broken relationships. Illness not only challenges the physical body, but frays families and business organizations, explodes preexisting coping patterns, and creates questions about relationship with the transcendent (Sulmasy, 2002). The treatment team, too, builds on a relational model where the patient and team collaborate in a process of discovery and dialogue, with the understanding that each may be transformed.

Spiritual care is interdisciplinary and interprofessional (Puchalski, 2006). The NCP guidelines suggest that the interdisciplinary team include professionals with skill in assessment of and response to spiritual and existential issues of patients with life threatening illness. This group of professionals should further have education and training in helping with spiritual issues that may arise. The board-certified chaplain is often the designated professional with such expertise who also manifests knowledge and skill in respecting diverse religious and spiritual backgrounds. However, in nursing homes, assisted living facilities, and hospitals, nurses and social workers should conduct brief spiritual assessments to determine if a chaplain is needed. The chaplain's role is to engage the one who suffers and help reframe his or her perspective of suffering and engender realistic hope. The chaplain is able to assess spiritual health, spiritual distress or struggle, and offer counseling at a profound level if desired. Spiritual care often includes coordination with religious leaders, pastoral counselors, or other informal religious or spiritual mentors in the community. However, the work of spiritual care is done by *all* team members.

Spiritual Care as a Collaborative Endeavor

Offering a compassionate presence, conducting a spiritual history, and integrating spiritual care into the treatment plan if desired by the patient, can be done by any team member. Further, some spiritual training and orientation should be offered to all formal caregivers, from housekeepers to interpreters, because the entire constellation of workers is ultimately responsible for the spiritual care provided. All team members should have knowledge of spiritual resources and some familiarity with cultural competency in spirituality that could influence care. Sometimes, one person may unexpectedly connect better spiritually with a patient because of a common faith tradition or compatible personality rather than formal professional expertise. However, even if a patient and formal caregiver share membership in the same religious tradition, their individual beliefs may vary greatly. A *Spiritual Care Bill of Rights* might be given to patients to offer protection against proselytization and support for referral to one's own faith community leaders. While pain is often termed "the fifth vital sign" in medical treatment, a sixth vital sign might include level of psychological or spiritual distress or eustress.

The spiritual care community is not only the treatment team, which includes both formal and informal caregivers (family, friends), but also the wider community of contact built by the patient throughout his or her life. For many older adults, this includes immediate family such as siblings and children, but as they age, these communities of support are likely to weaken and fade as individuals die. Certainly the religious or spiritual faith community may be a primary one; however, it would be an error to believe that even an individual with no clear spiritual interests lacks a spiritual community, as anyone who evinces caring may become a spiritual presence for the dying person.

Spiritual care for significant others. Spiritual care does not end with the death of the patient, but includes the bereavement process of family and significant others. Spiritual involvement after the death may include attendance at the wake, funeral, or memorial service; sending a condolence card; follow-up phone calls; providing grief manuals; and referral to bereavement support (Otis-Green, 2006). The palliative care team may facilitate rituals that make healing possible such as family members who prefer to bathe or dress the body. The memories created at this difficult time can offer solace and comfort. Symptoms of complicated grief and mourning should also be assessed for follow-up work if needed, particularly in the case of traumatic deaths. The spiritual care expert on the team should also be prepared to assist with reflection on the part of team members that helps prevent compassion fatigue among professionals who deal with deep loss on a daily basis.

Spiritual care as calling. The question of who is designated to provide spiritual care is one of both calling and preparation. Most spiritual care providers will have the education and training requisite for this task. However, the intuitive ability that some people carry lies beyond the limits of formal training. Further, some religious traditions do not require their leaders to have formal seminary training, but rather the skills learned on the job, through mentoring, a sincere and receptive heart, and vocation approved by the community. Whatever one has not yet dealt with on their own spiritual journey often arises in working with others. However, when one brings awareness of life as a spiritual journey and an ability to reflect on what makes meaning for oneself, one is better able to assist a patient. Professionals assisting in spiritual work should know that they, too, will be transformed as they work with others. One cannot work in death and dying and be unchanged, nor would one want to be.

SPIRITUAL CARE AT THE END OF LIFE: SPIRITUAL PRACTICES

In end-of-life work, there are many forms of helping activities that assist with the dying process. Not all of these need to be initiated by a clinician and some—such as music thanatology—require particular expertise. At the moment, most of these are not evidence based. In other words, they have not been subjected to randomized clinical trials with random selection of subjects to a treatment or a control group and data collected at all stages. However, they offer potential to help prepare for dying or living moment by moment. Above all, it is important to remember and use the foundation of any clinical helping work: offering the gift of full presence and attentiveness to what is, imparting acceptance, cultivating candor, inserting humor as a tool for modulating the emotional tone of the session, apportioning patience (particularly to oneself), recognizing the role to advocate when needed, and developing the courage to enter new territory beyond the boundaries of what is familiar.

Reflection and Reminiscence

One intervention includes engaging in a reflective process—either using journaling or oral reflections with a professional, family member, or friend—or even a voice recording device as legacy for those by whom one hopes to be remembered. This can enlist a form of narrative therapy where one's own life story is compared and contrasted to the dominant stories of the historical time in which they live. Stepping back, the client is able to witness the larger themes of his or her life and gain a new or different perspective on the meaning of particular events. The power of the telling is in remaking, revising, and reinterpreting the personal story with the added value of later insights. A video recording also offers a way for an older client to offer memories and life lessons as a legacy. Some individuals find that in gathering reflections for others, they are also able to reach a new level of understanding of the meaning of their own life.

Poetry

The Buddhist tradition offers death meditations to help prepare for the final transition. Zen death poems are a traditional means in the Japanese culture of coming to terms with death. The following two poems were among poems collected and published in a book by Hoffman (1998). They express simply and beautifully some essential truths about the relationship between living and dying.

Poem One

Empty-handed I entered the world
Barefoot I leave it.
My coming, my going—
Two simple happenings
That got entangled.

—Kozan

Source: Permission granted by Tuttle publishing.

Poem Two

Like dew drops
on a lotus leaf
I vanish.

—Senryu

Source: Permission granted by Tuttle publishing.

Poetry, either writing it or reading it, can help express the inexpressible. It is often in art forms that one is able to engage beauty in ways that are less common in routine life. Beauty is all around us, through every stage of the aging process, if one cultivates the eyes to see it. Writing poetry may help an individual distill elusive thoughts and images; reading it can be inspirational. It has been said that some of the great Zen masters recited poetry at the moment of death. Many Eastern and some Western religious traditions teach that how you die—holding an attitude of forgiveness and peace versus anger and rebellion toward God or the Divine—is critically important. Dying in hatred may invalidate a lifetime of virtuous acts. Conversely, a person who dies enveloped with prayer, can surround himself or herself with peace and light even in the most impoverished outer conditions.

Rituals for Dying

Ritual provides another way to publicly express difficult emotions and thoughts that are hard to discuss. A funeral or memorial service is a common community-based death ritual that serves as a rite of passage for the deceased and a transition for significant others left behind, but rituals may also be created to focus on living well. They are useful both for the dying and for creating a healing environment with loved ones or staff after the death. Denzin (1974) defines ritual as a

> joint activity given to ceremony, involving two or more persons, endowed with special emotion and often sacred meaning, focused around a clearly defined set of social objects, and when performed confers upon its participants a special sense of the sacred and out of the ordinary. (p. 272)

The flame of a candle, flowers, a pile of stones, a container of water, or objects specific to a faith tradition can help provide a focus. These can help individuals enter a space that is normally difficult for them to enter, to say things to each other like "I'm sorry," or "I'm sad." Music can also help to create a contemplative atmosphere or whatever environment individuals prefer. Music touches the emotions; giving a place to emotion can help release those that are difficult to shoulder. Rituals can serve to bring validation of the experience, reconciliation, and peace as individuals recognize their interdependence and help to dispel guilt, grief, or frustration that a desired future can no longer be attained (Running & Tolle, 2008). Passing a talking stick, as American Indian tribes do, gives individuals permission to express difficult thoughts and feelings. I have sometimes used a rain stick in hospice staff support groups. The gentle sounds of the seeds or stones falling in the hollow core of the cactus usually help people to pause and listen carefully to each other. This ritual could be used with family groups or professional groups to help mourn a loss.

Music Thanatology and Healing Instruments

Music thanatology unites music with medicine in palliative care. The music thanatologist engages the harp and sometimes her voice to create an environment that serves the physical, emotional, and spiritual needs of the dying person and those with him or her. The harpist plays prescriptively. That is, she observes the heart and respiration rates as well as facial expressions of the individual as she watches the chest rise and fall and chooses her repertoire accordingly. She also observes the mood of the client. If there is a need to slow the dying individual's pace, if he or she is agitated, for example, the harpist plays music slowly and softly. Music can thus help ease symptoms of pain and restlessness or labored breathing by offering calming, soothing sounds. There is no intention to entertain or distract the patient, but instead to help the patient let go and be at peace. The harpist thus enters into the situation with senses open to connect not just to the music but to the people present in an interactive and intuitive way. The deep resonance of the music is not only heard but felt as it vibrates through the air.

On a trip to Hong Kong in 2008, I saw an array of guzheng instruments displayed in neat rows in a music shop. These are Chinese harps or zithers, related to the Japanese koto, with movable bridges and 21 strings that create a four octave pentatonic scale. Despite the considerable difficulty of toting this back with me to the United States, I was very intrigued. With the help of a colleague and her husband, I left that store in the condition of being one guzheng lighter. As more than luck would have it, I found a teacher who lives 15 minutes away from my home and teaches in Chinatown as well. His uncle was a master of the guzheng in China and he is a patient and knowledgeable teacher for me. Although I am perhaps not the most skilled student he has had, I am sure I must be one of the most enthusiastic. The sound of this ancient stringed instrument penetrates my mind and body, leaving me with serene feelings. Indeed, my teacher tells me that this was one of the purposes of the original guzheng instrument: to create a sense of calm. Although I have yet to explore playing publicly, this does offer some possibilities. There are many opportunities for those willing to volunteer their musical talent.

Harpists, as well as those who play other types of instruments, such as a guitar, violin, flute, or cello, play not only for the clients but for the staff of hospice and palliative care units. Staff and patients in an ER have reported feeling calmer and more relaxed as they listened to harp music playing. Perhaps someday, this form of live music will be a routine encounter in public places of healing.

Facilitating Connectedness

At the end of life as at other times, loneliness can be a concern. Mental health practitioners can encourage visits from friends, family members, and others in the faith community or workplace if desired by the patient. Reviewing photo albums together and placing photographs in view of the patient can be helpful. Connecting with nature by hanging bird feeders near the window, placing flowers nearby, or moving the patient's bed so they can see a tree and witness the vibrancy in the outdoors can be important. Asking about and then locating meaningful spiritual symbols can also bring comfort (Burkhardt & Nagai-Jacobson, 2005; Meraviglia, Sutter, & Gaskamp, 2008).

COMMUNICATION AT THE END OF LIFE

Questions From the Soul

Patients at the end of life often identify soul-level questions that they want to discuss, whether they can find an answer or not. Some of these questions include the timeless questions about the human condition such as "Why am I here? What is the meaning of my life? Where am I going when I die? Is there a God or benevolent Force in the Universe? Will I be forgiven? Why do I suffer?" (Nelson-Becker, 2006). Some patients do find answers to their questions, but many do not. Palliative care professionals do well to be able to hear these difficult questions and the anguish and sorrow that lie underneath or behind them, as well as, sometimes, the joy (Byrne, 2007). Patients do not only communicate with words, they communicate their emotions in very tangible and sometimes intense ways. Practitioners need to be able to hear all of these expressions of grief, longing, and compassion. To do so means reflecting on and coming to terms with their own life questions and emotional repertoire. Spiritually sensitive palliative care practice does not condemn or seek to rationalize away patient beliefs, but rather asks questions and seeks understanding through that process. In spiritual care work, asking the right questions is almost everything. And it is important to understand that asking the right questions is not difficult work.

Creating an environment of trust with a dying patient and his or her significant others is done through communicating a genuine interest. Professionals can bring their own compassionate presence; pose open-ended questions about what beliefs and values a patient carries and what practices are comforting; reflect back to the patient what they hear and observe to foster new insight; and listen to the patient's story. However this is accomplished, it should be consistent with one's own style. Not every professional will approach spirituality the same way and this is a profound benefit for patients. Sometimes, a simple comment, such as "How are you doing with all of this—the big questions?" is enough to open up space. From a narrative therapy standpoint, patients who share their personal perspective and stories about their views of illness and interpretation of life events can experience a form of spiritual and emotional healing. This is a healing that is hope-inducing even where hope for the body's healing itself is absent. However, for some individuals spirituality is a private matter, or even an irrelevant one. Not everyone will want to discuss it, so it is always a wise course to follow the client's lead.

Communication about spiritual issues occurs in four ways: (1) identification of spiritual themes or spiritual distress in patient conversations; (2) offering response to patient-initiated statements about religious, spiritual, or existential concerns or values;(3) noticing patient nonverbal cues; or (4) formal spiritual assessment, screening, or religious/spiritual history taking.

At this phase of life, individuals will usually discuss what matters most to them. They may make references to God or a transcendent force, or mention meaningful practices such as reading devotional materials, praying, or meditating. They may also discuss the theodicy question—"If God is omnipotent, why must I (or my family) suffer?" A clinician might ask for details or encourage further conversation by saying, "Tell me more." Patients at this stage can easily be unintentionally shut down or discouraged from further discussion by an unaware attitude from the professional, so it is helpful for the practitioner to remain alert to religious or spiritual references. A practitioner might also notice religious symbols in the room or that the patient is wearing and comment on those. A prayer book, cross, rosary, prayer wheel, or Qur'an might rest on the bedside. Finally, using a formal spiritual history, such as the kind discussed in Chapter 6 on Spiritual Assessment, can also open up conversation about religious and spiritual values at this end-of-life time.

Above all, the best communication at the end of life is directed by the client. Merely sitting nearby and listening can encourage clients to find their own truth, a truth whose deep wisdom they may never have guessed they possessed. When a practitioner sits with a dying person, he or she can imagine that person whole and standing against a deep blue sky. In other words, they should look for that person's true nature as a column of light underneath a dark rain-inducing cumulonimbus or wispy cirrus cloud. Alternatively, they may imagine the individual as a shining mirror covered by the thin mist of their pain or suffering. The quality of the helper's presence matters. When you sit with a dying person and don't know what else to do, call on your own sacred sources of meaning for assistance for you to stay in that place of suffering with the dying. Many times, being there can be an inspiration for the helper. Generating hope with the dying person through assisting him or her to recall what he or she did well in life may bring peace. Further, encouraging the finding of forgiveness for self can also release feelings of sadness or depression, guilt or regret (Sogyal Rinpoche, 1992). Simple presence, sitting in silence, can be a boundless and noble support.

Death Preparation Tasks

Impending death is unquestionably difficult for everyone. Everyone lives their own life and likewise has their own death. As many ways as someone can be born into the world, are the ways an individual can leave it. We seldom talk about what people prefer in their dying time, as if to ask those words would indicate that we welcome death. However, this is a conversation that can carry great weight. Some people prefer to die in the company of family and friends, with someone holding their hand or touching them to offer comfort. Others prefer to die alone, with their own thoughts for company. One of my most challenging grief counseling cases was a woman who had left her dying husband's side to get some rest at home. He encouraged her to go, but then died after she left. She had great difficulty forgiving herself for failing to accompany him at this moment of passing. A young woman I counseled had inherited olivopontocerebellar atrophy. Her older sister had died of the illness alone in a nursing care facility, and the most pressing concern for her was fear of dying alone. Asking clients about their wishes in dying can open a valuable discourse and deflect later guilt among survivors. Rather than guessing what their loved one may have wanted or wished for, they know.

Life Completion Tasks

Some people die quickly in an accident or acute illness. In these cases, their life is their preparation for their death, however much or however little death held any specific interest or concern. Surviving loved ones can be comforted—though of course this would not be an initial consideration in the immediate shock and traumatic aftermath—that their life has been touched profoundly by the one lost. Over time, the memories left may be viewed as the primary legacy.

Other people have notice of impending death, uncertain though the timeline may be. If an individual receives a terminal diagnosis, the incredibly distressing aspect is that diagnosis. Still, this person has the opportunity to know and understand their remaining time will be brief. This gift opens space for life completion tasks. Certain communities, such as the Hutterites in South Dakota, in fact much prefer a prolonged death to a short sudden one for this reason (Cacciatore & Ong, 2011). Their rationale is largely religious; with a longer death, community members can confess sins and prepare for eternity.

Life completion tasks consist of four fundamental acts: (1) I love you; (2) I forgive you; (3) please forgive me; and (4) thank you (Byock, 2004). Sharing love, knowing one is beloved as well as loving others, expands the heart. It is one of the great learnings in life. It can be difficult to say these words in family groups that have no pattern for this, but love can also be expressed in acts of caring. Offering forgiveness as well as inviting it helps the dying individual and his or her significant others to release any lingering misunderstanding and pain. Saying, "You did not do what I wanted-expected-hoped you to do, but that's OK," or "I know I did not always do what helped you and in fact have hurt you," acknowledges the chasm that bursts open among individuals, but it also begins the bridging or emotional and spiritual healing process to be found in forgiveness. Further, sometimes it is the self that is most in need of healing, so self-forgiveness should be included under the umbrella of forgiveness. Voicing gratitude acknowledges the unearned abundance of life (see Table 11.6). This task completion process can eventually lead to joy and deeper appreciation. Forming relationships and connecting with people is the very essence of what it means to share humanity. Our words and how they are delivered carry this important capacity for healing.

There is one other last task that should be added: saying good-bye. There is always a last time, as much as we may wish a moment to last forever. I will never forget the poignant last image of my daughter asking for a private moment to say good-bye to her grandmother who lay dying. As her dad and I left the room, she bent down to say something to my mother who was in a semi-conscious state. When people leave us, we will miss them forever, but they enter a state free from pain and move on into the great adventure, whatever that may be. Anticipatory grieving for loved ones begins at any point in the dying trajectory among survivors. Saying good-bye may facilitate moving through anticipatory grief.

Table 11.6   Growing Through Loss Case Study
Karen attended the funeral service of her husband's now elderly godfather. She had never known him well, though she had met him a few times over the nearly 20 years of her marriage. At the service, his three grandchildren who had lived nearby stood up and in turn told the audience what he had meant in their lives. He loved cars and could build anything and often worked with them on his cars. As he taught them about life in his quiet way, he showed them how much he loved them. Clearly, each grandson had been affected in a powerful way by his presence in their lives, and everyone present was also touched by the deep feeling and appreciation expressed. Karen walked out, vowing to be a better mother, friend, and spouse. She told her husband how glad she had been to be present. She was moved to be more caring in the small interactions of daily life as this man had been. That evening she and her husband were at a café ordering dinner. After waiting a long time for their order to be taken, the server brought a bottle of wine and promptly spilled a few drops on Karen's new dress when he opened it. Karen felt herself become very impatient and began to angrily reprimand the server, when her husband leaned over and said, "It's just wine—we can clean it up." Ding. There was an instant reminder to Karen that she had failed in her earlier vow. How easy it is to forget the important things in life!
1. What experiences have you had that have taught you something important about loss, grief, death, dying, and living?
2. Can you share this with someone else?

SUMMARY

In this chapter about the end of life and aging, context was provided for perceptions of dying and death in the United States. The history of attitudes toward death was presented along with a brief history of the hospice and palliative care movements. Findings from a study about end-of-life resilience were discussed. A spiritual care model, components of spiritual care, as well as ideal communication practices between professionals and patients at the end of life were suggested. Loss, grief, and dying well are key areas of mental health need, but they remain wildly and widely under addressed.

QUESTIONS FOR DISCUSSION

1. How have societal views about death and dying changed over time? How is death respected in modern culture?

2. What is palliative care and how does it differ from other treatment models (e.g., aggressive care)?

3. What was Dame Cicely Saunders's contribution to end-of-life care, and in what way was it innovative?

4. What are the benefits/critiques concerning Kübler-Ross's stage theory about dying?

5. How can spiritual care be integrated into palliative care? Discuss the current standards and what could still be absent.

6. How can one best communicate with someone who is dying? What can get in the way?

ASSIGNMENT: SPIRITUALITY, RELIGION, AND LOSS

Think, pair, and share. Pair up with a partner, one to be the interviewer and one the interviewee. Switch roles halfway through the allotted time. You may also briefly write your responses before sharing them.

Ask each other the following:

1. Can you remember a loss or death when your religion, sense of spirituality, or practical philosophy helped you cope with grieving? How did it help you?

2. If you are part of an organized religion, what does that religion teach about death, afterlife, and suffering? If not, what are your own beliefs?

3. Was discussing your views on religion or spirituality and its relationship to loss useful? If so, in what way? If not, why not?

Write up your experience of interviewing someone about ideas on loss, spirituality, or religion in a short reflection paper with his/her permission. You can also interview someone informally outside the class and bring their responses to class. Or this can be done formally through an IRB approval process.

MEDITATION: REFRESHING THE SENSES

This exercise invites you to clear out any dark thoughts or stagnant or dark energy you may have acquired. In your mind, picture an object to use for this exercise. You may choose an eagle feather, holy water, magic hands, a magic stone, a magic wand, or other device to freshen and clean the senses. Or if you happen to have an object available, such as a talking stick sometimes used in group work, you may use it. Sit quietly and relax, releasing all tension. Take your assisting object and in your mind or your hand, touch it to your eyes, your ears, your mouth, your nose, and your fingertips. As it touches each part of you, ask it to remove anything that is unhealthy or stuck, and send it into an imaginary recycling well located in front of your feet. This well will take any of this energy that does not belong to you or should not belong to you and send it back somewhere. You don't need to worry about where it goes. Then take your object and touch it to the top of your head, allowing the cleansing properties to flow down your front, your right and left sides, and your back. Return when you are ready.

EXPLORING YOUR SPIRITUALITY: CREATING YOUR OWN OBITUARY—AN OPPORTUNITY FOR REFLECTION

Everyone will die. You will, too. It is helpful to face your mortality by thinking about how you want to be remembered—and writing about it in two or three pages. What is your authentic self and what do you want people to know about you? First place yourself 30 to 50 years into the future when you are well along your life course, reflect on the following questions, and then respond.

1. What mattered most in your life? How do you want others to remember you? What has been the major message or theme of your life?

2. What three or four words describe you best?

3. What were your accomplishments? What were your meaningful experiences? Are those the same or different?

4. Who did you love and care about? Who or what (e.g., ideas) supported you?

5. What was your relationship to the sacred?

6. What specific lesson, philosophical view, wisdom thought, or memory do you want to leave for family and friends?

7. How might the lives of others be better because of what you learned and contributed? What is your hope for those you leave behind?

8. Any other ideas that might be important to share?

After writing this essay, put it aside and look at it in two years or more. How does this writing reflect the essential you? Will the goals you have set for yourself now help you to develop into the person described in your obituary? This exercise is similar to an ethical will used in Judaism and described in Genesis 49:1–33: In this passage, Jacob, who is dying, gathers his sons and offers them his blessing. An ethical will, similar to a self-written obituary, addresses the need to be known, to be remembered, to have one's life make a difference, to bless, and be blessed.

EXPLORING YOUR SPIRITUALITY: PLAN YOUR MEMORIAL OR FUNERAL SERVICE

Consider how you hope to help attendees mourn and celebrate your life. First think about your life, highlighting the moments that meant a lot to you, where you learned or grew. Second, think about other people who have helped you (sometimes through the obstacles they presented) and how this has mattered. Also consider the supports offered generally in your own religious or spiritual tradition, if any.

1. How do you want to be remembered? What is the essence of you as best you can ascertain?

2. What visual, sensory, auditory, or other elements do you want to be present? Are there particular songs or hymns you might like to have used?

3. What would the nature of this service or ceremony look like?

4. Where might it be held? What would happen? How would the event flow? Are there certain people (perhaps choose someone younger than yourself) who you might encourage to participate in particular ways? Would you ask them in advance or leave instructions for this? What would be gained through each method?

5. What will planning this service contribute to you now and to those who will mourn you in the future? What do you hope will be accomplished through it?

6. How does this service reflect you and what you thought was important in your life?

7. What summative message do you want to leave as your legacy to those who attend?

EXPLORING YOUR SPIRITUALITY: A MEETING WITH DEATH

There are many things in life that we hold onto long after their usefulness wanes. There comes a time when it helps to declutter or dissolve ideas, possessions, or habits that no longer serve and expand us, but instead limit us. Ernst Becker (1973) suggests, "one of the great rediscoveries of modern thought [is] that of all things that move man, one of the principal ones is his terror of death" (p. 11). Most of us would agree that we live in a society that largely denies that we live in the face of our dying.

How can we prepare for letting go of what we need to release in our lives and for our ultimate end in death? Acknowledging that we will die can give poignancy and purpose to life. In fact, a Buddhist tenet is that when one faces what is feared directly, that fear can be dispersed, so Buddhist monks may meditate on their own death and particularly a moment when they might be murdered. To achieve equanimity under that condition, is to being able to apply it easily in less emotionally absorbing conditions.

With this in mind, prepare to participate in a meditation where you will meet Death and ask it/ him or her the question(s) that you carry. These questions may center on what needs to die within you, how you kill your own dreams, or participate in belittling the dreams others hold. You may ask Death what message death has for you today or what it wants from you. Then invite Death to tell you what you can do for it and thank it for the new understanding it has given you. Sometimes listening to music or a gentle drumbeat can facilitate this process.

1. Imagine a long hallway of some kind with a door at the end. Move down that hallway and open the door. You will find Death there. What does Death look like or feel like? How do you perceive it? Is it a friend or enemy? Take a moment and ask death your question(s). You may even want to ask how much time you will have until you meet Death at the end of your life.

2. Sit a moment with Death and let your fear dissolve, however long this may take.

3. Thank Death for spending this time with you and for the insights you have gained.

4. Travel back down the corridor to your present place.

5. Journal about this experience.

WEBSITES

Association for Death Education and Counseling (ADEC)

http://www.adec.org/adec/default.aspx

This organization offers certification in thanatology, has other resources and links, as well as sponsors an annual conference.

Caring Community: Wellness Through Life's End

http://caringcommunity.org/links/midbiolinks

This site has information about advanced care planning and other areas of interest in end-of-life care.

National Hospice and Palliative Care Organization: Caring Connections

http://www.caringinfo.org/

This site provides information for consumers of hospice care, such as choosing a hospice, and for caregivers on managing the illness and dealing with grief. (See Chapter 3 on Ethics for similar website resources.)

Caring Conversations: Making Your Wishes Known About End of Life Care

http://www.practicalbioethics.org/resources/caring-conversations

A downloadable workbook is available here in English and Spanish. (This is also listed in Chapter 3.)

Dying Well

http://www.dyingwell.com/

This website features articles, books, and discussion guides by Ira Byock, a physician who has been active in hospice and palliative care movements.

The GoWish Game

http://www.gowish.org/

This website offers a set of cards developed with the support of the Archstone Foundation. The cards help players find specific words to talk about what is important if they find themselves living a life that was shortened by serious illness.

National Hospice and Palliative Care Organization

http://www.nhpco.org/templates/1/homepage.cfm

This site has information about hospice and palliative care policy and statistics.

Sacred Dying

http://www.sacreddying.org/

This includes online fee-based training modules on sitting vigil with dying persons.

The Social Work in Hospice and Palliative Care Network

http://swhpn.org

This network holds an annual conference and is affiliated with the *Journal of Social Work* in end-of-life and palliative care.

RECOMMENDED READING

Altilio, T., & Otis-Green, S. (Eds.). (2011) *Oxford textbook of palliative social work*. New York, NY: Oxford University Press.

This is a recent text that offers a wealth of information about palliative care.

Brody, J. (2009). *Jane Brody's guide to the great beyond: Prepare now for a smooth ride to the end of life*. New York, NY: Random House.

Besides practical tips, this book has a chapter on communication and coping with spiritual issues.

Butler, K. (2013). *Knocking on heaven's door: The path to a better way of death*. New York, NY: Scribner.

This book details one woman's experience with caregiving and the unexpected discoveries. It includes a section on ways to facilitate natural death in a health care industry bent on doing all possible.

Byock, I. (1997). *Dying well: Peace and possibilities at the end of life*. New York, NY: Riverhead Books.

This edited book by a physician has much to offer about living with dying, suffering, and growing through the experience. Many of the chapters relate to aspects of spirituality useful for those working with older adults.

Byock, I. (2012). *The best care possible: A physician's quest to transform care through the end of life*. New York, NY: Avery/Penguin.

This is an important book about what can and often does diminish the experience of end of life.

Callanan, M., & Kelley, P. (1992). *Final gifts*. New York, NY: Simon & Shuster.

Two nurses discuss their experiences in working with dying patients.

Dalai Lama, & Hopkins, J. (2002). *Advice on dying and living a better life*. New York, NY: Atria.

Discussion of death preparation tasks as key to life enhancement is provided.

Ferrell, B., & Coyle, N. (Eds.). (2010). *Oxford textbook of palliative nursing* (3rd Ed.). New York, NY: Oxford Press.

This very extensive text on principles of care for the dying person is written for nurses and others.

Harris, D. L., & Winokuer, H. R. (2016). *Principles and practice of grief counseling* (2nd ed.). New York, NY: Springer.

This is a concise but well-written text on helping individuals grieve more fully and includes spirituality.

Holder, J. S., & Aldredge-Clanton, J. (2004). *Parting: A handbook for spiritual care near the end of life*. Chapel Hill: University of North Carolina Press.

This is a travel guide for meaningful companionship at life's end.

Lischer, R. (2013). *Stations of the heart: Parting with a son*. New York, NY: Knopf Press.

This book is a portrait of grief when an adult son dies too young.

Lynn, J., & Harrold, J. (2006). *Handbook for mortals*. New York, NY: Oxford University Press.

This book offers practical tips to patients about finding meaning in terminal illness and coping with illness and dying. It includes a chapter on talking with the physician and coping with events surrounding a death.

Rando, T. A. (1998). *Treatment of complicated mourning.* Champaign, IL: Research Press.

This is a classic text with many wise strategies for working with grief.

Shepherd, M. (2000). *Dying: A guide for helping and coping.* Sag Harbor, NY: Permanent Press.

Material is presented from interviews with dying patients who have a range of responses.

Sogyal, R., Gaffney, P., & Harvey, A. (1992). *The Tibetan book of living and dying.* San Francisco, CA: Harper.

This is a wonderful book on different ways of conceptualizing and preparing for death.

Yalom, I. (2009). *Staring at the sun: Overcoming the terror of death.* San Francisco, CA: Jossey-Bass.

Psychotherapist Yalom encourages us to confront our fear of death in this compelling book.

CHAPTER TWELVE

INTEGRATION

Let the beauty we love be what we do.
There are hundreds of ways to kneel and kiss the ground.

—Rumi

If the doors of perception were cleansed,
everything would appear to man as it is: infinite.

—William Blake

This chapter discusses a mélange of perspectives on integration. First it provides information on how religion and spirituality cohere or fail to cohere with professional practice disciplines and their foundational knowledge. Functions of religion are explored as well as a return to the discussion of societal changes in views toward religion presented in Chapter 1. Trends in spirituality are investigated and spiritual questions that vary by generation are posed. Spirituality as a practical life philosophy is theorized. Dissimilarity in spiritual orientations between clients and professionals and avenues for bridging that gap are presented. Addressed, too, is treating clients under great environmental duress during a backdrop of national disaster. Evaluation of practice as a necessary integrating element in the therapeutic process of engagement, assessment, and interventions is provided. The value of interprofessional practice related to spiritual care along with features of its complexity are displayed. Finally, attention is turned to mindfulness, self-care, and self-compassion methods for practitioners.

INTEGRATION OF RELIGION AND SPIRITUALITY WITH PROFESSIONAL PRACTICE

How well do religion and spirituality align with a broad array of professional disciplines serving older people, such as psychology, social work, counseling, nursing, pastoral care, occupational therapy, and art and music therapies? Two ways of assessing the relationships include considering characteristics of *congruence*—how well do religion and spirituality inform and relate to professional work—and *importance*—which domain should take priority in work with clients (Nelson, 2009). Congruence models range from separation, to conflict, to complement.

In *separation*, the assumption is that religion/spirituality and the discipline have different spheres of influence, different truth claims, and thus should be separate from clinical practice. The professional discipline has its own tools: a knowledge base and skill set enhanced through internships of one kind or another. Thus, it would be unreasonable to suggest—with the exception of the position of pastoral care as a profession—that it should entertain ideas about working with religious or spiritual issues that could arise in the context of life challenges. Neither the profession nor religion/spirituality can add any validity to the other. This principle of separation is largely evident in the political choice in the United States to separate church and state, thus preserving respect for and freedom of religion, and a partition between religion and government. In practice, this partition is not opaque and it is likely a good result where its boundaries continue to be considered and contested, sometimes in the courts, against the backdrop of other necessary freedoms.

Conflict, similar to arguments in the natural or physical sciences fields, advances the idea that there may be areas of common interest and overlap, but competing truth claims. Thus, one area cannot be proved or informed by the other and in fact, taken together, one may even diminish the validity of the other. Religion has been said to promote stereotypes, especially in gender roles and ideas about gender invariance. Further theological explanations may serve to keep people satisfied with unequal positions of power. Women in some faith traditions, such as Catholicism, have seen their sphere of influence limited to subordinate roles and doors into the highest positions of ecclesial authority sealed against them. Professional practice disciplines promote equal access to goods and services and support for the most vulnerable individuals of society. Most faith traditions, too, support social justice initiatives, although concepts about what constitutes social justice and the means to bring it about may be sources of dissent.

Finally, in the *complement* model, both religion/spirituality and professional practice viewpoints are required to create a whole and complete understanding of the phenomenon, even if there are areas lacking knowledge. In this latter model, both provide insight into human behavior. Thus, interaction can synergistically lead to better understanding. This view of complementarity is consistent with the Jesuit philosophy that God is in all things. In particular, Ignatian spirituality is defined as follows:

1. Finding God in everything

2. Becoming a contemplative in action

3. Looking at the world in an incarnational way (as if the spirit of Jesus were still present in it)

4. Seeking freedom and detachment (Martin, 2010, p. 10)

Endorsing the concept that God is in all things suggests that God is similarly, in some mysterious way, present in interactions between professionals and clients as they co-create better mental health in the client. Striving for the benefits of being a contemplative while active in the world, suggests reaching for balance that attends to the inner life while seeking service opportunities. Similarly, looking at the world incarnationally is a reminder beyond Christianity that people are connected to each other and to whatever source they deem to be sacred. Finally, the desire to seek freedom and detachment aligns with the Four Noble Truths of Buddhism, especially the Third Noble Truth. This latter Truth also addresses the value of recognizing impermanence and detachment and adjusting one's actions accordingly.

The question of the relative *importance* between religion/spirituality and professional disciplines can likely only be answered by personal preference. Two different people grounded in the same professional tradition would tend to have different viewpoints that depend on their background characteristics and experiences with faith or spirituality. However, similar to the question of congruence, importance elicits three standards: confessionalism, scientism, and dialogical integration (Nelson, 2009).

Confessionalism refers to a partisan orientation toward one domain above others. This principally refers to adherence to exact beliefs. This could be a primary orientation to one's profession and the values and beliefs that emanate from it such as particular beliefs about the nature of human behavior, though often in current usage the word usually implies orientation toward faith, or spiritual views. There is an emphasis on learning and following the traditional dogma absent appreciation of different interpretative frameworks. Sometimes individuals view their discipline in almost a confessional way, adhering to certain views that may, for instance, be labeled liberal and progressive or traditional. Although it is likely true that certain professions tend to elicit practitioners with more liberal views, harm can be done when people with more traditional or conservative views are not also welcomed into the profession. The greater the categorical diversity within a profession—ethnic, cultural, religious, spiritual, age, gender, and tenure—the better situated it is to respond to community need.

Scientism involves privileging empirically proven data over other forms, especially over religion. For instance, the existence of God, a Higher Power, or Sacred Source is beyond the power of any research design to accurately assess. It lies outside every attempt at reductionism. However, scientism would always assert that science triumphs over any theological perspectives about life and living. What has been proven? "Let's consider the statistics and the facts first," would be the response. The incompatibility of science and philosophical/theological thought also implies that each answers different questions, both kinds of which are important.

Dialogical integration seeks both forms of knowledge applied more or less equally, though in a specific instance, one form might be given preference over another. Science may someday suggest answers to the puzzle regarding causes of dementia and how it can be successfully treated. Does it come from auto-inflammation or other bioprocesses or structures of the aging brain? Research funding and intellectual resources are proceeding to this area in the form of study of nutrition, exercise patterns, education and other brain stimulation, and many additional behavioral applications as well as basic science, pharmacology, and biomedicine. Although those answers for the moment are elusive, professional practice provides interim responses, if not resolutions. Until successful treatment avenues emerge, spirituality and religion suggest that relational work with persons with dementia at every stage of the illness includes honoring the dignity and worth of the person. In this way, both the biological mechanics and the spiritual valuation are respected.

The congruence or lack of it between the professions and the field of religion and spirituality can in the end only be answered by the professional who stands in relationship to both. This may be a measure of how strongly one identifies with professional values, knowledge, and skills that could also be named the artistry of the profession, and the perceived role of the spiritual/religious domain. The absence or presence of spirituality or religion may influence the nature of the transformation. Although the mechanism is often not entirely clear, research continues to explore correlations and causal links among religion, spirituality, and behavior. The professional may engage spirituality/religion explicitly in the client encounter through assessment or intervention that addresses these domains. Second, either area may be implicitly involved if the professional uses a spiritual or religious lens himself or herself. If unimportant personally to the professional, it still may emerge if it is an important dynamic for the client.

FUNCTIONS OF RELIGION

Coherence With Professional Practice

Professional disciplines are sourced out of a combination of a critical knowledge base regarding human behavior and a particular public need. So, for instance, some professions such as mathematics have a knowledge base, but do not necessarily have a public audience. Other professions, such as landscape management or food distribution, meet a public need and do that through knowledge systems of marketing and labor distribution, but fail to have a scientific critical knowledge base aside from one rooted in economics. Religion, however, serves a number of different functions within the public sphere that complement the work of professional disciplines (Berger, 1974; Durkheim & Fields, 1995).

First, religion is a source of meaning and purpose. Many people find that religion answers their most salient and enduring questions about life. It may help them discover a larger level response to immediate concerns, particularly if they have a concept of life after death. They also may find within a religious faith the opportunity to engage in service that matters to them. Professional practitioners generally find meaning in their work and believe their work is important, even when secondary trauma or burnout symptoms provide stressors.

Second, religion reinforces social unity through providing a framework of belief. In many cases that framework has widened over the years to include both theistic and nontheistic perspectives. There is a move toward ecumenical and interfaith understanding echoed by interprofessional practice, even while religion also elicits narrow entrenched views that lead to warfare in certain areas of the world. Religion also reinforces unity by fostering social bonds, sometimes between people who would have no other way to meet. People who practice in professions also form a social bond with clients, offering their acceptance to clients and patients who may feel rejected because of perceived social, physical, developmental, or other deficits.

Third, religion fosters greater psychological and physical well-being. Studies such as those detailed in Chapter 8 have shown that older adults who are networked into a religious faith generally accrue positive benefits (George et al., 2013; Koenig et al., 2012; Moberg, 2005). Positive psychological—and in some cases, physical—well-being is also a primary goal of professional practice disciplines. Lastly, religion can offer a home for those who seek positive social change. The U.S. Civil Rights movement had a large base of support from churches in both Southern and Northern states, even when government was slow to legislate and safeguard rights. Professional practice disciplines often invite their members to support legislation that will affect the common good for client mental and social health.

What does this mean for older persons who are religious? Strengthening their continued interest in religious faith is an appropriate goal, except in rare cases where that faith expression may cause harmful effects. Older adults who can no longer drive may find transportation to religious meetings burdensome. This may be true whether they continue to live at home or whether they live at a congregate care facility. Finding ways to continue to facilitate their religious connection can provide psychological benefit and reduce loneliness (Green & Elliott, 2010). Sometimes this may be accomplished through linking them with those in their faith community who can either provide transportation or find others who can. Some religious communities will ask for volunteers or send religious representatives to conduct religious services in a senior housing or nursing care facility to which others are also invited as nonfaith members or guests. Municipal communities may foster free or reduced rate transportation to facilitate ongoing connection.

Trending Changes in the Societal Context of Religion

Current demographic patterns in the percentages of older adults who found religion important were detailed in Chapter 1. These included religious attendance, belief in God, and importance of religion. Surveys still indicate that older adults are, for the most part, the highest supporters by age group of formal faith organizations in the United States (Pew Forum on Religion & Public Life, 2013). However, religious research in third world nations tends to show that religious adherence is higher for all age groups in countries with lower per capita income (Almond, Appleby, & Sivan, 2003). With immigration, the hosting country thus may experience an uptick in those seeking to form and attend religious communities.

Overall in the United States, there is an increasing move toward secularization— probably—at least, that is the popular belief supported by some survey research. However, Stark (2015) suggests that there is a complication with survey data in Pew surveys that likely underreports belief with the rise of the *nones* or religiously nonaffiliated; he prefers to rely on Gallup world polls. He suggests fewer than 10% of those sampled in surveys participate, leading to skewed data. Further, those who report themselves nonreligious may not attend church but still subscribe to religious belief. In fact, the Baylor Religion Survey (2007) suggests that 60.5% of those surveyed *absolutely* believe in angels with another 20.9% believing angels *probably* exist. Surveys indicate a majority of adults in the United States, aged 18 and older, believe in God. In fact this is, at minimum, close to 93% (Pew Forum, 2008).

Berger (2012) likewise today does not support the secularization hypothesis; this represents a change from his early writing in the 1970s and somewhat later. He believes that increasing secularization is not an accurate prediction for two reasons. First, theories come from highly educated people who have somewhat different viewpoints from the common person and these intellectuals tend to influence each other, ignoring other data. Second, secularization is a Eurocentric view that is not representative of most of the rest of the world. Berger suggests that secularization was confused with pluralization, the increasing numbers of religions, denominations, and sects. Instead of modernity leading to greater secularity, it instead leads to greater plurality and awareness of that plurality as people make their home among others with competing ideas, values, and yes, religions. Instead, Berger (2012) submits that although some religious faiths like Islam and charismatic Christianity are expanding quickly, in other cases, religious and secular views coexist peacefully. In sum, his view is that many still-religious people advance rational arguments and "successfully alternate between secular and religious definitions of reality" (p. 315). For instance, if someone who is religious becomes seriously ill, he or she will pray, but this person will also arrange to be seen by medical specialist. An older person with an illness might draw on resources from his or her cultural heritage, such as a shaman or espiritista (spiritual healer). A rather seamless integration of several types of practices can take place. Further, this occurs with such fluency that this may not rise to the level of conscious thought or question.

About one-third of U.S. citizens endorse conservative religious denominations (Pew Forum, 2008). This indicates that conservatism remains a strong religious preference. People who are more educated and obtain higher incomes, which would tend to include professionals, are more likely to belong to more liberal religious groups, if they belong to any at all (Pew Forum on Religion & Public Life, 2008). This suggests an ongoing general disparity between religious views of professionals and clients they may serve—at least if their clients represent vulnerable diverse populations. In this time of multiple modernities with competing viewpoints, it makes sense that professional practitioners from every discipline should be the ones capable of stretching or setting aside personal views to be able to hear alternative stories of very different lives in the clients/consumers with whom they work.

TRENDS IN SPIRITUALITY

Amidst this cultural context of a changing religious landscape, what can be known about spirituality? By definition, spirituality is a more individual-level response to the question of what gives meaning and purpose, sparkling moments, and vibrancy to life. Please refer to Chapter 2 for the broad definitions and concepts provided earlier. In a course I took many years ago on practical theology taught by Don S. Browning in the Divinity School of the University of Chicago, he asked students to consider the question, "Who is God for me?" That made sense in the ecumenical and interprofessional environment, and students responded with a variety of answers based on the deep questions that brought them back to a seminary education; these were answers that rested on the premise of who they were and had been, their beliefs about the nature of the world. Follow-up questions ensued. A few questions were, "Who is God for the athlete in a competition?" "Who is God for the recovering alcoholic who was saved on the street?" "Who is God for the early career economics professor (at a very prestigious university) who left the academy to become a minister in the Unitarian Universalist fellowship?" And mine, "Who is God in the eyes of an aging person?" Browning met with each of us individually as we composed papers and pushed us to move more profoundly into our questions. Mine became the foundation of my dissertation question, much better articulated under his guidance. Spirituality remains at the expanding edge of people in their individual lives and is best accessed through their questions.

Religious and Spiritual Questions Asked by Each Generation

How do different generations address religion and spirituality and what are the spiritual questions that shape them? Some people have proposed that older adults grow more religious as they age, but this has not generally been proven. Intragenerational differences as well as flexibility in what constitutes a generation indicate that no one individual may fit the features of his or her group, but guided by data from the General Global Social Survey and what is suggested about some age cohorts, I have framed some questions to consider. These questions suggest very broadly what the concerns of this group may have been, are, or will be. This is important for two reasons. It suggests the spiritual thumbprint of those who are growing older and it suggests the spiritual gaps between younger professionals who serve older clients.

The "G.I. Generation" or the "Greatest Generation," the latter appellation given by newscaster Tom Brokaw, included people born from approximately 1900 to 1924. Nearly all were affected by World War II. As adults they either served in the military directly, fueled the growth in factory efficiency, or supported the effort in other ways. They lived through the stock market crash of 1929 and the Great Depression with its dust bowl–impaired harvests. They have largely been faith believers, committed to their communities and doing what they can now to sustain their faith traditions in times of falling numbers (Gay & Lynxwiler, 2013). They have, on the whole, petitioned God directly for answers to their religious and spiritual (R/S) questions and/or followed the lead of clergy. For a few, direct reading of sacred texts was discouraged—that was the province of the priest. On the whole, they are more likely than younger adults to believe literally in the Bible if they are Christian (Gay & Lynxwiler, 2013). Questions: "How can I serve God? How can I serve my faith?"

The "Silent Generation," those born from 1925 to 1945, was stamped by World War II, the Korean War, and the Vietnam War. They are also known as the "Swing Generation." Their interest was in sustaining their families and they were largely other directed, concerned about how others perceived them and adhering to social norms (Bellah, Madsen, Sullivan, Swidler, & Tipton, 1985; Gay & Lynxwiler, 2013). Their financial support fueled growth in religious participation and in building religious organizations and facilities. The Global Social Survey does not show they pray more than other generational groups (Gay & Lynxwiler, 2013). Any personal spiritual questions were largely overshadowed by war involvement and later prosperity. In some cases, individual spiritual questions were discouraged and they adopted values of their group. Questions: "How can I serve God and my community? What are the religious rules I should follow and how can I best do that?"

The "Baby Boom Generation" represents the period from post war 1946 to about 1964 (Pilcher, 1994). This is the generation just entering early older adulthood now. Bellah et al. (1985) wrote about the greater role of religious individualism in this group who largely broke free from worshipping out of a sense of duty or obligation. The Baby Boomers are a bridge generation spiritually. Many were raised in the faith of their parents, and some still keep that faith. Others have gone far afield in their spiritual explorations, studying nature-based spiritualities and more rare religions, such as Baháʼí, Jainism, Rastafarianism, Scientology, Wicca, and Zoroastrianism. Some call themselves atheist or agnostic. They were the first as a group to forge their own way spiritually, rejecting religious institutions as they also engaged in political and social protest. Questions: "Who or what is God? What is spirituality and where can I find it? What questions should I ask about God, religion, and the spiritual world? What are the spiritual and religious interconnections in life?"

Following the Baby Boomers is "Generation X," made up of those born from approximately 1965 to 1980. Generation X has not been highly visible in faith community settings; however, they may have a strong sense of social justice. They believe in God as much as the generations that precede them (Gay & Lynxwiler, 2013). This group and the generations following tend to be less committed to one faith or particular religious or spiritual group if affiliated, but will try out or "shop" different ones to meet changing interests and needs. In this sense, they may practice spiritual entrepreneurship, seeking out different spiritual or religious groups at different times. Questions: "What is the role of the faith community in promoting social justice for all? How can religion serve the needs of the poor and those hurting? What role do advances in science and astrophysics have on the meaning, efficacy, or the value of religious faith? How is spirituality a part of life?"

The "Millennial Generation" or "Generation Y" birth years range from the early 1980s to 2000 or so. This latter group, the digital natives, has been greatly affected by technological innovations with the Internet, cell phone, and the decrease in sense of personal security. Low on social trust, they also face economic challenges in the marketplace, more so than previous generations. Thus, they tend to distrust institutions including religious ones. They have the lowest faith tradition attendance rates of all these generational groups and are less religious, as suggested by responses on the General Social Survey (Gay & Lynxwiler, 2013), yet according to the Pew Research Center (2014b), they still believe in God to a large extent (86%). Greater educational achievement, represented by this age group, also decreases the odds of belief in God. The spirituality of the Millennial Generation is essentially shaped by the complex matrix of interrelationships. Questions: "What is the role of faith, if any, in my life and the lives of those about whom I care? What can I learn from people around me about spirituality? How can I connect with others in formulating my spiritual questions? What is the value of spirituality for me? What is my spiritual identity?"

There is a younger generation beginning to establish now: those born after 2000. This group is not included here because they are still working on personal identity issues. The question of their spiritual identity has likely not coalesced and won't as a generation, if it does at all, for an unknown number of years. The correlation of every generation to a specific range of years is somewhat flexible, based on historical events and the rise of movements and subcultures.

Scientific evidence and support for generational variability remain somewhat controversial. What we do know is that intragenerational variability is greater today than in previous generations (Pew Research Center, 2014b). Forty-three percent of Millennial adults correspond to an ethnic category that is nonwhite, the highest proportion of any generation (Pew Research Center, 2014b). Each cohort, besides being a chronological generation, is also a social generation because of the impact of the broad sweep of social events that unspooled over its course. It may also carry a common social consciousness. Each of these cohorts listed above and those that come after in generations yet to be born will, in turn, become older adults, though not all members will survive to that age. They are likely to have been shaped by their own generation's views on religion and spirituality as well as the questions asked by previous generations. All of this information available to them becomes their *spiritual capital*.

Spiritual capital is one of many cultural resources, but it takes a primary position because it moves to the heart of questions of life meaning and purpose. Spiritual capital is what connects people to the sacred; it consists of concepts or ideologies, religious/spiritual experiences, and practices, and it is influenced by religious structures within societies. Spiritual capital is affected by life trajectories and biography, life course development, generational transmission, and exchange of resources.

Later generations will consist of a greater diversity of faiths affected by immigration and greater access to knowledge of those faiths affected by proximity, both geographic and inhabiting shared workspaces, for example, than previous generations have held. Generally, the role of religious authority in their lives will weaken, apart from subgroups who will still subscribe to religious fundamentalism. However, people will gladly support and connect to religious and spiritual groups that share ideals and operationalize those ideals.

This topic has been developed here to provide very broad guidance for clinical work. Those in professional practice disciplines will often be younger than the older clients they serve. At times, they will find themselves looking over the generational divide to apprehend a different mindset. Building cross-generational relationships while engaged in professional work can be profoundly satisfying. Table 12.1 provides a summary of the key questions I attribute to each generation.

Table 12.1   Common Spiritual Questions Arising From Each Generation

Generational Term	Birth Years	Common Spiritual Questions
Greatest Generation	1900–1924	How can I serve God?
		How can I serve my faith?
Silent Generation	1925–1945	How can I serve God and my community?
		What are the religious rules I should follow?
		How can I best follow them?
Baby Boom Generation	1946–1964	Who or what is God?
		What is spirituality and where can I find it?
		What questions should I ask about God, religion, and the spiritual world?
		What are the spiritual and religious interconnections in life?
Generation X	1965–1980	What is the role of the faith community in promoting social justice for all?
		How can religion serve the needs of the poor and those hurting?
		What role do advances in science and astrophysics have on the meaning, efficacy, or the value of religious faith?
		How is spirituality a part of life?
Millennial Generation/ Generation Y	1981–2000	What is the role of faith, if any, in my life, and the lives of those about whom I care?
		What can I learn from people around me about spirituality?
		How can I connect with others in formulating my spiritual questions?
		What is the value of spirituality for me?
		What is my spiritual identity?

Note: Birth years are only approximate.

©Holly Nelson-Becker

Spiritual, but Not Religious

God may not be woven into the spiritual question at all, or may comprise a small part of it. Those who endorse survey questions that suggest they are "spiritual, but not religious" are an expanding group, beginning with the Baby Boom Generation (Pilcher, 1994). This characterization is endorsed even more strongly by following generations.

The "spiritual, but not religious" trend is not one that completely shuns religion, but it expresses more of a religion-as-marketplace mentality (Roof, 1999). In this view, certain individuals who endorse spirituality may also be completely comfortable sitting on the seat of pews or synagogue chairs at religious high points or ceremonial events such as marriage and Bar/Bat Mitzvahs. Beyond the Judeo-Christian culture also lays an increasing interfaith acceptability, largely among more progressive religious groups. The term *seekers* has been applied to this group of spiritual/religious questers, in contrast to the *dwellers*, those who have found a faith home. Roof (1999) has argued that seekers are "spiritual tourists," those who seek a sampling of different kinds of spiritual expression but lack a community to practice it. This stands in dialogical opposition to the concept of "spiritual pilgrims." Spiritual pilgrims follow the ancient tradition of the monks and mystics who seek the demanding work of spiritual growth. However, they may not follow the ancient ways, but instead incorporate modern and possibly new age understandings of the spiritual path. Eclecticism and syncretism, a process of combining aspects from different faith traditions, are also potential outcomes of the seeker movement.

It is important to note that some ethnic communities have long been shaped by a mixing of spiritual traditions, such as Daoism, Confucianism, Christianity, and Buddhism in China and Korea or Chinese-American and Korean-American communities. At times this blending may be somewhat idiosyncratic within families and especially their younger generations. An increasing, though still small group of adult Americans, are *not* religiously affiliated and this includes those who identify as atheists, agnostics, and many who describe their religion as "nothing in particular" (Pew Research Center, 2015). People who identify as unaffiliated, touched on earlier in the section on Trending Changes, are now called "the nones" and stand at about 23% of the adult population.

A PRACTICAL PHILOSOPHY OR PRACTICAL THEOLOGY

An anthropological or interpretive lens can be used to frame how religion—and spirituality where it, too, is endorsed—are applied to daily living. When talking with older adults and especially when conducting interviews with them, their view of life and living is often readily accessible. In my research I have learned that older people welcome such conversations, for in them they find a way to reinforce, but also understand and extend their thinking. They bring to their lifestyle greater consciousness as they speak of it. In clinical fields what is especially relevant is not only what their life view is, but also how well it functions for them. That may be known through the degree of life satisfaction, wellness, well-being, or happiness they espouse. When I spoke with older people about their life views, it became clear to me that what they revealed were their *practical philosophies* (Nelson-Becker, 2003). Practical philosophies was a term I developed out of Browning's (1991, 2007) idea of a practical theology. Practical philosophy was a more encompassing term that could also include under its umbrella those who were nonreligious and nonspiritual, though in my sample this was a small percentage.

Browning (1991) identified a four-part process of living faith/belief that may be interpreted as Faith with a capital *F* for a formal religious faith or faith with a small *f* for any faith or belief system that guides one's life. This process to uncover a way of living consistent with values begins with description, moves to history, to systematic theology, and finally to strategic practical theology; the latter is his term. Description should involve a thick description of practices embedded in life that includes one's pre-understandings that condition the choices one makes. Ultimately, what results is a critical correlational approach, or a middle way between historicity and normative traditions on the one hand and tradition-transcending approaches on the other. The central commonality of his process was developed in regard to theological reflection, but this holds merit for extra-theological reflection.

All that can be realized or thought about by a person at a given point in history and culture is widened when two people share their horizons of meaning. Thus when two people enter a dialogue, they form a *text* that results in a "fusion of horizons" that brings them both to a new place (Gadamer, 1999). People understand each other through their own lived experience and an imaginative reconstruction of the experience of the other. A horizon, in Gadamer's view, involves moving past the visible limit to see beyond it. "Working out of the hermeneutical situation means the achievement of the right horizon of inquiry for the questions evoked by the encounter" (Gadamer, 1997, p. 302). Two people in a therapeutic encounter form a hermeneutic circle. They are a text in themselves that is layered with the pre-understandings they each bring; what goes on in the circle is reinterpreted within the encounter and becomes new within and outside of it. This is the therapeutic encounter in psychology, counseling, social work, nursing, and pastoral care. People enter with their pre-understandings, which are the beliefs and biases they bring. When made conscious of those, they can be examined and/or altered. In the hermeneutic circle between practitioner and client, a text forms that is a new interpretation leading to new understanding and perhaps even a new way of life, a new practical philosophy—or practical theology for those more oriented toward religion.

SPIRITUAL ORIENTATION DISSIMILARITY BETWEEN CLIENT AND PRACTITIONER

The most frequent spiritual-religious situation is one where the practitioner will *not* match the client on spiritual or religious sensibility. This is not a situation to fear, but one to welcome. Lack of coherence in religious or spiritual views is one reason why creating a spiritually sensitive practice is beneficial. The principal precondition for the professional is having interest in hearing about spiritual and/or religious matters, intense and urgent or normative and woven into daily living routines. This type of shared space is often sacred space: intimate and revelatory through personal perception. Where difference exists, it offers great opportunity for increased learning in that space of not-knowing. What can happen is that people who share spiritual/religious interests may proceed with unexamined bias that conceals aspects that might be useful for both to know. Although it may not be necessary to the encounter to examine spiritual or religious beliefs in their full dimensions, this bias might preclude contemplation of the full range of solutions to a problem simply because these solutions are not seen.

How do we learn to speak about sacred sources of meaning with clients when we so often deny, defer, or delay reflection on our own inner journey? "The failure to integrate our sense of the spiritual with what emerges in daily life impedes progress to wholeness and keeps from our clients the best that we could offer" (Nelson-Becker, 2008, p. 13). We view our journeys as our own, completely separate from therapeutic space we share with clients. In fact, our journeys are influenced by all our connections to the outside world, our view of late life, our personal sense of purpose or life mission and vision, and unexpected events that arise. Work with clients can facilitate mutual growth.

Ongoing self-monitoring is essential whether a mental health practitioner is grounded in a faith tradition, a spiritual context, or neither. Self-observation reduces blind spots and biases, unconscious unresolved issues that could affect the direction of treatment, and any need for control or fear of working in ambiguous areas. The answers about what may be important to address aren't always immediately apparent but unfold in the relational context. "I think this is important to explore, but I don't know where this is going" is practitioner self-talk that may lead to collection of what later may be very useful client data. Client growth happens when the client is aware of positive contributions he or she is generating to make the relationship work for him or her. "If I am accepted here, then other will also accept the person I am." This may lead to an energizing affect, increased knowledge, and a broadened skill repertoire.

Individuals respond more openly when the person with whom they interact creates a zone of comfort. When an older adult is treated as a subject and author of his or her life, the relationship has the possibility of reaching authenticity. At times, older adults will throw up screens to distance others and keep their inner fears from being known. These screens can take the form of abusive language and obstinate, sometimes hurtful behavior. It may take courage on both sides of the professional-client relationship to learn how religion and spirituality may be valued, held in the background, ignored, disfavored, or despised. The reference point for the discussion will vary based on the relative positions of the professional and the client.

This dyadic relationship may prove the most challenging for a professional who is less religious or spiritual and who, in fact, may be completely unfamiliar with religious and spiritual traditions. One of the dangers is that if no assessment of religion or spirituality is routinely included in initial interactions, then the area may be neglected. As addressed in Chapter 1, this relative position is generally the most common: Mental health practitioners and other professionals are less religious than their clients (Hofmann & Walach, 2011; Sperry & Shafranske, 2005).

Three principal scenarios may unfold based on these positions: professional *less* religious/spiritual than client, professional and client *both* religious or spiritual or *both neither* religious or spiritual, or professional *more* religious/spiritual than client. Within each of these major positions lie countless variations, including a combination where the client and mental health practitioner are spiritual and/or religious, but in very different ways. Diversity may not feel comfortable, but it stretches and enriches our ideas, knowledge, and skills. The case detailed below provides one example of how a master's level student in a professional discipline worked with an older client around religion and spirituality. What follows is an excerpt from a very detailed paper that also includes the student's identification of her own orienting theories and her integration of discussions with pastoral care professionals, as well as thoughtful commentary on her own complicated spiritual journey.

Case of a Client Who Is Differently Religious Than a Professional

Ms. R is an 80-year-old widowed African American woman. Ms. R's story is full of heartbreak, tragedy, and loss. She was widowed 15 years ago after her husband suffered with cancer for years, a slow death that Ms. R stated was gut wrenching to watch. Following her husband's death, Ms. R devoted herself even more to steering her daughter and sons in the right direction. This *right path* was one that centered on living a godly life as she interpreted it. Tragedy struck again in 2009, when four female friends murdered one of Ms. R's three children. Less than two years after the murder of her daughter, Ms. R's youngest son was incarcerated after being found guilty of murder. Less than one year after that, Ms. R's remaining son was incarcerated for violating his house arrest. Ms. R's two remaining sons are still imprisoned, and she has continued contact with them via mail. The prison is too far away for her to easily visit. All of Ms. R's losses have challenged her belief in a God who is loving and just. She has not lost her faith, but she has difficulty assigning meaning to the losses that she has experienced. Ms. R identifies as nondenominational Christian and although she does not attend church services regularly, prayer and worship are a part of her daily routine.

Ms. R. grew up in a family that affiliated with the Southern Baptist denomination of Christianity. Ms. R's family attended church often and the ideas of prayer and worship were prominent throughout her upbringing. Her mother believed in the power of prayer and would often emphasize to the family their responsibility to pray for themselves and others. Ms. R continued to incorporate religion into her life although not necessarily with a focus on the Southern Baptists. Her beliefs evolved into a more general idea of a loving God as someone who is present and active in her life. "Despite all that I tried to do for my kids, the appeal of following God could never compete with the power and wealth my kids thought they were going to get out of gang life."

Ms. R is struggling with her idea of a loving God and how the events in her life reflect her place in God's plan. Despite her dedication to prayer, Ms. R reports feeling that the answers to her prayers often seem to be *No* more often than she believes her prayers are answered. Ms. R stated that even though her two sons strayed from the path that she wanted for them before their incarceration, their time in prison seems to have helped them refocus on what it means to be a good person in the eyes of God. Although each of her sons do not absolve themselves of their crimes, they understand a God who is forgiving and have embraced the chance to live a better life—even if this life has to be lived in prison.

My own struggles and experience may lend me insight in how to help Ms. R cope with hers. At the same time, it is important that I do not over identify with nor project my own feelings and issues onto Ms. R. It is a delicate balance between sharing experience and proselytizing, which some colleagues fear mention of religion may do implicitly. I think that this conflict can create a gray area, and may often be the reason why spiritually sensitive practice is not used more often. The situation becomes even more complicated in situations where the beliefs of a therapist differ significantly from the client. For example, it might be more difficult to relate and be spiritually sensitive to someone who is of significantly different religious background. This *is the very reason why there is a great need to incorporate spiritually sensitive work into practice* [emphasis added]. My spiritual framework is my commitment to serving Ms. R. Also, by helping Ms. R understand that all events have value in meaning, it is possible to help her reframe her current perspective on her own experiences so she can see the positive value that has come from them.

Spiritually sensitive work is dependent upon providing the client with a safe and open space to express her views in a nonjudgmental environment. Part of providing good spiritual care is to be aware of how my own beliefs may influence my interactions with Ms. R. It is important to remember not to over emphasize my own thoughts and instead to provide reflection for the things that Ms. R says in a way that may offer new perspectives that she had not previously seen. The way in which I achieve this is through the use of one-on-one therapy and creating an environment where Ms. R feels comfortable to share her story.

During my third meeting with Ms. R, she had stated that she could not find the scripture Psalms 23 in her Bible. Ms. R was convinced that the pages of the Bible were missing. Leveraging my knowledge of the scripture from my personal religious background, I asked her if she wanted me to assist her in finding the scripture. Ms. R took her Bible from the dais and stated that she would "really like that." When I found the scripture in her Bible, I pointed it out to her. Ms. R asked me if I minded reading it to her. Ms. R was most interested in Psalms 23:4, "Even though I walk through the darkest valley, I will fear no evil, for you are with me; your rod and your staff, they comfort me." Through the creation of a safe and open space for Ms. R to share her beliefs, she felt comfortable enough to ask me to help her. Pieces of my conceptual framework for spiritually sensitive practice may not always apply to each individual, but having a commitment to service and being open to creating a safe space for clients to explore their spiritual beliefs and the value they have, is of the upmost importance.

Historically, I have not viewed the Catholic religion in the most positive light due to my own feelings of discontent with the beliefs and practices I was exposed to being raised Catholic. I feel that my negative perspective could have an impact on how I serve those clients of mine who are Catholic. I would not treat them negatively, but I fear that I would be less likely to encourage them to open up about their spiritual beliefs. For my own development, I think it would be useful to take another look at the issues I had with Catholicism and try to reframe them in a way that allows me, if not to understand, at least to respect them. My own religious and spiritual journey has been one filled with ebbs and flows. . . . "Spiritually sensitive practice," to me, means not only incorporating spirituality into my work with older adults and giving it the respect that it is due, but also opening myself up to learning more about and valuing perspectives other than my own, whether they are other religious faiths, other forms of spirituality, or none at all. I have learned that the relationship needs to be built in order for clinically effective work to happen. To ignore religion and spirituality may be akin to ignoring the person and not providing the most complete care possible. It was important to me, and research shows, that studying spirituality is helpful in creating effective practice. One of the things that I have learned personally from my experiences

> with Ms. R throughout this course and my reflection is that the struggle to understand one's place in the world is universal.

Source: Catherine Stowers, MSW; used with permission.

The case above highlights a therapist and client who inhabit two kinds of spiritual spaces. Both have had life experiences that led them to questions about their religious faith, but they have reached different accommodations concerning their spiritual and religious views. The therapist's view is privately held, not shared with the client, but was related to me as a course instructor. Of the three different stances listed above, they share the category of both religious and spiritual. However, as can be noted from this example, there is a substantial spectrum within this category. After reading the case above, a student or professional might ask herself or himself the following questions to prepare for an initial meeting with a client.

QUESTIONS FOR SELF REFLECTION PRE- AND POST-INITIAL CLIENT SESSION

PRE-SESSION

1. How do I plan to engage and address spirituality and/or religion with my client?

2. What is my position regarding spirituality and religion? How might this be visible as I talk with this client?

3. What is my comfort level around spirituality and religion? Why?

POST-SESSION

4. In what way did my client assess the value of spirituality or religion? What else related to these areas emerged, if anything?

5. In what ways is this client's spiritual or religious view a struggle or a strength?

6. What did I learn from this session that will help me work with spiritual and religious issues in the future?

Holding a stance of curiosity about our own lives as well as the lives of our clients can open up new kinds of healing space. We stay connected, but notice and then liberate assumptions. We participate in the interaction, but de-center (divest ego) from it. When we can appreciate paradox and ambiguity in ourselves, we can also learn to appreciate them in clients. Integrating our own spiritual journey in our practice in a conscious way, even if we do it only by holding it in awareness, can help us understand wholeness in ways that will benefit our clients and everyone with whom we interact.

WORKING WITH SPIRITUAL
UNEASE AND DISTRESS IN DISASTERS

Suffering can emerge at many points in a life space. It can transpire from individual or family issues that arise, some of which may be connected with a change in health status and some of which may have more voluntary aspects, resulting from such issues as alcohol and drug addiction, for example. Separate from individual and family-level calamities are emergent issues that occur in times of disaster. Disasters pose a unique challenge for mental health practitioners because it invites them to respond to needs beyond what they have imagined and beyond what they feel prepared to do.

Disasters, when they occur, are usually medium to large scale and involve harm to many people. They are caused by ecological imbalance, technological accidents, lack of foresight and care such as occurred in Flint, Michigan water supplies, or economic collapse, among others. At times they are random and premeditated out of violent desires. Sometimes they also occur because of the greed of a few people. They result in injury or loss of great magnitude. Disasters share the following characteristics: (1) little forewarning, (2) quick occurrence, (3) large impact, (4) a geographical scope, and (5) an impact that endures (FEMA Emergency Management Institute, n.d.). Disasters also are marked by the need for outside intervention. People are vulnerable for reasons about which little can be done, such as the topographical places where cities have been built and travel that increases epidemiological health risk.

These tragedies are accompanied by a reaction of surprise, shock, and horror by those they directly impact; others who have tenuous links through family or friends, or those who only hear of the event still shudder with that news. They affect so many people that community service agencies and mental health community responses are greatly strained or completely overwhelmed (Nelson-Becker, Chapin, & Fast, 2013). Older adults may be drawn into these maelstroms through families they love or the places they reside. An additional concern that puts older adults at risk is that they find it more difficult to flee places in the path of danger. For instance, in 2014, there was a disastrous nursing care facility fire in L'Isle-Verte, Quebec that left 32 older people dead. Many people perished when they were unable to leave. On other occasions, older people find it emotionally difficult to disengage when they must leave for their safety.

Common Spiritual Concerns in Times of Duress

At these junctures, a number of spiritual and religious questions emerge for older people and sometimes for those who serve them as well. The spiritual questions and emotional forces that older people can experience include the following:

- wondering why I was saved when my . . . (friends, family) were not

- asking questions like *Why did God do this? Am I being punished*

- questioning justice, meaning, and purpose of life

- feeling estranged from previously held beliefs

- feeling abandoned by previous ideology that no longer offers comfort

- reconsidering core tenets of religious beliefs

- feeling a need to be cleansed or purified

- closing oneself off from loved ones *who will not understand*

- feeling despair and hopelessness, not knowing where to turn

- feeling guilt, or in some cases, shame

- feeling anxiety about the future of generations to follow

- wondering about life and death. (adapted from National Voluntary Organizations Active in Disaster, 2013, p. 6)

Although the first impulse many trained mental health professional might have would be to refer to a spiritual care professional or faith community leader, the latter two groups may be unavailable and find themselves also overwhelmed by the numbers of people requiring assistance and the depth of the immediate need. Older adults caught up in a disaster will be less likely to advocate for their needs to be met. They should be sought out and offered professional attention. It may be that, based on their prior life experiences, they will be fine and can be co-providers of help. In any community lie natural helpers with inherent resilience who are as likely to be older as younger. If they offer their help, find something for them to do to assist and the entire community will be better for their contribution.

How Can Mental Health Practitioners
Respond to Immediate Distress?

As addressed in previous chapters, it is critical to *provide a listening space* after addressing basic needs of food, clothing, or shelter. In fact a several-tiered community response could have immediate responders looking after basic material needs while mental health responders might circulate in a shelter to offer consolation. Consolation is not so much given by words of advice or counsel, but through helping people know and reach their fulcrum or point of stability in the immediate aftermath and in their doubt: their still point. Disaster survivors need to regain confidence in themselves, if they have lost it, and in the larger world. Questioning should not be foreclosed, but elaboration should also not be encouraged as people seek to regain balance/equipoise. Too large an aperture at this time can send people who are trying to regain balance into disequilibrium and disquietude. Later, they may desire to address some of their deeper questions. For now, there is no theory or practice so powerful as presence:

- being there

- respecting, honoring, and working with difference
  (e.g., in disability, faith beliefs, ethnic or racial variation)

- normalizing the need to seek help (especially important
  with older adults)

- watching, assessing for, and responding to dangerous reactions,
  e.g., suicidal thoughts

- reconnecting survivors to their natural networks or helping them
  form new temporary ones

- providing permission for and facilitation of spontaneous rituals,
  both those that may be spiritual and those embedded in a
  particular faith tradition

- supporting expressions of hope

- understanding that you may experience the unexpected; being ready for it

- recognizing your limits and paying attention to boundaries, but also distinguishing when it may be ok to loosen certain aspects of your typical professional demeanor, through use of touch—for example, a quick hug

- offering whatever you have to offer

- knowing in the end, it will be enough

- taking care of your own distress afterward, so you can be available a second day, and a third

- talking to professional peers about your experiences during and afterward

- keeping your focus on the need at hand

- releasing worry about your plans at home or at your office if you are a volunteer

- finding a moment to meditate or breathe meditatively at the end of your day

- reflecting and perhaps journaling about your immediate experience

- sharing your insights with others when you return, perhaps in a university class in your field

- finding yourself more generous, with greater understanding of your capacity for generosity

This experience for you, the mental health practitioner, will be about giving back what you are uniquely able to give and growing through the experience. There will likely be both benefit and discouragement as you thread your way through the remains of people's spiritual lives, seeking to repair the fabric of their essential selves. It is nothing, if not important work.

EVALUATION

Spirituality and religion often give access to information beyond ordinary sensory perception. Some practitioners might assume that because of this, they lie outside need for evaluation. However, as with other kinds of work completed by mental health practitioners and other professionals, clinical work with spirituality and religion do lie within the scope of necessary evaluation. In fact, because it could be possible for professionals to justify treatment that is not grounded in an evidentiary base and also do harm, it is *even more* important for evaluation to occur in practice addressing religious and spiritual issues. Evaluation follows engagement, assessment, and intervention and forms a key aspect of spiritually sensitive clinical work (Dudley, 2016). Evaluations may suggest areas of need for training and education for the particular discipline related to competency goals, evidence and support for inclusion of spirituality and religion in assessment and intervention in general, and whether specific approaches are effective for particular clients. Evaluation can also protect client safety.

Although many agree that there should be some form of evaluation or accountability in addressing spiritual and religious components of care, there is broad variability in how this might be achieved. Puchalski and Ferrell (2010) include a chapter on quality improvement (QI) in their book about integrating spirituality into patient care. When I worked on the project to improve spiritual care in palliative care (Puchalski et al., 2009), the workgroup to which I was assigned was the quality improvement workgroup. An insightful discussion ensued about the gap between the merit of accountability and difficulties in such measurement. Traditionally, QI looks for common standards of care that can be accepted across specific locations of care.

Quality Improvement in Health Care

Health care systems are included in this evaluation section because so many older people interface with health care. How religion and spirituality fit into the larger system and the role of their evaluation have been less visible. Development of the Donabedian conceptual framework resulted in improved patient outcomes through attention to both structures and processes of care (Marjoua & Bozic, 2012). Utilization Review committees were established by Medicare/Medicaid in the 1960s to ensure institutions delivered appropriate care and met their Conditions of Participation (Luce, Bindma, & Lee, 1994). Achieving limited success, these were superseded by Medicare's Professional Standards Review Organizations (PSROs) in 1972 to assess overuse, underuse and inappropriate use of services. Viewed as unsuccessful in improving quality and managing costs, and largely resisted by the American Medical Association, which found them intrusive, these were replaced by utilization and quality control Peer Review Organizations (PROs) in 1982. Their success was ensured when, beyond simply identifying problems, these groups were given authority to resolve them by implementing such practices as retrospective reviews, continued medical education requirements, disciplinary action, and loss of Medicare billing privileges.

The value of randomized clinical trials (RCTs) became clear as evidence for use of certain treatment protocols over others began to accrue (Chassin & Loeb, 2011; Marjoua & Bozic, 2012). These were used to develop recommendations, now known as clinical practice guidelines, for more effective clinical care in health. However, gradual understanding developed that different patients had differing risk factors and not everyone responded equally well to these guidelines. The Institute of Medicine (IOM) in 2001 reported that some patients were receiving inconsistent care that placed them at risk. Problems were recast as a patient safety issue. The National Quality Forum, a private nonprofit agency organized in 1999, was tasked with assessing both patient safety and health care quality. Ongoing problems have led Chassin and Loeb (2012) to call for a *collective mindfulness* to promote safety and for organizations to become high reliability organizations that eliminate medical errors. Financial incentives through reimbursement based on health care quality determinations and achievement as well as responsible leadership seem poised to promote ongoing improvement and adjustment to a changing knowledge base (Marjoua & Bozic, 2012).

System-level feedback has been incorporated in health care, but issues such as policy requirements, financial incentives/disincentives, and other regulation have only partially met treatment effectiveness goals. In the United States, The Joint Commission (2003) has mandated that spiritual values receive attention. Patients should have access to pastoral and other spiritual services, and religion/spirituality should be included in assessment, but there has been little guidance on how this standard can or should be met. What this means in practice is that due to variability in practitioner comfort with religion and/or spirituality, this domain is addressed to varying degrees regardless of the level of attention preferred by particular patients.

Quality Improvement in Spiritual and Religious Care

Establishing of quality improvement practices in spirituality and religion is challenging. Quantifying and measuring improvement in such areas as existential suffering, constructing greater meaning in life, increasing hope, and decreasing spiritual distress levels remains imprecise. Quantitatively, care that is given can be documented, but improvement is not necessarily amenable to actions by a care provider or mental health professional alone. Referrals can be provided and discussions around spiritual or religious issues mentioned in case notes within standards of confidentiality. Qualitatively, reflections by mental health practitioners may be documented and research interviews may be conducted around spiritual and religious issues on completion of standard research protocols and compliance with ethical measures through institutional review boards (IRBs).

What models exist for this kind of quality assessment? The Catholic Health Association of Canada (CHAC) and the Canadian Association for Pastoral Practice and Education (CAPPE) produced a booklet in 2000, *Standards of Spiritual and Religious Care for Health Services in Canada*, that suggest accountability and evaluation standards measurable both quantitatively and qualitatively:

- The service is involved in continuous quality improvement activities in the organization.

- Processes for monitoring and improving the quality and quantity of spiritual and religious care and services are developed and implemented by the Service in consultation with the Advisory Council, health care team(s) and care recipients.

- In the evaluation of spiritual and religious care services, priorities are identified considering the needs and expectations of the care recipients, and the current effectiveness of the service.

- Activities are undertaken to improve the identified priorities.

- Service staff is evaluated annually.

- Organizations offering Supervised Pastoral Education (SPE) maintain their accreditation with the Canadian Association for Pastoral Practice and Education (CAPPE).

- Spiritual and Religious Care Service meetings are held on a regular basis.

- Minutes of the Service staff meetings are reported, filed, and made available to administration.

- Meetings of the Spiritual and Religious Care Service Advisory Council are held at least quarterly.

- The Service functions within budgetary directives.

- The Service staff document their assessments, plans, interventions, and outcomes in the record of the care-recipient according to the established guidelines of the organization.

- The Service maintains a workload measurement system that records its activities.

- There are position descriptions for all staff.

- Scheduling of staff hours is consistent with care recipient and staff need.

Although most of these suggested standards are not controversial, they also seem to reflect general management practice and do not address many of the unique areas of evaluation that correspond to spiritual and religious domains.

A second model for assessing spiritual care is provided in a well-developed protocol for assessing spiritual care standards titled *Standards for Spiritual Care Services in the NHS in Wales 2010* (NHS Wales, 2010). This document addresses seven standards of spiritual and religious care. An opportunity for a self-audit is encouraged by asking such questions as, "How do you ensure that patients have had the opportunity for their spiritual and religious needs to be assessed and addressed? (Describe the process and how audited)." Outcomes sought include patient satisfaction with the service provided, but also the higher standard of a positive change in life quality where possible. As suggested in the original Donabedian framework of care for hospitals, standards in the models here also cover structures and processes for religious and spiritual care.

Chaplaincy and social work related to spirituality and religion have struggled to find their position as equal partners in the medical system, but they have both lent their voices to call for attending to evidence-based and research-informed work in the area of religion and spirituality (Moberg, 2005; Mowat, 2008; Nelson-Becker & Canda, 2009). The importance of testing the efficacy of practice has been emphasized by chaplains as well as not over-inflating evidence that should accrue to the work of the interprofessional team (Jankowski, Handzo, & Flannelly, 2011).

Feedback-Informed Practice

Aside from assessing spiritual and religious-related clinical work in large systems, especially medical systems detailed above, it is equally important to assess the effects of spiritual and religious engagement in agency or private clinical practice. This kind of feedback is relatively easy to obtain and is accomplished simply through inviting a client to share his or her experience of the helpfulness of the session or series of sessions. Why do some mental health practitioners seem to be more effective than others? Variability in outcomes between therapists equaled or exceeded the contribution of factors known to exercise a significant effect on the therapeutic success (Wampold & Brown, 2006). Quality of the therapeutic alliance accounted for 5% to 8% of difference, allegiance to the treatment approach accounted for 3% to 4%, and selection of the treatment model or method accounted for less than 1% of effects (Wampold & Brown, 2006). Some therapists were more effective than others because they made themselves vulnerable by asking about perceptions of what occurred during the session and what could be done better or differently.

Duncan et al. (2004) present a contextual model of change that suggests practitioners ensure sessions are: client-directed (fit), outcome-informed (effect), maintain emphasis on benefit over need (likely reflecting a penchant for solution-focused approaches), and lastly restore *real-life* functioning. This process helps practitioners fail successfully (Duncan et al., 2010). How does this happen? Practitioners first ask for feedback at the end of the session, and second they *incorporate the results of the feedback* into the next and following sessions. An example of simple feedback tools is provided by Scott Miller through his Outcome Rating Scale (ORS) and Session Rating Scale (SRS) available at http://www.scottdmiller.com/about-scott/.

Feedback can be obtained successfully about any kind of intervention or helping activity. Creating a single item global assessment scale anchored with 1 and 10 for any dimension including addressing a spiritual or religious problem can also work well. The value of welcoming feedback in this form is that it improves the therapeutic alliance. The therapeutic alliance has been shown to be an important factor in motivating clients to keep invested in their work when it is so easy for them to drop out of treatment. Clinicians are not particularly adept at identifying clients likely to drop out of care; or clients who deteriorate while in care (Duncan et al., 2010). Routinely seeking client feedback builds a bond with them. Reaching for feedback also provides clients with an opportunity to identify whether treatment has moved into an area of deep discomfort to them and they prefer the mental health practitioner to withdraw. Even if both agree this might be necessary work, it must be addressed through mutual agreement. The timing must fit the client's pace or he or she will be unable to fully engage and may leave prematurely before the work is done. Because of the intimacy of the topic, this can be a more likely risk with inclusion of religion and spirituality in the therapeutic work.

INTERPROFESSIONAL PRACTICE AND SPIRITUALITY

Much of the current thought on interprofessional practice comes out of the health literature and is not confined to work with older adults. It is in the health professions where the value of solving the complex needs requiring interdisciplinary expertise has come to the foreground. The health professions are also likely to include chaplains embedded in health care delivery models. However, it is equally important to note that the skill of interprofessional practice can be applied beyond health and mental health care. Interprofessionality has been defined as follows:

> The process by which professionals reflect on and develop ways of practicing that provides an integrated and cohesive answer to the needs of the client/ family/population . . . [I]t involves continuous interaction and knowledge sharing between professionals, organized to solve or explore a variety of education and care issues all while seeking to optimize the patient's participation . . . Interprofessionality requires a paradigm shift, since interprofessional practice has unique characteristics in terms of values, codes of conduct, and ways of working. (D'Amour & Oandasan, 2005, p. 9)

Interprofessional practice involves clear communication leading to well-articulated decisions. Especially in the area of spiritually sensitive practice, it involves some measure of self and team reflection. Synergistic professional collaboration should lead to a more thorough review of options and more comprehensive care. Mutual trust and respect within teams form an important foundation (Sangster, 2016).

Interprofessional teamwork is a further iteration that assumes professionals will work at least at some point on versatile, dynamic teams that adjust composition to meet client needs. Teamwork has been described as "the levels of cooperation, coordination and collaboration characterizing the relationships between professions in delivering patient-centered [or other client] care" (Interprofessional Education Collaborative Expert Panel, 2011, p. 2). There is recognition that the *process* of providing client care is as important as *what care* is provided. Interprofessional competencies include *complementary competencies*, which enhance what other professions may provide, *collaborative competencies*, which include skills professionals need to effectively interact in providing care, and *common overlapping competencies* (Barr, Koppel, Reeves, Hammick, & Freeth, 2005). Some competencies also exist that are unique to the profession and form their resident domain(s) of expertise.

The professional practice disciplines have rightly been accused of inhabiting *silos* of practice that fail to incorporate research findings and knowledge developed outside their own discipline. Certain settings of practice are better oriented to interprofessional and transdisciplinary work, particularly health care settings such as palliative care and hospice teams that characteristically function with interdisciplinary members. Operating in an interprofessional setting does not necessarily mean that these professionals know how to do this well. There has been great variability in perceptions of how well teams function; this is often dependent on how willing the team leader is to share authority in areas of shared knowledge and skill.

Advantages of interprofessional collaboration include shared expertise and greater ability to be responsive to multiple needs. When the case load is high, sometimes team members can fill gaps for each other. A clear and common goal can keep these professionals invested in their work. Typically they collaborate to solve problems and to deliver consistent care, often in the health or mental health sectors. Tenure with the team and in the field can affect both confidence and practice knowledge. One palliative care team I know operated on an authoritarian and hierarchal model that kept replacing interdisciplinary team members successively until a new physician finally curtailed the depletion by encouraging greater appreciation of interprofessional assets. Ideally, teams will develop a common identity through their shared work. Creating a *culture of collaboration* is the ideal approach to fostering interdisciplinary practice for spiritual care. This approach, whether done implicitly or explicitly, acknowledges both professional and personal strengths and limits in care provision.

Interprofessional practice begins with education, either on entry into the discipline at beginning or advanced levels or later through continuing education models. The Institute of Medicine (IoM) has called for mixed methods research on interprofessional education (IPE) and a best practices approach that includes educators, economists, and health services researchers (IoM, 2015). There is a beginning but growing research in this area (Sangster, 2016). One recent initiative brought medical, chaplaincy, and social work students together in a workshop format to teach spiritual assessment (Lennon-Dearing, Florence, Halvorson, & Pollard, 2012). No pretest was given, but 50 posttest evaluations showed high understanding and respect for separate roles and communication among clergy, social workers, and physicians. Understanding how to apply knowledge of a patient's spiritual and cultural beliefs was rated lowest among nine objectives.

Much practice-based learning in spiritual care provision is more likely to be informal rather than formal and it is probable that such informal learning experiences are not maximized for reflection and integration. The IoM (2014) report suggests a learning continuum model that recognizes enabling and interfering factors expressed in professional and institutional cultures. Learning outcomes should lead to collaborative behavior supported by attitudes, knowledge, and skills (p. 29). Discussion and recommendations on how to best integrate palliative care across a spectrum of medical care, including working with international contexts that may approach spirituality and religion with very different cultural lenses, are continuing areas of focus (Nelson-Becker & Sullivan, 2012; Puchalski, Vitillo, Hull, & Reller, 2014).

Chaplains should be recognized as spiritual care specialists and their guidance should be sought for interprofessional work in gerontological and geriatric practice. However, because of availability, practice needs, and personal affinity, there are times when other mental health practitioners from separate disciplines must conduct spiritual triage, spiritual assessment, or ongoing spiritual care provision within bounds of their discipline. Because interprofessional practice adds layers of complexity, there is an ongoing need to develop new models in this area, especially for interprofessional practice with older adults that may occur outside of standard medical settings. Further research is needed on what factors contribute to excellent outcomes by interprofessional teams.

SELF-CARE AND MINDFULNESS: SPIRITUAL AWARENESS

The concept of the wounded healer comes largely through the writings of Carl Jung. In mythology, Chiron was said to be the greatest of the centaurs. He was revered as a teacher and tutor and was known as a healer and an oracle. Poisoned by an arrow, the healer could not heal himself, but he willingly gave up his immortality so Prometheus might live and be healed. Jung (1947) wrote that it is his "own hurt that gives the therapist power to heal" (p. 181). The therapist, through awareness of his or her own vulnerabilities and losses, possesses the power to assist in restoration, cure, and/or growth. Mindfulness fosters the ability to turn vulnerabilities into strengths.

Although mindfulness meditation has been practiced for centuries in Eastern traditions and philosophies, it has often been separated from spiritual connections and repurposed for secular situations. Herbert Benson (1975) contributed to this movement with his relaxation response. Jon Kabat-Zinn (2004) developed mindfulness-based stress reduction (MBSR) at Massachusetts Institute for Technology. Even though he had studied Buddhism, he removed the Buddhist framework for his structured teaching. He taught the value of attention to the breath, body scan techniques to search for stress, sitting meditation, walking meditation, yoga, responding rather than reacting to stress, and working with physical and emotional pain. Overall, this method upheld the value of disciplined attention and practice through which one could better attend to the moment, the self, and others. This powerful set of practices, whether disengaged from spirituality or engaged with it, is no less useful for both older people and the professionals who work with them.

Mindfulness is an approach to life and to professional practice that invites practitioners and their clients to pause and refocus. Intractable problems and cognitions about them are not evaluated, but instead accepted. Under the condition of acceptance and nonjudgment, problems can be approached instead of avoided. There is room for novel nonalgorithmic appraisals rather than routines that categorize and limit thinking. Mindfulness has many parallels with the spiritual path, which often presents novel and unexpected opportunities and challenges. Spiritual awareness invites people to consider the larger purposes their lives may serve. Instead of feeling or being stuck in jobs that are no longer meaningful, relationships that are no longer supportive, or community affiliations that are life wresting rather than life enhancing, people can change their way of thinking, acting, or being, which then can change how others respond to them. Sometimes moving away from the situation entirely is required, but at other times a subtle shift in appraisal can change cognition, feeling, and subsequent activities. The term *mindfulness* has transmitted into English largely through Buddhism. Sharf (2014) explains that as understood in English, this has resulted in reduction of the richness of the concept. It derives from the Pali term *sati*, which means "skillful" or "bare attentiveness." Sati also means "to remember." This is a particularly salient word in aging.

Langer and Mindfulness

There are five components of mindfulness in Langer's (1997) definition: (1) openness to novelty; (2) alertness to distinction; (3) sensitivity to contextual difference; (4) implicit, if not explicit, awareness of multiple perspectives; and (5) a present-centered orientation. Being present sounds simple, but often proves arduous. It is a lifelong skill that is now being taught in many sectors of society, from youth in school systems to yoga sessions for older adults. The concept behind the practice is that it is only in the present moment that one can learn and create positive change through fluidity and acceptance as well as choosing what has personal and ultimate value.

What have we learned about mindful approaches? Langer's (1989) 18-month study of nursing care facility residents showed positive emotional and health benefits in those who were given plants to care for over a control group. When older people were offered the perception of control, their lives were enhanced. Older adults thrived who had plants for which they made decisions. *Mindfulness* invites one to be alert, attentive, present as fully as possible, and undistracted. Multiple perspectives are sought. In mindfulness one cultivates openness and releases any judgement or attempt to categorize experience. *Mindlessness*, its opposite, emerged from premature cognitive commitment or already knowing and so foreclosing opportunities to learn.

Models of mindfulness. Several models of mindfulness are relevant to professional practice. Bishop et al. (2004) describe a two-component model. The first component consists of *attentional aspects:* (1) self-regulation, such as the ability to sustain attentional focus; (2) capacity to switch attention at will to different objects; and (3) capacity to delay or constrain complex thought processing. The second component Bishop calls *orientation of experience*. This involves developing an attitude of investigation, curiosity, and acceptance of or engagement with what is being experienced in the moment. Further, this process allows one to decenter cognition and affect in favor of recognition of their impermanence. Impermanence mirrors the aging process itself as older adults often experience changes in health and housing status, even friendships when friends move away or die.

A second, but similar, model is posited by Shapiro, Carlson, Astin, and Freedman (2006) who identify "intention, attention, and attitude" as principal components. The added focus of intention suggests the purpose behind mindfulness practice. Attitude is specifically defined as acceptance, openness, and kindness along with other attitudes that tilt toward positivity. Shapiro et al. (2006) suggest that in this process the thinker no longer identifies with his or her thoughts as subject but becomes the object of his or her experience. This process of *reperceiving* leads to greater clarity and detachment. Further sequelae of these three components are (1) stability of internal functions and adaptability within a self-regulating process; (2) values clarification that reaches for authenticity; (3) cognitive, emotional, and behavioral flexibility; and (4) exposure, defined as witnessing present moment events. The latter process can result in greater ability to separate from the experience and be an observer. Mindfulness is not the same as meditation practice. Instead, mindfulness is a way of being in the world that demonstrates receptivity and equipoise (Cashwell & Young, 2011; Germer, Siegel, & Fulton, 2013). Meditation is one of many techniques or tools that results in mindful awareness.

Metacognition is the process of thinking about one's thinking patterns, thus opening them to view and thus making them potentially alterable. Cognition and affect in mindfulness practice are thus transient rather than permanent parts of the self. *Cognitive diffusion* refers to the ability to change the sensitivity, frequency, or type of thought that emerges, thus increasing overall adaptability and conscious choice over automatic reactions (Hayes, 2003).

Aging and Mindful Emotional Work

There can be great growth in aging, but acknowledging loss—naming and validating it—is one supportive task toward healing from those losses apparent in the aging experience. Attachment to anything we have loved facilitates healthy relationships, but balance is needed for being able to let go when the person leaves or the object disappears. This includes termination with clients with whom we have had deep experiences of helping and become invested through observing their growth. Grief can be enfolded in the joy of their success. Grief also can appear with all of the good-byes we haven't been able to give.

How is it possible to release attachments? This can occur through tending to emotions. As in the Kubler-Ross-identified stages of grief in the death experience, anger masks resistance to pain. Sorrow enables one to touch pain of loss in past events, experience that feeling, give it recognition, and then allow it fade. Meditation can unlock grief that we have kept at bay from fear; that form of grief often needs to be touched to be released. Acceptance as a product of mindfulness meditation can minimize fear. Grief, then, can be released in cathartic work, commencing and continuing healing in oneself and increasing one's availability to others.

CONTEMPLATIVE PRACTICES FOR RENEWAL

Mental health practitioners who work intensively with others also require attention to their own renewal. There are many active practices that can be incorporated as part of one's lifestyle or used intermittently. The goal of the Contemplative Mind in Society (www.contemplativemind.org) is to "create active learning and research environments to make education integrative, transformative, and communal" (see Figure 12.1). They suggest using this model as an opportunity to try out a practice for which one has an affinity. Practitioners can select one practice or try many. Keeping a journal of reflections, thoughts, and experiences while testing out a practice can help one enter into it more deeply. Joining a community of practitioners of a particular exercise will help foster the chosen exercise as a habit. It is often through repetition that one is able to reap the strongest benefit. The contemplative arts are listed in Figure 12.1 as one category on the tree. Any creative practice, such as playing an instrument; painting, drawing, or coloring with colored pencils; crafting; woodworking; or dancing gives expression to our sacred center.

SELF-COMPASSION

Some people are naturally drawn into the helping professions of nursing, social work, counseling, psychology and pastoral care. They are skilled at developing interpersonal connections and their focus is on service and helping people who suffer find their own healing. Often their clients are deeply in need of restoration and a new vision. Those in the mental health professions are also at risk to overgive or perhaps have not learned how to draw boundaries in a healthy way. In their desire to connect and assist, they give more of themselves away or do so at a greater pace than they can replenish energetically. They remain on the sidelines at parties or use their time to counsel friends rather than restore themselves. They pray for others, but do not include themselves in the prayer. Or, it can be that over years of clinical work, they have been vicariously traumatized by the suffering of their clients and so are on the verge of

Figure 12.1   Tree of Contemplative Practices

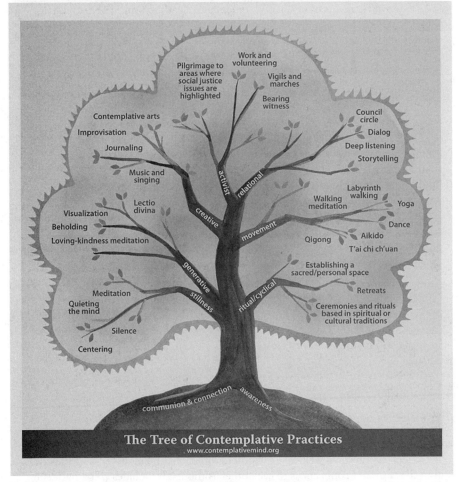

The Tree of Contemplative Practices
. www.contemplativemind.org

Source: © The Center for Contemplative Mind in Society. Concept & design by Maia Duerr; illustration by Carrie Bergman.

burnout or compassion fatigue. These professionals lie closer to an empathic expression rather than a compassionate ideal.

Self-compassion reduces the ego of the self and privileges love toward oneself. The person who practices self-compassion is at peace within himself or herself. The capacity for deep self-love includes forbearance of foibles and makes it possible to extend this love outward to enfold others. This is not about egoism, but humility. It is difficult to give away what one does not own. Loving self, however, lifts the spirit—and renews it. This kind of love increases capacity.

A simple way to remember and practice self-care is to place your hand on your heart and intentionally send yourself healing thoughts or your own healing energy. When I use this with classes, I remind students that it is a practice for both learning and teaching, one they can in turn teach clients. Other benefits are that it is simple, can be done quickly as a reminder anywhere and anytime, and if privacy is not possible, can still be performed in a casual manner that can conceal the intent. The only challenge might be to recall it. Like anything in the spiritual way, it can be used as a discipline or spiritual practice. I invite students to (1) take a moment and clear their mind of distracting thoughts and take a few deep breaths in and out; (2) touch their hand to their heart, resting it lightly there; (3) practice sending compassion to themselves for the work that they do and the way they engage in the lives of others; and (4) with repetition, they can also listen for any response, intuition, or insight that returns to them.

The nursing literature (Delaney, Barrere, & Helming, 2011; Jelonek, 2008) specifies a similar approach using an imaginal process tagged as the heart touch technique (HTT). As described in this literature, there is a strong God-centered component that would be useful with Christian, Jewish, or Muslim clients. First, participants were directed to center with a breath, imagine a circle of light in the forehead moving to the heart and expanding, and then recall a time when they felt loved or loving (Jelonek, 2008). Second, they were to send love heart-to-heart to an individual of their choice and third, they were asked to create a three-way connection with their higher power, God, or sacred source, all through imagination. A small evaluative study of volunteer nurses taught this technique cited that they reported it was a reminder to be aware, to focus, and was viewed as a means of feeling nurtured by God (Jelonek, 2008).

A study of patients with cardiovascular disease compared HTT with two other spiritual techniques: mindfulness meditation and prayer or reflection on nature (Delaney et al., 2011). Participants were placed in eight categories of different combinations of these three interventions to assess any difference in quality of life measures, depression, and anxiety. The numbers in each category (mostly single digits) were too small to evaluate much difference quantitatively, in my view, though there was very modest overall improvement. Qualitative data did suggest utility of the interventions. Study participants were predominantly Catholic.

In therapeutic practice with older people, it is important for practitioners to bear witness to suffering and hold hope for those who suffer. Compassion, the love and affection we are able to nourish and give, is of central importance in both our relations with others and our own well-being. Compassion opens an emotional door that diminishes fear and connects us to each other. Although it includes empathy, feeling for and with others, it also seeks relief of the pain others experience. Self-compassion permits us to pursue our own interests, while considering the effect of our behavior, inventions, and creative processes on others. It also serves as a way of creating sanctuary in the face of difficult environments.

A PERSONAL NOTE ON THE CHALLENGE OF SPIRITUAL INTEGRATION

I have long struggled with how to integrate what I know about spirituality and the spiritual path with academic or disciplinary work. If you consider yourself a novice in the spiritual world, wide-eyed and receptive to new kinds of information, that is a magnificent place to be. If you consider yourself a questioner and interrogator of life, believing that what we see before us in the world is all that there is, but wondering if there is more, that is good, too. If you are a bit further on the path, far enough along to be sometimes mired in the mud or caught in the thickets, that is when you know that growth may be ahead.

Is there anything in darkness? The answer in the objective world is, perhaps surprisingly, *yes*. It seems that 96% of the universe is made of dark matter and dark energy (Fermilab, 2014). What does dark matter and dark energy consist of? No one knows, yet there is evidence of it everywhere. Galaxies should be flying apart, yet something holds the stars in their orbits circling at about the same speed. The universe should either be moving at a constant rate or slowing down over time, but instead it is accelerating. (Nothing to worry about here, we won't fly off.) Its properties, though not observable, are inferred from gravitational effects. Evidence of dark energy was discovered in 1998 by researchers at Fermilab through the Sloan Digital Sky Survey (SDSS).

The metaphor here is clear. Darkness is not necessarily absence but presence. At the time we enter darkness, the way forward is unclear. Our thoughts center on all that the darkness may hold that scares us. However, there is a side or dimension over there, beyond the horizon, beyond the darkness, on which we can depend. Someday, looking back, the way through the darkness may become visible to our then-gaze. Or not. Perhaps it won't matter much because we will be so far beyond it. Yet, we will still hold it in our history, our story. There are parts of our stories we can forge, and parts that unfold totally beyond any dream, hope, our expectation we ever held. The spiritual path may be muddy and dark, but in the darkness perhaps lies a type of light beyond what we now know: dark energy—with its own category of beauty.

In 2004, I wrote a piece for a special issue of the *Reflections* journal that sought to integrate several disparate parts of myself. The special issue was titled "The Making of a Gerontologist," and it was edited by Molly Ranney. In that article, I wrote about how gerontology had chosen me before I chose it, through relationships I had formed with elder relatives and friends (Nelson-Becker, 2004c). "Later I came to fully recognize my place in the aging studies field, I began to understand how this vocation had always called to my soul and how the digressions from this path had only made the way more clear" (p. 14). However, much of my spiritual and religious side I still kept hidden from view, particularly the role that I carry in the local expression of my faith community where I serve as minister along with others. Ed Canda, who is my friend and mentor, wrote a bit about me and highlighted this aspect in the introduction to his text on spiritual diversity (Canda & Furman, 2010). In what I have kept dark or poorly integrated and in the light—what others may know about me—there have been many growth points.

When I attended The University of Chicago for my doctorate, intent on asking and learning about the religious and spiritual lives of older persons, I did find a way forward there. However, I was told by my dissertation chair and others that I should expect my work would always be marginalized, certainly not at the center of my profession of social work nor others. Several years later, when I served as a professor at the University of Kansas, I received an alumni letter from The University of Chicago. This was a relatively common strategic tool at the time, but this one was different. I was stunned to read that the university saw value in it and wanted to develop a plan to "build the spiritual infrastructure" of the university. At that point, I wondered if interest in spirituality was going mainstream. Perhaps it slowly has. It also faces rigorous review, as it should. What is particularly of note is that across time, it continues to fire the imaginations of countless seekers and sojourners. Something endures over generations.

I have found much support for spirituality and religion across the disciplines in gerontology. Increasingly, spirituality and/or religion are being added to many studies as investigatory variables. Still, these domains do hold a different place in the world of social science and social and psychological science practice. Because spirituality can veer off into the irrelevant and well as the irreverent, there are risks to building a career on this work alone. However, I have always returned to what older adults themselves have to say on the matter, and have found it a rich trove of concepts, practices, and signs of their resilience.

Today, I teach my courses with an implicit spirituality. I may not speak of spirituality except in the one course session in which spiritual assessment and intervention is explicit, but it is present with me as perennial approach to inquiry. I recognize it seeps into my classes from the comments my students make both during and after the course ends on the holistic approaches I employ, in-class exercises (the flipped classroom), and how I engage students to integrate their growing knowledge through their internship opportunities with clients.

Still, I am not unmindful of my position relative to multidimensional aspects of the field that I know less well. With advanced knowledge, the bounds of spirituality grow ever farther away and I know much less of the whole. I, too, see myself as a novice, while at the same time owning expert-level knowledge. The spiritual world is correctly viewed as a mosaic, with certain pieces advancing at one moment, then retreating, while others take a first level position. Everything remains there in the artwork, but overtime it remodels itself. Concomitantly, like a river, the spiritual runs deep through layer upon layer, farther than what can be seen, heard, touched, or intuited. Rather than touching our toe in the surface stream, sometimes it may be pivotal to plunge in to the unseen depth, confident that many gifts can come back with us, which is our best service to others. In fact, some traditions suggest that it is important to keep gifts moving, so that we do not become corroded by stagnant, stuck energy that turns back on itself. Learning how to do integration is a lifetime task. When done well, a state of heightened focus carries one forward, the flow—in Csikszentmihalyi's concept of flow—just flows. Unbidden, unexpected, it is there. This text is a beginning effort in integration.

SUMMARY

This chapter approached integration on many levels. Discussion developed around the present status of religion and spirituality in society; generational spiritual questions; personal, professional, and client spiritual orientations; attending to spirituality in times of national disaster; evaluation of religious and spiritual practice in larger clinical work; interprofessional practice; self-care and mindfulness; and my own challenges with professional and personal integration.

QUESTIONS FOR DISCUSSION

1. In your view, what is the relationship between professional knowledge, values, and skill and spiritual/religious domains? How would you characterize level of congruence, if any? How do you assess the importance of the spiritual domain in professional work?

2. What, in your experience, seem to be modern-day trends concerning spirituality and also religion? How has it emerged in the lives of your clients?

3. What is your generation's spiritual capital? What are the most important spiritual questions of the generation to which you belong?

4. Think of a situation when your spiritual or religious orientation was different from your client's orientation. How did this affect clinical work? What were the outcomes?

5. Why does evaluation matter in clinical practice? How can professionals evaluate their work with clients around spiritual and religious strengths or concerns?

6. In what ways can the professions serve as resources to each other? What has your interprofessional learning been like, particularly around spirituality and/or religion?

MEDITATION: COLOR

This exercise allows play with color using imagination. We all have certain colors that we find appealing, and others that we find repellant. Color can enhance different feelings. For instance, we may find the color orange helps us feel active and vibrant, while the color blue is soothing or restful.

Breathe in and out mindfully and slowly. Begin by visualizing a rainbow and then imagine yourself washed in each color separately. Move from red to orange to yellow to green to blue to violet, each time permitting your body to absorb as much of each color as it seems to want. Next, imagine yourself washed in a spectrum of color, perhaps visualizing a color wheel with one hundred colors. Think of the colors at the crown of your head flowing down together through your body and then into the ground. As the colors flow through you, absorb what you need. Come back to the moment when you are ready.

EXPLORING YOUR SPIRITUALITY: BALANCE AND EQUIPOISE

Achieving balance is important in life. The Buddhists refer to this as the middle way, or way of moderation. Around us, within us, and toward us we encounter experiences that challenge us, upset us, cause us to feel anger, grief, or pain. Satisfaction or joy also resides at the end of a continuum of experience. Pleasant as they are, they, too, can be disconcerting if we strive to re-create conditions to experience them where a result is that many other important facets of life are disregarded in an unyielding quest. Finding the *still point* or the quiet center within us is something we can strive for through practice. It does become easier. Buddhists practice this in zazen meditation, and Christians also look for the still point in centering prayer, as two examples (see Sue Monk Kidd, *Dance of the Dissident Daughter*, 1996). I sometimes think back to doing gymnastics in high school where I was able to lean back and turn upside down on the rings, holding my position there a short time. I would always think I couldn't do it, and then my head would tilt back, I would bring my knees up, and my body would follow. That tipping point felt wonderful.

1. Read the following from Chase (2011, p. 167):

   - Balance is to locate the still point at the center of complexity.
   - Balance is to be in a constant state of sensitive fine adjustments.
   - Balance requires exquisite sensitivity to inner and outer forces.
   - Balance appears spontaneous and improvisational, but is utterly responsible and devoted.
   - Balance is thwarted by pretense, also by insistence.
   - Balance knows both this and that, and prefers neither.
   - Balance is opportunistic.
   - Balance finds home anywhere, finds the center everywhere.
   - *Balancing* is a better descriptor, more in balance than *balanced*.
   - Complete balance is the aim of nature.

2. Think about each statement and its meaning, one by one. Can you think of an example of each? Which statements speak particularly to you?

3. What does balance mean to you? When have you known balance in your life? How did you recognize it? What was different about it from other experiences in daily living?

4. What has assisted you in achieving this state? In maintaining it? Is it simple, difficult, or both? Why?

5. When do you find yourself *out of balance* and what leads you into this condition? What warning signs have you learned to look for?

6. What does *being in balance* mean for you? What were the outcomes you experienced from being in a state of balance? How can you search for strategies to regain this state when desired?

7. Is it possible to stay in balance over long periods? Is balance a static state for you or a dynamic one, necessitating many small, but constant, adjustments to achieve?

8. Journal about your experiences with balance.

EXPLORING YOUR SPIRITUALITY: SELF-INTEGRATION

We are complex and multifaceted beings, *homo sapiens*. This latter term comes from the Latin *homo* (human being) plus *sapiens* (wise). Developing greater wisdom is a goal most of us would find worthy of pursuit. Despite this, we are often fragmented with multiple subparts: Some of these subparts are healthy and others less so. This can result in a condition we have often heard described as, "You are your own worst enemy." At times when we work to achieve something desired, we can get in our own way, placing obstacles to that achievement. This aspect of ourselves is sometimes referred to in Jungian terms as our "shadow" side. The shadow side describes our unconscious sublimated processes, what we deem inferior or unacceptable, in contrast to our preferred self. We deny or manage their expression because that is not who we consciously want to be. However, failure to acknowledge these aspects often causes them to pop up or emerge in unhealthy or hurtful behavior. People who deny their shadow selves stand in danger of *projecting* them onto others, thus further removing any possibility of bringing them to the light of awareness.

Examples of obstacles that get thrown up from our shadow side may involve absences from meetings we've agreed to attend, procrastination, or allowing any kind of interruptions to come between us and our goal. Alternatively, the presence of unhealthy use of alcohol, drugs, or other distracting activities can demand our attention and derail us from what we hoped to complete. This exercise involves guidance toward achieving self-integration or a development of a holistic self, access to our inner wisdom.

1. Identify a part of yourself that gets in your way. This may be a behavior or a feeling with which you are having difficulty, your shadow side. An assumption that you can make is that every subpart of you ultimately wants to achieve the same ultimate aim and holds a positive intention for your growth.

2. What does that part of your self achieve? What is the deeper need that it is trying to address? You may need to go into a meditation mode to retrieve this information. Once that part begins to *speak* to you or allows itself to be heard, make sure you offer it your gratitude. It is important not to argue with it but to accept what it tells you. Listen with kindness and write down what you learn. Ask the part, "What is it you really want?"

3. Go deeper. What is this part trying to balance for you? What does this part hope to bring to you? Stay with it and go as deep as you can, remembering to thank it each time. You may discover that the goal of this subpart is also joy, satisfaction, letting go, or peace, acceptance, and transcendence, although it has a different method.

4. You may have had previous experience when you have achieved satisfaction or a transcendent state, but this part is not aware of it and so is trying to achieve that for you in a different way. Bring this part to find or remember that state, so it knows you already know how to get there. Not all of our subparts know that we already have resources; we are already starting with the state we are trying to accomplish. Thus, this part can understand that the behavior it is generating is already accomplished. Invite this part back into the full self. This also works for positive behaviors. When we have fewer or less intense inner struggles, we are more aligned with ourselves and our actions in life become easier; they flow.

5. Bring this knowledge that you already know what to do, or have the resource, back to the original problem or challenge. How does already knowing you have the resource change how you act or feel? How might this affect you in the future?

6. Journal about your experience and your results. If this advanced exercise is completely foreign to your understanding, you may want to participate in it more than once.

WEBSITES

National Voluntary Organizations Active in Disaster (NVOAD).

http://www.nvoad.org/

This site has several features that offer guidance for disaster work, especially in attending to matters of faith. They would be a good organization with which mental health practitioners might partner during times of crisis.

Spiritual and Religious Care Competencies for Specialist Palliative Care

http://www.ahpcc.org.uk/wordpress/wp-content/uploads/2014/07/compaudittool.pdf

http://www.ahpcc.org.uk/wp-content/uploads/2014/07/spiritcomp.pdf

These resources provide beginning and advanced ideas about spiritual competencies for both staff and volunteers. Further, they ask whether the competency was met, what the evidence was for meeting the competency, and invite a review with comments. This evaluative aspect gives this instrumentation strong appeal.

RECOMMENDED READING

Germer, C., Siegel, R., & Fulton, P. (2013). *Mindfulness and psychotherapy* (2nd ed.). New York, NY: Guilford Press.

This is a very practical book that presents both practice information and research studies in the area of mindfulness.

Kimble, M. (1995). *Aging, spirituality, and religion: A handbook*. Minneapolis, MN: Fortress Press.

This book addresses many dimensions of aging, spirituality, and religion including both theological and social science perspectives.

Kimble, M., & McFadden, S. (Eds.). (2003). *Aging, spirituality, and religion: A handbook* (vol. 2). Minneapolis, MN: Fortress Press.

This second volume considers pastoral care, ethics, and the future of religion, spirituality, and aging, among other topics.

CHAPTER THIRTEEN

LESSONS FOR BUILDING SPIRITUAL RESILIENCE AND EPILOGUE

Come, my friends. 'Tis not too late to seek a newer world. . . .
Though much is taken, much abides; and though
We are not now that strength which in old days
Moved earth and heaven, that which we are, we are—
One equal temper of heroic hearts,
Made weak by time and fate, but strong in will
To strive, to seek, to find, and not to yield.

—Alfred, Lord Tennyson, "Ulysses"

As once the winged energy of delight carried you over
childhood's dark abysses, now beyond your own life build
the great arch of unimagined bridges.

—Rainer Maria Rilke

Addressed in this final chapter are metaphors for the aging experience and for mental health practice with older people. Resilience and the ability of symbols to translate and address spiritual needs are provided. This chapter closes with an Epilogue that provides recommendations and illuminations for therapists.

SECTION 1: LESSONS FOR BUILDING RESILIENCE

Resilience: The Hero's Journey

In the excerpt from Alfred Lord Tennyson's poem "Ulysses" above, the heroic structure of life is called forth through its particular articulation of aging. Much is required to attain an older age, but still, much remains. Acknowledging the glory of bygone days, "the strength that moved earth and heaven," there is acceptance of what is in place now, "heroic hearts made weak." However frail in physical form, the will of Ulysses and his fellow sailors continues to be sturdy, stout, and resilient. Purpose continues to infuse his days anew. There is more "to seek" and "to find." It is as if Tennyson is narrating Ulysses's life from a high promontory, where Ulysses now holds a clearer vision, although his actual eyesight may be dimming, to understand and appreciate the arc of his life. This is one spiritual assessment of the aging experience.

Aging as hero's journey. In many ways aging is the hero or heroine's journey. The most magnificent characteristic is that we each are the appointed hero of our own path. The concept of the hero's journey was formulated by Campbell (1968) as he sought to synthesize major myths across cultures. What he found particularly striking is that many of the major cultural and religious stories that have been conveyed through oral traditions across generations carry common themes. The hero metaphor reinforces ideas of power and choice, and the myth serves as an allegorical map for the inner journey of spirit.

This is similar to the modern problem-solving therapy model described by D'Zurilla and Nezu (2010), which proposes a cognitive-behavioral model of problem resolution through application of both a social problem-solving and a relational problem-solving model of stress and well-being. This is the hero's journey in old age. Social problem solving is a learning process that results in improved adaptability and performance in natural environments. Relational problem solving is needed in the person-environment relationship when effective coping is overwhelmed by stress. People face difficulties within themselves or in their environments that must be solved (D'Zurilla & Nezu, 2010; Gellis, McGinty, Horowitz, Bruce, & Misener, 2007). They appraise threats and implement solutions that hopefully become more nuanced and effective as learning increases over time. This is resiliency—bouncing back from difficulties. Problem-solving capacity is marred by impulsivity and avoidance in some older people just as when a hero faces a challenge and succumbs to an unhealthy choice.

The older person is entrenched in the *ordinary world*, which is typically a life space that includes some form of suffering for him or her that emerges out of the unique combination of person (individual characteristics) and environment (constraining or facilitating) variables. The older person has heard and responded to the *call to adventure*, which also enfolds belief that there is a way out of suffering (Mijares, 2003). The call is followed by the *challenge*, the *initiation*, and finally the *return*. The older person who is depressed may at first *refuse the call* due to fear. However, with the help of a mental health professional such as a social worker, counselor, psychologist, nurse, or chaplain and/or family and friends in his or her support network, he or she builds courage to *cross the threshold* into new territory. In this life phase, the *initiation* into late life encompasses *tests, allies, and enemies* as have appeared in earlier phases of life. The older person faces his or her *ordeal*, which may be the death of a spouse, partner, or friend; a health challenge; an unwanted relocation; and depression or anxiety. The *reward* is finding his or her own version of resilience, which may involve new kinds of learning. There lies ahead a *road back* that involves reintegration with ordinary life, but also new knowledge, self-understanding, and competence. This constitutes the *elixir*, the new skills acquired out of the struggle, which can strengthen the remainder of his or her life. In Western culture, the ideal hero does not follow a path set by others, but must locate his or her own path. That can be difficult in itself. However, some people find their choice constrained by relationships, acceptable behavior patterns of their time and locale, ageism, and other stereotypes that may negatively impact their ability to choose their own path.

When heroes fail or fall. A paradox surrounds aging itself. More people are living longer lives, yet at the same time, no one wants to be seen as old. People who are incontrovertibly old by any calculation of remaining lifespan think and talk about themselves as young. The face they recognize in the mirror is their former younger one, not the one that presents itself.

We have fewer geriatricians than we need (Peterson, Bazemore, Bragg, Xierali, & Warshaw, 2011). Many physicians choose other specializations because work with older people makes them sad, as well as the complexity of health problems at older ages, and lower pay than alternate specializations. In fact, in many of the professions, there are fewer graduates who choose to work with older adults and as a result less needed aging knowledge among professionals working in the field of aging (Scharlach, Simon, & Dal Santo, 2002).

Why are so many professionals walking away from older persons rather than toward them? One of the reasons that aging is so often viewed as worrisome rather than wonderful is that it is so often seen only as decline and death. In our market economy those who can produce or consume goods are usually deemed to hold the greatest value—at least with media and marketers (Nelson, 2009). When the dependence to independence ratio begins to slide more firmly into the side of dependence, some would-be professional helpers find the multiple complex issues older people face especially burdensome. The personhood of people living with dementia has been called into question, though strong voices such as Kitwood's have begun to consider how those with dementia can still be honored and engaged. These relationships can even be enjoyable when frustrations are thoughtfully countered.

Another issue concerns the fact that aging is regarded as a problem to be solved (Nelson, 2009). With increasing technological discoveries and skills, there have been many positive advances in health and other treatments. There are some who want to see whether the current boundaries of chronological age can be surpassed (Olshansky, Perry, Miller, & Butler, 2007). Although that may be a meaningful and important goal for some, what is the effect on those who are aging badly, for whatever reason? What happens to those who then are devalued because they are unable due to physical or developmental disability to perform at a particular level of functioning? How can we as a society uphold and validate the value of many kinds of aging experiences? Sometimes that is left to religion and spirituality to answer in the service that contemporaries of those who feel the arrow stings of aging, but are not so negatively affected, and their younger generational allies may provide. Much service is given from those already aged to other older adults.

The final concern lies directly with the older person himself or herself. Some older people enter old age and fail in the goal of becoming heroic, if they ever signed on to it in the first place. They are grumpy. They complain. They whine and they protest. They kick the would-be helper out of their room. They smoke, drink, or eat what they know they shouldn't. Longstanding personality disorders or other negative personal traits continue. They have known violence in their life, been abused, traumatized, grown up in an impossible family. They have suffered, and their response is to try to make others suffer. No one would call them resilient. These are the hardest clients to treat, and professionals do follow the client's expressed wish and allow themselves to be removed or rejected, reinforcing the client's beliefs. However, one professional may find a way to connect and there can still be a chance for change. As long as people live, life gives them an opportunity. The spiritual path tries not to leave others behind; in community everyone can be brought inside the circle of friendship.

Resilience in Aging

Older persons who come into contact with mental health practitioners may do so for reasons of personal growth, but it is more likely they come because of psychosocial or spiritual problems. Stress-related growth—growth because of life problems—and conscious aging are often a result of sorting through tangled situations (Moody, 2003; Park & Fenster, 2004). One definition of resiliency establishes it as the universal capacity to avoid, reduce, or overcome adversity (Monroe & Oliviere, 2007; Newman, 2004). However, many people might question whether the avoidance of adversity would meet a definition of resilience because avoidance may mean passively doing nothing rather than actively planning. If individuals develop a resilient response to life challenges when they are young, they will likely be able to maintain it into old age, evident in the idea of selective optimization with compensation (Baltes, 1993). Having a longer time horizon, they can benefit from this approach throughout their life. Resilience may grow increasingly expansive in later years.

> *Resilience involves the ability to access one's inner wisdom and strength enhanced by time and experience ... [It is] the ability to achieve growth through life challenges based on personal history and environmental assets, a capacity for generating hope, and the ability to transcend boundaries in optimal ways.* (Nelson-Becker, 2013, p. 324)

Instead of an extraordinary quality, resilience may reflect a normative response to difficulty. However, people hold vulnerabilities, which, when combined with adversity, may lead to negative outcomes, such as depression, fear, or anxiety. Because of a lifetime of experience, older adults also may hold a larger cumulative vulnerability if they have not achieved mastery of problems at earlier ages (Nelson-Becker, 2013). Bar-Tur and Levy-Shiff (2000) suggest several variables that affect resilience at older age. These include the patterns and interplay between cumulative risk and protective factors from behavior learned during stressful events; health determinants; history of behavioral, social, and economic events; and psychological and cultural factors. Aging-related loss may in fact be perceived as secondary to earlier trauma effects (Bar-Tur & Levy-Shiff, 2000). It is also possible that older people have a reservoir in their lived experience that buffers them from feeling the force of the impact of unfolding events in contrast to what others at different ages in the life course could experience (Baltes, 1993).

Resilience is generally discussed in biopsychosocial terms that are more easily incorporated into scientific investigation. However, in this text, it is helpful to be more explicit about how spirituality affects the person. Drawing on past research with older persons that explored their use of religion and spirituality in coping with life events (Nelson-Becker, 2004b, 2005a), spiritual resilience is an ability to be nurtured by one's inner spiritual self, outer spiritual and other social relationships, and to live with ambiguity, trusting the goodness of the universe when that goodness might be only faintly perceived (Nelson-Becker, 2013).

Figure 13.1 Resilience Quotient Transforming Over Time depicts a model of resilience that considers challenging events and situations over the life course. Coincidentally it is also drawn in a spiral form. Multiple points of distress and eustress, that is, positive stress, lead to new insight. The crash point continuum reflects the bioemotional spectrum of feelings from distress to joy. Arcs vary in length, representing different degrees of stress, though the drawing shows them the same length. These effects rotate forward with time passing, but for simplicity are drawn at the same height and depth. Each arc captures the learning achieved from prior historic points. Although learning always moves forward, people can make choices that seem to contradict forward movement. Self-doubt, suffering, and fear can cause individuals to remain at a standstill or deteriorate to an earlier developmental position (Nelson-Becker, 2013). Resilience capacity is informed by variables that shift over time.

Engaging Symbols for Resilience

Direct experience of reality can be conceived as a type of "first experiencing moment" (Smith, 2014). "We do not need symbols, concepts, cognitive categories, and language to experience reality. But in most cases we do need them to represent, clarify, cognize,

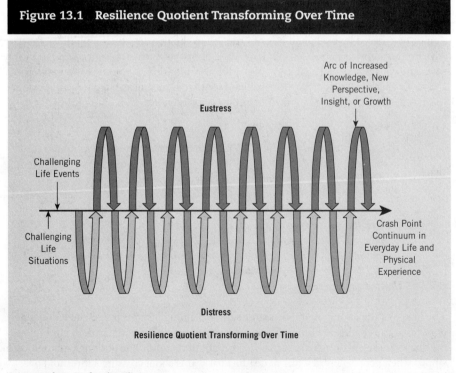

Figure 13.1   Resilience Quotient Transforming Over Time

Arc of Increased Knowledge, New Perspective, Insight, or Growth

Eustress

Challenging Life Events

Challenging Life Situations

Crash Point Continuum in Everyday Life and Physical Experience

Distress

Resilience Quotient Transforming Over Time

Source: Nelson-Becker (2013).

interpret, express, and discuss our experiences of reality" (p. 181). Direct experience is just that, direct and unmediated. It happens between you and that thing that you experience. The only meaning it keeps is through, in Smith's terms, "the second hermeneutical moment." (See Chapter 12 for discussion of the hermeneutical text.) The second hermeneutical moment refers to knowledge gained from reflection, evaluation, and articulation/communication of the experience to others. Symbols used to create meaning lead to a sense of resilience.

Narrative therapy, as discussed in Chapter 7, is one of the approaches most likely to help older clients integrate their own experience of the spiritual with their unique struggles and the context of their everyday life. Narrative knowing and the unfolding of that knowing is filtered through the self in relationship to the audience to whom the story is told. Coherent stories contain both a type of sequencing of events and the emotional meaning of those events; many events that occur in life cannot be completely understood, accounted for, or known in their entirety. That is why we need the language of metaphor, allegory, and symbols. Culture "denotes a . . . pattern of meanings embodied in symbols, a system of inherited conceptions expressed in symbolic forms, by means of which men communicate, perpetuate, and develop their knowledge about and attitudes toward life" (Geertz, 1973, p. 89). Meaning is made for some, though not for all, older people in symbolic interfaces. There are several common symbols beyond explicitly religious symbols that convey rich content. Some of this symbolism emerges through objects and some through words that signify meaning. Discussed here are the door, the spiral, art, and poetry.

The door. A door has physical purpose: to unlock and open a space when one stands on the threshold of entry. It also has metaphorical purpose when one crosses the threshold into something new. Or, sometimes, one searches for a door and fails to find it. The way out seems forever hidden. Merton (1975) writes about the three doors that are one door. The first is the door of emptiness. He suggests that this kind of no-door opening cannot be entered by a self, and it is of little use to the person who is ambitious, for it does not go anywhere. The second door is the door that carries no sign to call attention to itself. It has no posting that says "Not a Door" or "No Exit." Nothing points to it and says, "Here is the door!" The third kind of door is the unexpected door. This door was not desired, but it is not a trap door. This door is endless; it has no purpose; it has no key.

> *When you have asked for a list of all the doors, this one is not on the list. When you have asked the numbers of all the doors, this one is without a number. Do not be deceived into thinking this door is merely hard to find and difficult to open. When sought, it fades. Recedes, diminishes. Is nothing. There is no threshold. No footing. It is not empty space. It is neither this world nor another. It is not based on anything. Because it has no foundation, it is the end of sorrow. Nothing remains to be done. Therefore there is no threshold, no stop, no advance, no recessing, no entry, no non-entry. Such is the door that ends all doors: the unbuilt, the impossible, the undestroyed, through which all the fires go when they have "gone out."* (Merton, 1975, p.177)

The image of the door is an important one for explaining insights that come unbidden— or never arrive at all. Sometimes the closed door is a reminder of the path that is blocked, the divine Source who fails to hear, the dark night of the soul. The door metaphor is also tapped when people describe fear of death. That fear is about crossing a threshold over which no one has ever returned. Death remains a great unknown. However, it is a door

Figure 13.2 The Door to Nowhere

© Photo by Alexa Gummow. Used with permission.

each one of us will pass through in our own timing. It is human nature for people to fear what they do not understand. Yet there are many doors that do open as people age through the life cycle. For monk and writer Merton, the door was God himself. This is also true for other older adults who stand fully or partially in a faith tradition.

> *As soon as man is fully disposed to be alone with God, he is alone with God no matter where he may be—in the country, the monastery, the woods, or the city. . . . Although he is a traveler in time, he has opened his eyes, for a moment, in eternity.* (Merton, 1975, p. 112)

Spiritual and religious coping at older ages may be avenues to open a door. That door may appear in unexpected places, as did the door in Figure 13.2. The older person, as the inner child experiencing, may stomp his or her feet, cross her or his arms and walk only grudgingly through. What will appear on the other side? Approaching the unknown door in a state of readiness and anticipation can help older people align with what remains vital, vibrant, and utterly meaningful in their lives. When therapists work with clients to visualize doors where before they only saw walls, resilience is enhanced.

The spiral. The spiral is found frequently in nature and as a symbol brims with conceptual density. The mathematical definition of an Archimedean spiral is given by the equation $r = a\theta$, in which a is a constant, r is the length of the radius from the center, or beginning, of the spiral, and θ is the angular position (amount of rotation) of the radius (Encyclopedia Britannica, 2015). In this model, distances between the intersection points along an imaginary line from the edges of the spiral through the origin are the same. Another spiral form is logarithmic, or equiangular: a spiral that appears to widen as it moves outward. Yet a third common form of the spiral is the helix, a three-dimensional or cylindrical spiral. If the point is narrowest at the bottom, it can appear as a tornado.

The coiled shape seems to have been recognized from ancient times as containing unusual meaning. The spiral is found abundantly at Newgrange in County Meath Ireland, a Neolithic monument recognized as a UNESCO World Heritage Site that dates from approximately 3000 B.C. Spirals are also used to depict some galaxies, as in the spiral galaxy, and are famously depicted in van Gogh's 1889 painting, *The Starry Night*. One well-known version comes from the 8th–9th century manuscript the *Book of Kells*, now at Trinity College in Dublin (see Figure 13.3). The entwined triple spirals are a form of Archimedean spiral.

As depicted above, the spiral is an ancient design that illustrates the enfolding and unfolding of spirituality (Jung, 2001). It suggests that the way to transformation *travels both inward and outward*. The spiral illustrates a complex geometry that is found in nature through substances as diverse as the nautilus seashell, the pinecone,

Figure 13.3   Triple Spiral From the *Book of Kells*

Spiral ornament, with key-pattern border, from the Book of Kells

Source: Allen (1904).

the spiral nebulae, and an ammonite fossil. It describes a spirituality small as a microcosm and vast as the great mystery of universe, an unfailing yet unknowable presence. Depicted in three forms through the triple spiral, it also may represent the cycles of life: birth, death, and rebirth, or the unity of body, mind, and spirit that gather into an overall center or wholeness of the person. As we age, the power of this symbol can speak to us in compelling ways and serve as a reminder of our own unique and powerful spiritual paths. The spiral marks the path from external consciousness such as ego and perception to the essence of what is unseen but formidable: inner awareness or soul. The movements between the macrocosm and the micro-world can be mapped through the spiraling activity. The spiral is both strong and resilient. In Figure 13.4 are images of an unfurling fern and ammonite fossil. The spiral found in forest ferns unfolds as they grow, adding another layer of symbolic meaning.

The spiral in nature has been transmuted to contemporary built environments. In the Community of Christ faith tradition, the spiral is engineered into a stainless steel spire in the temple (designed by Gyo Obata) in Independence, Missouri. This nautilus-shell shape was intended to be a symbol resonant to all cultures and nations. In design it is closest to the logarithmic spiral. Figure 13.5 is the view from the inside looking upward.

Figure 13.4   Spiral Shapes in Nature

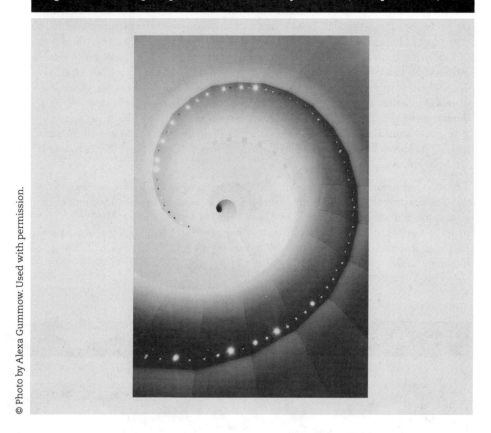

Figure 13.5   Temple Spire From Community of Christ, Independence, MO

© Photo by Alexa Gummow. Used with permission.

The spiral is also evident in most labyrinth shapes, as discussed in Chapter 7. There is a cadence between moving toward the center, perhaps giving something up along the way, and then taking new knowledge outward. It is important to keep learning in motion through a rhythmic pattern of integrating inner and outer knowledge and sending that knowledge outward into the world in positive peaceful ways. The spiral provides evidence of resilience in aging as people participate by moving into the center of their own knowledge and then turning outward to share their knowledge or supportive actions with their communities.

Aikido, spiral in motion. Aikido is a modern Japanese martial art form that has a dual goal of defense and protecting the attacker from harm. It is mind-body-spirit training in the way of harmony. In the practice of Aikido, movements tend to be circular or spiraling, large and flowing, rather than contracting and tightening as a boxer's punch might do. The discipline requires practice in timing, balance, focus, and leverage. Aikido is concerned with decentering the partner and redirecting the momentum of that person's energy. As in many spiritual practices, successful practice involves staying aware, flexible, and connected. One is more easily able to sidestep the energy of an opponent—or a difficult client—in a fluid state. Once the opponent has begun the energy of an action, it is much harder for them to control. The person who would receive the adverse action can move off the line of attack into a place of safety. For older persons, Aikido practice, like yoga, can enhance mobility, keep them more flexible, and help them learn to fall safely. In Asian cultures, older people often practice martial arts as well as gentler movement forms, like Ta'i Chi Chuan, in very late age.

In a contentious situation, rather than taking a defensive position, a response with a more satisfying outcome is to deflate or sidetrack that energy by agreeing with what you can agree with and suggesting alternatives. If translated to mental sparring, it represents a way to bring peace to anger and hate. Practice of *ki* seems to carry parallels with a Daoist or Zen Buddhist approach. Older adults may not be able to practice Aikido if they have physical limitations, but they could use its principles in oral interactions. Mental health professionals likewise, can use the principles and metaphors of Aikido in their therapeutic practice. Aikido suggests the capacity of older people to react resiliently to adverse situations and to model their own resilience for others.

Art. Aging may bring with it surprising capacity and wisdom. Aging is not necessarily synonymous with wisdom, which also is present at young ages. In fact, some older people bring into their aging experience all of the difficulties, misunderstandings, and confusion they lived with earlier or created. However, in aging there is greater opportunity for attaining wisdom. Although not everything can be altered and some events are not controllable, engaging in practice of the arts can be substantially satisfying. Below two kinds of artistic opportunities are discussed: print-making and poetry.

Katsushika Hokusai (1760–1849) was a preeminent artist in the Edo period of Japan. The Edo period lasted from 1615 to 1868 and brought unprecedented stability, which likely facilitated artistic and cultural freedom and innovation. Power was ceded to the *shogun*, who was a military dictator ceremonially appointed by the emperor. The emperor had limited authority himself, but the shogun in this administrative system held nearly absolute power. The shogun directed lords of each region who were served, in turn, by *samurai*. The samurai respected a code of conduct called *Bushido* (The Way of the Warrior), which stressed mastery of martial arts, frugality, loyalty, courage, and honor. In fact, Bushido, although it was not recognized that way in those times, represented an early spiritual code for the best way to live one's life.

Against this backdrop, Hokusai made a remarkable series of prints, all views of Mount Fuji. Mount Fuji has been considered a sacred location for centuries. Until 1868, women were not allowed there. From ages 64 through 72, Hokusai produced what is known as *The Thirty-Six Views of Mount Fuji*. In many perspectives, Mount Fuji is dwarfed by towering waves and represents a point of stability in the midst of chaos (see Figure 13.6).

At an older age, Kathsushika Hokusai wrote the following concerning his life:

> *From the time that I was 6 years old I had the mania of drawing the form of objects. As I came to be 50, I had published an infinity of designs. All I have produced before the age of seventy is not worth taking into account. At seventy-three I have learned a little about the real structure of nature, of animals, plants, trees, birds, fishes and insects. In consequence when I am eighty, I shall have made still more progress. At ninety I shall penetrate the mystery of things; at one hundred I shall certainly have reached a marvelous stage; and when I am a hundred and ten, everything I do, be it a dot or a line, will be alive. I beg those who live as long as I to see if I do not keep my word. Written at the age of seventy five by me, once Hokusai, today Gwakyo Rojin.*
> (Calza & Katsushika, 2003)

Hokusai used at least 30 pseudonyms during his lifetime, and Gwakyo Rojin meant "the old man mad about drawing." It was as if it was only at older ages that he deemed his life worthwhile. It seemed that everything he had done previously in his life was simply prelude.

The stigma of aging is so prevalent that younger adults often see older age as having nothing to recommend it. Gwakyo Rojin escaped that limited assumption by making it untrue. He expressed confidence that with time he would "penetrate the mystery of things" and "everything I do will be alive." The symmetry, beauty, and arresting nature of his woodblock prints gave example of this view. Reportedly, when he died, he thought his work was still in progress, not complete. Yet his influence has penetrated several centuries already. Rather than thinking of increasing age as decline, he saw it as providing *increasing vitality*. This idea is echoed centuries later by May Sarton's comment given in Chapter 7 that it wasn't until old age that she finally became herself. A woman living with dementia discussed in Chapter 10 observed that she was becoming *something* that was not necessarily less than what she was. These individuals who have charted their path ahead of us who follow did not see the vulnerabilities of aging as the entire story of the period. Instead, there were openings for light.

As older adults engage their full creativity in the arts as in other areas of their life, they showcase resilience. If they do not allow others to set limits on their own perceived capacity, their ability to influence the lives of nearby support networks as well as larger groups—the macrosociety—can be boundless. Older adults also teach us that in art, we should pause for beauty. That pause to either create or appreciate art of any kind can lift us out of ordinary time into the timeless. In the space of timelessness, people of any age can find restoration and energy for renewed engagement.

Poetry. In the world of poetry where words are sparse and critically selected, deeper insight is expressed and received. David Whyte and Mary Oliver, both poets of our century,

Figure 13.6 Thirty-Six Views of Mount Fuji: The Great Wave Off the Coast of Kanagawa

Source: Hokusai. K. (19th c.). *The Great Wave Off the Coast of Kanagawa* [Painting]. Retrieved from https://commons.wikimedia.org/wiki/File:Katsushika_Hokusai_-_Thirty-Six_Views_of_Mount_Fuji-_The_Great_Wave_Off_the_Coast_of_Kanagawa_-_Google_Art_Project.jpg.

suggest the world is waiting for us at every age of life. Anything can happen in any moment. How to prepare for that? With a nod to Rumi's writing, we ought to open every door and window of our house so the wind can sweep in the keys to deeper being. We should welcome all guests, whether they arrive with joy or sorrows. Our task is to be accessible, available. Then, beauty will rain down and flowers will unfold around us, even if we are sitting in what a moment before could only be termed mire. A part of our work is to see what is there before us in the frame. So much of it we miss. Part of the reason people enjoy pictures is that there is far more detail in the picture than they can take in at the moment or recall. Seeing what is present and acting on it is the hero's journey into resilience.

The ancient tradition of alchemy was the search to make gold out of base objects. The gold sought then was mostly thought to make one rich in goods and property. However, metaphorically alchemical work is a project of the inner psychic world. It is about refining the inner self while living in the outer world. It could be said that the alchemical goal is to work on the soul. That is what we should make rich, however we might guess at the definition and meaning of it. Perhaps if practitioners or their clients are successful in making true gold, they have found the nature of God, the spiritual, or connected with their unique purpose in their multi-storied, multi-motivated lives. They have created, or are creating, their preferred future. They are seeing what is just a step before them, even if partly in fog.

"Late Fragment" (available at https://allpoetry.com/Late-Fragment) was the final poem in Mr. Carver's last published book as he lay dying from cancer. It is both profound and hopeful, while sharing what is elemental. Did you get what you wanted from life? Of course, each person will design their own response to that question. The beauty in Carver's thoughts is that his answer to the query—even if he was the one who posed it—could stand for many older people who may not have had the opportunity to respond to such a similar question. Why? Because no one ever asked them. We do great service by the questions we think to ask. Carver did not identify his writing, or the numbers of readers who must have been fans of his work, or any other achievement as having lasting significance. What mattered, simply, was being loved during the time that he lived. It was not what he did, but who he was, knowing how he was valued by others, that held remarkable significance for him. This exemplifies a hero's journey into the heart of finding what resilience means to that person.

Many older people engage in writing reflections, memoirs, and poetry. At times the audience and the beneficiaries are only themselves. However, occasionally those texts become available to others. In the latter way, resilience is passed on to generations that follow.

SECTION 2: EPILOGUE

Review of Chapters

This book was designed to provide greater knowledge for anyone desiring to increase his or her capacity and comfort with gerontological practice, specifically around spiritual and religious issues. To that end, it began with a chapter on the importance of these areas to older people. Second, it explored definitions of these and related terms that can often be confusing and, as signifiers, can contain meanings differently understood. A foundation for ethical practice in these areas was presented in Chapter 3. Chapter 4 explored theories and perspectives on aging with particular interest for spirituality and religion. Chapter 5 explored eight different world religions or philosophies and provided some integration with aging across each tradition presented. Chapter 6 discussed the important area of assessment and what practitioners may expect to discover when asking questions about these domains.

Chapter 7 addressed inclusion of spirituality and religion in clinical practice. This was an expansive topic, and what is presented here is just a beginning exposure rather than a depth treatment. Chapter 8 considered spirituality and health, with a close look at Judaism, Christianity, and Islam. Caregiving needs were presented. Chapter 9 looked at mental health, the meaning of emotions, depression, the period known as the dark night of the soul, and anxiety. Chapter 10 addressed the spiritual possibilities in working with persons living with dementia. Chapter 11 considered religion and spirituality at the end of life. Chapter 12 looked at integration of religion and spirituality from quite a number of sociological and practice perspectives. Chapter 13 provides the conclusion to the book and a nod to the importance of resilience.

Recommendations for the Aging Field in Spirituality and Religion

There are a number of recommendations that can be made for mental health practitioners who want to gain greater knowledge about spirituality, religion, and aging and include spirituality and religion in their professional practice to a deeper extent. Of course, it can be very useful to hold knowledge of many faith traditions and different spiritual and religious practices, but therapists do not need to be experts in religious sociology. Integration with clinical work should also not be accomplished for its own sake or for curiosity, but where it is invited by clients.

First, we need to be open to question our assumptions about spirituality and religion. These domains are not unequivocally positive or negative for our clients and communities. Studies have shown that clinician judgment is unfavorably affected by knowledge of client beliefs (O'Connor & Vandenberg, 2005). Spirituality and religious belief does sustain many older people, as I have shown through this text, but there can also be much turbulence in faith expressions, at the extreme end serving as a rationale for war. As practitioners, we don't need to match our clients on their religious or spiritual views in order to assist. In fact, sometimes those who stand at opposite ends of a traditional to contemporary/liberal spiritual or religious perspective from a client or inside/outside a spiritual or religious community or tradition from a client's stance can best see how to effectively work with particular spiritual or religious problems. No one should edit herself out of at least learning basic, respectful spiritually sensitive practice.

Second, although research in these areas has gained a greater visibility and profile in recent years, there is much we don't know about the mechanisms and how they work to the benefit of some people and to the detriment of others. More than just correlations, such as "people who attend church have better mental health," *we need to explore the specifics* of who and what is included in these studies and who is omitted or self-selected out. A recent 10-year study of 75,000 women suggests that women who attend church live longer (Shanshan, Stampfer, Williams, & VanderWeele, 2016), explained partially by social support, less smoking, less depression, and optimism. That's intriguing, but we need to know more about what "attendance" means—what people participate in and what they receive—and how that enhances physical and mental health. Better studies and randomized controlled trials should continue to understand mechanisms of the brain and religious behavior. Harold Koenig's Duke Center for Spirituality, Theology, and Health e-newsletter *Crossroads* is one good resource for learning about current developments, particularly related to health and health systems. There is a greater need for practitioners who work with client spiritual and/or religious issues, particularly spiritual distress, to be involved in practice research or consult with those who are doing it. We need to learn more about use of spiritual and religious interventions.

Third, we need to know more about how religion and spirituality can safely and respectfully be supported among older people and by the mental health and health professions. What should be the ethical boundaries of inclusion of these areas? What protocols should be put in place for ensuring older people's spiritual and religious needs are addressed, especially in large institutions or systems where they may be easy to overlook. How should practice in these areas be evaluated? These are important areas for further specification and reflection in clinical work. For many therapists, though likely for fewer than the clients they serve, the areas of spirituality and religion may carry both personal and professional interest.

Illuminations for the Therapist

This text has promised illuminations about practice with older people, and I hope that the reader agrees the contract has been met. In this section, several ideas are offered to accentuate major points.

Empirical knowledge is important. All professions need a repository of empirical work as evidence and rationale for the therapeutic approaches they engage. The disciplines rely on and advance from their knowledge base. Throughout this text, the research literature has been used to showcase important observations and measures that apply to work with older adults. This side of practice is very well represented in the literature. However, there is another side to the prism of knowledge that has been largely unaddressed, yet has equal value. "There is also the knowledge of how to be and behave, how to grow and mature through life's sometimes turbulent journey. For those awake to the spiritual dimension, this is transcendent, sacred knowledge; and sacred knowledge is wisdom" (Culliford, 2011, p. 49). This more intuitive and artful side has typically been underaddressed in professional practice.

Who should tell whose story? In clinical practice, learning is dependent on many forms of knowledge, not the least of which is interesting cases that may be used for teaching. The cases developed for this text are based on true stories, but as with all good practice, names and circumstances have been altered and, in a few cases, details from two or more cases have been merged. As suggested in the ethics section in Chapter 3, integrity comes from empathy that is not exploited. It is also the case that many older people will delight in an invitation to share their story. They view it as a type of service, or a generational responsibility for certain kinds of knowledge to remain visible, so that generations following will remember and the knowledge does not disappear. Our task as professionals is to bear responsible witness, to share what is essential and true. The integrity we practice will give courage to others to do the same. Ultimately, we tell each other's stories through what we hold in our memories, our actions, and our hearts.

Find the middle way. Most faith traditions address the need for balance. This doesn't mean that one should or can necessarily avoid the ends of the spectrums of life: celebration or burgeoning effects of bad decisions. But the truth of learning is that it often materializes out of the ordinariness of daily living. Master Chuang Tzu has suggested, "A sage steers by the bright light of confusion and doubt. In this way, rather than relying on your own distinctions, you dwell in the ordinary. This is called illumination" (Hinton, 1997, p. 25). The middle way calls for finding the still point that provides a place of peace. Part of its appeal is that swirling around this point is a dynamic energy. As long as people have life, they will be a part of that swirling, spinning movement. "Except for the point, the still point, there would be no dance, and there is only the dance" (Eliot, 1970, p. 77). We are part of the dance, and though we wouldn't want it otherwise, finding the still point, the middle way that may be uniquely our own, is an excellent method to rest from the frenetic pace of the dance. And then we step in again.

From whence comes healing? Older people carry an innate, resilient, self-righting mechanism. In many cases, people can and do heal themselves. Still, there are instances when capacity is completely overwhelmed. People can find no comfort, no ledge of safety, no shelter on the mountain they are climbing. So just where can healing emerge? As suggested above, sometimes it comes from opening a new door, from losing oneself in artistic expression, from volunteering in service to others, from merely living through the pain. Every religious faith and every religious philosophy has its methods or pathways to healing worth exploring. Some people only need find one. A common one is prayer—or laughter. Others may require healing practices from several faith traditions. Culliford (2011) shares the following: "Thus, I concluded that the spirituality necessary for healing was not identical with any specific religion or professed set of beliefs, but rather a set of qualities that could be developed within any individual who sought them" (Schermer, 2003, p. 35 as cited in Culliford, 2011, p. 48). That is an important assessment. As shown in Chapter 5, the subsection on Religious Integration, faith traditions all value and respect older persons. Acceptance of aging and a guide to aging well is to be found in them. Many individuals find healing surrounded by the natural world, including older people. Described in Chapter 8 on Spirituality and Health, slow medicine offers promise for healing in its use of time as tincture. "In the quiet, everything is connected and you have all the time you need" (Sweet, 2012, p. 61). But most important, healing comes from others who first notice, and then act. It comes from those who encourage rather than disparage, ridicule, or shun. It comes out of the sacred encounter between helper and client.

Dwell comfortably in paradox. Great mystery is present in the center of some encounters. Things transpire that are difficult to understand. The Dao, sacred writing of Daoism, placed unusual emphasis and confidence in the self-reliance that results in a sense of completeness, but within a culture that values interconnectedness. "To be ordinary is to be self-reliant; to be self-reliant is to move freely; and to move freely is to arrive. That's almost it, because to arrive is to be complete. But to be complete without understanding how—that is called Tao" (Hinton, 1997, pp. 23–24). Individuals are invited to sense that so much more is possible than we can imagine. If we can stay with that sensibility, then we can better operationalize yet-unrealized promise. "Move in the boundless, and the boundless becomes your home" (p. 34). When we dwell in possibility, we can see new potential and accomplish things we did not think achievable. We knock at the door. The door opens, and we walk through. "This is called the treasure-house of heaven. Pour into it, and it never fills up. Pour from it, and it never empties out. And never understanding where it all comes from—that is called inward radiance" (p. 28). We don't always need to know from whence comes our help. Sometimes it just shows up.

Benediction

We all hold the power to bless each other, whether we are religious, spiritual, or simply proponents of living out the human condition in the most authentic and self— and—other aware way available to each one of us in our moment in time. The word *benediction* implies speaking or pronouncing a blessing. The origin of the word comes from the circa 1400 Latin *benedicere*, to say well, and *benedictio*, meaning to speak well of or to bless well. Listening well, sharing the best of what we can do for each other and for our clients is the beginning of blessing. When we listen well, we tell our interaction partners what they have to say is worth hearing. They matter.

Martin (2011) shares a story about the best of the best sometimes failing in this listening task. His friend met an elderly priest renowned for his skill at spiritual direction:

The priest asked, *So Kevin, where are you from? Boston,* answered Kevin. Then Kevin decided to ask an important question, *Father, what would you say is the most important part of spiritual direction?* The priest answered, *That's easy Kevin, it's listening. You have to be a good listener to be a good spiritual director. Thanks, Father, that's really helpful,* replied Kevin. And the priest asked, *So Kevin, where are you from?* (p. 143)

Sometimes even "experts" fall short. When we listen, we begin to sense the nature of the blessing needed. The more specific we can make the blessing, the better it may be received. Many of the chapters in this book have addressed listening, yet even so, its depths have not been fully probed.

Although giving and receiving blessings are common (or should be) in a religious environment, they should not be limited to that. A healthy spirituality suggests that in the dynamics of life, we all stand in need and everyone should be blessed. The second part of blessing beyond awareness is in the offer and the acceptance. The blessings parents can bestow on their children in modeling best practices in living a life are at the same time burden and gift. Everyone needs to follow their own thread through the maze. The blessing *older adults* can confer on the generations that follow in their approach to the frailties and endowments of aging, is matchless. Why do we so often choose to hurt each other by saying the unkind word when we all carry this great power inside?

Mental health professionals are critical in their capacity to unlock this potential to give blessing rather than perpetrate pain. Further, we don't have to be fully healed to bless. Blessings may come out of any direction or any person with any kind of past. Like so many things, blessing is simple, though it may seem byzantine or antiquated. At some occasions, for example, graduation at Loyola University Chicago, the whole assembly has been invited to raise their hand in blessing of students. That is not mere rote action; the energy sent and received can be palpable.

Parting Thoughts

The work of a gerontologist and mental health practitioner is to be a multifaceted teacher to older persons, their support network if invited, and other allied professions who may not hold necessary knowledge in aging. This text has provided both knowledge about spirituality, religion, and aging, and suggestions for accompanying and working with clients in these domains. The opening quote to this chapter implies that this set of knowledge, professional values, and skills can assist in constructing bridges: "now beyond your own life build the great arch of unimagined bridges." There are quite a number of ways to build the "unimagined bridges." One is the bridge across time as older generations link back to grandchildren, even those who may not be related by genetics. This generation is also their future and the future of the planet. Younger generations tenderly remember the times when they were cared for as youth and share their mutual affection with the departing generations of elders. Another bridge is the bond of teaching and learning that both generations can share bidirectionally, especially when one generation is gadget-proficient and the other is life-proficient. "When you help, you see life as weak. When you fix, you see life as broken. When you serve, you see life as whole. Fixing and helping may be the work of the ego, and service the work of the soul" (Remen, 1999, p. 1). Complaints about aging will always be present, but busting through stereotypical thinking and seeing the possibilities in aging can be enlightening.

Achieving necessary balance between our inner and outer work is key to staying in the field of mental health practice. Giving attention to the self is not ego, but increasing capacity to give and to serve. Within yourself you can find adequate room for sanctuary. In the end the questions we carry about our identity—who we are, our work and who it benefits, and what our clients most need—may have few direct answers. However, in those intersections, in the interstitial spaces between concerns, we often figure out what we need to know. The answer lies somewhere in acceptance of the mystery of life and in the living of it—as best we can—with courage. "I keep giving myself away to the next moment, and the next moment receives me. I just have to step through" (Moon, 2010, p. 171). We are puzzles who must ultimately solve ourselves. We can move out of problem-saturated stories and make the choice to change.

"Adieu, dit le renard. Voici mon secret. Il est très simple: on ne voit bien qu'avec le coeur. L'essentiel est invisible pour les yeux" (Go with God [or goodbye], said the fox. This is my secret. It is very simple. One only sees rightly with the heart. What is essential is invisible to the eyes; de Saint-Exupéry, p. 72). Whatever your beliefs and your experience, understand that your path is not a solitary one. Whether you live mostly in the everyday world of the visible or partly in the world of the invisible, there will be others, both seen and unseen, to guide you on your path as you give your best service to the world. As you stand on the bluff, and look out into the distance both near and far, may what you find there bring you peace.

QUESTIONS FOR DISCUSSION

1. In what way is aging a hero's journey?

2. How can aging be a time of resilience?

3. Why is the spiral a symbol for the spiritual path? How can this metaphor be used with older clients? What other metaphors might be useful?

4. How will you engage older adults around spirituality and religious needs?

5. What is the key lesson you will take from this book?

ASSIGNMENT: VISIONING

Visioning involves the process of seeing what is not yet and making it visible and real through the creation of that vision. Visioning encourages a stepwise process whereby actions open new possibilities, new steps that lead to other new steps previously hidden. All strong visions are contingent, open to change, yet also have a timeless quality. Visions can keep clients and therapists motivated—especially through tough economic times when social service organizations are pressured by limited funds. Yet visions are not just about seeing; they are dynamic constellations of cognition and sensory perceptions joined with imagination.

Visioning is a transformative process that extends beyond immediate objectives to craft excellence at all levels—for therapists or mental health practitioners, for the clients they treat, for the organization in which they work and for external stakeholders and nonstakeholders. This form of visioning is intertwined with meaning making. It has the power to capture the hearts and minds of anyone who participates. It can be done at personal levels (What do I have to give in the workplace?) and beyond (How am I or my organization making a difference in the wider world?) The rewards gained are both intrinsic (I'm happy with my accomplishment here) and extrinsic (how other groups may find benefit).

In a human resources course in an administration track of social work, "Strengthening Staff Performance in a Diverse Workplace," I added a segment on visioning and leadership. I sensed a gap between how students perceived themselves at the end of their second year master's classes and what they still needed in order to move confidently into their future career with a sense of what they could contribute to the work and their workplace. I have long had an interest in how people view themselves in relation to the work they perform: it is important for work to be fulfilling in some measure in order to prevent turnover and keep people invested in their work.

For this assignment, students were asked to create a vision statement that would guide their future work. This was to be a combination of their personal mission as well as what they could bring to their organization and/or profession. The purpose of the assignment was to anticipate the future and prepare to thrive in new environments or in environments with a measure of chaos or flux. The task was short, the equivalent of a 250-word abstract. In this brief space, they should choose to make every word matter in a crisp, almost poetic writing style. Expectations were that the writing should reflect the writer, say something meaningful by the writer that would matter individually to him or her and be composed without a lot of extra feathers or fill. Further, this concise yet spirited statement could be one students would return to, reminding them of their essential self-selected purpose. It could be revised as needed or expanded from time to time as circumstances in their future might shift.

The following items were required:

1. Description of your mission or goal;

2. Future orientation—what you see as your potential gift in self-development that will also contribute to the lives of others;

3. Personal aspects, show evidence of passion—can you own this?

4. Connection of your personal vision to your work or anticipated work.

Other elements were optional:

5. Why would someone want to work in your envisioned workplace?

6. How do hope and elements of the possible play a role?

7. What is universal or lasting about your vision?

8. Are there any symbols that might convey your meaning well?

9. Is there a theme that emerged from your thoughts?

Besides serving to sum up their work on developing administrative skills for the workplace, this short exercise became a capstone assignment. The following is an example, shared with permission: "My Vision," by Amber Weaver, MSW KU Graduate 2008.

My Vision

I will have the ability to see strength,

Strength in a person, in a community, in a situation, and in myself,

I will use my inner strength, my drive, and my motivation to help others,

I will take action, not just discuss it,

Swim against the current regardless of what others think,

I will defend the defenseless,

Fight against injustice and oppression for those who cannot or will not,

Challenge the status quo,

I will educate others,

Lead change movements,

Force others to contemplate their points of view, opinions, outlooks, and beliefs,

Change the system when it is damaged,

Create hope for the hopeless,

Help families find their strength, find safety, find shelter,

I will be a leader worth following, personally and professionally,

Be a role model to young and old, lead by example,

Speak for the voiceless,

I will enjoy life and love with all I have,

Be an optimist,

Be passionate in work and play,

Celebrate the good,

Be true to my beliefs

And be true to myself.

MEDITATION: A MEDITATION WITH MUSIC—THE GREAT BELL CHANT

Watch the video of the Great Bell Chant at http://www.onbeing.org/blog/great-bell-chant-meditation/3905. This beautiful visual and auditory meditation features the words of Vietnamese Zen Buddhist monk Thich Nhat Hanh as a bell is slowly and intermittently rung. Because we are all wired differently, students and others may have varying reactions. If you are listening with a group, it can deepen learning to process this experience afterward. The entire chant lasts about seven minutes.

1. How did the sound of the bell and the words of Thich Nhat Hanh help you in focusing your attention?

2. In what ways did the cinematography of sweeping, aerial vistas and intimate portraits aid you in your focus on nature and fellow people?

3. Did you find that Phap Niem's fluid chanting helped you in letting go and being more aware of the compassion inside you? Please explain.

4. How did/didn't the combination of visuals and audio help guide you in this exercise? Did you find them more distracting then helpful? (Gilliss, 2010)

MEDITATION: A MEDITATION WITH MOVEMENT—FIVE AGES DANCING

Watch the video at http://www.onbeing.org/blog/five-ages-dancing-remembering-sage-cowles/6086. This beautiful meditation, just over one minute in length, follows each of five women from different generations sharing in the same meditative dance, but at different intervals.

MEDITATION: A MEDITATION USING HANDS OR FINGERS

Meditations with the fingers are called *mudras*. The following site offers detailed instructions on paying attention to the position of the fingers and hands: http://www.wildmind.org/posture/hands.

MEDITATION: MBSR MINDFULNESS EIGHT-WEEK COURSE

The Palouse Mindfulness-Based Stress Reduction (MBSR) course (http://palousemindfulness.com/index.html) is an online course that appears to be completely free and was developed by a certified MBSR instructor. It is modeled on the program by Jon Kabat-Zinn at the University of Massachusetts Medical School. Comments on the website as recently as June 2016 are very positive. I can't find any objection to exploring it. It contains within it many types of meditations, including one led by Tara Brach, who is well known in meditation circles.

EXPLORING YOUR SPIRITUALITY: WORKING WITH LIGHT

The body and the spirit are not as separate as we often think in our dualistic world. They engage and nourish each other. Breathing in light can be a practice to relax and heal our darker parts, those places where we hold pain, self-doubt, or worry.

1. Begin by finding a quiet place to sit and relax. Notice any parts of your body where you feel tense and intentionally release that tension. You can do this by thinking that part of your body to relax or by contracting and releasing the muscle. If you feel as though anything is in your space that does not belong to you, any energy or negativity from another person for example, send it to a recycling well in front of your feet to return to that other person. As you sit in stillness, begin to imagine a light above your head and all around you. You may want to think of this as the light of your soul, or not.

2. With each inward breath, bring that light into your body and circulate it, paying particular attention to those parts of your body where you find it difficult to release tension. Send that light to that place of tension, with gratitude for how that part of your body supports you.

3. With each outward breath, exhale any tension, pain, self-doubt, or worry, which you may also think of as dispelling darkness. Are there any neglected places or places of suffering?

4. Notice how you feel both physically and emotionally. Do you feel more whole?

5. If you wish, you may also send this light into other situations or to a client for example, trusting that they have the choice to accept this light or not. If not, it will return to you.

6. Journal about your experience. What wisdom did your body share with you? Far from being separate, your body knows and responds to you. In what way do you feel more integrated, if you do? If you do not, what blocks or obstructions seem to be present?

Participation is about keeping energy moving. It is concerned with being involved in cycles of reciprocity: giving and receiving. Older adults especially have a need to continue their active participation, lest they overbenefit or underbenefit from social support that is offered. In caregiving situations, there is a danger that an older person will always be in a position of receiving care and will begin to view himself or herself as having little to offer the care provider. If the elder overbenefits, reciprocity is impaired. This unequal equation can lead to an imbalance in feelings of worth and contribution. Further, an older person who either volunteers excessively and always seeks to provide for others or isolates herself may underbenefit from social relationships. In the first case, they give, but do not allow themselves to be given to. In the second case, there is very little engagement coming into their lives.

We often think of giving related to religious and charitable organizations in terms of financial donations. This is one type of giving, but focus on this aspect alone is impoverished. Giving is a multidimensional action that takes many forms, including giving of our time through active listening. Listening well involves openness to receive, to enliven our being through what we hear, and maybe—to change.

In Sufism, dervishes whirl to the honor of God in an act of service that unites elements of simultaneous giving and receiving. The right hand is lifted upward to receive divine energy while the left hand is pointed downward to convey this energy into the world. Our biological selves, too, participate in this reciprocal exchange. We are nourished and stay vital through inhalation (inspiration) and exhalation (expiration). We take in oxygen through our lungs and we release carbon dioxide, which in turn nourishes plant life in an amazing web of biodiversity.

In our Western culture, there has been a strong focus on acquisitions. Media behemoths suggest there is something more we should want and happiness lies just around the corner of purchasing the item. However, a part of living lightly on the earth, as American Indian tribes suggest, is to transmit what is given to us. Sometimes we will do this in proximate time and sometimes in distal time. We should act as conduits rather than repositories of goods. In fact, people who become adept at building personal repositories often fall into hoarding: seeking possessions for the sake of ownership alone regardless of their value. Some older people who have had many years to acquire things suffer from this and have piles of stuff, more than they can ever use, in their houses. Kept in houses, stuff becomes stagnant.

The key to participation in life is to keep spirit and vitality flowing. This involves phases of giving and receiving, separately or within the parameters of a single interchange. It means times of clearing off the shelves of our lives where we have stored old ideas alongside old objects, so that something new can be placed there. It involves being mentored by others as a novice would be, but also mentoring others as a master would do. In the spaces opened by reciprocity and sharing, we both give and receive. We participate in the ancient rhythm of life.

1. Think about the times and situations in your life where you over-give. Name them and consider the consequences of this over-giving. How do you feel when you do this? How can you begin to let go of some of the ways you over-give—and change? Are there ways you can invite others to help support this change?

2. Think about the times and situations where you mostly receive. Define them. Who gives to you? What have you been given that has stayed with you? This can be an actual object or an idea. Why do you think you recall this?

3. How can you create a healthy reciprocity to keep energy moving in your life, allowing new things to enter and releasing things that are stale? What are the benefits to you when things both come into your life and leave it? What do you choose to hold onto long term that benefits you?

4. Has there been a time or situation when you both gave and received and these actions seemed undifferentiated?

5. Journal about your thoughts.

EXPLORING YOUR SPIRITUALITY: LAUGHTER AND JOY

Traditionally many religious faiths discouraged laughter. In recent past centuries, one idea of religion was to scare people into right action through the idea of a punishing God. Hell was grim and that was what awaited most people, especially those who hid their sins. But as time has moved on, new ideas have come to the foreground. Laughter leads to joy and becoming a joyful people is what Christians are taught to pursue. Joy is not the province of Christians, Jews, Muslims, or other theist religions alone. The Dalai Lama has written many books on happiness and at public talks he is often seen making jokes and laughing. Arriving at joy enriches our lives. Of course, laughter can be used two ways—to lighten our lives or to be the target of jokes, being mocked or laughed at. Working with older people, it is easy to fall into the sadder moments of life as they experience unwanted change. However, genuine laughter can be a great antidote to that. A randomized control trial of older women with depression showed that laughter yoga showed as much improvement on mood as exercise, significantly more than a control group (Shahidi et al., 2011). There are clubs whose goal is to facilitate laughter in community. The opportunity for table fellowship, sharing conversation at mealtimes, can potentially be a source of mirth.

Where is the humor in holy texts? The book of Jonah can be read in a humorous way (Martin, 2012). When Jonah finally reached Nineveh and the people unexpectedly (to him) repented, even the cows were said to don sackcloths (What, they gorged on too much green grass?). Jonah is soothed by the shade of a miraculously appearing tree, he complains petulantly to God of his discomfort when that same tree suddenly withers. God's response is to suggest that his care for the people of Nineveh (which came about because of Jonah's reluctantly delivered message) is far more meaningful than providing the tree as relief against the heat for one person. Because of the cultural location of

humor, the arrow of what may have seemed funny in earlier times completely shoots past us now, making us hunt for—or yearn for—more humorous interpretations.

What can humor bring us? Martin (2012) suggests several possibilities. Among others, several are particularly useful to those who are spiritual, religious, or neither. Humor can keep us humble, especially when we tell jokes about our own flaws. Humor can put events that happen in a broader perspective by communicating a truth we have overlooked. Humor can expand our relationship with God or other people. If we can laugh with others, we allow ourselves to be fully known. Humor heals. There is a physiological response to laughing that releases endorphins in our brains, serves as a natural analgesic to pain, causes enlargement of blood vessels facilitating blood flow, and removes stress-induced cortisol from our bodies. Thus, with laughter comes a higher pain threshold. It feels good to laugh. Finally, humor opens our understanding and spiritual insight when we recognize we have acted from our vulnerability and humanity instead of our strength.

1. Consider the role of humor in your life. Would friends call you a person with a good sense of humor? One who is over-serious? Think about your relationship with what is funny in the world.

2. How do you notice what is humorous. Some of us have a more skilled humor detector than others. What works for you?

3. Think about some incidents in your life that were the object of much humor, if not at the time, at least in the retelling. What did you think was so funny? What made you laugh?

4. How do you propose to look for and incorporate humor in your life going forward?

WEBSITE

The Conscious Elders Network

http://www.consciouselders.org/

"Our vision is to initiate a cultural shift wherein conscious elders reclaim our place in providing education, wisdom, and guidance within our communities. We become catalysts of a social movement in which all generations collaborate in evolving changes for our common betterment. In so doing, we find a new and rewarding sense of meaning in our lives, and we create a new elder culture in the process." This site offers many interesting links, stories, and opportunities for civic involvement.

RECOMMENDED READING

Whyte, D. (2001). *Crossing the unknown sea: Work as a pilgrimage of identity.* New York, NY: Riverhead Books.

This book discusses ways to build identity through the experience of work as it provides opportunity for rediscovering, shaping, and nurturing our personal lives.

APPENDIX

Older Adult Definitions

A discussion of meanings would not be complete without a brief consideration of definitions delivered by adults themselves. The material that follows is a summary of some of the findings from my research. In the following study (Nelson-Becker, 1999), I invited older adults ($n = 79$) to identify up to three of the most difficult problems (called "life challenges" in the study) they had faced in their life. I asked them how they coped with these problems and analyzed both life challenge and coping responses using qualitative methods. I then asked them separate questions about the importance of religion and spirituality in their lives, using a 4-point Likert scale. Table A.1 illustrates how they defined their stance toward each.

Table A.1 Participant Ratings of the Importance of Religion and Spirituality in their Lives ($n = 79$)			
Category	Jewish American $n = 37$	African American $n = 42$	Total 79
Religion and spirituality are important.	48%	95.0%	73%
Religion, not spirituality, is important.	26%	2.5%	14%
Spirituality, not religion, is important.	12%	0.0%	5%
Neither religion nor spirituality is important.	14%	2.5%	8%
Total Percentage	100%	100%	100%

BRIEF LOOK AT THE SAMPLE

The participants in this spiritual and religious coping study were primarily African American (AA) and Jewish American (JA; Nelson-Becker, 2005). There were many kinds of views expressed. This sample was community dwelling and tended to be generally healthy. Age range was 58 to 92, with a median of 78 years. Out of the 79 older people, 66 were female, 37 were JA and 42 were AA. Ninety percent of the sample earned less than $15,000 per year. Table A.2 describes the sample.

Patterns in synagogue/church attendance varied significantly among participants. Only 8% of Jewish American respondents attended synagogue/church weekly or more, in contrast to 50% of AA respondents who attended religious activities weekly or more. Fifty-four percent of Jewish American respondents reported they never attended synagogue/church; 17% of AAs never attended church. Religious affiliation of the total sample included 16% Baptist and 24% Jews who attended synagogue. See Table A.3 and Figure A.1 for the range of religious denominations. Twelve denominations were represented, including African Methodist Episcopal (AME), Catholic, and Buddhist.

Table A.2 Sample Demographics (n = 79)

Item	North Number	North Percentage	South Number	South Percentage	Total Number	Total Percentage
Sites (*n*=79)	37	100	42	100	79	100
Age in years						
(mean)	79		76		77 (mean)	
(median)	81		75		78 (median)	
Race					79	
African American	1	2.7	41	97.6	42	53
Predominantly Jewish	36	97.3	1	2.4	37	47
Gender					79	
Female	31	83.8	35	83.3	66	84
Male	6	16.2	7	16.6	13	16
Education in years						
(mean)	11.86		11.36		11.59 (mean)	
(median)	12		12		12 (median)	
Income						
Under $5000	3	8.1	7	16.7	10	12.6
$5000-$10,000	13	35.1	26	61.9	39	49.4
$10,000-$15,000	14	37.8	9	21.4	23	29.1
Over $15,000	4	10.8	—		4	5.1
No Response	3	8.1	—		3	3.8
Children						
One Child	9	24.3	6	14.3	15	19.0
Two Children	14	37.8	9	21.4	23	29.1
Three Children	6	16.2	2	4.8	8	10.1
Other Children	2	5.4	8	19.0	10	12.7
None	5	13.5	17	40.5	22	27.8
Missing	1	2.7	—		1	1.3
Attend Church						
Weekly or more	3	8.1	21	50.0	24	30.4
1–3 Times Month	—	—	6	14.3	6	7.6
6–11 Times Year	6	16.2	3	7.1	9	11.4
2–3 Times Year	8	21.6	5	11.9	13	16.5
Never[a]	20	54.1	7	16.7	27	34.2

a. Includes those not affiliated with a religion.

Table A.3 Religious Affiliation Characteristics

	Number	Percentage of Total
No Affiliation	11	13.9
Denomination		
African Methodist Episcopal	3	3.8
Apostolic Church of God	1	1.3
Baptist	13	16.4
Buddhist	1	1.3
Catholic	4	5.0
Community Church	6	7.6
Congregational Church	1	1.3
Jehovah's Witness	1	1.3
Jewish (attending)	19	24.1
Jewish (cultural, nonattending)	14	17.7
Lutheran	1	1.3
Pentecostal	1	1.3
Unity	1	1.3
Total	79	100

Figure A.1 Sample Religious Affiliation by Percentage (*n* = 79)

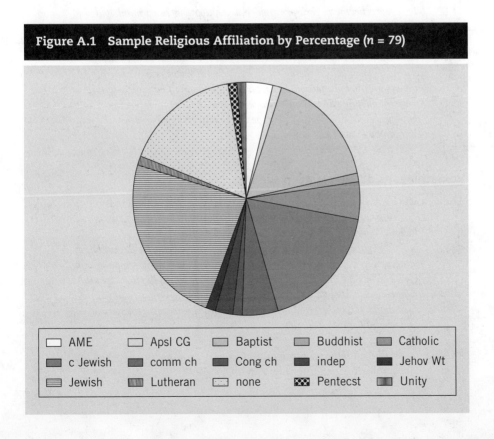

AME	Apsl CG	Baptist	Buddhist	Catholic
c Jewish	comm ch	Cong ch	indep	Jehov Wt
Jewish	Lutheran	none	Pentecst	Unity

One limit of the study was that this was not a large dataset; however, it was large for many qualitative studies, which tend to have sample sizes of 40 and under. The rich specific wording of their beliefs would not have been easy to capture in a quantitative study. A sample of respondent definitions was independently validated by a peer reviewer to ensure rigor.

RELIGION

The following common themes are discussed below: religion is belief or trust, something personal, right behavior, moral code, heritage, faith, and a particular way of thinking. Some criticism of religion as insincere and not true to its teaching was also expressed by participants in the study.

Religion is Belief, Trust in God

While religion as an institution has value, many older adults separated personal belief from institutional doctrine. "Religion is a belief in God. To me it's trying to live the best you can, doing the right thing for everyone. You don't hate," advised one AA woman. "There are so many different religions, you know. I think some religions are phony, not true to what they say. I believe in God," asserted another AA woman. A third AA interviewee distinguished between religion and trust. "Religion is only a duty. I don't accept religion. I would say, 'Trust in the Lord and He will make everything alright.' You have to have faith." The AA respondent below identified several components of religious faith.

> *I suppose believing in basic principles that develop your heart mind, soul and body. It's something you believe in strongly and get satisfaction out of practicing. That's about as deep as I can go. I believe there are so many different faiths and I get something out of all of them that I have intertwined with . . . I don't believe there is any perfect one. If you believe in something, it helps give you satisfaction. You treat people better. You have peace within yourself and peace and harmony among people. That's the bottom line. You have peace within—you can still cope with whatever is going on around you. You can have love . . .*

Something Inside, a Feeling in the Heart

The following AA woman suggested there are many shared aims across religious faiths.

> *Religion comes from your heart. Your belief. That's my religion: my belief. I believe a Catholic has as much religion as a Baptist. I believe a Baptist has as much as a Methodist. They all read the same Bible; they all worship the same God. I believe a German, a Japanese or a Chinaman [sic] has just as much religion as me. How can I explain it? Nowadays people keep changing from one religion to another. It's got to be within you. God is God. He's spirit. It's universal. That's your religion.*

A JA woman described religion as something from the soul as well as belief, but she seemed to be employing the term belief as faith.

Religion is something that comes from your own soul that has nothing to do with Bibles and temples and magnificent churches. It's a belief that either you form or you don't form, but it doesn't depend on your background. It depends on you as an individual. I believe in God, personally, as much as I believe in nature. So name your own God. It's what you believe in.

Right Behavior, Moral Code, Opportunity to Socialize

An AA woman highlighted the value of the code of behavior that many religions teach. "The way I look at religion is being truthful to yourself and being truthful to anybody else. I try to live my life in such a way that I treat everybody the same way I would love for them to treat me." A Jewish American male recognized hypocrisy in people who would use religion for secondary purposes:

You'd be surprised how many people call themselves Catholic or Jewish but they are falling away. They don't practice it. People have various ideas. They go to church for various reasons. People move into town and go to church to get acquainted, for socializing—that's a big point.

Religion as Heritage, Faith

One JA woman mused on her own relationship to religion and her history of sustained religious practice.

Sometimes I believe in it and sometimes I don't. I go to temple on all of the holidays; that's something I've been doing all my life. But I don't know if I believe in it because if there was a God in heaven, he wouldn't do the things he does. Wars and—He wouldn't give so much sorrow to so many people. They call it the golden years, but I don't know what they meant.

Religion as Insincere

Similar to the woman above, another JA woman expressed conflicted feelings about her own relationship to religion. Further she expressed doubts about the ability of religion to assist people in dealing with problems.

I'm not raised a very religious person and yet I guess I am. I don't know. I'm not religious I guess because I don't go to church, but I have a very bad attitude about religion. I think religion has become a very commercial type of thing. I look on religion frankly as a crutch. I think it's almost as bad as the guy who believes his answer lies at the bottom of a whiskey bottle is the guy who believes the answer lies at the cross.

Lastly, a JA woman summarized her own views by deliberating about the darker side of religion.

Finally, in the name of religion, more people have been killed than in any other cause on the face of the earth. It's an excuse for money, power and to keep people mollified. I do not believe in any omnipotent being. I never will. It's all right here. Make the best of it.

Table A.4 Content Analysis of Religious Definitions (n = 79)	
Category	Percentage
Belief * (8)	38
Personal, within, comes from your heart* (14)	18
Doing the golden rule* (4)	9
Heritage	6
Faith * (1)	6
Basic principles, a guide	5
A way of thinking	4
Duty	3
Going to synagogue, church	3
Denominations don't matter	3
A con game, a make-believe story	3
Involvement in community	1
Spirit	1
Never discuss religion	1
Total**	**101**

*The number in parentheses denotes the same definition given for spirituality.

**Represents rounding error.

This illustration of respondent viewpoints provides a perspective on the span of ideas expressed. These older adults, representing two different ethnic groups, twelve faith or philosophical traditions including Buddhism, and two types of nonreligious positions, generally held stances of acceptance towards other faiths. Religion was meaningful to them through self-referencing their own belief system. While many saw the value of religion, they could also be somewhat cautious toward religion and suspicious of religious leadership. What is important to note is that their views on religion were not stereotypically what some people would assume of an aging population: blind, unexamined faith. See Table A.4 for further information about the themes and percentages of endorsements for each theme.

SPIRITUALITY

Older adults in the same study cited above found it more difficult to define spirituality and especially to distinguish it from religion (Nelson-Becker, 2003). For many older persons, this term was newer and not part of their lexicon. Some older people thus gave similar responses for spirituality that they had provided for religion, or could not say what it was at all. Major themes were a feeling in the heart, connection with God, beliefs, relationships, and forgiveness. The individual quality of spirituality and connection with nature were also noted by several people.

A Feeling Inside, In the Heart, Embedded in Being

Several respondents spoke about the numinous quality of spirituality and an intimate connection with Spirit. One AA woman explained,

> *The Spirit sometimes tells me to do or not to do something. It's in my mind. And sure enough if I don't do it, I be so happy that I didn't do it. Because something [would have happened] that I would have been very unhappy about. I call that spirituality.*

"Spirituality is embedded in your being, in your soul," reported another AA woman. Another response included, "Spirituality comes from the heart. You have to believe in it very deeply." A woman from a JA couple who reconnected with their religious heritage after immigration from Russia stated simply and eloquently, "It is my soul." An AA woman who was also a minister in a storefront church related her thoughts.

> *Spirituality is something you think—something within. That's the way I feel about it. It's different from religion. Religion is a big word; spirituality is something within. As you know we're made up of three parts: spirit, soul, and body. The body is the outer appearance; the temple of God is within you.*

A JA female instructed,

> *Spirituality is a gift. And not everyone is blessed with having it unfortunately. It's not that it isn't there, but it is a gift. Sometimes you are born with it. Sometimes you come by it through various means. Trials and tribulations give a lot of people spirituality that they might never have come by.*

Connection With God

"Spirituality is being in tune with the Higher Presence," stated an AA female. A different AA female reported, "I think my relationship with God helps me solve problems. Only by believing, it gives me peace and comfort." Another AA female suggested what she saw as a key characteristic of spirituality and then distinguished it from religion. "Spirituality is the knowing of God and feeling his presence. Believing him. Religion is just attributes of it—like going to church." A JA female explained spirituality directly in terms of a connection, "There are times when you feel spiritual but not especially religious. You connect." [Researcher: "What is it you connect to?"] "You connect to another Higher Being. I can't explain it. Only from the standpoint of I have felt it."

Beliefs

Similar to definitions specified for religion, belief was prominently mentioned. "Spirituality is a teaching, a learning, a self-feeling, your beliefs," offered one AA female. "Spirituality is belief in a thing," affirmed a JA female. An 89-year-old AA female who suffered from chronic health problems and pain, especially in the morning, postulated,

> We each one of us come along with a different spirit and a different life. I can't get angry at you because you believe in this religion and I believe in that one. There is but one God. We have to turn around and say, Hey, ain't but one God so we all got to depend on Him because He's the one who's made this world and made it so beautiful for us to live in. Some mornings I get up and look out there with all those beautiful colors. Man didn't do that. God did it. So we've got to be thankful. Maybe I might not be thankful this morning but I've got to get to it this afternoon.

"What is spirituality? I know the difference between right and wrong. If I do wrong it bothers me. I have a very deep conscience," admitted one JA female.

Relationships and Forgiving

Constructing and maintaining relationships was another area where older adults spoke about how spirituality was included. "I believe spirituality is to be forgiving. That's all I can say," detailed a JA female. Others spoke about friendships with "soul-friends" who would listen to them deeply as they would listen in return.

"Connection with nature." A JA female who was a Holocaust survivor stipulated,

> Spirituality is more in touch with nature, the soul, the better part of a human being. Being whole and not necessarily having a religious belief, being in tune with nature. Nature gives me a lift. What I see out my window [the lake] gives me a sense of eternity and my place in it.

A second JA female who described herself as an atheist articulated her thoughts as follows:

> I would say that it's a form of communication with nature, or natural things or other creatures of the earth. I think man as an entity treats other living beings in a horrifying manner. Really. We destroy everything we touch. I think spirituality is the ability to communicate. Communication is the essence of human endeavor.

Struggle to Distinguish Between Spirituality and Religion

One AA male suggested, "I can't think of a definition. I don't know. Spirituality and the way you deal with things, as opposed to a set building. I think that's religion. Go over there and sit down in a pew and pray." An AA woman told me, "I'd give the same answer as for religion." A JA male answered, "I don't know what spirit is. Religion was built into me from day one." "'I haven't the slightest idea,' would be my answer," verbalized a JA woman. "Spirituality? That is religion," firmly instructed a second JA female.

Overall, while some older respondents expressed a clear understanding of spirituality and how they saw it separately from religion, a fairly large number of individuals either did not distinguish it, found the term confusing, or just couldn't say what it was (see Table A.5). In a sense, the perspective individuals provided represented their practical

Table A.5 Content Analysis of Spirituality Definitions (n = 79)

Category	Percentage
A feeling inside, in the heart, embedded in Being*(14)	18
Connection with God	15
Beliefs*(30)	10
Relationships, forgiving	8
Same as religion	6
The way you live*(7)	5
Individuality, what you think	4
Communication with nature	3
A higher form of something	1
I avoid these conversations	1
Don't know	29
Total	100

*The number in parentheses denotes the same definition given for religion.

philosophy for living. Although I was asking for definitions and meanings, what people gave me was the life philosophy that they had built over many years and circumstances that represented their way of being in the world. It felt like such a privilege to be invited into what existed as private space and to be generously given what felt like intimate responses.

As I asked about their interest in talking about religion and spirituality, individuals told me that had I not directly asked, they would never have spoken of such things. This provides evidence for the value of asking about religion and spirituality in assessment with all older people. If they are nonreligious and nonspiritual and their views about these domains are not a problem for them, then nothing further needs to be addressed in this area. Several people who I had earlier invited to participate and who had declined at the time, asked to be included later in the study. I was told this occurred due to the safe space created for previous interviewees. This seems to emphasize the importance of the therapeutic relationship, perhaps even revisiting religion and spirituality later in the relationship once an individual feels more comfortable. At any age, it appears that people enjoy reflecting on and responding to the deep questions that reappear across the centuries.

REFERENCES

Aboriginal Health and Medical Research Council (AHMRC). (n.d.). *Definition of aboriginal health*. Retrieved from http://www.ahmrc.org.au/index.php?option=comcontent&view=article&id=35&Itemid=37

Abraham, A., Kutner, J., & Beaty, B. (2006). Suffering at the end of life in the setting of low physical symptom distress. *Journal of Palliative Medicine, 9*(3), 658–665.

Achenbaum, W. A. (2014). Robert N. Butler, MD (January 21, 1927–July 4, 2010): Visionary leader. *The Gerontologist, 54*(1), 6–12.

Ackerman, D. (2007). *The zookeeper's wife: A war story*. London, UK: W. W. Norton.

Addams, J. (1981). *Twenty years at Hull-House with autobiographical notes*. New York, NY: MacMillan. Original work published 1910

Address, R. (2012). Contemplating a theology of healthy aging. In J. Levin & K. Meador (Eds.), *Healing to all their flesh: Jewish and Christian perspectives on spirituality, theology, and health* (pp. 26–51). West Conshohocken, PA: Templeton Press.

Administration on Aging. (2009). *Profile of older Americans*. Retrieved from http://www.aoa.gov/aoaroot/aging_statistics/Profile/2009/2.aspx

Administration on Aging. (2012). *A profile of older Americans: 2012*. Retrieved from http://www.aoa.gov/Aging_Statistics/Profile/2012/docs/2012profile.pdf

Ahmed, S., & Amer, M. M. (2012). *Counseling Muslims: Handbook of mental health issues and interventions*. New York, NY: Routledge.

Ai, A. (2006). Daoist spirituality and philosophy: Implications for holistic health, aging and longevity. In E. Mackenzie & B. Rakel (Eds.), *Complementary and alternative medicine for older adults* (pp. 149–160). New York, NY: Springer.

Ai, A. L., Ardelt, M., & Wink, P. (2010). Spirituality in aging: A journey for meaning through deep interconnection in humanity. In J. C. Cavanaugh & C. K. Cavanaugh (Eds.), *Aging in America* (Volume III, pp. 222–246). Westport, CT: Praeger.

Ai, A. L., & McCormick, T. R. (2009). Increasing diversity of American's faiths alongside baby boomer's aging: Implications for chaplain intervention in health settings. *Journal of Health Care Chaplaincy, 16*(1–2), 24–41.

Ai, A. L., Tice, T. N., & Kelsey, C. L. (2009). Pathways of deep interconnectedness and struggle to PTSD and PTG in responses to 9/11. In M. Morgan (Ed.), *The impact of 9/11 on psychology and education: The day that changed everything?* (pp. 115–138). New York, NY: Palgrave.

Ai, A. L., Tice, T. N., Peterson, C., & Bu, H. B. (2005). Prayers, spiritual support, and positive attitudes in coping with the 9–11 national crisis. *Journal of Personality, 73*(3), 763–791.

Ainsworth, M. D. S. (1968). Object relations, dependency, and attachment: A theoretical review of the infant mother relationship. *Child Development, 40*, 969–1025.

Algase, D. L., Beck, C., Kolanowski, A., Berrent, S., Richards, K., & Beattie, E.

(1996). Need-driven dementia-compromised behavior: An alternative view of disruptive behavior. *American Journal of Alzheimers Disease & Other Dementias, 11*, 10–19.

Al-heeti, R. (2007). Why nursing homes will not work: Caring for the needs of the aging Muslim American population. *The Elder Law Journal, 15*(1), 205–231.

Allen, J. R. (1904). *Celtic art in pagan and Christian times*. Retrieved from https://commons.wikimedia.org/wiki/Category:Triple_spiral#/media/File:Celtic_Art_p287.jpg

Almond, G. A., Appleby, R. S., & Sivan, E. (2003). *Strong religion: The rise of fundamentalisms around the world*. Chicago, IL: University of Chicago Press.

Allport, G. (1950). *The individual and his religion: A psychological interpretation*. Oxford, UK: Macmillan.

Alzheimer's Association. (AA). (2015). Alzheimer's disease facts and figures. *Alzheimer's & Dementia, 11*(3), 3–32.

American Association of Professional Chaplains. (2005). *Common standards for professional chaplaincy*. Retrieved from http://www.professionalchaplains.org

American Holistic Nurses Association (AHNA). (n.d.). *What is holistic nursing?* Retrieved from http://www.ahna.org/About-Us/What-is-Holistic-Nursing

American Indian Relief Council. (n.d.). *History and culture: Boarding schools*. Retrieved from http://www.nrcprograms.org

American Nurses Association (ANA). (2004). *Nursing: Scope and standards of practice* (2nd ed.). Washington, DC: Author.

American Psychiatric Association. (1994). *Diagnostic and statistical manual of mental disorders* (4th ed.). Washington, DC: Author.

American Psychiatric Association. (2000). *Diagnostic and statistical manual of mental disorders* (4th ed., text rev.). Washington, DC: Author.

American Psychiatric Association. (2013). *Diagnostic and statistical manual of mental disorders* (5th ed.). Arlington, VA: Author.

American Psychological Association. (n.d.). *Division 36.* Retrieved from http://www.apa.org/about/division/div36.aspx

American Psychological Association. (2010). *Ethical principles of psychologists and code of conduct: Including 2010 amendments.* Retrieved from https://www.apa.org/ethics/code/index.aspx

American Psychological Association. (2013). *Guidelines and principles for accreditation of programs in professional psychology.* Retrieved from http://www.apa.org/ed/accreditation/about/policies/guiding-principles.pdf

Ammerman, N. T. (2013). Spiritual but not religious? Beyond binary choices in the study of religion. *Journal for the Scientific Study of Religion, 52*(2), 258–278.

The Analects by Confucious, Part 2. (n.d.). Retrieved from http://classics.mit.edu/Confucius/analects.1.1.html

Anandarajah, G., & Hight, E. (2001). Spirituality and medical practice: Using HOPE questions as a practical tool for spiritual assessment. *American Physician, 63*(1), 81–88.

Anderson, N. B., & Kazak, A. E. (2015). Guidelines for psychological practice with transgender and gender nonconforming people. *American Psychologist, 70*(9), 832–864.

Angelica, J., Gordon, N., & Koepke, D. (2015, March). *Meeting the mystery of Alzheimer's: Healing when there is no cure.* Presentation at the 2015 American Society on Aging Conference, Chicago, IL.

Arbesman, S. (2012). *The half-life of facts: Why everything we know has an expiration date.* New York, NY: Current.

Ardito, R. B., & Rabellino, D. (2011). Therapeutic alliance and outcome of psychotherapy: Historical excursus, measurements, and prospects for research. *Frontiers in Psychology, 2,* 270. Retrieved from http://doi.org/10.3389/fpsyg.2011.00270

Arinzon, Z., Peisakh, A., & Berner, Y. N. (2008). Evaluation of the benefits of enteral nutrition in long-term care elderly patients. *Journal of the American Medical Directors Association, 9*(9), 657–662.

Aries, P. (1981). *The hour of our death.* New York, NY: Alfred Knopf.

Ark, P. D., Hull, P. C., Husaini, B. A., & Craun, C. (2006). Religiosity, religious coping styles, and health service use: Racial differences among elderly women. *Journal of Gerontological Nursing, 32*(8), 20–29.

Aronowitz, R., Deener, A., Keene, D., Schnittker, J., & Tach, L. (2015). Cultural reflexivity in health research and practice. *American Journal of Public Health,105*(S3), S403–S408. doi:10.2105/AJPH.2015.302551

Ars, B., & Montero, E. (2004). *Suffering and dignity in the twilight of life.* The Hague, Brussels: Kugler European Institute of Bioethics.

Association for Spiritual, Ethical and Religious Values in Counseling. (n.d.) *Historical development of the Association for Spiritual, Ethical and Religious Values.* Retrieved from http://www.aservic.org/about/history

Association for Spiritual, Ethical, and Religious Values in Counseling. (2016). *Competencies for addressing spiritual and religious issues in counseling.* Retrieved from http://www.aservic.org/wp-content/uploads/2010/04/Spiritual-Competencies-Printer-friendly1.pdf

Association of Religion Data Archives. (n.d.). Retrieved from http://www.thearda.com/

Association of Religion Data Archives. (2008). Retrieved from http://www.thearda.com/Archive/Files/Analysis/GSS2004/GSS2004_Var570_1.asp

Assous, A. B. (2013). Cultural and Islamic values in relation with death. *European Scientific Journal, 9*(5), 280–300.

Atchley, R. C. (1999). *Continuity and adaptation in aging: Creating positive experiences.* Baltimore, MD: Johns Hopkins University Press.

Aufauvre, B. V. (2003). Depression and spiritual desolation. *The Way (Society of Jesus) Publications, 42*(3), 47–56.

Awofeso, N. (2005). Redefining health. *Bulletin of the World Health Organization.* Retrieved from http://www.who.int/bulletin/bulletin_board/83/ustun11051/en/

Aylor, A. (2008). End of life review. *American Journal of Hospice and Palliative Medicine, 25*(3), 233–236.

Baetz, M., Griffin, R., Bowen, R., Koenig, H. G., & Marcoux, E. (2004). The association between spiritual and religious involvement and depressive symptoms in a Canadian population. *The Journal of Nervous and Mental Disease, 192*(12), 818–822.

Balboni, T., Vanderwerker, L., Block, S., Paulk, M., Lathan, C., Peteet, J., & Prigerson, H. (2007). Religiousness and spiritual support among advanced cancer patients and associations with end-of-life treatment preferences and quality of life. *Journal of Clinical Oncology, 25*(5), 555–560.

Baltes, P. B. (1993). The aging mind: Potential and limits. *The Gerontologist, 33*(5), 580–594.

Banerjee, M. M. (2005). Applying Rawlsian social justice to welfare reform: An unexpected finding for social work. *Journal of Sociology & Social Welfare, 32*(3), 35–47.

Barbour, I. G. (2000). *When science meets religion: Enemies, strangers, or partners?* San Francisco, CA: Harper.

Barclay, A. (2012). Psalm 88: Living with Alzheimer's. *Journal of Religion, Disability and Health, 16*(1), 88–101.

Barg, F. K., Huss-Ashmore, R., Wittink, M. N., Murray, G. F., Bogner, H. R., & Gallo, J. J. (2006). A mixed-methods approach to understanding loneliness and depression in older adults. *The Journals of Gerontology. Series B, Psychological Sciences and Social Sciences, 61*(6), 329–339.

Barker, S. L. (2007). The integration of spirituality and religion content in social work education: Where we've been, where we're going. *Social Work & Christianity, 34*(2), 146–166.

Barnum, B. S. (2006). *Spirituality in nursing: From traditional to new age.* New York, NY: Springer.

Barnum, B. S. (2011). *Spirituality in nursing: The challenges of complexity.* New York, NY: Springer.

Barr, H., Koppel, I., Reeves, S., Hammick, M., & Freeth, D. (2005). *Effective interprofessional education: Argument, assumption and evidence.* Oxford, England: Blackwell.

Barrett, A. M., Orange, W., Keller, M., Damgaard, P., & Swerdlow, R. H. (2006). Short-term effect of dementia disclosure: How patients and families describe the diagnosis. *Journal of the American Geriatrics Society, 54*(12), 1968–1970.

Bar-Tur, L., & Levy-Shiff, R. (2000). Coping with losses and past trauma in old age: The separation-individuation perspective. *Journal of Personal and Interpersonal Loss, 5,* 263–281.

Basting, A. D. (2009). *Forget memory, creating better lives for people with dementia.* Baltimore, MD: John Hopkins University Press.

Baumeister, R. F., Bratslavsky, E., Muraven, M., & Tice, D. M. (1998). Ego depletion: Is the active self a limited resource? *Journal of Personality and Social Psychology, 74*(5), 1252–1265.

Baylor Religion Survey. (2007). *Belief in angels.* Retrieved from http://www.thearda.com/quickstats/qs_74.asp

Beard, R. L. (2004). In their voices: Identity preservation and experiences of Alzheimer's disease. *Journal of Aging Studies,18,* 415–428.

Beauchamp, T., & Childress, J. (2013). *Principles of biomedical ethics* (7th ed.). New York, NY: Oxford University Press.

Beck, A. T., & Alford, B. A. (2009). *Depression: Causes and treatment.* Philadelphia: University of Pennsylvania Press.

Becker, E. (1973). *The denial of death.* New York, NY: Free Press.

Bellah, R., Madsen, R., Sullivan, W., Swidler, A., & Tipton, S. (1985). *Habits of the heart: Individualism and commitment in American life.* Berkeley: University of California Press.

Beng, T., Chin, L., Guan, N., Yee, A., Wu, C., Jane, L., & Meng, C. (2015). Mindfulness-based supportive therapy (MBST). *American Journal of Hospice and Palliative Medicine, 32*(2), 144–160.

Bengston, V. L., & Allen, K. R. (1993). The life course perspective applied to families over time. In P. G. Boss, W. J. Doherty, R. LaRossa, W. R. Schumm, & S. K. Steinmetz (Eds.), *Source book of family theories and methods: A contextual approach* (pp.469–499). New York, NY: Plenum Press.

Bensen, H. (1975). *The relaxation response.* New York, NY: HarperCollins.

Berger, P. L. (1974). Some second thoughts on substantive versus functional definitions of religion. *Journal for the Scientific Study of Religion, 13*(2), 125–133.

Berger, P. (2012). Further thoughts on religion and modernity. *Society, 49*(4), 313–316.

Berger, P. L., & Luckmann, T. (1971). *The social construction of reality: A treatise in the sociology of knowledge.* Middlesex, England: Penguin.

Bern-Klug, M., Gessert, C., & Forbes, S. (2001). The need to revise assumptions about the end of life: Implications for social work practice. *Health and Social Work, 26*(1), 38–48.

Bertalanffy, L. (1969). *General system theory: Foundations, development, applications.* New York, NY: G. Braziller.

Berti, V., Pupi, A., & Mosconi, L. (2011). PET/CT in diagnosis of dementia. *Annals of the New York Academy of Sciences, 1228,* 81–92.

Bessinger, D., & Kuhne, T. (2002). Medical spirituality: Defining domains and boundaries. *Southern Medical Journal, 95*(12), 1385–1388.

Beuscher, L., & Beck, C. (2008). A literature review of spirituality in coping with early-stage Alzheimer's disease. *Journal of Clinical Nursing, 17*(5a), 88–97.

Beuscher, L., & Grando, V. (2009). Using spirituality to cope with early-stage Alzheimer's disease. *Western Journal of Nursing Research, 31*(5), 583–598.

Beversluis, J. (Ed.). (2000). *Source book of the world's religions.* Novato, CA: New World Library.

Bialon, L., & Coke, S. (2012). A study on caregiver burden: Stressors, challenges, and possible solutions. *The American Journal of Hospice & Palliative Care, 29*(3), 210–218.

Biberman, J., & Whitty, M. (2007). *At work: Spirituality matters.* Scranton, PA: University of Scranton Press.

Bier, W. C. (1975, August*). PIRI— Bridge between the AICPA and the APA Division 36.* Presidential address, meeting of the American Psychological Association, Chicago , IL.

Bircher J. (2005). Towards a dynamic definition of health and disease. *Medicine, Health Care, and Philosophy, 8,* 335–41.

Biron, L. (2015, June 30). How do you solve a puzzle like neutrinos? *Symmetry Magazine.* Retrieved from http://www .symmetrymagazine.org/article/june-2015/how-do-you-solve-a-puzzle-like-neutrinos

Bishop, A. J. (2008). Stress and depression among older residents in religious monasteries: Do friends and God matter? *The International Journal of Aging and Human Development, 67*(1), 1–23.

Bishop, S. R., Lau, M., Shapiro, S., Carlson, L., Anderson, N. D., Carmody, . . . & Devins, G. (2004). Mindfulness: A proposed operational definition. *Clinical Psychology: Science and Practice, 11,* 230–241.

Blake, W. (1975). *The marriage of heaven and hell.* London, UK: Oxford University Press.

Blazer, D. (2002). *Depression in late life.* New York, NY: Springer.

Blazer, D. G. (2003). Depression in late life: Review and commentary. *The Journals of Gerontology. Series A, Biological Sciences and Medical Sciences, 58*(3), 249–65.

Borg, M. J. (1987). *Jesus: A new vision.* San Francisco, CA: Harper.

Bormann, J., Warren, K. A., Regalbuto, L., Glaser, D., Kelly, A., Schnack, J., & Hinton, L. (2009). A spiritually based caregiver intervention with telephone delivery for family caregivers of veterans with dementia. *Family & Community Health, 32*(4), 345–353.

Bowker, J. (1997). *The Oxford dictionary of world religions.* New York, NY: Oxford University Press.

Bowker, J. (2014). *God: A very short introduction.* Oxford, UK: Oxford University Press.

Bowland, S., Edmond, T., & Fallot, R. D. (2012). Evaluation of a spiritually focused intervention with older trauma survivors. *Social Work, 57*(1), 73–82.

Bowlby, J. (1969). Attachment and loss, Vol. 1: *Attachment.* New York: Basic Books.

Brassen, S., Gamer, M., Peters, J., Gluth, S., & Büchel, C. (2012). Don't look back in anger! Responsiveness to missed chances in successful and nonsuccessful aging. *Science. 336*(6081), 612–614.

Brawer, P. A., Handal, P. J., Fabricatore, A. N., Roberts, R., & Wajda-Johnson, V. A. (2002). Training and education in religion/spirituality within APA-accredited clinical psychology programs. *Professional Psychology: Research and Practice, 33,* 203–206.

Breitenfeld, T., Jurasic, M., & Breitenfeld, D. (2014). Hippocrates: The forefather of neurology. *Neurological Sciences, 35*(9), 1349–1352. doi:10.1007/s10072–014–1869–3

Brennan-lng, M. (Ed.). (2013). Spirituality and religion among older lesbian, gay, bisexual, and transgender adults [Special issue]. *Journal of Religion, Spirituality and Aging, 25*(2).

Breytspraak, L., & Badura, L. (2015). *Facts on aging quiz.* Retrieved from http://info.umkc .edu/aging/quiz/

Briggs, L., & Macleod, A. (2006). Demoralisation—A useful conceptualisation of non-specific psychological distress among refugees attending mental health services. *International Journal of Social Psychiatry, 5*(6) 512–524.

Bronstein, M. (1999). Healing: A Jewish word. *Tikkun, 14*(2), 39–40.

Brown, S. F. (2014b). *Introduction: Protestantism.* Retrieved from http://wro.factsonfile.com .flagship.luc.edu/world-religions-online/protestantism/sections/introduction-the-protestant-world.aspx

Browning, D. (1991). *A fundamental practical theology: Descriptive and strategic proposals.* Minneapolis, MN: Fortress Press.

Browning, D. S. (1995). *A fundamental practical theology: Descriptive and strategic proposals.* Minneapolis, MN: Fortress Press.

Browning, D. (2007). *Equality and the family: A fundamental, practical theology of children, mothers, and fathers in modern societies* (Religion, marriage, and family series). Grand Rapids, MI: Wm. B. Eerdmans.

Bruni, F. (2009; updated 2011, November 17). Memoirs and memory. *Huffington Post.* Retrieved from http://www.huffingtonpost.com

Buber, M. (1958). *I and thou.* New York, NY: Scribner's. Original work published 1923

Bulkeley, K. (2005). *Soul, psyche, brain: New directions in the study of religion and brain-mind science.* New York, NY: Palgrave Macmillan.

Bull, M. (2014). Strategies for sustaining self used by family caregivers for older adults with dementia. *Journal of Holistic Nursing, 32*(2), 127–135.

Bullis, R. K. (1996). *Spirituality in social work practice.* Washington, DC: Taylor & Francis.

Burkhardt & Nagai-Jacobson, (2005). Reawakening spirit in clinical practice. *Journal of Holistic Nursing, 12*(1), 9–21.

Bursell, J., & Mayers, C. A. (2010). Spirituality within dementia care: Perceptions of health professionals. *British Journal of Occupational Therapy, 73*(4), 144–151.

Burtless, G. (2013). *The impact of population aging and delayed retirement on workforce productivity.* Chestnut Hill, MA: Center for Retirement Research at

Boston College. Retrieved from http://crr.bc.edu/wp-content/uploads/2013/05/wp_2013–111.pdf

Butler, R. N. (2002). Declaration of the rights of older persons. *The Gerontologist, 42*(2), 152.

Byock, I. (2004). *The four things that matter most: A book about living.* New York, NY: Free Press.

Byrne, L., & MacKinlay, E. (2012). Seeking meaning: Making art and the experience of spirituality in dementia care. *Journal of Religion, Spirituality & Aging, 24*(1–2), 105–119.

Byrne, M. (2007). Spirituality in palliative care: What language do we need? *International Journal of Palliative Nursing, 13*(3), 118–124.

Cacciatore, J., & Ong, R. (2011). Through the touch of God: child death and spiritual sustenance in a Hutterian colony. *Omega, 64*(3), 2011–2012.

Calza, G., & Katsushika, H. (2003). *Hokusai.* New York, NY: Phaidon.

Campbell, J. (1968). *The hero with a thousand faces* (2nd ed.). Princeton, NJ: Princeton University Press.

Campbell, J. (1988). *The power of myth: With Bill Moyers.* New York, NY: Doubleday.

Camus, A. (1991). *The myth of Sisyphus and other essays* (Justin O'Brien, Trans.). New York, NY: Vintage Books.

Canadian Hospice Palliative Care Association. (2013). *A model to guide hospice palliative care.* Ottawa, ON: Author.

Canda, E. (1986). *A conceptualization of spirituality for social work: Its issues and implications.* Unpublished dissertation. The Ohio State University.

Canda, E. R. (1988). Conceptualizing spirituality for social work: Insights from diverse perspectives. *Social Thought, 14*(1), 30–46.

Canda, E. R., & Furman, L. D. (1999). *Spiritual diversity in social work practice.* New York, NY: Free Press.

Canda, E. R., & Furman, L. D. (2010). *Spiritual diversity in social work practice: The heart of helping* (2nd ed.). New York, NY: Oxford Press.

Canda, E. R., Ketchell, A., Dybicz, P., Pyles, L., & Nelson-Becker, H. (2006). *Health through faith and community: A study resource for faith communities to promote social well-being.* Binghamton, NY: Haworth Press.

Carstensen, L. L., & Mikels, J. A. (2005). At the intersection of emotion and cognition: Aging and the positivity effect. *Current Directions in Psychological Science, 14*(3), 117–121.

Cashwell, C., & Young, J. (2011). *Integrating spirituality and religion into counseling: A guide to competent practice* (2nd ed.). Alexandria, VA: American Counseling Association.

Catholic Health Association of Canada (CHAC) and the Canadian Association for Pastoral Practice and Education (CAPPE). (2000). *Standards of spiritual and religious care for health services in Canada.* Retrieved from http://www.chac.ca/alliance/online/docs/brochure_standards_en.pdf

Centers for Disease Control and Prevention (CDC). (2013). *The state of aging and health in America, 2013.* Retrieved from http://www.cdc.gov/

Chakravarti, S. S. (1991). *Hinduism, a way of life.* Delhi: Motilal Banarsidass.

Chan, C. H., Chan, T. H., & Chan, C. L. (2014). Translating Daoist concepts into integrative social work practice: An empowerment program for persons with depressive symptoms. *Journal of Religion & Spirituality in Social Work: Social Thought, 33*(1), 61–72.

Charmaz, K. (1991). *Good days, bad days: The self in chronic illness and time.* New Brunswick, NJ: Rutgers University Press.

Chase, S. (2011). *Nature as spiritual practice.* Grand Rapids, MI: Wm B. Eerdman's.

Chassin, M., & Loeb, J. (2011). The ongoing quality improvement journey: Next stop, high reliability. *Health Affairs (Project Hope), 30*(4), 559–568.

Chatterton, W., Baker, F., & Morgan, K. (2010). The singer or the singing: Who sings individually to persons with dementia and what are the effects? *American Journal of Alzheimer's Disease and Other Dementias, 25*(8), 641–649.

Chittister, J. (2008). *The gift of years: Growing old gracefully.* New York, NY: BlueBridge.

Chittister, J. (2011). *The monastery of the heart: An invitation to a meaningful life.* Katonah, NY: BlueBridge/United Tribes Media.

Chodron, P. (1997). *When things fall apart.* Boston, MA: Shambhala.

Choi, N. G., & McDougall, G. (2007). Comparison of depressive symptoms between homebound older adults and ambulatory older adults. *Aging & Mental Health, 11*(3), 310–322.

Choi, G., Tirrito, T., & Mills, F. (2008). Caregiver's spirituality and its influence on maintaining the elderly and disabled in a home environment. *Journal of*

Gerontological Social Work, 51(3–4), 247–259.

Chow, E. O, & Nelson-Becker, H. (2011). Spiritual distress to spiritual transformation: Stroke survivor narratives from Hong Kong. *Journal of Aging Studies, 24*(4), 313–324.

Chung, D. K. (2000). Taoism. In J. Beversluis (Ed.), *Source book of the world's religions* (pp. 105–107). Novato, CA: New World Library.

Cicirelli, V. G. (2002). Older adults' fear and acceptance of death: A transition model. *Ageing International, 28*(1), 66–81.

Clark, D. (1999). "Total pain," disciplinary power and the body in the work of Cicely Saunders, 1958–1967. *Social Science & Medicine, 49*(6), 727–736.

Clark, D. (2005). *Cicely Saunders: Founder of the hospice movement.* New York, NY: Oxford University Press.

Clark, P. A. (2003). Addressing patient's emotional and spiritual needs. *Joint Commission Journal on Quality and Safety, 29*(12), 659–670.

Clarke, D. M., & Kissane, D. W. (2002). Demoralization: Its phenomenology and importance. *Australian and New Zealand Journal of Psychiatry, 36*(6), 733–742.

Clarke, P. B., Giordano, A. L., Cashwell, C. S., & Lewis, T. F. (2013). The straight path to healing: Using motivational interviewing to address spiritual bypass. *Journal of Counseling & Development, 91*(1), 87–94.

Cohen, G. (2005). *The mature mind: The positive power of the aging brain.* New York, NY: Basic Books.

Cohen-Mansfield, J., Golander, H., & Arnheim, G. (2000). Self-identity in older persons suffering from dementia: Preliminary

results. *Social Science & Medicine, 51*, 381–394.

Cohn-Sherbok, D. (2012). Judaism. In M. Cobb, C. M. Puchalski, & B. Rumbold (Eds.), *Oxford textbook of spirituality in healthcare* (pp. 63–68). New York, NY: Oxford University Press.

Coleman, P. (2011). *Belief and ageing: Spiritual pathways in later life.* Portland, OR: Policy Press.

Coleman, P. G., Ivani-Chalian, C., & Robinson, M. (2004). Religious attitudes among British older people: Stability and change in a 20-year longitudinal study. *Ageing and Society, 24*(2), 167–188.

Coleman, P. G., & O'Hanlon, A. (2004). *Ageing and development: Theories and research.* London, UK: Arnold.

Community of Christ. (n.d.). *Yearning for God.* Retrieved from https://cofcspiritualformationcenter.files.wordpress.com/2015/02/yearningforgod.pdf

Corey, G., Corey, M., & Callanan, P. (2003). *Issues & ethics in the counseling profession* (6th ed.). Pacific Grove, CA: Brooks/Cole.

Corr, C. A., Nabe, C. M., & Corr, D. M. (2006). *Death and dying, life and living.* Belmont, CA: Thomson Wadsworth.

Coryell, W. (2007). The facets of melancholia. *Acta Psychiatrica Scandinavica. Supplementum, 433*, 31–36.

Cotrell, V., & Hooker, K. (2005). Possible selves of individuals with Alzheimer's disease. *Psychology & Aging, 20*, 285–294.

Council for Social Work Education. (2008).) *Educational policies.* Retrieved from http://www.cswe.org/File.aspx

Cowley, A. S. (1993). Transpersonal social work: A theory for the 1990s. *Social Work, 38*(5), 527–534.

Cribbs, J., Byers, L., & Moxley, D. (2009). Serving older Native Americans: Challenges facing gerontological social work in Indian country. *Journal of Ethnic and Cultural Diversity in Social Work, 18*(4), 261–275.

Crider, G. (2014). Stricken by grief, finding solace in a robin. *New York Times.* Retrieved from http://www.nytimes .com/2014/11/08/opinion/ stricken-by-grief-finding-solace- in-a- robin.html

Crowther, M. R., Parker, M. W., Achenbaum, W. A., Larimore, W. L. (2002). Rowe and Kahn's model of successful aging revisited: Positive spirituality—the forgotton factor. *The Gerontologist, 42*(5), 613–620.

Culliford, L. (2011). Beware! Paradigm shift under way. *Mental Health, Religion & Culture, 14*(1), 43–51. doi:10.1080/13674676.20 10.492591

Cumming, E. (1963). Further thoughts on the theory of disengagement. *International Social Science Journal, 15*(3), 377–393.

Cumming, E., & Henry, W. E. (Eds.). (1961). *Growing old: The process of disengagement.* New York, NY: Basic Books.

Cummings, S. M., Cooper, R L., & Cassie, K. M. (2009). Motivational interviewing to affect behavioral change in older adults. *Research on Social Work Practice 19*(2), 195–204.

Curran, S., & Wattis, J. P. (Eds.). (2008). *Practical management of affective disorders in older people: A multiprofessional approach.* Oxford, UK: Radcliffe.

Daaleman, T. P., & Nease, D. E., Jr. (1994). Patient attitudes regarding physician inquiry into spiritual and religious issues. *Journal of Family Practice, 39,* 564–568.

Dahlsgaard, K., Peterson, C., & Seligman, M. E. P. (2005). Shared virtue: The convergence of valued human strengths across culture and history. *Review of General Psychology, 9*(3), 203–213.

Dalai Lama. (2002). *Advice on dying and living a better life.* London, UK: Random House.

Dalai Lama. (2010). *Toward a true kinship of faiths: How the world's religions can come together.* New York, NY: Random House.

Dalai Lama, & Ekman, P. (2008). *Emotional awareness: Overcoming obstacles to psychological balance and compassion.* New York, NY: Henry Holt.

Dalai Lama, & Norman, A. (2011). *Beyond religion: Ethics for a whole world.* New York, NY: Houghton, Mifflin Harcourt.

Dalal, A. S. (Ed.). (2001). *A greater psychology: An introduction to the psychological thought of Sri Aurobindo.* New York, NY: Jeremy P. Tarcher/Putnam.

Dalby, P., Sperlinger, D. J., & Boddington, S. (2011). The lived experience of spirituality and dementia in older people living with mild to moderate dementia. *Dementia, 11*(1), 75–94.

Damjanovic, A., Yang, Y., Glaser, R., Kiecolt-Glaser, J., Nguyen, H., Laskowski, B., . . . Weng, N. (2007). Accelerated telomere erosion is associated with a declining immune function of caregivers of Alzheimer's disease patients. *Journal of Immunology, 179*(6), 4249–4254.

D'Amour, D., & Oandasan, I. (2005). Interprofessionality as the field of interprofessional practice and interprofessional education: An emerging concept. *Journal of Interprofessional Care, 19*(Supplement 1), 8–20.

Darnley-Smith, R., & Patey, H. (2003). *Music therapy.* London, UK: Sage.

Davies, P. (1995). *About time: Einstein's unfinished revolution.* New York, NY: Simon & Schuster.

Davison, S. N., & Jhangri, G. S. (2010). Impact of pain and symptom burden on the health- related quality of life of hemodialysis patients. *Journal of Pain and Symptom Management, 39*(3), 477–485.

Dawson, M. M. (1915). *The ethics of Confucious.* New York, NY: Putnam. Retrieved from http://www.sacred- texts.com/cfu/ eoc/eoc09.htm

de Beauvoir, S. (1972). *The coming of age.* New York, NY: W. W. Norton.

De Medeiros, K. (2014). *Narrative gerontology in research and practice.* New York, NY: Springer.

De Raedt, R., & Van Der Speeten, N. (2008). Discrepancies between direct and indirect measures of death anxiety disappear in old age. *Depression & Anxiety (1091–4269), 25*(8), E11-E17. doi:10.1002/ da.20336

de Saint Exupéry, A. (2000). *Le petit prince.* Paris, France: Gallimard.

De Sousa, A. (2011). Spirituality and geriatric psychiatry: A review. *Indian Journal of Gerontology, 25*(3), 345–354.

Dean, S. N. (Trans.). (1903). *St. Anselm: Basic writings. Proslogium or discourse on the existence of God, Chapter II.* Retrieved from http://www.sacred-texts.com/chr/ans/ans008.htm

Dearmer, P. (1909). *Body and soul: An enquiry into the effect of religion upon health.* New York, NY: E. P. Dutton and Co. Retrieved from http://babel.hathitrust.org/cgi/pt?id=njp.32101067128932;view=1up;seq=3

Dein, S. (2006). Religion, spirituality and depression: Implications for research and treatment. *Primary Care & Community Psychiatry, 11*(2), 67–72.

Delaney, C., Barrere, C., & Helming, M. (2011). The influence of a spirituality-based intervention on quality of life, depression, and anxiety in community-dwelling adults with cardiovascular disease: a pilot study. *Journal of Holistic Nursing: Official Journal of the American Holistic Nurses' Association, 29*(1), 21–32.

Denzin, N. K. (1974). The methodological implications of symbolic interactionism for the study of deviance. *British Journal of Sociology, 25,* 2269–282.

Department of Health and Human Services (DHHS). (2010). *Health people 2020.* Retrieved from http://www.healthypeople.gov/2020/topics-objectives/topic/older-adults/objectives

Dhar, N., Chaturvedi, S. K., & Nandan, D. (2013). Spiritual health, the fourth dimension: A public health perspective. *WHO South-East Asia Journal of Public Health, 2,* 3–5.

Didion, J. (2006). *The year of magical thinking.* New York, NY: Alfred A. Knopf.

Diehl, M., Elnick, A. B., Bourbeau, L. S., & Labouvie-Vief, G. (1998). Adult attachment styles: Their relations to family context and personality. *Journal of Personality and Social Psychology, 74*(6), 1656–1669.

Diener, E., Oishi, S., & Ryan, K. L. (2013). Universals and cultural differences in the causes and structure of happiness: A multilevel review. In C. L. Keyes (Ed.), *Mental well-being: International contributions to the study of positive mental health* (pp. 153–176). New York, NY: Springer.

Dillon, M., & Wink, P. (2007). *In the course of a lifetime: Tracing religious belief, practice, and change.* Berkeley: University of California Press.

Dowling, E. M. (2005). Religious theory, developmental systems view. In E. M. Dowling and W. G. Scarlett (Eds.), *Encyclopedia of religious and spiritual development* (pp. 381–384). Thousand Oaks, CA: Sage. Retrieved from http://dx.doi.org.flagship.luc.edu/10.4135/9781412952477

Downey, M. (1997). *Understanding Christian spirituality.* Mahwah, NJ: Paulist Press.

Drywater-Whitekiller, V. (2006). What the dominant society can't give me: Perceptions of Native American elders teaching native traditions. *The Journal of Baccalaureate Social Work, 12*(1), 71–86.

Dudley, J. R. (2016). *Spirituality matters in social work.* New York, NY: Routledge Press.

Dudley, R., O'Brien, J., Barnett, N., McGuckin, L., & Britton, P. (2002, January 01). Distinguishing depression from dementia in later life: A pilot study employing the emotional stroop task. *International Journal of Geriatric Psychiatry, 17*(1), 48–53.

Duggleby, W., Williams, A., Holtslander, L., Cunningham, S., & Wright, K. (2012). The chaos of caregiving and hope. *Qualitative Social Work, 11*(5), 459–469.

Duncan, B. L., Miller, S. D., & Sparks, J. A. (2004). *The heroic client: A revolutionary way to improve effectiveness through client-directed, outcome-informed therapy.* San Francisco, CA: Wiley Press.

Duncan, B. L., & Miller, S. D., Wampold, B. E., & Hubble, M. A. (2010). *The heart & soul of change: What works in therapy* (2nd ed.). Washington, DC: American Psychological Association.

Dupuis, S. L., Wiersma, E., & Loiselle, L. (2012). Pathologizing behavior: Meanings of behaviors in dementia care. *Journal of Aging Studies, 26*(2), 162–173.

Duran, E. (2006). *Healing the soul wound: Counseling with American Indians and other Native peoples.* New York, NY: Teacher's College.

Durkheim, E. (1965). *The elementary forms of the religious life.* New York, NY: Free Press. Original work published 1915

Durkheim, E. (2008). *The elementary forms of the religious life.* London, UK: Oxford Press. Original work published 1915

Durkheim, E., & Fields, K. (1995). *The elementary forms of religious life.* New York, NY: Free Press.

Dybicz, P. (2012). The ethic of care: Recapturing social work's first voice. *Social Work, 57*(3), 271–280.

D'Zurilla, T. J., & Nezu, A. M. (2010). Problem-solving therapy. In K. Dobson (Ed.), *Handbook of cognitive-behavioral therapies* (3rd ed., pp. 197–225). New York, NY: Guilford Press.

Ekerdt, D. J., & Sergeant, J. F. (2006). Family things: Attending the household disbandment of older adults. *Journal of Aging Studies, 20*(3), 193–205.

Elder, G. (2001). Life course. In G. L. Maddox (Ed.), *The encyclopedia of aging* (3rd ed.; pp. 593–596). New York, NY: Springer.

The Elders. (2007, July 18). *Nelson Mandela introduces the Elders, Johannesburg, 18 July 2007* [Video file]. Retrieved from https://www.youtube.com/watch?v=9AGz5P4SI3k

The Elders. (2014). *Who are the Elders?* Retrieved from http://www.theelders.org/about

Eliade, M. (1958). *Patterns in comparative religion.* New York, NY: The New American Library.

Eliade, M. (1987). *The sacred and the profane: The nature of religion.* San Diego, CA: Harcourt Brace Jovanovich.

Eliade, M., & Trask, W. R. (1965). *Rites and symbols of initiation: The mysteries of birth and rebirth.* New York, NY: Harper & Row.

Eliot, T. S. (1970). Four quartets: Burnt Norton. *Collected Poems 1909–1962.* New York, NY: Harcourt, Brace & World.

Elkins, D. N., Hedstrom, L. J., Hughes, L. L., Leaf, J. A., & Saunders, C. (1988). Toward a humanistic-phenomenological spirituality: Definition, description, and measurement. *Journal of Humanistic Psychology, 28*(4), 5–18.

Ellor, J. (2013). Religion and spirituality among older adults in light of the DSM-5. *Social Work & Christianity, 40*(4), 372–383.

Emerson, R. W. (1890). *Essays.* New York, NY: Houghton Mifflin.

Emmons, R. A. (2005). Sacred emotions. In K. Bulkeley (Ed.), *Soul, psyche, brain: New directions in the study of religion and brain-mind*

science (pp. 93–112). New York, NY: Macmillan.

Encyclopedia Britannica. (2015). *Spiral math.* Retrieved from http://www.britannica.com/topic/spiral-mathematics

Ensrud, K., Ewing, S., Cawthon, P., Fink, H., Taylor, B., Cauley, J., ... Cummings, S. (2009). A comparison of frailty indexes for the prediction of falls, disability, fractures, and mortality in older men. *Journal of the American Geriatrics Society, 57*(3), 492–498.

Epel, E., Blackburn, E., Lin, J., Dhabhar, F., Adler, N., Morrow, J., & Cawthon, R. (2004). Accelerated telomere shortening in response to life stress. *Proceedings of the National Academy of Sciences of the United States of America, 101*(49), 17312–17315.

Erikson, E. H. (1950). *Childhood and society.* New York, NY: W. W. Norton.

Erikson, E. H. (1982). *The life cycle completed: A review.* New York, NY: W. W. Norton.

Erikson, E. H., & Erikson, J. M. (1997). *The life cycle completed: Extended version.* New York, NY: W. W. Norton.

Erikson, E. H., Erikson, J. M., & Kivnick, H. Q. (1986). *Vital involvement in old age.* New York, NY: W. W. Norton.

Ernecoff, N. C., Curlin, F. A., Buddadhumaruk, P., & White, D. B. (2015). Health care professionals' responses to religious or spiritual statements by surrogate decision makers during goals-of-care discussions. *JAMA, Internal Medicine, 175*(10), 1662–1669. doi:10.1001/jamainternmed.2015.4124

Esposito, J. (2011). *What everyone needs to know about Islam.* New York, NY: Oxford University Press.

Esposito, J. L., Fasching, D. J., & Lewis, T. (2012). *Religions of Asia today.* New York, NY: Oxford University Press.

Estes, C. P. (1992). *Women who run with the wolves. Myths and stories of the wild woman archetype.* New York, NY: Ballentyne Books.

Fahey, C. J., & Lewis, M. A. (1990). Principles of integrating spiritual concerns into programs for the aging. *Generations, 14*(4), 59.

Faiver, C., Ingersoll, R., O'Brien, E., & McNally, C. (2001). *Explorations in counseling and spirituality: Philosophical, practical, and personal reflections.* Belmont, CA: Wadsworth/Thompson.

Fast, B., & Chapin, R. (2000). *Strength-based care management for older adults.* Baltimore, MD: Health Professions Press.

Federal Interagency Forum on Aging-Related Statistics. (2012). *Older Americans: Key indicators of well-being.* Retrieved from http://www.agingstats.gov

FEMA Emergency Management Institute. (n.d.). *Why define disaster?* Emergency Management Institute. Washington, DC: US Government. Retrieved from https://training.fema.gov/

Fermilab. (2014). *Dark matter and dark energy.* Retrieved from http://www.fnal.gov/pub/science/particle-physics/experiments/dark-matter-and-dark-energy.html

Ferngren, G. B. (2012). Medicine and religion: A historical perspective. In M. Cobb, C. M. Puchalski, & B. Rumbold (Eds.), *Oxford textbook of spirituality in healthcare* (pp. 3–10). Oxford, UK: Oxford University Press.

Fetzer Institute. (1999). *Multidimensional measurement of*

religiousness/spirituality for use in health research. Kalamazoo, MI: Author.

Fick, D. M., Steis, M. R., Waller, J. L., & Inouye, S. K. (2013). Delirium superimposed on dementia is associated with prolonged length of stay and poor outcomes in hospitalized older adults. *Journal of Hospital Medicine, 8*(9), 500–505.

Fischer, K. (1998). *Winter grace: Spirituality and aging.* Nashville, TN: Upper Room.

Fitchett, G. (1993). *Assessing spiritual needs: A guide for caregivers.* Minneapolis, MN: Augsburg Press.

Fletcher, J. (1997). *Situation ethics: The new morality.* Louisville, KY: Westminster John Knox Press.

Forsyth, J. (2003). *Psychological theories of religion.* Upper Saddle River, NJ: Prentice-Hall.

Fowler, J. W. (1981). *Stages of faith.* San Francisco, CA: Harper & Row.

Frame, M. W. (2003). *Integrating religion and spirituality into counseling: A comprehensive approach.* Pacific Grove, CA: Thompson/Brooks-Cole.

Frank, J. D., & Frank, J. B. (1993). *Persuasion and healing: A comparative study of psychotherapy.* Baltimore, MD: Johns Hopkins University Press.

Frankl, V. (1972). *Why believe in others?* [Video]. Retrieved from https://www.ted.com/talks/viktor_frankl_youth_in_search_of_meaning

Frankl, V. (1984). *Man's search for meaning.* New York, NY: Washington Square Press.

Frankl, V. (1992). *Man's search for meaning: An introduction to logotherapy* (4th ed.). Boston, MA: Beacon Press.

Fredrickson, B. L. (2001). The role of positive emotions in positive psychology: The broaden-and-build theory of positive emotions. *American Psychologist, 56*(3), 218–226.

Fredrickson, B. L. (2013). Updated thinking on positivity ratios. *American Psychologist, 68*(9), 814–822.

Fredriksen-Goldsen, K. I. (2011). Resilience and disparities among lesbian, gay, bisexual, and transgender older adults. *Public Policy & Aging Report, 21*(3), 3–7.

Freeman, S. J., & Francis, P. C. (2006). Casuistry: A complement to principle ethics and a foundation for ethical decisions. *Counseling and Values, 50*(2), 142–153.

Freud, S. (1989). *The future of an illusion* (Vol. 21). New York, NY: Norton Press. Original work published 1927

Fukui, S., Okada, S., Nishimoto, Y., & Nelson-Becker, H. (2010). The repeated appeal to return home in older adults with dementia: Developing a model for practice. *Journal of Cross Cultural Gerontology, 26*(1), 39–54.

Gadamer, H. (1999). *Truth and method* (2nd rev. ed., Trans. Joel Weinsheimer and Donald G. Marshall). New York, NY: Continuum Press.

Galek, K., Flannelly, K. J., Vane, A., & Galek, R. (2005). Assessing a patient's spiritual needs: A comprehensive instrument. *Holistic Nursing Practice, 19*(2), 62–69.

Galenson, D. W. (2010). Understanding creativity. *Journal of Applied Economics, 13*(2), 351–362.

Gallagher, T. H., Waterman, A. D., Ebers, A. G., Fraser, V. J., & Levinson, W. (2003). Patients' and

physicians' attitudes regarding the disclosure of medical error. *Journal of the American Medical Association (JAMA), 289*(8), 1001–1007.

Gallup. (2014a). *Americans still believe in God.* Retrieved from http://www.gallup.com/poll/193271/americans-believe-god.aspx

Gallup. (2014b). *Majority still says religion can answer today's problems.* Retrieved from http://www.gallup.com/poll/171998/majority-says-religion-answer-todayproblems.aspx

Ganss, G. E. (1992). *The spiritual exercises of Saint Ignatius: A translation and commentary.* St. Louis, MO: The Institute of Jesuit Sources.

Garrett, M., Brubaker, M., Torres-Rivera, E., West-Olatunji, C., & Conwill, W. (2008). The medicine of coming to center: Use of the Native American centering technique—Ayeli—to promote wellness and healing in group work. *The Journal for Specialists in Group Work, 33*(2), 179–198.

Garrett, M., Garrett, J. T., & Brotherton, D. (2001). Inner circle/outer circle: A group technique based on Native American healing circles. *Journal for Specialists in Group Work, 26*(1), 17–30.

Gaspar, C. (2007). *Aging Muslim communities.* Retrieved from http://worldmuslimcongress.blogspot.com/2007/04/aging-muslim-communities.html

Gay, D., & Lynxwiler, J. P. (2013). Cohort, spirituality, and religiosity: A cross-sectional comparison. *Journal of Religion and Society, 15*, 1–17.

Geertz, C. (1973). *The interpretation of cultures.* New York, NY: Basic Books.

Gellis, Z. D., McGinty, J., Horowitz, A., Bruce, M. L., & Misener, E. (2007). Problem-solving therapy for late-life depression in home care: A randomized field trial. *The American Journal of Geriatric Psychiatry, 15*(11), 968–978.

General Social Survey. (2004). Retrieved from http://www.thearda.com/Archive/Files/Analysis/GSS2004/GSS2004_Var570_1.asp

General Social Survey. (2012). Retrieved from http://sda.berkeley.edu/quicktables/quicksetoptions.do;jsessionid=E8DBE1E1534DDEBACC95F4D4B047B72B?reportKey=gss12%3A1

George, L., Kinghorn, W., Koenig, H., Gammon, P., & Blazer, D. (2013). Why gerontologists should care about empirical research on religion and health: Transdisciplinary perspectives. *The Gerontologist, 53*(6), 898–906.

Germer, C. K., & Siegel, R. D. (Eds.). (2012). *Wisdom and compassion in psychotherapy: Deepening mindfulness in clinical practice.* New York, NY: Guilford Press.

Germer, C., Siegel, R., & Fulton, P. (2013). *Mindfulness and psychotherapy* (2nd ed.). New York, NY: Guilford Press.

Gerzon, R. (1997). *Finding serenity in the age of anxiety.* New York, NY: Macmillan.

Gethin, R. (1998). *The foundations of Buddhism.* Oxford, UK: Oxford University Press.

Gibbons, M. B., Crits-Christoph, P., Levinson, J., Gladis, M., Siqueland, L., Barber, J. P., & Elkin, I. (2002). Therapist interventions in the interpersonal and cognitive therapy sessions of the treatment of depression collaborative research program. *American Journal of Psychotherapy, 56*(1), 3–26.

Gilligan, C. (1977). In a different voice: Women's conception of the self and of morality. *Harvard Educational Review, 47*(4), 481–517.

Gilligan, C. (2014). Moral injury and the ethic of care: Reframing the conversation about differences. *Journal of Social Philosophy, 45*(1), 89–106.

Gilliss, T. (2010). *The great bell chant: A meditation.* Retrieved from http://www.onbeing.org/blog/great-bell-chant-meditation/3905

Glazner, G. M. (2014). *Dementia arts: Celebrating creativity in elder care.* Baltimore, MD: Health Professions Press.

Global Spirit (Producer). (n.d.). *Stories to remember* [video]. Retrieved from http://www.cemproductions.org/globalspirit/stories-to-remember/

Golant, S. M. (2003). Conceptualizing time and behavior in environmental gerontology: A pair of old issues deserving new thought. *Gerontologist, 4*(5), 638–648.

Gold, J. M. (2010). *Counseling and spirituality: Integrating spiritual and clinical orientations.* Upper Saddle River, NJ: Prentice Hall.

Gone, J. P. (2010). Psychotherapy and traditional healing for American Indians: Exploring the prospects for therapeutic integration. *Counseling Psychologist, 38*(2), 166–235.

Goodkind, J., Gorman, B., Hess, J., Parker, D., & Hough, R. (2015). Reconsidering culturally competent approaches to American Indian healing and well-being. *Qualitative Health Research, 25*(4), 486–499.

Gordon, M. (2002). *Islam: Origins, practices, holy texts, sacred persons, sacred places.* New York, NY: Oxford University Press.

Gordon, P. (2014). *Part I: Dementia: The "epidemic" of metaphors.* Retrieved from https://holeousia.wordpress.com/2014/01/01/part-i-dementia-the-epidemic-of-metaphors/

Gozalo, P. L., & Miller, S. C. (2007). Hospice enrollment and evaluation of its causal effect on hospitalization of dying nursing home patients. *Health Services Research, 42*(2), 587–610. doi:10.1111/j.1475-6773.2006.00623.x

Granqvist, P., Mikulincer, M., & Shaver, P. R. (2010). Religion as attachment: Normative processes and individual differences. *Personality and Social Psychology Review, 14*(1), 49–59.

Greeley, A. (2001). The future of religion in America. *Society, 38*(3), 32–37.

Green, M., & Elliott, M. (2010). Religion, health, and psychological well-being. *Journal of Religion & Health, 49*(2), 149–163.

Greenberg, G. (2013, April 23). Does psychiatry need science? *The New Yorker.* Retrieved from http://www.newyorker.com/tech/elements/does-psychiatry-need-science

Grof, C., & Grof, S. (Eds.). (1989). *Spiritual emergency: When personal transformation becomes a crisis.* Los Angeles, CA: Jeremy P. Tarcher.

Gupta, S., & Bonanno, G. A. (2011). Complicated grief and deficits in emotional expressive flexibility. *Journal of Abnormal Psychology 120*(3), 635–643.

Halifax, J. (2008). *Being with dying: Cultivating compassion and fearlessness in the presence of death.* Boston, MA: Shambhala.

Hallenbeck, J. (2003). *Perspectives on palliative care*. New York, NY: Oxford University Press.

Han, J., & Richardson, V. E. (2010). The relationship between depression and loneliness among homebound older persons: Does spirituality moderate this relationship? *Journal of Religion and Spirituality in Social Work*, 29(3), 218–236.

Hanh, T. (1991). *Peace is every step: The path of mindfulness in everyday life*. New York, NY: Bantam Books.

Hanh, T. N. (1995). *Living Buddha, living Christ*. New York, NY: Riverhead Books.

Hanh, T. N. (2002). *Interbeing: Fourteen guidelines for engaged Buddhism*. Berkeley, CA: Parallax Press.

Hanh, T. N. (2012). *Making space: Creating a home meditation practice*. Berkeley, CA: Parallax Press.

Hank, K., & Schaan, B. (2008). Cross-national variations in the correlation between frequency of prayer and health among older Europeans. *Research on Aging*, 30(1), 36–54.

Hanks, G. (2010). *Oxford textbook of palliative medicine* (4th ed.). New York, NY: Oxford University Press.

Hartley, C. (2011). Disability and justice. *Philosophy Compass*, 6(2), 120–132.

Hartz, P. R. (2014). *Introduction: Native American religions*. Retrieved from http://wro.factsonfile.flagship.luc.edu/world-religions-online/native-american-religions.aspx

Havens, B. J. (1968). An investigation of activity patterns and adjustment in an aging population. *The Gerontologist, 8*, 201–206.

Hawley, K. (2012). *Trust: A very short introduction*. Oxford, UK: Oxford University Press.

Hayes, S. C. (2003). Mindfulness: Method and process. *Clinical Psychology: Science & Practice*, 10(2), 161–165.

Hayes, S. C., Strosahl, K. D., & Wilson, K. G. (2012). *Acceptance and commitment therapy: The process and practice of mindful change* (2nd ed.). New York, NY: Guilford Press.

Heard, G. (1963). *The five ages of man*. New York, NY: The Julian Press.

Hebert, L. E., Weuve, J., Scherr, P. A., & Evans, D. A. (2013). *Alzheimer disease in the United States (2010–2050) estimated using the 2010 census*. Philadelphia, PA: Lippincott Williams & Wilkins.

Higginson, I. J., & Sen-Gupta, G. J. A. (2000). Place of care in advanced cancer: A qualitative systematic literature review of patient preferences. *Journal of Palliative Medicine*, 3(3), 287–300.

Hill, P. C., & Hood, R. W. (1999). *Measures of religiosity*. Birmingham, AL: Religious Education Press.

Hindu History. (2015). *ReligionFacts.com*. Retrieved from http://www.religionfacts.com/hinduism/history.htm

Hinton, D. (Trans.). (1997). *Chuang Tzu: The inner chapters*. Washington, DC: Counterpoint.

Hodge, D. R. (2004). Working with Hindu clients in a spiritually sensitive manner. *Social Work*, 49(1), 27–38.

Hodge, D. R. (2005). Spiritual assessment tools. *Health and Social Work*, 30(4), 314–323.

Hofmann, L., & Walach, H. (2011). Spirituality and religiosity in psychotherapy: A representative survey among German psychotherapists. *Psychotherapy Research*, 21(2), 179–192.

Hoffman, E. (Ed.). (1996). *Future visions: The unpublished papers of Abraham Maslow*. Thousand Oaks, CA: Sage.

Hoffman, Y. (1998). *Japanese Death Poems: Written by Zen monks and haiku poets on the verge of death*. Hong Kong, China: Periplus Editions.

Hoobler, T., & Hoobler, D. (1993). *Confucianism*. New York, NY: Brown.

Hooyman, N. R., & Kiyak, H. A. (2008). *Social gerontology: A multidisciplinary perspective*. Boston, MA: Pearson Education.

Horne-Thompson, A., & Grocke, D. (2008). The effect of music therapy on anxiety in patients who are terminally ill. *Journal of Palliative Medicine, 11*, 582–590.

Hummert, M. L. (1990). Multiple stereotypes of elderly and young adults: A comparison of structure and evaluations. *Psychology and Aging*, 5(2), 182–193.

Huxley, A. (2004). *The perennial philosophy*. New York, NY: Perennial Classics.

Hwang, K. K. (2001). The deep structure of Confucianism: A social psychological approach. *Asian Philosophy*, 11(3), 179–204.

Hybels, C. F., Blazer, D. G., Pieper, C. F., Landerman, L. R., & Steffens, D. C. (2009). Profiles of depressive symptoms in older adults diagnosed with major depression: Latent cluster analysis. *The American Journal of Geriatric Psychiatry*, 17(5), 387–396.

Ibrahim, I. A. (2002). *How do Muslims treat the elderly?* Retrieved from http://www.islam-guide.com/ch3-15.htm

Idler, E. L., Hudson, S. V., & Leventhal, H. (1999). The

meanings of self-ratings of health: A qualitative and quantitative approach. *Research on Aging, 21,* 458–476.

Ignatius of Loyola. (1951). *The spiritual exercises of St. Ignatius: Based on studies in the language of the autograph* (L. J. Puhl, Trans.). Chicago, IL: Loyola University Press.

Indian Health Service. (2006). *Indian Health Service strategic plan 2006–2011.* Retrieved from https://www.ihs.gov/planningevaluation/documents/IHSStrategicPlan20062011.pdf

Inhorn, M. C., & Serour, G. I. (2011). Islam, medicine, and Arab-Muslim refugee health in America after 9/11. *The Lancet, 378*(9794), 935–943.

Institute of Medicine. (2001). *Crossing the quality chasm: A new health system for the 21st century.* Washington, DC: National Academies Press.

Institute of Medicine. (2011). *The health of lesbian, gay, bisexual, and transgender people: Building a foundation for better understanding.* Washington, DC: National Academy of Sciences.

Institute of Medicine. (2015). *Measuring the impact of interprofessional education on collaborative practice and patient outcomes.* Washington, DC: National Academies Press.

International Council of Nurses. (2012). *The ICN code of ethics for nurses.* Retrieved from http://www.icn.ch/images/stories/documents/about/icncode_english.pdf

Interprofessional Education Collaborative Expert Panel. (2011). *Core competencies for interprofessional collaborative practice: Report of an expert panel.* Washington, DC:

Interprofessional Education Collaborative.

Irving, K., Fick, D., & Foreman, M. (2006). Delirium: a new appraisal of an old problem. *International Journal of Older People Nursing, 1*(2), 106–112.

Jacobs, A. (Ed.). (2008). *Native American wisdom: A spiritual tradition at one with nature.* London , UK: Watkins.

James, W. (1961). *The varieties of religious experience.* Cambridge, MA: Harvard University Press. Original work published 1902

Jankowski, K. B., Handzo, G. F., & Flannelly, K. J. (2011). Testing the efficacy of chaplaincy care. *Journal Of Health Care Chaplaincy, 17*(3/4), 100–125. doi:10.1080/08854726.2011.616166

Jelonek, W. M. (2008). Nurses' experiences of practicing the heart touch technique for one month. *Journal of Holistic Nursing, 26*(4), 271–282.

Jensen, J. P., & Bergin, A. E. (1988). Mental health values of professional therapists: A national interdisciplinary survey. *Professional Psychology: Research and Practice, 19*(3), 290–297.

Jeste, D. V., Blazer, D. G., & First, M. (2005). Aging-related diagnostic variations: Need for diagnostic criteria appropriate for elderly psychiatric patients. *Biological Psychiatry, 589*(4), 265–271.

Jewell, A. (2011). *Spirituality and personhood in dementia.* London, UK: Jessica Kingsley.

Johnson, R. W., Tilghman, J. S., Davis-Dick, L. R., & Hamilton-Faison, B. (2006). A historical overview of spirituality in nursing. *The ABNF Journal 17*(2), 60–62.

Johnstone, M., & Kanitsaki, O. (2009). Ethics and advance care

planning in a culturally diverse Society. *Journal of Transcultural Nursing, 20*(4), 405–416.

The Joint Commission on Accreditation of Hospital Organizations. (2003). *Joint commission resources' 2003 comprehensive accreditation manual for hospitals: The official handbook.* Oakbrook Terrace, IL: Author.

Jordens, C., Little, M., Kerridge, I., & McPhee, J. (2005). Ethics in medicine, from advance directives to advance care planning: Current legal status, ethical rationales and a new research agenda. *Internal Medicine Journal, 35,* 563–566.

Jung, C. (1939). *Modern man in search of a soul.* New York, NY: Harcourt Brace.

Jung, C. G. (1947). *Psychology of the unconscious.* New York, NY: Dodd, Mead, and Co.

Jung, C. (1963). *Memories, dreams, and reflections.* New York, NY: Vintage Books.

Jung, C. G. (2001). *Modern man in search of a soul* (Trans. W. S. Dell & C. F. Baynes). New York, NY: Routledge.

Kabat-Zinn, J. (2004). *Full catastrophe living: How to cope with stress, pain and illness using mindfulness meditation* (15th anniversary ed.). London, UK: Piatkus.

Kabat-Zinn, J. (2005). *Coming to our senses.* New York, NY: Hyperion.

Kant, I., & Ellington, J. (1983). *Ethical philosophy: The complete texts of grounding for the metaphysics of morals, and metaphysical principles of virtue, part II of the metaphysics of morals.* Indianapolis, IN: Hackett.

Kashdan, T. B., & Biswas-Diener, R. (2014). *The upside of your dark side.* New York, NY: Plume.

Kass, L. R. (1980). Ethical dilemmas in the care of the ill: What is the patient's good? *JAMA, 244*(17), 1946–1949.

Katsuno, T. (2003). Personal spirituality of persons with early-stage dementia: Is it related to perceived quality of life? *Dementia, 2*(3), 315–335.

Katz, S. (1983). Assessing self-maintenance: Activities of daily living, mobility and instrumental activities of daily living. *Journal of the American Geriatrics Society, 31*(12), 721–726.

Kaufman, Y., Anaki, D., Binns, M., & Freedman, M. (2007). Cognitive decline in Alzheimer disease: Impact of spirituality, religiosity, and QOL. *Neurology, 68*(18), 1509–1514.

Kellems, I. S, Hill, C. E., Crook-Lyon, R. E., & Freitas, G. (2010). Working with clients who have religious/spiritual issues: A survey of University Counseling Center therapists. *Journal of College Student Psychotherapy, 24*(2), 139–155. doi:10.1080/87568220903558745

Kelly, E. W. (1997). Relationship-centered counseling: A humanistic model of integration. *Journal of Counseling and Development, 75*(5), 337–345. doi:10.1002/j.1556–6676. 1997.tb02349.x

Kelsey, M. T. (1987). *Encounter with God.* New York, NY: Paulist Press.

Kelsey, M. T. (1995). *Healing and Christianity.* Minneapolis, MN: Augsburg Fortress Press.

Kenyon, G. M. (2003). Telling and listening to stories: Creating a wisdom environment for older people, responsible guidelines for intervention. *Generations: The Journal of the Western Gerontological Society, 27,* 30–33.

Kerner, F. F. (1991). Judaism. In *Religious worlds: Primary readings in comparative perspective* (pp. 281–349). Chicago, IL: Kendall/Hunt.

Keshavarzi, H., & Haque, A. (2013). Outlining a psychotherapy model for enhancing Muslim mental health within an Islamic context. *The International Journal for the Psychology of Religion, 23*(3), 230–249. doi: 10.1080/10508619.2012.712000

Keyes, C. L. M. (2013). *Mental well-being: International contributions to the study of positive mental health.* Dordrecht, NED: Springer.

Khirfan, G. (2012). *Muslim elders' issues in aging.* Retrieved from http://ginakhirfan.blogspot .com/2012/09/muslim-elders-issues-in-aging.html

Killick, J. (2006). Helping the flame to stay bright celebrating the spiritual in dementia. *Journal of Religion, Spirituality & Aging, 18*(2–3), 73–78.

Killick, J., & Craig, C. (2012). *Creativity and communication in persons with dementia: A practical guide.* London, UK: Jessica Kingsley.

King, D. E., & Bushwick, B. (1994). Beliefs and attitudes of hospital inpatients about faith healing and prayer. *Journal of Family Practice, 39,* 349–352.

Kirkpatrick, L. (2005). *Attachment, evolution, and the psychology of religion.* New York, NY: Guilford Press.

Kitwood T. (1997) *Dementia reconsidered: The person comes first.* Buckingham, UK: Open University Press.

Kitwood, T. (1998). Toward a theory of dementia care: Ethics and interaction. *The Journal of Clinical Ethics, 9*(1), 23–34.

Kivnick, H. Q., & Murray, S. V. (2001). Life strengths interview guide: Assessing elder clients' strengths. *Journal of Gerontological Social Work, 34*(4), 7–32.

Kleinfield, N. R. (2016, April 30). Fraying at the edges: Her fight to live with Alzheimer's. *New York Times.* Retrieved from http://www.nytimes.com/ interactive/2016/05/01/nyregion/ living-with-alzheimers.html

Kleinman, A. (2013). From illness as culture to caregiving as moral experience. *New England Journal of Medicine, 368*(15),1376–1377.

Klostermaier, K. (1999). *A short introduction to Hinduism.* Oxford, UK: Oneworld.

Knight, T., Davison, T. E., McCabe, M. P., & Mellor, D. (2011). Environmental mastery and depression in older adults in residential care. *Ageing and Society, 31*(5), 870–884.

Koenig, H. (1994). *Aging and God: Spiritual pathways to mental health in midlife and later years.* New York, NY: Routledge Press.

Koenig, H. G. (2002). *Spirituality in patient care: Why, how, when, and what.* Philadelphia, PA: Templeton Foundation Press.

Koenig, H. G. (2005). *Faith and mental health: Religious resources for healing.* Philadelphia, PA: Templeton Press.

Koenig, H. G. (2012). Religion, spirituality and health: The research and clinical implications. *International Scholarly Research Notices Psychiatry,* 1–33. doi:10.5402/2012/278730

Koenig, H. G. (2015). Religion, spirituality, and health: A review and update. *Advances in Mind-Body Medicine, 29*(3), 19–26.

Koenig, H., King, D., & Carson, V. (2012). *Handbook of religion and health* (2nd ed.). New York, NY: Oxford University Press.

Koenig, H. G., McCullough, M. E., & Larson, D. B. (2001). *Handbook of religion and health.* New York, NY: Oxford University Press.

Kohlberg, L. (1984). *The psychology of moral development: The nature and validity of moral stages.* San Francisco, CA: Harper & Row.

Kontos, P., & Martin, W. (2013). Embodiment and dementia: Exploring critical narratives of selfhood, surveillance, and dementia care. *Dementia, 12*(3), 288–302.

Krause, N., Emmons, R., & Ironson, A. (2015). Benevolent images of God, gratitude, and physical health status. *Journal of Religion and Health, 54*(4), 1503–1519.

Krishnan, V., & Nestler, E. J. (2010). Linking molecules to mood: New insight into the biology of depression. *The American Journal of Psychiatry, 167*(11), 1305–1320.

Kübler-Ross, E. (1969). *On death and dying.* New York, NY: Simon & Schuster.

Kupfer, F. (1996). Everything but the truth. *Women's Review of Books, 13*(0/11), 291–293.

Lama, D. (2010). *Toward a true kinship of faiths.* New York, NY: Three Rivers Press.

Langer, E. J. (1989). *Mindfulness.* Reading, MA: Addison-Wesley.

Langer, E. J. (1997). *The power of mindful learning.* Reading, MA: Addison-Wesley.

Lao-Tzu, & Mitchell, S. (Trans.). (2008). *Tao te ching.* Radford, VA: Wilder.

Laszlo, V. (Ed.). (1993). *The basic writings of C. G. Jung.* New York, NY: Random House.

Lawler-Row, K. A. (2010). Forgiveness as a mediator of the religiosity-health relationship. *Psychology of Religion and Spirituality, 2*(1), 1–16.

Lebow, V. (1955, Spring). Price competition in 1955. *The Journal of Retailing,* p. 1–7. Retrieved from http://hundredgoals.files .wordpress.com/2009/05/journal-of-retailing.pdf

Lecso, P. A. (1989). Aging through Buddhist eyes. *Journal of Religion and Aging, 5*(30), 59–65.

Lee, M. Y., Ng, S., Leung, P., & Chan, C. (2009). *Integrative body-mind-spirit social work: An empirically-based approach to assessment and treatment.* New York, NY: Oxford University Press.

Legge, J. (Trans.). (1893). *The analects of Confucious.* London, UK: Clarendon Press. Retrieved from http://nothingistic.org/library/ confucius/analects/analects18 .html

Lemmer, C. M. (2005). Recognizing and caring for spiritual needs of patients. *Journal of Holistic Nursing, 23*(3), 310–322.

Lennon-Dearing, R., Florence, J. A., Halvorson, H., & Pollard, J. T. (2012). An interprofessional educational approach to teaching spiritual assessment. *Journal Of Health Care Chaplaincy, 18*(3/4), 121–132. doi:10.1080/08854726.2 012.720546

Levin, J. S. (2001). Religion. In G. L. Maddox (Ed.), *The encyclopedia of aging* (3rd ed., pp. 866–869). New York, NY: Springer.

Levin, J., & Meador, K. (2012). *Healing to all their flesh: Jewish and Christian perspectives on spirituality, theology, and health.* West Conshohocken, PA: Templeton Press.

Levin, J., & Prince, M. F. (2011). Judaism and health: Reflections on an emerging scholarly field. *Journal of Religion and Health, 50,* 765–777.

Lewinsohn, P. M., & Libet, J. (1972). Pleasant events, activity schedules, and depressions. *Journal of Abnormal Psychology, 79*(3), 291–295.

Lewis, B. (2009). *Islam: The religion and the people.* Upper Saddle River, NJ: Pearson.

Lewis, C. S. (1955). *Surprised by joy: The shape of my early life.* New York, NY: Harcourt Brace.

Lieblich, A., McAdams, D., & Josselson, R. (2004). *Healing plot: The narrative basis of psychotherapy.* Washington, DC: American Psychological Association.

Littleton, C. S. (1996). *Eastern wisdom.* New York, NY: Henry Holt.

Litz, B. T., Stein, N., Delaney, E., Lebowitz, L., Nash, W. P., Silva, C., et al. (2009). Moral injury and moral repair in war veterans: A preliminary model and intervention strategy. *Clinical Psychology Review, 29,* 695–706.

Lobjanidze, N., Akiashili, N., Beridze, M. & Janelidze, M. (2015). The role of inflammation and free radicals in Alzheimer's disease type dementia. *Alzheimer's & Dementia: The Journal of the Alzheimer's Association, 11*(7), P643.

Lockenhoff, L., & Carstensen, L. (2004). Socioemotional selectivity theory, aging, and health: The increasingly delicate balance between regulating emotions and making tough choices. *Journal of Personality 76*(6), 1395–1424.

Lomawaim, K. T. (1999). *The unnatural history of American Indian education.* Retrieved from http://files.eric.ed.gov/fulltext/ ED427903.pdf

Luce, J. M., Bindma, A. B., & Lee, P. R. (1994). A brief history of health care quality assessment and improvement in the United States. *Western Journal of Medicine, 160,* 263–268.

Ludtke, P. R. (2005). *Policy recommendations for Native elders.* Grand Forks: University of North Dakota School of Medicine and Health Sciences.

Lukoff, D., Lu, F. G., & Turner, R. (1998). From spiritual emergency to spiritual problem: The transpersonal roots of the new SM-IV category. *Journal of Humanistic Psychology, 38*(2), 21–50. doi:10.1177/00221678980382003

MacKinlay, E. (2006a). Spiritual care: Recognizing spiritual needs of older adults. *Journal of Religion, Spirituality, and Aging, 18*(2/3), 59–71.

MacKinlay, E. (2006b). *Spiritual growth and care in the 4th age of life.* London, UK: Jessica Kingsley.

MacKinlay, E. (2010). *Ageing and spirituality across faiths and cultures.* London, U.K.: Jessica Kingsley.

Mackler, A. (2007). Eye on religion: A Jewish view on miracles of healing. *Southern Medical Journal, 100*(12), 1252–1254.

Macnicol, J. (2010). *Ageism and age discrimination: Some analytical issues.* Retrieved from http://www.ilcuk.org.uk/index.php/publications/publication_details/ageism_and_age_discrimination_some_analytical_issues

MacRae, H. (2010). Managing identity while living with Alzheimer's disease. *Qualitative Health Research, 20*(3), 293–305.

Malcolm, L., & Ramsey, J. (2006). Teaching and learning forgiveness: A multidimensional approach.

Teaching Theology & Religion, 9(3), 175–185.

Marjoua, Y., & Bozic, K. J. (2012). Brief history of quality movement in U.S. healthcare. *Current Reviews in Musculoskeletal Medicine, 5*(4), 265–273. Retrieved from http://doi.org/10.1007/s12178–012–9137–8

Marquez-Gonzalez, M., Lopez, J., Romero-Moreno, R., & Losada, A. (2012). Anger, spiritual meaning and support from the religious community in dementia caregiving. *Journal of Religion and Health, 51*(1), 179–186.

Martin, E., Jobin, G., Büla, C. J., Rochat, E., Monod, S. M., & Spencer, B. (2010). The spiritual distress assessment tool: An instrument to assess spiritual distress in hospitalised elderly persons. *BMC Geriatrics, 10*(1), 88.

Martin, J. (2010). *The Jesuit guide to (almost) everything: A spirituality for real life.* New York, NY: HarperCollins.

Martin, J. (2011). *Between heaven and mirth: Why joy, humor, and laughter are at the heart of the spiritual life.* New York, NY: HarperCollins.

Martin, J. (2012). *Between heaven and mirth: Why joy, humor, and laughter are at the heart of the spiritual life.* New York, NY: HarperOne.

Marty, M. E. (1980). Social service: Godly and godless. *Social Service Review, 54*(4), 463–481.

Maslow, A. (1963). The need to know and the fear of knowing. *Journal of General Psychology 68,* 111–125.

Maslow, A. (1964). *Religion, values, and peak experiences.* Columbus: Ohio State University Press.

Maslow, A. H. (1968). *Toward a psychology of being* (2nd ed.).

New York, NY: Van Nostrand Reinhold.

Maslow, A. H. (1970). *Religion, values and peak experiences.* New York, NY: Viking Press.

Maslow, A. H. (1971). *The farther reaches of human nature.* New York, NY: Viking Press.

Mattingly, C., & Garro, L. (2000). *Narrative and the cultural construction of illness and healing.* Berkeley: University of California Press.

May, G. G. (2004). *The dark night of the soul: A psychiatrist explores the connection between darkness and spiritual growth.* New York, NY: HarperCollins.

May, R. (1950). *The meaning of anxiety.* New York, NY: The Ronald Press.

May, R. (1953). *Man's search for himself.* New York, NY: W.W. Norton and Company.

McAdams, D. (1997). *The stories we live by: Personal myths and the making of the self.* New York, NY: Guilford Press.

McAdams, D., & McLean, K. (2013.). Narrative identity. *Current Directions in Psychological Science, 22*(3), 233–238.

McCann, R., & Giles, H. (2002). Ageism in the workplace: A communication perspective. In T. D. Nelson (Ed.), *Ageism: Stereotyping and prejudice against older persons* (pp.163–199). Cambridge, MA: MIT Press.

McClung, E., Grossoehme, D. H., & Jacobson, A. F. (2006). Collaborating with chaplains to meet spiritual needs. *MEDSURG Nursing: Official Journal of the Academy of Medical-Surgical Nurses, 15*(3), 147–156.

McCormick, T., Hopp, F., Nelson-Becker, H., Ai, A., Schlueter, J., &

Camp, J. (2012). Ethical and spiritual concerns near the end of life. *Journal of Religion, Spirituality, and Aging, 24*(4), 301–313.

McCubbin, H. (1999). *The dynamics of resilient families.* Thousand Oaks, CA: Sage.

McCullough, M., Pargament, K., & Thoresen, C. (2000). *Forgiveness: Theory, research, and practice.* New York, NY: Guilford Press.

McCullough, M. E., Root, L. M., & Cohen, A. D. (2006). Writing about the benefits of an interpersonal transgression facilitates forgiveness. *Journal of Consulting and Clinical Psychology, 74*(5), 887–897.

McDowell, I., Xi, G., Lindsay, J., & Tierney, M. (2007). Mapping the connections between education and dementia. *Journal of Clinical and Experimental Neuropsychology, 29*(2), 127–141.

McEwan, M. (2005). Spiritual nursing care: State of the art. *Holistic Nursing Practice, 19*(4), 161–168.

McFadden, S. (1995). Religion and well-being in aging persons in an aging society. *Journal of Social Issues, 51*(2), 161–175.

McFadden, S. H. (1996). Religion, spirituality and aging. In J. E. Birren & K. W. Schaie (Eds.), *Handbook of the psychology of aging* (4th ed., pp. 162–177). San Diego, CA: Academic Press.

McFadden, S. H. (2005). Points of connection: Gerontology and the psychology of religion. In R. F. Paloutzian & C. L. Parks (Eds.), *Handbook of the psychology of religion and spirituality* (pp. 162–176). New York, NY: Guilford Press.

McFadden, S. H. (2015). Spirituality, religion, and aging: Clinical geropsychology and aging people's need for meaning. In P. A. Lichtenberg & B. T. Mast (Eds.), *APA handbook of clinical geropsychology* (Vol. 1, pp. 473–496). Washington, DC: American Psychological Association.

McGaa, E. (2004). *Nature's way: Native wisdom for living in balance with the earth.* New York, NY: HarperCollins.

McGoldrick, M., Gerson, R., & Shellenberger, S. (1999). *Genograms: Assessment and intervention* (2nd ed.). New York, NY: W. W. Norton.

McGoldrick, M., Giordano, J., & Garcia-Preto, N. (2005). *Ethnicity and family therapy* (3rd ed.). New York, NY: Guilford Press.

McPherson, C. J., Wilson, K. G., & Murray, M. A. (2007). Feeling like a burden to others: A systematic review focusing on the end of life. *Palliative Medicine, 21*(2), 115–128.

Mehrotra, C. M., & Wagner, L. S. (2009). *Aging and diversity* (2nd ed.). New York, NY: Routledge.

Melton, J. G. (Ed.) (2009). Eastern family, part II: Buddhism, Shinto, Japanese, new religions. *Melton's Encyclopedia of American Religions* (8th ed.). Detroit, MI: Gale.

Mencius. (n.d.). Retrieved from http://www.sacred-texts.com/cfu/menc/menc10.htm

Meraviglia, M., Sutter, R., & Gaskamp, C. D. (2008). Providing spiritual care to terminally ill older adults. *Journal of Gerontological Nursing 34*(7), 8–14.

Merel, S., Demers, S., & Vig, E. (2014). Palliative care in advanced dementia. *Clinics in Geriatric Medicine, 30*(3), 469–492.

Merton, T. (1975). *The Asian journal of Thomas Merton.* (Ed. N. Burton, B. Hart, & J. Laughlin). New York, NY: New Directions.

Merton, T. (2008). *Choosing to love the world: On contemplation* (Ed. J. Montaldo). Boulder, CO: Sounds True.

Mijares, S. G. (Ed.). (2003). *Modern psychology and ancient wisdom: Psychological healing practices from the world's religious traditions.* Binghamton, NY: Haworth Press.

Miller, S. D., Duncan, B. L., Brown, J., Sorrell, R., & Chalk, M. B. (2006). Using formal client feedback to improve retention and outcome: Making ongoing real-time assessment feasible. *Journal of Brief Therapy, 5,* 5–22.

Miller, W. R. (1999). *Integrating spirituality into treatment: Resources for practitioners.* Washington, DC: American Psychological Association.

Miller, W. R. (2014, July). *Motivational interviewing and quantum change.* Ruth Knee invited lecture on Spirituality and Social Work at the University of Chicago, School of Social Service Administration.

Miller, W. R., & Rollnick, S. (2002). *Motivational interviewing: Preparing people to change.* New York, NY: Guilford Press.

Miller, W. R., & Rollnick, S. (2013). *Motivational interviewing: Helping people change.* New York, NY: Guilford Press.

Miller, W. R., & Thoreson, C. E. (2003). Spirituality, religion, and health: An emerging research field. *American Psychologist, 58*(1), 24–25.

Miranti, J. G. (n.d.). *Historical development of the Association for Spiritual, Ethical and Religious Values.* Retrieved from http://www.aservic.org/about/history/

Mitchell, S. (Trans.). (1988). *Tao te ching.* New York, NY: Harper & Row.

Moberg, D. O. (1979). *Spiritual well-being: Sociological perspectives.* Washington, DC: University Press of America.

Moberg, D. (2005). Research in spirituality, religion, and aging. *Journal of Gerontological Social Work, 45*(1–2), 11–40.

Molyneaux, V. J., Butchard, S., Simpson, J., & Murray, C. (2012). The con-construction of couplehood in dementia. *Dementia, 11*(40), 483–502.

Monod, S., Martin, E., Spencer, B., Rochat, E., & Büla, C. (2012). Validation of the Spiritual Distress Assessment Tool in older hospitalized patients. *BMC Geriatrics, 12,* 13.

Monroe, B., & Oliviere, D. (Eds.). (2007). *Resilience in palliative care: Achievement in adversity.* Oxford, UK: Oxford University Press.

Montagne, R. (2014, May 19). *Silver tsunami and other terms that can irk the over-65 set.* National Public Radio Morning Edition. Retrieved from http://www.npr .org/2014/05/19/313133555/ silver-tsunami-and-other-terms- that-can-irk-the-over-65-set

Monti, D., & Beitman, B. (2010). *Integrative psychiatry.* New York, NY: Oxford University Press.

Moody, H. R. (2003). Conscious aging: A strategy for positive change in later life. In J. Roch & J. Goldfield (Eds.), *Mental wellness in aging: Strength-based approaches* (pp. 139–160). Baltimore, MD: Health Professions Press.

Moon, S. (2010). *This is getting old: Zen thoughts on aging with humor and dignity.* Boston, MA: Shambhala.

Moore, T. (1993). *Care of the soul: A guide for cultivating depth and sacredness in everyday life.* New York, NY: HarperCollins.

Moore, T. (1998). *Care of the soul: How to add depth and meaning to your everyday life.* (Illustrated ed.). New York, NY: HarperCollins.

Moore, T. (2004). *Dark nights of the soul: A guide to finding your way through life's ordeals.* New York, NY: Gotham Books.

Morano, C. L., & King, D. (2005). Religiosity as a mediator of caregiver well-being: Does ethnicity make a difference? *Journal of Gerontological Social Work, 45*(1/2), 69–84.

Morrow-Howell, N., Hinterlong, J., & Sherraden, M. (Eds.). (2001). *Productive aging: Concepts and challenges.* Baltimore, MD: Johns Hopkins University Press.

Moskowitz, C. (2011). *What's 96 percent of the universe made of? Astronomers don't know.* Retrieved from http://www.space .com/11642-dark-matter-dark- energy-4-percent-universe-panek. html

Mowat, H. (2008). *The potential for efficacy of healthcare chaplaincy and spiritual care provision in the NHS (UK): A coping review of recent research.* Retrieved from http:// www.ukbhc.org.uk/sites/default/ files/The%20potential%20 for%20effiicacy%20for%20 healthcare%20chaplaincy.pdf

Muangpaisan, W., Petcharat, C., & Srinonprasert, C. (2012). Prevalence of potentially reversible conditions in dementia and mild cognitive impairment in a geriatric clinic. *Geriatrics & Gerontology International, 12*(1), 59–64.

Mukamel, D. B., Caprio, T., Ahn, R., Zheng, N. T., Norton, S., Quill, T., et al. (2012). End-of-life quality-of-care measures for nursing homes: Place of death and hospice. *Journal of Palliative Medicine, 15*(4), 438–446. doi:10.1089/jpm.2011.0345

Murphy, M. (1992). *The future of the body: Explorations into the further evolution of human nature.* Los Angeles, CA: J. P. Tarcher.

Nadir, A., & Dziegielewski, S. (2001). Islam. In M. Van Hook, B. Hugen, & M. Aguilar (Eds.), *Spirituality within religious traditions in social work practice* (pp. 146–162). Pacific Grove, CA: Brooks/Cole.

Nakamura, H., Kobayashi, S., Ohashi, Y., & Ando, S., (1999). Age-changes of brain synapses and synaptic plasticity in response to an enriched environment. *Journal of Neuroscience Research, 56*(3), 307–315.

Nakasone, R. (2008). A brief review of literature of Buddhist writings on spirituality and aging. *Journal of Religion, Spirituality, and Aging, 20*(3), 220–226.

National Alliance for Caregiving (NAC). (2015). *Caregiving in the U.S. 2015.* Retrieved from http://www.caregiving.org/wp- content/uploads/2015/05/2015_ CaregivingintheUS_Executive- Summary-June-4_WEB.pdf

National Association for Home Care & Hospice. (n.d.). *Hospice: An HAA/NAHC historical perspective.* Retrieved from http://www.nahc .org/Haa/history

National Association of Social Workers. (2005). *NASW standards for social work practice in health care settings.* Retrieved from http://www.socialworkers .org/practice/standards/ naswhealthcarestandards.pdf

National Association of Social Workers. (2008). *Code of ethics of the National Association of Social Workers.* Retrieved from https:// www.socialworkers.org/pubs/ code/code.asp

National Center on Elder Abuse, Administration on Aging. (2014).

Statistics/Data. Retrieved from http://www.ncea.aoa.gov/Library/Data/

National Consensus Project for Quality Palliative Care. (2009). *Clinical practice guidelines for quality palliative care* (2nd ed.). Retrieved from http://www.nationalconsensusproject.org/Guideline.pdf

National Hospice and Palliative Care Organization. (October 2008). *NHPCO facts and figures on hospice care in America.* Retrieved from http://www.nhpco.org/files/public/Statistics_Research/NHPCO_facts-and-figures_2008.pdf

National Hospice and Palliative Care Organization. (2015). *NHPCO facts and figures on hospice care in America.* Retrieved from http://www.nhpco.org/sites/default/files/public/Statistics_Research/2015_Facts_Figures.pdf

National Institute of Mental Health. (2012). *Major depression among older adults.* Retrieved from http://www.nimh.nih.gov/health/statistics/prevalence/major-depression-among-adults.shtml

National Interfaith Coalition on Aging. (1980). A definition of spiritual well-being. In James A. Thorson & Thomas C. Cook (Eds.), *Spiritual well-being of the elderly* (pp. xiii). Springfield, MO: Charles C. Thomas.

National Quality Forum. (2006). *A national framework and preferred practices for palliative and hospice care: A consensus report.* Washington DC: Author. Retrieved from http://www.qualityforum.org/publications/reports/palliative.asp

National Voluntary Organizations Active in Disaster (NVOAD). (2013). *Light our way: A guide for spiritual care in times of disaster for disaster response volunteers, first responders and disaster planners*

(1st ed., 2nd revision). Retrieved from http://www.nvoad.org

Neihardt, J. G. (1979). *Black Elk speaks: Being the life story of a holy man of the Oglala Sioux.* Lincoln: University of Nebraska Press. Original work published 1932

Neimeyer, R. A., Torres, C., & Smith, D. C. (2011). The virtual dream: Rewriting stories of loss and grief. *Death Studies, 35*(7), 646–672.

Nelson, J. (2009). *Psychology, religion, and spirituality.* New York, NY: Springer.

Nelson, P. L. (2000). Mystical experience and radical deconstruction. In T. Hart, P. L. Nelson, & K. Puhakka (Eds.), *Transpersonal knowing: Exploring the horizon of consciousness* (pp. 55–84). Albany: State University of New York Press.

Nelson-Becker, H. B. (1999). Spiritual and religious problem-solving in older adults: Mechanisms for managing life challenge. Doctoral dissertation, The University of Chicago. *Dissertation Abstracts International*, 60–08, 253p.

Nelson-Becker, H. (2003). Practical philosophies: Interpretations of religion and spirituality by African-American and Jewish elders. *Journal of Religious Gerontology, 14*(2–3), 85–99. doi:10.1300/J078v14n02_01

Nelson-Becker, H. (2004a). Meeting life challenges: A hierarchy of coping styles in African-American and Jewish-American older adults. *Journal of Human Behavior in the Social Environment, 10*(1), 155–174.

Nelson-Becker, H. (2004b). Spiritual, religious, nonspiritual, nonreligious narratives in marginalized older adults: A typology of coping styles. *Journal*

of Religion, Spirituality, and Aging, 17(1/2), 21–38.

Nelson-Becker, H. (2004c). Wisdom-bearers and story-tellers: Older adults as guides and friends. *Reflections, 10*(2), 14–21.

Nelson-Becker, H. (2005a). Religion and coping in older adults. In H. R. Moody (Ed.), *Religion, spirituality, and aging: A social work perspective* (pp. 51–68). Binghamton, NY: Haworth Press.

Nelson-Becker, H. B. (2005b). Development of a spiritual support scale for use with older adults. *Journal of Human Behavior in the Social Environment, 11*(3/4), 195–212.

Nelson-Becker, H. (2006). Voices of resilience: Older adults in hospice care. *The Journal of Social Work in End-of-Life and Palliative Care, 2*(3), 87–106.

Nelson-Becker, H. (2008). Integrating spirituality in practice: From inner journey to outer engagement. *Journal of Geriatric Care Management, 18*(2), 10–15.

Nelson-Becker, H. (2011). Research in spirituality, religion, and aging: An emerging area. *Generations Review, 21*(3).

Nelson-Becker, H. (2013). Resilience in aging: Moving through challenge to wisdom. In D. S. Becvar (Ed.), *Handbook of family resilience* (pp. 339–357). New York, NY: Springer. doi:10.1007/978–1–4614–3917–2_20

Nelson-Becker, H., Ai, L. A., Hopp, F., McCormick, T. R., Schlueter, J. O., & Camp, J. K. (2013). Spirituality and religion in end-of-life care: The challenge of interfaith and cross-generational matters in changing environments. *British Journal of Social Work*, 1–16. doi:10.1093/bjsw/bct110

Nelson-Becker, H., & Canda, E. R. (2008). Research on religion, spirituality, and aging: A social work perspective on the state of the art. *Journal of Religion, Spirituality, & Aging, 20*(3), 177–193.

Nelson-Becker, H. & Canda, E. R. (2009). Spirituality, religion and aging research in social work: State of the art and future possibilities. In J. W. Ellor (Ed.), *Methods in religion, spirituality, and aging* (pp. 169–184). New York, NY: Routledge Press.

Nelson-Becker, H., Canda, E. R., & Nakashima, M. (2015). Spirituality in professional helping interventions. In B. Berkman & D. Kaplan (Eds.), *The Oxford handbook of social work in health and aging* (2nd ed., pp.73–84). Boston, MA: Oxford Press.

Nelson-Becker, H., Chapin, R., & Fast, B. (2009). The strengths model with older adults: critical practice components. In D. Saleebey (Ed.), *The strengths perspective in social work practice* (5th ed., pp.161–180). Boston, MA: Allyn & Bacon.

Nelson-Becker, H., Chapin, R., & Fast, B. (2013). The strengths model with older adults: Critical practice components. In D. Saleebey (Ed.), *The strengths perspective in social work practice* (6th ed.). Boston, MA: Allyn & Bacon.

Nelson-Becker, H. B., Nakashima, M., & Canda, E. R. (2007). Spiritual assessment in aging: A framework for clinicians. *Journal of Gerontological Social Work, 48*(3/4), 331–347.

Nelson-Becker, H., & Sangster, K. (2015). Spirituality and religious participation in later life. In N. Pachana (Ed.), *Encyclopedia of geropsychology* (pp.1–11). New York, NY: Springer. doi:10.1007/978–981–287–080–3_71–1

Nelson-Becker, H., & Sullivan, M. (2012). Social care. In M. Cobb, C. Puchalski, & B. Rumpold (Eds.) *Oxford textbook of spirituality in healthcare* (pp. 409–417). London, UK: Oxford University Press.

Neugarten, B. L. (1974). Age groups in American society and the rise of the young-old. *Annals of the American Academy of Political and Social Science, 415,* 187–198.

Neugarten, B., & Maddox. G. (2001). Kansas City studies of adult life. In G. L. Maddox (Ed.). *The encyclopedia of aging* (3rd ed.; pp. 576–577). New York, NY: Springer.

Newberg, A. B., & Waldman, M. R. (2009). *How God changes your brain: Breakthrough findings from a leading neuroscientist.* New York, NY: Ballantine Books.

Newman, T. (2004). *What works in building resilience?* Ilford, UK: Barnado's Press.

Newstein, N. P., & Frumer, J. (2006). Jewish aging services. *Journal of Jewish Communal Service, 82*(3/4), 231–238.

NHS Wales (2010). *Standards for spiritual care services in the NHS in Wales 2010.* Retrieved from http://gov.wales/docs/dhss/publications/100525spiritualcarestandarden.pdf

99 names of God. (2014). Retrieved from http://simple.wikipedia.org/wiki/99_Names_of_God

Nuland, S. B. (1993). *How we die: Reflections on life's final chapter.* New York, NY: Knopf-Doubleday.

O'Brien, K. F. (2011). *The Ignatian adventure: Experiencing the spiritual exercises of Saint Ignatius in daily life.* Chicago, IL: Loyola Press.

O'Brien, M. E. (2008). *Spirituality in nursing: Standing on holy ground* (3rd ed.). Sudbury, MA: Jones and Bartlett.

O'Brien, M. E. (2011). *Spirituality in nursing: Standing on holy ground* (4th ed). Sudbury, MA: Jones & Bartlett.

O'Connor, S., & Vandenberg, B. (2005). Psychosis or faith? Clinicians' assessment of religious beliefs. *Journal of Consulting and Clinical Psychology, 73,* 610–616.

Ødbehr, L., Kvigne, K., Hauge, S., & Danbolt, L. (2014). Nurses' and care workers' experiences of spiritual needs in residents with dementia in nursing homes: a qualitative study. *BMC Nursing, 13*(1), 12.

O'Donnell, W. H. (1994). *The collected works of W. B. Yeats. Vol. V: Later essays.* New York, NY: Simon & Schuster.

O'Donohue, J. (n.d.). *The inner landscape of beauty* [Audio podcast]. Retrieved from http://www.onbeing.org/program/john-o-donohue-the-inner-landscape-beauty/203/audio

O'Donohue, J. (2004). *Anam Cara: A book of Celtic wisdom.* New York, NY: HarperCollins.

Oldstone-Moore, J. (2003). *Taoism: Origins, beliefs, practices, holy texts, sacred places.* New York, NY: Oxford University Press.

Oliver, M. (1995). Maybe. In R. Bly (Ed.), *The soul is here for its own joy: Sacred poems from many cultures* (p. 15). Hopewell, NJ: Ecco Press.

Olshansky, S. J., Perry, D., Miller, R. A., & Butler, R. N. (2007). Pursuing the longevity dividend. *Annals of The New York Academy Of Sciences, 1114*(1), 1–13. doi:10.1196/annals.1396.050

Olson, D. M., & Kane, R. A. (2000). Spiritual assessment. In R. L. Kane & R. A. Kane (Eds.), *Assessing older persons* (pp. 300–319). New York, NY: Oxford University Press.

Ortiz, L. P., & Langer, N. (2002). Assessment of spirituality and religion in later life: Acknowledging clients' needs and personal resources. *Journal of Gerontological Social Work*, *37*(2), 5–21.

Otis-Green, S. (2006). The transitions program: Existential care in action. *Journal of Cancer Education*, *21*(1), 23–25.

Overbye, D. (2016, February 11). Gravitational waves detected, confirming Einstein's theory. *New York Times*. Retrieved from http://www.nytimes.com/2016/02/12/science/ligo-gravitational-waves-black-holes-einstein.html

Padmakara Translation Group. (2008). Shantideva. In *The way of the Bodhisattva* (p. 130). Boston, MA: Shambhala.

Pagels, E. (2003). *Beyond belief: The secret gospel of Thomas*. New York, NY: Random House.

Paley, J. (2008a). Spirituality and nursing: A reductionist approach. *Nursing Philosophy*, *9*(1), 3–18.

Paley, J. (2008b). Spirituality and secularization: Nursing and the sociology of religion. *Journal of Clinical Nursing*, *17*(2), 175–186.

Palmer, P. J. (2004). *A hidden wholeness: The journey toward an undivided life: Welcoming the soul and weaving community in a wounded world*. San Francisco, CA: Jossey-Bass.

Paloutzian, R., & Park, C. (Eds.). (2005). *Handbook of the psychology of religion and spirituality*. New York, NY: Guilford Press.

Pargament, K. I. (1997). *The psychology of religion and coping. Theory, research, practice*. New York, NY: Guilford Press.

Pargament, K. I., & Mahoney, A. (2005). THEORY: Sacred matters: Sanctification as a vital topic for the psychology of religion. *The International Journal for the Psychology of Religion*, *15*(3), 179–198.

Pargament, K. I., Van Haitsma, K. S., & Ensing, D. S. (1995). Religion and coping. In M. A. Kimble, S. H. McFadden, J. W. Ellor, & J. J. Seeber (Eds.), *Aging, spirituality and religion: A handbook* (pp. 47–67). Minneapolis, MN: Fortress Press.

Park, C. L., & Fenster, J. R. (2004). Stress-related growth: Predictors of occurrence and correlates with psychological adjustment. *Journal of Social and Clinical Psychology*, *23*(2), 195–215.

Patient Self-Determination Act, 42 U.S.C. 1395 (1990).

Paukert, A. L., Phillips, L., Cully, J. A., Loboprabhu, S. M., Lomax, J. W., & Stanley, M. A. (2009). Integration of religion into cognitive-behavioral therapy for geriatric anxiety and depression. *Journal of Psychiatric Practice*, *15*(2), 103–112.

Pausch R. (2008). *The last lecture*. New York, NY: Hyperion Press.

Perissinotto, C. M., Stijacic, C. I., & Covinsky, K. E. (2012). Loneliness in older persons: A predictor of functional decline and death. *Archives of Internal Medicine*, *172*(14), 1078–1083.

Periyakoil, V. J. (2015). Pitfalls for proxies. *Opinionator New York Times*. Retrieved from http://opinionator.blogs.nytimes.com/author/vj-periyakoil/

Perkins, H. S. (2007). Controlling death: The false promise of advance directives. *Annals of Internal Medicine*, *147*, 51–57.

Peterson, C., & Seligman, M. E. P. (2004). *Character strengths and virtues: A handbook and classification*. New York, NY: Oxford University Press.

Peterson, L. E., Bazemore, A., Bragg, E. J., Xierali, I., & Warshaw, G. A. (2011). Rural-urban distribution of the U.S. geriatrics physician workforce. *Journal of the American Geriatrics Society*, *59*(4), 699–703. doi:10.1111/j.1532-5415.2011.03335.x

Pew Forum on Religion & Public Life. (2007). *U.S. religious landscape survey: Chapter 3. Religious affiliation and demographic groups*. Retrieved from http://religions.pewforum.org/reports# and http://www.pewforum.org/topics/religious-beliefs-and-practices/2007

Pew Forum on Religion & Public Life. (2008). *U.S. religious landscape survey*. Washington, DC: Pew Research Center.

Pew Forum on Religion & Public Life. (2013). *U.S. religious landscape survey: Reports: report 1: religious affiliation. Summary of key findings*. Retrieved from http://religions.pewforum.org/reports

Pew Research Center. (2009). *Growing old in America: Expectations versus reality*. Retrieved from http://www.pewsocialtrends.org/files/2010/10/Getting-Old-in-America.pdf

Pew Research Center. (2014a). *America's changing religious landscape*. Retrieved from http://www.pewforum.org/2015/05/12/americas-changing-religious-landscape/

Pew Research Center. (2014b). *Millennials in adulthood*. Retrieved from http://www.pewsocialtrends.org/2014/03/07/millennials-in-adulthood/

Pew Research Center. (2014c). *Religious landscape study: Religious composition of adults ages 65 and older.* Retrieved from http://www.pewforum.org/religious-landscape-study/age-distribution/65/

Pew Research Center. (2015). *U. S. public becoming less religious.* Retrieved from http://www.pewforum.org/2015/11/03/u-s-public-becoming-less-religious/

Pickard, J., & Nelson-Becker, H. (2011). Attachment and spiritual coping: Theory and practice with older adults. *Journal of Spirituality in Mental Health, 13*(2), 138–155. doi: 10.1080/19349637.2011.565239

Piercy, K. (2007). Characteristics of strong commitments to intergenerational family care of older adults. *The Journals of Gerontology. Series B, Psychological Sciences and Social Sciences, 62*(6), S381–387.

Pilcher, J. (1994). Mannheim's sociology of generations: An undervalued legacy. *British Journal of Sociology, 45*(3), 481–495.

Polkinghorne, D. (1988). *Narrative knowing and the human sciences.* Albany: SUNY Press.

Polkinghorne, J. (2002). *Quantum theory: A very short introduction.* Oxford, UK: Oxford University Press.

Porter, K. E., Ronneberg, C. R., & Witten, T. M. (2013). Religious affiliation and successful aging among transgender older adults: Findings from the Trans Metlife survey. *Journal of Religion, Spirituality & Aging, 25*(2), 112–139.

Post, B. C., & Wade, N. G. (2009). Religion and spirituality in psychotherapy: A practice-friendly review of research. *Journal of Clinical Psychology, 65/2,* 131–46.

Potter, G. G., Plassman, B. L., Burke, J. R., Kabeto, M. U., Langa, K. M., Llewellyn, D. J., . . . Steffens, D. C. (2009). Cognitive performance and informant reports in the diagnosis of cognitive impairment and dementia in African Americans and whites. *Alzheimer's & Dementia, 5*(6), 445–453.

Power, B. A., & Watson, N. M. (2011). Spiritual nurturance and support for nursing home residents with dementia. *Dementia, 10*(1), 59–80.

Powers, R. (2005). Counseling and spirituality: A historical review. *Counseling and Values, 49*(3), 217–225.

Pratchett, T. (2015, March 14). "A butt of my own jokes": Terry Pratchett on the disease that finally claimed him. *The Guardian.* Retrieved from http://www.theguardian.com/books/2015/mar/15/a-butt-of-my-own-jokes-terry-pratchett-on-the-disease-that-finally-claimed-him

Prest, L., Russel, R., & D'Souza, H. (1999). Spirituality and religion in training, practice, and personal development. *Journal of Family Therapy, 21,* 60–77.

Priggen, E. (Producer), & Fox, L. (Director). (2007). *The story of stuff* [Video]. Retrieved from http://storyofstuff.org

Prochaska, J., DiClemente, C., Norcross, J., & Fowler, R. D. (1992). In search of how people change. *American Psychologist, 47*(9), 1102–1114.

Pronk, T. M., Karremans, J. C., Overbeek, G., Vermulst, A. A., & Wigboldus, D. H. J. (2010). What it takes to forgive: When and why executive functioning facilitates forgiveness. *Journal of Personality and Social Psychology 98*(1), 119–131.

Pruter, K. (1985). *The teachings of the great mystics.* San Bernardino, CA: Borgo Press.

Puchalski, C. M. (2006). Spiritual assessment in clinical practice. *Psychiatric Annals, 36*(3), 150.

Puchalski, C., & Ferrell, B. (2010). *Making health care whole: Integrating spirituality into health care.* West Conshohocken, PA: Templeton Press.

Puchalski, C., Ferrell, B., Virani, R., Otis-Green, S., Baird, P., Bull, . . . Sulmasy, D. (2009). Improving the quality of spiritual care as a dimension of palliative care: The report of the consensus conference. *Journal of Palliative Medicine, 12*(10), 885–904.

Puchalski, C. M., & Romer, A. L. (2000). Taking a spiritual history allows clinicians to understand patients more fully. *Journal of Palliative Medicine, 3,* 129–137.

Puchalski, C. M., Vitillo, R., Hull, S. K., & Reller, N. (2014). Improving the spiritual dimension of whole person care: Reaching national and international consensus. *Journal of Palliative Medicine, 17*(6), 642–656. doi:10.1089/jpm.2014.9427

Puhakka, K. (2000). An invitation to authentic knowing. In T. Hart, P. L. Nelson, & K. Puhakka (Eds.), *Transpersonal knowing: Exploring the horizon of consciousness* (pp. 11–30). Albany: SUNY Press.

Rabins, P. V. (2005). *Getting old without getting anxious: Conquering late-life anxiety.* New York, NY: Penguin Group.

Rachels, J. (1999). *The elements of moral philosophy* (3rd ed.). New York, NY: McGraw-Hill.

Ramsey, J. L., & Blieszner, R. (1999). *Spiritual resiliency in older women: Models of strength for* challenges through the life span. Thousand Oaks, CA: Sage.

Rando, T. (1993). *Treatment of complicated mourning.* Champaign, IL: Research Press.

Rasmussen, J. L. (2014). *Defending the correspondence theory of truth.* Cambridge, UK: Cambridge University Press.

Rassool, G. H. (2000). The crescent and Islam: Healing, nursing and the spiritual dimension. Some considerations towards an understanding of the Islamic perspectives on caring. *Journal of Advanced Nursing, 32*(6), 1476–1484.

Rawls, J. (1971). *A theory of justice.* Cambridge, MA: Harvard University Press.

Rawls, J. (2001). *Justice as fairness: A restatement.* Edited by E. Kelly. Cambridge, MA: Belknap Press of Harvard University Press.

Reamer, F. G. (1995). *Social work values and ethics.* New York, NY: Columbia University Press.

Remen, R. N. (1999, September). Helping, fixing or serving? *Shambhala Sun.* Retrieved from http://www.lionsroar.com/helping-fixing-or-serving/

Reuder, M. E. (1999). A history of Division 36 (Psychology of Religion). In D. A. Dewsbury (Ed.), *Unification through division: Histories of the divisions of the American Psychological Association* (Vol. 4, pp. 91–108). Washington, DC: American Psychological Association.

Reynolds, K., Henderson, M., Schuylman, A., & Hanson, L. C. (2002). Needs of the dying in nursing homes. *Journal of Palliative Medicine, 5*(6), 895–901.

Ricard, M. (2010). *Why meditate: Working with thoughts and emotions.* New York, NY: Hay House.

Richards, M. (2010). *Caresharing: A reciprocal approach to caregiving and care receiving in the complexities of aging, illness, or disability.* Woodstock, VT.: Skylight Paths.

Richards, P. S., & Bergin, A. E. (2005). *A spiritual strategy for counseling and psychotherapy* (2nd ed.). Washington, DC: American Psychiatric Association.

Richmond, M. E. (1917). *Social diagnosis.* New York, NY: Russell Sage Foundation.

Riemer, J., & Stampfer, N. (Eds.). (1991). *So that your values live on: Ethical wills and how to prepare them.* Woodstock, VT: Jewish Lights.

Riley, K. P., Snowdon, D. A., Desrosiers, M. F., & Markesbery, W. R. (2005). Early life linguistic ability, late life cognitive function, and neuropathology: Findings from the Nun Study. *Neurobiology of Aging, 26*(3), 341–347. doi:10.1016/j.neurobiolaging.2004.06.019

Rilke, R. M. (1954). *Letters to a young poet.* New York, NY: Norton.

Rilke, R. M. (1984). As once the winged energy of delight. In S. Mitchell (Ed.), *The selected poetry of Rainer Maria Rilke* (p. 261). New York, NY: Vintage Books.

Risse, G. B. (1999). *Mending bodies, saving souls: A history of hospitals.* New York, NY: Oxford University Press.

Ritchie, J. E. (2014). *Self-compassion for women in later midlife: A feminist approach to conscious aging.* Unpublished dissertation, Saybrook University, San Francisco, CA.

Robbins, S. P., Chatterjee, P., & Canda, E. R. (2006). *Contemporary human behavior theory* (2nd ed.). Boston, MA: Pearson.

Rogers, C. (1961). *On becoming a person: A therapist's view of psychotherapy.* London, UK: Constable.

Rohr, R. (2011). *Falling upward: A spirituality for the two halves of life.* San Francisco, CA: Jossey-Bass.

Roof, W. (1999). *Spiritual marketplace: Baby boomers and the remaking of American religion.* Princeton, NJ: Princeton University Press.

Rosenberg, E. L. (1998). Levels of analysis and he organization of affect. *Review of General Psychology, 2*(3), 247–270.

Rosmarin, D. H., Auerbach, R. P., Bigda-Peyton, J. S., Björgvinsson, T., & Levendusky, P. G. (2011). Integrating spirituality into cognitive behavioral therapy in an acute psychiatric setting: A pilot study. *Journal of Cognitive Psychotherapy, 25*(4), 287–303. doi:10.1891/0889–8391.25.4.287

Roth, A., & Fonagy, P. (2006). *What works for whom? A critical review of psychotherapy research.* New York, NY: Guilford Press.

Rothberg, D. (2000). Spiritual inquiry. In T. Hart, P. L. Nelson, & K. Puhakka (Eds.), *Transpersonal knowing: Exploring the horizon of consciousness* (pp. 161–184). Albany: State University of New York Press.

Rowe, J. W., & Kahn, R. L. (1998). *Successful aging.* New York, NY: Pantheon Books.

Rowles, G. D., & Bernard, M. (2013). The meaning and significance of place in old age. In G. D. Rowles & M. Bernard (Eds.), *Environmental gerontology: Making meaningful places in old age* (pp. 3–24). New York, NY: Springer.

Rugkåsa, J., Canvin, K., Sinclair, J., Sulman, A., & Burns, T. (2014).

Trust, deals and authority: Community mental health professionals' experiences of influencing reluctant patients. *Community Mental Health Journal, 50*(8), 886–895.

Running, A., & Tolle, L. W. (2008). When there is nothing left to do, there is everything left to do. *American Journal of Hospice and Palliative Medicine, 24*(6), 451–454.

Rupp, D. E., Vodanovich, S. J., & Crede, M. (2005). The multidimensional nature of ageism: Construct validity and group differences, *The Journal of Social Psychology, 145*(3), 335–362.

Russ, C. (2014). Cholinesterase inhibitors should not be prescribed for mild cognitive impairment. *Evidence-Based Medicine, 19*, 101. doi:10.1136/eb-2013-101687

Russell, S. R., & Yarhouse, M. A. (2006). Increasing the diversity of internship training—Training in religion/spirituality within APA-accredited psychology predoctoral internships. *Professional Psychology, Research and Practice, 37*(4), 430.

Rybak, C., & Decker-Fitts, A. (2009). Theory and practice: Understanding Native American healing practices. *Counseling Psychology Quarterly, 22*(3), 333–342.

Sabat, S. R. (2006). Mind, meaning, and personhood in dementia: The effects of positioning. In J. C. Hughes, S. J. Louw, & S. R. Sabat (Eds.), *Dementia: Mind, meaning, and the person* (pp. 287–305). New York, NY: Oxford University Press.

Sabat, S. R., & Collins, M. (1999). Intact social, cognitive ability, and selfhood: A case study of Alzheimer's disease. *American Journal of Alzheimer's Disease, 14*, 11–19.

Sacks, O. (2007). *Musicophilia: Tales of music and the brain.* New York, NY: Alfred A. Knopf.

Sage-ing International. (2012). *Vision, mission, & values.* Retrieved from http://sage-ing.org/the-mission-of-the-sage-ing-guild

Saint John of the Cross. (ca. 1500). *The dark night of the soul* (E.A. Peers, Trans.). [Scanned document]. Retrieved from http://www.ccel.org/ccel/john_cross/dark_night.txt

Saint John of the Cross. (2010). *The dark night of the soul* (E.A. Peers, Trans.). Retrieved from http://books.google.com

Saleebey, D. (Ed.). (2009). *The strengths perspective in social work practice* (5th ed.). Boston, MA: Allyn & Bacon.

Salzberg, S. (2010). *Real happiness—The power of meditation: A 28-day program.* New York, NY: Workman.

Sangster, K. (2016). *Exploring the relationships between spiritual well-being, team regard and turnover intention of hospice social workers: The mediating role of job satisfaction.* Doctoral dissertation. Retrieved from ProQuest UMI Dissertations Publishing (11552).

Saracci, R. (1997). The World Health Organization needs to reconsider its definition of health. *British Medical Journal, 314*(7091), 1409–1410.

Sarton, M. (1974). *Collected poems, 1930–1973.* New York, NY: W. W. Norton.

Sartre, J. P. (2003). *Being and nothingness* (Hazel E. Barnes, Trans.). London, England: Routledge Press. Original work published 1958

Sauer, J., Brewer, N., Zweck, T., & Weber, N. (2010). The effect of retention interval on the confidence-accuracy relationship for witness identification. *Law and Human Behavior, 34*, 337–347.

Saunders, C. M. (1983). *Beyond all pain: A companion for the suffering and bereaved.* London, UK: SPCK.

Saunders, C. (1999). Origins: International perspectives, then and now. In I. B. Corless & Z. Foster (Eds.), *The hospice heritage: Celebrating our future* (pp. 1–8). New York, NY: Haworth Press.

Saunders, D. (2001). Social work and palliative care: The early history. *The British Journal of Social Work, 31*(5), 791–799.

Saylor, C. (2004). The circle of health: A health definition model. *Journal of Holistic Nursing, 22*(2), 98–115.

Scharlach, A., Simon, J., & Dal Santo, T. (2002). Who is providing social services to today's older adults? Implications of a survey of aging services personnel. *Journal of Gerontological Social Work, 38*, 5–17.

Schineller, P. (2000). A distinctive Christian world vision. *African Ecclesial Review, 42*(1/2), 81–99.

Schmall, V., & Pratt, C. (1996). *What do you know about aging? Facts and fallacies.* Retrieved from http://www.cswe.org/File.aspx?id=17527

Schnittker, J. (2001). When is faith enough? The effects of religious involvement on depression. *Journal for the Scientific Study of Religion, 40*(3), 393–412.

Scholl, J. M., & Sabat, S. R. (2008). Stereotypes, stereotype threat and ageing: Implications for the understanding and treatment of people with Alzheimer's disease. *Ageing and Society, 28*(1), 103–130.

Schön, D. (1983). *The reflective practitioner: How professionals think in action.* New York, NY: Basic Books.

Schulz, K. (2011.) *Don't regret regret*. Retrieved from https://www.ted.com/talks/kathryn_schulz_don_t_regret_regret?language=en

Seager, R. H. (2009). *Buddhism in America*. New York, NY: Columbia University Press.

Sedley, R. D. (2012). *TAG institute for social development*. Retrieved from http://wwww.taginstitute.org

Seligman, M. E. P. (1975). *Helplessness: On depression, development, and death*. San Francisco, CA: W. H. Freeman.

Seligman, M., & Csikszentmihalyi, M. (2000). Positive psychology: An introduction. *American Psychologist, 55*(1), 5–14.

Sessanna, L., Finnell, D., & Jezewski, M. A. (2007). Spirituality in nursing and health-related literature: A concept analysis. *Journal of Holistic Nursing, 25*(4), 252–262.

Shafranske, E. P., & Gorsuch, R. L. (1984). Factors associated with the perception of spirituality in psychotherapy. *Journal of Transpersonal Psychology, 16*(2), 231–241.

Shafranske, E. P., & Malony, H. N. (1990). Clinical psychologists' religious and spiritual orientations and their practice of psychotherapy. *Psychotherapy, 27*, 72–78.

Shahidi, M., Mojtahed, A., Modabbernia, A., Mojtahed, M., Shafiabady, A., Delavar, A., & Honari, H. (2011). Laughter yoga versus group exercise program in elderly depressed women: A randomized controlled trial. *International Journal of Geriatric Psychiatry, 26*(3), 322–327.

Shanshan, L., Stampfer, M. J., Williams, D. R., & VanderWeele, T. J. (2016). Association of religious service attendance with mortality among women. *JAMA Internal Medicine, 176*(6), 777–785. doi:10.1001/jamainternmed.2016.1615

Shapiro, S., Carlson, L., Astin, J., & Freedman, B. (2006). Mechanisms of mindfulness. *Journal of Clinical Psychology, 62*(3), 373–386.

Sharf, R. S., (2008). *Theories of psychotherapy and counseling* (4th ed.). Belmont, CA: Thomson Brooks/Cole.

Sharf, R. (2014). Mindfulness and mindlessness in early Chan. *Philosophy East and West, 64*(4), 933–964.

Shim, W., & Nelson-Becker, H. (2009). Korean older intimate partner violence survivors in North America: Cultural considerations and practice recommendations. *Journal of Women and Aging, 21*(3), 213–218. doi:10.1080/08952840903054773

Siegel, D. J. (2006). An interpersonal neurobiology approach to psychotherapy: Awareness, mirror neurons, and neural plasticity in the development of well-being. *Psychiatric Annals, 36*(4), 248–258.

Siegel, D. (2012). *The developing mind: How relationships and the brain intersect to shape who we are.* New York, NY: Guilford Press.

Siegler, I., Poon, L., Madden, D. J., & Dilworth-Anderson, P. (2004). Psychological aspects of normal aging. In D. Blazer, D. C. Steffens, & E. W. Busse (Eds.), *Textbook of geriatric psychiatry* (pp. 121–123). Arlington, VA: American Psychiatric Association.

Singer, T., Seymour, B., O'Doherty, J., Kaube, H., Dolan, R., & Frith, C. (2004). Empathy for pain involves the affective but not sensory components of pain. *Science, 303*(5661), 1157-1162.

Sloan, R. P., & Bagiella, E. (2002). Claims about religious involvement and health outcomes. *Annals of Behavioral Medicine, 24*, 14–21.

Smale, A. (2015, July 15). Oskar Gröning, Ex-SS soldier at Auschwitz, gets four-year sentence. *The New York Times.* Retrieved from http://www.nytimes.com/2015/07/16/world/europe/oskar-groning-auschwitz-nazi.html?rref=homepage&module=Ribbon&version=origin&region=Header&action=click&contentCollection=Home%20Page&pgtype=Blogs

Smith, C. (2014). What is a person? And why it matters in religious ethics. *Journal of Religious Ethics, 42*(1), 180–186. doi:10.1111/jore.12051

Smith, D. (2012, January 14,). It's still the "age of anxiety." Or is it? *The New York Times.* Retrieved from http://opinionator.blogs.nytimes.com/2012/01/14/its-still-the-age-of- anxiety-or-is-it/

Smith, H. (1958). *The religions of man*. New York, NY: Harper and Row.

Smith, H. (1994a). The Confucian project. In *Illustrated world's religions: A guide to our wisdom traditions*. San Francisco, CA: Labyrinth.

Smith, H. (1994b). Islam. In *The illustrated world's religions: A guide to our wisdom traditions*. London, UK: Labyrinth.

Smith, H. (1994c). *World religions*. New York, NY: HarperCollins.

Smith, H. (2009). *Tales of wonder*. New York, NY: HarperCollins.

Smith, W. C. (1979). *Faith and belief*. Princeton, NJ: Princeton University Press.

Snodgrass, J. L., & Noronha, K. (2015). Responding to explicit and implicit spiritual content in pastoral counseling. In E. A. Maynard & J. L. Snodgrass (Eds.), *Understanding pastoral counseling* (pp. 139–160). New York, NY: Springer.

Snowden, D. A. (1997). Aging and Alzheimer's disease: Lessons from the Nun Study. *The Gerontologist, 37*(2), 150–156.

Snowdon, D. (2001). *Aging with grace: What the Nun Study teaches us about leading longer, healthier, and more meaningful lives.* New York, NY: Bantam Books.

Snyder, L. (2003). Satisfactions and challenges in spiritual faith and practice for persons with dementia. *Dementia, 2*, 299–313.

Snyder, C., Ilardi, R., Cheavens, S., Michael, S., Yamhure, J., & Sympson, S. (2000). The role of hope in cognitive-behavior therapies. *Cognitive Therapy and Research, 24*(6), 747–762.

Society for the Psychology of Religion and Spirituality. (2014). Retrieved from http://www.apa.org/about/division/div36.aspx

Sogyal Rinpoche. (1992). *The Tibetan book of living and dying.* San Francisco, CA: Harper.

Sperry, L., & Shafranske, E. (2005). *Spiritually-oriented psychotherapy.* Washington DC: American Psychological Association.

Spiegel, M. C. (1996). Spirituality for survival: Jewish women healing themselves. *Journal of Feminist Studies in Religion, 12*(2), 121–137.

Spilka, B., Hood, R. W., Hunsberger, B., Gorsuch, R. (2003). *The psychology of religion: An empirical approach* (3rd ed.). New York, NY: Guilford Press.

Stallard, J. M., Decker, I. M., & Sellers, J. B. (2002). Health care for the elderly: A social obligation. *Nursing Forum, 37*(2), 5–15.

Stanley, M. A., Bush, A. L., Camp, M. E., Jameson, J. P., Phillips, L. L., Barber, C. R., . . . Cully, J. A. (2011). Older adults' preferences for religion/spirituality in treatment for anxiety and depression. *Aging & Mental Health, 15*(3), 334–343.

Stark, R. (2015). *The triumph of faith: Why the world is more religious than ever.* Wilmington, DE: Intercollegiate Studies Institute Books.

Steen, R. L., Engles, D., & Thweatt, W. T. (2006). Ethical aspects of spirituality in counseling. *Counseling and Values, 50*(2), 108–118.

Stemmler, S. (2009). Commentary: Tribal voices. *American Indian Culture and Research Journal, 33*(3), 107–109.

Strohminger, N., & Nichols, S. (2015). Neurodegeneration and identity. *Psychological Science.* doi:10.1177/0956797615592381

Stuckey, J. C. (2001). Blessed assurance: The role of religion and spirituality in Alzheimer's disease caregiving and other significant life events. *Journal of Aging Studies, 15*, 69–84.

Sulmasy, D. P. (2002). A biopsychosocial-spiritual model for the care of patients at end of life. *The Gerontologist, 42*(2), 24–33.

Sweet, V. (2012). *God's hotel: A doctor, a hospital, and a pilgrimage to the heart of medicine.* New York, NY: Riverhead Books.

Swinton, J. (2012). *Dementia: Living in the memories of God.* Grand Rapids, MI: William B. Eerdmans.

Tang, S. T., Liu, T. W., Lai, M. S., & McCorkle, R. (2005). Discrepancy in the preferences for place of death between terminally ill patients and their primary family caregivers in Taiwan. *Social Science Medicine, 61*(7), 1560–1566.

Tay, L., & Diener, E. (2011). Needs and subjective well-being around the world. *Journal of Personality and Social Psychology, 101*(2), 354–365.

Taylor, R. (2004). *Religions of the world: Confucianism.* Philadelphia, PA: Chelsea House.

Temel, J., Greer, J., Muzikansky, A., Gallagher, E., Admane, S., Jackson, V., . . . Lynch, T. (2010). Early palliative care for patients with metastatic non-small-cell lung cancer. *New England Journal of Medicine, 363*(8), 733–742.

Tennyson, A. T. (1859). Ulysses. In *Idylls of the King* (6th ed.). London, UK: Edward Moxon & Co.

Thibault, J. (2009, November). A psycho-spiritual intervention for late-life suffering. In *Religion and spirituality: From definition and variable to practice application.* Symposium conducted at the 62nd annual meeting of the Gerontological Society of America, Atlanta, GA.

Thompson, L. G. (1989). *Chinese religion* (4th ed.). Belmont, CA: Wadsworth.

Tillich. P. (1952). *The courage to be.* New Haven, CT: Yale University Press.

Torges, C., Stewart, A., & Nolen-Hoeksema, S. (2008). Regret resolution, aging, and adapting to loss. *Psychology and Aging, 23*(1), 169–180.

Tornstam, L. (1982). *Aging and life course transitions: An interdisciplinary perspective.* New York, NY: Guilford Press.

Tornstam, L. (1996). Gerotranscendence: A theory about maturing into old age. *Journal of Aging and Identity, 1*(1), 37–50.

Tornstam, L. (1997). Gerotranscendence: The contemplative dimension of aging. *Journal of Aging Studies, 11*(2), 143–154.

Tornstam, L. (1999). Gerotranscendence and the functions of reminiscence. *Journal of Aging and Identity, 4*(3), 155–166.

Tornstam, L. (2005). *Gerotranscendence: A developmental theory of positive aging.* New York, NY: Springer.

Toropov, B., & Buckles, L. (2011). *The complete idiot's guide to world religions.* Royersford, PA: Alpha.

Tracy, J. C., Sandee, H. M., & Phyllis, M. (2011). What's so big about the 'little things': A phenomenological inquiry into the meaning of spiritual care in dementia. *Dementia, 10*(3), 399–414.

Tröster, A. I. (1998). *Memory in neurodegenerative disease: Biological, cognitive, and clinical perspectives.* Cambridge, UK: Cambridge University Press.

Turner, V. W. (1969). *The ritual process.* London, UK: Routledge.

Tyas, S. L., Salazar, J. C., Snowdon, D. A., Desrosiers, M. F., Riley, K. P., Mendiondo, M. S., & Kryscio, R. J. (2007). Transitions to mild cognitive impairments, dementia, and death: Findings from the Nun Study. *American Journal of Epidemiology, 165*(11), 1231–1238.

United Nations. (1991). *U.N. Resolution 46/91 on the implementation of the international plan of action on ageing and related activities.* Retrieved from http://www.monitoringris.org/documents/norm_glob/ARES461.pdf

United Nations. (2002). *Political declaration and Madrid international plan of action on ageing.* Madrid, Spain. Retrieved from http://www.un.org/en/events/pastevents/pdfs/Madrid_plan.pdf

United Nations General Assembly. (2015). *Follow-up to the International Year of Older Persons: Second world assembly on ageing.* Retrieved from http://daccess-dds-ny.un.org/doc/UNDOC/GEN/N15/230/71/PDF/N1523071.pdf?OpenElement

Valliant, G. E. (2002). *Aging well.* New York, NY: Little, Brown, and Company.

Valliant, G. E. (2008). *Spiritual evolution: A scientific defense of faith.* New York, NY: Broadway Books.

van Gennep, A. (1960). *The rites of passage.* Chicago, IL: University of Chicago Press.

van Kan, G. A., Rolland, Y. M, & Morley, J. E. (2008). Frailty: Toward a clinical definition. *Journal of the American Medical Directors Association Long Term Care—Management, Applied Research and Clinical Issues, 9*(2), 71–72.

Vance, D., Brennan, M., Enah, C., Smith, G., & Kaur, J. (2011). Religion, spirituality, and older adults with HIV: Critical personal and social resources for an aging epidemic. *Clinical Interventions In Aging, 6,* 101–109.

Van Hook, M. P., Hugen, B., Aguilar, M. (2001). *Spirituality within religious traditions in social work practice.* Pacific Grove, CA: Brooks/Cole.

Västfjäll, D., Slovic, P., Mayorga, M., & Peters, E. (2014).

Compassion fade: Affect and charity are greatest for a single child in need. *PloS One, 9*(6), E100115.

Wagner, N., Hassanein, K., & Head, M. (2010). Computer use by older adults: A multi-disciplinary review. *Computers in Human Behavior, 26* (5), 870–882.

Walshe, M. O. (Ed. & Trans.). (1979). *Meister Eckhart: Sermons & treatises.* Longmead, UK: Element Books.

Wampold, B., & Brown, J. (2006). Estimating variability in outcomes attributable to therapists: A naturalistic study of outcomes in managed care. *Journal of Consulting and Clinical Psychology, 73*(5), 914–923.

Weaver, H. (2013). Native Americans: Overview. In *Encyclopedia of social work.* New York, NY: Oxford University Press.

Webster, J., Bohlmeijer, E., & Westerhof, G. (2010). Mapping the future of reminiscence: A conceptual guide for research and practice. *Research on Aging, 3*(4), 527–564.

Weston, A. (2011). *A practical companion to ethics.* New York, NY: Oxford University Press.

White Bison. (n.d.). *White Bison wellbriety movement.* Retrieved from http://www.whitebison.org/white-bison/white-bison-philosophy.php

Who we are: Bureau of Indian Affairs. (n.d.). Retrieved from http://www.bia.gov/WhoWeAre/index.htm

Whyte, D. (1997). *The house of belonging. Poems.* Langley, WA: Many Rivers Press.

Wilber, K. (2000). *Integral psychology: Consciousness, spirit, psychology, therapy.* Boston, MA: Shambhala.

Wilber, K. (2001). *The eye of spirit: An integral vision for a world gone slightly mad.* Boston, MA: Shambhala.

Wilber, K. (2005). *Introduction to the Integral Approach and the AQAL Map.* Retrieved from http://www .kenwilber.com/Writings/PDF/ IntroductiontotheIntegral Approach_GENERAL_2005_ NN.pdf

Williams, A. (2006). Perspectives on spirituality at the end of life: A meta-summary. *Palliative and Supportive Care, 4,* 407–417.

Williams, K., Herman, R., Gajewski, B., & Wilson, K. (2009). Elderspeak communication: Impact on dementia care. *American Journal of Alzheimer's Disease and Other Dementias, 24*(1), 11–20.

Williams, K., Kemper, S., & Hummert, M. L. (2003). Improving nursing home communication: An intervention to reduce elderspeak. *Gerontologist, 43,* 242–247.

Williams, P. T., & Thompson, P. D. (2014). Increased cardiovascular disease mortality associated with excessive exercise in heart attack survivors. *Mayo Clinic Proceedings, 89*(9), 1187–1194.

Williams, R. R. (2010). Space for god: Lived religion at work, home, and play. *Sociology of Religion, 71*(3), 257–279.

Wilson, K., Chochinov, H., Mcpherson, C., Lemay, K., Allard, P., Chary, S., . . . Fainsinger, R. (2007). Suffering with advanced cancer. *Journal of Clinical Oncology: Official Journal of the American Society of Clinical Oncology, 25*(13), 1691–1697.

Winokuer, H. R., & Harris, D. L. (2012). *Principles and practice of*

grief counseling. New York, NY: Springer.

Wolterstorff, N. (2011). *Justice in love.* Grand Rapids, MI: Eerdmans.

Woodhead, H. (1992). *The American Indians: The spirit world.* Alexandria, VA: Time-Life Books.

Woodward, J. (2008). *Valuing age: Pastoral ministry with older people.* London, UK: Ashford Colour Press.

World Health Organization. (1946). *Preamble to the Constitution of the World Health Organization as adopted by the International Health Conference, New York, 19–22 June, 1946.* Retrieved from http://www .who.int/about/definition/en/ print.html

World Health Organization. (1990). *Cancer pain relief and palliative care. Report of a WHO expert committee.* Geneva, Switzerland: Author.

World Health Organization. (1995). *Redefining health.* Retrieved from http://www.who .int/bulletin/bulletin_board/83/ ustun11051/en/

World Health Organization. (2002). *WHO definition of palliative care.* Retrieved from http:// www.who.int/cancer/palliative/ definition/en/

Worldometers Real Time World Statistics. (2014). *World population by region.* Retrieved from http:// www.worldometers.info/world- population/#growthrate

Worthington, E. L. (2003). *Forgiving and reconciling: Bridges to wholeness and hope.* Downers Grove, IL: InterVarsity Press.

Worthington, E. (Ed.) (2005). *Handbook of forgiveness.* New York, NY: Routledge.

Wulff, D. M. (1997). *Psychology of religion: Classic and contemporary*

(2nd ed.). New York, NY: John Wiley & Sons.

Wuthnow, R. (1998). *After heaven: Spirituality in America since the 1950s.* Berkley: University of California Press.

Wyatt, K. (2012, November 6). Finding Maria: Spiritual care and Alzheimer's disease. *Huffington Post.* Retrieved from http://www.huffingtonpost .com/karen-m-wyatt- md/ alzheimers-disease_b_2078673 .html

Young, E. (2010). Narrative therapy and elders with memory loss. *Clinical Social Work Journal, 38,* 193–202.

Young, J. S., Cashwell, C., Wiggins-Frame, M., & Belaire, C. (2002). Spiritual and religious competencies: A national survey of CACREP-accredited programs. *Counseling and Values, 47*(1), 22–33.

Zarit, S., & Zarit, J. M. (2011). *Mental disorders in older adults: Fundamentals of assessment and treatment* (2nd ed.). New York, NY: Guilford Press.

Zeilig, H. (2014). Dementia as a cultural metaphor. *Gerontologist, 54*(2), 258–267.

Zhao, Q. (2010). *Do nothing and do everything: An illustrated new Taoism.* St. Paul, MN: Paragon House.

Zimmerman, F. (1995). The history of melancholy. *The Journal of the International Institute, 2*(2). Retrieved from http://quod.lib .umich.edu/cgi/t/text/text- idx?c=jii;view=text;rgn=main;id no=4750978.0002.205

Zinnbauer, B., Pargament, K., Cole, B., Rye, M., Butter, E., Belavich, T., . . . Kadar, J. (1997). Religion and spirituality: Unfuzzying the fuzzy. *Journal for the Scientific Study of Religion, 36*(4), 549–564.

INDEX

interventions, 273–275
natural, 272, 274
sacred, 272
spiritual interventions, 274–275
toxic, 272, 274
types, 271–273
websites, 279
APA. *See* American Psychological Association
Apathy, 57
APC. *See* Association of Professional Chaplains
Aphasia, 283
Apraxia, 283
Archetypal stories, 199–200
Archetypes, 95
Archimedean spirals, 382, 382 (figure)
Aristotle, 59, 60 (figure)
Arjuna (Prince), 132–133, 201
Ars moriendi, 315
Art, 212–213, 385–386, 386 (figure)
Arts-based interventions for dementia, 299, 302–304
Asclepius (Greek god), 226
ASERVIC. *See* Association for Spiritual, Ethical, and Religious Values in Counseling
Ashramas, 135–136
Ask-tell-ask method, 290
Assessment. *See* Clinical assessment; Mental health assessment; Spiritual assessment
Association for Religion Data Archives, 8
Association for Spiritual, Ethical, and Religious Values in Counseling (ASERVIC), 16, 46, 47–48 (table)
Association of Professional Chaplains (APC), 49, 50 (table)
Astin, J., 365
Attachment, 267
Attention, focused, 182–183
Attentional aspects of mindfulness, 365
Aufauvre, B. V., 265
Autonomy versus shame and doubt stage, 98 (table)
Awareness, 152, 364–366
Ayeli, 237–238

Baby Boom Generation, 347–348, 349 (table)
Bagiella, E., 240
Balance, 223, 371–372
Baltes, P. B., 5, 59, 107, 136
Barbour, I. G., 12
Barg, F. K., 267
Bargaining, 317, 318 (table)
Bar-Tur, L., 378
Basting, Anne, 304
Baylor Religion Survey, 345
Beauty, 212–213
Beauty Way song, 127
Beck, A. T., 268

Beck, C., 294
Becker, Ernest, 313–314, 337
Beginner's mind, 166
Behavior, spiritual, 174 (table), 176
Behavioral therapy, 268–269
Behaviorism, 15, 96
Being-realm, 102, 103 (table)
Belaire, C., 46
Beliefnet website, 10
Belief-O-Matic quiz, 10
Beliefs:
    faith versus, 193
    in God, 8, 8 (table)
    rapid assessment instrument protocols, 179
    religious, 9–10
    spiritual, 174 (table), 176
Bellah, R., 347
Benediction, 390–391
Benevolence, 140, 141
Benson, Herbert, 364
Berger, P. L., 30, 38, 346
Bergin, A. E., 164–165
Berrent, S., 294
Bessinger, D., 223
Bettie, E., 294
Beyond Belief (Pagels), 193
Bhagavad Gita, 132–133, 201
Bhakti yoga, 133, 134
Bible:
    ethics, 61
    healing, 232, 233, 234–235 (table)
    Hebrew, 120, 201
    psalms, 302
Binns, M., 298
Biopsychosocial spiritual model of care for hospice, 40
Bishop, S. R., 365
Bistami, Abu Yazid al-, 29, 30
Black Elk (healer), 127
Blake, William, 35
Blessing Way, 127
Blieszner, R., 267
Boarding schools for American Indians, 195
Body scan, 51
Bogner, H. R., 267
Bohlmeijer, E., 201
Bohr, Niels, 167
Book of Kells, 382, 382 (figure)
Boundaries in ethical practice, 70–73
Bowland, S., 268
Brahma, 133
Brain, 20–21, 253
Brawer, P. A., 48
Breathing, 23
Bridges, unimagined, 391

"Late Fragment" (Carver), 387
Lau, M., 365
Laughter, 397
Lemmer, C. M., 162
Lesbian, gay, bisexual, transgender, or gender
    nonconforming (LGBT-NC) individuals,
    11–12
Leuba, James, 15, 171
Levy-Schiff, R., 378
Lewis, C. S., 102
LGBT-NC individuals. *See* Lesbian, gay, bisexual,
    transgender, or gender nonconforming
    individuals
Li, 140
Liberation phase, 109
Life, social investment in, 321
Life completion tasks, 334–335
Life course perspective, 93–94
Lifemaps, spiritual, 178
Life review, 201
Lifespan developmental theory, 96–97, 98 (table)
Life stages, 202–203
Light, working with, 395
Liminal space, 31
Linked lives, 94
Listening, 188, 390–391
Loeb, J., 359
Logarithmic spirals, 382, 383, 384 (figure)
Logotherapy, 64, 104–105
Loiselle, L., 294–295
Loneliness, 5–6
Long-term memory, 283
Losses, 261, 335 (table)
Love, 98 (table)
Low emotions, 63–64
Luckmann, T., 30
Lukoff, David, 168

MacArthur Foundation, 107–108
MacKinlay, E., 299
MacRae, H., 294
Madrid International Plan of Action
    on Ageing, 80–82
Madsen, R., 347
Mahayana Buddhism, 138
Mahoney, A., 39
Major depressive disorder (MDD), 260, 262
Maladies of the soul, 254–255
Malcolm, L., 196
Malony, H. N., 48
Mandela, Nelson, 19, 64
Marshall Plan, 78–79
Martin, J., 390–391, 397
Martin, W., 294
Marty, Martin, 13

Maslow, Abraham:
    humanism, 101, 102, 103 (table), 104
    peak experiences, 102, 116, 313
    religion and spirituality, 13
Master Chuang (Chuang Tzu), 143
Master storytellers, 302
Maybe (Oliver), 35
McCullough, M. E., 194
McGoldrick, M., 178
MDD. *See* Major depressive disorder
Meaning, 179, 245, 344
Measures of Religiosity, 181
Mecca, pilgrimage to, 130, 153
Medical spirituality, 223
Medicare, 324, 359
Medicine:
    assessment, religion and spirituality in, 164
    fast, 225–226
    integrative, 238
    slow, 226
Medicine wheels, 127
Meditation:
    about, 23
    anxiety and, 275
    as religious practice, 205
    as spiritual practice, 206
    See also Meditation exercises
Meditation exercises:
    attention, focused, 182–183
    awareness, present moment, 152
    breath, 23
    bringing your self together, 216
    color, 371
    hands or fingers, 395
    Mindfulness-Based Stress Reduction course, 395
    movement (Five Ages Dancing), 395
    music (Great Bell Chant), 394
    relaxation, 51
    seasons, changing of the, 83–84
    self-compassion with movement, 277
    senses, refreshing the, 336
    taste, 246–247
    tree planted on day you were born, 115
    walking, 305
    See also Meditation
Melancholia, 260–261
Memoir writing, 284
Memorial, planning your, 337
Memory, 282–284
    See also Dementia
Mencius, 140, 141
Mental health, 245
Mental health assessment, 165–169
Merton, T., 380, 381
Metacognition, 365

Method, 98 (table)
MI. *See* Motivational interviewing
Michael, S., 193
Middle Ages, 226–227, 229, 315
Middle way, 389
Mikels, J. A., 5–6
Mild cognitive impairment, 285–286
Millennial Generation, 348, 349 (table)
Miller, S. D., 361
Miller, Scott, 361–362
Miller, W. R., 46, 190
Mindfulness:
   about, 58
   attentional aspects of, 365
   collective, 359
   emotional, 183–184
   spiritual awareness and, 364–366
   as spiritual practice, 206
   training for, 189
Mindfulness-Based Stress Reduction course, 395
Minor depression, 261
Mitchell, Stephen, 143
Mixed dementias, 287 (table)
Moberg, David O., 43
Moksha, 133
Monastic hospitals, 226–227
Moods, 253
Moody, H. R., 18
Moore, T., 265, 277
Moral hierarchy, 62
Moral injury, 62–63
Morality, 62
Moses (Biblical figure), 201
Motivational interviewing (MI), 190–191, 274–275
Movement, 152–153, 206, 214–215, 277, 395
Mudras, 395
Muhammad (Prophet), 129
Murphy, Michael, 20
Murray, G. F., 267
Murray, Les, 37
Music, 205, 213–214, 303–304, 394
Musical instruments, healing, 331–332
Music and Memories program, 304
Music thanatology, 331–332
Muslims. *See* Islam
My Life in France (Child), 197
Mythic-literal faith, 99, 100 (table)
"My Vision" (Weaver), 394

Nadir experiences, 102
Nagarjuna, 139
Nakashima, M., 174–175 (table), 176
Narrative therapy, 198–202, 380
National Association of Social Workers, 49, 164
National Congress of American Indians, 128

National Consensus Project for Quality Palliative Care (NCP), 164, 325–326, 326–327 (table)
National Institute of Mental Health, 5
National Interfaith Coalition on Aging, 43
Native Americans, as term, 125
   See also American Indian religion/spirituality
Natural anxiety, 272, 274
Nature:
   connecting with, 25, 163
   spiral shapes in, 382–383, 383 (figure)
   as spiritual practice, 206
Nazism, 65–66
NCP. *See* National Consensus Project for Quality Palliative Care
Need-driven, dementia-compromised behavior, 294–297
Needs, 102, 103 (table), 162–164
Needy, support of the, 130
Negative emotions, 63–64
Neimeyer, R. A., 208–209, 209–210 (table)
Nei-tan (inner elixir), 144
Nelson-Becker, H. B., 174–175 (table), 176, 180–181 (table)
Neugarten, Bernice, 11
Neurocognitive disorder, 285
Nezu, A. M., 376
Niebuhr, Reinhold, 207
Nightingale, Florence, 14
Noble Eightfold Path, 137
Nonfinite losses, 261
Nonviolence, 63, 138
Norcross, J., 190
Normal pressure hydrocephalus, 287 (table)
Normative ethics, 64
North American Association of Christians in Social Work, 13–14
"Now I Become Myself" (Sarton), 215
Nuland, S. B., 312
Nun Study, 20
Nursing, 14, 46, 164, 368
Nursing homes, 131

Obituary, creating your own, 336–337
Objects of meaning and memory, 52–53
"Ode to a Grecian Urn" (Keats), 213
O'Donoghue, John, 35
O'Hanlon, A., 201
Olan, Kay, 200
Older adults:
   demographics, 10, 11
   hope in, 192–193
   in hospice care, 319–321, 320 (table), 322 (figure)
   philosophical approaches to therapy with, 188–190
   rights of, 79–80 (table)
   terms for, 11

as workers, 5
See also Aging; *specific topics*
Oliver, Mary, 35
Olson, D. M., 180
Om, 136
Opportunity, fair equality of, 65
Oppression, 121, 125–126
Organizational religiousness, 179
Orientation of experience, 365
Orthodox Church, 123
Ortiz, L. P., 173
Overbeek, G., 194

Pagels, Elaine, 193
Pain, 229–230
Palliative care, 322–323, 324–325, 325 (figure)
    See also Hospice care
Panentheism, 37
Panic disorder, 271
Paradox, 390
Parents, in Islam, 131
Pargament, K. I., 39, 59, 177
Parker, D., 237
Parker, M. W., 108
Parkinson's disease dementia, 286 (table)
Participation, 79–80 (table), 396
Pathology, aging as, 91
Pathways, 191
Pausch, Randy, 109
Peak experiences, 102, 116, 313
Perennial Philosophy, The (Huxley), 35
Periyakoil, V. J., 75
Persecution, 121
Persistent depressive disorder (dysthymia), 261
Personal control, 94
Person-centered care, 69, 292
Peterson, C., 173
Pew Religious Landscape Survey, 160
Pew Research Center, 11, 345, 348
Peyote, 126–127, 227
Philosophical approaches to therapy with older
    adults, 188–190
Philosophies, practical, 350–351
Photography, 212
Physical pain, 229
Physical well-being, 345
Physician Orders for Life Sustaining Treatment
    (POLST), 74
Picasso, Pablo, 213
Pilgrimages, 153–154, 198, 206
Pilgrims, spiritual, 350
Plains Indians Sun Dance, 126
Planck, Max, 159, 160
Plateau experiences, 102
Plato, 59, 60 (figure)

Poetry, 330–331, 386–387
Policy Recommendations for Native Elders, 128
Positive aging, 109
Positive emotions, 63–64, 253
Positive psychology, 59, 60 (figure), 63–64
Positive self-talk, 273–274
Powers, R., 16
Practical philosophies, 350–351
Practical theology, 350–351
Pratchett, Terry, 299
Prayer:
    clients, use with, 72–73
    dementia and, 297
    health and, 243
    intercessory, 72
    Islam, 129–130
    religious and spiritual practices, 205, 207–208
    as religious practice, 205
Pre-contemplation, 190
Pre-egoic phase, 105
Preparation for change, 190
Primary memory, 283
Principles for Older Persons, 79–80 (table)
Print-making, 385–386, 386 (figure)
Private religious practices, 179
Procedural memory, 283
Prochaska, J., 190
Production, 98 (table)
Profane, as term, 52
Professionalization and secularization phase, 17
Professionals, suffering of, 230
Pronk, T. M., 194
Proselytizing, 70–71
Prospective memory, 283
Protestantism, 123–124
Protocols, clinical assessment:
    domains of spirituality tool, 174–175 (table), 176
    Fitchett's 7x7 model for spiritual assessment,
        176–177, 177 (table)
    God images, 177–178
    spiritual ecomaps, 178
    spiritual genograms, 178
    spiritual history/spiritual lifemaps, 178
    spiritual screening tools, 172–173, 173 (table)
Psalms, 302
Psychodynamic perspectives, 94–95
Psychological well-being, 345
Psychology:
    assessment, religion and spirituality in, 164–165
    positive, 59, 60 (figure), 63–64
    spirituality, history of, 14–15
    standards of care, 48–49
    transpersonal, 104–106, 106 (figure)
Psychotherapeutic approaches to depression,
    268–269

Psychotherapy, as term, 34, 95
Puchalski, C., 359
Puja, 244
Purpose, 98 (table), 245, 344
Pyramid model of forgiveness, 196

Qigong, 144
Quality improvement:
  in health care, 359–360
  in spiritual and religious care, 360–361
Questions:
  formulating, 165–167
  for self reflection pre- and post-initial client
    session, 355
  from the soul, 332–334
Qur'an, 129, 130, 131, 235, 236

Rachels, J., 56
Raisin meditation, 246–247
Raja yoga, 134
Ramadan, 130
Ramsey, J. L., 196, 267
Rando, T., 203–204 (table)
Rapid assessment instrument protocols, 178–181
Rawls, John, 65
REACH model of forgiveness, 196
Reading, 205, 206
Reality, 30–31
Recall, 283
Reciprocity, 396
Reciting, 205
Recognition, 283
Redefinition of self, 319–320
Reevaluation phase, 109
Reflection, 330
Regret, 201–202, 277–278
Reincarnation, 133
Relapse, 191
Relationships, 140–141, 320–321
Relaxation, 51
Religion:
  abuse in, 73, 162
  aging and, 161
  aging field, recommendations for, 388–389
  assumptions about, 17–18
  attendance by age, 7 (table), 8
  beliefs about, 9–10
  clinical assessment and, 160–165
  defined, 6, 37–39
  depression and, 266–267
  domains of, 38–39
  early historical inquiries about, 171–172
  ethics and, 32, 61
  functions of, 344–346
  importance of, 8, 9 (table)

myths about, 5
negative effects of, 73, 162
older client and therapist concerns in discussing,
    167–168
professional/organizational stances on,
    164–165
professional practice, coherence with, 344–345
science and, 12
shadow sides of, 73
societal context of, 345–346
spirituality, intersection with, 33–34, 34 (figure)
spirituality versus, 5
statistics, 7–9, 7 (table), 8 (table), 9 (table)
as term, 31
training practitioners on, 40–41
See also specific religions and topics
Religion, Values and Peak Experiences (Maslow), 104
Religion and Public Life Survey, 7 (table),
    8, 8 (table), 9 (table)
Religious and spiritual practices:
  about, 205–207
  art, 212–213
  dementia, principles for, 299–302
  movement, 206, 214–215
  music, 205, 213–214
  photography, 212
  prayer, 205, 207–208
  writing therapy and restorative language, 208–210,
    209–210 (table), 211 (table), 212
Religious and spiritual texts, 302
Religious care, quality improvement in, 360–361
Religious conversion, 70–71
Religious history, 179
Religious Landscape survey, 5
Religious preference/affiliation, 179
Religious support, 179
Reminiscence, 201–202, 330
Remorse, 277
Renewal, contemplative practices for,
    366, 367 (figure)
Renewal of interest phase, 17
Renunciation, 98 (table), 135–136
Reperceiving, 365
Reserve capacity, 223
Resilience:
  in aging, 378–379, 379 (figure)
  art as symbol for, 385–386, 386 (figure)
  defined, 378
  door as symbol for, 380–381, 381 (figure)
  hero's journey, 376–378
  poetry as symbol for, 386–387
  spiral as symbol for, 382–385, 382 (figure),
    383 (figure), 384 (figure)
  symbols for, 379–387
  website, 397–398

Smith, D. C., 208–209, 209–210 (table)
Smith, Huston, 18–19, 21, 122, 139
Smith, W. C., 32
Snyder, C., 193
Social gerontology theories, 91–94
Social investment in life, 321
Social phobia, 271
Social support, 175 (table), 176
Social unity, 344–345
Social work, 12–14, 49, 164
Society for Spirituality and Social Work, 13
Society for the Psychology of Religion and
      Spirituality, 14–15
Socioemotional selectivity theory, 111
Sorrow, chronic, 261
Soul:
   about, 34–35
   dark night of the, 264–265
   maladies of the, 254–255
   questions from the, 332–334
Sound, 305–306
Source memory, 283
Sparks, J. A., 361
Spirals, 382–385, 382 (figure), 383 (figure),
    384 (figure)
Spirit, as term, 33
Spirits, discernment of, 270
Spiritual affiliation, 174 (table), 176
Spiritual and existentialist/humanist ethics, 62–63
Spiritual and religious practices:
   about, 205–207
   art, 212–213
   dementia, principles for, 299–302
   movement, 206, 214–215
   music, 205, 213–214
   photography, 212
   prayer, 205, 207–208
   writing therapy and restorative language, 208–210,
     209–210 (table), 211 (table), 212
Spiritual assessment:
   defined, 169–170
   ethical practice and, 70
   Fitchett's 7x7 model, 176–177, 177 (table)
   National Consensus Project guidelines,
     326–327 (table)
Spiritual awareness, 364–366
Spiritual behavior, 174 (table), 176
Spiritual beliefs, 174 (table), 176
Spiritual bypass, 73
Spiritual capital, 348–349
Spiritual care:
   about, 45
   as calling, 329
   as collaborative endeavor, 328–329
   end-of-life issues, 328–332

quality improvement in, 360–361
   for significant others, 329
Spiritual concerns, 43–45, 44 (table)
Spiritual consolation, 270
Spiritual desolation, 270
Spiritual discovery, 255, 258, 258 (figure)
Spiritual Distress Assessment Tool (SDAT), 181
Spiritual ecomaps, 178
Spiritual-ethical wills, 84
Spiritual experiences, 174 (table), 176, 179
Spiritual freedom, 255, 258 (figure)
Spiritual genograms, 178
Spiritual health, 222
Spiritual history:
   about, 178
   defined, 169–170
   developing, 115–116
   rapid assessment instrument protocols, 179
   as spirituality domain, 175 (table), 176
Spirituality:
   aging field, recommendations for, 388–389
   assumptions about, 17–18
   brain and, 20–21
   in caregiving methods, 242–243
   defined, 7, 39, 41–42, 326 (table)
   dementia and, 292–294
   dimensions of, 33, 63
   emotional qualities of, 174 (table), 176
   emotion and, 255, 258–259, 258 (figure)
   history across disciplines, 12–17
   Ignatian, 343
   interprofessional practice and, 362–364
   Islam, 132
   medical, 223
   older client and therapist concerns in discussing,
     167–168
   professional/organizational stances on, 164–165
   religion, intersection with, 33–34, 34 (figure)
   religion versus, 5
   shadow sides of, 73
   as term, 33
   training practitioners on, 40–41
   trends in, 346–350, 349 (table)
   visual, 212–213
   See also Exploring Your Spirituality; *specific topics*
Spiritual journeys, clinical aspects of, 21–22
Spiritual lifemaps, 178
Spiritually sensitive practice, 45, 67
Spiritual needs, 162–164
Spiritual orientation dissimilarity between client and
    practitioner, 351–355
Spiritual pilgrims, 350
Spiritual places, 184–185, 217
Spiritual reminiscence, 201–202
Spiritual screening, 169, 172–173, 173 (table)

Time, 300
Tipton, S., 347
Tonglen practice, 306–307
Torah, 120, 121
Tornstam, L., 97, 99
Torres, C., 208–209, 209–210 (table)
Torres-Rivera, E., 237
Touch, 247–248
Tourists, spiritual, 350
Toxic anxiety, 272, 274
Training practitioners on religion and
    spirituality, 40–41
Transcendence, 37, 39–40, 59, 60
Transcending boundaries/integration phase, 17
Transcranial magnetic imaging, 269
Transegoic phase, 105
Transformation, archetypes of, 95
Transpersonal psychology, 104–106, 106 (figure)
Trask, W. R., 203
Trauma, intergenerational, 195–196
Traumatic brain injury, 287 (table)
Traumatic stress, secondary, 58
Tree planted on day you were born, 115
Tripitaka (Pali Canon), 137–138
True mind, 189
Trust, 69
Trust versus mistrust stage, 98 (table)
Turner, V. W., 31

"Ulysses" (Tennyson), 375, 376
United Nations, 78, 79–80 (table), 80–82
Unity, social, 344–345
Universalizing faith, 99–100, 100 (table)
University of Chicago, 369
Upanishads, 132
U.S. Department of Energy, Office of Science, 37
U.S. Department of Health and Human Services, 239
Utilitarianism, 66

Valliant, G. E., 108
Values:
    across religious faiths, 146, 149 (table)
    ethics, 69–70
    rapid assessment instrument protocols, 179
    as spirituality domain, 174 (table), 176
Van Gennep, A., 202
Vascular dementia, 286 (table)
Vascular depression, 261
Vedas, 132
Vermulst, A. A., 194
Virtual dreams, 208–209, 209–210 (table), 211 (table)
Virtue ethics, 58–60, 60 (figure)
Virtues, 59, 60 (figure), 97, 98 (table)
Vishnu, 133
Vision, 84

Visioning, 393–394
Visual spirituality, 212–213

Wai-tan (outer elixir), 144
Wajda-Johnson, V. A., 48
Wald, Florence, 316
Wales, 361
Walking meditation, 305
Walther, Thomas, 194
Wanderer above the Sea of Fog (Friedrich), 391
Wealth, spiritual, 82
Weariness, 223
Weaver, Amber, 394
Websites:
    clinical assessment, 185
    defining religion and spirituality, 53
    dementia, 307–308
    emotion, depression, and anxiety, 279
    end-of-life issues, 338–339
    ethics, 86–87
    health, 249–250
    integration, 373
    religion, 154–155
    religious/spiritual interventions with clients,
        218–219
    resilience, 397–398
    spirituality and religion, importance for
        gerontology, 25–27
    theories, 116–117
Webster, J., 201
Wei wu wei (doing not doing), 143
Well-being:
    existential, 42
    physical, 345
    psychological, 345
    spiritual, 42–43, 175 (table), 176
Westerhof, G., 201
West-Olatunji, C., 237
White Bison movement, 195–196
White House Conference on Aging, 42–43
WHO. *See* World Health Organization
Whole-being, 63–64
Wiersma, E., 294–295
Wigboldus, D. H. J., 194
Wiggins-Frame, M., 46
Wilber, Ken, 21, 34, 105–106, 106 (figure)
Williams, R. R., 212
Willpower, 98 (table)
Wills, ethical, 84, 108–109
Wisdom, 59, 98 (table), 108
Wittink, M. N., 267
Women:
    archetypal stories, 200
    Confucianism, 141–142
    ordination of, 9–10